Clipper Ships

[WARTIME CHANGES CENSORED]

WORLD AIRWAYS

# PAN AMERICAN'S
# PACIFIC PIONEERS
## THE REST OF THE STORY

A Pictorial History of Pan Am's Pacific First Flights 1935-1946
Jon E. Krupnick

*"The Last Clipper"* by Bob Jenny - Painted expressly for cover of book

•

ISBN – 1-57510-076-2

•

Cover, layout, and graphics by
Fred Wolfe – sfwgraphic@aol.com

•

Printed by Super Color
Hollywood, Florida

•

Bindery by Bind-Tech Binding Technology Inc.
Nashville, Tennessee

•

**Contact author Jon E. Krupnick**
**Visit the new web site for this book to post**
**comments, supplements and additions.**
Web site at: http//www.pacificpioneers.com
e-mail: jonpac@aol.com
**(954) 763-8181  FAX: (954) 763-8292**
**700 S.E. 3rd Ave.,**
**Fort Lauderdale, FL 33316**

•

Published and distributed for Jon E. Krupnick by
Pictorial Histories Publishing Co. Inc.
713 South Third Street West
Missoula, Montana 59801
Telephone: 888-763-8350 • FAX: 406-728-9280
e-mail: phpc@montana.com
Web site: http://www.montana.com/phpc/stancvr.htm

•

For each book sold the author
will donate one dollar to
Pan Am Historical Foundation
52 Vanderbilt Avenue
New York, New York 10017
Email: foundation@panam.org
Home Page:  www.panam.org

*Pan Am Clippers Unite the Pacific Rim*
*by Bob Jenny*

This exciting painting by renowned aviation artist, Bob Jenny, brings together in flight for the first and only time the three Pan Am Clippers that pioneered Pacific flight. Overhead is the Sikorsky S-42 that flew the early survey flights to Hawaii, the mid-Pacific islands and New Zealand. Taxiing into view is the Martin M-130 that made the first flight to Manila in 1935 and to Hong Kong in 1937. Seen breaking the water with the Oakland Bay Bridge in the background is the mighty Boeing B-314 that made its maiden Pacific flight in March of 1939. This Boeing Clipper raised air travel to a level of luxury and comfort that has never again been equalled. These three Clipper ships opened the Pacific to the world and they have finally been united in this painting.

3

# Foreword

## E-MAIL FROM

# JIMMY BUFFETT

## Singer - Song writer
## Best selling author

*Jimmy showing his Albatross flying boat to author Jon Krupnick on right and the author's son Jack on left.*

**From:** margaritaville .com-jimmy buffett
**To:** jonpac@aol.com-jon krupnick

Remember Address | Download Later | Download Now | Reply | Forward

**Subject:** Re: Pacific Pioneers-The Rest of the Story

**Date Sent:** March 17, 2000 - 10:35 PM

At this moment, I am high above the Pacific on a 747 on my way to Hong Kong for the first time. We are four times as fast and five miles higher than the route taken by the China Clipper, but I can't help but wander back to the pages of photos and mementoes in Jon's book.

I have been fortunate enough to do a lot of things and see a lot of the world in my lifetime, but if I had one wish, it would be to have been able, just once, to ride aboard a Pan Am Clipper. That will never happen, but Jon Krupnick's book gives us a wonderful glimpse into one of the great time periods in all of aviation.

In an era of fast planes and high tech theme parks, it is truly refreshing to be able to be taken back in time by the pages of a book.

**Jimmy Buffett**
Somewhere over the Pacific

### Reply

Thanks Jimmy for the nice words.

I have enjoyed your music for over 25 years and it has been part of our family's good times. I am pleased that you have enjoyed Pan Am's Pacific Pioneers as much as I have enjoyed your music.

Best wishes
**Jon Krupnick**
jonpac@aol.com

Delete

## TABLE OF CONTENTS

# DEDICATION

This book is dedicated to all of the men and women who worked together to help Pan Am pioneer flight in the Pacific. I especially want to thank two men who personally shared with me their memories of Pan Am's pioneering flights: Captain Harry Canaday, who was the junior flight officer on the first flight to Hawaii in 1935, and Dr. Myron "Ken" Kenler, who was Pan Am's doctor on Wake Island when the bases were built. Their sharing with me of their scrapbooks and their memories was really the beginning of my desire to write a book on this exciting history.

Now, unfortunately, with the passage of time, it is the children of these early pioneers who are sharing their father's stories and saved mementoes. Alex Vucetich loaned me his father's log from the Kingman Reef expedition in 1937 and the scrapbooks of his father's adventures on Pan Am's ships, the North Wind, North Haven and Southern Seas.

Then Catherine Berst Lytton shared the stories of her father, Phil Berst, who started as a young mechanic in Miami before being transferred in 1935 to Honolulu to oversee the maintenance of all of the Pacific bases.

*Captain Harry Canaday*

*Dr. Ken Kenler*

*Danilo (Dan) Vucetich*

*Phil Berst with family-1935*

The family of Almon Gray shared their father's photo albums and flight covers from the time he started as a radio operator on Wake Island in mid-1935 up until the early 1940s when he served as a radio flight officer on the first flights of the Boeing B-314 Clippers.

Finally, Tim Young, the son of Colonel Clarence Young, Pan Am's director of the Pacific division from its founding in 1935 up to the 1960s, shared with me not only his father's scrapbooks and picture albums, but also his priceless mementoes of a lifetime of service with Pan Am, such as the prop from the China Clipper made into a wall plaque and a lamp and even a piece of the Philippine Clipper, with a bullet hole, that was hit by Japanese gunfire at Wake Island at the outbreak of WWII.

*Almon Gray*          *Clarence Young*

I made a promise to all of these people, that if they would share their parents' stories and their saved souvenirs, I would keep alive the memory of their fathers' contributions to this great adventure. I hope they are all pleased with my effort, because without their generosity and without their good will, I never could have told the "**REST OF THE STORY**".

*Jon and family, Key West, Florida - March 2000*

I also dedicate this book to my family, my life's greatest achievement and the source of constant joy and happiness.

To my wife, Elaine, thanks for a lifetime of love, help, encouragement and good counsel.

To my son Jack and his wife Florence and their children, Jackson, Katie and Jon; to my son Mike and his wife Kim; to my daughter Laura and her husband Robert, and their children Ivo and Austin - you all have taught me how to enjoy life and you are all also a constant reminder of what is really important in this life.

I thank you all for having made such wonderful and productive lives for yourselves and for your families. You have made your parents very proud.

# INTRODUCTION

*Flying boats are like no other machines. They were created out of the same desire to explore that drove the early pathfinders from Columbus to Captain Cook. The giant Sikorsky and Boeing flying boats that took to the skies and the seas more than half a century ago created a mysterious and romantic kind of flying that can never be duplicated. The designers and engineers who brought these flying boats to life built more than airplanes. They created art. But their time was short. Runways built for World War II were the concrete stakes that pierced the heart of the giant flying boat.*

*From the book* **A Pirate Looks at Fifty** *by* **Jimmy Buffett**. *Copyright© 1998 by Jimmy Buffett. Reprinted with permission of Random House , Inc. - Quotation from page 22 of* **A Pirate Looks at Fifty**.

They all tell a story - these old envelopes that collectors call "flight covers". The more you learn about the airplanes and crews that flew them, the better story they can tell you. The more you learn about the airline companies and the national and world politics that shaped their fate, the better stories the covers can tell you. The purpose of this book is to give you some of the background of the people and of the airplanes so that souvenir flight covers can come alive and tell you the story they want to share with you.

How did I get started collecting flight covers? Well, the winters were long in Cleveland, Ohio where I grew up in the 1940s and 1950s. To help fill the time between Christmas and the beginning of baseball season, I would get out the family atlas and find some small islands in the Pacific that were claimed by the United States. I would then write a note to the postmaster on a particular island, put a couple of two cent postcards addressed back to me in an envelope, put a three cent stamp on the envelope addressed to a far away island and lob it somewhere out in the mid-Pacific. Many of my envelopes came back with "no post office", stamped in purple. But a few of my envelopes found their mark and the postcards inside came back cancelled from some remote island like Wake or Midway and my little collection of postmarks and postcards from the U.S. Pacific islands began to grow.

*Postcards from Wake and Canton Islands sent back to me in 1954*

Then came spring and baseball and the postcards and covers went back into the shoe box in the back of the closet until the next winter.

About this time, however, I found out about girls - and then high school became more serious than junior high had been - and you know about college - and then law school - marriage - three kids - a new job with a move to Florida and then a new house - and suddenly twenty years had gone by. I had almost forgotten about the shoe box I had left in my closet many, many years before.

Somehow, however, through all the house cleanings, Mom hadn't thrown it out. When she was getting ready to sell the house she found the shoe box and sent it to me here in Fort Lauderdale, Florida where I had settled with my wife Elaine and our three children to start my law career and raise my family. The postcards and envelopes in the shoe box contained a lot of memories of a simpler time and they renewed my interest in the Pacific islands.

After work and dinner with the family there was some quiet time. So once again I took up my old hobby and sent out letters to the postmasters on the same remote islands claimed by the United States to see what new postmarks might have shown up in the last 20 years.

I joined stamp groups, like the Pacific Islands Study Circle of Great Britain, the War Cover Club and others. I started picking up any items I could from Wake, Midway, Canton and the other Pacific islands. Soon the little collection in the shoe box moved into a small four drawer filing cabinet as my collection grew.

In 1978 L.J. Crampon was writing a book *"Aerophilatelic Flights - Hawaii and Central Pacific - 1913 to 1946"*. He somehow heard about my collection of covers from the United States Pacific Islands and he wrote me asking if I had any unusual flight covers that might help his research. Until I got his letter, I had never paid any attention to whether my covers from Wake and Midway were flight covers or not. But, after checking my collection, I discovered several items that I thought might be of interest to him including a cover I had just picked up postmarked from Kingman Reef, a little known U.S. possession in the mid-Pacific.

*Cover flown to Kingman Reef on first New Zealand survey flight*

After receiving my letter he wrote back excitedly that the Kingman Reef cover might be the missing and long sought after flight cover from Pan American's first survey flight to New Zealand in March of 1937 that had been flown by the famous pilot, Edwin Musick. He went on to explain that souvenir flight covers had been prepared by the crew members of the Pan Am flights for all of the previous Pacific survey flights and first scheduled flights. But up until that time no flown covers had ever surfaced from this very important March 1937 survey flight to New Zealand that used Kingman Reef as an overnight stopover. Collectors knew that survey flight covers from the 1937 New Zealand survey flight should exist, but none had been discovered.

I had never heard of flight covers - never heard of survey flights or first flights - never heard of back stamped, cachets or legs of a flight. I didn't even know what aerophilatelic meant, let alone how to spell it. All I did know was that the cover I had picked up simply because "Kingman Reef" was a U.S. possession was causing Pan Am flight cover collectors to become excited about a unique find. I figured if I really had the rarest Pan American flight cover from the Pacific, I had better learn something about the flight cover side of the cover collecting hobby.

The more I learned about the Pan Am flights in the Pacific, the more fascinated I became. I was hooked! Why? Because the flight covers told a far better story when I knew the exciting aviation history that went with the covers than they had ever told me when I didn't know the history.

Without realizing it, I had become a collector of Pan Am first flight covers of the Pacific.

In the beginning, it was hard for me to find the information in one place about the history of the flights. I wanted to know what planes were used to make the flights and what dates were important. Crampon's book was a good start, for it included most of the Pan Am Pacific first flights that had occurred between 1935 and 1946. **The Airpost Journal** and the **Jack Knight Air Log** also had timely and informative articles covering the period.

But the real knowledge and the real excitement started when I met the Pan Am people who were involved in the actual flights.

The first person I met was Harry Canaday. Harry Canaday was Pan Am's junior flight officer on all four of the Pacific survey flights leading up to the November 1935 first scheduled flight across the Pacific. I was fortunate in that he had retired to nearby Coral Gables, Florida. When I contacted him, he invited me down for a visit.

Captain Canaday worked closely with Pan Am Captains Edwin Musick, Sullivan, Tilton and all the rest. Captain Canaday generously shared his pictures, his souvenir covers, and his memories of this exciting time. I also met Overton Snyder, the station manager at Miami in the 1930s and 1940s. He, too, shared his memories and his flight covers.

*First flight to Manila - November 22, 1935*

Admiral Jesse Johnson, a Navy pilot who served in the Pacific during the mid-1930s and flew many of the historic Navy flights became a friend by mail. From time to time he would sell me flight covers for much less than their true market value, because he knew that at the time I couldn't afford expensive covers and because he also knew that I loved the history of the early flights. He would share not only the cover but also the story behind the cover. My knowledge and my collection continued to grow.

But, what brought it all together was meeting Dr. Myron "Ken" Kenler, who had been Pan Am's doctor in 1935 on Wake Island when Pan Am was building the Pacific bases and flying the 1935 Pacific survey flights.

His scrapbook of his year with Pan Am, his flight covers, and his memories brought to life the hardship and difficulty faced by Pan Am in building the Pacific bases and in bridging the Pacific with the first flights. Over the time that we spent together, he really made the history come alive. He helped me to fully understand and appreciate the exciting story that each of my covers had to tell.

I also realized that for fellow cover collectors and future cover collectors, there simply would not be any more Dr. Kenlers or Captain Canadays or Admiral Jesse Johnsons to help share the memories and to help build the knowledge about these flights. They were, unfortunately, all passing on as the years slipped away. So I made a promise to Dr. Kenler that if he would share his covers with me, I would share them with others to keep his memories alive of that exciting time.

So that's where the idea came from for writing a book. My first book, **Pan Am's Pacific Pioneers**, was published in May of 1997. One of the nice things about writing a book about Pan Am flying boats is that you get to meet an awful lot of nice people who share your love of the romantic old Pan Am clippers. I was very fortunate that some of these people that I met were the children of Pan Am pioneers who had passed away. These children wanted the efforts of their parents to be recognized and their memories to be kept alive. They wanted me to tell "The Rest Of The Story" about their parents' role in Pan Am's early Pacific flights.

Once I decided to tell their stories, I decided it would be fun and helpful to other collectors if I gathered together in one place enough information about the aircraft and the historic flights to give new collectors an understanding of the history, so they could more easily enjoy the story behind their covers.

I purposely left out a value guide, because once you find a cover or a piece of Pan Am history and once you know the history, whether you paid $5 or $500 for it, it becomes priceless to you. I have not attempted to give detailed information on the legs of the flights or postal rates. The **American Air Mail Catalogs** do that far better than I could ever do it. I have tried to give the dates of historic flights so that by checking the postmarks you can hopefully find some historical flight covers that have not been previously identified. There are still a lot of covers to be found. I have also tried, by using color, to make the covers more exciting for both the beginner and advanced collector.

*First flight Boeing B-314 - March 1939*

I also discovered that Pan Am's timetables, annual reports, postcards and brochures provided valuable information about the flights and further helped me in understanding and in recapturing the excitement and romance of these Pacific pioneer flights. Therefore, I have included pictures of these colorful items from my collection.

I have tried to write the book as if you were a guest in my home and I was showing you my collection and sharing with you the stories that I have learned from meeting some of the people who were actually involved in these flights. Remember - it's the story that counts - the story that each flight cover wants to tell you about the airplane, airline and flight crew that made that historical flight possible.

I hope by telling the **"Rest of The Story"**, you have a better understanding of the challenges faced by these Pan Am Pacific pioneers.

*Best wishes*

*Jon E Krupnick*

*April 2000*

11

# CHAPTER ONE
# Dr. KEN KENLER'S SCRAPBOOK

I have been collecting Pan American Airways flight covers from the Pacific area for over twenty years. Whenever I visit a stamp show, I make the rounds of the dealers asking if they have anything in my area of interest. About five years ago at the Fort Lauderdale, Florida stamp show, one of the dealers said he might have something I would enjoy - a card signed by the doctor on Wake Island in 1935.

After a little negotiating I was happy to purchase it from him for $5. However, before I left his table, I noticed to my surprise, that the back of the card contained a printed advertisement for a recent stamp show in our area. I pointed out to the dealer that the card with Dr. Kenler's signature was not old, but of more recent vintage. With a smile, he said he never told me it was old, only that it was signed by Pan Am's doctor on Wake Island - which it was. He went on to explain that Dr. Kenler was a delightful gentlemen who had come to a Hollywood, Florida stamp club meeting a year or so before and had shared with them his experiences on Wake Island as Pan Am's doctor when the bases were being built. It was at that meeting that he got him to sign the card. He said the doctor had great stories to tell and that he might be willing to share some of his memories with me if I gave him a call.

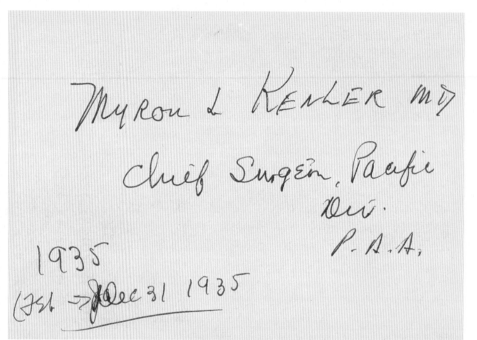

*Card signed by Dr. Kenler*

With the card in hand I checked the local telephone listings under Kenler and my first call met with success. Dr. Myron "Ken" Kenler greeted me warmly and he had a good laugh over my story of how I had purchased his recent autograph for $5. He also invited me over to his condominium to see his scrapbook from his Pan Am adventure.

Early on a rainy Saturday morning I arrived at his apartment and met Ken and his lovely wife Roselyn, for what would be the beginning of a very enjoyable, but all too short friendship.

*Dr. Kenler showing me two of his souvenir covers*

He had the worn scrapbook on the table when I arrived. I was, of course, anxious to see what it contained. However, before we opened the scrapbook to relive Dr. Kenler's Pan Am experience, we spent a little time getting to know each other better.

Dr. Kenler was born in Brooklyn in 1906. He was always a good student and in 1925 he entered Columbia University to study chemical engineering. Quickly his interests changed to medicine, so he transferred to Johns Hopkins, graduating with his medical degree in 1933. He started his medical internship at Jamaica Hospital in Queens.

In early 1935 the head of the Pathology Department mentioned to him that Pan American Airways was interviewing for a doctor and he might want to give them a call. He put on his best suit and summoned up all his courage and rode the trolley downtown to the Chrysler Building for the interview. He had never taken an elevator in a skyscraper before in his life and his first ride was to the 58th Floor where Pan Am's offices were located. When he entered he saw that the waiting room was filled with older, more experienced doctors and he didn't think he had a chance of landing the position with the airline.

The interview was a bizarre experience. They wouldn't tell him where they intended him to go; and they wouldn't tell him the purpose of the project. All they told him was that it would be like a *"National Geographic"* adventure and that everything had to be kept secret. It was stressed that he could not talk to the newspaper reporters without the full approval of the public relations department. They specifically asked him if he was afraid of giant crabs or reptiles.

*Dr Kenler's scrapbook*

In reply to these unusual questions, he merely wanted to know whether or not other men would be going along on the expedition or if he would be alone. When they told him others would be going, he told them he was certain he could do as well as the others under the circumstances. To his surprise, he was selected. They told him he was chosen because he was young and they felt he could stand up to the rigors of the travel involved. The pay would be $100 a month. This was less than they would be paying some of the carpenters and plumbers, but far more than he had hoped to earn over the next few years as a young doctor.

Once he had been hired, they revealed to him that he would be the only doctor for an expedition that would be building five seaplane bases across the Pacific and he would be responsible for the health and welfare of the 125 men involved in the project.

His work started immediately and in early February of 1935 he reported to the Chrysler Building to give physicals to the applicants for the project. For each person selected he had to certify that they would "not break down" under a year of hard work. One young man he wanted to reject, because he felt that his health was too frail for the mission. This decision was overruled by Pan Am because the applicant was the brother of the Pacific Division Manager. Therefore, the young man was permitted to join the expedition. This proved to be a fateful decision, for the young man died of illness while in the Pacific.

By the end of February 1935 his work in New York was completed. He flew to California to Pan Am's new seaplane base in Alameda on San Francisco Bay, where he continued to examine applicants.

After our nice talk, it was time to open the well worn scrapbook put together by Dr. Kenler when he was a young doctor upon his return from the Pacific almost 60 years before. The black album pages were crumbling from age and many of the pictures were small and faded, but in Dr. Kenler's hands they told a vivid story of the hardship, loneliness, isolation and ultimate success of Pan Am's mission to bridge the Pacific.

For the Pacific expedition, Pan Am had chartered the 3000 ton freighter, the S.S. North Haven from the Northland Transportation Company in Seattle. It was to serve as the mother ship to transport the construction crew and material to the Pacific Islands. On March 22, 1935 the North Haven, under the command of Captain Borklund,

**DIES**

WILLIAM F. YOUNG.

## W. F. Young Dies at Guam

### Speedy Mid-Ocean Trip Unavailing.

William F. Young of Valley Junction, whose illness aboard a vessel in mid-Pacific called a navy transport to his aid, died Thursday in a hospital on the island of Guam.

Young, 36, was stricken three weeks ago with influenza abroad the North Haven, carrying a Pan American Airways expedition en route to establish air bases on Pacific islands.

### Vessel Came 1,000 Miles.

By wireless the navy transport, Henderson, was summoned across more than 1,000 miles of water so Young could have hospital treatment.

Young, who was a brother of Col. Clarence M. Young, now an executive directing Pan America's development of a United States-Orient airline, was transferred in mid-Pacific from the North Haven to the Henderson, which then steamed to Guam, 11 days away.

### Brothers Here.

The mission of mercy proved futile, however, because Young's influenza developed into pneumonia.

Word of Young's death came Friday by cable to three of his brothers here. The brothers are Ralph Young, deputy Iowa industrial commissioner, and Harry H. Young and George Young of Valley Junction.

*The North Haven ready to depart at pier 22 in San Francisco*

arrived in San Francisco from Seattle and tied up at pier 22. Over the next five days, all the supplies to build two villages, one on Wake and one on Midway, and to outfit three other bases in Honolulu, Guam and Manila, were loaded on board.

Just before midnight on March 26, 1935, the North Haven left the dock to the goodbyes of friends, wives and sweethearts whom they would not see for the next four months.

The vessel anchored in San Francisco Bay until morning and got underway again at 10:00 a.m. passing under the Golden Gate Bridge with a course for Honolulu.

The 44 technicians and 73 construction workers on board had quite a task ahead of them. Pan Am intended to start the survey flights in mid-April. The crew had to hurry if they were going to keep this tight schedule. It took them a week to reach Honolulu. When they arrived on April 4, 1935 they let it be known that they needed a couple of extra construction workers. Honolulu was still in the depths of the Depression and over a thousand men showed up hoping to find work.

The S.S. North Haven, with 118 men and 6,000 tons of equipment, is about ready to depart. From left to right, Karl Lueder, station manager at Wake; William S. Grooch, director of the expedition and author of the book which told the story of building the Pacific bases; Skyway to Asia, William Van Dusen, Pan Am's public relations director; Captain L.L. O'Dell; H.E. Ward; Dr. Myron Ken Kenler, doctor for the expedition and the doctor for Wake Island.

Rear row - left to right, William G. Taylor; A.A. Mittag; and John S. Borger, junior engineer who served on Wake.

North Haven Crew and Pan-Am Construction Workers

One of the six who was hired was Bill Mullahey, who was a lifeguard and surfer at Waikiki Beach. Like Dr. Kenler, he had attended Columbia University. He never took his studies seriously and as the cold weather approached, he always found himself dropping out of school and drifting back to Honolulu and the beach life that he enjoyed. He was an excellent swimmer and he was hired to assist the man in charge of dynamiting the coral heads out of the lagoon. Bill Mullahey and Dr. Kenler quickly became good friends.

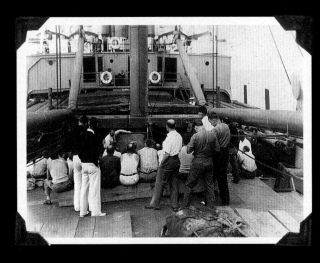

Morning lecture

Dr. Kenler giving shots

Docking at Honolulu-April 4, 1935

North Haven at Honolulu-April 1935

After off loading the supplies necessary for the seaplane base at Pearl Harbor, the North Haven departed Honolulu on April 8 for Midway, where their real work would begin.

It took the North Haven four days to reach Midway and they arrived on April 12. The men on board the North Haven at Midway took time out from their construction work to listen to the radio broadcast and to cheer the Clipper and its crew as the Clipper neared Honolulu in the early morning hours of April 17 on the first survey flight to Honolulu. They also knew they had to complete their work as quickly as possible if they were going to stay on schedule and be ready for the June survey flight to Midway.

The North Haven was too large to enter the lagoon at Midway Island, so it had to anchor more than a mile off shore in the open ocean to off load supplies. While they were unloading a 60 foot pole that was to be used for a radio antenna, the crane operator mistook a signal and the load came crashing down on the barge. One workman had to dive overboard to avoid injury, but another was not so fortunate and his hand was badly smashed between the pole and the barge. Using a landing net and boom they got him aboard the North Haven and from the extent of the injury, there was fear that he would lose his hand.

Dr. Kenler had been trained in general surgery and he ordered the North Haven to circle in the ocean so as to create a relatively calm area of water so he could attempt surgery on the hand. With the assistance of construction men serving as anesthesiologists and nurses, and while operating under the most primitive conditions in the ship's galley, the hand of the worker was saved with only slight loss of movement. This was the most serious injury that Dr.Kenler had to deal with during the expedition.

Sam - 1935

Brother Sam stayed in Midway

1935

I stayed on Wake

The top brass-I'm front row third from left

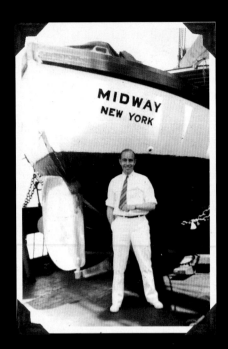

Dr.Kenler

Lueder-Midway

Bicknell-Wake

Station managers left to right Gregory-Guam,
Bicknell-Wake, Lueder-Midway, Dr.Kenler

Onboard the North Haven

Building temporary radio shack
for Wake

"Hula maidens" - Colonel George
Bicknell; Karl Lueder, with broom

First mate Pedersen
S.S. North Haven

During the three weeks that the North Haven was at Midway, Karl Lueder, the station manager at Midway, Col.George Bicknell, station manager at Wake and Dr. Kenler would spend the night on board the North Haven. During one of their evening talks, they began to discuss what souvenir flight covers would be appropriate to commemorate the survey flights to their remote island bases.

First flight cover collecting was quite popular in the mid 1930s and the Pan Am managers didn't want to miss the chance to prepare some unique covers for these historic flights. William Mullahey, the surfer and lifeguard from Honolulu, was something of an artist and he joined in their efforts to create an interesting design. They would each try their hand at a sketch - discuss the merits of each - then select the favorite - trace it on a wood block and give it a try. To fill time on board, many wood blocks were designed, carved and discarded in the process. By the time they departed Midway on May 1, 1935, three completed wood carved blocks were left on Midway with the station manager Karl Lueder. He promised to use the blocks to make souvenir covers and send the covers on to Dr. Kenler, Col. Bicknell and Bill Mullahey, who were going on to Wake island. The three designs are shown below.

Closed beak

*Cachet used on Midway survey flight covers*

Open beak

*Seen on only one cover on Midway survey flight*

*Used on August 1935 flight - Midway to Wake*

One of the three (the gooney bird with the open beak) has only been found on one Midway survey flight cover.

On May 1, 1935 the North Haven departed Midway for Wake Island leaving behind thirty-five construction workers, including Dr. Kenler's brother, Samuel, and twelve Pan Am personnel. When they arrived at Wake on May 9, Col. Bicknell, Dr. Kenler and William Mullahey again had time to sketch designs for the souvenir covers and to carve the cachet designs out of the wooden blocks. As on Midway, several different designs were carved into the wooden blocks for the Wake survey flight planned for August.

*Selected design for Wake survey flights*

*Rejected design*

The hermit crab design, inspired by the thousands of hermit crabs seen on Wake Island beaches, was rejected by the station manager for use on survey flight covers from Wake. Therefore, it has only been seen used on two envelopes from Wake. One of the envelopes with the hermit crab cachet was prepared

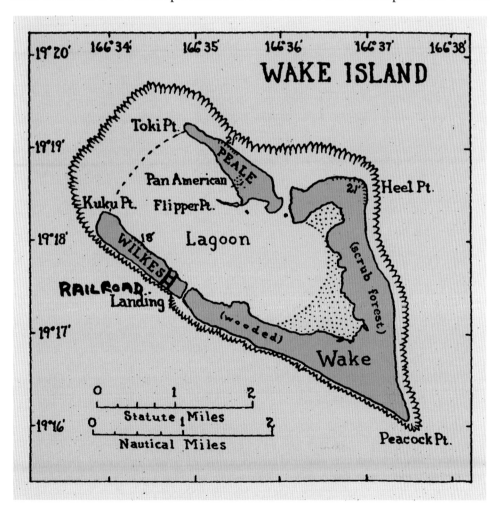

by the radio operator on Wake, Almon Gray, and sent back to himself at Pan Am's Alameda base on the August 1935 survey flight. The other hermit crab cachet envelope was on a personal letter mailed from Wake by the cachet's designer, William Mullahey.

These five different cachet designs were carved from wood blocks at Wake or Midway and applied at Wake or Midway by the men who designed them. All other cachet designs seen by collectors on the Midway and Wake survey flight covers were prepared and applied to the covers by the office staff at Pan Am's offices at Alameda, California or New York City.

At Wake, the sea plane base had been planned for Wilkes Island, but when Dr. Kepler and the other members of the landing party from the North Haven went ashore on Wilkes,

they found that driftwood had been thrown up from the ocean onto the area where they were to construct buildings, clearly indicating that water routinely washed over the area. So the site of the base was moved across the lagoon to Peale Island. A track was laid across Wilkes from the ocean to the lagoon to assist in getting supplies to the base being built on Peale. The workmen joked that the 300 foot Wake Island railroad was the shortest railroad in the world.

After it was decided to relocate the Pan Am buildings to Peale Island, rather than locate them on Wilkes Island as originally planned, it was necessary to do a new and much more accurate survey of previously uninhabited Wake Island. This July 31, 1935 survey was Pan Am's first detailed mapping of the island.

If you look carefully you can see that the channel they had to dig by hand into the cement-hard coral was two feet deep at high tide and 25 feet wide. A lot of sweat under the hot sun went into hand digging that barge channel. The path of the Wake Island railroad - the shortest railroad in the world - can also be seen.

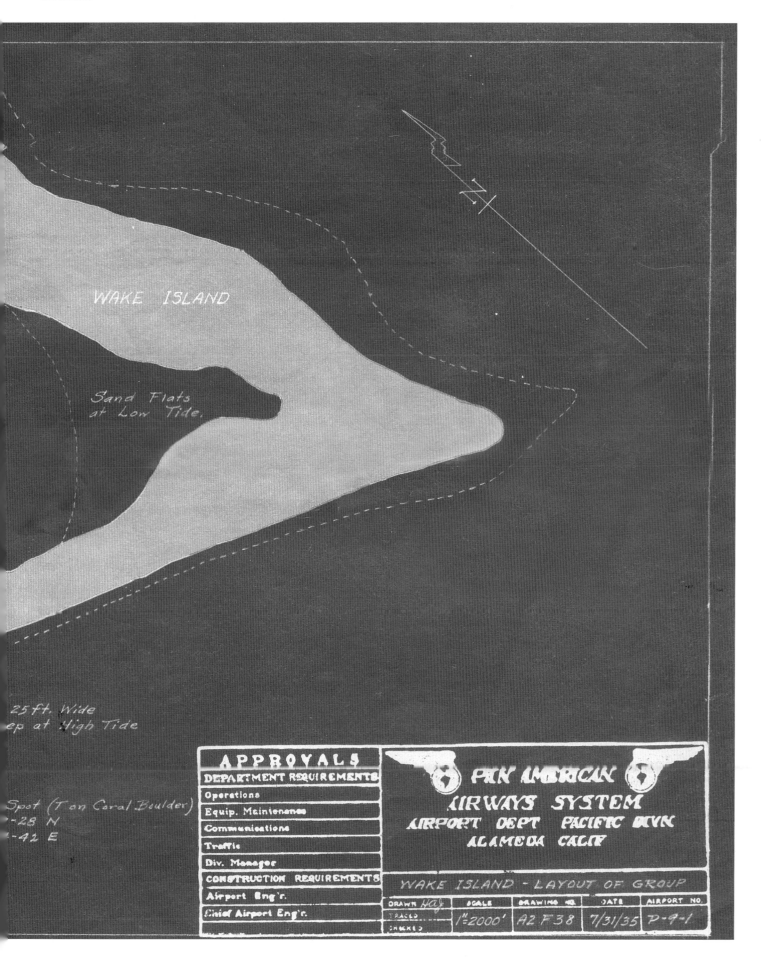

WAKE ISLAND

Sand Flats at Low Tide.

25 ft. Wide
ep at High Tide

Spot (T on Coral Boulder)
-28 N
-42 E

| APPROVALS | | | | |
|---|---|---|---|---|
| **DEPARTMENT REQUIREMENTS** | | | | |
| Operations | | | | |
| Equip. Maintenance | | | | |
| Communications | | | | |
| Traffic | | | | |
| Div. Manager | | | | |
| **CONSTRUCTION REQUIREMENTS** | | | | |
| Airport Eng'r. | | | | |
| Chief Airport Eng'r. | | | | |

**PAN AMERICAN AIRWAYS SYSTEM**
**AIRPORT DEPT   PACIFIC DIVN**
**ALAMEDA CALIF**

| WAKE ISLAND - LAYOUT OF GROUP | | | | |
|---|---|---|---|---|
| DRAWN Hay | SCALE | DRAWING NO. | DATE | AIRPORT NO. |
| TRACED | 1"=2000' | A2 F38 | 7/31/35 | P-9-1 |
| CHECKED | | | | |

Again, the North Haven had to anchor off Wake and the difficult and dangerous task of off loading equipment in the open ocean was repeated. After three weeks of back breaking work, on May 29, the North Haven left Wake for Guam and the Philippines, leaving behind 35 construction workers and 18 Pan Am support people, including Dr. Kenler. One of the first buildings completed by the construction crew was his infirmary, which was a small shack underneath one of the radio antennas in the middle of the tent village.

Wake railroad

Off loading supplies at Wake from North Haven

Dr Kenler's infirmary being barged across lagoon to Peale Island

Dr. Kenler's
Wake home

Wake Generator

Infirmary below radiotower

Airport office and radioroom

Wake - June 1935 - listening to broadcast of survey
flight to Midway

The Wake crew William Mullahey standing without tie.
I'm seated front Left

I took a picture of the entire Wake population - standing left
to right: Brewer; Neidiger; Woodbridge; Gray; Bicknell; Tatum;
Kuhn; Borger; Mullahey; Zeigler; McGill; Sitting: VanWye; Benny;
Stuhrman; Willinger; Makota; Sadler;

27

Going to lunch at Wake

Wake village November 1935

Wake beachcombers: George Kuhn with pipe;
John Borger, junior engineer; Colonel Bicknell,
airport manager; Walt Zeigler, chief mechanic.

Bill Mullahey cleaning
swimming goggles

Communications staff - KNBI - Wake - October 1935:
left to right: A.A. Gray, operator in charge; W. Brewer,
assistant; E.L. Stuhrman, direction finder engineer

Another view of
Wake village

Pan Am office
on Wake

Streets on Wake
with watertowers
in background

Movies at Wake

End of the day - Wake - 1935

On June 12 the second Pacific Pan Am Clipper survey flight under the command of Capt. Musick left San Francisco for Midway, where they were welcomed on June 15 by the Pan Am staff and the construction workers including Dr. Kenler's brother, Samuel, who had been left to complete the base at Midway.

The crew spent June 16 on Midway and then on June 17 they returned at 5:30 p.m. to Honolulu. To commemorate this first flight to Midway the hand carved cachet designed by station manager Karl Lueder, William Mullahey and Dr. Kenler was first used on souvenir flight covers.

In his scrapbook Dr. Kenler had saved about a dozen envelopes and letters from his eight months in the Pacific. As we sat and talked and got to know each other better, he took the old envelopes from the scrapbook where they had rested for almost 60 years and shared them with me one by one. Each cover was unique in some way. As he told me the story behind each cover, the excitement of his pioneering days with Pan Am came alive. He not only shared the covers with me, but he shared the personalities of those involved in making them and in making the survey flights. As he talked you could almost smell the salt air and hear the surf at Wake and Midway.

*Envelope to Sam Kenler stationed at Midway*

The first cover he showed me was posted May 15, 1935 at New York City, addressed to his brother, Sam Kenler in care of Pan American Airways, Honolulu, Hawaii. This letter undoubtedly arrived in Honolulu by regular ground and sea post to the Pan Am office in time to be placed aboard the June 15, 1935 survey flight from Honolulu to Midway. The Pan Am newsletter stated that about 20 pounds of mail was placed aboard the Clipper in Honolulu and delivered to the Pan Am staff and construction workers on Midway. When the letter arrived at Midway on the June survey flight, the gooney bird cachet was applied to show that it travelled on the Clipper. This appears to have been the only envelope that has been saved from that first inward flight.

The next item that Dr. Kenler shared with me was a menu for the meal served to the crew in celebration of their arrival, also utilizing the "gooney bird" cachet.

The staff at Midway was proud that they could serve the flight crew such an impressive meal - including the ice cream - on this remote island.

SOUVENIR MENUE.

FIRST FLIGHT

MIDWAY 35

JUNE 15, 1935. DINNER 6:P.M.

FRESH FRUIT COCKTAIL

GREEN OLIVES                    COLD SLAW

CREAM OF TOMATO SOUP

ENTREE

FILET MIGNON

STRING BEANS               POTATOES AU GRATIN

ICE CREAM                         CAKE

WINE                          COFFEE-TEA

NUTS&RAISINS

*Menu for dinners served to crew the evening they arrived at Midway June 15, 1935*

*Sam Kenler on Midway writes to his brother on Wake*

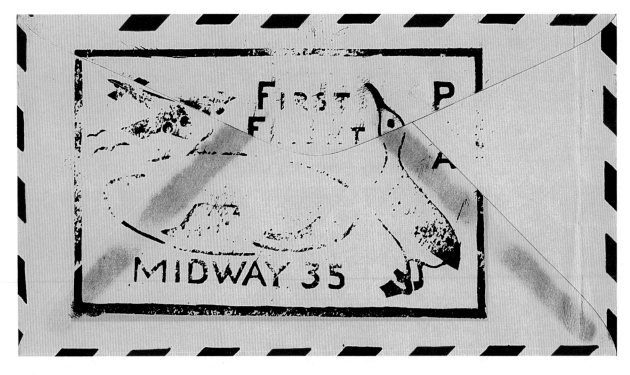

*Reverse*

The cover shown above is one of my favorites.

Sam Kenler, stationed on Midway, sent a letter to his brother, Dr. Kenler, stationed on Wake. The cover was flown back to Honolulu on June 17, 1935 by Clipper and sent on to Wake on the August 13, 1935 survey flight. It has to be the only surviving commercial mail between the two islands during this period. I wish the letter between the brothers had been saved, but the envelope tells a great story by itself.

A little over a month after departing, the North Haven reappeared off Wake and on July 3, 1935 picked up the construction workers to return them to their homes in Honolulu and the mainland. With the North Haven's departure the small group of 17 men settled into the quiet routine of isolated island life.

Blasting coral heads          Setting charges

One of the main tasks of the construction crew was to clear the lagoon of coral heads so that Clippers could land safely and taxi to the landing and boarding platform.

Bill Mullahey's September 7, 1935 letter in the envelope with the crab cachet states *"It's been a great trip all the way thru Midway and the early days at Wake. Am stationed at Wake for 6 or 8 months more ...Am still blasting coral heads out of the landing area in the lagoon, been at it over two months now - beginning to look like a lifetime job"*.

Dr. Kenler was in charge of the cooks and sanitation for Wake island. He also collected marine and insect specimens for the Bishop Museum and helped with the meteorological readings.

The third Pacific survey flight destined for Wake departed San Francisco on August 9, 1935 arriving at Wake on August 17. Captain Ed Musick was in Baltimore test flying the Martin M-130 in preparation for the first scheduled Transpacific flight in November. The Wake survey flight was under the command of Captain R.O.D. Sullivan, who had been the first officer on the first two survey flights. This was the first time Dr. Kenler had seen one of the great Clipper ships in flight and he described for me the thrill that he experienced in watching it settle gently onto the lagoon. This was also the first time that Dr. Kenler had gotten to meet other flight crew members who had made the first two survey flights to Honolulu and Midway.

Station manager Colonel George Bicknell got out the carved wooden block and prepared unofficial souvenir flight covers for the crew members, Pan Am staff and friends who were collecting the survey flight covers.

*Captain Sullivan was happy to sign the souvenir covers for Dr. Kenler*

*Front*

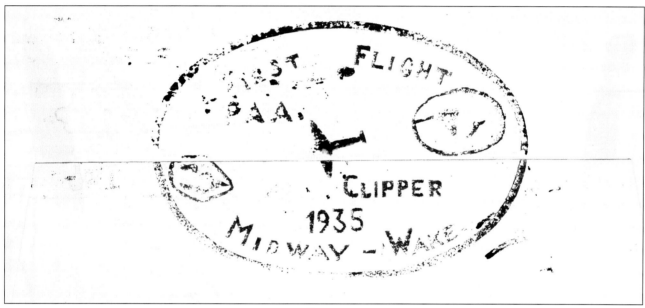

*Reverse*

The next cover in Dr. Kenler's scrapbook was the one that Karl Lueder promised he would send on the first flight from Midway to Wake, using the oval cachet that the men had designed for the first Midway to Wake flight

It carried no postage because it never went back to Honolulu and it was only a souvenir. Neither Wake nor Midway had any postal facilities at this time and for men making only $100 a month, there was no reason to waste three or six cents on needless postage stamps.

The fourth and final survey flight to Guam, again under the command of Captain Sullivan, left San Francisco on October 5, 1935. After several stops it arrived on Wake October 12. Dr. Kenler vividly recalled how happy they were to get the newspapers and mail at Wake. Unfortunately, none of this mail shipment from the Guam survey flight survived in his scrap book. On the return flight of the Guam survey flight to Wake, the Clipper was required to make a night landing and the landing lights were lit and ready for its arrival. Dr. Kenler related how excited they were when they spotted the approaching Clipper in the distance. After watching it for several minutes, they realized it wasn't moving. They were embarrassed to admit they had been watching Venus, thinking it was the Clipper ship, while the Clipper was still far out at sea. Minutes later the Clipper did appear and the first night landing of the Clipper in the Pacific went smoothly as the Pan Am clipper settled gently onto the water of the Wake Island lagoon.

By this time, Dr. Kenler was becoming bored with his isolated life on Wake. He felt that he was not advancing his medical training and that life was passing him by. He had been gone seven months and had been on Wake for almost five months. It was time to leave. So when Captain Sullivan departed Wake to return to California, Dr. Kenler gave him a personal letter to deliver to Pan Am back in San Francisco, asking if he could return to Honolulu on the first scheduled airmail flight which was to take place in November. He received word that his request had been granted, so he knew he had about a month to remain on Wake before returning to civilization.

The progress of the survey flights was being enthusiastically reported by the press and the excitement of the country heightened as the date approached for the first official airmail flight. By November of 1935 the nation's excitement was equal to what was experienced in the late 1960s when the first flights were being scheduled to the moon. It is estimated that over 125,000 people lined the banks of San Francisco harbor on November 22, 1935 when the new Martin M-130 China Clipper, now under the command of Captain Musick, took off from San Francisco for the first scheduled flight across the Pacific. The radio announcement of the departure was carried live nationwide.

On Tuesday, November 26 at 1:30 p.m. the Martin M-130 came into view over Wake Island. Minutes later it settled smoothly onto the lagoon and taxied up to the pier; Dr. Kenler was among the welcoming party along with all the Pan Am personnel. He described the sight as overwhelming. The China Clipper was larger and sleeker than anything they had seen in their lives. Friendships were renewed with First Officer Sullivan, Navigation Officer Noonan and the other crew members who had flown on the two previous survey flights to Wake and Guam. Dr. Kenler found Ed Musick to be as serious as he had been described. His nick names of "Uncle Ed" and the "Jeweler" for his serious nature and meticulous preparation had been well earned. The crew was smartly dressed. The station manager at Wake, Col. Bicknell, and the entire staff were outfitted in their white dress uniforms. The island had the air of a military installation.

Because the China Clipper would be leaving early the next morning, Dr. Kenler had to take care of his souvenir covers the afternoon of the Clipper's arrival.

This is the first time he had to concern himself with postal rates. The rate had been established as 25 cents for each of the three legs between the mainland and Honolulu, Guam and Manila. Dr. Kenler's pay was less than 50 cents an hour so he did not want to be wasting his limited income by over posting his souvenir covers. He also had never seen the stamp that was issued for the first flight covers and he was able to purchase the ones he needed from the crew. His souvenir covers were carefully prepared and addressed and freshly stamped with the new commemorative Clipper stamp sold by the crew to Dr. Kenler. This small collection of flight covers prepared by Dr. Kenler may be unique because they were posted from Wake Island rather than the regular post offices and because they were also personally mailed by Captain Musick.

The cover given to Captain Musick mailed Guam to Wake was posted from Guam and received by Dr. Kenler on Wake Island.

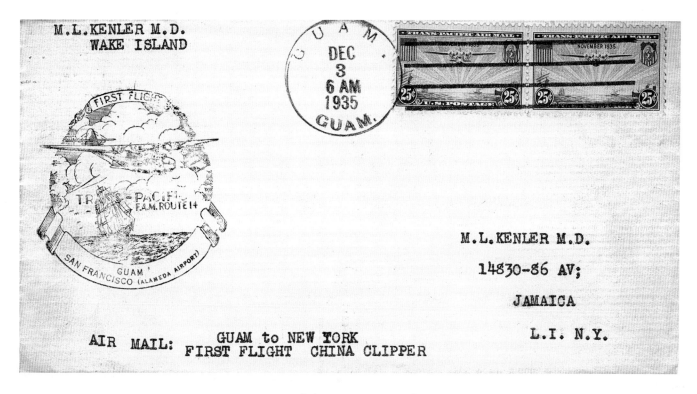

*Mailed Guam to New York*

The last of the covers posted by Captain Musick for Dr. Kenler was sent from Guam to the doctor's home on Long Island, New York. It too carried the correct postage of two 25 cent stamps for the two official legs that it was flown.

Meeting Captain Musick at Wake on east bound flight

Colonel Bicknell on left, Captain Musick center, Dr. Kenler on right

When Dr. Kenler departed Wake for the return flight to Honolulu at 6:45 a.m. on December 4, 1935 he carried an envelope with him for writing a letter to his family while in flight.

Imagine the excitement felt by a young man who was now flying as one of the world's first passengers on a scheduled Transpacific flight back to his family. He is clearly filled with awe and wonder as he writes. Take a moment and share that excitement with him.

Dr. Kenler's December 5, 1935 letter home.

December 5, 1935

*Darlings- all of you-*

*Progress in speed has assumed regular scheduled transportation over these former vast expanses of water. Indeed it was a privilege and pleasure to return aboard the China Clipper on it's maiden voyage, It somewhat compensates the trials and difficulties experienced creating the mid-Pacific bases, making this remarkable voyage possible. Too, this trip finally took me out of the isolated tropical dot of land in the great ocean.*

*Strange as it may seem, I left Wake Island at sunrise on December 4th, flew 1150 miles over the ocean among the clouds and reached Midway on December 3rd. The day before I left. Then next morning aboard the famous giant liner to home 1250 miles to the Hawaiian Islands. Arriving in the late afternoon of December 4, 1935. I did not send a cable or radiogram particularly to keep some of you from worrying. And with the present air mail service this should reach you only one day behind cable service. After being away for  months, a few more hours will make little difference.*

*As a matter of fact, I have decided to spend a week on these islands for a little vacation among humans again, just to get used to clothes, people, autos, stores, etc. Will write you from the ship when I leave Hawaii for California. At that time will tell you more. May as well make a grand spree of it now. For once I settle down God knows when the next carefree vacation will present itself.*

*A word about the giant airliner. No doubt you have read considerably about it in the newspapers. The China Clipper is the flying miniature hotel weighing about 61,000 pounds loaded. There is room for about 50 passengers. It accommodates 16 large size berths. There are arrangements for complete steward service. The lounge room is large - over 6 feet of head clearance. Comfortable seating in club room style. Very spacious. Free to walk about. Noise of motors diminished to a hum so that conversation is easily carried on in a voice not much louder than normal talk.*

*So the great history making period is about over. I have made several acquaintances at these islands and expect to have a nice vacation at my own expense. From now on my return voyage will be in the leisurely service manner, either boat or train. Regards to all.*

*Love, Ken*

The China Clipper arrived in Honolulu from Midway at 3:02 p.m. on Wednesday, December 4, 1935. The mail was off loaded and taken to the Honolulu post office, where it was posted the next afternoon, December 5 at 2:00 p.m. in time to be put on the continuation flight of the China Clipper scheduled for departure at 3:00 p.m. Thursday, December 5. On December 8 it arrived in New York at the Penn Terminal and was stamped in at 3:30 p.m. Even though it was a Sunday, because it was special delivery, it was taken immediately to the Jamaica, Long Island post office, where it arrived just an hour and a half later for a 5:00 p.m. date stamp. A letter that left Wake Island on Wednesday, December 4, 1935, was delivered on Long Island four days later. This is a feat that would be hard to duplicate today and was absolutely astonishing in 1935.

Dec 1935 - Ready to leave Wake island

Leaving Honolulu 1935

ARRIVE Pearl Harbor Dec 1935

# Tropical Isle Thrills Trail-Blazing Doctor

ISLAND DOCTOR

## Dr. Myron L. Kenler of Jamaica Discovers on Return From Wake Island That He's Just Beginning to Enjoy Experiences

### By LEW SHEAFFER

For an hour the words of Dr. Myron L. Kenler had been of strange deep sea fish, of quick tropical squalls and far-away Pacific islands. He was obviously unaware of the chill January rain beating against the window of his home at 148-30 86th Ave., Jamaica, last night as told of his experiences on Wake Island in the middle of the Pacific.

"Do you know," he said with a puzzled smile," I'm just beginning to enjoy my seven-month stay on that island."

He had talked with pleasurable gusto of his experience and it was with surprise that he realized the excitement that the reminiscing brought. He has just returned home from a position as staff physician to the expedition sent out by the Pan American Airways line to establish island bases for the trans-pacific service recently established.

### Found It a Strange Life

"Why, I wasn't a tenth as excited when I faced the prospect of going," Dr. Kenler said, "as I feel now in thinking of my time out there.

"It was a strange life, but we were too busy working during the expedition to think of the excitement or glamour. Of course, there was much that we enjoyed at the time it happened. But the scene of work changed so rapidly for a while and things happened in such quick order that we lived for the day—the hour, more truthfully.

"The voyage from Honolulu to Wake Island took us 15 days on the North Haven, a freighter of the air line. But the same distance was made on the return trip in about 17 hours. I came back with the China Clipper on her maiden flight from the Philippines.

"The airship raced time and won. Leaving Wake Island on Dec. 4, the plane arrived at Midway Island, over 1,100 miles away, on Dec. 3. The joker is that the international date line is crossed during the flight and a day gained."

### Found Barren Isle

A barren coral island with scrubby brush and jagged boulders greeted the expeditionary ship when she anchored off the Wake Island last Spring.

"But the place was well on the way to being completely organized by the time I left in December," the doctor said. "An electric generating plant, repair shop, mess hall, quarters for the employes, storage huts, all are up now and even a clinic, which I built and is still standing."

"It wasn't all work, though," he continued. "The men were generally through with their work by 4 or 4:30 in the afternoon and they had their choice of baseball, horse shoes, ping pong and, of course, swimming. We had no trouble from the sharks, which were plentiful, but only because we were careful. One man stood on watch when the others were in the water. And some of the men carried knives with them while swimming.

### Moaning Birds at Midway

"A popular sport was fish-spearing. The fish were very plentiful and we would dive underwater, wearing goggles, of course, to spear them. Another recreation—this will be surprising—was talking pictures. We had full equipment and showed movies twice a week.

"When we stopped off at Midway Island we had a bad time of it with a type of bird known as the "moaning bird." Its cry sounds exactly like the crying and wailing of a person at a wake. A superstition popular among South Sea islanders is that the souls of drowned sailors are embodied in the birds.

"But all that seems far away now. I'm returning in a few days to my post as clinic assistant at Wyckoff

The leis gives the scene away as Honolulu. Dr. Kenler was on the way out to Wake Island.

Heights Hospital and intend to open an office shortly here in Jamaica."

A graduate of Richmond Hill School, Dr. Kenler was graduated from John Hopkins University and the University of Maryland. Before taking the position with the Pan American expedition, he was an interne at the Wyckoff Heights institution. He has worked for the health department of Baltimore as assistant city obstetrician and was interne for a time at Jamaica Hospital. He lives at the Jamaica address with his sisters, Mrs. Molly Sorkin and Rose Kenler.

*The local newspapers reported his return.*

When Dr. Kenler entrusted me with these unique envelopes, I promised him that I would try to make them come alive for other collectors, as his stories and scrapbook made his adventures come alive for me. I am sorry that he will be unable to share in the excitement once again, but I do hope that with this book I have kept my promise to him and that the retelling of his story makes the adventure of the first Pacific flights memorable for all of you.

Dr. Kenler was a kind and gentle man, who enjoyed bringing happiness to others. He is greatly missed by his family and remembered with love by those who knew him.

44

# CHAPTER TWO
# AIRCRAFT THAT BRIDGED THE PACIFIC

When Pan Am was founded in October of 1927, airplanes were small, primitive machines and airports were merely grassy pastures on the outskirts of towns.

Juan Trippe, the founder of Pan Am, knew that passenger service would never flourish until aircraft were big and roomy so that passengers would feel safe and comfortable. He also knew, when others didn't, that the future of aviation was not in mail, or cargo, but in carrying passengers. So with his vision of transoceanic travel, he challenged the aviation manufacturers to build bigger and more comfortable aircraft to serve this untapped market.

Although the aircraft industry was ready to build larger aircraft, air fields did not exist that could handle these heavier and more spacious planes. However, large harbors existed throughout the world and the large flying boats could use these protected harbors for their take offs and landings. The giant Clipper ship, half boat/half plane was conceived to meet the need for world wide travel before airports had been developed. Pan Am's ability to develop its Pacific air routes from 1935 to 1941 was made possible by three great models of seaplanes, each a significant improvement over its predecessor.

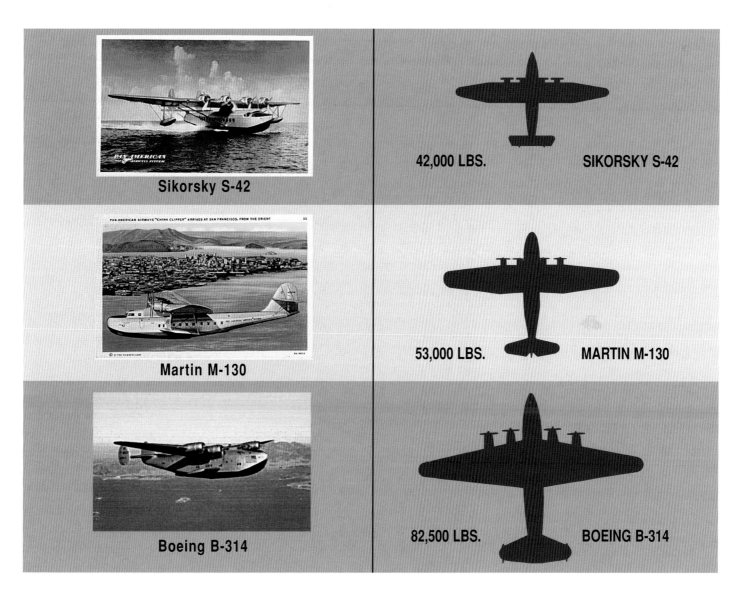

Sikorsky S-42

42,000 LBS.        SIKORSKY S-42

Martin M-130

53,000 LBS.        MARTIN M-130

Boeing B-314

82,500 LBS.        BOEING B-314

# SIKORSKY S-42

The Sikorsky S-42 was built by Igor Sikorsky, an immigrant from the Ukraine, who fled to the United States during the Bolshevik revolution in 1917. He was an aeronautical engineer and his dream was to build big airplanes. By 1923 he had the financial backing to form the Sikorsky Aero Engineering Corporation. In early 1929 Pan Am contracted with Sikorsky to build the S-40, Pan Am's first four engine amphibian airplane, and by November of 1931 it flew its maiden flight with passengers aboard to Panama, with Charles A. Lindbergh at the controls.

*S-42 about to break clear of water*

Shortly after Charles Lindbergh completed his epic solo flight across the Atlantic, Juan Trippe asked him to become involved with Pan Am, both as a pilot and as a technical advisor. What Trippe really wanted was Lindbergh's star quality. He knew that Lindbergh's value in public relations far exceeded whatever salary Pan Am would have to pay the young aviator. Lindbergh rightly believed that Trippe shared his passion for aviation and that through Pan Am he could best promote commercial flight. Therefore, he passed up many higher paying offers to work with Pan Am in an advisory capacity. The salary was $10,000 a year plus stock options for 10,000 shares of Pan Am stock at $15 per share and 30,000 shares at $30 a share. Although no one could have predicted it at the time, the stock options ultimately made Lindbergh financially independent. His presence undoubtedly helped Pan Am in the company's development. Lindbergh began what became a lifelong relationship with Pan Am and by the early 1960's he was a director who enjoyed flying around the world each year on Juan Trippe's annual inspection flight conducted for the directors.

Trippe, however, was always the astute businessman. He was fearful that if anything happened to Lindbergh while working for Pan Am, a resulting lawsuit could wipe out the corporation. Therefore, before the deal was finalized, Trippe had a letter agreement drafted that Lindbergh was required to sign before he became a technical advisor, waiving any legal claims against Pan Am in the event of injury related to his work. Trippe even went so far as to change the rather vague language, "suggesting" that no lawsuit would be filed, to the stronger statement that "Lindbergh states" that no lawsuit would be filed in the event Lindbergh was injured or killed while working for Pan Am.

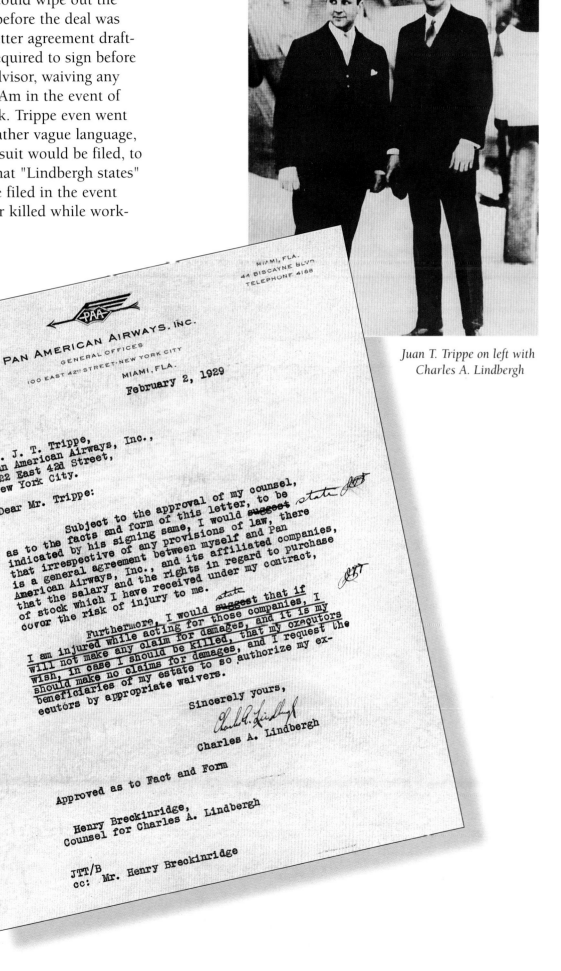

*Juan T. Trippe on left with Charles A. Lindbergh*

*Pan Am issued card - 1929 showing Lindbergh as "Technical advisor to Pan Am"*

*First commercial airmail flight to the Canal Zone flown by Charles Lindbergh – two days after signing the letter waiving any claim if an accident resulted while working for Pan Am*

*Postcard of Lindbergh flown from Canal Zone to Miami on the return flight of the first airmail flight flown by Lindbergh for Pan Am*

Pictured is a young Charles Lindbergh with his new wife, Anne Morrow Lindbergh. They both signed a picture to William VanDusen, Pan Am's public relations director. The innocence in their faces would soon disappear with the constant pressure of the press, and later with the kidnapping of their young son.

Lindbergh test flew the S-40 and in his capacity as a technical advisor, he worked with Sikorsky on the specifications for the next generation of Clippers.

In 1931, with the help of Lindbergh, Pan Am issued specifications for a transoceanic flying boat and asked the airline manufacturers for bids. Only two bids were submitted, one from Sikorsky for the S-42 and one from the Glenn Martin Aviation Corporation of Baltimore, Maryland, for the Martin M-130. When faced with the two bids, Trippe decided to accept both of them. So in early 1932 contracts were entered into with Sikorsky to build three of the Sikorsky S-42s and with Martin to build three Martin M-130s.

*Prototype of S-42 - December 1932*

By December of 1932, Sikorsky had begun work on the prototype of the S-42. In a press release of December 11, 1932, Pan Am's public relations department stated:

*Clipper Ships for Trans-oceanic Travel – the Sikorsky model S-42, of the new trans-oceanic "Clipper Ships" which had been designed for Pan Am Airways on specifications of Colonel Charles A. Lindbergh, head of the Pan American Airways technical committee. The model was designed after 18 months of work and is specifically designed for possible trans-oceanic travel with passengers, airmail and freight. The four motored plane will be able to carry 50 passengers. The seaplane is tremendously advanced over any transport craft so far developed and will carry the hopes of this country's aviation industry to win back for the U.S. the "blue ribbon" of the Merchant Marine Service.*

*S-42 at liftoff*

*S-42 departing San Francisco with Oakland Bay Bridge below.*

By 1934 the Sikorsky S-42 was ready for its test flights but the Martin M-130 was still nine months behind the S-42 in development. Although the Martin M-130 was clearly the aircraft best suited for the Pacific flights, Trippe was impatient and he could not wait for its completion. Therefore in April of 1935 the first of the Pacific survey flights was flown in the Sikorsky S-42 from San Francisco to Honolulu.

*Cutaway view of S-42*

Fully loaded for passenger service, the Sikorsky S-42 carried 32 passengers and a crew of five, with a range of 1200 miles. Equipped with extra fuel tanks for the Pacific survey flights and limited to an 800 pound payload and without a stiff head wind the range could be stretched to 3,000 miles - enough to reach Hawaii, the longest leg of the Transpacific route. Eight fuel tanks held a total of 1,240 gallons of fuel. The standard crew of five called for two pilots, an engineer, a radio operator and a steward. For the survey flights a junior flight officer and a navigator were added and the steward omitted. The craft was powered by four Pratt & Whitney Hornet engines. Its contract price was $242,000 equal to at least $4,000,000 today.

To meet the rugged conditions of ocean flight, Sikorsky designed the S-42 with high wing loading of 30 pounds per square foot, because his studies had shown that the heavy loading gave greater stability in rough weather. However, this heavy wing loading produced difficult takeoffs and fast landings that Sikorsky tried to minimize by a large wing flap configuration.

54:-PAN-AMERICAN CLIPPER. BALTIMORE. MD. TO BERMUDA

47336

A "Clipper Ship of the Sky"

Clipper Over the Ocean

*Postcards of S-42-round windows and twin tail fins identify the S-42*

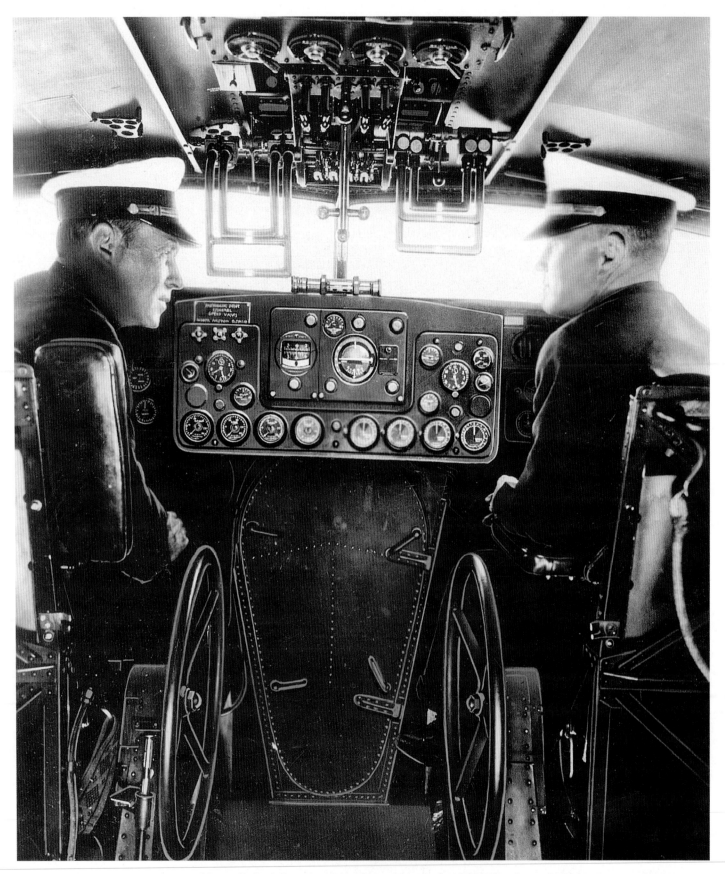

*Captain Musick on the left and first officer Sullivan on the right at the controls of the Sikorsky S-42 Pan American Clipper in preparation for the first Pacific survey flight*

Captain Musick commanded the first flight to Hawaii in April of 1935 and the next flight to Midway in June of 1935 in this aircraft. Captain Sullivan took over command on the third survey flight to Wake in August and the fourth survey flight to Guam in October of 1935. At the time of the Wake and Guam survey flights, Captain Musick was in Baltimore, awaiting delivery of the Martin M-130 that would make the first airmail flight across the Pacific in November of 1935.

When completed in March of 1934, the Sikorsky S-42 was the largest aircraft ever built in the United States. In one series of test flights with Lindbergh, and Pan Am's chief pilot, Edwin Musick, and Igor Sikorsky, 10 world speed and altitude records were set.

*Licensing of S-42 at Bridgeport Connecticut, March 1934. Pictured L to R - Captain Edwin Musick, Andre Priester - Pan Am's chief engineer, Charles Lindbergh - Juan Trippe - President Pan Am, Igor Sikorsky, E.L. Vidal, director of U.S. Air Commerce Dept. and F. R. Neilson, president of Sikorsky Aircraft*

*Signed by crew-Charles Lindbergh, Edwin Musick and Boris Sergievsky*

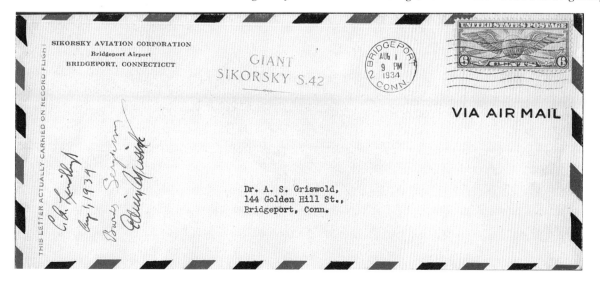

A different model, the S-42B, with slightly longer wings and other modifications to increase the range, flew the survey flights to New Zealand in March of 1937. Even with these changes the S-42 configuration simply had too low a payload for the long range Pacific flights. Of the ten S-42s delivered to Pan Am, only three would ever serve in the Pacific. In the Pacific the S-42s were used either for survey flights without passengers or for the short Manila to Hong Kong shuttle flights where long range and high pay loads were not necessary.

*Specifications for the S-42B- the S-42B made the survey flights to New Zealand in 1937*

*NC 16734 Pan American Clipper II/ Hong Kong Clipper/ Samoan Clipper - at Sikorsky's Bridgeport, Connecticut factory*

*Travel agent's desk model of Sikorsky S-42*

The die cast highly detailed model of the Sikorsky S-42 was distributed by Pan Am to its travel agents across the country. The soft glow from its interior light was intended to excite the traveler of the mid 1930s with visions of palm trees and Caribbean beaches.

The last of the Sikorsky S-42s with their proud wings removed ended their careers as houseboats along the Miami River. Unfortunately, not a single aircraft was saved for history.

# The three Sikorsky S-42s serving in the Pacific

| MODEL AIRCRAFT | REGISTRATION | OTHER NAMES | DELIVERY |
|---|---|---|---|
| S-42 Pan American Clipper | NC 823M | West Indies Clipper | December 1934 |

Initially christened the West Indies Clipper, it went into service in 1934. In 1935 it was renamed the American Clipper, flown to the Pacific and was modified with on board fuel tanks to increase its range. It was then used for the four survey flights starting in April of 1935 with the first survey flight to Honolulu, followed in June by the flight to Midway, in August to Wake, and in October to Guam. After completing these survey flights it was returned to the Caribbean and it sank at Antilla, Cuba on August 7, 1944.

| MODEL AIRCRAFT | REGISTRATION | OTHER NAMES | DELIVERY |
|---|---|---|---|
| S-42B Pan Am Clipper II | NC 16734 | Hong Kong Clipper April 1937<br><br>Samoan Clipper December 1937 | September 1936 |

Originally christened the Pan Am Clipper II, the new S-42B model had slightly longer wings and a greatly increased fuel capacity than the original S-42 model. It was specifically designed for the survey flights to New Zealand. It made the first successful flight to New Zealand in March of 1937. In April of 1937, it was renamed the Hong Kong Clipper and it was used to complete the last leg of the San Francisco to Hong Kong flights by flying the Manila to Hong Kong route. In December of 1937 it was brought back to Honolulu and was renamed the Samoan Clipper. In December of 1937 it made the second flight to New Zealand under the command of Capt. Musick. By agreement, twice monthly service was to be maintained after that date. Unfortunately on the next flight, which was the third flight to New Zealand, after taking off from the harbor at Pago Pago, American Samoa, it developed a fuel leak and while attempting to dump fuel and return to Samoa, an explosion occurred and the plane and its entire crew under the command of Capt. Musick was lost on January 11, 1938.

| MODEL AIRCRAFT | REGISTRATION | OTHER NAMES | DELIVERY |
|---|---|---|---|
| S-42B Hong Kong Clipper II | NC 16735 | Bermuda Clipper | September 1936 |

Christened the Bermuda Clipper, it flew the New York to Bermuda run until 1940 when it was transferred briefly to Alaska. In September 1941 it was transferred to the Manila to Hong Kong shuttle route and re-christened the Hong Kong Clipper II. At the outbreak of WW II on December 8, 1941 it was moored in the Hong Kong harbor, where it was destroyed by enemy fire.

# MARTIN M-130

Even as Trippe was awarding a contract for the building of Sikorsky S-42, he realized that for transoceanic flight to be financially successful, Pan Am needed a faster craft with greater range, and more importantly, far greater long range payload capacity.

*Classic Clyde Sunderland photo of China Clipper above San Francisco.*

Basically Pan Am wanted an aircraft that had the capacity to carry a payload equal to its weight, for a distance of 3,000 miles, far enough to reach either Hawaii or Europe. In response to these specifications, Glenn Martin Aviation Corporation of Baltimore, Maryland designed and developed the Martin M-130. It had an overall length of 90 feet and a wing span of 130 feet. Four Pratt & Whitney Wasp engines provided its power.

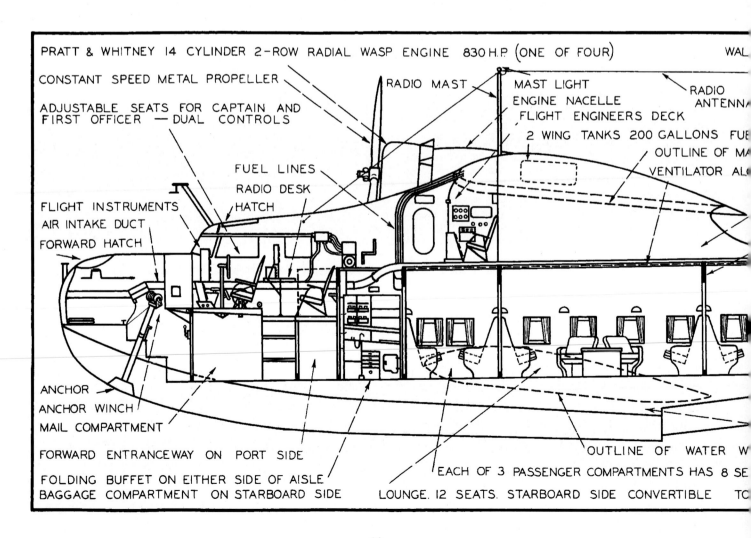

PRATT & WHITNEY 14 CYLINDER 2-ROW RADIAL WASP ENGINE 830 H.P. (ONE OF FOUR)          WAL

CONSTANT SPEED METAL PROPELLER          RADIO MAST          MAST LIGHT          RADIO
                                                            ENGINE NACELLE          ANTENNA
ADJUSTABLE SEATS FOR CAPTAIN AND                            FLIGHT ENGINEERS DECK
FIRST OFFICER — DUAL CONTROLS                               2 WING TANKS 200 GALLONS FUE

                        FUEL LINES                                    OUTLINE OF MA

                        RADIO DESK                                    VENTILATOR AL

FLIGHT INSTRUMENTS      HATCH

AIR INTAKE DUCT

FORWARD HATCH

ANCHOR

ANCHOR WINCH

MAIL COMPARTMENT

FORWARD ENTRANCEWAY ON PORT SIDE                    OUTLINE OF WATER W

FOLDING BUFFET ON EITHER SIDE OF AISLE          EACH OF 3 PASSENGER COMPARTMENTS HAS 8 SE

BAGGAGE COMPARTMENT ON STARBOARD SIDE       LOUNGE. 12 SEATS. STARBOARD SIDE CONVERTIBLE      TO

*Cutaway View of Martin M-130*

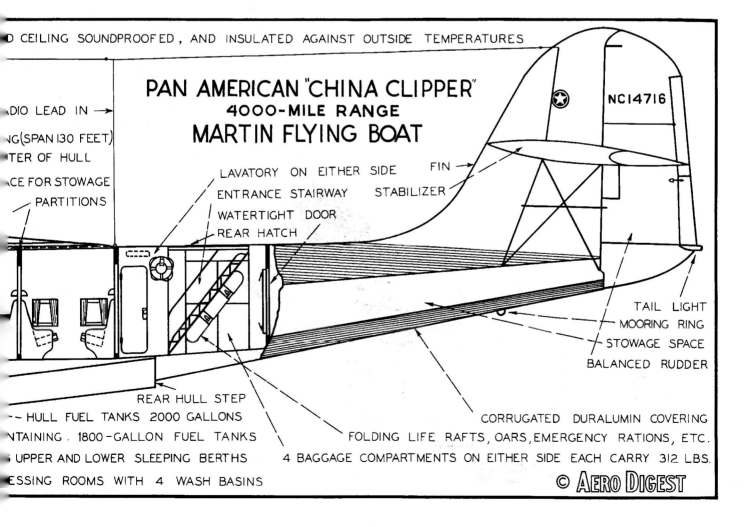

D CEILING SOUNDPROOFED, AND INSULATED AGAINST OUTSIDE TEMPERATURES

PAN AMERICAN "CHINA CLIPPER"
4000-MILE RANGE
MARTIN FLYING BOAT

NC14716

DIO LEAD IN →

NG (SPAN 130 FEET)

TER OF HULL

CE FOR STOWAGE

PARTITIONS

LAVATORY ON EITHER SIDE    FIN →
ENTRANCE STAIRWAY    STABILIZER
WATERTIGHT DOOR
REAR HATCH

TAIL LIGHT
MOORING RING
STOWAGE SPACE
BALANCED RUDDER

REAR HULL STEP

HULL FUEL TANKS 2000 GALLONS

NTAINING . 1800-GALLON FUEL TANKS

UPPER AND LOWER SLEEPING BERTHS

ESSING ROOMS WITH 4 WASH BASINS

CORRUGATED DURALUMIN COVERING
FOLDING LIFE RAFTS, OARS, EMERGENCY RATIONS, ETC.
4 BAGGAGE COMPARTMENTS ON EITHER SIDE EACH CARRY 312 LBS.

© AERO DIGEST

*Interior of Martin M-130*
    *During a stopover in Hawaii on the first revenue passenger flight in October of 1936, Charles Lindbergh chatted with passenger and world traveler, Clara Adams. Fellow passenger, Lewis Weinzheimer, who joined the flight in Honolulu, is also pictured.*

*Private passenger cabin of M-130*

*Dining in comfort on the M-130*

*At Martin plant, Middle River Maryland. Rear, left to right: Unknown, Ralph Dahlstrom, Sam P. Crago, Captain Edwin Musick, William Miller, Ralph Belcher, Chan Wright, flight engineer*
*Front: T. Ray Runnells, Radio Operator, Floyd Penning, J.C. McCarty, Martin project engineer*

Over a year behind schedule, on October 9, 1935, the Martin Aviation Corporation finally delivered the China Clipper to Pan Am at its Baltimore factory in Middle River, Maryland. Pictured at Middle River just before a test flight on October 7, 1935, are the following from left to right: Unknown, Ralph Dahlstrom (Pan Am captain), Sam Crago (Pan Am mechanic), Captain Edwin Musick (Pan Am's chief pilot), William Miller (CAA representative), Ralph Belcher (division engineer), Chan Wright (flight engineer).

Front kneeling: T.R. Runnells (Pan Am radio operator), Floyd Penning, J.C. McCarty (the Martin project engineer for the M-130).

After testing was completed, Pan Am formally accepted the China Clipper and it was flown on October 9, 1935 to Miami for an overnight stay.

*Martin M-130 at Miami*

The M-130 had spacious and luxurious accommodations for 46 day passengers or 18 to 30 passengers overnight with berths for sleeping. The crew size was seven. Each wing carried 950 gallons of fuel and other tanks brought the total fuel capacity up to 4,000 gallons. The contract called for a total of three planes to be delivered in 1934 at a cost of $430,000 each. This was a remarkable sum in 1934 - it was five times more than the cost of the largest contemporary airliner built at the time - the Douglas DC-2 and it was almost twice as much as the Sikorsky S-42 being developed at the same time for Pan Am.

*Cockpit of M-130-Captain Musick on left*

Even though the Sikorsky S-42s were successfully completing the four survey flights across the Pacific between April and October of 1935, regularly scheduled Pacific flights could not take place until the Martin M-130 was ready to make the flights.

*China Clipper - Miami*

Pictured is the China Clipper at Pan Am's Dinner Key facility, which was Pan Am's Miami base and Pan Am's gateway to Central and South America for all of the Clipper flights. Its arrival created a lot of local excitement and crowds lined the seawalls to get a glimpse of the new giant of the skies.

After leaving Miami the China Clipper flew to Acapulco, Mexico. After an overnight stop it proceeded up the west coast of Mexico, for an overnight stopover at Los Angeles, California.

*Welcoming ceremonies – San Pedro Harbor near Los Angeles – November 10, 1935*

Pictured is the China Clipper at the Los Angeles Terminal Island base in San Pedro Harbor. Los Angeles held a welcoming ceremony for the Clipper upon its arrival. The next day the China Clipper flew on to San Francisco to begin the final preparations for the first scheduled Transpacific flight in aviation history.

Merry Christmas from.
"The Gang"
Alameda, California
Dec 25, 1936.

Pictured is the maintenance and operations personnel for Pan Am in Alameda in 1936. This group picture did not include the management people or the office staff. It is hard to imagine that it required this many people at the Alameda base, just to keep three aircraft flying the Pacific. When we also consider that sizable crews were maintained in Honolulu, Midway, Wake, Guam and Manila, it is easy to understand why the Pacific operations were not profitable for Pan Am in the early years.

*Hawaii Clipper at Alameda –
platform used to remove the craft
from the water*

*Close up of the platform used to
remove the Clipper from the water*

*Boarding China Clipper at Honolulu – 1937 (note the broad red stripe on the wing rearward)
The stripe was added to commemorate the first flight to Hong Kong in April 1937*

*Routine maintenance and servicing of the China Clipper*

*China Clipper at Honolulu – November 23, 1935*

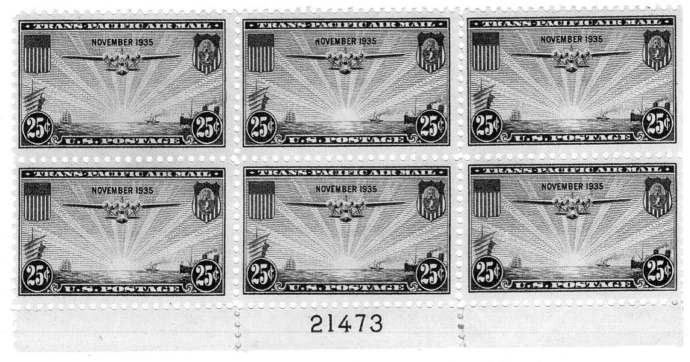

*Postage stamps issued especially for November 22, 1935 first flight of China Clipper*

A month after the China Clipper was delivered to Pan Am, Martin Aviation delivered the second M-130, the Philippine Clipper. Now that Pan Am had two aircraft in readiness, they were prepared to announce the November 1935 departure date for the long anticipated Transpacific flight.

The Post Office Department issued a special Clipper stamp in anticipation of the first scheduled air mail. The rate per half ounce was 25 cents to Honolulu, 50 cents to Guam, and 75 cents to Manila in the Philippines.

Due to the publicity generated by the first four survey flights, the American public was excited and collectors of flight covers were sending hundreds of thousands of letters to Pan Am to be carried on the flight. On November 22, 1935, with great pomp and formality and with 150,000 people watching, the China Clipper departed its Alameda base for its first Transpacific flight.

The Glenn Martin Corporation claimed to have lost money on the initial order of three aircraft, but with the successful flights they were confident that a reorder would make the development of the Martin M-130 profitable, but the reorder never occurred.

*Postcards of the China Clipper*

Tragically, all three of the Martin M-130s were lost in crashes. First the Hawaii Clipper disappeared after departing Guam for Manila in July of 1938. It was always suspected but never confirmed that the aircraft had been highjacked or shot down by the Japanese.

Secondly, on January 21, 1943 the Philippine Clipper on service to the Navy, was being flown with a Pan Am crew when it hit a California mountain in foggy weather, with the loss of all aboard.

The China Clipper, after the start of the war was transferred from the Pacific back to Miami in 1943. On January 8, 1945, while on a flight from Miami to Africa by way of Trinidad, the China Clipper hit a submerged object and sank while attempting to land in the harbor at Port of Spain, Trinidad. The last of the Martin M-130s was removed from the harbor to the scrap yard and cut up for salvage-a sad end for each of these three historic pioneers.

# The three Martin M-130s serving in the Pacific

| MODEL AIRCRAFT | REGISTRATION | OTHER NAME | DELIVERY |
|---|---|---|---|
| M-130 China Clipper | NC 14716 | | Oct. 9, 1935 |

The China Clipper's maiden flight was the first scheduled Transpacific flight on November 22, 1935. The China Clipper was also used for the press flight in October of 1936 and the first scheduled mail flight to Hong Kong in April of 1937. At the outbreak of WW II the China Clipper was transferred to the Caribbean and on a scheduled flight to Africa, it sank at Port of Spain, Trinidad on January 8, 1945. When it sank it was the last of the three Martins still in operation.

| MODEL AIRCRAFT | REGISTRATION | OTHER NAME | DELIVERY |
|---|---|---|---|
| M-130 Philippine Clipper | NC 14715 | | Nov. 14, 1935 |

The Philippine Clipper made the second of the scheduled airmail flights across the Pacific on December 9, 1935. It was also used on the VIP flight with Juan Trippe on board, which made the first flight into Hong Kong in October of 1936. On December 7, 1941 it was leaving Wake when it learned of the attack on Pearl Harbor. It returned to Wake to pick up Pan Am staff, was caught on the lagoon and hit several times by enemy fire, but was still able to depart. In their haste to leave, they left one Pan Am employee on Wake, who was ultimately taken prisoner. At the outbreak of WW II it continued to make the Honolulu to San Francisco run. On a flight to California on January 21, 1943 in bad weather, it hit a mountain and all on board were killed.

| MODEL AIRCRAFT | REGISTRATION | OTHER NAME | DELIVERY |
|---|---|---|---|
| M-130 Hawaii Clipper | NC 14714 | Hawaiian Clipper | March 30, 1936 |

The Hawaii Clipper was put into service on May 2, 1936, when it made its first scheduled flight to Manila. On October 21, 1936 it was used for the first scheduled passenger flight across the Pacific and it completed the flight successfully on November 4,1936. On July 29, 1938 it was lost without a trace east of Manila. Although there was speculation that it had been brought down by enemy fire, there was never any confirmation.

# BOEING B-314

The Boeing Corporation was founded by William Boeing in 1916 as the Pacific Aero Products Company. The new company concentrated on manufacturing military aircraft and it did not pursue the earlier civilian contracts with Pan Am. In 1936 however, Boeing engineers were working on the giant military aircraft, the B-15 bomber, and they thought they could adapt its 150 foot wings to the giant seaplane being proposed by Pan Am

*Boeing B-314 California Clipper departing Treasure Island base*

After preliminary studies and discussions, Boeing and Pan Am entered into a contract on July 21, 1936 for the construction of six huge and totally revolutionary flying boats. The mighty aircraft being proposed would accommodate 74 passengers and have a cruising speed of 180 mph. Its gross take off weight of 82,500 pounds gave it five times the payload of the Martin M-130. Its range of 3500 miles was easily suitable for either Transpacific or Transatlantic flight. Its four engines could produce 1500 horsepower at take off, which was almost twice the horsepower provided by the engines for the Martin M-130.

*Flight deck B-314*

*Main lounge of B-314*

Furthermore, comfort, spaciousness and even luxury would be provided for the passengers. The passenger deck was divided into nine sections, with plush seats for 74 and sleeping berths for 36. Also provided was a separate dining room, a deluxe compartment for VIPs, separate men's and women's bathrooms and dressing rooms and a separate lounge that became the social center for the aircraft. The roomy luxury of the Boeing 314 has never been equalled in commercial aviation. The cost was $4,000,000 - equal to more than $50,000,000 today and an extravagant amount in the late 1930s.

By June of 1938 the first Boeing 314 was undergoing test flights. The original single tail design, similar to that seen on the Martin M-130, proved to be unstable.

*After the single fin tail proved unstable, the double fin shown above was tested - The triple tail was finally selected for all Boeing 314s*

A double tail was tested without success and after further testing a conversion was made to the triple tail design for the aircraft.

Boeing delivered the first of the Boeing 314s, the California Clipper, on January 27, 1939. The new Clipper was rushed immediately into Pacific service on February 23, 1939 to meet the severe shortage of aircraft that had existed on the Pacific routes since the loss of the M-130 Hawaii Clipper in July of 1938.

*Postcards of Boeing B-314*

*Passenger certificate for
Phil Berst
Note Boeing B-314 on
certificate - certificate is
10 inches by 12 inches*

*Travel brochure - 1939-1942*

*Blotter - 1939-1942*

*The cutaway view of the Boeing B-314 shows the spaciousness of its luxurious interior - Never before or since have air passengers had so much room and so much comfort while flying*

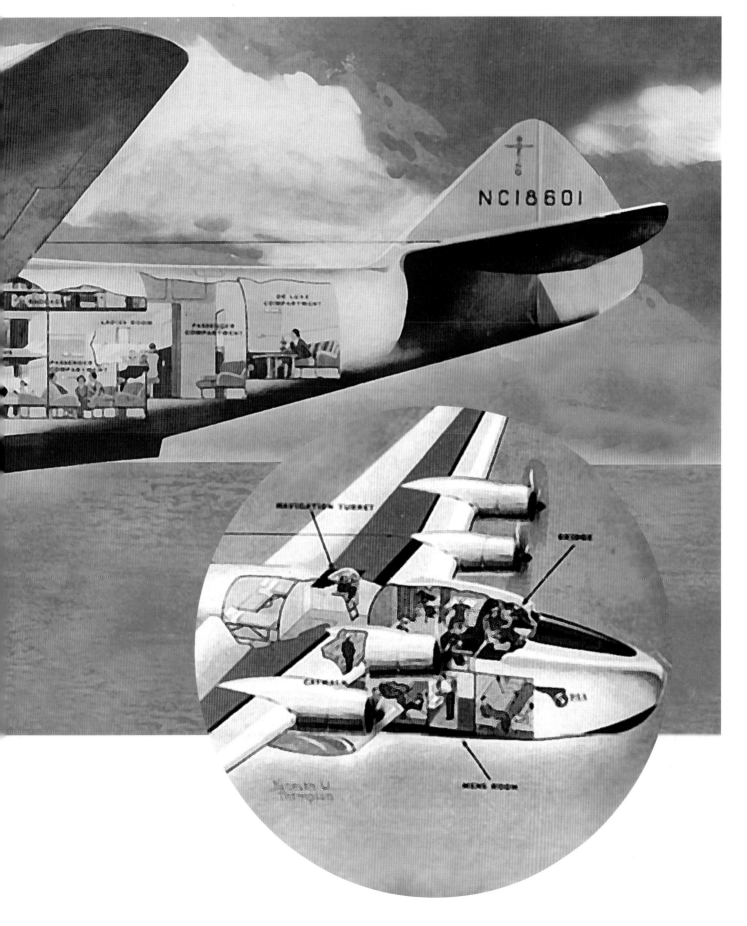

The handbook of instructions and maintenance of the Boeing Model 314 flying boat contains a wealth of information on this revolutionary aircraft. My copy was published in July of 1939 and it provides detailed pictures that cannot be found in any other book.

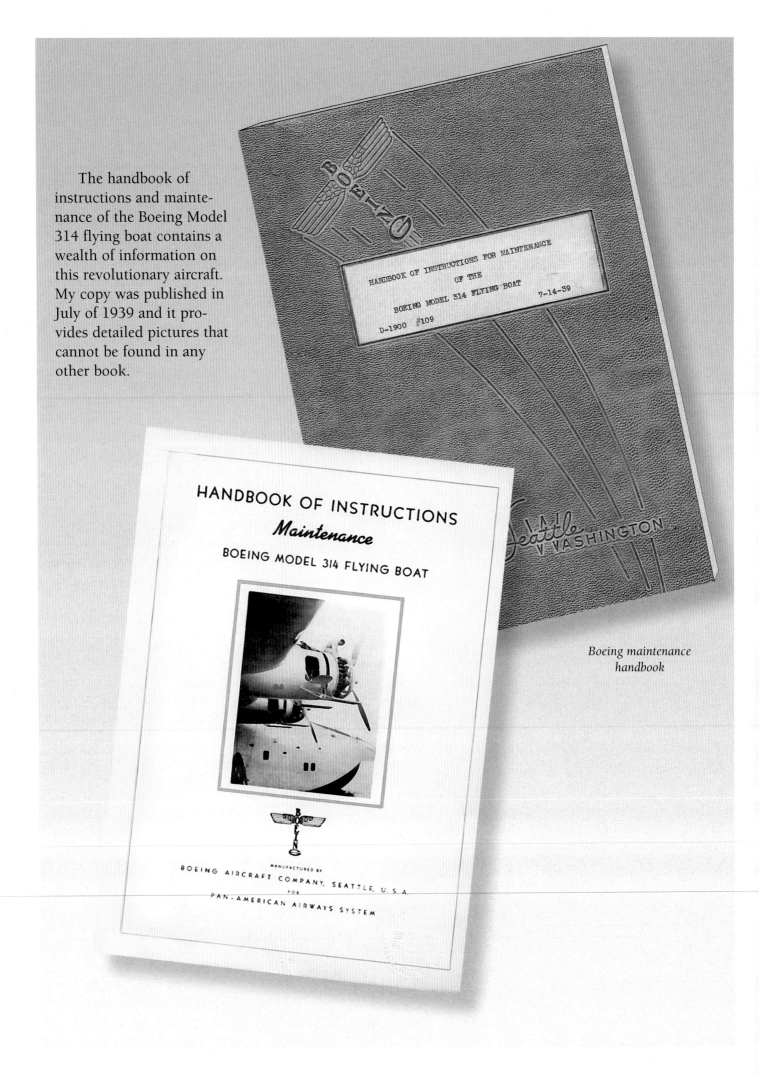

*Boeing maintenance handbook*

FIG. 17 COMPARTMENT No. 4 INTERIOR

PORT SIDE

STBD. SIDE

FIG. 18—STANDARD NIGHT ARRANGEMENT

FIG. 19 DINING SALON

PORT SIDE

STBD. SIDE

FIG. 21—DeLUXE COMPARTMENT

*Honeymoon suite*

FIG. 22 GALLEY AND MEN'S ROOM

FIG. 20—SPECIAL AND LADIES' COMPARTMENTS

From the original July 1936 order for six Boeing 314s three of them were ultimately delivered to Pan American's Pacific Division. The California and Honolulu Clippers were delivered in January of 1939 and the American Clipper was delivered in June of 1939.

Pan Am was so pleased with the performance of the Boeing 314s that six more were ordered in October of 1939.

*Cutaway of Boeing B-314-in 1939 round trip to Hawaii was $500 and to Hong Kong was $1400*

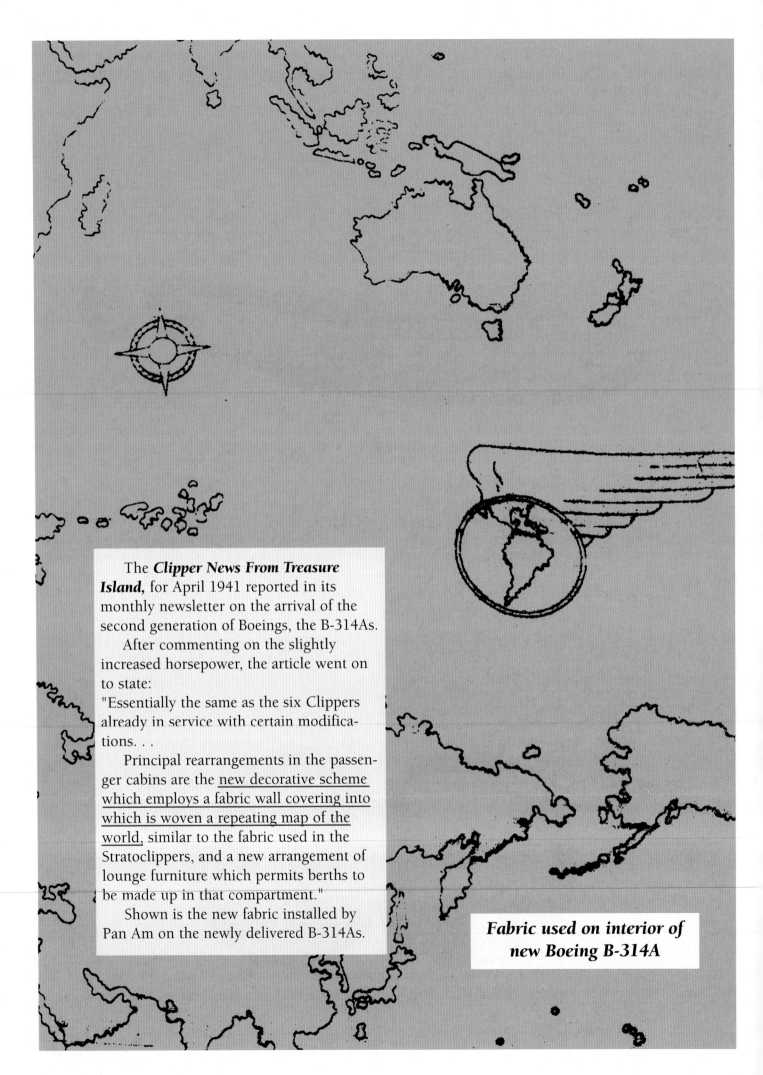

The **Clipper News From Treasure Island,** for April 1941 reported in its monthly newsletter on the arrival of the second generation of Boeings, the B-314As.

After commenting on the slightly increased horsepower, the article went on to state:

"Essentially the same as the six Clippers already in service with certain modifications. . .

Principal rearrangements in the passenger cabins are the <u>new decorative scheme which employs a fabric wall covering into which is woven a repeating map of the world,</u> similar to the fabric used in the Stratoclippers, and a new arrangement of lounge furniture which permits berths to be made up in that compartment."

Shown is the new fabric installed by Pan Am on the newly delivered B-314As.

**Fabric used on interior of new Boeing B-314A**

On the new order Boeing increased the plane's fuel efficiency and take off horsepower. New fuel tanks held an additional 1200 gallons of fuel, bringing the total capacity up to 5,450 gallons. These changes permitted quicker take offs and greater payload capacity over a greater cruising range.

The new aircraft also received a new model designation, the Boeing B-314A.

Two of the new B-314A models, the Pacific Clipper and Anzac Clipper were delivered to the Pacific division just before World War II. The changes made in the new models proved to be so effective that Boeing modified the earlier B-314s to bring them up to the performance level of the new generation of Boeing Clippers.

With the outbreak of World War II, three of the Boeing 314s ordered by Pan Am were sold to the British The nine Pan Am Boeing B-314s in service were sold to the Navy and joined the war effort in the Pacific and Atlantic, carrying essential military cargo, mail and key military personnel, including President Roosevelt to the war conferences in Europe.

At war's end the Navy offered the craft back to Pan Am. But by 1946 largely as a result of the war effort, airports around the world had been built that could handle large land based planes. So Pan Am declined the offer to repurchase the aircraft and the Boeing 314s were transferred to the War Assets Department and sold off to various airlines.

Salt water, salt air and rough water landings took a heavy toll. By the early 1950s all the Boeing 314s had been sunk or scrapped. Although one fatal crash occurred in the Atlantic with a loss of 24 people, a fatal accident involving the Boeing B-314 operating in the Pacific never occurred while flying in the harshest salt water environment. They proved their worth in peace and in war.

However, the era of the flying boat was coming to an end and with it, one of the most exciting and glamorous periods in aviation history. In the short period between November of 1935 and December of 1941 world scheduled passenger service went from being a dream to a reality. The mighty Boeing B-314s changed world travel forever.

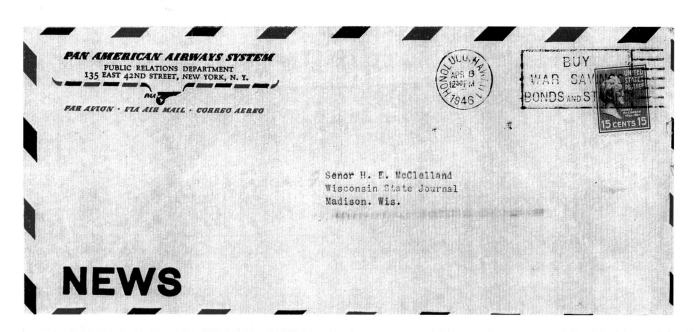

*Cover from last flight of Pan Am Clipper flying boat April 1946*

William VanDusen, Pan Am's Public Relations Director, wrote to the newspaper editors across the country on a regular basis to keep them advised of Pan Am's developments. These became known as "Dear Senor" letters. In the "Dear Senor" letter dated April 10, 1946 he told them about the inauguration of the land based Super Constellation service to Hawaii and the last flight of Pan Am's Clipper ship. He closed his letter with a salute to all Pan Am Clippers and a sentimental farewell to the era of the flying boats with these emotional words:

"Well, Senor, that's progress. But we couldn't let those grand old ladies pass out of the picture without a little visit. We're going to miss 'em! Why, they had more sex and glamour in five minutes than we can build into a land plane in five years! They were big - - too big to go wrong timid passengers used to be convinced. And comfortable. Why, their lounge was so cozy as that corner by the fireplace back home! More than that, they were chummy. You got around and visited with your fellow travelers, have a rubber of bridge or a spasm of gin rummy or swapped a yarn or two over a Scotch or three. There was something about them....

From the flying man's side, we're losing something, too. Those boats made America first on the airways of the world. We can't very well - - and shouldn't - - forget that.

They contributed a chapter in the annals of flying that'll still be thrilling reading for generations to come. They bred a new breed of airmen - - who talked and thought and worked in the lingo of the air-sea. They left an indelible mark. .
And they'll take with them some of that glory, some of that sense of accomplishment, some of that excitement of the "first", some of that thrill of "managainst-the-sea", some of that bold adventure of the explorer and pioneer. . yes, some of the faith and the hope and the courage of all of those who fly...

So Hail, old timers, Hail and Farewell.....
Salud!*

# The Six Boeing B-314s serving in the Pacific

| MODEL AIRCRAFT | REGISTRATION | OTHER NAME | DELIVERY |
|---|---|---|---|
| B-314  California Clipper | NC 18602 | *Pacific Clipper | January 27, 1939 |

The California Clipper was the first of the Boeing B-314s delivered to Pan Am and it made its inaugural flight on February 23, 1939 from the newly constructed Treasure Island base. August 22, 1939 the California Clipper made the first survey flight over the new route to New Zealand. On May 3, 1941 it inaugurated regular service to Singapore. On November 30, 1941 it completed the last regular flight to New Zealand before the outbreak of WW II. Throughout WW II it continued to fly the Honolulu - San Francisco route. At the end of the war it was sold to War Assets Department. In 1946 they sold it to World Airways and it was scrapped in 1950.

*In May of 1941, when the California Clipper was transferred temporarily to the Atlantic Division, the name California Clipper was loaned to the newly delivered Boeing Clipper NC 18609. Later in the year, when Clipper NC 18602 was returned from the Atlantic to the Pacific Division, the name California Clipper was restored and Clipper NC 18609 was named the Pacific Clipper.

| B-314  Honolulu Clipper | NC 18601 | | January 27, 1939 |
|---|---|---|---|

The Honolulu Clipper's inaugural flight was March 15, 1939. At the outbreak of WW II, it made the Honolulu to San Francisco flights. On November 4, 1945 the Honolulu Clipper on a flight from Honolulu to San Francisco developed engine trouble and landed successfully and safely at sea. The Navy vessel that saved the passengers and crew tried to take it under tow, but the plane hit the towing vessel and the clipper had to be sunk at sea on November 7, 1945.

| MODEL AIRCRAFT | REGISTRATION | OTHER NAME | DELIVERY |
|---|---|---|---|
| B-314 American Clipper | NC 18606 | | June 1939 |

The American Clipper's inaugural flight was also the inauguration of regularly scheduled airmail service to New Zealand July 12, 1940. Several months later the American Clipper made the first passenger flight to New Zealand on September 11, 1940. This Clipper had the distinction of making the last Pan American Clipper flight when it carried the mail from Honolulu to San Francisco on April 8, 1946. With that flight the era of the flying Clippers for Pan Am was closed and land based planes took over the Pacific routes. At the end of the war it was purchased by the War Assets Department and sold to World Airways and it, too, was scrapped in 1950.

| MODEL AIRCRAFT | REGISTRATION | OTHER NAME | DELIVERY |
|---|---|---|---|
| B-314A Pacific Clipper | NC 18609 | *California Clipper | May 1941 |

The Pacific Clipper's inaugural flight was May 21, 1941 to Singapore. The Pacific Clipper was also used on the first flight to Fiji in November 1941. At the outbreak of WW II the Pacific Clipper was on the New Zealand route and after reaching New Zealand it was given orders to proceed west bound around the World, ultimately arriving in New York, the first commercial flight around the World by a single airplane. At the end of the war it too was purchased by the War Assets Department and sold to Universal Airlines in 1946. It was damaged in a storm and salvaged for parts.

*In May of 1941, when the California Clipper was transferred temporarily to the Atlantic Division, the name California Clipper was loaned to the newly delivered Boeing Clipper NC 18609. Later in the year, when Clipper NC 18602 was returned from the Atlantic to the Pacific Division, the name California Clipper was restored and Clipper NC 18609 was named the Pacific Clipper.

| MODEL AIRCRAFT | REGISTRATION | OTHER NAME | DELIVERY |
|---|---|---|---|
| B-314A Anzac Clipper | NC 18611 | | June 1941 |

This was the last Boeing B-314 delivered to Pan Am for Pacific service. It went into service on the Manila run on June 15, 1941. At the end of the war, it was purchased by the War Assets Department in 1946, and sold to American International Airways in 1947 and sold again in 1951 and destroyed in Baltimore later in 1951.

| MODEL AIRCRAFT | REGISTRATION | OTHER NAME | DELIVERY |
|---|---|---|---|
| B-314 Dixie Clipper | NC 18605 | | April 1939 |

This Boeing B-314 was originally put into service on the North Atlantic run and transferred to the Pacific run in April of 1943 after the loss of the Philippine Clipper. The Dixie Clipper made 293 Transatlantic crossings and was the first U.S. commercial aircraft to dock at an African port. In January of 1943 the Dixie Clipper carried President Roosevelt to Africa for the historic Casablanca conference. At war's end the Dixie Clipper was sold to World Airways and scrapped in 1950.

# CHAPTER THREE
# PAN AM'S 50 HISTORIC AND FIRST FLIGHTS

*Pan American Clippers unite the Pacific rim*

Dr. Ken Kenler's memories of the early Pacific flights are the soul of my book and the 50 historic flights are, without question, the heart. Each flight either celebrates a triumph - the successful crossing of a new frontier - or memorializes a tragedy - a constant reminder of the risks faced by any pioneer.

The 50 historic flights, when taken together, tell a gripping story of the Pan Am Clippers' remarkable eleven years from April 1935 to April 1946 when transoceanic flights became a reality.

I hope you enjoy your trip back through time.

# " PAN AMERICAN CLIPPERS UNITE THE PACIFIC RIM "
## 1935-1946

The exciting painting by renowned aviation artist, Bob Jenny, brings together for the first time the three most famous Pan American Clippers that pioneered the Pacific air routes and united the Pacific rim between 1935 and 1941.

With the Oakland Bay Bridge in the background, the painting shows the Sikorsky S-42 American Clipper circling over Pan American's Treasure Island base. The S-42, with a length of 69 feet and a wing span of 114 feet, was the largest airplane built in the United States up to the time of its delivery to Pan Am in 1934. On April 16,1935, under the command of Captain Ed Musick, this S-42 made the historic first flight from San Francisco to Honolulu. This successful flight was followed by additional survey flights to Midway in June, to Wake in August, and to Guam in October of 1935.

The world's first scheduled Transpacific flight however would not be made by the S-42. This honor would go to the famed Martin M-130 China Clipper that is seen taxiing into view in the painting. The Martin M-130 China Clipper was 90 feet long with a wing span of 130 feet and a range of up to 3,200 miles. On November 22,1935 with Captain Ed Musick in command, the China Clipper made history by making the first scheduled Transpacific flight from Pan Am's San Francisco base to Manila. This epic flight made Captain Musick and the entire crew worldwide celebrities. In April of 1937, the China Clipper inaugurated the first scheduled Transpacific flight from San Francisco to Hong Kong, uniting the United States with China.

Seen breaking the water with mist streaming from its sea wings is the third of the pioneering Clippers - the mighty Boeing B-314 California Clipper. Delivered to Pan Am in early 1939, the California Clipper had a length of 108 feet and a wing span of over 150 feet. Its engines produced twice the power and five times the payload of the Martin M-130s. In September of 1939, under the command of Captain Tilton, this Boeing B-314 California Clipper flew the first survey flight over the new route to New Zealand. Later in 1941 the California Clipper would also make the initial flight to Singapore.

These three famous Clippers - the Sikorsky S-42 American Clipper, the Martin M-130 China Clipper and the Boeing B-314 California Clipper opened the Pacific rim to the world and they have been united once again in this painting.

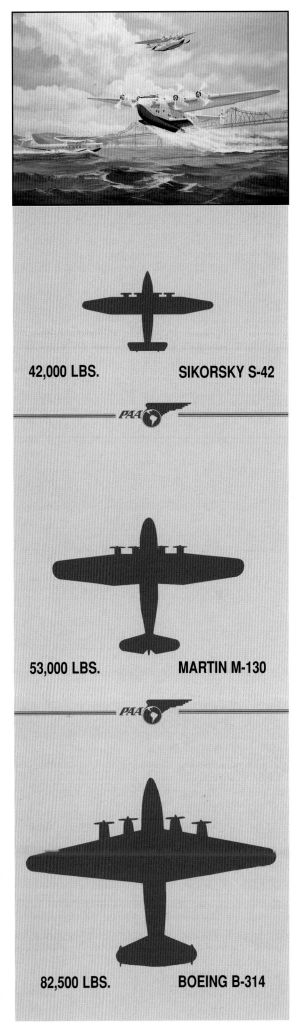

**42,000 LBS.**     **SIKORSKY S-42**

**53,000 LBS.**     **MARTIN M-130**

**82,500 LBS.**     **BOEING B-314**

# 1935

| | NAME | PAGE | DATE | AIRCRAFT | CAPTAIN/1st OFFICER |
|---|---|---|---|---|---|
| 1 | Survey 1 Honolulu | 94 | April 16 - 23 | S-42 Pan Am Clipper | Musick/Sullivan |
| 2 | Survey 2 Midway | 119 | June 12-22 | S-42 Pan Am Clipper | Musick/Sullivan |
| 3 | Survey 3 Wake | 128 | August 9-29 | S-42 Pan Am Clipper | Sullivan/Tilton |
| 4 | Survey 4 Guam | 140 | October 5-24 | S-42 Pan Am Clipper | Sullivan/Tilton |
| 5 | 1st Scheduled Mail Flight - Manila | 149 | November 22- December 6 | M-130 China Clipper | Musick/Sullivan |
| 6 | 1st Flight Philippine Clipper | 174 | December 9 -26 | M-130 Philippine Clipper | Tilton/Dahlstrom |

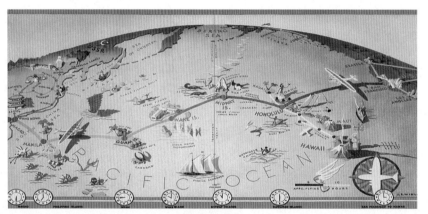

# 1936

| | NAME | PAGE | DATE | AIRCRAFT | CAPTAIN/1st OFFICER |
|---|---|---|---|---|---|
| 7 | Resumed Service to Manila & 1st Air Express Cargo | 177 | February 22 - March 9 | M-130 China Clipper | Musick/DeLima |
| 8 | 1st Flight Hawaii Clipper | 187 | May 2-16 | M-130 Hawaii Clipper | Musick/LaPorte |
| 9 | Press Flight to Manila | 195 | October 7-24 | M-130 China Clipper | Dahlstrom/Lewis |
| 10 | Public Relations VIP Flight to Hong Kong | 199 | October 14 - November 2 | M-130 Philippine Clipper | Tilton/Ralph |
| 11 | 1st Revenue Passenger Flight to Manila | 220 | October 21 - November 4 | M-130 Hawaii Clipper | Musick/Gray |

# 1937

| | NAME | PAGE | DATE | AIRCRAFT | CAPTAIN/1st OFFICER |
|---|---|---|---|---|---|
| 12 | Survey 1 to New Zealand | 235 | March 17 - April 9 | S-42B Pan Am Clipper II | Musick/Briggs |
| 13 | Transfer Flight S-42 to Manila | 275 | April 18-22 December 9-11 | S-42B Hong Kong Clipper Return Manila to Honolulu | LaPorte/Nixon |
| 14 | Survey - Manila - to Hong Kong | 280 | April 23-24 | S-42B Hong Kong Clipper | LaPorte/Briggs |
| 15 | 1st Scheduled Mail Flight to Hong Kong | 284 | April 21-27 | M-130 China Clipper (Alameda to Manila) | Cluthe/Cone |
| | | | April 28-29 | S-42B Hong Kong Clipper (Manila - Hong Kong) | LaPorte/Briggs |
| | | | April 30 - May 3 | M-130 China Clipper Manila - Honolulu) | Cluthe/Cone |
| | | | May 3-4 | M-130 China Clipper Honolulu - San Fran. | Lorber/Culbertson |
| 16 | 1st Revenue Passenger Service to Hong Kong | 293 | April 29 to May 12 | M-130 Hawaii Clipper (to Manila) | Dahlstrom/Culbertson |
| | | | | S-42 Hong Kong Clipper II (to Hong Kong) | LaPorte/Nixon |
| 17 | 1st Mail Flight from New Zealand | 296 | December 23 January 3, 1938 | S-42B Samoan Clipper (to Honolulu) | Musick/Culbertson |
| | | | January 5, 1938 | M-130 Philippine Clipper (Honolulu to San Fran.) | Cluthe |

# 1938

| | NAME | PAGE | DATE | AIRCRAFT | CAPTAIN/1st OFFICER |
|---|---|---|---|---|---|
| 18 | Last Flight of Samoan Clipper | 304 | January 9-11 | S-42B Samoan Clipper | Musick/Sellers |
| 19 | Last Flight of Hawaii Clipper | 322 | July 23 - 29 | M-130 Hawaii Clipper | Terletzky/Walker |

# 1939

| | NAME | PAGE | DATE | AIRCRAFT | CAPTAIN/1st OFFICER |
|---|---|---|---|---|---|
| 20 | 1st Flight to Treasure Island | 326 | January 24-31 | M-130 China Clipper | Nixon |
| 21 | 1st Flight from Treasure Island | 330 | February 5-14 | M-130 China Clipper | Cluthe/Bierer |
| 22 | 1st Flight of California Clipper | 332 | February 23 - March 14 | B-314 California Clipper | Cluthe/Bierer |
| 23 | 1st Flight of Honolulu Clipper | 342 | March 15 - April 5 | B-314 Honolulu Clipper | McGlohn |
| 24 | 1st Survey to New Zealand New Route | 344 | August 22 - September 6 | B-314 California Clipper | Tilton/Cluthe |
| 25 | 2nd Proving Flight New Zealand New Route | 361 | November 19-30 | B-314 Honolulu Clipper | Cluthe/McGlohn |

# 1940

| | NAME | PAGE | DATE | AIRCRAFT | CAPTAIN/1st OFFICER |
|---|---|---|---|---|---|
| 25a | 3rd Survey Flight to Canton Island | 362 | February - 16-17 | B-314 California Clipper | K. Beer |
| 26 | 1st Mail Flight New Zealand | 364 | July 12 - 24 | B-314 American Clipper | Tilton/Martin |
| 27 | 1st Flight Honolulu to Los Angeles | 379 | July 23 - 24 | B-314 American Clipper | Tilton/Martin |
| 28 | Preview Press Flight to New Zealand | 383 | August 10 - 15 September 4 - 10 | B-314 California Clipper (Return H.K. to San Fran.) | Cluthe/Barrows |
| 29 | VIP Flight to New Zealand | 386 | August 24 - September 7 | B-314 American Clipper | Nixon/Searles |
| 30 | 1st Revenue Passenger Flight to New Zealand | 388 | September 11-23 | B-314 American Clipper | Beer |

# 1941

| | NAME | PAGE | DATE | AIRCRAFT | CAPTAIN/1st OFFICER |
|---|---|---|---|---|---|
| 31 | 1st Air Mail to Singapore | 392 | May 3-20 | B-314 California Clipper | Barrows/Howard |
| 32 | 1st Revenue Passenger Flight to Singapore & 1st Flight Pacific Clipper | 401 | May 21 June 4 | B-314A Pacific Clipper | Blackmore |
| 33 | 1st Flight Anzac Clipper | 402 | July 15-29 | B-314A Anzac Clipper | Blackmore |
| 34 | 1st Regular Shuttle L.A.- San Francisco-Hon. | 403 | August 10-13 | B-314A Anzac Clipper | Tilton |
| 35 | 1st Flight Hong Kong Clipper II (Manila to H.K.) | 404 | September 22-23 | S-42B Hong Kong Clipper II | Ralph Strickland |
| 36 | 1st Flight to Fiji | 405 | November 5-17 | B-314A Pacific Clipper | Tilton/Wilson |

| NAME | PAGE | DATE | AIRCRAFT | CAPTAIN/1st OFFICER |
|------|------|------|----------|---------------------|

# LAST FLIGHTS BEFORE WORLD WAR II

| | NAME | PAGE | DATE | AIRCRAFT | CAPTAIN/1st OFFICER |
|---|------|------|------|----------|---------------------|
| 37 | Honolulu Clipper | 412 | October 20-23 | B-314 Honolulu Clipper | Ford |
| 38 | California Clipper | 412 | November 17-30 | B-314 California Clipper | Lodeesen |
| 39 | American Clipper | 413 | December 2-5 | B-314 American Clipper | |
| 40 | Pacific Clipper | 414 | December 1-8 (N.Y.C. Jan 6, 1942) | B-314A Pacific Clipper | Ford/Mack |
| 41 | Anzac Clipper | 420 | December 6-8 | B-314A Anzac Clipper | Turner/Sommers |
| 42 | China Clipper | 422 | November 19 - December 6 | M-130 China Clipper | McGlohn |
| 43 | Philippine Clipper | 427 | December 3-11 | M-130 Philippine Clipper | Hamilton/Moss |
| 44 | Hong Kong Clipper II | 440 | December 6 | S-42B Hong Kong Clipper II | Ralph/Strickland |

## 1942

| | NAME | PAGE | DATE | AIRCRAFT | CAPTAIN/1st OFFICER |
|---|------|------|------|----------|---------------------|
| 45 | NATS Pacific Survey | 442 | Mid-August to September 18 | PBM-3R Martin Mariner | Tilton/Chase |

## 1943

| | NAME | PAGE | DATE | AIRCRAFT | CAPTAIN/1st OFFICER |
|---|------|------|------|----------|---------------------|
| 46 | 2nd Flight Around the World | 449 | January 14 to February 23 | B-314A Capetown Clipper B-314A Anzac Clipper | Masland/Auten |
| 47 | Last Flight Philippine Clipper | 454 | January 20-21 | M-130 Philippine Clipper | Elzey/Judd |

## 1944

| | NAME | PAGE | DATE | AIRCRAFT | CAPTAIN/1st OFFICER |
|---|------|------|------|----------|---------------------|
| 48 | Transfer from Treasure Island to Mills Field | 455 | September 15 | | |

## 1945

| | NAME | PAGE | DATE | AIRCRAFT | CAPTAIN/1st OFFICER |
|---|------|------|------|----------|---------------------|
| 49 | Last Flight Honolulu Clipper | 457 | November 3-4 | B-314 Honolulu Clipper | Robbins/Reid |

## 1946

| | NAME | PAGE | DATE | AIRCRAFT | CAPTAIN/1st OFFICER |
|---|------|------|------|----------|---------------------|
| 50 | Last Clipper Flight in Pacific | 459 | April 8-9 | B-314 American Clipper | Terrell |

# PAN AMERICAN AIRWAYS PACIFIC FLIGHTS 1935 - 1946

| Survey 1 Honolulu | April 16 - 23, 1935 | S-42 Pan Am Clipper | Musick/Sullivan |
|---|---|---|---|

| Outbound Flight Schedule | | Inbound Flight Schedule | |
|---|---|---|---|
| San Francisco - Honolulu | April 16 - 17 | Honolulu - San Francisco | April 22 - 23 |

Four survey flights preceded the first scheduled Transpacific flight of November 1935. The first of these flights from San Francisco to Honolulu was planned for mid April 1935. In February of 1935 modifications for the Sikorsky S-42 Pan American Clipper had been completed and the plane was sent to Miami for endurance flights in the Caribbean. Crew members Musick, Sullivan, V. Wright, Noonan, Canaday and Jarboe flew a non stop round trip from Miami to the Virgin Islands and return, simulating the San Francisco to Honolulu run.

Pictured above in Miami is the crew selected for the first flight after having completed the test flights in the Caribbean with the Pan American Clipper shown in the background.

After leaving Miami, the Clipper proceeded to Acapulco, Mexico for an overnight stop. The next stop was Los Angeles, where they were warmly greeted.

*Above - Postcard of Clipper at Acapulco March 29, 1935*

*Clipper at Los Angeles - San Pedro Harbor - March 30, 1935*

At the microphone welcoming the crew is Los Angeles Mayor Frank Shaw. From left to right in front of him is Captain Musick, with crew members Sullivan, Wright, Noonan, and Jarboe.

95

*Arrival of Pan Am Clipper at new Alameda base-March 31, 1935 - This is first in a long series of outstanding*
*Pan Am photos taken by San Francisco photographer Clyde Sunderland*

On March 31, 1935 the Pan American Clipper arrived at the end of its delivery flight at Pan Am's new base at Alameda on San Francisco Bay. Pictured is the Clipper on its approach with excited onlookers lining the shore.

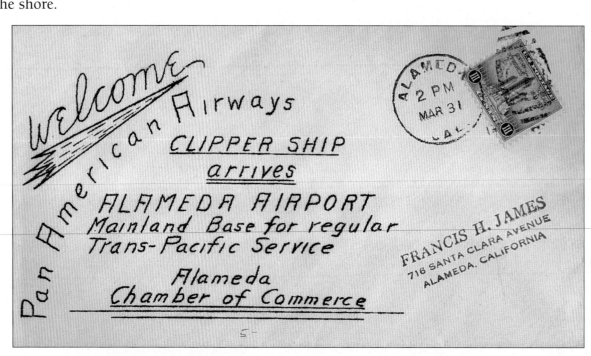

*Souvenir for Clipper's arrival - March 31, 1935*

Waiting to greet the crew in Alameda was Colonel Clarence M. Young, the recently appointed director of Pan Am's newly formed Pacific division. Colonel Young was in the inner circle of Pan Am's

*Hanger at Alameda - the first office for the new Pacific division*

management. He had attended Yale, as had Pan Am's President, Juan Trippe. Both men belonged to the Yale Flying Club and they shared a passion for flying. Trippe's wealthy friends from Yale, who invested the money to form Pan Am in 1927, were also close friends of Colonel Young. If anyone had the power and the influence to get Pan Am to commit the money and equipment necessary to make the Pacific operation a success, it was Colonel Clarence Young.

Colonel Young was born and raised in Iowa. In 1910 he graduated from Yale. When the United States entered World War I he enlisted and was shot down while piloting an Italian bomber. He made a dramatic escape by hiding in a boxcar that took him back to Allied territory.

After the war he returned to Iowa to practice law. In 1926, he was appointed as Chief of Air Regulation in the newly formed aeronautics branch of the United States Department of Commerce. In 1927 he was appointed Assistant Secretary for Aeronautics in charge of all commercial aviation in the rapidly expanding airline industry.

Aviation was the glamour industry of the 1930s when **Time** Magazine, in March of 1932, put Colonel Young on its cover. In their cover story, **Time** stated:

*"Today Colonel Young enjoys enormous popularity in the industry and practically universal respect. Utterly conscientious in administering his job, he is incapable of political ball playing. Many a manufacturer or transport operator has learned that 'the Chief' may submit to being called by his first name, but is quick to meet each and every request for an easy or lax interpretation of government rules with: 'The Air Commerce Act says no!".*

*Colonel Young works long hours. He is tall, bronzed, 42, not married and he lives alone at the Hay-Adams House across Lafayette Square from the White House. He smokes cigarettes furiously, curses lustily."*

FIFTEEN CENTS

March 14, 1932

# TIME
### The Weekly Newsmagazine

**COL. CLARENCE MARSHALL YOUNG**
"The Air Commerce Act says 'No'"
(See Aeronautics)

Volume XIX

Number 11

Circulation this issue more than 550,000

*Colonel Young*

# LOIS MORAN BRIDE OF NOTED AIRMAN

### Actress and Col. C. M. Young on Honeymoon Here. Wed Yesterday.

Lois Moran, stage and screen star, and Col. Clarence M. Young, former Assistant Secretary of Commerce for Aeronautics, are honeymooning at the Hay-Adams House here today following their unannounced marriage yesterday afternoon while en route from New York to Washington.

Col. Young, now an aviation consultant to Pan-American Airways and other aeronautical groups, had planned a business trip to Washington and last week made several appointments with business and personal acquaintances here for today.

Miss Moran told the Associated Press last night that she and the colonel made up their minds to be married while the colonel was preparing to leave New York for Washington yesterday morning.

It was said that plans of the couple are indefinite, except that they will go to San Francisco soon. The bride indicated that she might "make another picture or two if the chance comes."

**Bride 25, Young Is 45.**

Mrs. Young, whose home was in Pittsburgh, will be 25 years old next month. Col. Young is 45 years old and a native of Colfax, Iowa.

The bride, born and reared in Pittsburgh, started her stage career as a dancer in the Paris National Opera. She was the star of motion pictures of a few years ago, among them "Stella Dallas," "God Gave Me 20 Cents," "The Road to Mandalay" and "The Music Master," but returned to the stage several years ago.

Since her return to the stage she has appeared here as co-star with William Gaxton and Victor Moore in "Of Thee I Sing" and its sequel, "Let 'em Eat Cake."

Col. Young, a graduate of Drake and Yale Universities, began his flying career in the Army Air Service in the World War and was so proficient in his ground training that he was one of three men selected from his class for duty overseas. During the World War he landed a crippled plane in a marsh in front of a nest of Austrian machine guns and spent five months in a prison camp.

Young played a vital part in the establishment of Federal control over civil aeronautics and when William P. MacCracken res... succeeded him a... holding office... Hoover and Roo... was abolished in... ization which le... the present Bure...

## Col. Young and Bride

From all accounts, Colonel Young was a hard driving administrator who followed the rules and expected strict adherence to all government regulations. Colonel Young left government in 1933 when President Roosevelt took office and he used his extensive contacts in the aviation industry to become an aviation consultant to Pan Am and to other airlines.

In late 1934 he accepted Juan Trippe's challenge of starting the new Pacific division, with the exciting objective of being the first airline to fly the Pacific. In February of 1935, before moving from Washington, D.C. to San Francisco to set up Pan Am's new division, he wed Miss Lois Moran, a young and beautiful actress who starred both in films and on Broadway. Their son, Tim Young, has shared with me his father's most treasured mementoes of his long and distinguished career as the manager of Pan Am's Pacific division, and they are illustrated throughout this book.

Clarence Young's wife, Lois Moran Young, was the leading lady of Pan Am's Pacific division

After Colonel Young met the crew of the Pan Am Clipper on their arrival in Alameda on March 31, 1935, he and his bride departed immediately on the S.S. Lurline for Honolulu to inspect the proposed landing areas that had been chosen by his staff for the historic Clipper flight. It was also very important to him to be in Honolulu to meet the Clipper on the successful completion of the first commercial Pacific flight in history.

### HONOLULU STAR-BULLETIN,
## PACIFIC DIVISION PAA CHIEF ARRIVES

Col. Clarence M. Young, Pacific division manager of Pan American Airways, arrived on the Lurline today to continue surveys for a Hawaiian landing spot for the forthcoming transoceanic service of his company. He was accompanied by Mrs. Young, the former Lois Moran of stage and screen fame. They will remain at the Royal Hawaiian hotel from 10 days to two weeks.—Star-Bulletin photo.

*Below:*
*Clarence Young and his bride at the Royal Hawaiian Hotel- April 20, 1935 - The announcement of the marriage appeared in the* **Honolulu Star-Bulletin**

Back in San Francisco, the Sikorsky S-42, Captain Musick and the crew were ready for an April 9, 1935 departure for Honolulu.

Collectors of souvenir first flight covers, however, did not have enough advance notice to prepare their covers for the flight and mail them to San Francisco. In response to their complaints, the post office (who had sanctioned mail for this survey flight) along with Pan Am, agreed to delay the clipper's departure from April 9 to April 16, 1935.

The announcement from Second Assistant Postmaster General, Harllee Branch, officially authorized the postponement of the epic first survey flight to Honolulu. It is hard now to imagine how important the concerns and wishes of flight cover collectors were both to Pan Am and to the Post Office Department. First, there were a lot of cover collectors in the mid-1930s. Secondly, and much more importantly, they increased the general public's awareness of airmail in general and specifically the Pacific airmail service that would soon be authorized. Without the public's support, the airmail service would be unprofitable for the Postal Service and Pan Am. The seven day delay in Alameda that was requested by the Post Office Department gave the flight crew added time to rest and prepare for the difficult flight that they knew would take more than 20 hours. The night before their April 16 departure, the crew stayed at the Hotel Claremont in Berkeley, California. Fred Noonan, the famous navigator who would disappear in 1937 with Amelia Earhart on her failed attempt to be the first woman to fly around the world, had time to write one last postcard to his good friend, Pan Am employee Marvel Brown from Miami. His postcard to her read:

*"Berkeley, California - April 15, 1935. Received your welcome letter and was greatly pleased to hear from you. We leave at four p.m. tomorrow. Everything is fine. Regards to you . . . Fred Noonan."*

It is postmarked 11:30 p.m. in Berkeley and it is probably the last note that Noonan wrote before the historic flight of the next day.

(See postcard from Noonan to Brown at top of next page)

POST OFFICE DEPARTMENT
Second Assistant Postmaster General

Division of Air Mail Service

April 6, 1935.

A N N O U N C E M E N T

Trans-Pacific Flight Postponed

Pan American Airways have received so many requests from philatelists and others who are interested in the transmission of covers on the flight to Honolulu that they have decided, due to the short notice that was given to the public, to postpone the flight one week and the time for the receipt of covers by them has been extended from 5:00 p.m., April 8 to 5:00 p.m., April 15th.

Harllee Branch
HARLLEE BRANCH,

Second Assistant
Postmaster General.

*Post office announcement moving departure to April 16, 1935*

Noonan's postcard to Brown

Harry Canaday, one of the crew members, also shared a page with me from his personal scrapbook depicting the crew in Alameda on the afternoon of April 16, 1935, just before take off.

When I met Harry Canaday in his Coral Gables, Florida home in 1979, he was kind enough to also sign one of his personal photos for me showing him as a young officer about to depart as the Junior Flight Officer on the April 1935 survey flight. Many of my covers for these first four survey flights are from his personal collection. His willingness to share his stories with me was really the beginning of my great interest in these Pan Am flights.

The afternoon of April 16 was clear and bright as the Sikorsky S-42 lifted off from the water to set its course for Honolulu. Pictured is the Clipper passing over the Oakland Bay Bridge that was still under construction.

Even with the vast improvement in directional finders and radios in the years just before the flight, the success of the trip also depended to a large measure on the skill of the navigator. Pictured below is Fred Noonan working at the chart table on the Pan American Clipper.

*Above-Junior Flight officer Harry Canaday*

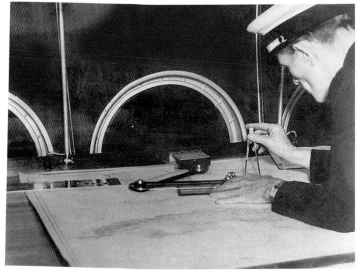

*Left - Navigator Fred Noonan at chart table of Sikorsky S-42*

*Right - Clipper departs for Honolulu-passing over Oakland Bay Bridge-April 1935*

*Classic picture of Clipper arriving at Diamondhead, Honolulu, April 17, 1935 - Signed by entire crew*

Eighteen hours and 37 minutes after takeoff the crew arrived in Honolulu, bettering by six hours the record crossing from California to Honolulu set by the Navy fliers the year before. Even with the one week delay in the flight's departure to accommodate collectors of souvenir flight mail, many collectors who wanted flight covers did not get their requests to San Francisco in time. Nevertheless, over 15,000 pieces of souvenir mail were carried.

The welcoming ceremonies for the arriving crew in Honolulu were planned for 8:00 a.m. Captain Musick, however, arrived over Honolulu at 7:00 a.m. Therefore in order to accommodate the welcoming crowd, he circled Honolulu for an hour so that his arrival would be precisely at the 8:00 a.m. scheduled time. Captain Musick insisted on doing everything "by the book".

*Arrival Ford Island - April 17, 1935*

*Crowd at the ramp - welcoming the Clipper*

As promised, Colonel Young was in Honolulu awaiting the Clipper's arrival at the end of the epic flight. Colonel Young was the first person to greet Captain Musick as he emerged from the hatch. Phil Berst, the superintendent of maintenance, can also be seen reaching in the window of the Clipper to congratulate First Officer Sullivan.

*Captain Musick followed by first officer Sullivan and navigator Noonan come ashore*

*Captain Musick being greeted by the press - A nation wide radio audience listened to the arrival ceremonies*

*The crew with Hawaii's Governor Poindexter*

*Colonel Young with Mrs. Poindexter*

*Mrs. Lois Moran Young on the left,
in white - with Mrs. Poindexter at
welcoming ceremonies*

Upon arrival in Honolulu, Captain Musick and the crew of the Pan Am Clipper strike a lighthearted football pose. Pictured is the crew, from left to right, W.T. Jarboe, radio officer; Harry Canaday, junior flight officer; R.O.D. Sullivan, first officer; Edwin C. Musick, captain; Fred J. Noonan, navigation officer; Victor A. Wright, engineering officer. Standing in the second row, from left to right, are J. Parker VanZandt, Pan Am station manager; Postmaster John H. Wilson, who was later mayor of Honolulu; Roy A. Vitousek, speaker of the house, Hawaii; Donald Ross, district manager of Standard Oil Company; Col. Clarence M. Young, Pacific division manager (covered in leis); Rear Admiral Harry E. Yarrnell, Commandant 14th Naval District; Hawaii Governor Joseph P. Poindexter; Major General Hugh A. Drum; Commander Hawaiian Department; Col. Daniel VanVoohis, Chief of Staff, Hawaii Department; Fred Wright, mayor of Honolulu; Commander E. Wayne Todd, fleet air base; John R. Galt, president Hawaii chapter Aeronautical Association; Col. Deloss Emmons, Commander 18th Composite Wing. Every official in Honolulu wanted to be part of the welcoming ceremonies for this great event.

**MAIL SCHEDULE**
STEAMER MAIL
From Coast—Lurline, Tues., 9 p. m.
From Coast—Lurline, Jan. 11 a. m.
From Orient—Tes. Tatt, Jan. 21
From Orient—Mariposa, Jan. 19
From Australia—Niagara, Jan. 26
AIR MAIL
From Coast—Phil. Clip., Tues, a. m.
From Coast—China Clip, Fri., 11 a. m.
From Orient—China Clip. Thurs. p. m.
From Australia—Niagara, Jan. 26
From Orient—China Clip, Thurs. p. m.

# Honolulu Star-Bulletin EXTRA

Evening Bulletin, Est. 1882, No. 19179
Hawaiian Star, Vol. XLV., No. 14163

16 PAGES—HONOLULU, TERRITORY OF HAWAII, U. S. A., WEDNESDAY, APRIL 17, 1935—16 PAGES

★ PRICE FIVE CENTS

# HAWAII IS LINKED TO COAST BY AIR

## PAN AMERICAN'S GIANT CLIPPER SHIP OF THE AIR OPENS PACIFIC SERVICE TO HAWAII

## Navy Replies To Protests Over Airline

### Purely Commercial, Says Swanson, Denying 'Hidden Motives'

### COAST TESTS TODAY

### Ship Due at Noon With Technicians, Equipment For Island Bases

(United Press by Radio)
WASHINGTON, April 3.—Attempting to dissipate foreign fears of "hidden motives," Secretary of Navy Claude Swanson reiterated today that the projected air line from California to China, planned by American interests, was strictly a commercial venture.

"There is nothing exclusive even to Pan-American Airways about this line, but there have been no other applications for a similar service," Swanson said.

Notice that the navy department had granted Pan-American permission to establish bases on the mid-Pacific islands of Midway, Wake and Guam brought rumblings of protest from some quarters that the United State was using the enterprise as a commercial veil to hide an alleged purpose of strengthening her control in the Pacific.

Much unofficial objection was raised in Japan, though the Foreign Office emphasized that Japan did not oppose any venture of such nature that was strictly commercial.

### RADIO PERMITS

Pan-American was authorized today by the Federal Communications commission to establish immediately radio stations at Hawaii, Midway, Wake and Guam islands for use in connection with the projected transpacific air service.

It was understood Pan-American was ready to rush construction of the stations in preparation for experimental test flights to be made over the projected transpacific route during the summer months.

### TESTS START TODAY

ALAMEDA, Cal., April 3.—Businesslike preparations for the Pan-American Clipper ship's first flight to Honolulu were proceeding tonight on the eve of a series f coastwise test hops.

Tomorrow the powerful Sikorsky flying boat will engage in "water" tests, taxiing around San Francisco bay with the crew getting the feel of surface conditions, determining the prevailing winds and other technicalities involved in the takeoff. Pilots said they must know the conditions also.

Officials expected the first coastwise test flight would start Friday.

Meanwhile, land technicians were also working on schedule, ready to give the ship's direction finder the first test. Over-water test of the apparatus, which was developed exclusively in Pan - American's Miami laboratories, will begin soon.

Pilots have already tested the direction finder apparatus with Miami, Port Au Prince, Puerto Rico and other Caribbean stations. The over-water test will consist of contacting ships at sea, under all weather and flying conditions.

Above, the Pan American Clipper as it appeared in Pearl Harbor shortly after 8 a. m. today when it completed its flight from Alameda to Honolulu. Below, transpacific air mail becomes a reality. At the left Victor A. Wright, Clipper engineering officer, and Capt. Edwin C. Musick with the last of three bags of postal matter loaded on the plane just before it left Alameda at 1:21 p. m. Tuesday, Honolulu time. Photo by NEA Service. Right, Postmaster John H. Wilson receives the mail bag from members of the Clipper crew here slightly more than 18 hours later. It was the fastest mail delivery ever recorded between California and Hawaii. Upper picture and picture at the right by The Star-Bulletin, the picture from Alameda came on the plane. The NEA Service photographer took the picture less than 5 minutes before the plane left Alameda, and handed the plateholder, addressed to The Star-Bulletin, to Capt. Musick as the latter got into the plane.

## PAA PLANE IS TO BEGIN NEW ERA IN TRAVEL

### Weather Conditions Favorable For Takeoff of Big Plane For Hawaii

### Is Expected To Land Wednesday Morning At Pearl Harbor Navy Yard

(Associated Press by Wireless)
LOS ANGELES, April 16.—Laura Ingalls hopped off at 5:10 a. m. today in an attempt to shatter Amelia Earhart's transcontinental speed record.

She hoped to reached New York in 14 hours or less via Albuquerque, Kansas City and Cleveland.

(Associated Press by Wireless)
ALAMEDA, Cal., April 16.—A new era in transoceanic transportation will begin when the Pan American Airways Pioneer Clipper leaves her base at 4 p. m. today (1:30 p. m. Honolulu time) on the first leg of a commercial air service route to the Orient.

The commander of the big seaplane planned to hold to the scheduled takeoff time unless weather over the Pacific changed suddenly. This morning the reports were favorable.

There was no announcement today of the expected airspeed, but at Honolulu but the Clipper has a cruising speed of 130 to 160 miles an hour, which should carry her to Hawaii by Wednesday morning.

### May Take Slower Pace

There were reports, however, that she might travel much more slowly in order to study conditions and minimize fuel consumption.

The Clipper carries sufficient fuel to fly 800 miles past her destination. Commanded by Capt. Edwin Musick, a veteran of 23 years' flying, the big seaplane weighs 41,000 pounds, including 3,000 gallons of fuel, engineering equipment and special flight covers dispatched by philatelists.

A large crowd is expected to watch the huge aircraft begin the inaugural flight of transpacific service which later this year will be extended to the Orient.

While Capt. Musick and the five man crew who will make the flight with him received orders to sleep as long as they could this morning, the ground crew gave a final grooming to the plane which if all goes well should alight to a rousing welcome at Pearl Harbor.

### 3,000 Gallons of Fuel

The plane was wheeled from her hangar and fueled with 3,000 gallons of gasoline and 300 gallons of oil before noon. Then she was taxied to the water's edge, her landing gear was removed and the

## Airline Heads Check Flight

### Clipper Reports Regularly All Night

As methodically as if they were stock quotations over a market ticker, came position reports from the Clipper to Pan-American headquarters in the Young hotel last night.

Each half-hour a radio report relayed by the night operator in the hotel suite occupied by airline executives. Each varied from the other only in that another degree or so of longitude had been checked off, marking the Clipper's steady eastward flight.

So there was none of the excitement at headquarters that attended clocking of the westward flight a week ago. For that westward trip had revealed the ocean flight for what it is, at least to Pan-American Airways—just a matter of routine.

### NO NERVOUSNESS

Only Col. Clarence M. Young and Mrs. Young, J. Parker Van

(Continued on Page 10, Col. 7)

## Capt. Musick's Own Story Tells Graphically Of Hop To New East-West Record

Any honor due Pan American Airways for its inaugural commercial flight from the mainland to Honolulu must be shared by all aviation, Capt. Edwin Musick said after he brought the Pan American Clipper ship to a landing at Pearl Harbor this morning. Dismissing the plaudits of the crowd for himself and his crew:

"Therefore, the aviation industry of the United States combined should share in the results of this hop.

"For those of us in aviation, there are not many thrills left. But on this journey we can thrill to the tremendous advance which is being made in aviation.

"We made a regular flight," he said, "following the 15,000 miles we had flown in preparation for the journey.

"We had no difficulty during any portion of the trip and we were able to accomplish the scientific experiments and observation assigned to us.

"When we think of the others who have made this trip across the Pacific with a singled motor plane, what courage it must have taken to fly as they did with no communi-

(Continued on Page 7, Col. 4)

### EQUIPMENT HERE TODAY

J. Parker Van Zandt, local representative for Pan-American Airways, announced yesterday that the freighter North Haven, under charter to the company, would arrive at noon today from San Francisco and would dock at Pier No. 8.

The vessel is bringing equipment and technicians for the establishment of air bases at Kanohe, Midway and Wake Islands for PAA.

After discharging local equip-

## NO DIFFICULTY MET BY PAA'S CLIPPER PLANE

### Big Plane Flies Above Fog And Clouds; Crew Enjoys Sunset, Moonlight

(Associated Press by Wireless)
WASHINGTON, April 17.—The successful flight of the Clipper Pioneer to Honolulu indicates the practicability of long range passenger flights over great water areas, Secretary of War George H. Dern said today.

"Thus it hastens the time of transoceanic airline operations," he said.

SAN FRANCISCO, April 17.—Mayor Angelo Rossi radioed congratulations to Capt. Edwin Musick today.

(Associated Press by Wireless)
ALAMEDA, Cal., April 17.—Soaring above clouds and fogs at speeds ranging from 110 to more than 130 miles an hour and at altitudes ranging from 6,000 to 7,300 feet, the Pan American Clipper Tuesday night and early this morning was rapidly approaching her goal, Honolulu.

The Clipper reported itself as being 316 miles out at sea at 5:30 p. m. PST (3 p. m. Honolulu time). It was then flying at a speed of 151 miles an hour, at an elevation of 6,000 feet. Visibility was limited, but everything aboard was "Okeh."

The Clipper was 476 miles out at 6:30 p. m. PST (4 p. m. Honolulu time), flying at 6,100 feet with clear weather.

At 7:30 p. m. PST (5 p. m. Honolulu time) the Clipper sent out the following message: "Sailing above the clouds. The sun is just setting. Beautiful weather."

### Beautiful Moonlight

The Clipper ship was 712 miles out of Alameda at 8:30 p. m. PST (6 p. m. Honolulu time), enjoying beautiful moonlight and with its speed averaging 152 miles an hour.

The plane airliner moved into the great circle course at 9:30 p. m. PST (7 p. m. Honolulu time), at which time it was 866 miles out at sea. Weather and visibility were reported as good, and the ship was flying over clouds at a speed of 155 miles an hour.

The Clipper was 1,030 miles out, flying at an altitude of 7,000 feet and 3,500 feet above the clouds, and making 156 miles an hour at 10:30 p. m. PST (8 p. m. Honolulu time).

The halfway mark was passed by the big ship at 11:40 p. m. PST (9:10

(Continued on Page 4, Col. 8)

## INTER-ISLAND HOPS PLANNED FOR BIG PLANE

### Personnel To Study Terrain of All Coasts, Weather Conditions Here

The Pan American Clipper while in Hawaii is scheduled to be used in the exploratory project for the annotation of flight maps and to enable her crew to familiarize themselves with terrain and marine characteristics of the Hawaiian islands, it was officially announced by a Pan American headquarters here today.

Several exploratory flights will be made over the islands for this purpose. No time schedule has been set for the program and the project will be advanced as conditions permit.

## GIANT CLIPPER HERALDS NEW TRAVEL TREND

### Makes Alameda-Honolulu Experimental Flight In 17 Hours, 44 Minutes

### Thousands See Big Plane In Circle Over City Before Landing At 8 A. M.

Through facilities furnished by the navy under orders issued by Rear Admiral H. E. Yarnell, the general public may visit the fleet air base and view the PAA Clipper ship up until 6 p. m. today and from 8 a. m. to 4 p. m. Thursday.

Visitors should go to the main gate, where they will be given directions for reaching Hancock landing. Boats will be provided at the landing for taking parties across to the fleet air base on Ford Island. Visitors should not take cameras with them.

Riding out of the cloud-filled sky, the silver monarch of the air, Pan American Airways Pioneer Clipper, roared over Honolulu today, 17 hours and 44 minutes out of Alameda, Cal., establishing a new transpacific flight record for east-west flight and heralding the approach of a new era in transportation.

The plane averaged 136 miles an hour across nearly a direct route from the coast here and was forced to circle the city to prevent an early landing.

The silver bird headed in to Makapuu, then sped across the city to Pearl Harbor, circled Ford island and doubled back on the course, killing time so that she settled precisely at 8 a. m. on the channel at Pearl Harbor. She reached Pearl Harbor 18 hours and 38 minutes after the takeoff, 2,400 miles away.

Capt. Edwin Musick brought the plane with calm skill and as she settled on the water, there was no perceptible jar.

Despite the arduous trip, members of the crew smiled broadly with little apparent fatigue as they stepped from the plane and were mustered into the center of a curious horde while they were greeted officially over the air by leading officials of civil and military life.

Upon culmination of the flight, Col. Clarence M. Young, Pacific division manager of PAA said, "Results of this trip are tremendously satisfactory and we appreciate fully the hearty welcome given the plane and its crew by the people of Honolulu.

"However, Pan American officials consider this flight to be a routine movement in the steady construction of transoceanic airlines.

"It was undertaken only after careful preparation, and for the purpose of concluding further surveys in the islands, and was in no way intended to be a stunt flight."

At two minutes of eight, the huge Clipper hung on the horizon at sea off Pearl Harbor entrance after completing its circle of the city, turned gracefully and slowly towards its landing spot while underneath, a flock of fast pursuit planes shot by in formation.

The Clipper then had the aerial stage alone and as the first roar of its motors could be heard at Ford Island, there was a quiet hum over spectators broken only by the mutter of this historic event.

While a crowd of several hundred, predominantly military men, flocked to the landing raft at the fleet air base, the huge Clipper circled over the base at 12 minutes after 7. It was led by five planes of VP 10 squadron and flanked by 12 planes of the 13th pursuit group.

A large part of the crowd remained at the fleet air base to watch the huge plane being towed up the landing ramp and wheeled up beside one of the hangars.

Small children walked beneath the wings of the plane as it was wheeled along, touching it and apparently hoping that they could obtain souvenirs.

Meanwhile, the six members o
(Continued on Page 4, Col. 4)

Pictured is the happy, but tired crew covered by the traditional leis of welcome to the Hawaiian Islands. Aloha! From left to right are pictured Jarboe, Canaday, Sullivan, Captain Musick, Noonan and Wright.

Souvenir covers for collectors were flown, either on the Honolulu or San Francisco portion of the trip, or on the round trip to both Honolulu and back to San Francisco.

Pictured is a round trip cover that was signed by the crew. Also pictured is a cover from Hawaii to California from Fred Noonan to his friend, Marvel Brown of Coconut Grove, Florida, who had received the postcard mailed by Noonan the evening before his departure from Alameda.

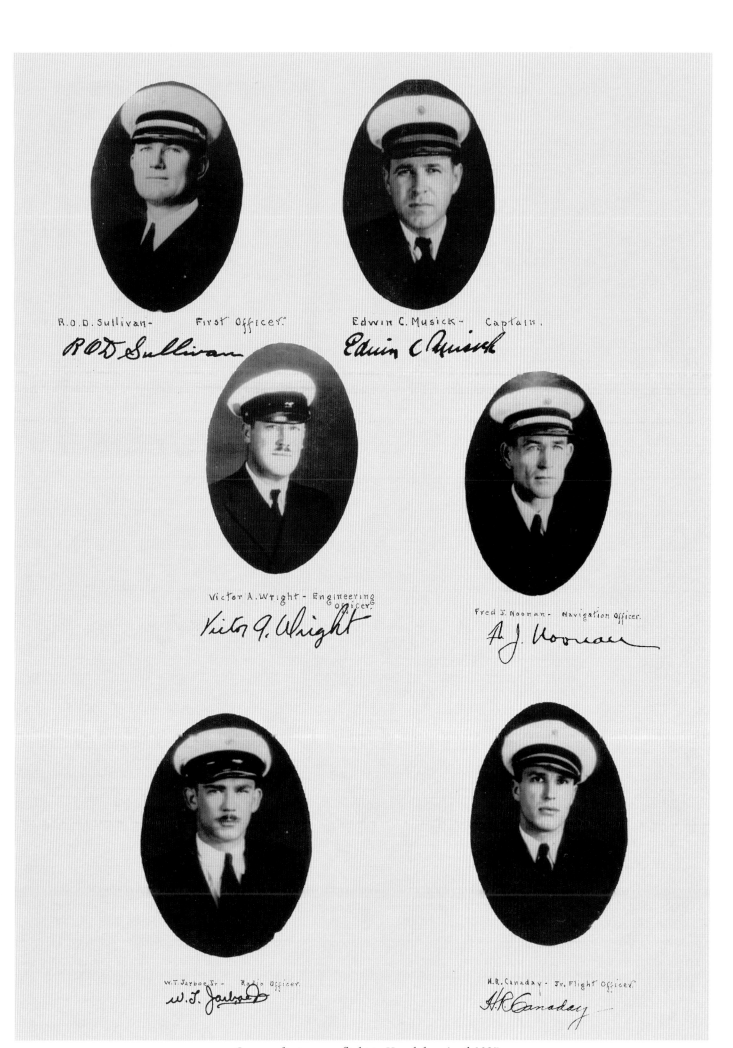

R.O.D.Sullivan -          First Officer.

*R O D Sullivan*

Edwin C. Musick -    Captain.

*Edwin C Musick*

Victor A. Wright - Engineering Officer

*Victor A. Wright*

Fred J. Noonan -   Navigation Officer.

*F. J. Noonan*

W.T.Jarboe Jr -    Radio Officer.

*W.T. Jarboe*

H.R.Canaday -   Jr. Flight Officer.

*H R Canaday*

*Crew on first survey flight to Honolulu - April 1935*

J. T. TRIPPE
CHRYSLER BUILDING
NEW YORK

June 6, 1935

Dear Amon:

Only this morning have I received back from
California the two first flight covers which I sent out
to Eddie Musick asking that he sign them so that I
could send them to you for your son and daughter.

I am only sorry that they were addressed to
me personally rather than direct to them for they would
have been more interesting additions to their collections.

Now that the Navy maneuvers are nearly completed
our next survey flight to Hawaii and Midway will shortly
get under way.  I am still looking forward to your
company as a fellow voyager on that first through passenger
flight to the Far East.

With best regards,

Sincerely,

Amon G. Carter, Esq.
Fort Worth Star-Telegram
Forth Worth, Texas

An interesting personal note from Juan Trippe dated June 6, 1935, addressed to his friend Amon G. Carter, the owner and editor of the ***Fort Worth Star-Telegram***, not only enclosed flight covers that Ed Musick signed for Mr. Carter's children, but it also again showed the close cooperation that existed between Pan Am and the Navy in coordinating the scheduling of these early flights across the Pacific.

Another interesting note from Ed Musick, dated May 5, 1935 on the letterhead of the Hotel St. Francis where Musick and the other crew members were staying in San Francisco while awaiting the June survey flight to Midway, shows us that the crew-signed flight covers were not necessarily signed the day of the flight. Requests for signed covers were being honored by the accommodating Captain Musick well after the flight's completion.

Between the arrival of the Clipper on the morning of April 17 and its departure on April 22, the crew rested and attended celebrations in their honor. The Clipper was also fully serviced. During this layover period in Honolulu, on April 19 Fred Noonan wrote another postcard to his friend in Coconut Grove:

*"Honolulu - April 19, 1935 - Dear Friend: Had a pleasant flight out and enjoying our visit here. Expect return Alameda the first of next week. . . Kindest wishes to you, Fred Noonan".*

It was postmarked April 20, 1935 - two days before the April 22 departure on the flight back to San Francisco.

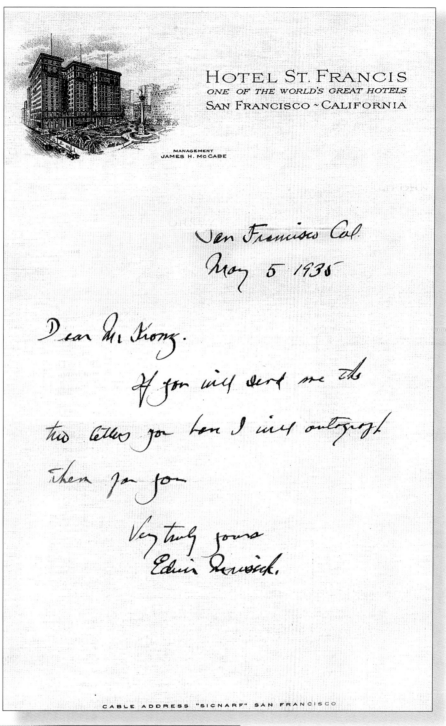

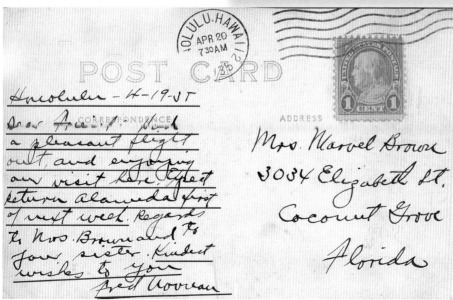

It is interesting that Fred Noonan did not just carry the postcard back with him on the flight to San Francisco so that it would also have been a flight souvenir cover before mailing it on to Coconut Grove, Florida. But that would have violated the regulations of both the post office and Pan Am. Because the postcard went by sea, Fred Noonan and the Clipper were back in California many days ahead of his postcard to Marvel Brown.

*Note -Pan Am envelope from Midway station manager Lueder used for Navy flight*

*Combination of May 1935 Naval flight and April 1935 Pan Am survey*

After the April survey flight to Honolulu in April of 1935, the Navy flights to Midway referred to by Trippe in his letter to Amon Carter took place between May 9 and May 24, 1935 and involved 46 Navy planes. By this time Karl Lueder, Pan Am's station manager at Midway, was on Midway along with the construction crew and Lueder used one of the Pan Am envelopes that he had with him to send a souvenir cover for the Navy flight that returned from Midway to Honolulu on May 25. It's a nice Navy-Pan Am combination. Another combination Navy-Pan Am cover used the April survey flight cover and added the May 22, 1935 Navy flight cachet.

The Pan Am Clipper's return flight from Honolulu to San Francisco took much longer and was more difficult than the survey flight over. Captain Musick had to contend with head winds and cross winds and the plane arrived over five hours overdue and its fuel tanks were virtually dry. It was close to being a disaster. The flight took 23 hours and 41 minutes.

*Travel agent model of Sikorsky S-42 with crew signed Pan Am navigation chart actually used on return flight*

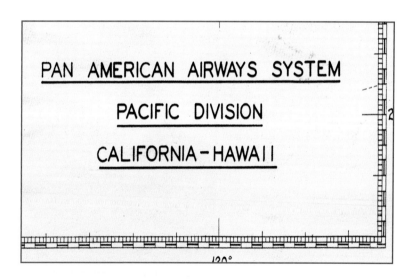

PAN AMERICAN AIRWAYS SYSTEM

PACIFIC DIVISION

CALIFORNIA – HAWAII

An actual navigation chart for this first survey flight signed by the crew charts the Clipper's progress from Honolulu back to San Francisco for the first 14 hours of the return flight. In spite of the near disaster in almost running out of fuel, Pan Am did not want to alarm the public and Captain Musick was quoted as saying, *"A fine trip without major trouble and satisfactory in all particulars. We could do it again tomorrow if it were necessary, I think the flight has removed the element of chance in Transpacific journey"*.

Pictured is a relieved Captain Musick leaving the Clipper after completing the survey flight. Captain Musick's duties, however, were not complete. He had to sign one more souvenir cover for a very special collector. President Franklin D. Roosevelt fully supported and closely followed Pan Am's pioneering efforts and he was to receive this special envelope.

From the look in Captain Musick's eyes, it appears that he is enjoying this last duty from the first survey flight.

San Francisco, California - President Roosevelt received a special souvenir of the flight of the Pan American Clipper from Honolulu to San Francisco. It was a special cover bearing all of the stamps issued by the U.S. Government, a special flight cachet and the signatures of the Clipper crew. The cover was flown east from San Francisco and delivered to the White House by a United Airlines stewardess. Left to right: Captain Ed Musick, pilot of the Clipper, autographs the cover at the request of Miss Ruth Fisher.

*Ruth Fisher holding first flight cover for F.D.R. being signed by Captain Musick*

| Survey 2 Midway | June 12 - 22, 1935 | S-42 Pan Am Clipper | Musick/Sullivan |
|---|---|---|---|

| **Outbound Flight Schedule** | | **Inbound Flight Schedule** | |
|---|---|---|---|
| San Francisco - Honolulu | June 12-13 | Midway - Honolulu | June 17 |
| Honolulu - Midway | June 15 | Honolulu - San Francisco | June 21-22 |

On June 12 the Pan American Clipper departed San Francisco bound for Midway on the second survey flight. On the first survey flight to Honolulu, because of severe weight restrictions, only the six crew members actually flying the plane made the trip. There were no passengers. However, on this second survey flight to Midway, once the Clipper reached Honolulu, the next leg of the flight to Midway was so short that added flight personnel could be carried. Therefore, making the flight from

Honolulu to Midway was Phil Berst, the Section Maintenance Supervisor and T.W. Winter, Pan Am Radio Service Engineer. Pictured is Section Maintenance Supervisor Phil Berst, with his wife and young daughter, Catherine. Berst had joined Pan Am in 1928 as an airplane mechanic in Miami. He was selected in early 1935 to head up the maintenance department in Honolulu and to supervise the head mechanics at bases on Midway, Wake, Guam and Manila. He arrived in Honolulu by the ocean liner S.S. Lurline in March, 1935.

*Phil Berst and Family in Honolulu - 1935 after completion of survey flight*

*On the landing float at Midway - left to right - Chief Mechanic H.S. de Nourie, Engineering Officer V.A. Wright - Capt. Edwin Musick, Radio Operator W.T. Jarboe, Jr. - Navigation Officer Fred Noonan - Airport Manager Karl Luede -, and First Officer R.O.D. Sullivan*

Phil Berst made the three survey flights to Midway, Wake and Guam. In each case he joined the crew in Honolulu and remained in Honolulu on the plane's return trip. From official Pan Am news releases it appears that he was considered a full fledged crew member on at least some of these three survey flights. Therefore, Phil Berst was the forgotten crew member of the survey flights to Midway, Wake and Guam and he was also the first passenger on any Pan Am flight in the Pacific. All of Phil Berst's scrapbooks, photos and flight covers were shared with me by his daughter, Catherine Berst Lytton - the very cute little girl in the 1935 photo of her family on the preceding.

The crew on the Midway flight from San Francisco to Honolulu was exactly the same crew that had flown the first survey flight to Honolulu. After their June 13 arrival, the plane was serviced for the flight to Midway and they departed early in the morning on June 15.

Phil Berst reported on how primitive the conditions were on Midway: *"The Midway taxi was the large diesel tractor pulling a sled. Whenever it started most of us were thrown off because of the fast start. The night we arrived the Pan Am staff made a fine dinner. The next night men from the cable company on the other end of the island had a dinner in our honor. Everyone was happy to see us. It was the first mail they had received since the departure of the North Haven at the end of April 1935".*

Conditions on Midway were primitive. Station manager Karl Lueder is standing in front of Pan Am's first office on the island.

Direction finder

Clearing building site

Also pictured is
Midway's dock
and launch

Midway launch,
lost in storm
December 1935

Roadbuilding at Midway

Movie night at Midway

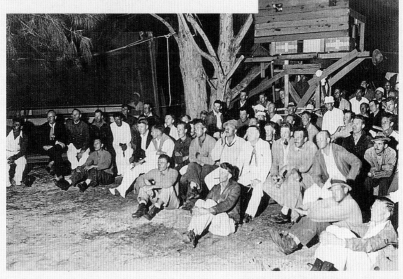

Midway village

On this flight Pan Am and the Post Office did not encourage souvenir mail. The only commemorative flight covers from the Midway survey flight contain the cachets that were hand carved out of a wooden block by the station manager at Midway, Karl Lueder, assisted by the station manager at Wake, Col. George Bicknell, Dr. Kenler and William Mullahey while they were all together on the North Haven. Virtually all of the covers seen contain the gooney bird with the closed beak and the words "first flight".

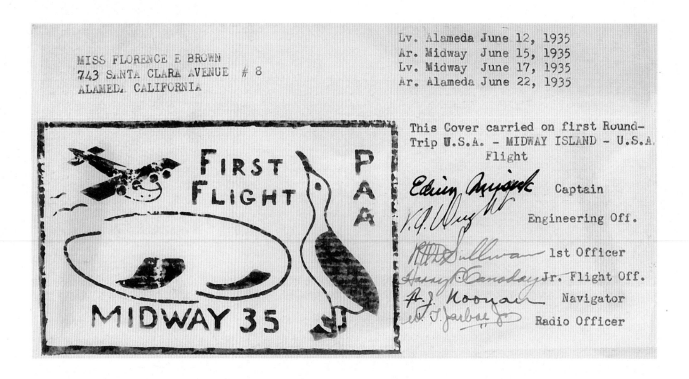

Miss Florence Brown was the fiancee of the radio operator on Wake Island, Almon Gray who later became his wife. He made sure she got a souvenir flight cover from the Midway flight signed by the entire crew. Almon Gray's widow and his daughter also kindly shared his scrapbooks and flight covers with me so that this book would tell a more complete story of these Pacific pioneers.

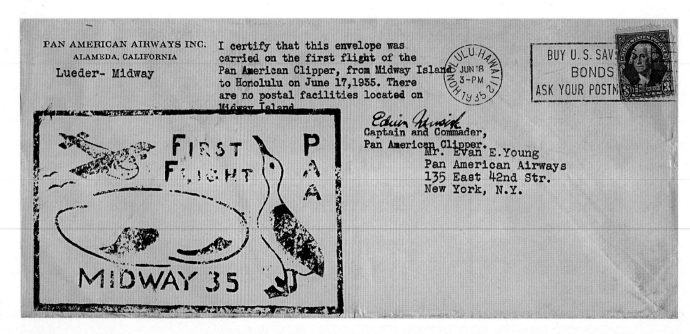

Illustrated above is a cover with the typical gooney bird cachet signed by Captain Musick as a favor for one of the directors of Pan Am, Evan Young.

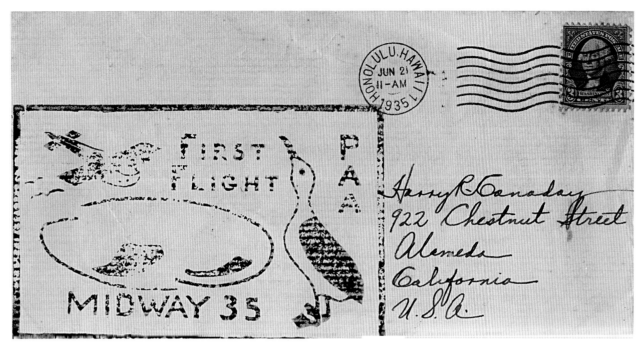

*Souvenir cover Harry Canaday sent to himself*

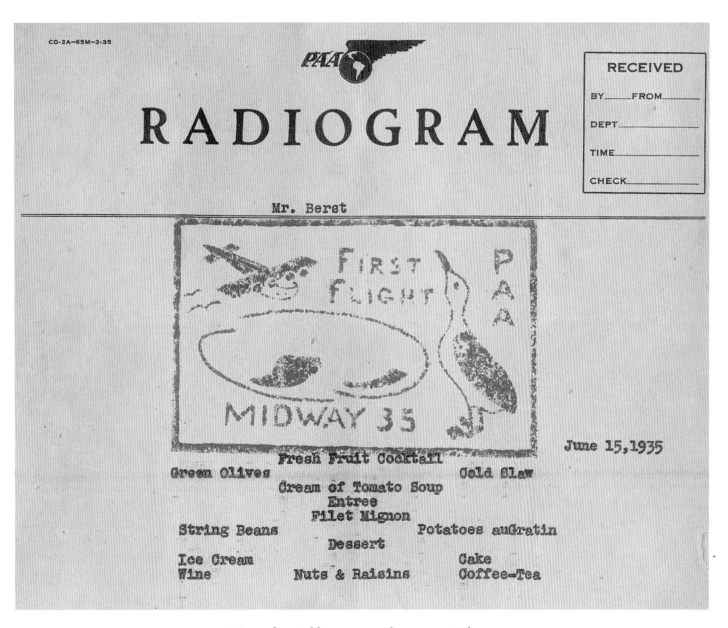

*Menu of special banquet served to crew at Midway*

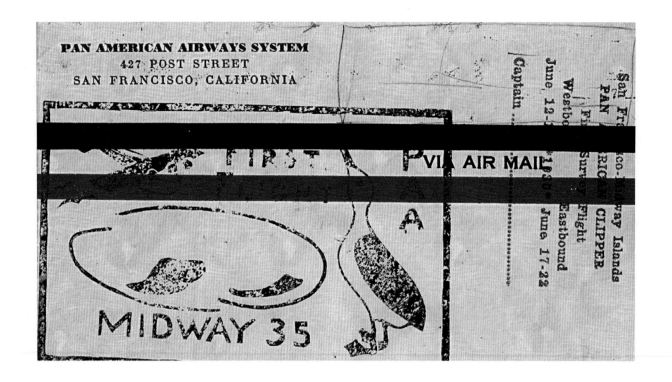

Note the hand stamp at the right side of the cover that is illustrated above. This cover may not have been flown. It is believed that this hand stamp with the arrival time and a place for the captain to sign was made up by the station manager at Alameda. This is the only cover I have seen with this printed cachet.

By far the most interesting Midway survey flight cover I have seen depicts the gooney bird with its mouth open and the words "First Air Mail" rather than "First Flight". This is undoubtedly one of the cachets carved by Karl Lueder and the others while they were at Midway. It obviously was not the design chosen to be used by the station manager for the Midway survey flight souvenir covers, perhaps, because it says "Air Mail", when airmail was not authorized. However, Lt. Johnson, being such an avid collector of covers, was undoubtedly favored with at least one example of this unique cachet. Based on the handwriting and the return address, the cover to Lt. Johnson was addressed to Karl Lueder, Midway's station manager.

This cover is from the collection of Bob Wilcsek. If any others exist, I would appreciate copies.

*Rare cachet - beak open - first airmail*

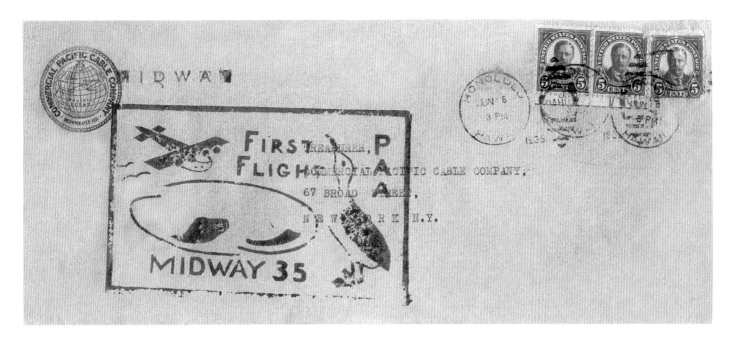

About twenty men lived and worked on Midway with the Commercial Pacific Cable Company. Even though commercial mail was not supposed to be carried on this survey flight, the Pan Am crew accommodated the cable company's Midway manager by carrying this envelope on the return flight to Honolulu, where it was placed in the regular mail on the next ship to California. It is one of the very few truly commercial letters carried on this survey flight from Midway to Honolulu.

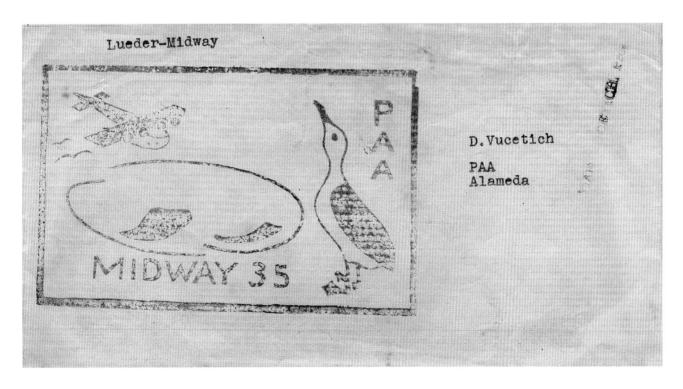

Another interesting cover showing the gooney bird cachet in red is addressed to Dan Vucetich at Pan Am's Alameda base. Vucetich was the supercargo on the supply ship North Haven and he, of course, knew Pan Am's Midway manager, Karl Lueder. The words "First Flight" have been removed from this cachet. Therefore, this envelope was flown back to Alameda, either on the return flight of the Wake Island survey flight in August of 1935, or the return flight of the Guam survey flight in October of 1935.

After November of 1935, when the airmail contracts went into effect, all personal mail going back to Alameda had to be properly stamped with the new airmail stamps in accordance with postal regulations. Therefore, this unusual cover was flown before the November 1935 airmail contracts went into effect.

With the success of the Midway survey flight, Pan Am was much more confident that they could truly cross the Pacific with mail and eventually with passengers. These were exciting days for Pan Am.

| Survey 3 Wake | August 9 - 29, 1935 | S-42 Pan Am Clipper | Sullivan/Tilton |
|---|---|---|---|

| Outbound Flight Schedule | | Inbound Flight Schedule | |
|---|---|---|---|
| San Francisco - Honolulu | Aug. 9-10 | Wake - Midway | Aug. 21-20* |
| Honolulu - Midway | Aug. 13 | Midway - Honolulu | Aug. 22 |
| Midway - Wake | Aug. 16-17* | Honolulu - San Francisco | Aug. 28-29 |

*Dateline - Gain day outbound - Lose day inbound

The third Pacific survey flight was from San Francisco to Honolulu and on to Wake. It departed San Francisco on August 9, and after stops at Honolulu and Midway, arrived at Wake on August 17. Shown above is the crew for the Wake flight. From left to right are Jarboe, Canaday, Sullivan, Wright, Webber, Noonan and Tilton. Captain Musick, who had captained the first two survey flights, was in Baltimore familiarizing himself with the Martin M-130 that would be making the first scheduled airmail flight in November.

Tilton, who was on his first survey flight, went on to become the chief Pan Am pilot in the Pacific after Musick's tragic accident in January of 1938.

*Captain Sullivan*

Phil Berst, who was the first passenger ever to fly the Pacific in a commercial aircraft, was listed officially by Pan Am as a crew member on this flight. In a Pan American Airways newsletter for July and August of 1935, it states:

> *"In the crew were J.H. Tilton, First Officer; Victor A. Wright, Engineering Officer; Fred Noonan, Navigation Officer; W. Turner Jarboe, Radio Officer; M.C. Webber, Jr. Flight Officer; H.R. Canaday, Second Navigation Officer; and (from Honolulu) Philip Berst, Second Engineering Officer".*

In spite of the fact that he was listed officially by Pan Am as a flight officer, I have been unable to locate a single picture where he appears with the other crew members in any official photographs. He

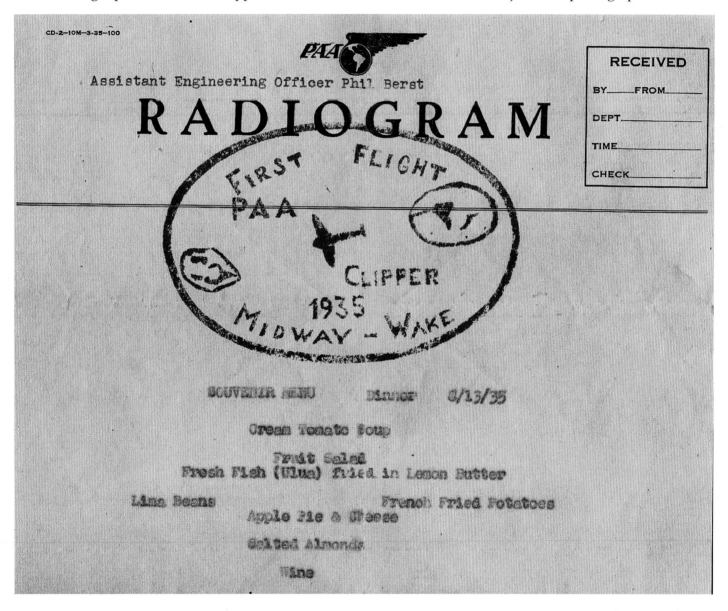

never signed a souvenir flight cover with the other crew members. Whether his omission was due merely to inadvertence or whether it was intentional on the part of the other crew members that had flown from Alameda to Honolulu is not known. Perhaps they felt he did not deserve the recognition of those who made the complete flight. But, in any event, it appears that he remains the forgotten crew member of these survey flights.

Pictured above is a souvenir dinner menu from the Wake survey flight that was served to the crew on the day of their arrival at Midway on August 13 on the outbound second leg of the Wake flight. Three days later, on August 16, the crew along with Phil Berst would make the final leg of the trip from Midway to Wake.

Pan Am Clipper arrives at
Wake-August 17, 1935

Landing at Wake lagoon

Crew arrives by launch at
Wake base

Mess hall

Airport office with flag
Wake September 1935

General view of Wake
village showing barrels
of fuel

Wake transmitters KNBI -
Western Electric 14-A
PAA100-G2

All important direction finder

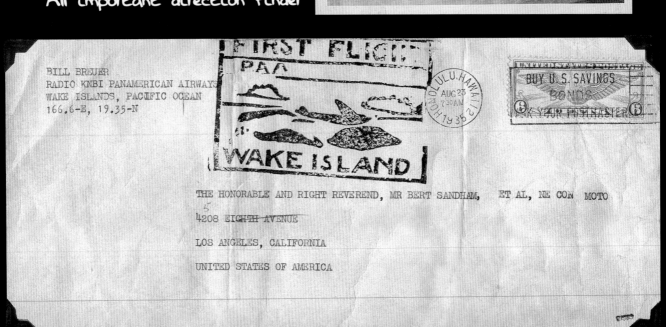

Wake pioneer, Bill Brewer, the assistant radio operator, sent the
first commercial airmail letter from Wake Island Radio Station
KNBI on August 21, to Reverend Bert Sandham in Los Angeles -
Commercial mail was not supposed to be carried on the flight

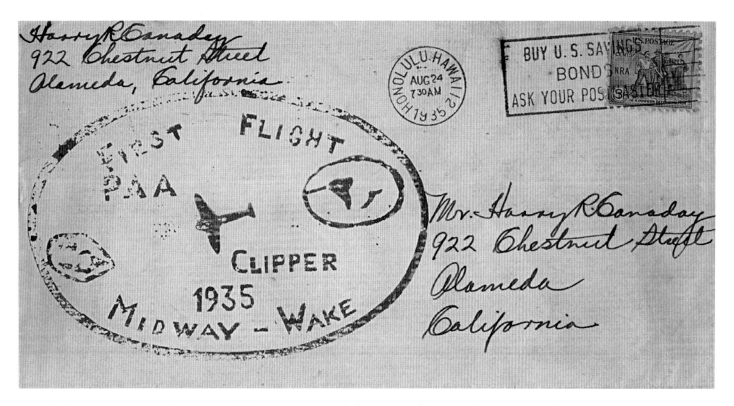

Flight covers were discouraged by Pan Am and the post office on these survey flights. The Pan Am crew members and personnel, however, wanted lasting mementoes of their hard work and their accomplishments. In spite of the regulations, a few souvenir covers were prepared.

The cover shown above uses the oval cachet, which Karl Leuder and the others carved from the wood block at Midway while on the North Haven. It commemorates the first flight between Midway and Wake and it is seen on both stamped and unstamped envelopes that traveled between the two islands.

The cover shown below was cancelled at Wake Island, with the words: **WAKE ISLAND AUG 20 1935** This cancel makes the cover unique, because Wake Island did not have a post office and envelopes were not supposed to be cancelled on Wake in this fashion. The cover was also date stamped on the reverse on August 16 when it was carried from Midway to Wake and on August 20, when it was flown back from Wake to Midway. Therefore, it is also an unusual first flight round trip flight cover between Midway and Wake.

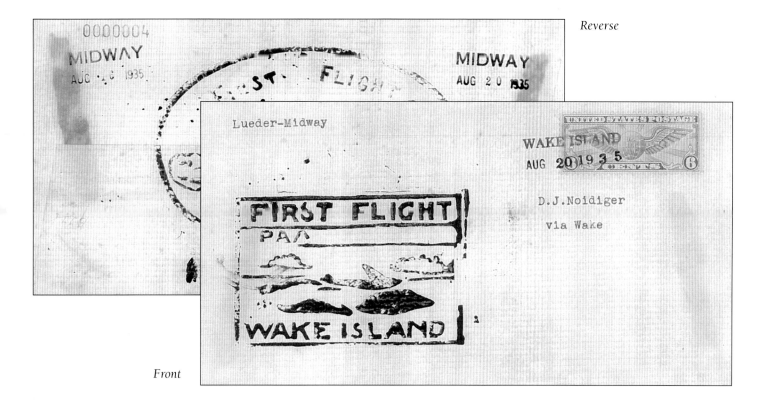

*Reverse*

*Front*

Harry R Canaday
922 Chestnut Street
Alameda, California

BUY U. S. SAVINGS
BONDS
ASK YOUR POST...

FIRST FLIGHT
PAA
WAKE ISLAND

Mrs. Harry R Canaday
922 Chestnut Street
Alameda
California

Alexander Young Hotel
HONOLULU
HAWAII

The next illustrated cover was sent to Mrs. Canaday by her husband, who was the junior flight officer on all four of the survey flights. When I was preparing the envelope for this book, I found that it contained a very touching letter from Canaday to his wife on the six month anniversary of their marriage. This note makes us aware of the long periods of separation faced by the crew members and their families. It is also very unusual to find a personal letter in the survey mail. As of 1999 Captain Canaday and his bride of 65 years are still living happily together in Florida. He reports that he plays golf at least twice a week.

August 23rd, 1935.

My dear wife:

Six months ago today, in fact, six months to this very minute we were married. It is 3:30 p.m. here. That would make it 9:00 p.m. in Miami.

They have been the happiest, most contented six months of my life. And you have made that possible. I love you with my whole heart, body, & soul. There'll never be another, but you.

Your own adoring husband,
Harry.

*More common black cachet*

The cachet of the Clipper flying over the chain to California is seen in both red and black and its use is surrounded by some question and controversy. It was not prepared on Wake or Midway, but instead by the station crew back in Alameda. Before the flight an official request was made by Pan Am that it not be used on souvenir mail. Nonetheless, it was.

*Rarely seen red cachet*

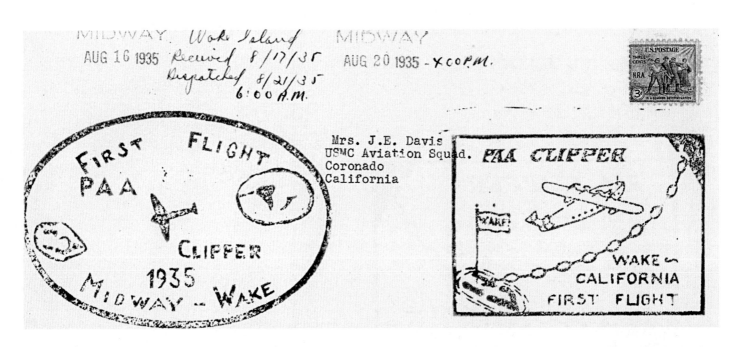

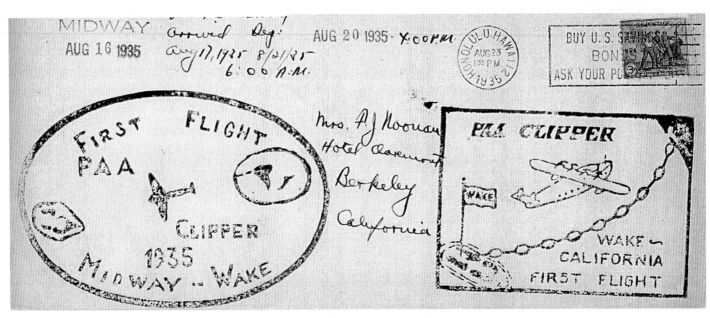

The only three known covers with two cachets are from the collections of John Johnson, Allen Klein and Bob Wilcsek.

The next cover depicted was printed by Pan Am and all of them are addressed to Juan Trippe in New York. Most are also signed by Captain Sullivan. The cachet was applied after the flight was completed, either at Pan Am's Alameda office, or perhaps even at the New York office, to make the envelopes a more attractive souvenir.

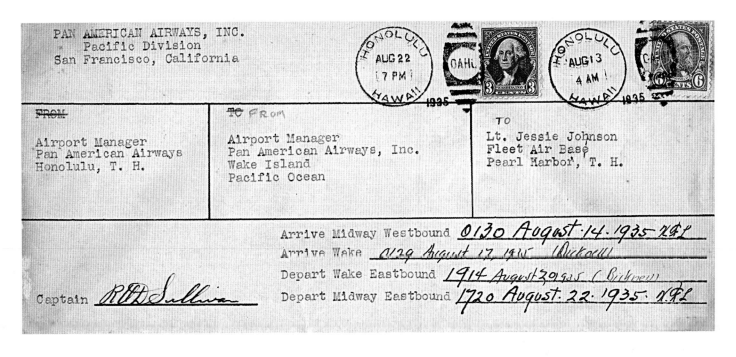

Lt. Jesse Johnson, a Navy aviator and avid collector stationed in Honolulu, saw the covers before they were sent out on the Wake survey flight. He undoubtedly prepared his own covers in a similar but larger format, addressed to himself back in Pearl Harbor. It never went to Pan Am's office, but was delivered directly to him. Therefore, his cover does not contain the blue cachet and it is the only one I have seen of this type that is not addressed to Trippe in New York.

Wake radio operator Almon Gray also made sure that his fiancée, Florence Brown, who later became his wife, received two very nice souvenirs of the Wake flight signed by Captain Sullivan. One of them traveled by air back to Honolulu and then by ship back to Alameda. The other was carried back by the crew and the cachet with the chain of islands leading to Wake was applied in Alameda and given to Miss Brown.

The cover at the bottom of the page is a rare inward commercial letter from Pan Am's New York office to the station manager on Wake. It was mailed August 7 by domestic air mail, addressed to the Alameda base of Pan Am. It arrived just in time to be placed on the Clipper to Alameda before the S-42 departed in the late afternoon of August 9 for the Wake survey flight.

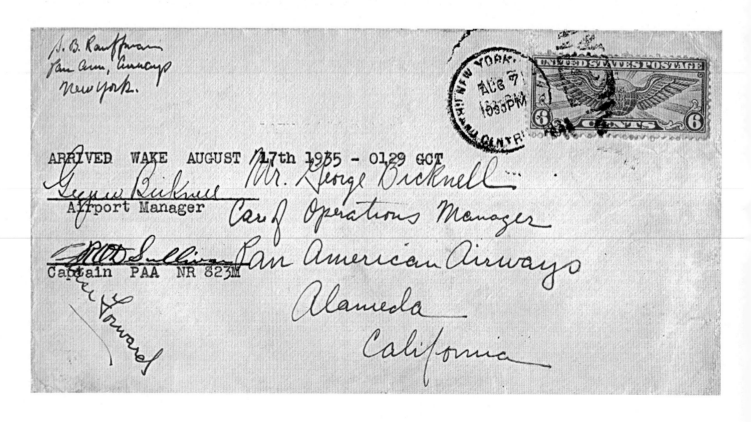

Shown again are covers with the hermit crab cachet that was prepared on Wake Island. This hermit crab design, although rejected by the station manager, George Bicknell, for use on souvenir mail, has only been seen on these two envelopes. The first is addressed by Almon Gray, Wake's radio operator, to himself at Pan Am's Alameda base. At this point in time Mr. Gray knew he would be returning to Alameda on the inbound flight of the Guam survey flight scheduled for October. He obtained one of these envelopes from its designer, Bill Mullahey, and prepared his own souvenir to be carried back to California by one of the survey flight's crew members as a part of the company mail and given to his fiancee, Florence Brown, a secretary in Pan Am's Alameda office.

The only other envelope seen with the hermit crab cachet was sent by its designer, Bill Mullahey, to his friends from his lifeguarding days on Long Island. Mailed two months after the August survey flight, it clearly did not travel by air.

The Wake Island survey flight covers display a greater variety of cachets than any of the other early survey flights and I find covers from this flight to be the most interesting of any of the first four survey flights.

Pan Am was very pleased with both the flight's success and also their preparations for the planned November flight to Manila. Everything was going according to plan.

*Hermit crabs on Wake beach*

*Rare hermit crab cachet carved by William Mullahey*

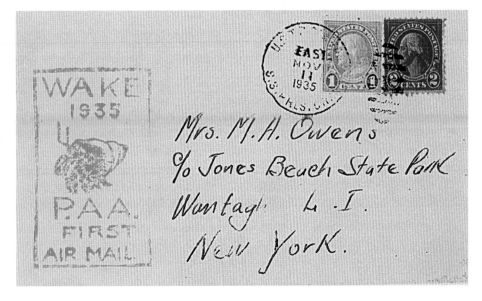

139

| Survey 4  Guam | October 5 - 24, 1935 | S-42 Pan Am Clipper | Sullivan/Tilton |
|---|---|---|---|

| Outbound Flight Schedule | | Inbound Flight Schedule | |
|---|---|---|---|
| San Francisco - Honolulu | Oct. 5-6 | Guam - Wake | Oct.16 |
| Honolulu - Midway | Oct. 10 | Wake - Midway | Oct. 18-17* |
| Midway - Wake | Oct. 11-12* | Midway - Honolulu | Oct. 19 |
| Wake - Guam | Oct. 13 | Honolulu - San Francisco | Oct. 23-24 |

*Dateline - Gain day outbound - Lose day inbound

The fourth and last Pacific survey flight went from San Francisco to Guam. It was hailed by Pan Am as the longest over-ocean airplane flight ever made. In their newsletter for September / October 1935 they proudly stated:

> *Going confidently westward with that same effortless precision that had characterized the pioneering of the greatest airway in history, the Pan American Clipper dramatically removed from the unknown with the longest over ocean airplane flight ever made, the long 1,500 mile stretch of heretofore unflown Pacific that lies between Wake Island and Guam, and cleared the way for the first scheduled Transport flight across the world's greatest ocean . . . Favorable conditions of wind and weather over practically the entire route enabled them to make the best time yet recorded for the crossing.*

### CREW OF "PAN AMERICAN CLIPPER" ON LONGEST OCEAN FLIGHT

*Left to right: Radio Officer W.T. Jarboe, Jr., Second Officer M. Lodeesen, Junior Flight Officer H.R. Canaday, Engineering Officer V.A. Wright, Captain R.O.D. Sullivan, First Officer J.H. Tilton, and Navigating Officer Fred Noonan*

Pictured above is the crew for the Guam survey flight as they were shown in the company newsletter. Once again, district maintenance supervisor Phil Berst joined the crew in Honolulu for the flight west, as he had done on the Midway and Wake survey flights.

Upon landing at Apra Harbor at Guam, it was determined that none of the ground personnel had enough experience in docking the Clipper to do it successfully. So a Navy launch was sent out to the plane and Phil Berst was brought to the docking area to coordinate the mooring of the Clipper.

*Pan Am base at Guam*

These six rare picture postcards from Phil Berst's scrapbook, taken at Guam upon the Clipper's arrival, capture the excitement felt by this lonely and isolated outpost that was finally to be connected to the rest of the world.

*Crowd awaiting Clipper's arrival*

*Launch assisted in mooring*

*Navy Governor and crew*

Standing proudly in the middle of the flight crew in his white dress uniform is Naval Governor George A. Alexander, Governor of Guam. To his left is Captain Sullivan with the rest of the crew gathered around.

*Phil Berst and friends*

Phil Berst is shown in this picture, second from the right, in a white Pan Am uniform.

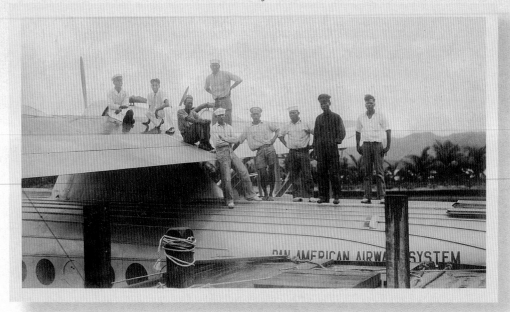

*Mooring crew for Clipper*

Once moored, the clipper was taken charge of by airport manager I.P. Gregory and his crew.

After the welcoming at the harbor, the people on Guam had celebrations planned for the crew.

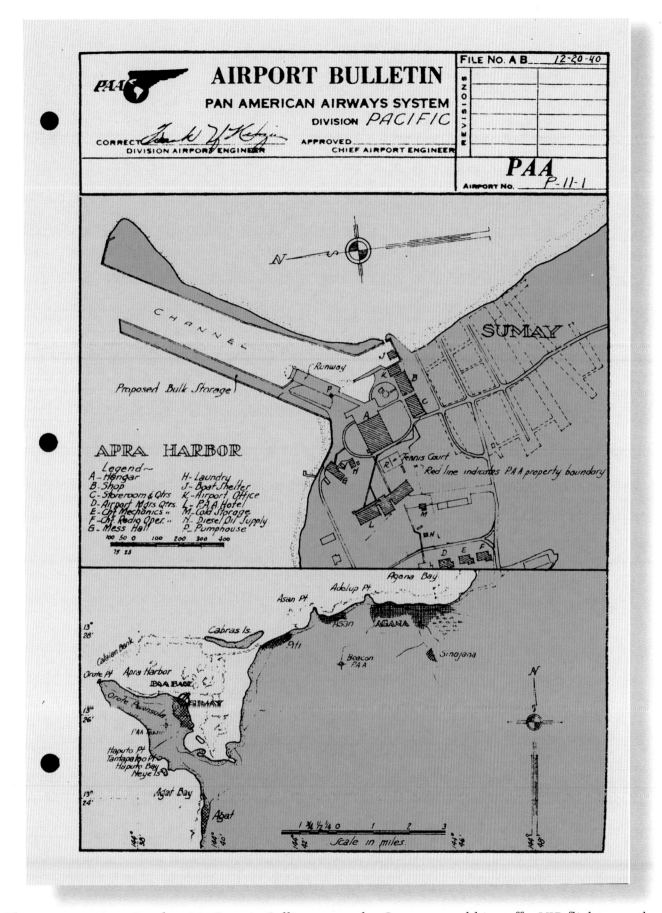

**AIRPORT BULLETIN**
PAN AMERICAN AIRWAYS SYSTEM
DIVISION *PACIFIC*

CORRECT_____
DIVISION AIRPORT ENGINEER

APPROVED_____
CHIEF AIRPORT ENGINEER

**PAA**
AIRPORT NO. ____ P-11-1

REVISIONS

CHANNEL

*Proposed Bulk Storage*

SUMAY

*Runway*

*Tennis Court*

*Red line indicates PAA property boundary*

**APRA HARBOR**

Legend—
A- Hangar        H- Laundry
B- Shop          J- Boat Shelter
C- Storeroom & Qtrs   K- Airport Office
D- Airport Mgrs Qtrs  L- PAA Hotel
E- Cht Mechanics "    M- Cold Storage
F- Cht Radio Oper. "  N- Diesel Oil Supply
G- Mess Hall     P- Pumphouse

100 50 0   100   200   300   400
75 25

Agana Bay
Adelup Pt.
Asan Pt.
Asan    AGANA
Sinajana
Cabras Is.
Calalan Bank
Piti
Beacon PAA
Orote Pt.    Apra Harbor
PAA BASE
Orote Peninsula    SUMAY
PAA Radio
Haputo Pt.
Tantapalao Pt.
Haputo Bay
Neye Is.
Agat Bay
Agat

1 ¾ ½ ¼ 0    1    2    3
Scale in miles.

The next morning, October 14, Captain Sullivan gave the Governor and his staff a VIP flight over the island. At this same time they made a survey of the approaches for the Apra harbor landing area, completing the mapping assignment of their flight project.

In the afternoon, at the Governor's invitation, the crew took a motor tour about the island and they were enthusiastically greeted everywhere by the native people. In late afternoon there was a reception hosted by the Governor at the Government House honoring the flight crew.

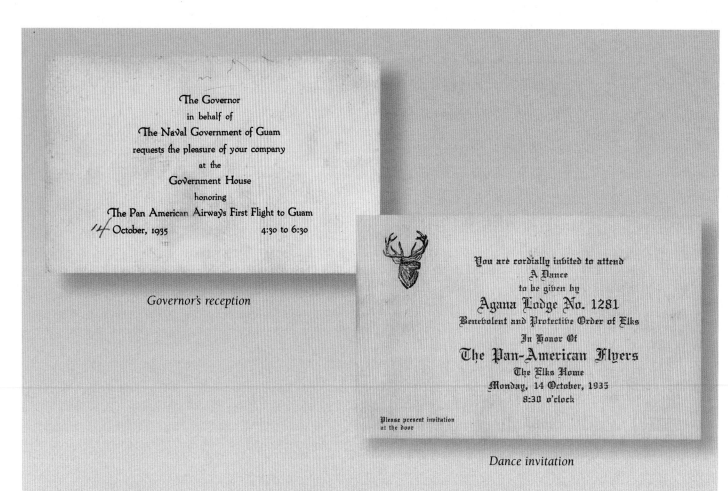

The Governor
in behalf of
The Naval Government of Guam
requests the pleasure of your company
at the
Government House
honoring
The Pan American Airways First Flight to Guam
14 October, 1935                    4:30 to 6:30

*Governor's reception*

You are cordially invited to attend
A Dance
to be given by
Agana Lodge No. 1281
Benevolent and Protective Order of Elks
In Honor Of
The Pan-American Flyers
The Elks Home
Monday, 14 October, 1935
8:30 o'clock

Please present invitation
at the door

*Dance invitation*

But their day wasn't over yet! The ladies of Guam had planned a dance in their honor, complete with a dance program that included twelve fox trots and four waltzes.

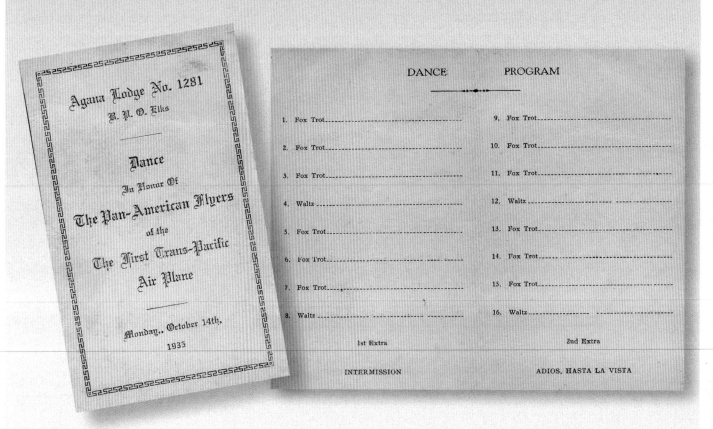

Agana Lodge No. 1281
B. P. O. Elks

Dance
In Honor Of
The Pan-American Flyers
of the
The First Trans-Pacific
Air Plane

Monday, October 14th,
1935

DANCE         PROGRAM

1. Fox Trot_____        9. Fox Trot_____
2. Fox Trot_____        10. Fox Trot_____
3. Fox Trot_____        11. Fox Trot_____
4. Waltz_____         12. Waltz_____
5. Fox Trot_____        13. Fox Trot_____
6. Fox Trot_____        14. Fox Trot_____
7. Fox Trot_____        15. Fox Trot_____
8. Waltz_____         16. Waltz_____

1st Extra                       2nd Extra

INTERMISSION                    ADIOS, HASTA LA VISTA

When the Clipper departed Guam on October 16 heading back to Wake and ultimately San Francisco, Phil Berst was not aboard. He remained on Guam to train the new mechanics in preparation for the first scheduled flight in November.

## ARMY AMATEUR RADIO SYSTEM
### SIGNAL CORPS
### A. R. L.
# RADIOGRAM

| CITY OF ORIGIN | STATION OF ORIGIN | NUMBER | DATE | CHECK |
|---|---|---|---|---|
| AGANA GUAM | K6FKB | 131 | OCT 25 | |

TO MRS PHIL B BERST

1630 MAKIKI ST
(STREET AND NUMBER, OR PHONE)

HONOLULU T.H.
(PLACE)

THIS MESSAGE WAS RECEIVED AT

AMATEUR RADIO STATION Amateur Radio Station K6EWQ
OWNER _____ Phone: Schofield 354,
STREET ADDRESS 21st Brigade Headquarters, PHONE
CITY AND STATE Schofield Barracks, Hawaii

EVERYTHING FINE HERE WRITE A LETTER AND LEAVE IT AT THE OFFICE

IT WILL COME OUT ON CLIPPER STOP ADDRESS IT P A A MANILA PI

STOP LEAVING HERE SATURDAY OR SUNDAY LOVE

PHIL

Sender's Address and
Phone Number for Reference:

| Rec'd | FROM STATION | LOCATED AT | DATE | TIME | OPERATOR |
|---|---|---|---|---|---|
| | K6FKB | AGANA GUAM | OCT 24 | 9P | HO |
| Sent | TO STATION | | | | |

The Army Amateur Radio System is a nation-wide network of patriotic expert amateur radio operators voluntarily affiliated with the Signal Corps, U. S. Army. It affords rapid emergency communication to the American Red Cross in time of disaster.
998—Ft. Monmouth, N. J.—6-23-33—100M

UNITED STATES ARMY TRANSPORT "U. S. GRANT"

**FIRST CLASS**

Guam 10-26-35
Place          Date

Received $ 75 as deposit to cover cost of subsistence.

O.E. Jrefele
Quartermaster Agent

Manila-3-21-35-3000

UNITED STATES ARMY TRANSPORT "U. S. GRANT"

| Name | **FIRST CLASS** | Stateroom |
|---|---|---|
| BERST PHIL B. COMM.PASSENGER. | | 309 |

First
Sitting { 
Second

Table No. 21
Seat Nos. 148

Please present this card to dining room steward at first meal served after sailing.

On October 24, 1935 Phil Berst sent a telegram to his wife in Honolulu telling her that he was about to leave by boat for the Philippines. He asked her to write to him and take the letter to the Pan Am office in Honolulu for delivery on the first mail flight to Manila in November of 1935. On October 26, Phil Berst took the U.S. Grant, an Army Transport, to Manila to arrange the mooring and maintenance facilities for the November flight. Pan Am was about to cross the North Pacific and the excitement was building.

Unlike the survey flights to Midway and Wake, where souvenir mail was carried privately by the crew, often times in violation of both post office and company procedures, the mail on the flight to Guam was sanctioned by the post office. In a brochure to collectors issued by Pan Am, they state the cost was $1.25 for each cover going one way and $2.50 for each round trip cover. Pan Am specifically said that special requests for signatures or special stamps could not be met, but as was always the case, some special covers were created.

| The available legs with the number of flown covers for each leg are: | |
|---|---|
| 1. San Francisco to Guam | 1,043 |
| 2. Honolulu to Guam | 300 |
| 3. Guam to Honolulu | 215 |
| 4. Guam to San Francisco | 563 |
| 5. San Francisco - Guam - San Francisco | 4,132 |
| 6. San Francisco - Guam - Honolulu | 149 |
| 7. Honolulu - Guam - San Francisco | 87 |
| 8. Honolulu - Guam - Honolulu | 313 |

Because of the advance notice given to collectors, many covers exist from this flight. However, some of the legs of the flight are quite rare. To determine the legs flown by a cover, the postmarks should be read from right to left across the top of the cover.

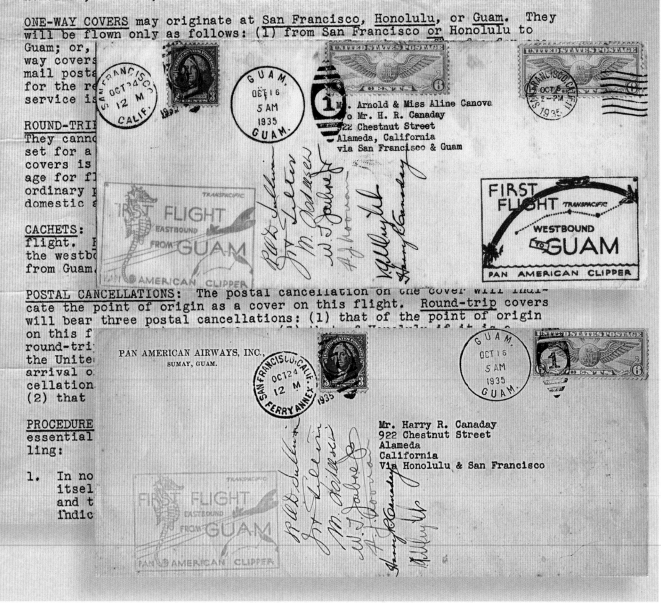

# PAN AMERICAN AIRWAYS SYSTEM
## PACIFIC DIVISION
### TRAFFIC DEPARTMENT, 427 POST STREET, SAN FRANCISCO, CALIFORNIA

## SPECIAL INFORMATION

Telephone
DOuglas 8500

ANNOUNCEMENT -- FIRST COVERS -- SAN FRANCISCO-GUAM

SPECIAL SURVEY FLIGHT

In response to many requests the Second Assistant Postmaster General on August 27, 1935, sanctioned the carrying of philatelic mail on the round-trip Pan American Airways survey flight from California, via Honolulu, to Guam, to be made shortly after September 15th, 1935.

ONE-WAY COVERS may originate at San Francisco, Honolulu, or Guam. They will be flown only as follows: (1) from San Francisco or Honolulu to Guam; or,
way cover
mail post
for the re
service is

ROUND-TRI
They canno
set for a
covers is
age for f
ordinary
domestic

CACHETS:
flight.
the westb
from Guam.

POSTAL CANCELLATIONS: The postal cancellation on the cover will indi- cate the point of origin as a cover on this flight. Round-trip covers will bear three postal cancellations: (1) that of the point of origin on this f
round-tri
the Unite
arrival o
cellation
(2) that

PROCEDURE
essential
ling:

1. In no
itsel
and t
indic

Harry Canaday again provided me with unique souvenirs from this flight. The first cover is typical of the round trip covers and it contains the complete crew autographs.

The second cover was prepared by Mr. Canaday while he was at Guam, using the station manager's envelope.

This cover addressed to Juan Trippe, flown from Honolulu to Guam and back to San Francisco, is the most difficult of the eight legs of the flight to find, because only 87 were flown.

The cover below is unusual because it flew to Shanghai and survey mail was rarely posted to a foreign destination.

*The duties of each crew member are identified beneath their signatures on this nice survey cover*

The two covers on this page contain a hand stamp "via San Francisco, California and Guam". One is addressed to William Snyder, station manager in Miami, and it contained a note from the public relations director of Pan Am, William VanDusen.

This additional hand stamp "via San Francisco" was also applied by Pan Am. The cover illustrated below contains the same hand stamp "via San Francisco" in two different colors matching the color of the two cachets. This raises several interesting questions as to when the "via San Francisco" stamp was applied and how Pan Am was able to print "via San Francisco" in one color and "Guam" in another color, when it appears that it was a single rubber stamp. Does anyone have the answer as to how it was applied?

| 1st Scheduled Mail Flight Manila | November 22-December 6, 1935 | M-130 China Clipper | Musick/Sullivan |
|---|---|---|---|

| Outbound Flight Schedule | | Inbound Flight Schedule | |
|---|---|---|---|
| San Francisco - Honolulu | Nov. 22-23 | Manila - Guam | Dec. 2 |
| Honolulu - Midway | Nov. 24 | Guam - Wake | Dec. 3 |
| Midway - Wake | Nov. 25-26* | Wake - Midway | Dec. 4-3* |
| Wake - Guam | Nov. 27 | Midway - Honolulu | Dec. 4 |
| Guam - Manila | Nov. 29 | Honolulu - San Francisco | Dec. 5-6 |

*Dateline - Gain day outbound - Lose day inbound

The first scheduled mail flight from San Francisco to Manila fully captured the imagination of the American public and was a public relations triumph for Pan Am in all regards. There were over 125,000 people lining the shore and with a nationwide radio hookup literally millions of people listened to the departure of the China Clipper.

Those listening to the radio broadcast heard the commentator say, "The China Clipper, a beautiful sight resting on quiet waters of Pan American's enclosed base here is turned towards the opening in the break water." It was 3:25 p.m. when Trippe stated, "China Clipper are you ready?" Capt. Musick replied, "Pan American Airways China Clipper is standing by for orders, sir." Trippe stated, "Stand by, Captain Musick, for station reports." When Honolulu, Midway, Wake, Guam and Manila had all replied in the affirmative, Juan Trippe stated, "Stand by, all stations. Post Master General Farley, I have the honor to report, sir, that the

*China Clipper before departure November 22, 1935 at Alameda*

Transpacific Airway is ready to inaugurate mail service of the United States Post Office from the mainland, across the Pacific to the Philippines by way of Hawaii, Midway, Wake and Guam islands." By Post Master Farley, "Mr. Trippe, it is an honor and a privilege for me as Post Master General of the United States of America, to hereby order the inauguration of the first scheduled service on foreign air mail route #14 at 3:28 p.m. Pacific Standard Time, on this date which will forever mark a new chapter in the glorious history of our nation, a new era in the world of transportation, a new and binding bond that will link for the first time in history the peoples of the east and west." Juan Trippe stated, "Captain Musick . . . you have your sailing orders. Cast off and depart for Manila in accordance therewith." The engines roared and the Clipper moved slowly into the bay. The national anthem played. At 3:46 p.m. the Clipper broke free of the water heading to Hawaii.

*Postmaster General James A. Farley (facing camera next to the stacks of mail) supervises the final loading of Transpacific mail aboard the China Clipper shortly before take-off. Left to right: Captain Musick, Captain Sullivan, James Farley, Harllee Branch (assistant postmaster in charge of first flight ceremonies), Juan Trippe and Colonel Young (director of the Pacific division for Pan Am).*

*View of official ceremonies for take off*

© CLYDE SUNDERLAND
OAKLAND

The China Clipper, heavily loaded with mail and fuel, almost met with disaster. After lifting off, as Captain Ed Musick flew the Clipper towards the unfinished Oakland Bridge, he realized he could not gain enough altitude to clear the bridge, so he dropped the Clipper back towards the water in a desperate attempt to avoid the maze of wires hanging from the unfinished structure. Somehow he found a clear path and avoided catastrophe. The small planes, that were following the Clipper's take off, believed that Musick's maneuver was intentional, therefore, they also followed the Clipper under the bridge. The dangerous stunt was definitely unintended by the cautious Musick and it was never repeated.

*A few moments later the Clipper was over the still unfinished Golden Gate Bridge on its first flight to Honolulu*

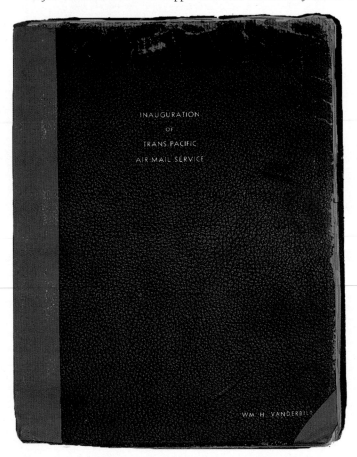

Each of the directors was given a beautiful leather bound volume to commemorate the historic event.

The book in my collection was given to Director William Vanderbilt.

152

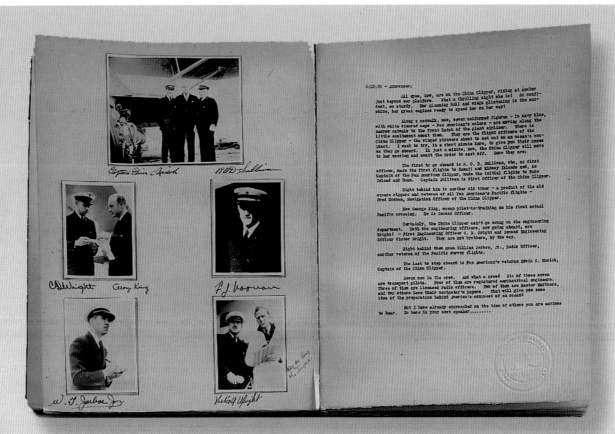

The book opens with these lofty words:

*"And so - God speed the China Clipper, across the aged and unconquered sea for you alone, since time began, can end forever, NOW, those barriers of time and distance - which too long have kept both west and east full half the world apart - to join these neighbors close in friendship and in peace"*

MUSICK

SULLIVAN

NOONAN

JARBOE

V. WRIGHT

C. WRIGHT

KING

*China Clipper arrives at Pan Am's Pearl City base*

154

*Honolulu welcome! Aloha!*

YOU are cordially invited to be present to welcome the "China Clipper" on its First Landing in Hawaii, inaugurating the Trans-Pacific Air Mail Service of Pan-American Airways, on Saturday, November 23, 1935, at 8:30 A.M., at the new operating base on the Pearl City Peninsula, midway between the Yacht Club and ferry landing.

Plane due to arrive 9 A.M.
(Present This Card)                                    (Reserved Section)

*The skipper of the China Clipper,*
*Captain Edwin Musick, who*
*piloted the flying boat on her*
*flight from California, broadcasts*
*the story of her crossing -*
*In Honolulu the crew received a*
*wildly enthusiastic and typically*
*Hawaiian welcome*

Following the Guam survey flight in October, Phil Berst, Pan Am's chief mechanic in the Pacific, sailed to Manila onboard the U.S. Grant. He was working frantically so that the arrival of the China Clipper would go without a hitch. By November 28, the landing barge that he had built in Manila was anchored inside the seawall, awaiting the Clipper's arrival.

*Phil Berst (center) supervising construction of barge-Manila*

*Above and left:*
*Berst on barge day of*
*Clipper's arrival*
*November 29, 1935*

*Barge under construction*

*The official photographs taken from the air of the China Clipper landing in Manila harbor capture the excitement of the day*

(0526-1595N-6)(11-29-35-3P)(10-1000) ARRIVAL OF P.A.A. "CHINA CLIPPER", 3:00 P.M., NOV.29,1935. OVER MANILA BAY, MANILA, P.I.

*Approach*

*Touchdown*

(27-1595N-6)(11-29-35-3:40P)(10-900) "CHINA CLIPPER" TAXIING TO LANDING STAGE UPON ARRIVAL AT MANILA P.I. NOV. 29, 1935.

*At barge in harbor*

(0533-1595N-6)(11-29-35-3:50P)(10-1100) GENERAL VIEW OF RECEPTION TO CHINA CLIPPER UPON ARRIVAL AT MANILA P.I. NOV.29,1935.

Crowd at harbor

*China Clipper at barge*

MABUMAY - Welcome!

If anything, the people of the Philippines were even more excited than the people of the United States about the first scheduled flight across the Pacific. It is estimated that 300,000 people lined the shore in Manila to witness the sight of the Clipper landing at Manila harbor.

*Clipper flies over Manila Harbor*

*The final approach*

*Seconds from touch down*

In addition to the official photos taken of the landing, Pan Am's maintenance supervisor, Phil Berst, took these personal pictures of the Clipper's triumphant arrival.

*The moment of touch down!*

*China Clipper safely moored at the barge that Berst had completed just in time for the Clipper's arrival*

*The primitive hand crank used for pumping fuel can be seen between the 55 gallon barrels of aviation fuel stored on the barge*

*Servicing continues*

Phil Berst was also in charge of servicing the Clipper at the end of the historic flight. Work was performed with the Clipper moored to the barge in Manila Bay. Berst also took these rare photos in Manila of the maintenance procedures.

*Servicing the China Clipper at barge in Manila Harbor*
*November, 1935*

*The China Clipper rests at the barge in Manila Harbor at the end of its history making flight - Crowds line the shore as sightseeing boats circle for a closer look - The Manila Hotel is in the background*

*Military aircraft fly in salute over the China Clipper moored in Manila Bay at the end of the first commercial airline flight across the Pacific*

The banquet at the Presidential Palace in Manila in honor of the crew on Saturday evening, November 30, was the highlight of their four day stay in Manila. Phil Berst saved not only his invitation to the banquet, but also the Pan Am name badge he and other Pan Am personnel wore at the celebrations in Manila for the Clipper's arrival. I have never seen this name tag with the Clipper and silk ribbon before. Because it is so fragile, I doubt if any others survived. Although it depicts the Sikorsky S-42 rather than the Martin M-130 that actually made the flight, it does show the careful preparation of Pan Am not only in planning the flight but also in planning the celebrations after the flight.

Mr. Berst

P. A. A.
STAFF.

FIRST
TRANS-PACIFIC
FLIGHT
P. A. A.
"CHINA CLIPPER"

MANILA
NOV. 29th., 1935

BANQUET

*in honor of*

*The Aviators of the "China Clipper"*

*on its Maiden Flight*

*Inaugurating the Trans-Pacific Air Service*

*of the*

*Pan-American Airways Company*

*at the*

*Manila Hotel*

*on Saturday evening, November the thirtieth*
*nineteen hundred and thirty-five*
*at eight-thirty o'clock*

Mr. *D. BERST*

Mr. Berst

*Tag on back of badge*

*Above-Postmaster Farley delivers letters from President Roosevelt to the crew for delivery to president of Philippines.*
*Harllee Branch assistant postmaster and Juan Trippe watch the proceedings*

Souvenir flight mail was a very important part of the first scheduled flight. Illustrated is a crew signed cover containing two blank lines - one for the second flight officer and one for an assistant radio officer. Pan Am had actually intended to carry a larger crew, but with the tremendous interest in the flight covers, the weight of the mail bags forced them to reduce the crew on the flight from San Francisco to Honolulu by two men. Harry Canaday, who had made all four of the survey flights, was very disappointed that the weight of the mail resulted in him being left off the crew for the first scheduled flight.

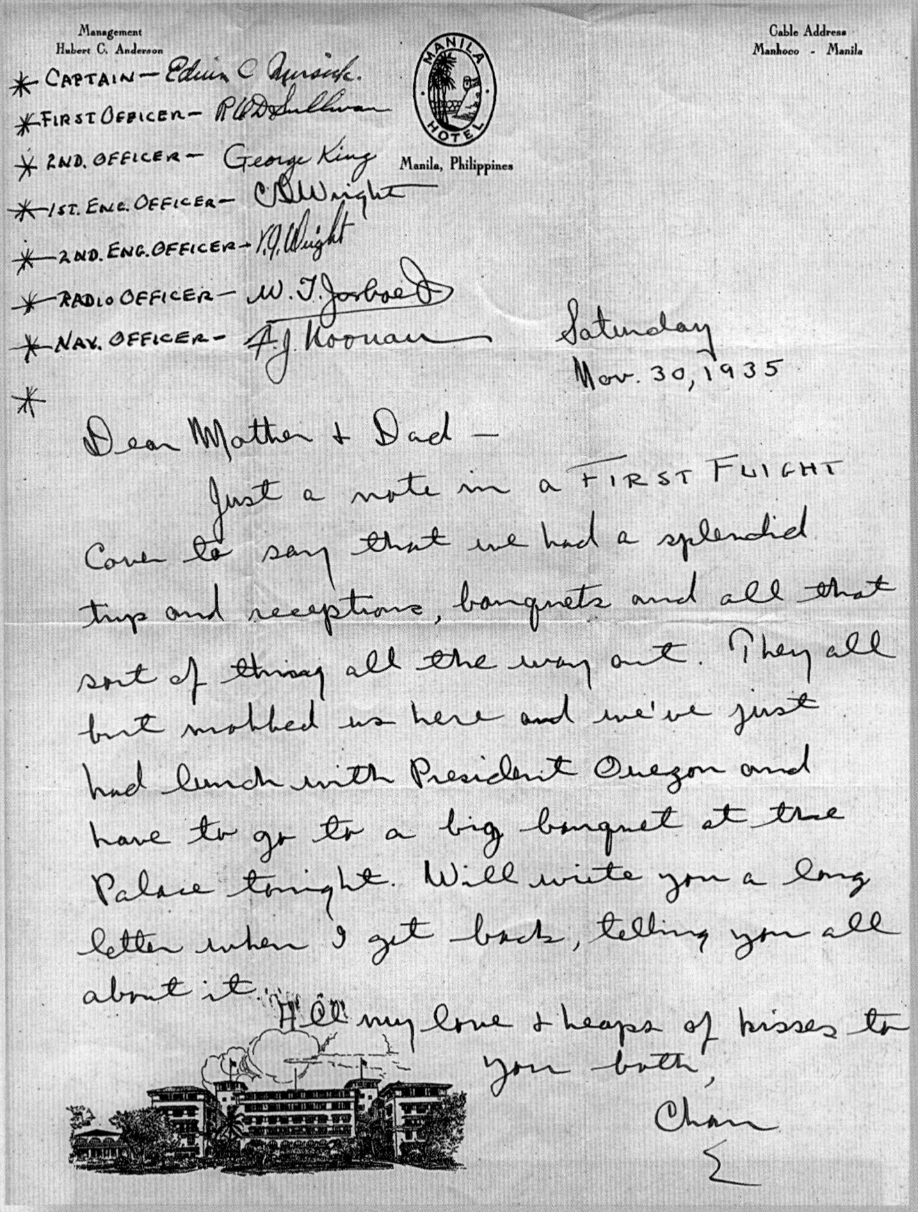

Management
Hubert C. Anderson

MANILA HOTEL
Manila, Philippines

Cable Address
Manhoco - Manila

* CAPTAIN — Edwin C Musick.
* FIRST OFFICER — R O D Sullivan
* 2ND. OFFICER — George King
* 1ST. ENG. OFFICER — C B Wright
* 2ND. ENG. OFFICER — V. J. Wright
* RADIO OFFICER — W. T. Jarboe Jr
* NAV. OFFICER — F. J. Noonan
*

Saturday
Nov. 30, 1935

Dear Mother & Dad —

Just a note in a FIRST FLIGHT Cover to say that we had a splendid trip and receptions, banquets and all that sort of thing all the way out. They all but mobbed us here and we've just had lunch with President Quezon and have to go to a big banquet at the Palace tonight. Will write you a long letter when I get back, telling you all about it.

All my love & heaps of kisses to you both,

Chan

S. FRANCISCO NOV 22 1 PM 1935 CALIF.

Captain Edwin C Musick
R O D Sullivan
F J Noonan
W. T. Jarboe Jr
George King
V. J. Wright
C B Wright

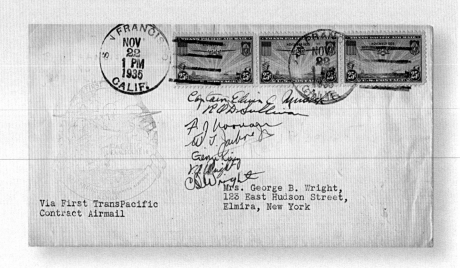

Via First TransPacific
Contract Airmail

Mrs. George B. Wright,
123 East Hudson Street,
Elmira, New York

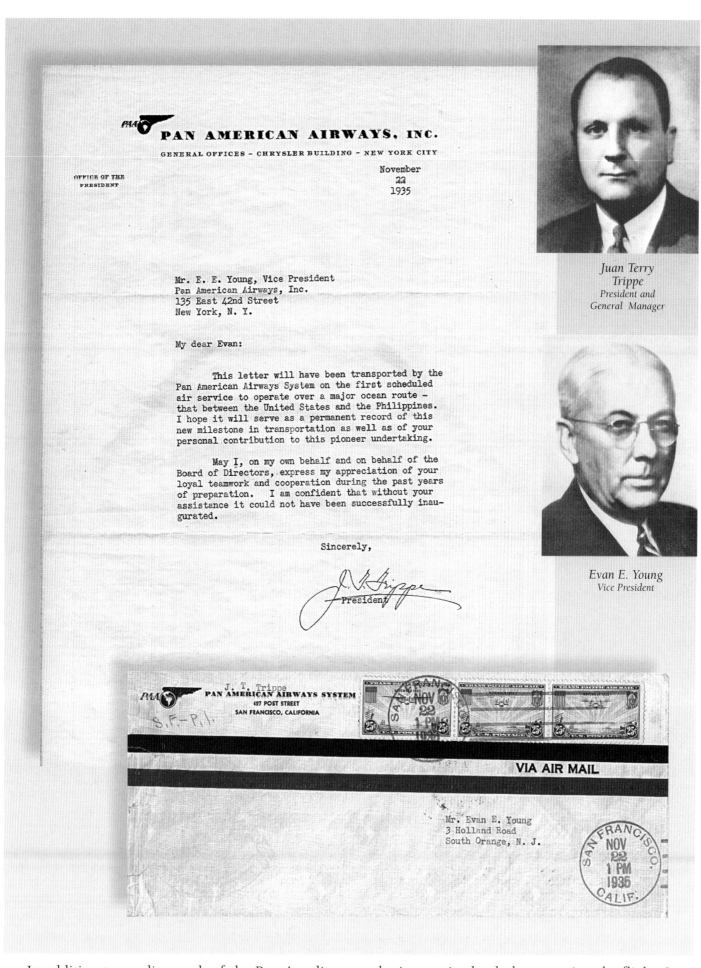

PAN AMERICAN AIRWAYS, INC.
GENERAL OFFICES - CHRYSLER BUILDING - NEW YORK CITY

OFFICE OF THE
PRESIDENT

November
22
1935

*Juan Terry*
*Trippe*
President and
General Manager

Mr. E. E. Young, Vice President
Pan American Airways, Inc.
135 East 42nd Street
New York, N. Y.

My dear Evan:

    This letter will have been transported by the
Pan American Airways System on the first scheduled
air service to operate over a major ocean route -
that between the United States and the Philippines.
I hope it will serve as a permanent record of this
new milestone in transportation as well as of your
personal contribution to this pioneer undertaking.

    May I, on my own behalf and on behalf of the
Board of Directors, express my appreciation of your
loyal teamwork and cooperation during the past years
of preparation. I am confident that without your
assistance it could not have been successfully inaugurated.

Sincerely,

President

*Evan E. Young*
Vice President

J. T. Trippe
PAN AMERICAN AIRWAYS SYSTEM
487 POST STREET
SAN FRANCISCO, CALIFORNIA

S.F.-P.I.

VIA AIR MAIL

Mr. Evan E. Young
3 Holland Road
South Orange, N. J.

SAN FRANCISCO
NOV
22
1 PM
1935
CALIF.

    In addition to sending each of the Pan Am directors the impressive book documenting the flight, Juan Trippe, Pan Am's President, also wrote each of them a personal letter using an envelope that had been carried on the first flight. My collection includes the letter to Director Evan Young.

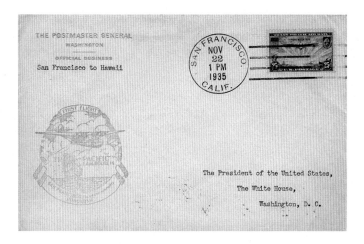

Postmaster General James Farley also made sure that the most famous stamp collector of the day received some nice souvenirs of the first flight. Shown is a letter to the President on the Postmaster's embossed letterhead and another using a White House envelope.

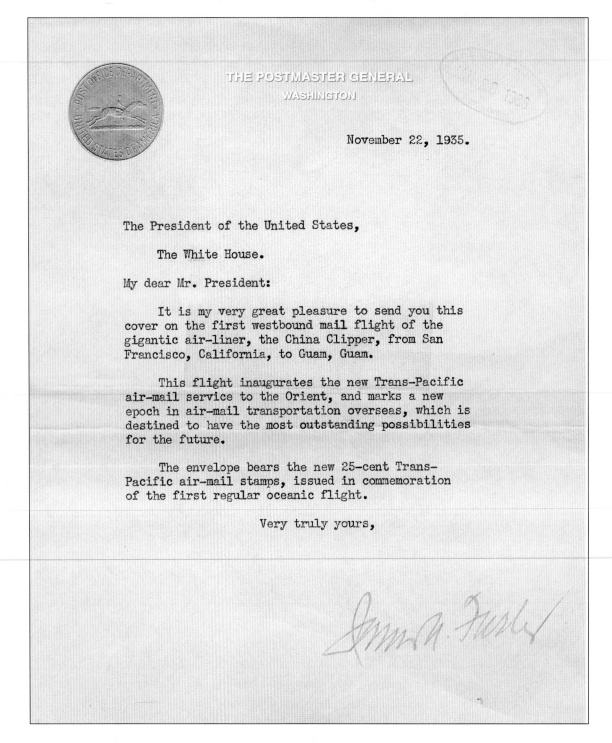

**THE POSTMASTER GENERAL**
WASHINGTON

November 22, 1935.

The President of the United States,

The White House.

My dear Mr. President:

It is my very great pleasure to send you this cover on the first westbound mail flight of the gigantic air-liner, the China Clipper, from San Francisco, California, to Guam, Guam.

This flight inaugurates the new Trans-Pacific air-mail service to the Orient, and marks a new epoch in air-mail transportation overseas, which is destined to have the most outstanding possibilities for the future.

The envelope bears the new 25-cent Trans-Pacific air-mail stamps, issued in commemoration of the first regular oceanic flight.

Very truly yours,

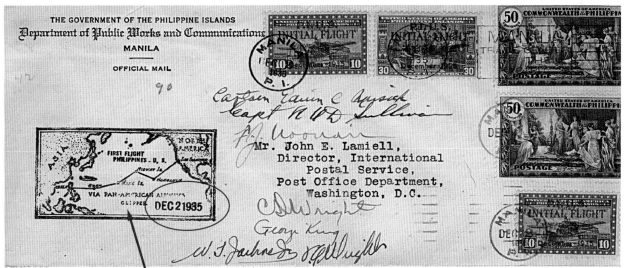

*Note: The word CLIPPER in cachet is directly under the word AMERICAN*

*Note: The word CLIPPER in cachet is directly under the word PAN*

*Note: The word CLIPPER in cachet is directly under the word PAN*

The three flight covers canceled in Manila for the east bound flight all contain cachets showing Asia and North America with the route of the Clipper in between. However, in the lower right hand corner of the cachet is a date stamp for the departure of the flight on December 2 and there are at least three varieties and sizes of the date stamp that can be found. Note the size and shape of the number "2". Also, note there are two varieties of cachets. In the top cover **Clipper** is to the right of the words "Pan American" and on the two bottom covers **Clipper** is directly below the words Pan American.

Another very interesting letter sent to the President from this first flight was from his Secretary of War, George H. Dern, who just "happened" to be onboard the Chester off of Wake Island when the China Clipper made its inaugural return eastbound flight with a stopover at Wake. Although the letter talks about the Thanksgiving holiday, there is no question that war tensions in the Pacific were growing in regards to the Japanese, and the first flight of the China Clipper was a good cover for the Secretary of War to be in the North Pacific near Japan inspecting the bases at Guam, Wake and Midway in anticipation of any possible conflict in the Pacific. As a member of Roosevelt's Cabinet, he was already supporting the President's 1936 re-election efforts. Therefore a political speech was planned in California before he returned to Washington. This souvenir letter to the President from the Secretary of War actually contained a lot more information about the current state of affairs in the Pacific than appears on the surface.

From:
Honorable George H. Dern,
Secretary of War,
Wake Island.

AIR MAIL via "CHINA CLIPPER"
on its first return Trans-
Pacific Flight.

Honorable Franklin D. Roosevelt,
President of the United States,
The White House,
Washington, D. C.

WAR DEPARTMENT
WASHINGTON

WAKE ISLAND,
November 28, 1935.

The President,

    The White House.

Dear Mr. President:

    Today is Thanksgiving Day. This morning I attended a special church service on board the CHESTER at which your Thanksgiving Day proclamation was read. Then we went fishing and I caught a forty inch barracuda. Next we came ashore and had a fine American Thanksgiving dinner with the personnel of the Pan American Airways. The dinner included roast turkey with cranberry sauce, sliced fresh tomatoes, ice cream made in Honolulu, plum pudding, and all the other trimmings. I understand it was brought from Honolulu by plane at a cost of probably a dollar an ounce.

    We had our Thanksgiving dinner at one o'clock p.m. Thursday, November 28th, and I suppose it was the first Thanksgiving dinner eaten anywhere this year in the world, because at that hour it was nine p.m. Wednesday in Washington. We are out where the days begin.

    My principal purpose in writing you is to send you a letter from this tiny American island and have it go to you by the China Clipper on the return trip of its first regular trans-Pacific flight. Unfortunately, there is no post office on Wake Island and no stamps can be obtained. The best I can do is to write this letter here and mail it at Honolulu, which will still be in time for the China Clipper. Perhaps the stamp on this envelope will be worth adding to your collection.

    We are still having a very delightful cruise, and are all feeling fine. We are due at San Francisco on December 11th, but will have to wait there for Mary and Betsy who will arrive on the Army transport GRANT about the 15th. I must spend a couple of days in Salt Lake City - hence I shall probably not reach Washington until the twenty-second or twenty-third.

    I have received your reply to my radio message and have advised Chairman Olson of the Democratic State Committee that I will make a speech in California if he still desires me to do so.

    My wife joins me in kindest regards to yourself and Mrs. Roosevelt.

Very sincerely yours,

Secretary of War.

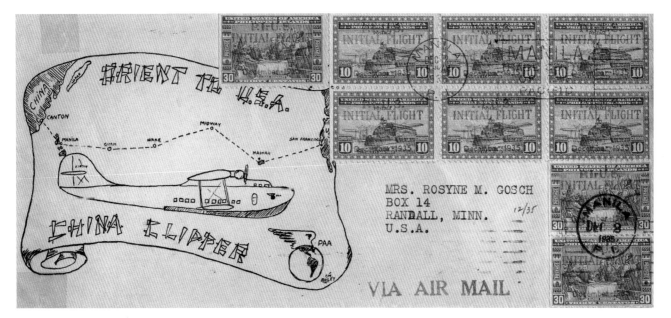

Because of the popularity of the flight, literally dozens of different private cachets were printed on envelopes for collectors.

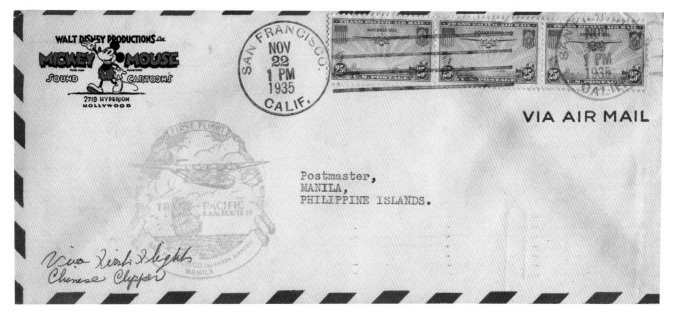

It appears that even Mickey Mouse was a cover collector in the mid-30s. Everyone was caught up in the hobby.

*Juan Trippe and Captain Musick celebrate the upcoming flight at a banquet in Oakland - November 20, 1935*

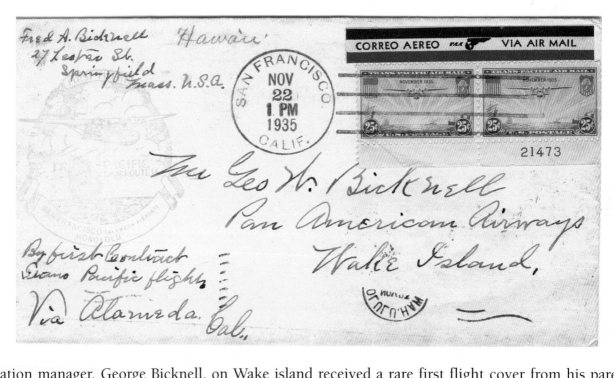

Station manager, George Bicknell, on Wake island received a rare first flight cover from his parents in Springfield, Massachusetts addressed to that remote island base.

The volume of mail on the first scheduled air mail flight overwhelmed the postmaster at Guam, J.H. Underwood. He is pictured holding the first of many airmail bags on the first flight, while the Pan Am manager for Guam, I.P. Gregory, looks on.

A whole book could be written on the variety of covers from this historic flight.

As captain of the China Clipper on the first scheduled flight, Ed Musick became a world wide celebrity. His picture was on the cover of *Time* magazine and at year's end he was awarded the Harmon Trophy as the world's outstanding aviator for the year. This clearly put him in a class with Charles Lindbergh and Amelia Earhart as one of the three most prominent pilots of his time. The year of 1935 was a year of triumph and celebration for Pan Am. The world took notice of its tremendous accomplishments.

173

| 1st Flight<br>Philippine Clipper | December 9 - 26, 1935 | M-130 Philippine Clipper | Tilton/Dahlstrom |
|---|---|---|---|

| Outbound Flight Schedule | | Inbound Flight Schedule | |
|---|---|---|---|
| San Francisco - Honolulu | Dec. 9-10 | Manila - Guam | Dec. 22 |
| Honolulu - Midway | Dec. 12 | Guam - Wake | Dec. 23 |
| Midway - Wake | Dec. 13-14* | Wake - Midway | Dec. 24-23* |
| Wake - Guam | Dec. 15 | Midway - Honolulu | Dec. 24 |
| Guam - Manila | Dec. 16 | Honolulu - San Francisco | Dec. 25-26 |

*Dateline - Gain day outbound - Lose day inbound

The second Transpacific flight was also the first flight of the Philippine Clipper -NC 14715. It was originally scheduled to depart San Francisco on November 29, a week before the anticipated return of the China Clipper. However, to accommodate collectors, the Post Office again requested that the flight be moved back a week. Then, because of bad weather, a later departure date of December 6 was finally announced. That date changed as well. The actual departure was on Monday, December 9, 1935.

*Martin M-130 Philippine Clipper on first Transpacific flight*

SAN FRANCISCO CHRONICLE, TUESDAY, DECEMBER 10, 1935

# SPEEDING TO SOUTH SEA ISLES

Here is the crew of the Philippine Clipper, which took off for Manila today on the second Transpacific crossing of the new air mail service to the Orient. Left to right: (Front row) Ralph Dahlstrom, first officer; Captain J. H. Tilton, S. P. Crago, first flight officer, and J. H. Fiske, first engineering officer; back row—T. R. Runnells, radio officer; M. C. Weber, second officer; J. H. Ingram, first navigating officer; E. B. Abarr, second engineering officer, and H. R. Canaday, second navigating officer.

Chronicle A. P. Photo

*Multiply "happy landing" by six and you have the spirit of this photo, showing wives of officers of the Philippine Clipper waving adieu to their men as they hopped on their Manila flight, which brought them uneventfully to Honolulu today.*

*Left to right are (with parentheses indicating mate's posts) Mrs. Ethel Ingram, (first navigation officer) Mrs. Helen Crago (junior flight officer), Mrs. Blanche Dahlstrom (first officer),*
*Mrs. Margaret Fiske (first engineering officer), Mrs. Lucille Canaday (second navigation officer), and Mrs. Leona Runnells (radio officer) snapped at Alameda takeoff.*

# CLIPPER 'SEXTET FROM ALAMEDA'
## Their Pioneer Husbands Now Spanning Pacific

F. A. M. ROUTE No. 14
SAN FRANCISCO, CALIF.,
DEC. 6, 1935
The arrival of the "China Clipper" from Manila and the departure of the "Philippine Clipper" for Manila on its first trip occurred on this date. This was the first time in history of an arrival and a departure of planes over a Trans-Pacific route from the same airport.

Flight Postponed

Philippine Clipper Crew

Because of the changes in the departure date, the printed message on the crew signed cover announces a December 6 departure. Even the cancel date on the cover of December 8 is the day before the actual December 9, 1935 departure.

Although the Post Office anticipated a heavy demand from collectors, this flight did not attract much attention and official cachets were not provided.

Because of the many changes in the departure date, it is difficult to find a cover with the correct date, December 9 1935, such as the one shown above.

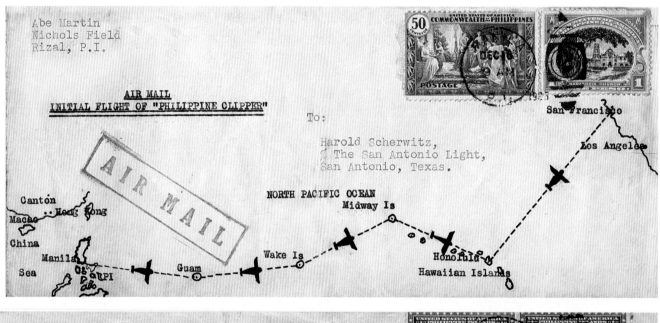

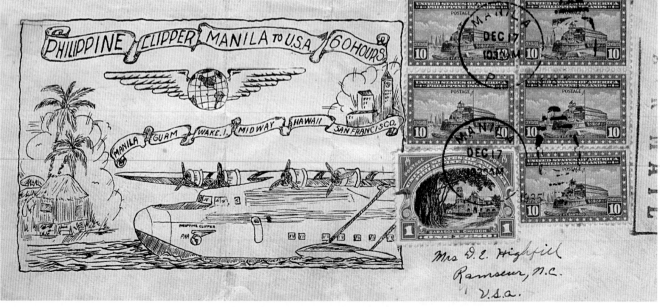

*Cachet prepared by crew of U.S.S. Black Hawk stationed in Manila*

| Resumed Service to Manila & 1st Air Express Cargo | February 22-March 9, 1936 | M-130 China Clipper | Musick/DeLima |
|---|---|---|---|

| Outbound Flight Schedule | | Inbound Flight Schedule | |
|---|---|---|---|
| San Francisco - Honolulu | Feb. 22-23 | Manila - Guam | March 4 |
| Honolulu - Midway | Feb. 25 | Guam - Wake | March 5 |
| Midway - Wake | Feb. 27-28* | Wake - Midway | March 6-5* |
| Wake - Guam | Feb. 29 | Midway - Honolulu | March 6 |
| Guam - Manila | March 1 | Honolulu - San Francisco | March 8-9 |

*Dateline - Gain day outbound - Lose day inbound

After the first two flights had been completed, it was obvious to Pan Am that the engines needed to be re-worked and they were returned to Pratt & Whitney in Hartford for this purpose. After all the publicity leading up to the flights, Juan Trippe was embarrassed by this delay, so he pressured the manufacturer to complete the modifications as quickly as possible.

Pan Am's chief engineer, Andre Priester, reported directly to Trippe on these problems. In Priester's memo of January 31, he suggests that a spare engine must be kept at each base along the route so that they could deal with an engine failure if the problem were to reoccur.

A follow up telegram to Trippe informed him that Pan Am flights could be resumed on February 5. As it turned out, this proved to be overly optimistic and the actual departure of the China Clipper occurred on February 14. However, this flight encountered strong head winds and had to return to San Francisco. Therefore the actual departure date for the resumption of service was February 22, 1936.

*Piston head of China Clipper presented to Trippe*

The Piston was used on the first Scheduled
Trans Pacific Flight San Francisco to Manila
Nov 22-29 1935 by Pan American Airways.
Presented to
J.T. Trippe

**Pratt & Whitney**
**Twin Wasp**

**Martin**
**China Clipper**

In reworking the engines, Pratt & Whitney removed the piston heads from the China Clipper's original engines. One of the piston heads was polished, engraved and embossed with Pratt & Whitney's flying eagle logo and presented to Juan Trippe at a banquet sometime later. This was undoubtedly done by Pratt & Whitney to appease Trippe's anger and disappointment in having the Clippers pulled out of service after only two flights.

# PAN AMERICAN AIRWAYS, INC.

### GENERAL OFFICES - CHRYSLER BUILDING - NEW YORK CITY

January 22, 1936

Mr. M. W. Finch
P. O. Box 288
West Warwick, R. I.

Dear Mr. Finch:

In answer to your recent letter, the China Clipper has made one round-trip flight from California to the Philippines leaving on November 22 and returning December 6th. The Philippine Clipper has also made one round-trip, leaving San Francisco December 9th and returning the 26th.

The Hawaiian Clipper is still at Baltimore, Maryland and will soon start to the coast for the trans-Pacific service. This is the ship which you have reference to, not a Sikorsky plane. It is a sister ship of the China Clipper built by Glenn L. Martin. No Sikorskys are to be used on the trans-Pacific route at present.

New engines are being installed in both the China and Philippine Clippers, which is the reason for the present delay.

I think the daily newspapers and perhaps the magazine, "Aviation," will be the best sources for up-to-date material on the progress of this service.

Very truly yours,

A. Hovgard

P.S. The address of Aviation Magazine is 330 W. 42nd, New York City.

A. H.

CONTRACTORS TO THE UNITED STATES AND FOREIGN GOVERNMENTS FOR AIR MAIL SERVICE BETWEEN THE UNITED STATES AND THE WEST INDIES, MEXICO, CENTRAL AND SOUTH AMERICA
RATES AND SCHEDULES OBTAINABLE AT ANY U. S. OR FOREIGN POST OFFICE, OR AT ANY OFFICE OF THE PAN AMERICAN AIRWAYS SYSTEM

In response to a letter to Pan Am, a member of the public relations department explained the reasons for the suspension of service that occurred in January of 1936. At this point in time, all three of the Martin M-130s were in Baltimore.

Thanks to the power of eBay, the internet auction site that I discovered in 1998 while working on my second book, I have acquired a companion piece to the China Clipper's piston head. Pictured is a lamp made out of a portion of the propeller also used on the China Clipper's first flight in November of 1935. In early 1938, Hamilton-Standard's constant speed controllable propellers were replaced by the newly developed variable pitch propellers that gave the Clippers increased fuel savings and, therefore, greater range and payload. The China Clipper's propellers that had made the first Pacific flight in November of 1935 were removed and stored at the back of the machine shop at the Alameda base, where they caught the eye of Pacific Division Manager Colonel Clarence Young. He had his mechanics cut off a portion of the historic, but now discarded, propeller and make it into a lamp that Colonel Young presented to his son on his second birthday.

The engraving tells the story. The propeller and the piston head of the China Clipper's first Pacific flight have now been reunited almost 65 years after the epic flight.

*Tim Young with his mother Lois Moran Young at Treasure Island - 1939*

Pictured at Treasure Island is Tim Young, at about age two, with his mother, Lois Moran Young. This picture was taken shortly after young Tim was given the lamp made out of the propeller blade from the China Clipper.

FLIES TO ORIENT

ON INSPECTION TRIP! Col. Clarence Young, manager of the Pacific division of Pan-American Airways, with his wife, the former Lois Moran of the movies, and their son, Timmy. Young is flying on the Clipper to Manila on an inspection trip. Mrs. Young and Timmy flew with him to Los Angeles.
—Post-Enquirer photo.

Pictured are Colonel and Mrs. Young with their son, Tim, who by this time was about four years old. The July 1941 *"Clipper News from Treasure Island"*, the monthly newsletter of the Pacific division, briefly reviewed Miss Moran's career and also mentioned her son's growing collection of Pan Am flight covers:

> *After winning stardom in Hollywood, Miss Moran went on the New York to achieve even greater recognition in musical comedy, particularly in 'Of Thee I Sing' and 'Let Them Eat Cake'. In the former production, she established a record by never missing a single appearance in the long run of 86 weeks with 8 performances a week.*
> *Retiring from the stage upon her marriage to Colonel Young, Lois Moran undertook a new career as wife and mother . . .'Timmie' Young is now four years old (and the possessor of an enviable collection of 'first flight covers' on Pan American Airway's routes).*

Many of the unique flight covers that I have recently added to my collection are from Tim Young's collection started by his father, Colonel Clarence Young.

Tim Young has now shared with me the wall plaque presented to Colonel Young by his Pan Am Pacific staff in 1943. It used the top half of the same propeller blade that was used to make the lamp given to young Tim. At the top of the blade is embedded Colonel Young's personal badge for Treasure Island. In addition to the inscription, there are 24 signatures of the most instrumental people in the early history of Pan Am in the Pacific. The signature of Ed Musick was added, even though he had passed away in 1938 with the loss of Samoan Clipper and the signature of K.A. Kennedy was added, even though he disappeared as a passenger on the Hawaii Clipper in July of 1938. Other signatures include John Tilton, chief pilot in the Pacific, John Leslie, the chief engineer for the Pacific division, George Bicknell, who served as station manager at Wake and Honolulu, and Bill Mullahey, who started as a construction worker blowing up coral heads and ultimately became station manager in Honolulu.

## To
## COLONEL CLARENCE M. YOUNG

THIS IS TO EXPRESS OUR APPRECIATION
FOR THE PRIVILEGE OF SERVING WITH YOU
IN YOUR GREAT WORK IN THE PIONEERING OF
THE WORLD'S FIRST TRANSOCEANIC AIRLINE.

YOUR SOUND LEADERSHIP
WISE COUNSEL AND SYMPATHETIC UNDERSTANDING
WILL BE REFLECTED IN THE FUTURE ACHIEVEMENTS OF
AIR TRANSPORTATION IN THE PACIFIC AREA

*Twenty four signatures
engraved on blade*

AUGUST 1943-Piece of propeller from original "China Clipper"

*The above inscription plus the signatures of 24 Pacific Pioneers were engraved on this piece of the propeller from the original "China Clipper"*

This resumption of Pacific service on February 22, 1936 also marked an important date for Pan Am, if they ever hoped to turn a profit on the Transpacific flights – the commencement of air express cargo service. The most interesting and unique souvenir of this flight is the documentation for the first air express cargo shipment sent from Honolulu to the mainland. A company newsletter tells us that Pan Am's general agent in Honolulu, Inter-Island Steam Navigation Company, promoted the new express service by telling customers that a special cachet stating <u>Inaugural Trans-Pacific Air Express P.A.A. "Clipper" R.E.A.</u> showing the Clipper would be applied to all shipments. In spite of this incentive, only 30 packages were shipped from Honolulu to California on this inaugural express flight. These interesting items are from the collection of John Johnson, a fellow collector who always generously shares his time and unsurpassed knowledge of Pacific flights.

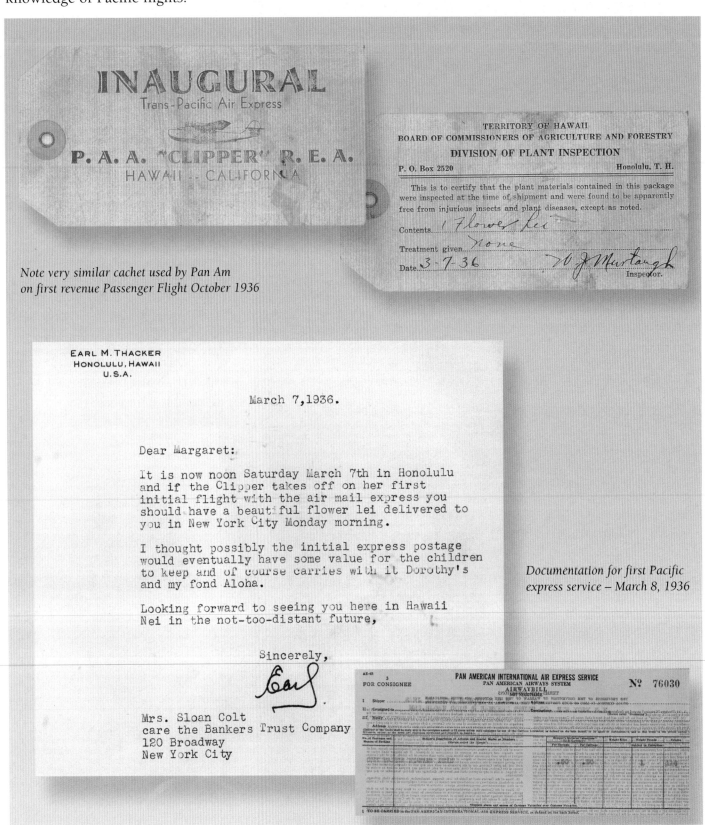

*Note very similar cachet used by Pan Am on first revenue Passenger Flight October 1936*

*Documentation for first Pacific express service – March 8, 1936*

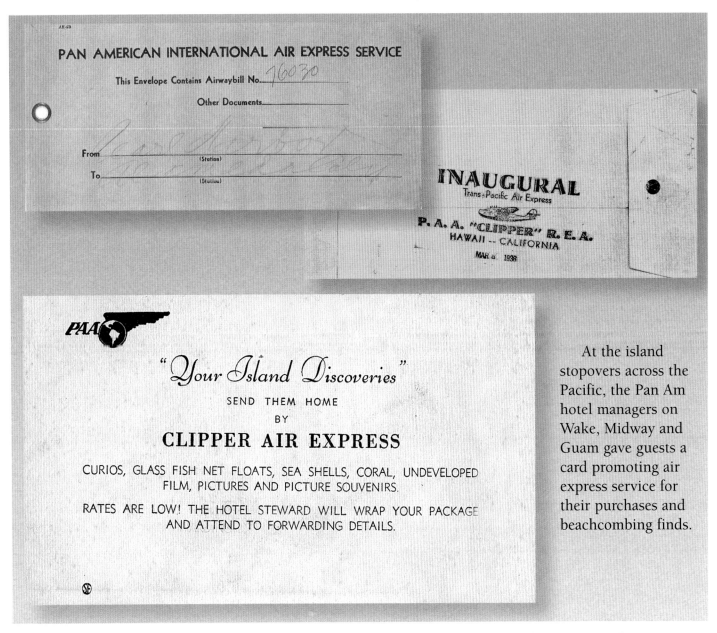

At the island stopovers across the Pacific, the Pan Am hotel managers on Wake, Midway and Guam gave guests a card promoting air express service for their purchases and beachcombing finds.

After the change of engines, very few collectors learned of the resumption of service and the commencement of air express service in time to send a souvenir cover for the flight. The cover below was sent by collector Jesse Johnson from Alameda in time for the original departure date of February 14, 1936. It is correctly back stamped in Manila on March 3, 1936.

With the passage of time, there was heavy promotion by Pan Am for Pacific air freight and it eventually became a more profitable undertaking. This large 12 x 14 inch envelope was carried as air freight by Royal Netherlands Indies Airways (KNILM) from Java to Manila, where it was turned over to Pan Am's freight office for the flight across the Pacific. On the back of the large envelope, completely hidden under a customs label, I found a Pan Am air express sticker that had not been seen before on a Pan Am express package. This type of sticker came into use in September of 1938 and finding it was a welcome surprise that made a nice addition to my collection.

| 1st Flight Hawaii Clipper | May 2 - 16, 1936 | M-130 Hawaii Clipper | Musick/LaPorte |
|---|---|---|---|

| Outbound Flight Schedule | | Inbound Flight Schedule | |
|---|---|---|---|
| San Francisco - Honolulu | May 2-3 | Manila - Guam | May 10 |
| Honolulu - Midway | May 4 | Guam - Wake | May 12 |
| Midway - Wake | May 5-6* | Wake - Midway | May 14-13* |
| Wake - Guam | May 7 | Midway - Honolulu | May 14 |
| Guam - Manila | May 8 | Honolulu - San Francisco | May 15-16 |

*Dateline - Gain day outbound - Lose day inbound

The third and last of the Martin M-130s, the Hawaii Clipper, was delivered to Pan Am at Glenn Martin's factory in Baltimore, Maryland on March 30, 1936. After the delivery ceremonies in Baltimore, it was flown to Alameda by way of Miami, Acapulco and San Diego.

It made its maiden flight on May 2 and was christened with coconut milk upon its arrival in Honolulu on May 3, 1936.

*The christening in Honolulu on May 3, 1936*

*Crew departing after christening of Hawaii Clipper*

*The Hawaii Clipper is pictured at the dock in Wake lagoon on its first flight*

Collectors showed little interest in this flight. The only cover I have located from this flight was mailed from New York on April 24 for the as yet unnamed Clipper. It was correctly back stamped on May 8 in Manila upon its arrival at the completion of the inaugural flight.

*Carried on Inaugural flight of*
*Hawaii Clipper*

*Cancellation stamp on reverse*

Other souvenir flight covers for the inaugural flight of the Hawaii Clipper, including the one illustrated below, were privately prepared and were not even flown on the inaugural Pacific flight.

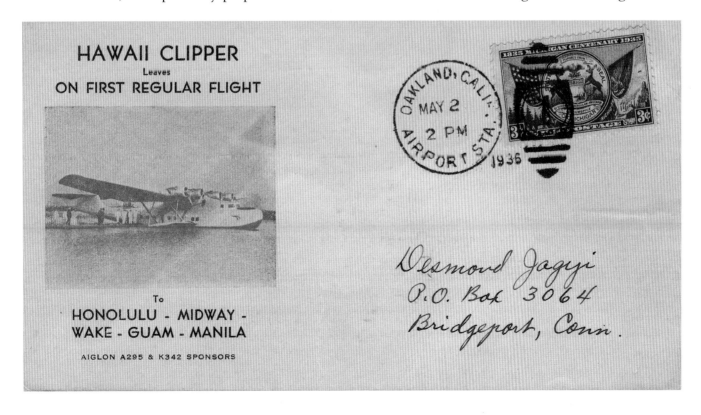

ALL SET!

THE PAN AMERICAN AIRWAYS

SHOWERS GREETINGS TO GUAM

AND WISHES THE

GUAM FAIR

EVERY SUCCESS

MAY 8 - 9 - 10, 1936

Good wishes,

"Scruggs"

Although cover collectors showed little interest in the first flight of the Hawaii Clipper, these humorous leaflets were flown on the Clipper's maiden flight. After Captain Musick arrived at Guam on May 7, 1936 in the Hawaii Clipper, he picked up the leaflets and took off again in the Clipper, circled the island and dropped these leaflets to publicize Guam's biggest event of the year, the Guam Fair. Evidently "Scruggs" was at the naval hospital and he claims to have retrieved one of the first leaflets dropped. He saved it as a souvenir of the Hawaii Clipper's first flight. Although most cover collectors would probably disagree, I think this unique item qualifies as a "flight cover" from the maiden flight of the Hawaii Clipper.

*Clipper at barge - Manila harbor - note wave action*

Pictured above is one of the Martin M-130 Clippers at the barge in Manila Harbor. Although the barge was located behind the breakwater, the harbor was still quite exposed to high wave action. With the approach of typhoon season it was obvious that the Manila Harbor would be an unsuitable landing and mooring area for the Clippers. Therefore, plans were made for the duration of the typhoon season to move the Pan Am seaplane base from the Manila Harbor to the more secure location across the bay at Cavite, the site of the United States Navy's main Philippine base. When the Hawaii Clipper returned to Manila on its second flight on June 7, 1936, it landed as usual at the Manila Harbor in front of the Manila Hotel.

However, after discharging the mail and cargo at the offshore landing float, the Hawaii Clipper flew to the calmer and more protected Cavite location. The new Cavite base proved to be so satisfactory that "temporary" quickly became "permanent" and all future flights after the Hawaii Clipper's June 7 flight used Cavite as their landing area and maintenance facility.

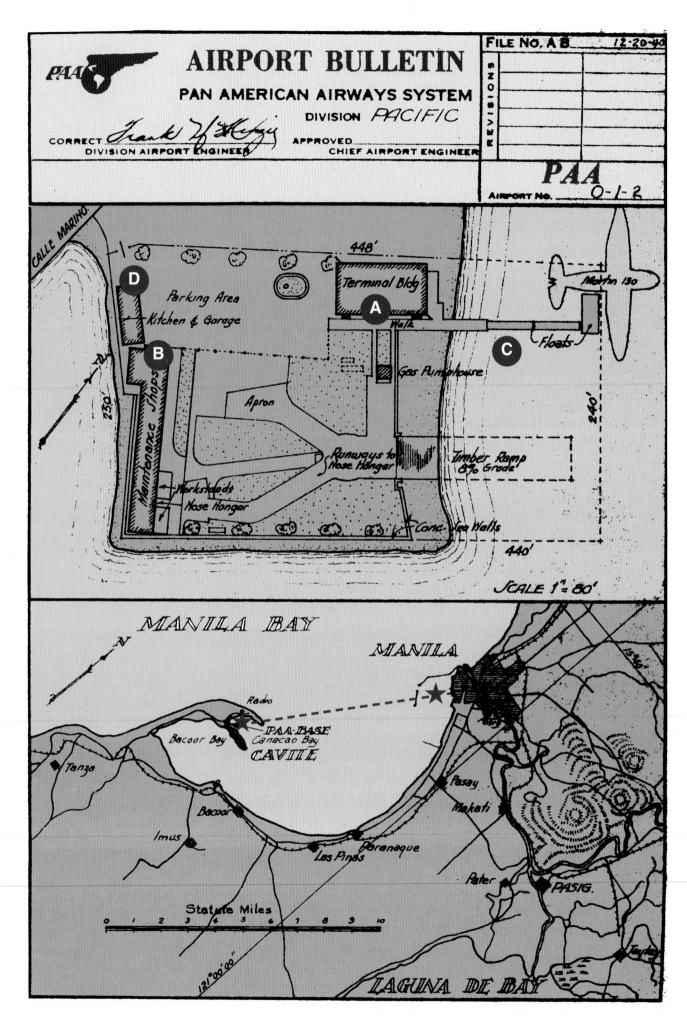

*June 7, 1936 - Pan Am base moved to Cavite*

*Views of new Cavite base - letters refer to location of photograph on the Pan Am survey*

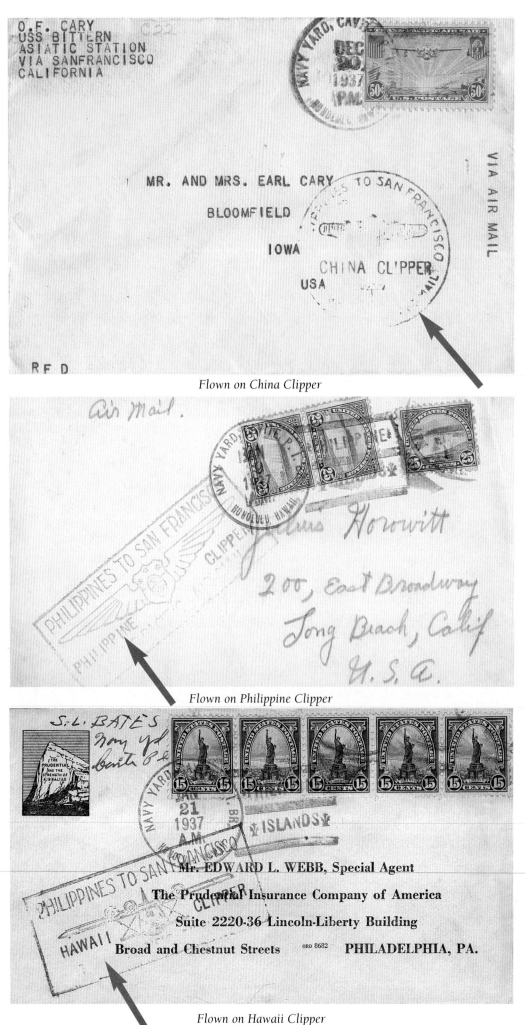

O.F. CARY
USS BITTERN
ASIATIC STATION
VIA SANFRANCISCO
CALIFORNIA

MR. AND MRS. EARL CARY

BLOOMFIELD

IOWA

USA

RFD

VIA AIR MAIL

*Flown on China Clipper*

*Flown on Philippine Clipper*

S.L. BATES

Mr. EDWARD L. WEBB, Special Agent

The Prudential Insurance Company of America

Suite 2220-36 Lincoln-Liberty Building

Broad and Chestnut Streets    ORD 8682    PHILADELPHIA, PA.

*Flown on Hawaii Clipper*

The Philippine post office maintained a branch at Cavite and after the transfer of Pan Am's base to Cavite, Clipper mail is found cancelled at the branch of the Honolulu post office.

Because of the large Navy base, the Honolulu post office also maintained a branch office at Cavite in the Philippines. Therefore, United States stamps could be used for Clipper mail sent to the United States. The postal clerk at the Cavite Naval base had a seperate rubber stamp prepared for each of the three Martin M-130 Clippers. Because the clerk knew which of the three aircraft would actually carry the mail back to the United States, he would carefully apply the rubber stamp to each envelope before the mail was placed on board the Clipper for the flight to San Francisco.

For the remainder of Clipper flights to Manila up until the outbreak of WWII, the Pan Am base at Cavite proved itself to be a well protected facility very suitable for use by the Clippers.

| Press Flight to Manila | October 7-24, 1936 | M-130 China Clipper | Dahlstrom/Lewis |
|---|---|---|---|

| Outbound Flight Schedule | | Inbound Flight Schedule | |
|---|---|---|---|
| San Francisco - Honolulu | Oct. 7-8 | Manila - Guam | Oct. 20 |
| Honolulu - Midway | Oct. 9 | Guam - Wake | Oct. 21 |
| Midway - Wake | Oct. 10-11* | Wake - Midway | Oct. 22-21* |
| Wake - Guam | Oct. 14 | Midway - Honolulu | Oct. 22 |
| Guam - Manila | Oct. 17 | Honolulu - San Francisco | Oct. 23-24 |

*Dateline - Gain day outbound - Lose day inbound

Juan Trippe was well aware of the powerful influence the press had upon forming public opinion in our country. Therefore, in order to generate as much favorable publicity as possible, his public relations director, William VanDusen, hosted a press flight across the Pacific before the inauguration of regular passenger service. On October 7, 1936 the China Clipper departed San Francisco for Manila with William VanDusen and five newsmen representing various news agencies in the United States. Once they reached Honolulu, other newsmen joined the group. Included were Harry W. Frantz of **United Press**, C.B. Allen of

the **New York Herald Tribune**, Lauren D. Lyman of the **New York Times**, W.W. Chaplin of **Universal Services**, Charles E. Harner of **Associated Press**, Earl M. Welty of **Pan American Press**, and John Williams a photographer and reporter for the **Honolulu Star-Bulletin**. Pictured upon their arrival are the reporters who traveled with VanDusen from San Francisco. VanDusen is on the far right; C.B. Allen of the **New York Herald Tribune** is on the far left.

After leaving Honolulu, they visited the new bases on Midway and Wake and sent back glowing reports of Pan Am's success in transforming these remote islands into pleasant stopovers for the Clipper passengers.

On Tuesday, October 14, the China Clipper, under the command of Captain Dahlstrom, arrived at Guam, making this Pacific outpost the center of world news, at least for a day. They were met by the governor and the representatives of the Guam Congress and given a quick tour of the island and an official reception at the governor's mansion.

On Wednesday, October 15, the plane took off for Manila. But, only 350 miles out adverse weather forced the plane back to Guam. The American community on Guam was delighted. They arranged for an open house at the officer's club and more tours of the island. The bad weather continued and the press group was unable to leave until the morning of October 17. However, the forced layover did not dampen the enthusiasm of the reporters, who continued to send back favorable reports on Guam and on the Clipper flight throughout their forced layover. The morning of October 17 they successfully took off for Manila. In Manila, two additional reporters joined their group – Miss Dorothy Kilgallen of **International News** and Mr. Leo Kiernan of the **New York Times**.

Each passenger and crew member was presented with a special certificate by VanDusen when the Clipper crossed the international dateline. The one illustrated was for crew member Briggs. It was signed by all of the reporters onboard. Unfortunately it has been damaged over the years.

*Cover signed by crew and newsman on flight from San Francisco to Wake*

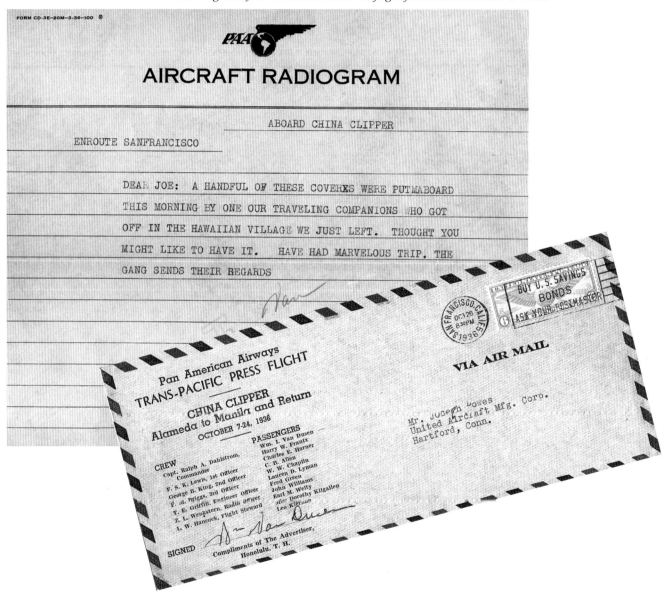

Many souvenir flight covers were prepared to commemorate this flight. Illustrated at the top of the page is a cover that flew westbound from San Francisco to Wake Island that was signed by the entire crew and Wake's airport manager, Stu Saunders.

Also shown is a cover prepared by the **Honolulu Advertiser** for the final inboard portion of the flight from Honolulu to Alameda. William VanDusen enclosed a seldom seen Pan Am radiogram in the envelope he sent to a friend in Hartford Connecticut as a souvenir of this flight.

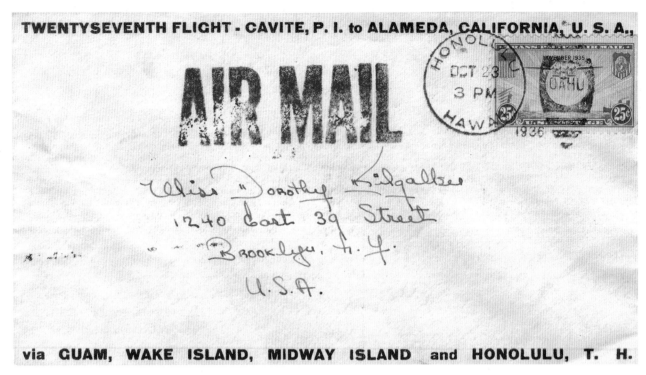

*A Whipple Hall designed and printed cover*

A printer in Manila, Whipple Hall, prepared souvenir covers for the first Clipper flights and the information he provided on the back of his envelopes has been helpful in better understanding the early flights. Dorothy Kilgallen, a journalist and panelist on the early television program "What's My Line?", addressed a Whipple Hall printed cover to herself and had the other journalists and Captain Dahlstrom sign her souvenir cover. Miss Kilgallen joined this flight in Manila on the last portion of her eastbound trip around the world by commercial airlines. When she completed the flight she became the first person to have completed an around the world flight by commercial aircraft.

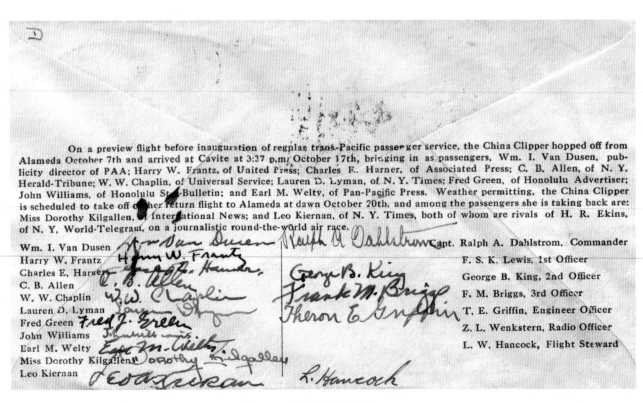

*Reverse of Whipple Hall cover*

| Public Relations VIP Flight to Hong Kong | Oct. 14-Nov. 2, 1936 | M-130 Philippine Clipper | Tilton/Ralph |
| --- | --- | --- | --- |

| Outbound Flight Schedule | | Inbound Flight Schedule | |
| --- | --- | --- | --- |
| San Francisco - Honolulu | Oct. 14-15 | Hong Kong - Manila | Oct. 24 |
| Honolulu - Midway | Oct. 16 | Manila - Guam | Oct. 25 |
| Midway - Wake | Oct. 17-18* | Guam - Wake | Oct. 29 |
| Wake - Guam | Oct. 19 | Wake - Midway | Oct. 30-29* |
| Guam - Manila | Oct. 20 | Midway - Honolulu | Oct. 31 |
| Manila-Macao-Hong Kong | Oct. 23 | Honolulu - San Francisco | Nov. 1-2 |

*Dateline - Gain day outbound - Lose day inbound

By October of 1936 Pan Am had completed the hotels for passengers on Wake and Midway and the Martin M-130 Clippers had been flying mail successfully over the route from San Francisco to Manila for almost a year. Pan Am's President, Juan Trippe, felt that it was now time to open the Pacific flights to revenue passengers. However, before the first revenue passenger flight across the Pacific route, he wanted to visit the facilities himself. On his personal flight of inspection and celebration he took his wife and some of his closest business and political friends. They departed on October 14, 1936, and, if he found that everything was up to his high standards for luxury and comfort, the first revenue passengers would leave a week later on October 21, 1936. Therefore, by October of 1936, all was in readiness for Juan Trippe and his wife Betty to survey his Pacific kingdom.

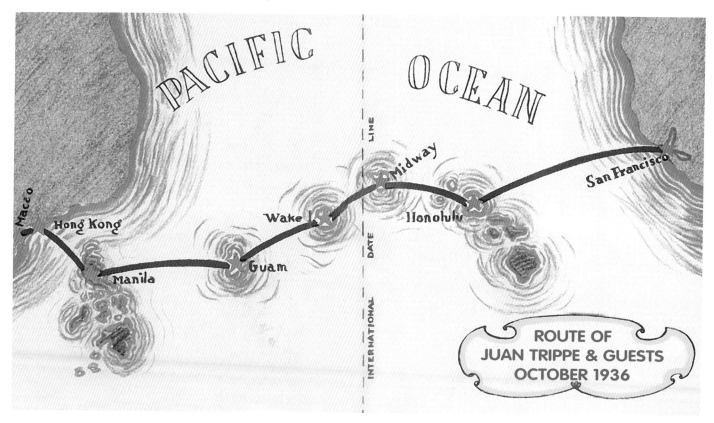

ROUTE OF
JUAN TRIPPE & GUESTS
OCTOBER 1936

Although the Martin Clippers were advertised as being able to carry 32 passengers, on the long 2400 mile flight from San Francisco to Honolulu, so much fuel had to be carried that only 8 passengers could fly that portion of the flight. Beyond Honolulu, because of much shorter distances between the island bases, 20 passengers or more could be carried. Therefore, only Juan Trippe and several of his business associates made the first portion of the flight from San Francisco to Honolulu. His wife, Betty, and the wives of two others in his group, plus the rest of his party would travel by steamer to Honolulu to join him for the remainder of the flight.

*Juan Trippe, center, Senator McAdoo, Director Whitney depart on VIP flight from Alameda*

*Newlyweds Charles and Anne Lindbergh and Betty and Juan Trippe - 1929*

*Juan and Betty Trippe and children - 1941*

Juan and Betty Trippe were married on June 16, 1928. They were good friends with newlyweds Anne and Charles Lindbergh. The two couples were considered among the most glamorous in the exciting new industry of commercial aviation. At the time of this VIP trip in 1936 the Trippes had two children: Missy, age four and Charles, not quite two. By the time this family picture was taken in 1941, the Trippe's had four beautiful children. In the photograph, Charles to the left was seven and young Missy on the right was nine.

Betty Trippe was a keen observer of the historic events going on around her and she is best able to capture the thrill and excitement of this VIP passenger trip. She kept an informative log of the exciting journey. So let us have Betty Trippe's impressions recreate for you this memorable flight.

# Betty S. Trippe

**October 11, 1936:**
We departed San Francisco to meet Juan and the Philippine Clipper in Honolulu.

**October 14, 1936:**
Now, after so many years of hard work and planning, it seemed hard to believe that we were actually going to fly to China, the first passengers to fly across the Pacific. This is the culmination of what at times has seemed an impossible dream; there were so many obstacles to overcome. Following Juan's vision that planes could be designed to fly long distances over the ocean, there were the years of planning to put the pieces of the puzzle together that would make it happen. . . This is now being accomplished because Juan has gathered together a wonderful,

*S.S.Lurline took us to Honolulu*

dedicated group of highly capable, confident men. When the enormous technical problems had been solved, there were still many who doubted the capability of the Martin flying boats to fly the long distances across the ocean. Two members of the Board of Directors of Pan American actually resigned, not wishing to be associated with such a venture. Onboard the Clipper with Juan for the inaugural passenger flight across the Pacific are Amon Carter, Publisher of the Fort Worth Star-Telegram; Roy Howard, Publisher of the Scripps Howard Papers; Paul Patterson, Publisher of the Baltimore Sun; Senator William McAdoo, Chairman of the U.S. Senate Commerce Committee; and Sonny Whitney, Chairman of Pan American Airways. Also onboard, but flying only as far as Honolulu, are Wallace Alexander and William Roth, of the Matson Steamship Company . . . Traveling by steamship from San Francisco to meet the plane in Honolulu in addition to myself are: Gee Whitney - wife of Director Sonny Whitney - Mrs. McAdoo - Eddie McDonnell - Pan Am Director - Graham Grosvenor -

*Amon Carter in cowboy hat - Juan on right arriving in Honolulu*

editor of the National Geographic and a Pan Am Director - Bob Lord, Juan's secretary- - Ed Swasey of the United Press - Jimmy Stahlman - publisher of the Nashville Banner - Tom Beck of Collier Publishing. We are all sailing over to Honolulu on the S.S. Lurline, a beautiful and very luxurious ship.

**October 15, 1936:**

At sea just off Honolulu. Captain invited us to join him on the bridge early in the morning to see the Philippine Clipper fly over the Lurline. Then we heard the roar of the four motors. As I held my

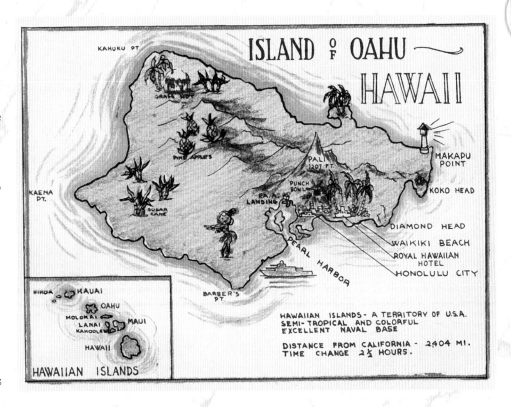

movie camera focused on the plane, tears of joy were streaming down my cheeks. It was an overwhelming moment. Their flight was an astonishing reality. Later, as we approached our dock I spotted Juan. What a thrill to see him. They were all there to meet us, those who had flown from San Francisco. More leis were put around our necks. Hugs and kisses on both cheeks and alohas, our welcome to Hawaii.

We stayed at the Royal Hawaiian Hotel overlooking a lush tropical garden with surf beyond rolling onto the beach of the Waikiki.

*We meet our group in Honolulu*

**October 16, 1936: Honolulu to Midway**

*Pan Am's Honolulu base at Pearl City*

We were called at 4:00 a.m. We drove to the Pan Am base at Pearl Harbor where there is a little passenger station among the palms. There were "leis and alohas" even at this early hour. Finally we were off. Fighting the earth's gravity the four 800 h.p. motors pulled us off the water. I couldn't believe it. We were on our way to China.

*Honolulu base among the palms*

The Clipper is unbelievably comfortable and luxurious. There is a big central lounge wider than a club car on a Pullman where meals are served and a cozy compartment aft seating 8 passengers. There were four berths made up, which we all took turns using for naps during the flight. There are separate lavatories, one for the ladies and one for the men. The toilets don't flush, of course, but there is a blue chemical in the water to purify the air. Forward is the chart room where the crew of 9 can rest when taking their shifts in the cockpit on the long flights, so as to never be overtired when on duty. They are all outstanding looking men. The noise was not bad - you only had to raise your voice a little to be heard. The day passed pleasantly with meals, books, sleep and good conversation while some played cards.

At last, at the end of ten hours in the air, the tiny, sandy island of Midway appeared ahead. Great breakers pound against the reef that almost surrounds the island. Inside the reef the water is calm.

Today on this remote island there are electric lights, radio communication facilities, hot and cold running water, a small first class hotel, furnished in excellent taste with bamboo furniture from Gumps in San Francisco with private baths and good beds. We had a delicious dinner, beautifully served. After dinner we went to see a movie with the men of the company.

The spirit of enthusiasm and pride in their work among all men here was marvelous. I got a real thrill seeing Juan's picture hanging on the wall of the administration building, as the men had put it up of their own accord.

*Midway's Gooney birds*

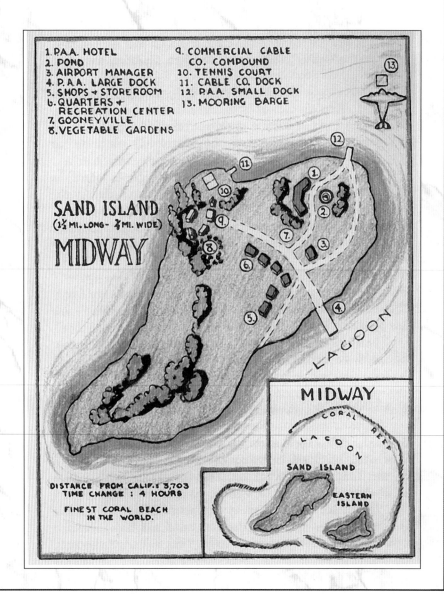

1. P.A.A. HOTEL
2. POND
3. AIRPORT MANAGER
4. P.A.A. LARGE DOCK
5. SHOPS + STORE ROOM
6. QUARTERS + RECREATION CENTER
7. GOONEYVILLE
8. VEGETABLE GARDENS
9. COMMERCIAL CABLE CO. COMPOUND
10. TENNIS COURT
11. CABLE CO. DOCK
12. P.A.A. SMALL DOCK
13. MOORING BARGE

SAND ISLAND
(1½ MI. LONG- ⅔ MI. WIDE)
MIDWAY

LAGOON

DISTANCE FROM CALIF.: 3,703
TIME CHANGE : 4 HOURS

FINEST CORAL BEACH
IN THE WORLD.

MIDWAY
CORAL REEF
LAGOON
SAND ISLAND
EASTERN ISLAND

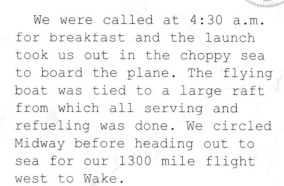

## October 17 - Midway to Wake.

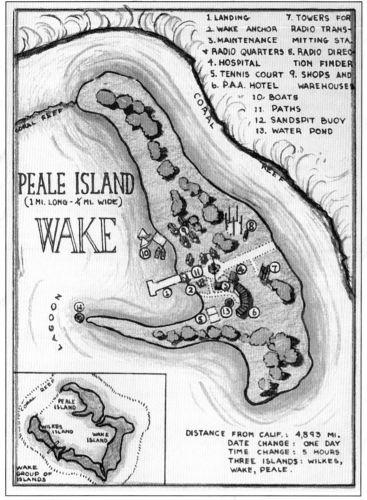

1. LANDING
2. WAKE ANCHOR
3. MAINTENANCE
4. RADIO QUARTERS
4. HOSPITAL
5. TENNIS COURT
6. P.A.A. HOTEL
7. TOWERS FOR RADIO TRANS-MITTING STA.
8. RADIO DIREC-TION FINDER
9. SHOPS AND WAREHOUSES
10. BOATS
11. PATHS
12. SANDSPIT BUOY
13. WATER POND

PEALE ISLAND
(1 MI. LONG - ¼ MI. WIDE)

WAKE

CORAL REEF

LAGOON

PEALE ISLAND
WILKES ISLAND
WAKE ISLAND
WAKE GROUP OF ISLANDS

DISTANCE FROM CALIF.: 4,893 MI.
DATE CHANGE: ONE DAY
TIME CHANGE: 5 HOURS
THREE ISLANDS: WILKES, WAKE, PEALE.

We were called at 4:30 a.m. for breakfast and the launch took us out in the choppy sea to board the plane. The flying boat was tied to a large raft from which all serving and refueling was done. We circled Midway before heading out to sea for our 1300 mile flight west to Wake.

We landed at Wake 9 hours after leaving Midway. We had crossed the dateline and gained a day. It is now October 18. We have seen that name on the company maps for so long and our attention was focused so much on the activities here, that it is a shock to see what a tiny bit of land Wake Island actually is. With much joking the crew insisted that I put my foot ashore as the first woman to set foot on Wake.

It was hot enough to blow your head off, but the hotel, a duplicate in plan to that on Midway, had a cool porch where we sat and had some delicious cool drinks. We had a delicious dinner with champagne brought along by Roy Howard. Amon Carter made a very serious speech about the difficulties overcome in the feat of Pan Am conquering the Pacific. One by one he called on the men to say a few words. These speeches were solemn enough for any large banquet and made our group of nine passengers seem even smaller.

Enough sleep was a rare treat. Six hours on Wake was wonderful. Our flight of ten hours to Guam has not seemed tedious as the time passes quickly with reading, conversation and meals. At the landing we were greeted by a Navy band and girl scouts presented bouquets of faded flowers. We walked across the plaza surrounded by Pan Am company buildings to an attractive little house on the water's edge in a grove of palms – the passenger lounge and dining room. We sat in comfortable bamboo chairs on the porch and had iced tea, beer and salad. It was a cool welcome spot as the heat and humidity were terrific. The same style of hotel is here as on the other islands, but the setting at Guam is particularly attractive, with a lovely view through the palms. In the afternoon we toured the island. We had dinner at the Governor's palace. After dinner we went to a party at the officer's club where we stood in line to receive about 50 Navy officers and their wives stationed in Guam. We almost passed out with the heat and exhaustion from lack of sleep.

ISLAND OF GUAM
(30 MI. LONG - 7 MI. WIDE)

CALLED "LATEEN SAILS ISLAND"
DISCOVERED BY MAGELLAN IN 1521
POSSESSION OF SPAIN IN 1565
CEDED TO U.S.A. IN 1898
A COMMONWEALTH IN 1935

DISTANCE FROM CALIF. 6,401 MILES
TIME CHANGE FROM CALIF. 6 HOURS

Guam base

208

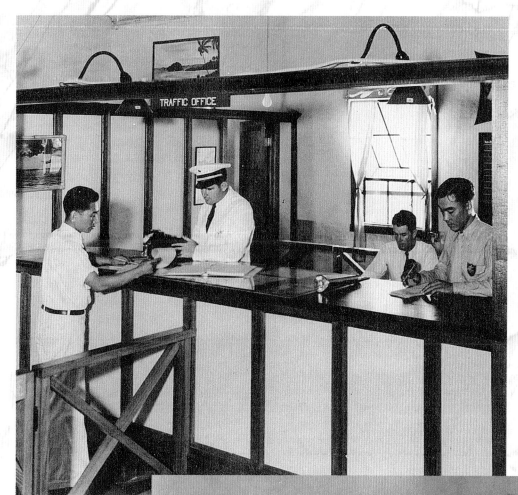

*Station
Manager Bill
Mullahey
at Guam*

*Pan Am's new
office at
Guam*

Called again at 4:00 - we are on our way to Manila on the last lap of the flight across the Pacific. We landed just before dark at Cavite. Hundreds of people, a band, photographers, and government officials dressed in immaculate white greeted us as we landed. Newspaper reporters gathered around asking each of us our impressions and experience as the first passengers to fly the Pacific.

We were guests of President Quezon at the Manila Hotel and had an enormous bedroom and sitting room. We felt like royalty, our room filled with boxes and flowers and tropical fruit. The flowers that pleased me most were a corsage of white orchids from "Captain Tilton and the crew" which they had radioed ahead. After dinner at the hotel we went to the Santa Ana, the largest dance hall in the world. The "taxi girls" of various colors, shapes and sizes sit at a little table on one side of the dance floor waiting to be selected to dance. They charge ten centavos a dance (which is about 5 cents U.S.) and they must share 50% of this with the management. When the fleet is in, we were told, the dance hall is wild and crowded with sailors.

General Douglas McArthur is Governor of the Philippines. He was away at the time but his assistant, Major Dwight Eisenhower, received us at Government House. Major Eisenhower has been most helpful in obtaining landing rights for Pan American in the Philippines.

Breakfast at 3:30

*Juan and I arriving at Cavite*

210

*Macao Harbor*

a.m. was a hilarious affair, as many of our fellow passengers were still
very high and some of our new Filipino friends came by on their way home
from the party to say good bye. The crew, seated at one end of the table,
was in contrast, serious rested and businesslike.

Once aboard we all curled up and tried to catch up on sleep.

*The old and the new - The Philippine Clipper and the Macao sampan*

*Landing at Macao*

Macao thrilled us more than anything seen so far. There were hundreds of sampans with their colorful sails.

*Landing barge - Macao*

212

*Pan Am's office at Macao*

Great rugged mountains rising out of the sea and the irregularity
of the coastline made it a fascinating, fantastic sight from the
air.Swarming crowds lined the shore. It was the first time the
Clipper had been to Macao. It was our first sight of the real
orient, rickshaws, coolie boys, old Chinese faces, and young
Chinese flappers in high heeled European shoes and to our surprise,
quite a number of Indians. A mechanic, a Sikh with a turban

*Leaving Clipper at Macao*

covering his long locks, in white Pan Am overalls, made us realize what a world-wide organization the company now is.

The Chinese gave Macao many years ago to the Portuguese in gratitude for wiping out the pirates, which were so numerous along this part of the coast. The Chinese, we were told, today regret this act of generosity.

We lunched with the Governor of Macao and Madam Barbosa. The beautiful table setting and delicious food were followed by a flowery speech by the Governor and a response by Juan.

We took off from Macao right after lunch and in 20 minutes we were over Hong Kong. Abiding by reciprocal landing rights granted only a day or two before the British gave Pan Am temporary permission to land in Hong Kong. The harbor was crowded with ships from the four corners of the world along with great Chinese junks and sails of orange matting.

Juan prepared a broadcast to London and we dressed for dinner at the Government House.

While the VIPs returned from Hong Kong with Captain Tilton on the Philippine Clipper, the Trippes continued on their westbound trip around the world – and what a trip it was! First they flew 3,000 miles to inspect the China National Air Corporation's routes throughout China. After returning to Hong Kong, they boarded the British Imperial Airways "Dorado" for the ten day flight to London. At Penang, they transferred to the Imperial Airways "Aurora" and continued on to London, where they stayed with the Lindberghs, who had moved to the English countryside to avoid the American press. After a short visit, they flew to Holland to discuss air routes and then to Germany for more business talks.

The press in Germany hounded the Trippes about their flight across the Pacific, so to avoid publicity, they assumed the names of "Mr. and Mrs. Brown". In Frankfurt the "Browns" boarded the Zeppelin, the *Hindenburg*, for the four day flight to Rio de Janeiro, where they again flew by Pan Am Clipper back to Dinner Key in Miami. They completed their trip from Miami to New York on an Eastern Airlines flight. Since leaving New York on October 10, 1936 for California to start the VIP flight, they had traveled for 53 days and covered 36,000 miles in 38 days of flying. Dorothy Kilgallen, who flew on the eastbound portion of Pan Am's press flight in early October of 1936, was the first person to fly by commercial airlines eastward around the world. The Trippes, with this flight, completed the first westbound trip around the world by commercial airlines.

The immigration and visa stamps in the well-traveled passport they carried with them on this historic flight tells a great story of their adventure. In the 1930s a married woman traveled on her husband's passport. Juan Trippe listed his occupation as "commercial air transportation".

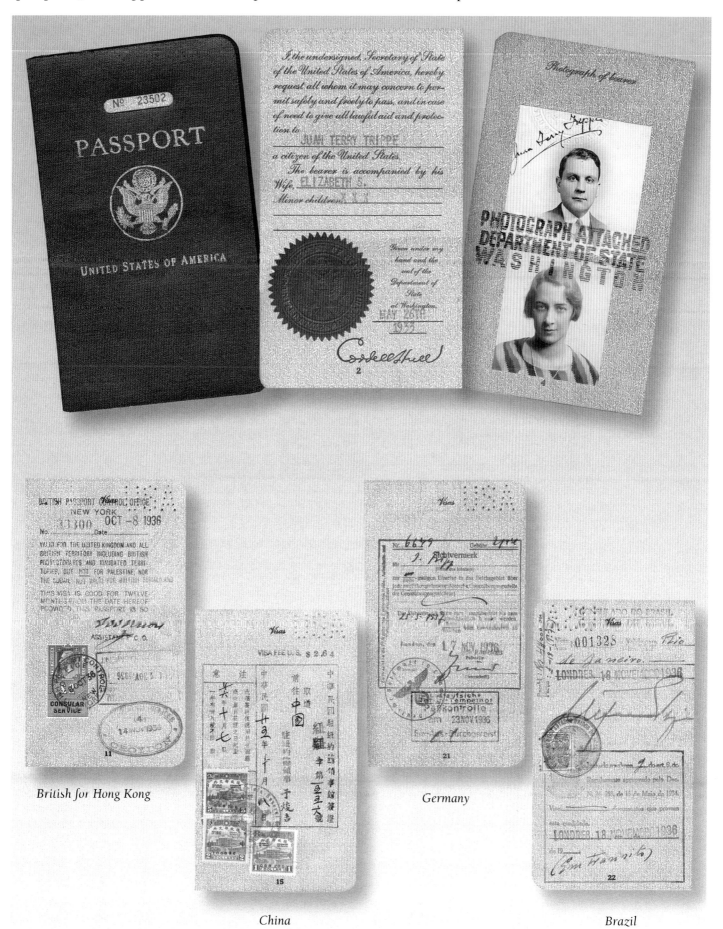

British for Hong Kong

China

Germany

Brazil

The VIPs on their return flight, arrived at Guam on October 25, 1936. For several days, the weather prevented them from flying on to Wake. While they were on Guam the westbound Hawaii Clipper with the first revenue passengers also arrived. For one night, tiny Guam had to entertain and provide for 30 passengers and Pan Am crew members. It was quite a strain on the limited facilities. This marked the first time that both the Philippine Clipper and the Hawaii Clipper were together at Guam.

While Amon Carter's VIP flight was held up for three days at Guam by bad weather, he wrote a letter to a friend in Detroit, telling him about his great adventure. His letter, however, was mailed too late to be placed on his flight home from Guam, so it remained on the island until the inbound return flight of the first revenue passengers returned from Manila to Guam. Amon Carter's letter reached San Francisco on November 4, 1936, two days after his return on the Philippine Clipper. Therefore, his letter to his friend in Detroit is a unique souvenir of both the VIP flight and the first revenue passenger flight.

*Actual text of Amon Carter's letter mailed from Guam*

*Guam – October 26, 1936: Dear Rusty: Well, here we are on our way home. Dandy trip by plane from Fort Worth to Hong Kong, China, 10,642 miles. The trip from Manila to Hong Kong was a first flight. We are tied up here on account of weather. The Hawaii Clipper arrived here this p.m. with the first paid commercial flight – Our trip with Pan Am officials was the final inspection trip before starting the first scheduled commercial passenger flights. These new Pan Am Clippers are great. Good berths and food. We should arrive S.F. Friday the 30th ahead of this letter, as the mail on our ship having been closed – hope you are well. I bet $1,500 even on Roosevelt before leaving San Francisco.* **(He won his bet - Roosevelt was relected)**

The publisher Amon Carter also prepared most of the souvenir covers for the VIP inspection flight. Let's take a look at three of his efforts.

*Amon Carter prepared cover*

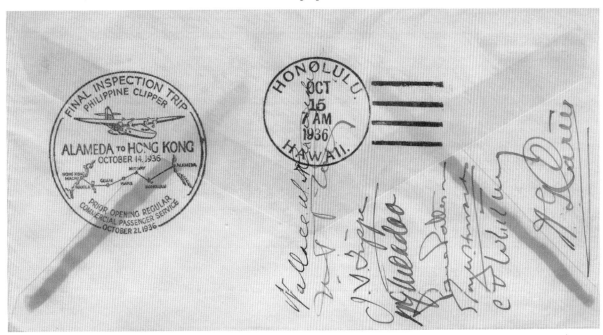

*Amon Carter cover for return flight from Manila*

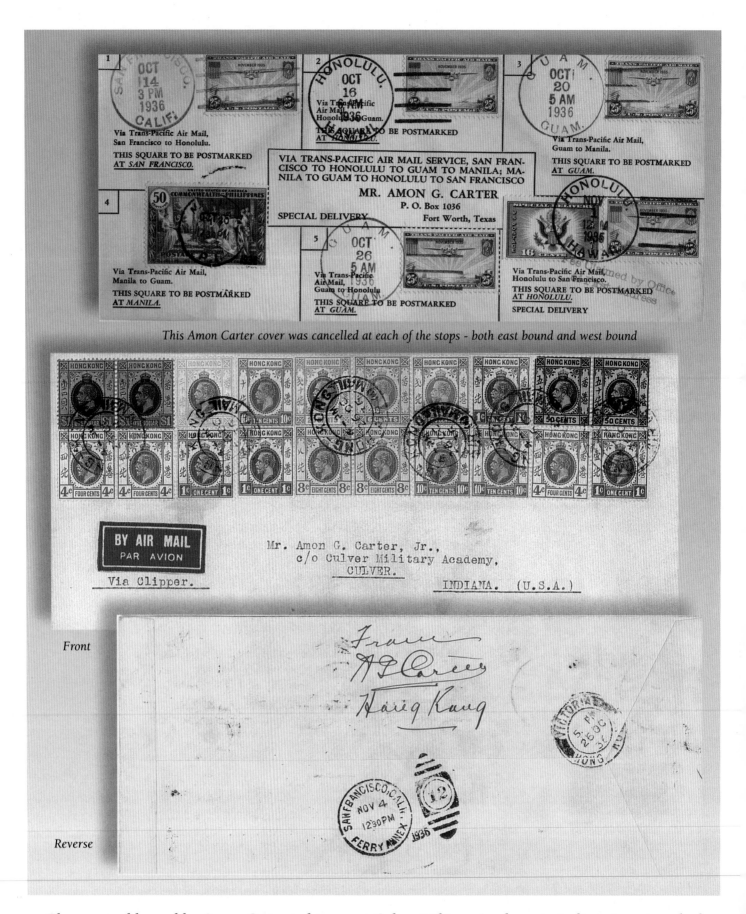

*This Amon Carter cover was cancelled at each of the stops - both east bound and west bound*

Front

Reverse

The cover addressed by Amon Carter to his son at Culver Military Academy in Indiana is postmarked October 24 in Hong Kong. It is back stamped November 4, 1936 in San Francisco. At this point in time there were not any connecting flights for mail between Hong Kong and Manila. Therefore it undoubtedly went by ship to Manila and it was placed onboard the Hawaii Clipper that was returning to San Francisco on the first revenue passenger flight. At this point in time Hong Kong had a special rate of $4.20 per one half ounce for mail sent by sea to Manila and onward to the United States by Pan Am Clipper. The cover carries the correct postage. I have now seen two airmail covers from Hong Kong from this flight.

Amon Carter was not the only person on the VIP flight writing letters to a son in prep school back in the states. William VanDusen, Pan Am's public relations director, had hosted the press corps flight that had laid over at Wake on October 21 and he had caught a large barracuda while fishing in Wake's lagoon. When the VIP flight passed through Wake on the inbound flight a week later, the station manager, Stew Saunders, mailed him a letter telling him about his dad's great catch.

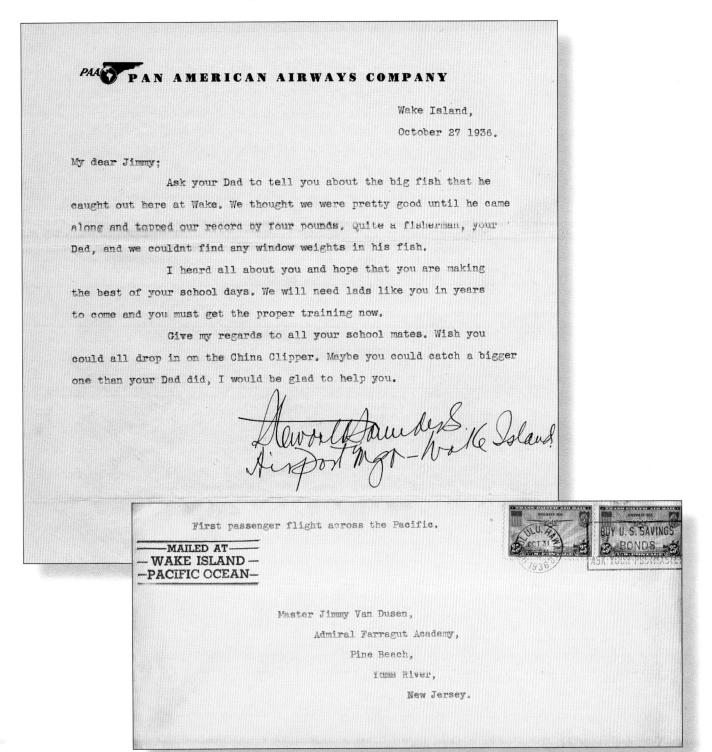

PAA ⟨logo⟩ PAN AMERICAN AIRWAYS COMPANY

Wake Island,
October 27 1936.

My dear Jimmy;

Ask your Dad to tell you about the big fish that he caught out here at Wake. We thought we were pretty good until he came along and topped our record by four pounds. Quite a fisherman, your Dad, and we couldnt find any window weights in his fish.

I heard all about you and hope that you are making the best of your school days. We will need lads like you in years to come and you must get the proper training now.

Give my regards to all your school mates. Wish you could all drop in on the China Clipper. Maybe you could catch a bigger one than your Dad did, I would be glad to help you.

⟨signature⟩ Stew Saunders
Airport Mgr - Wake Island

First passenger flight across the Pacific.

——MAILED AT——
— WAKE ISLAND —
—PACIFIC OCEAN—

Master Jimmy Van Dusen,
Admiral Farragut Academy,
Pine Beach,
Toms River,
New Jersey.

Juan Trippe's ploy of playing Hong Kong off of Macao worked! Once they had seen the Clipper, the British and Hong Kong's business men were fearful that they would lose out to Macao if they did not extend landing rights in Hong Kong to Pan Am. Therefore, in less than six months' time, the previously insurmountable political details were fully resolved and Pan Am established mail and passenger service directly to Hong Kong. Juan Trippe's VIP flight achieved his goal of opening service from California to China. The famous China Clipper would finally be able to fly to China. Reaching China was Trippe's goal from the time he conceived the bold plan to cross the Pacific.

| 1st Revenue Passenger Flight to Manila | October 21 - November 4, 1936 | M-130 Hawaii Clipper | Musick/Gray |
|---|---|---|---|

| Outbound Flight Schedule | | Inbound Flight Schedule | |
|---|---|---|---|
| San Francisco - Honolulu | Oct. 21-22 | Manila - Guam | Oct. 31 |
| Honolulu - Midway | Oct. 23 | Guam - Wake | Nov. 1 |
| Midway - Wake | Oct. 24-25* | Wake - Midway | Nov. 2-1* |
| Wake - Guam | Oct. 26 | Midway - Honolulu | Nov. 2 |
| Guam - Manila | Oct. 27 | Honolulu - San Francisco | Nov. 3-4 |

*Dateline - Gain day outbound - Lose day inbound

When Pan Am was ready to inaugurate passenger service across the Pacific, they posted an announcement in their office window at 427 Post Street, San Francisco. R.F. Bradley, manager of the Standard Oil Company of California's aviation department, was walking past the office, noticed the advertisement, and inquired if any of the seven tickets were still available. To his surprise, he received the first ticket issued by Pan Am for Pacific travel. Bradley is pictured proudly holding his ticket issued by V.A.

*Passenger number one Richard F. Bradley with Pan Am ticket manager*

Kropff, Pan Am's San Francisco traffic manager. Kropff is using the travel agent model of the Martin M-130 to explain the features of the Clipper. The one way fare to Manila was $950, an incredible amount in the depression years.

On October 21, 1936, the Martin M-130 Hawaii Clipper NC 14714, under the command of Capt. Musick, departed San Francisco on the first revenue passenger flight in history across the Pacific.

In a newsletter Pan Am identified the first passengers, left to right, as follows:

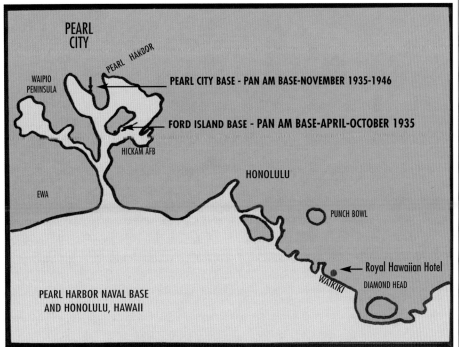

Proud possessor of ticket #1, Mr. R.F. Bradley, aviation manager of Standard Oil's San Francisco office; Wilbur May, Los Angeles department store executive and an excellent pilot in his own right; Mrs. Clara Adams of Stroudsburg, Pennsylvania, globe trotter, lecturer and well known 'first flighter'; Colonel Charles Bartley of Chicago, head of a large wholesale grocery firm; T.F. Ryan III, a San Francisco capitalist and an aviation executive; Alfred Bennett of Hightstown, New Jersey, manager of flying schools and airplane sales companies; and Zetta Averill, world traveler and aviation enthusiast of Aberdeen, Washington.

When the group arrived in
Honolulu on the early morning of
October 22 they were transferred by
Pan Am from the base at Pearl City on
Pearl Harbor back to Honolulu's best
hotel, the Royal Hawaiian at Waikiki
Beach. Pan Am's ticket to Manila
included all transfers to the hotel,
rooms and meals. The hotel's brochure
for 1935 states that a room with meals
cost $10 daily, but in the high season
the same room with meals went up
to $12.

*First revenue passengers at Honolulu*

*Royal Hawaiian Hotel*

The next day they flew to Midway and stayed at the newly completed hotel built for the Pan Am passengers. The architect's drawing for the Midway base showed tall palm trees shading the walkways and gardens for the Pan Am village near the hotel. The architects' expectations were never fulfilled. Palm trees never grew on Midway. As it turned out, it was easier to draw palm trees than to grow them in the desert-like conditions that existed at Midway.

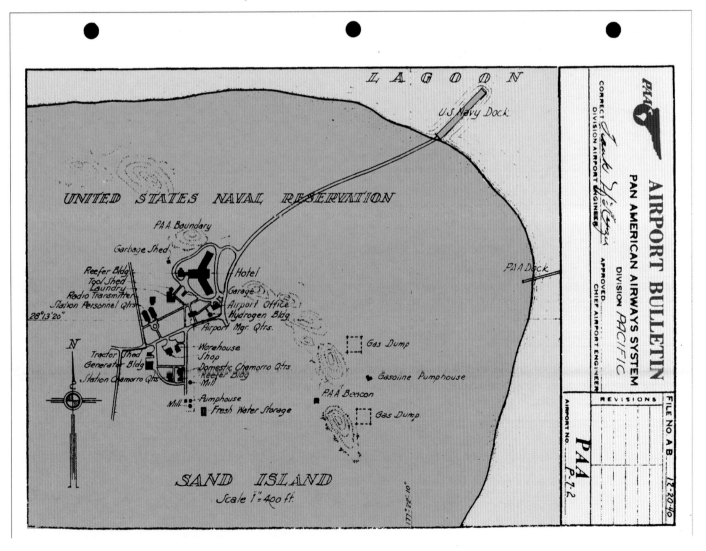

*Passenger waiting room - Cavite*

The next morning they departed Midway for Wake. They were taken from the landing barge and pier to a hotel identical to the one they had stayed in at Midway.

The next day they flew on to Guam where they finally saw some of the palm trees that were promised to them at Wake and Midway.

The next day they left Guam for Manila where they landed at the new base at Cavite. Once again they were transferred to the best hotel, the Manila Hotel, on the harbor in the heart of the old city.

*Navigator Noonan, left and Captain Musick departing Clipper at Cavite*

*Manila Hotel*

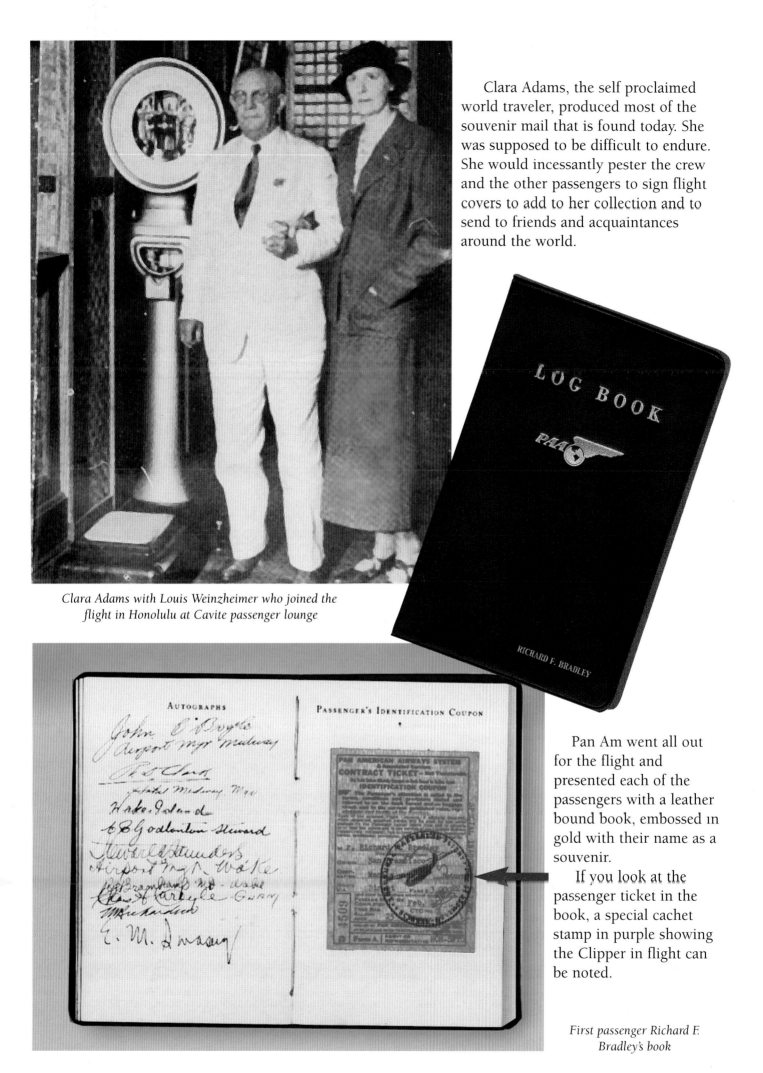

Clara Adams, the self proclaimed world traveler, produced most of the souvenir mail that is found today. She was supposed to be difficult to endure. She would incessantly pester the crew and the other passengers to sign flight covers to add to her collection and to send to friends and acquaintances around the world.

*Clara Adams with Louis Weinzheimer who joined the flight in Honolulu at Cavite passenger lounge*

Pan Am went all out for the flight and presented each of the passengers with a leather bound book, embossed in gold with their name as a souvenir.

If you look at the passenger ticket in the book, a special cachet stamp in purple showing the Clipper in flight can be noted.

*First passenger Richard F. Bradley's book*

Before departure, Colonel Clarence Young, director of the Pacific division, congratulates Richard F. Bradley of Standard Oil for being the holder of the #1 Transpacific ticket. In Bradley's left hand he holds the actual ticket and in his right hand he holds an enlargement of the logo that Pan Am designed to commemorate the first commercial passenger flight in history across the Pacific.

That same logo designed by Pan Am for use on the ticket of the first passengers was also used on the illustrated souvenir cover. It is the only example of this logo I have seen used on any flight covers as a souvenir of the first revenue passenger flight.

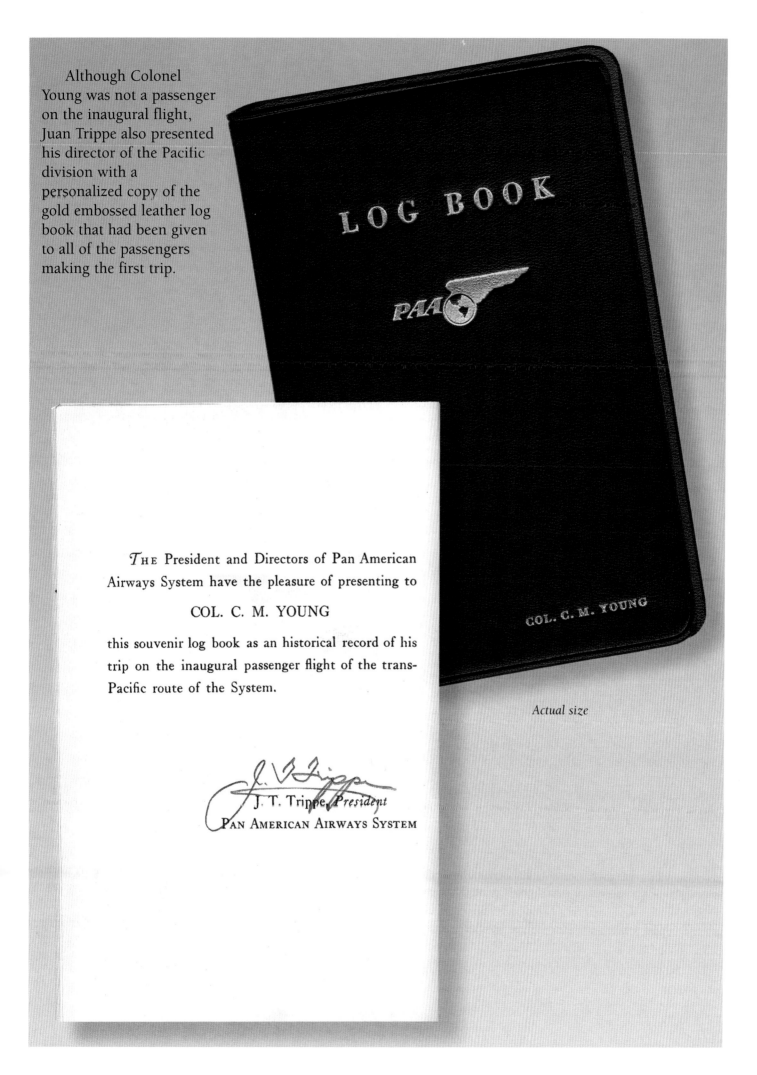

Although Colonel Young was not a passenger on the inaugural flight, Juan Trippe also presented his director of the Pacific division with a personalized copy of the gold embossed leather log book that had been given to all of the passengers making the first trip.

LOG BOOK

PAA

COL. C. M. YOUNG

*THE* President and Directors of Pan American Airways System have the pleasure of presenting to

COL. C. M. YOUNG

this souvenir log book as an historical record of his trip on the inaugural passenger flight of the trans-Pacific route of the System.

J. T. Trippe, *President*
PAN AMERICAN AIRWAYS SYSTEM

*Actual size*

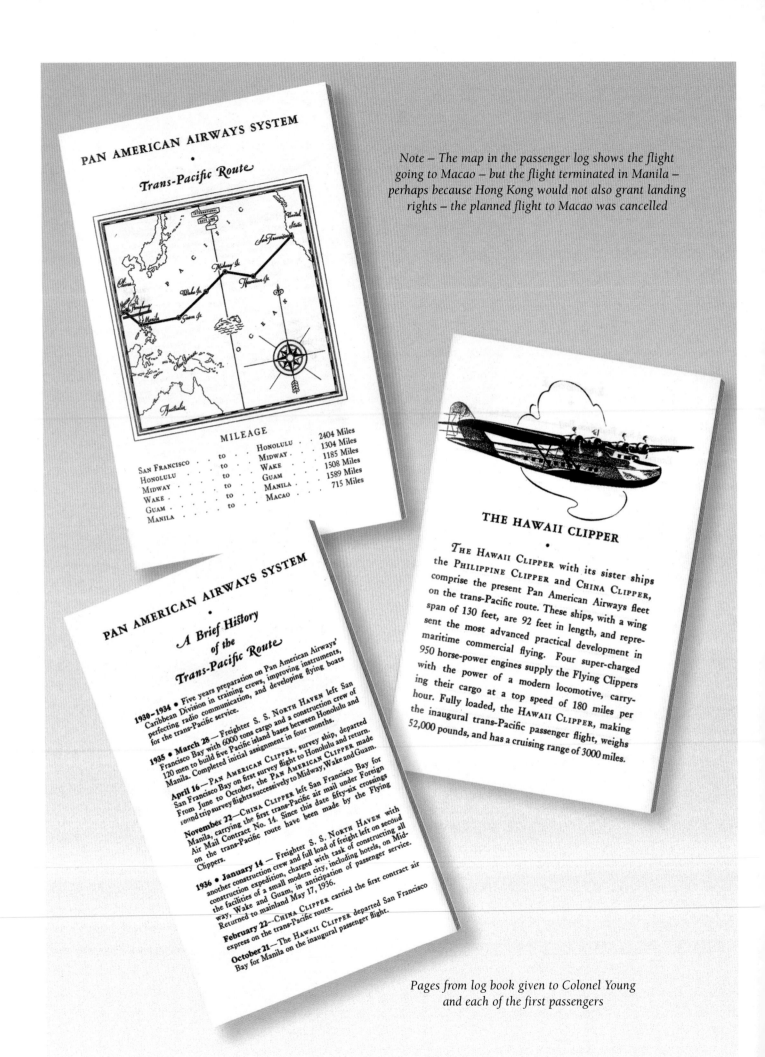

*Note – The map in the passenger log shows the flight going to Macao – but the flight terminated in Manila – perhaps because Hong Kong would not also grant landing rights – the planned flight to Macao was cancelled*

**PAN AMERICAN AIRWAYS SYSTEM**

*Trans-Pacific Route*

**MILEAGE**

| | | | |
|---|---|---|---|
| SAN FRANCISCO | to | HONOLULU | 2404 Miles |
| HONOLULU | to | MIDWAY | 1304 Miles |
| MIDWAY | to | WAKE | 1185 Miles |
| WAKE | to | GUAM | 1508 Miles |
| GUAM | to | MANILA | 1589 Miles |
| MANILA | to | MACAO | 715 Miles |

**THE HAWAII CLIPPER**

THE HAWAII CLIPPER with its sister ships the PHILIPPINE CLIPPER and CHINA CLIPPER, comprise the present Pan American Airways fleet on the trans-Pacific route. These ships, with a wing span of 130 feet, are 92 feet in length, and represent the most advanced practical development in maritime commercial flying. Four super-charged 950 horse-power engines supply the Flying Clippers with the power of a modern locomotive, carrying their cargo at a top speed of 180 miles per hour. Fully loaded, the HAWAII CLIPPER, making the inaugural trans-Pacific passenger flight, weighs 52,000 pounds, and has a cruising range of 3000 miles.

**PAN AMERICAN AIRWAYS SYSTEM**

*A Brief History of the Trans-Pacific Route*

**1930–1934** • Five years preparation on Pan American Airways' Caribbean Division in training crews, improving instruments, perfecting radio communication, and developing flying boats for the trans-Pacific service.

**1935** • March 28 — Freighter S. S. NORTH HAVEN left San Francisco Bay with 6000 tons cargo and a construction crew of 120 men to build five Pacific island bases between Honolulu and Manila. Completed initial assignment in four months.

April 16 — PAN AMERICAN CLIPPER, survey ship, departed San Francisco Bay on first survey flight to Honolulu and return. From June to October, the PAN AMERICAN CLIPPER made round trip survey flights successively to Midway, Wake and Guam.

November 22 — CHINA CLIPPER left San Francisco Bay for Manila, carrying the first trans-Pacific air mail under Foreign Air Mail Contract No. 14. Since this date fifty-six crossings on the trans-Pacific route have been made by the Flying Clippers.

**1936** • January 14 — Freighter S. S. NORTH HAVEN with another construction crew and full load of freight left on second construction expedition, charged with task of constructing all the facilities of a small modern city, including hotels, on Midway, Wake and Guam, in anticipation of passenger service. Returned to mainland May 17, 1936.

February 22 — CHINA CLIPPER carried the first contract air express on the trans-Pacific route.

October 21 — The HAWAII CLIPPER departed San Francisco Bay for Manila on the inaugural passenger flight.

*Pages from log book given to Colonel Young and each of the first passengers*

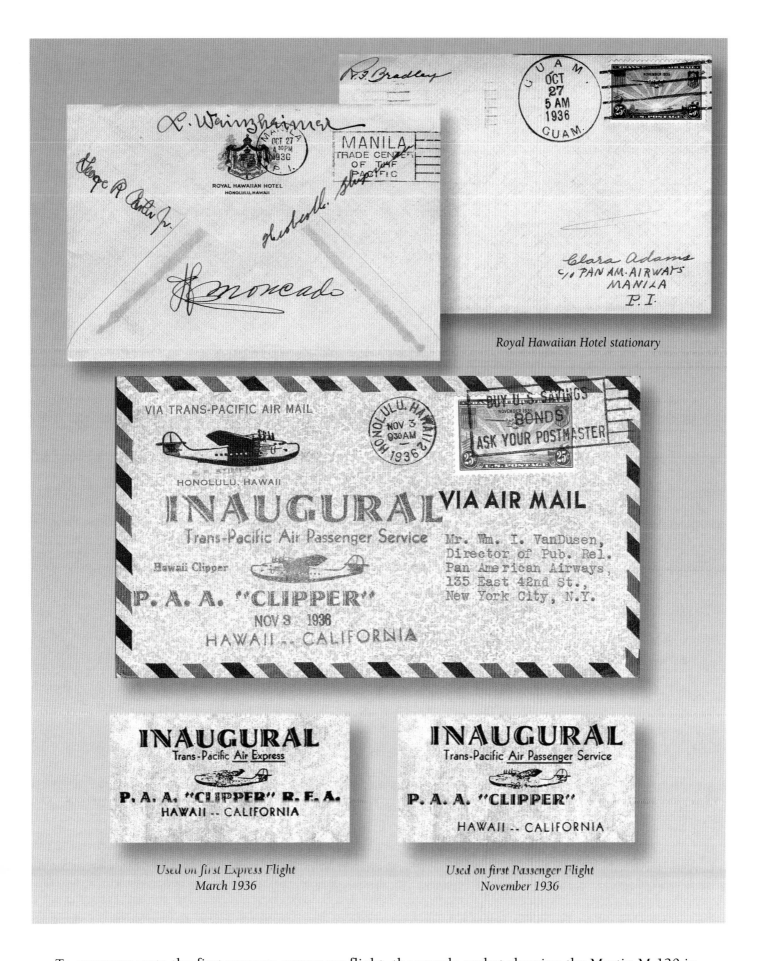

*Royal Hawaiian Hotel stationary*

INAUGURAL
Trans-Pacific Air Express

P. A. A. "CLIPPER" R. F. A.
HAWAII -- CALIFORNIA

*Used on first Express Flight*
*March 1936*

INAUGURAL
Trans-Pacific Air Passenger Service

P. A. A. "CLIPPER"

HAWAII -- CALIFORNIA

*Used on first Passenger Flight*
*November 1936*

To commemorate the first revenue passenger flight, the purple cachet showing the Martin M-130 in flight, was applied in Honolulu by Pan Am's general agent, the Inter-Island Steam Navigation Company, Ltd. In a slightly modified form the same purple cachet was applied by Pan Am's general agent in Honolulu to the first shipment of air express packages from Honolulu carried by Pan Am in March of 1936.

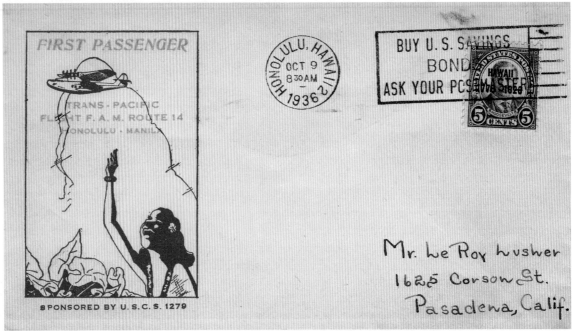

*Signed by Passenger #1 Bradley-Wake posting*

INAUGURATION
**TRANS-PACIFIC**
PASSENGER SERVICE

VIA CLIPPER

*The* FIRST CLIPPER
HELD AS MANY AS THE
"MAYFLOWER"

R U.S. MANILA
No. 2795

OCT
30
1936

Mr. Walter R. Carroll,
469 Franklin Street,
Buffalo,
New York, U.S.A.

*Reverse*

Return to P. O. Box 610
Manila, P. I.

Inaugurating the commercial trans-Pacific passenger service, the Hawaiian Clipper left Alameda October 21st and landed at Cavite at 2:58 p. m. October 27th. She brought eleven passengers including two women. At daybreak today, October 30th, she started on her return flight to the United States via Guam, Wake Island, Midway Island and Honolulu, taking the first paying passengers from Manila.

R. F Bradley, San Francisco, Calif.
Wilbur May, Los Angeles, Calif.
T. F. Ryan, San Francisco, Calif.
Mrs. Clara Adams, Stroudsburg, Penna.
G. R. Carter, Jr., Honolulu
Edward B. Brier, Honolulu
Herbert Shipman, Hilo, Hawaii
Dr. Hilario Camino Moncado, Manila
Dr. Bolivar Falconer, Marlin, Texas
E. M. Bachrach, Manila
Mrs. B. M. Lauritzen, Manila

Capt. Edwin C. Musick, Commander
H. F. Gray, 1st Officer
V. E. Bierer, 2nd Officer
M. C. Weber, Navigator
F. J. Noonan, Asst. Navigator
C. D. Wright, Engineer
T. R. Runnells, Radio Officer
L. R. Merrill, Flight Steward

AIR MAIL

China Clipper
First passenger flight

Rec'd at
Midway, Pacific Ocean
Oct. 23, 1936
2:19 p.m.
R. S. Clark, Mgr.
Hotel
P.A.A. Midway

Clara Adams
c/o Pan Am. Airways
MIDWAY ISLAND
U.S. TERRITORY
IN THE PACIFIC

*Clara Adams mailed this envelope to herself from New York on October 9, 1936 to Midway - received it when she arrived at Midway on October 23, 1936*

*Mailed to Wake from San Francisco*

*Amelia Earhart's navigator Fred Noonan who disappeared with Earhart in Pacific in 1937 signed this cover for Adams*

I recently found an envelope from this first revenue passenger flight that was sent by a passenger other than the irrepressible Clara Adams. Zetta Averill, the only other woman making the first flight, wrote a letter to her children after she completed the first leg of the flight from San Francisco to Honolulu. Zetta was, by all accounts, a pleasant and easy going traveler. Her letter captured her joy and excitement at being a part of this historic event. Illustrated below is her souvenir envelope and her letter that was enclosed. It was written on an envelope from the Saint Francis Hotel in San Francisco, where she spent the night before departing for Manila.

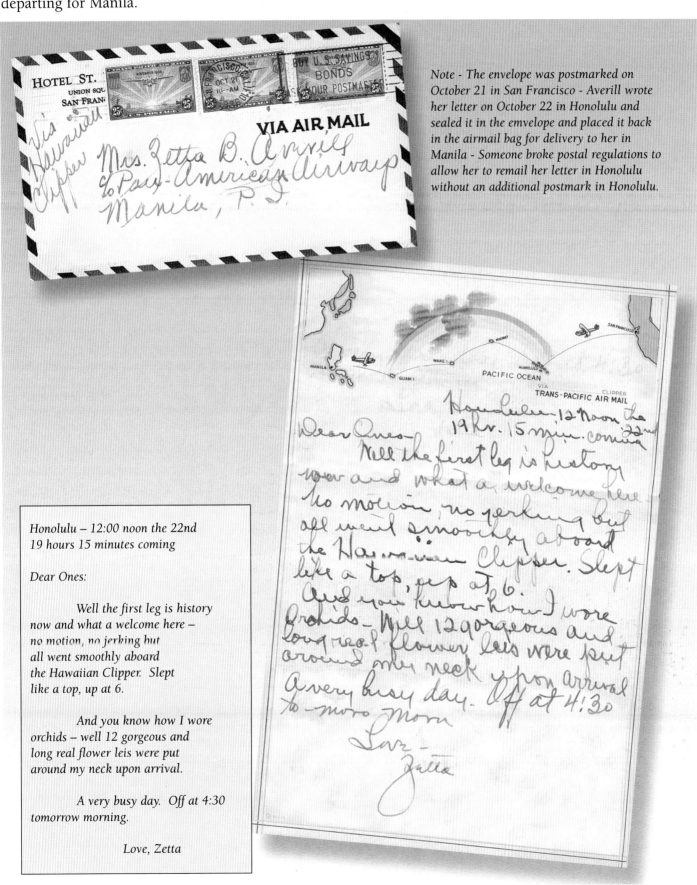

Note - The envelope was postmarked on October 21 in San Francisco - Averill wrote her letter on October 22 in Honolulu and sealed it in the emvelope and placed it back in the airmail bag for delivery to her in Manila - Someone broke postal regulations to allow her to remail her letter in Honolulu without an additional postmark in Honolulu.

Honolulu – 12:00 noon the 22nd
19 hours 15 minutes coming

Dear Ones:

Well the first leg is history now and what a welcome here – no motion, no jerking but all went smoothly aboard the Hawaiian Clipper. Slept like a top, up at 6.

And you know how I wore orchids – well 12 gorgeous and long real flower leis were put around my neck upon arrival.

A very busy day. Off at 4:30 tomorrow morning.

Love, Zetta

*Collier trophy*

The first revenue passenger flight caught the interest and imagination of the world. It was another triumph for Pan Am and it produced a wide variety of interesting souvenir covers for the growing number of flight cover collectors.

Pan Am's accomplishments in 1936 were remarkable. In the young company's eighth year of existence, they had crossed the Pacific for the first time in history on a commercial flight, built accommodations for passengers on remote Pacific islands, and successfully initiated passenger service to the Philippines. They well deserved the Collier Trophy that was presented to them for their accomplishments in commercial aviation during 1936.

*August 1937 – President Roosevelt joined with Thomas H. Beck, President of Crowell-Collier Publishing to present the Collier Trophy to Juan Trippe for Pan Am's accomplishments in 1936. The award had been established by the Collier Publishing Company and it was presented annually by the National Aeronautic Association for achievement in aviation in America.*

| Survey 1 San Fran. to New Zealand | March 17 - April 9, 1937 | S-42B Pan Am Clipper II | Musick/Briggs |
|---|---|---|---|

| Outbound Flight Schedule | | Inbound Flight Schedule | |
|---|---|---|---|
| San Francisco - Honolulu | March 17-18 | Auckland - Pago Pago | April 4-3* |
| Honolulu - Kingman Reef | March 23 | Pago Pago - Kingman Reef | April 8 |
| Kingman Reef - Pago Pago | March 24 | Kingman Reef - Honolulu | April 9 |
| Pago Pago - Auckland | March 28-29* | | |

*Dateline - Gain day outbound - Lose day inbound

Juan Trippe's desire to expand Pan Am's routes into Europe was stymied by the foreign governments refusal to allow landing rights to the American carrier. The closing of the European markets forced Pan Am to look aggressively to the Pacific for its further expansion. Although it was a tremendous achievement for Pan Am to reach Manila in November of 1935, the economic market there was weak and Pan Am's real goal was to fly on to Hong Kong and mainland China. Furthermore, once Pan Am made the commitment to expand into the Pacific, Trippe wanted to add Australia and New Zealand to his air routes to take advantage of those untapped markets. However, once again British interests with Imperial Airways put pressure on Australia and New Zealand not to grant landing rights to the American carrier. But New Zealand's isolation finally got the best of them and in negotiations carried on by Harold Gatty, Pan Am's representative in New Zealand, permission was finally granted for Pan Am to establish scheduled service to New Zealand, provided they could do so no later than the end of 1936.

In determining the air route to New Zealand, Pan Am discovered that all the potential islands that could be used for suitable landing areas for the Clipper were under British or French control, with the exception of American Samoa and some uninhabited islands and specks of land that were of so little value up until this point in time that no one really cared who owned them. Suddenly, they were very important to Pan Am and, with a little lobbying and political pressure, they were also important to the U.S. Government as well. To support Pan Am's efforts, our government authorized the colonization of the "disputed" islands by colonists - mainly Hawaiian high school graduates who were sent to the islands to fly the flag and strengthen the U.S. claim to ownership. Every three months the Coast Guard would deliver water, food and other supplies.

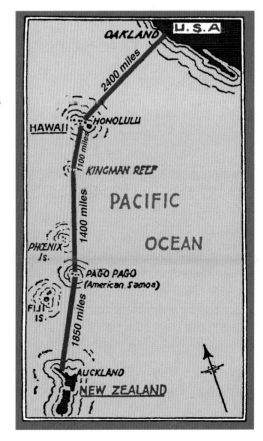

Harold Gatty was given the responsibility by Pan Am to visit the islands and determine which ones would be suitable for overnight stopovers on the route to New Zealand. In late 1935, Gatty joined Dr. Francis Coman on the two masted schooner Kinkajou and sailed to Howland, Jarvis, Baker and Christmas Islands and Kingman Reef. Gatty found that Howland, Jarvis and Baker did not have lagoons suitable for seaplanes, so they were rejected. Christmas Island was suitable but inhabited with workers at a successful coconut plantation so Great Britain would dispute sovereignty. So, in desperation, Kingman Reef was chosen as a mid-Pacific base for the planned flights to New Zealand.

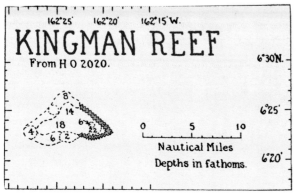

Kingman Reef did form a mid-ocean lagoon and it was 1100 miles south of Honolulu in the exact position for an overnight stay. But at Kingman Reef there was only a sliver of land - about 100 yards long and 60 yards wide - that was above high tide. When Gatty visited Kingman Reef on the Schooner Kinkajou in 1935, he built a small monument on the dry land. Then he sailed south 1400 miles to Pago Pago, American Samoa to survey the harbor as a landing site for the second stopover point to New Zealand. At Pago Pago he found 2000 foot high hills surrounding a small, beautiful harbor.

Gatty determined that if Kingman Reef was to be used as a stopover on the route to New Zealand, a supply boat would have to be stationed there. Furthermore, any pilot landing at Pago Pago harbor would have to come in low over the hills and drop in steeply to the harbor for a quick, short landing. It would be difficult and dangerous, but it could be done by a very well qualified pilot. Gatty knew that the proposed Kingman Reef - Pago Pago stopovers from Honolulu to New Zealand were much less than desirable, but Pan Am was desperate and world politics closed the other suitable islands. So he reported back to Trippe that a route to New Zealand with adequate stopovers was available if Pan Am was willing to risk using Kingman Reef and Pago Pago harbor.

Based on Gatty's report, Pan Am promised New Zealand that the company would start regular air service by the end of 1936. But the problems on the north Pacific route simply wouldn't go away. First, the engines had to be shipped back to the manufacturer and that took a couple of months to resolve. Then other maintenance problems developed. It became obvious that Pan Am did not have the time or the planes available to fly the New Zealand survey route by the end of 1936, so Gatty was forced to negotiate a one year extension of the agreement with New Zealand. In early 1937, New Zealand reluctantly gave Pan Am until December 31, 1937 to fulfill their promise of regular flights or they would lose the right to land in New Zealand. If Pan Am lost New Zealand, Trippe's dream of Pacific and world dominance would fail. Regardless of the difficulties faced, Pan Am was determined not to risk losing the New Zealand service. Therefore, Pan Am promised New Zealand that mail service would commence by the end of 1937, but first the survey flight to New Zealand by way of Kingman Reef and American Samoa would have to be a success.

The craft chosen to make this survey flight was a new model of the S-42 that had a four-foot longer wingspan and increased onboard fuel capacity. This S-42B, NC 16734 was initially called the Pan American Clipper II and later it became the Hong Kong Clipper and finally the Samoan Clipper.

For the difficult New Zealand flight, Pan Am wanted the most experienced crew possible. Only the famed pilot, Captain Edwin Musick, could be trusted with making this survey flight. The other experienced crew members included Harry Canaday and Victor Wright from the first four survey flights across the North Pacific in 1935.

Pictured is the crew about to depart on the first New Zealand survey flight from right to left: Captain Edwin Musick, first officer Frank Briggs, second officer (navigator) Harry Canaday, flight engineer Vic Wright, radio officer Ray Runnells, third officer Morgan Holsenbeck, purser/clerk Ivan Parker. Not pictured is junior flight engineer John Stickrod, who was added to the crew in Honolulu.

Once New Zealand agreed to the one year extension, Pan Am rushed ahead with the first survey flight. In order to have enough range for the 2400 mile leg of the flight from San Francisco to Honolulu, the Pan American Clipper II had to use its onboard fuel tanks. Therefore, the interior of the plane was reeking with gas fumes when it departed San Francisco under the command of Captain Musick on March 17, 1937. When they were just hours out of Honolulu an oil leak developed in the number two engine. It was immediately shut down. If the leak had developed earlier in the flight Captain Musick would have turned back to the Alameda base and dumped his excess fuel before landing to have the problem fixed. In this case, because they were within two hours of Honolulu, he had no choice but to push on with three engines and hope for the best. On landing, Captain Musick publicly doubted the viability of the rushed and dangerous survey flight to New Zealand. Uncharacteristically he showed his growing frustration when he told the reporter for the Honolulu Advertiser: *"The continuation of the flight to New Zealand, via Kingman Reef and American Samoa is undecided. We will await orders from Alameda. How long we will be in reaching Auckland depends entirely upon orders from Alameda and weather conditions."*

Pan Am, however, planned to open the all important scheduled service from Manila to Hong Kong on April 21, 1937. They needed this airplane, the Pan American Clipper, back in Honolulu by April 12, so that it could be serviced and flown to Manila for the Manila to Hong Kong shuttle flights. They also wanted Captain Musick to serve as chief pilot to fly the inaugural flight to Hong Kong. Therefore, if the survey trip to New Zealand were cancelled, or if it were even delayed for any extended period of time, due to the engine oil leaks or bad weather, there was no telling when it could be rescheduled. To cancel the New Zealand survey flight would be a public embarrassment and would once again jeopardize the New Zealand landing rights concession that had recently been extended. Furthermore, if the opening of the Hong Kong route were delayed or canceled, it would be more than an embarrassment. It would jeopardize the entire Pacific operation. Juan Trippe did not like to be embarrassed. Time was too short and equipment too scarce to permit any lengthy delay of the New Zealand survey flight. Therefore, Captain Musick was ordered by Pan Am to have emergency repairs made in Honolulu and to continue on to

KINGMAN REEF
LOG

*PAA*

MARCH 11-APRIL 14
1937

Danilo Vecutich
Dr. William O. French M.D.

*Newly discovered log*

237

New Zealand as quickly as possible. It is quite interesting and significant that this oil leak and the failed engine that occurred on the flight from Honolulu was never mentioned by Pan Am in any of the glowing reports made at the conclusion of the New Zealand survey flight. This oil leak that resulted in the failed engine, however, was a predictor of the tragic problems that lay ahead for Captain Musick with this Sikorsky S-42B Pan American Clipper II on the third flight to New Zealand in January of 1938.

After Captain Musick arrived in Honolulu, it took five days for the engine problem to be located and repaired and for the other regular maintenance to be completed. Because of this mechanical problem, Captain Musick announced that John Stickrod, age 22 from Honolulu, would be added as a junior flight engineer for the trip south.

On this survey flight, Ivan Parker, who normally served as a purser on Clipper flights, was designated by Pan Am as the crew's clerk. During the five day layover in Honolulu, one of his duties as clerk was to gather the personal mail addressed to the Pan Am staff serving on the North Wind at Kingman Reef so that the mail could be delivered to the North Wind on the Clipper's flight south. Parker also had time to visit Pan Am's general agent in Honolulu, the Inter-Island Steam Navigation Company, to see if they had any letters that they wanted carried to New Zealand.

Pan Am knew that this flight to New Zealand would be so difficult and so dangerous that they did not want to draw extra attention to it in case it failed or was canceled. Therefore, they did not alert the public or flight cover collectors as to the exact date of the Clipper's expected departure and they did not accept any souvenir mail from collectors who wanted covers carried on the first flight.

For over 60 years since the 1937 New Zealand survey flight there have been many unanswered questions as to why souvenir flight covers, which had been prepared for all the previous survey flights, were unknown for this epic first flight to New Zealand. A personal log kept by two of Pan Am's employees stationed on the North Wind at Kingman Reef for the March 1937 flight has now been discovered. This log not only answers all of those questions about flight covers and souvenir mail, but it also provides previously unknown details of the difficult and dangerous flight. Let's examine this very detailed log to see what it tells us about the flight and about why souvenir flight covers have been such elusive finds over these many years.

*Danilo (Dan) Vucetich-Supercargo*

Heading up Pan Am's six man crew stationed on the North Wind at Kingman Reef was Danilo (Dan) Vucetich. He held the title of supercargo and he had the responsibility for provisioning the vessel, loading the supplies and handling any problems that arose with the ship during the expedition. He made sure that the North Wind carried a spare Hornet engine, high test aviation gasoline, oil of various types, a launch, skiff and the all important radio direction finder. Dan Vucetich had served as the supercargo on the North Haven in 1935 when the bases at Wake and Midway were constructed. He had served again on the North Haven in 1936 when the hotels were built on those remote islands. It was his son, Alex (Sandy) Vucetich, who shared his father's log with me. Alex followed in his father's footsteps and retired as Captain from Pan Am with over 30 years experience. He still lives in his family's home in San Francisco.

Assisting Dan Vucetich with writing the log was Dr. William O. French, M.D. from the Alsop Clinic in Honolulu. Dr. French had practiced medicine in Oakland until 1932 when he moved to Honolulu. The log's entries reveal that Dan Vucetich greatly loved his wife and his only child, Alex, and that he was a poet who saw good in everyone. Dr. French, on the other hand, reveals by his log entries that he was a man with many personal and family problems, who was a pessimist and obviously fighting depression and melancholy. Their contrasting views of life at Kingman Reef make for interesting reading.

The third man in Pan Am's crew on board the North Wind was Stewart Saunders, the station manager for Pan Am at Wake Island. He had been picked up at Wake by the North Wind in February of 1937 and he acted as station manager at Kingman Reef.

Freeman Lang was the radio officer and chief photographer for the expedition. He was a well-known expert in radio transmission who lived in the Los Angeles, California area. He was temporarily living in Honolulu working for RCA when he was recruited by Pan Am to be responsible for the radio transmissions at Kingman Reef. He had a most important job, for if the Clipper crew was to find tiny Kingman Reef in the middle of the ocean, an experienced radio operator would have to lead them to their landing area.

*Dr. French-Expedition doctor*

*Stewart Saunders-Station manager at Wake Island and Kingman Reef*

*Freeman Lang-Radio officer and chief photographer*

239

*Harold Walsh - Radio technician*

*Joe Copeland - Mechanic and boatman*

Harold Walsh was a radio technician from Vermont who was interested in mathematics. He did calculus problems for fun and read Einstein's *Theory of Relativity* for bedtime reading.

Completing the Pan Am group at Kingman Reef was Joe Copeland from Texas. He was the head mechanic and boatman for the group. Dr. French described him as a plodding individual who was the salt of the earth.

The North Wind, a three hundred foot 2,000 ton Alaskan freighter, was under a four month charter from the Northland Transportation Company of Seattle, Washington to the Pan American Aviation Supply Corporation, a subsidiary of Pan Am set up to handle the supplying of bases in the Pacific. Captain Borklund, a Swede, was in command. He also commanded the North Haven when the Pan Am bases were built at Wake and Midway in 1935 and 1936. He had a crew of ten to assist him. The total charter fee for the vessel and the crew was $350 a day.

*Captain Borklund*

*S.S. North Wind at Honolulu - March 10, 1937*

*S.S. North Wind leaving Pier 25 in Honolulu for Kingman Reef - March 11, 1937*

Captain Borklund pulled the North Wind away from Pier 25 in Honolulu at 6:00 a.m. on March 11, 1937.

After a five and a half-day trip to cover 1100 miles they sighted Kingman Reef on the morning of March 16, 1937.

Over the next several days they built a beacon light on the little land that existed at Kingman Reef so that they could use the light at night as a fix to tell if they were dragging anchor. By their measurement the highest point above sea level on Kingman Reef was five feet and the portion of the reef above high tide was only 220 feet long by 197 feet wide. The entire land area was less than the size of a football field. They speculated that if Kingman Reef were ever to be used as a permanent base, a concrete pier would have to be built out into the lagoon to house the living quarters and the maintenance areas.

Dan Vucetich's log entry for March 19, 1937 appears to make fun of this small reef in the middle of the ocean that they were attempting to use for a seaplane base.

Kingman Reef - March 19, 1937

Visited the Island in the afternoon. Joe Copeland had built a tripod to which a coal oil lantern was attached, which at night is plainly visible from the ship. For our picture taking we used the newly erected beacon lamp tripod as background, the American Ensign and the PAA House Flag played an important role - There we were, good patriots indeed, sole temporary inhabitants of these tiny isles. Some of us were pioneers of every Trans-Pacific air base expedition. We walked around our tiny kingdom and surveyed the property carefully, whereupon a general discussion ensued about possibilities of claiming the entire area of real estate at high and low tides, all waterfronts including, up to the legal three mile limit. There, said Dr. French, is a wonderful site for my hospital and drug store. Near that yonder shoal, the Joe Copeland School could be built, Dan Vucetich insisted that a grand hotel could be built and named after his little boy to be known as the Hotel Alexander Vucetich. We drew a rough sketch of the town site. A prominent corner was given to Harold Walsh and Stew Saunders to use as a service station and garage - the main street in town is to be known as ALI BABA Avenue and that is where our financial institutions are to be erected - Saunders Trust Company - French Walsh Trust Company - Vucetich First National Bank - Copeland Factors, Inc. Ltd. With the plans for our town we returned to the ship.

-Danilo Vucetich

*Standard bearer Vucetich at Kingman Reef proudly displaying Old Glory to the world*

Kingman Reef from distance - at this point five feet above sea level,
land area not much bigger than a football field-tripod built by
Joe Copeland

*North Wind at sunset in the lagoon at Kingman Reef*

Joe Copeland

Joe Copeland built a tripod for
coal oil lantern on Kingman Reef.
Highest spot is about 5 feet above
water-size of a large city lot

Dr. French in front of tripod

From left: Dr. French, Joe Copeland, S.A. Saunders, Dan Vucetich and Harold
Walsh - Photo taken by Freeman Lang

All the humor about building a town in the middle of the Pacific pointed out the foolishness of
Pan Am in attempting to use this speck of land in the middle of the ocean 1100 miles south of Honolulu
as an overnight stop on the route to New Zealand.

Finally on March 22 Stew Saunders, the station manager at Kingman Reef, radioed Honolulu that all was in readiness, and he received back the word they had waited for - the oil leak had been repaired and the Clipper would depart, weather permitting, the morning of Tuesday, March 23, l937.

The log entries for Dr. French and for Dan Vucetich recapture the excitement and the danger of that historic day, as Captain Musick and his navigator, Harry Canaday, tried to find this football field sized island in the middle of the Pacific.

Kingman Reef, March 23, 1937:
    Should write a long note on the arrival of the Clipper NC #16734. We knew the night before that the Clipper was going to arrive the next day.  Got up at the usual time but got busy watching the radio boys keep in touch with the Clipper. At noon we realized the plane would arrive in a short time. At this time we were having many rain squalls. At 1:00 P.M., it was raining very hard, visibility was bad, however, she kept coming through. About 1:20 P.M. she came over flying low. Visibility was so bad that Captain Musick passed over quite low and circled out to sea and did not land until 1:47 - the boys all came aboard in an equinoxal storm very much drenched. The mail came on board. I received several letters and glanced through two or three of them reading one more carefully, then went out and gassed the plane. The evening was beautiful after the heavy rain. I sat part of the time in the cabin of the Clipper and then on the wing. The moon was nearly full and many stars were out.  It gave me much pleasure to sit up there and think of that which means much to me.
                                    - Bill French

*Clipper anchored at Kingman Reef*

246

Kingman Reef - March 23, 1937:

A red letter day at Kingman Reef aboard the good ship North Wind in the waters of the lagoon wherein we lay at anchor. The Clipper arrived, on its first survey flight to New Zealand, Captain Edwin Musick in command. The mail bag was open, it seemed like Christmas and I was Santa Claus. Almost everyone onboard had a letter or two. I received three, one from my wife, one from my son Sandy and one from a friend.

Accommodations on this Alaskan Freighter are poor. We did our very best to satisfy the flight crew, the boys who deserve the best, sturdy navigators of the air and plucky pioneers. I surrendered my humble little cabin to Captain Musick, Saunders and Dr. French surrendered theirs to the other boys. I had two leis in my cabin, one of which I received one evening in Honolulu while attending a luau in the Hawaiian Village and the other presented to me on the dock the morning of our departure for Kingman Reef. When Captain Musick stepped on board in the midst of a torrential downpour I placed these leis around his neck and welcomed him and the men aboard. I wore my hat and borrowed Captain Borklund's cravanette which was leaking badly through the seams. The lads were happy, the food was very good. All expressed their appreciation and because of that we also felt happy and turned in for the night.

- Danilo Vucetich

*Captain Edwin Musick boarding North Wind at Kingman Reef in the midst of torrential downpour being welcomed by Dan Vucetich-Observe leis worn by Captain Musick*

In spite of the good meal of steak and freshly caught fish and the good conversation with the Pan Am staff on the North Wind, Captain Musick did not want to stay a minute longer at Kingman Reef than was absolutely necessary. It was a miserable place to spend the night and a miserable place to use as a seaplane base. Therefore, the next morning, Wednesday, March 24, he had the flight crew up and out into the North Wind's launch by 6:00 a.m. to take them the 1000 feet in the lagoon to the anchored Clipper that was fully gassed and ready to go. The log entries for March 24 tell the tale.

Kingman Reef, March 24, 1937:

Came in from standing anchor watch at 5:30 A.M. Then went out in a heavy rainstorm to put the Clipper crew aboard. It was raining and blowing hard until we returned. Captain Musick took nearly an hour to warm up the engines of his plane, he finally got away about 7:00 A.M. Made a beautiful takeoff. I came back to the ship, Joe Copeland, Steve Walsh and I went out fishing.

— Bill French

Dr. French caught a tuna and a barracuda

During the plane's departure early this morning the downpour never did let up. The sky was overcast, the sheets of rain swept by the wind obscured all visibility. It must have been hard on Captain Musick and his men. — Suddenly like a gigantic eagle the Clipper took off and disappeared into the rainloaded clouds. In constant communication with our radio the Clipper reported more favorable weather after crossing the equator. It landed at Pago Pago late this afternoon. Another stretch successfully accomplished. The excitement was over, up since early this morning, I did not fish, I did not read, just went to bed early.

—Dan Vucetich.

Once airborne the weather cleared for the Clipper. Captain Musick, who had a reputation for being overly serious, did take time out for some lighthearted celebrating. The crew's approach to the Equator on the first survey flight to New Zealand was the first time that a Pan Am plane had crossed the Equator in the open Pacific. Therefore, to celebrate this memorable occasion Captain Musick initiated First Officer Frank Briggs into the Realm of Neptunis Rex. This is a tradition that had long been followed by sailors when a seaman crossed the Equator for the first time, and it was also adopted enthusiastically by Pan Am's Clipper crews.

KNOW YE, THAT ON THIS TWENTY-FOURTH DAY OF MARCH IN THE YEAR OF OUR LORD ONE THOUSAND NINE HUNDRED AND THIRTY-SEVEN AT 1013 IN THE MORNING FRANK M. BRIGGS DID ENTER THE REALM OF NEPTUNIS REX. IN THE GOOD SHIP "PAN AMERICAN CLIPPER" NC 16734

164° 57' WEST LONG.

Captain Edwin Musick
Imperial Plenipotentiary

*Certificate prepared by Captain Musick on March 24, 1937 for Frank Briggs on the first survey flight to New Zealand*

*Officer Frank Briggs*

Pictured as they approach the equator is Officer Briggs taking a noon latitude fix just before he was presented the hand-drawn certificate from the Imperial Plenipotentiary - Captain Edwin Musick welcoming him into the Realm of Neptunis Rex.

When the exhausted crew finally reached American Samoa, they had to make a very difficult approach over the 2,000 foot hills that surround the harbor at Pago Pago. After the bad weather they had experienced since leaving Honolulu and after the sleepless and worrisome night they spent on the rocking North Wind at Kingman Reef, this was a challenging landing, but they completed it successfully and finally were able to tie up on the tranquil waters of Pago Pago harbor. It had taken the Clipper ten hours to cover the 1400 miles between Kingman Reef and American Samoa. It would take the crew a lot longer to recover from the two days of rough flying they had just completed.

*Crew quarters at Pago Pago-Sadie Thompson Inn made famous in Somerset Maugham's story* **"Rain"**

*Postcard of Clipper at American Samoa*

As the crew rests in American Samoa, let us examine the very few pieces of mail that they had carried south with them on this historic flight.

From the log kept by Dr. French and Dan Vucetich we know that the Clipper crew carried the personal mail that they had picked up in Honolulu to the Pan Am staff on the North Wind at Kingman Reef. This was not mail that had been sent by collectors as souvenirs of a first flight. This was the personal mail from wives, children and friends addressed to the six Pan Am staff members onboard the North Wind who had been away from home for weeks and in some cases even months. Because the letters and envelopes were not intended to be collector's items, most of the envelopes were discarded soon after they were received. Therefore, it is not surprising that for many years after the flight, no covers from this survey flight had been found.

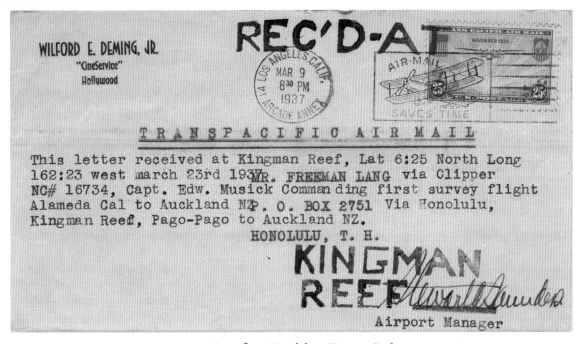

*Cover flown Honolulu to Kingman Reef*

The first envelope that did surface from this New Zealand survey flight was the one addressed to Freeman Lang from a friend in Los Angeles, Freeman Lang's home town. I had acquired this cover many years ago even before I collected Pan Am history merely because it had been sent to the little known United States possession of Kingman Reef. This is the cover that ultimately got me started collecting Pan Am flight covers. It was addressed to Freeman Lang's post office box in Honolulu and it was undoubtedly picked up by Ivan Parker as a part of his duties as clerk while the Clipper crew was in Honolulu.

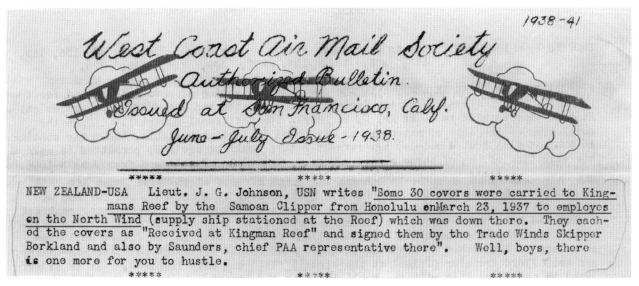

Inside the envelope when I acquired it was a note from Lt. Jesse Johnson, writing in a bulletin for cover collectors in June of 1938. Jesse Johnson was a Navy aviator who was also an avid cover collector. He stated that approximately 30 letters had been carried to Kingman Reef by the Pan Am Clipper to the

Pan Am employees on the North Wind. After reading the log kept by Dan Vucetich and Dr. French, it appears that Lt. Jesse Johnson was absolutely correct - all of the mail carried on the flight to Kingman Reef was personal mail and not mail that had come from cover collectors. With 16 people on board the North Wind, his count of 30 letters is probably also correct.

When I wrote my first book in 1997, the cover to Freeman Lang was the only cover known that was a souvenir from the first flight to Kingman Reef. However, since then one more envelope carried south from Honolulu to Kingman Reef on the Clipper has surfaced and it was addressed to one of the creators of the log, Dr. William O. French. The envelope is from his mother, who lived in Oakland, California, next to her son's former home in Oakland. This letter from his mother had not arrived in Honolulu until after Dr. French had left Honolulu on March 11 onboard the North Wind for Kingman Reef. Therefore, it was brought to the Pan Am office or picked up by purser Ivan Parker during the Clipper crews' five day layover in Honolulu. After Dr. French received the letter at Kingman Reef carried to him on the Clipper's flight, he typed an explanation on the envelope about its arrival on the first flight to Kingman Reef, and had it signed by the station manager, Stew Saunders, and by his fellow log writer, Dan Vucetich, who as supercargo was in charge of the Pan Am staff. So now after more than 60 years it appears that two letters have survived from the 30 that were carried to Kingman Reef on board the clipper. I now imagine that the other 28 envelopes were either discarded immediately or have been lost or destroyed over time because they were not intended as collector items, and they did not end up in the safekeeping of collectors. These only two surviving covers flown to Kingman Reef by Captain Musick are interesting and rare souvenirs of Pan Am's first flight to this remote mid-Pacific reef.

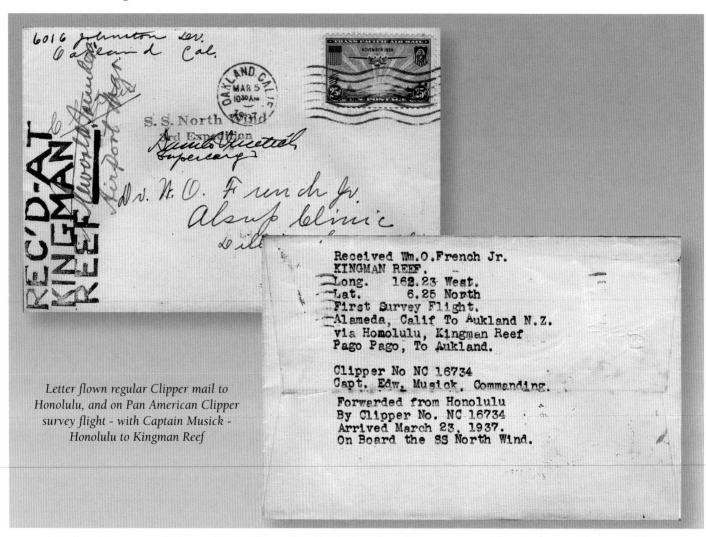

*Letter flown regular Clipper mail to Honolulu, and on Pan American Clipper survey flight - with Captain Musick - Honolulu to Kingman Reef*

But these two envelopes are not the only envelopes that have survived from the southbound flight to New Zealand. Ivan Parker, the purser/clerk, also prepared a very special souvenir flight cover for President Franklin Roosevelt. Roosevelt was not only an enthusiastic stamp and cover collector, but he was also vitally interested in these early Clipper flights from a national defense standpoint. For this souvenir envelope, Parker selected a colorful envelope of Pan Am's general agent in Honolulu, the

Inter-Island Steam Navigation Company. He then applied the rubber stamp showing the Martin M-130 in flight. This purple cachet of the Martin M-130 first appeared on mail for the inaugural air express flight in March of 1936 and the cachet reappeared for a second time on some souvenir covers for the first revenue passenger flight in November of 1936. Pan Am's general agent in Honolulu coordinated both the first air express flight and the first passenger flight. Therefore, for President Roosevelt's souvenir cover, Ivan Parker used the same rubber stamp showing the Martin M-130 and inserted the words "PROJECT FLIGHT HAWAII – NEW ZEALAND". He also applied the date that the Clipper departed Honolulu – March 23, 1937.  He carried the souvenir flight cover for President Roosevelt with him when the Clipper left Honolulu on the southbound survey flight. Then, when the Clipper arrived in American Samoa late on the afternoon of March 24, 1937, Parker signed the cover and had the post office cancel it to show its arrival date at Samoa. Ivan Parker created a very special Pan Am flight cover for a very special and important collector.

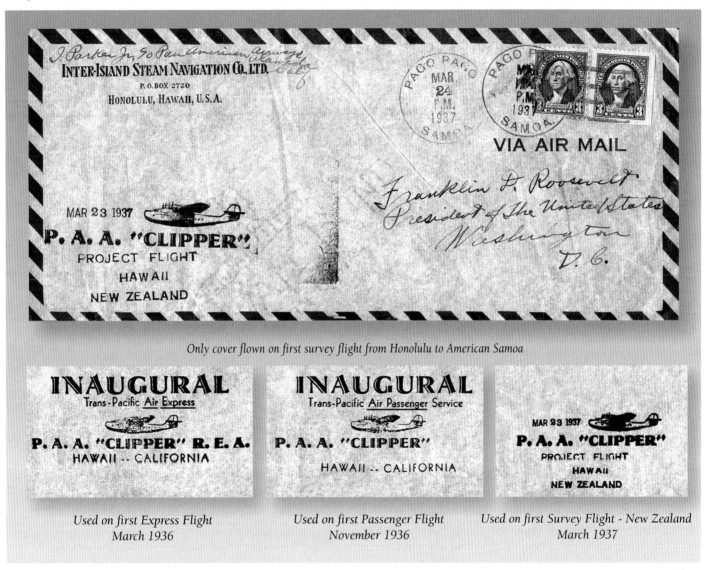

*Only cover flown on first survey flight from Honolulu to American Samoa*

*Used on first Express Flight*
*March 1936*

*Used on first Passenger Flight*
*November 1936*

*Used on first Survey Flight - New Zealand*
*March 1937*

A year after President Roosevelt's death in the Spring of 1945, this cover was sold along with most of President Roosevelt's collection by H.R. Harmer Auction House in New York City. It was apparently sold with a large group of President Roosevelt's flight covers, and it is believed that this historic cover sat undiscovered and unappreciated with a bundle of other covers wrapped up by a rubber band at the bottom of some collector's storage cabinet until it reappeared at an auction in the late 1990s.

Of the four flight covers known from the southbound New Zealand survey flight, this is the only one created solely as a souvenir flight cover for a collector. It is also the only cover carried from Honolulu to American Samoa on this flight. Because of its rarity and because it was created as a gift for the President of the United States, it is one of the most interesting souvenirs of Pan Am's pioneering flights across the Pacific.

After a good five day rest at American Samoa and after the weather cleared, on the morning of March 28 1937, the American Clipper lifted off from beautiful Pago Pago harbor for the final 1850 mile leg of the flight to Auckland, New Zealand. The anticipation in New Zealand had been growing day by day as the plane made its slow trip south from Honolulu. When the crew finally arrived in Auckland twelve days after leaving San Francisco, they received a tremendous welcome.

*Auckland welcomes Captain Musick and crew at Auckland Harbour - March 29, 1937*

*Captain Musick surrounded by crew - addresses crowd upon arrival at Auckland*

*Crowd at Auckland Harbour to welcome Captain Musick on arrival*

Pan Am's representative Harold Gatty is pictured accompanying Captain Musick and the crew as they step off the Clipper in Auckland. This picture was given to me by Harry Canaday, the navigator on this survey flight. He was kind enough to identify the members of the crew as they walk up the gangplank to the dock. From left to right: engineer Vic Wright; clerk/purser Ivan Parker; junior flight engineer John Stickrod; radio officer Ray Runnels; third officer Morgan Holsenbeck; navigator Harry Canaday; first officer Frank Briggs; Harold Gatty and Captain Musick. This was a crowning achievement for Harold Gatty. He had worked hard in finding the island stop-over bases at Kingman Reef and Pago Pago and in negotiating the agreement with New Zealand that permitted Pan Am to make this historic flight.

*Harold Gatty is pointing to Auckland on the New Zealand map - Captain Musick is seated right and navigator Harry Canaday is kneeling on far left*

New Zealand
postcards

Pan American Clipper
at Auckland

Pan American Clipper
at Auckland
March 29, 1937

257

FIRST SURVEY FLIGHT
FROM UNITED STATES OF AMERICA
TO NEW ZEALAND
BY
PAN-AMERICAN AIRWAYS

LUNCHEON

TENDERED TO
CAPT. EDWIN C. MUSICK
AND OFFICERS

BY CHAIRMAN AND MEMBERS
OF THE AUCKLAND HARBOUR
BOARD.

31st MARCH, 1937

In Auckland, luncheons and dinners were held in honor of Captain Musick and the crew. All of New Zealand celebrated what they hoped would be the end of their isolation and the start of regular scheduled flights. Pictured is the program for a luncheon honoring the crew put on by the Auckland Harbour Board.

*Program for luncheon*

While in New Zealand, Captain Musick and the crew were asked to prepare a short handwritten log of their flight that is now in a museum in Auckland. The Museum of Transportation in Auckland was kind enough to send a color copy of this log to me so that it could be included in this book.

Members of the crew of the Sikorsky Pan American Clipper Flying Boat which arrived in Auckland on 30th March 1937 on the first survey flight from U.S.A. to New Zealand.

| | Miles | Hours | Mins |
|---|---|---|---|
| First stop Honolulu. | 2400 | 18 | 48 |
| Second stop Kingman Reef. | 1100 | 8 | 5 |
| Third stop Pago Pago. | 1400 | 10 | 35 |
| Last stop Auckland. N.Z. | 1850 | 11 | 52 |
| | 6750 | 49 · 20 |

Captain Edwin C. Musick

Frank M. Briggs

Harry R. Canaday

T. R. Runnells

Ivan H. Parker Jr.

*Log prepared at luncheon*

WAR DEPARTMENT

Supply Officer,
30th Bomb Sq GHQ-AF
March Field, California.

OFFICIAL BUSINESS

Captain Edwin C. Musick

The only letter
Carried on First Survey
Flight to New Zealand

San Francisco - Honolulu
Kingman Reef - Pago Pago
Auckland

PENALTY FOR PRIVATE USE TO AVOID
PAYMENT OF POSTAGE; $300

Please forward.

Mr. Harold Gatty
C/o Colonel Clarence M. Young
Pan American Airways
Alameda, California.

Grand Hotel
Auckland

*The only letter carried on the southbound first survey flight from San Francisco to Auckland, New Zealand*

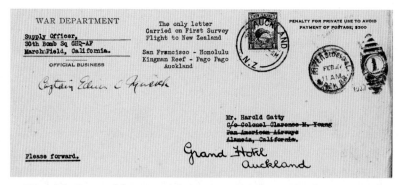

## A SINGLE LETTER

### CLIPPER'S AIR-MAIL

N. Z. Herald March 31, 1937

### ADDRESSED TO MR. GATTY

It was perhaps appropriate that the only letter carried on the Pan-American Clipper on her flight from San Francisco to Auckland was one addressed to Mr. Harold Gatty, the company's representative in New Zealand, and the man who, more than any other, has striven to bring into being a commercial airway spanning the greatest ocean of the world.

Owing to the fact that the flight was made solely for survey purposes, no ordinary mails were placed on board the Clipper at San Francisco. However, a friend of Mr. Gatty, from the American Army squadron with which the Australian-born airman was associated during his service with the United States Government, addressed a letter to him at Alameda, California. This was brought to Auckland by Captain Musick and handed to Mr. Gatty yesterday afternoon.

Mr. Gatty is making suitable arrangements to have the letter stamped with yesterday's date and later signed by Captain Musick, as the only "first cover" in the first flight by a commercial aircraft across the Pacific. The letter will be added to Mr. Gatty's already extensive collection of first-flight covers, which includes envelopes which were carried round the world when he made his memorable flight with the late Wiley Post.

The last few days have been an exceptionally exacting time for Mr. Gatty. Although he has had a staff of experts with him, he has been personally responsible for directing all the arrangements in connection with the Clipper's arrival. His expression when the giant flying-boat landed on the Waitemata Harbour yesterday afternoon was sufficient to show the pride which he can justifiably feel in the culmination of months of hard work.

*New Zealand Herald - March 31, 1937*

Harold Gatty, like President Roosevelt, was also an avid flight cover collector. Therefore, it was particularly surprising that a flight cover for this survey flight organized and planned by Gatty did not exist. However, a single flight cover addressed to Harold Gatty has now been found.

Let us examine this unique cover in detail. It is a personal letter from a friend of Harold Gatty's whom he knew from their association together in the U.S. Army Air Corps. It was postmarked February 27, 1937 at Riverside California in plenty of time to reach Pan Am's Alameda base for an uncertain departure date of the New Zealand survey flight. The flight actually departed Alameda on March 17, 1937. By sending the envelope c/o Clarence Young, the Division Manager for Pan Am's Pacific Operations, the sender knew it would reach Captain Musick before his departure from Alameda, regardless of the actual date chosen for the departure. Gatty was so busy planning the flight that he probably did not have time to prepare or request souvenir covers for himself. Therefore, this personal letter to him that was sent to Pan Am's California base was carried as a favor by Captain Musick to Harold Gatty on the survey flight south. When I showed a copy of the cover to my friend Harry Canaday, who was a crew member on the flight, he recalled that Captain Musick carried a letter for Harold Gatty.

When Musick delivered the letter to Gatty in Auckland, he signed it as Captain of the Clipper's survey flight. Then Gatty, in his own hand, crossed out the Pan Am address in California and wrote in his own Auckland address at the Grand Hotel.

As a first flight collector, Gatty knew when Captain Musick signed the cover and presented it to him, that the cover should immediately be canceled in New Zealand to prove that it was actually flown on the survey flight. According to the newspaper article, Gatty wanted it back canceled with the date of the Clipper's arrival at Auckland, March 29, 1937. The post office, however, would only apply the actual date and time that Gatty took it to the post office, that being March 31, 1937 at 11:00 a.m. With Captain Musick's autograph, and with the New Zealand postmark safely applied, cover collector Gatty had his unique souvenir first flight cover from the flight he worked so hard to make possible. Harold Gatty not only had a treasured souvenir of the flight, but also a memento of his own achievement in negotiating the landing agreement and in finding the island bases for the Clipper's flight.

Without question, this is my favorite cover from the Pan Am Pacific flights. It tells a wonderful story of apparent success over adversity. However, because of the tragedy that befell Captain Musick and the Samoan Clipper just two flights later over this route, it also reminds us of the incredible risks that were taken by these true pioneers of Pacific air travel.

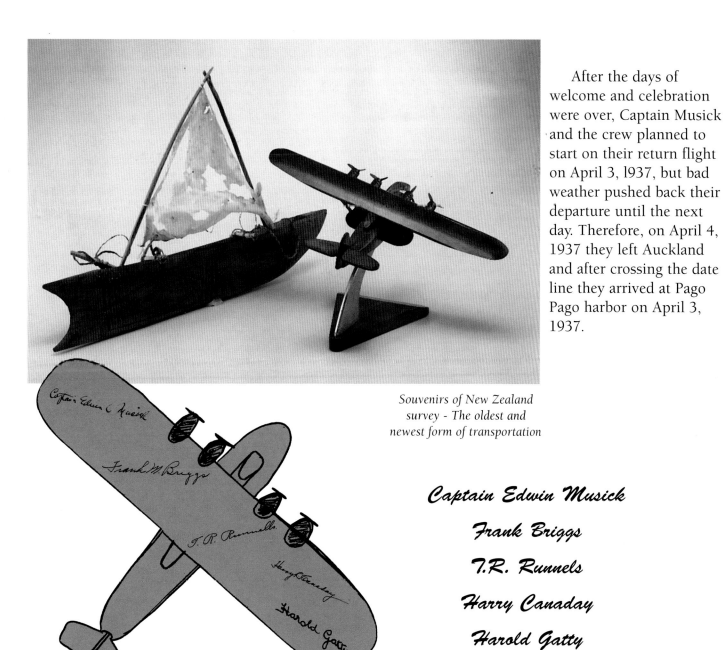

After the days of welcome and celebration were over, Captain Musick and the crew planned to start on their return flight on April 3, l937, but bad weather pushed back their departure until the next day. Therefore, on April 4, 1937 they left Auckland and after crossing the date line they arrived at Pago Pago harbor on April 3, 1937.

*Souvenirs of New Zealand survey - The oldest and newest form of transportation*

*Captain Edwin Musick*

*Frank Briggs*

*T.R. Runnels*

*Harry Canaday*

*Harold Gatty*

First Officer Briggs purchased the sailing canoe in Samoa on the flight south, and he brought the model of the flying boat with him to New Zealand. Harold Gatty and the crew signed the wing of the plane for his personal souvenir of the survey flight.

For two weeks the crew of the North Wind had been waiting very impatiently at Kingman Reef for the return of the Clipper from New Zealand. Dr. French planned to send a few souvenir flight covers on the return flight from Kingman Reef to Honolulu, to commemorate the historic flight and to have mementoes of the time he had spent on Kingman Reef. He knew that Pan Am discouraged souvenir mail on these survey flights before the airmail contracts were in effect. But, he also knew that, in the past, Pan Am had permitted a few souvenir covers to be carried by the flight crew on these survey flights. However, on this flight, mail carried on the return flight was also subject to the postal regulations of New Zealand and New Zealand prohibited any personal or souvenir mail on survey flights. Colonel Young, Pan Am's Pacific manager, was adamant that there would not be any personal mail of any type on the return survey flight to the United States. Colonel Young was fearful that any violation of the postal regulations of New Zealand might jeopardize the future airmail contracts for Pan Am. Therefore, Colonel Young notified the men on the North Wind that he was strictly enforcing the rule that forbid personal mail on this survey flight from New Zealand. Again, the log kept by Dr. French and Dan Vucetich tells the tale of their frustration with Colonel Young's decision to forbid all personal mail on the return flight from New Zealand.

Dr. French and the other members of the Pan Am crew on Kingman Reef were very disappointed that the Clipper would not carry their souvenir mail back to Honolulu. They had been gone from home for more than three weeks. The boredom of being anchored in the middle of the Pacific was beginning to mount. They express their growing impatience, frustration and boredom in the log.

Kingman Reef,  March 26, 1937:
   This afternoon dozed and read and intended to write some letters, but will let it go for manana. However, I am in no hurry as we learned tonight that we could not send any letter back by Clipper and that is a disappointment. I am going to get all of the letters written that I want to and mail them when I get back, as that will not be violating any of the company's rules and regulations. However, what is can't be helped. It seems to me that our government is seeming too paternalistic.If there is not a change I am afraid that what has happened to other great nations through all history will also happen to us.
                    -Bill French
Kingman Reef, March 31, 1937
   Should write some letters, but manana. Tomorrow and tomorrow. Will write a few in case the Clipper decides to take our mail out. Don't suppose there is a chance.
                    -Bill French
Kingman Reef, April 2, 1937:
   Today has been windy, stormy and everyone has had to stay in. The plane did not take off from Auckland today because of bad weather. We will probably be here four or five days longer. The men are all anxious to get back.
                    -Bill French

*Fishing, with hand lines, Kingman Reef*

Kingman Reef, April 3, 1937:

The Clipper left Auckland this morning and arrived in Pago Pago shortly after six p.m. - tomorrow it is supposed to arrive here, weather permitting, and we will all be busy getting her ready for the trip into Honolulu. From there I understand she will fly to Manila and take up the shuttle run from Manila to Macao.

*A good catch*

Today started out windy and squally.  Went out on the launch a couple of times.  Poor luck fishing. Just one bonita.
    -Bill French

Kingman Reef, April 4, 1937:

Today has been a stormy day all day, nothing but squalls and at times high winds.  Fortunately the Clipper stayed over at Pago because of the difficulty of fueling at night. Don't know whether she will come through tomorrow. If she does, I hope that it is better weather. Stew Saunders is sending and receiving messages, yet he has not said positively whether she is coming thru.

*Launch for North Wind at Kingman Reef*

Kingman Reef, April 5, 1937:

The usual squally, windy day at Kingman Reef, which we have been having for the past week. Reading as usual.

Captain Musick will probably take off tomorrow. We will have guests aboard again for a few hours. They will then fly to Honolulu and we shall start ourselves arriving there several days later.

-Bill French

Kingman Reef, April 6, 1937:

Still here, perhaps the Clipper will come through tomorrow. Today has been the best day as far as weather is concerned for about ten days. We caught about 75 pounds of fish, including barracuda and ulua. Joe Copeland, Freeman Lang and I were out this morning. Joe and I went out this afternoon. Stew is staying close to the ship because of weather conditions and to report every three hours.

-Bill French

*A good catch!*

*Big barracuda*

Kingman Reef, April 6, 1937:

Patiently we are awaiting the plane's arrival from Pago Pago and not until it arrives and departs for Honolulu will we be able to weigh anchor and proceed towards the same direction. The coffee supply is getting short, personally I'd rather pass up the hotcakes, the pies and the cakes, but a cup of coffee, most everyone aboard will agree, is invigorating, it is almost a necessity.So let us hope the cook knows how to make it last.

-Danilo Vucetich

Kingman Reef, April 7, 1937:

Rained all day. Played pinochle. Read and went to bed early. Nothing much to write about for that reason. When I retired we were waiting to hear if the plane was going to leave.

Kingman Reef, April 8, 1937:

Yesterday's log was rather short and did not have anything to say. Today started with much rain and wind. The lagoon was quite choppy. However, we received word that the NC 34 had taken off so we were all busy getting ready to receive her. Captain Musick has decided that he would refuel from the ship rather than from the launch as heretofore. Joe Copeland was busy with this and with checking the anchor buoy. Stew Saunders, Harold Walsh and Freeman Lang were kept busy on the radio. Dan fixed up his correspondence and was generally busy getting ready company mail for the plane. (No personal mail) The plane arrived at 5:40 P.M. Stew and Lang were in the launch taking pictures and ready to receive the plane. Walsh was in the radio shack. I was on the bridge. Musick brought her in and made a beautiful landing, then taxied around into position to tie up at the stern of the North Wind. As soon as she was tied up they started to gas by passing a 150-foot long hose from the ship to the plane. After dinner I relieved Stew and handled the nozzle on the plane until we finished fueling about 8:30 P.M. Joe and I stood the anchor watch and as a result I only got 3 hours sleep. All in all, I had a busy day and enjoyed it. Didn't mind the watch as the weather had cleared and it was beautiful sitting there. I took my last look at the Southern Cross and wondered when I would see it again.

                              -Bill French

Dr. French had prepared souvenir flight covers for himself and his friends on the North Wind for Captain Musick to take with him on the flight back to Honolulu from Kingman Reef. He also prepared a hand carved rubber stamp with the words "Kingman Reef" so that it could be applied to the flight covers. He probably even had another rubber stamp that said "First Flight" so that the cover would read "First Flight From Kingman Reef". But when Colonel Young absolutely forbid any mail to be taken by Captain Musick, other than official company mail, Dr. French had to change and alter the already prepared souvenir covers and remove any indication that the prized envelope had ever been flown by Captain Musick on the Clipper. Although disappointed, he would reluctantly follow company regulations.

On the three covers illustrated, any reference to "flight" or "the Clipper" has been crossed off or omitted. Captain Musick either would not or did not sign the covers to be carried back on the North Wind. One of the three, the one from Dan Vucetich to his son, was dated the day the Clipper departed Kingman Reef on April 9 and it was postmarked on the day that the North Wind arrived back in Honolulu April 14, 1937 and it is the only one of the three that was flown on any portion of its trip. It did travel by regular Clipper mail from Honolulu to young Sandy Vucetich back home in San Francisco.

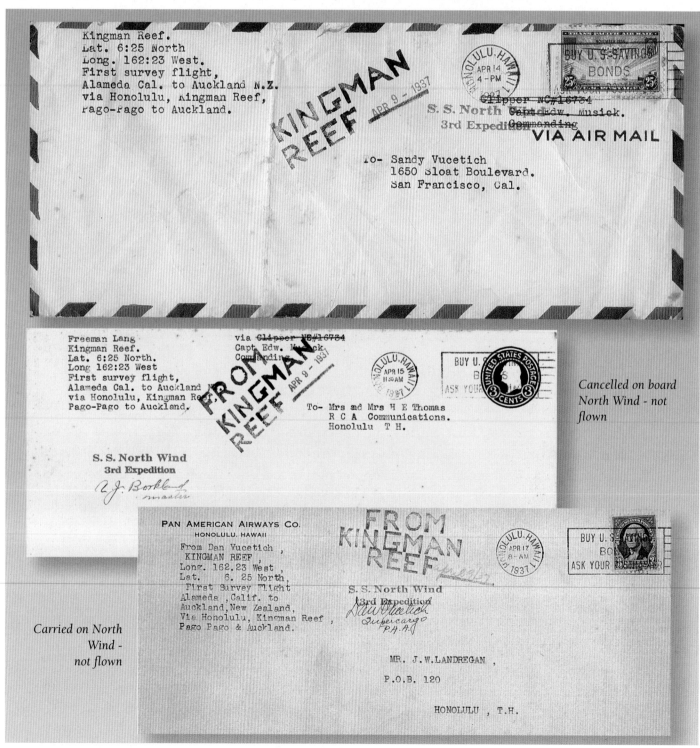

266

Again, after spending a sleepless night on board the North Wind, Captain Musick could not wait to get away from the exposed anchorage at Kingman Reef. He again had his flight crew up before dawn for the 1100 mile, eight hour flight. Dr. French's log documented the takeoff.

Kingman Reef, April 9, 1937:

Today has been a busy day, especially this morning. The flight crew had breakfast and the launch was taken back to the plane. Joe and I took the launch, picked up the crew and put them onboard the plane. Yesterday Walsh received word that he was to return to Honolulu by plane. He was naturally excited and was all ready to go when she took off. Walsh is a good scout and a good radio technician.

At 5:30 they began to warm up the engines and then taxied down the lagoon a short distance and took off. A beautiful bird took to the air. In a moment or so they were out of sight flying almost directly north. As soon as the plane was away, Joe, Stew and I went onboard the North Wind. We then got in the launch and took a bottle out to the islands. Joe and Lang took it over and took some pictures of placing it on the island.

At 10:20 Stew came up to the bridge and told Dan we could leave. The anchor was brought up and we steamed out of the lagoon at half speed. By 11:30 we were out of the lagoon and headed north full steam ahead. We were only making 7 knots due to rough seas, headwind and light load in the vessel.

The NC 34 left Kingman at 5:38 a.m. and was in Honolulu at 2:30 p.m. that afternoon. We left at 10:20 a.m. the same day (which is Friday) and won't arrive there until some time Wednesday. Thus has science and man's inventive genius shortened time. All this time the plane was in the air she was in contact with the entire world through radio.

With all the luxury, speed, breaking down of distance and communications is the world any happier than it was 50 years ago? Will all this lengthen life and add to our enjoyment of life? I wonder. Will miss Dan,

*Joe Copeland leaves bottle with note on Kingman Reef*

Five days after the Clipper departed Kingman Reef, the North Wind traveling at 7 to 8 knots wallowed into Pearl Harbor. The tired, and probably seasick, Pan Am crew had been gone over a month.

For more than sixty years, cover collectors have believed that first flight covers simply did not exist for the return survey flight of Captain Musick from New Zealand to the United States in April of 1937.

Recently, however, Tim Young, the son of Pan Am's Pacific Division Manager Clarence M. Young, found buried in his father's papers the long sought after flight covers. These unique covers were addressed to New Zealand collectors, Robert C. Cording and C.V. Smith. If I were going to solve the mystery of why the survey flight covers had not surfaced before now and why they were so rare, I would have to learn as much as I could about Mr. Cording and Mr. Smith.

I contacted the Auckland City Library and asked for help. Fortunately a top-notch researcher, Keith Giles, came to my aid. Giles quickly determined that in the late 1930s C.V. Smith from Dunedin, a town a thousand miles south of Auckland, was one of the most influential men in New Zealand. He

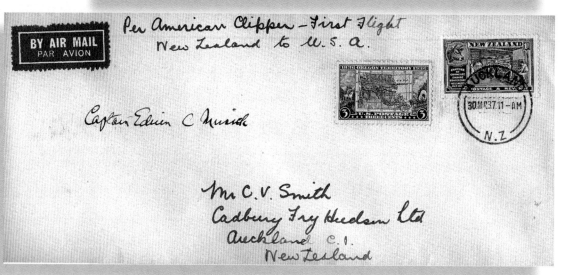

*Shown above are two first flight covers signed by Captain Musick and carried to the United States by him on the return survey flight in April of 1937*

was chairman of Cadbury Fry Hudson Ltd., the largest biscuit and candy maker in New Zealand. Finding out the identity of Mr. Robert C. Cording was a more challenging task. The Auckland city directory for 1937 listed Cecil Cording, as a salesman living at 5 Tirohanga Avenue in Auckland, at the same address as the cover addressed to Robert C. Cording. Robert C. Cording, however, was not listed. Therefore, it was assumed that Robert was the young son of Cecil Cording.

A book written by C.V. Smith on the history of Cadbury Fry Hudson Ltd. revealed that Cecil Cording was his sales manager for Cadbury Fry Hudson in the Auckland area. Therefore, it was established that there was a connection between the Cording and Smith flight covers.

Giles also learned that young Robert Cording had gone on to become a dentist. By checking the records of the dental school in Dunedin, Giles further discovered that Dr. Robert C. Cording had moved to the United States in the 1950s and that he had established a dental practice in Michigan. I was even provided with the Michigan telephone number for Dr. Cording's dental office.

Shortly before Christmas in 1999, I called Dr. Cording's office and was told that he had retired. Lena, his very protective former secretary, told me that if I would send a letter stating the purpose for my inquiry, she would pass it along to Dr. Cording. I was tantalizingly close to solving the mystery and I hoped my good luck would continue.

I quickly mailed off not only a letter explaining the purpose of my research, but also a copy of my first book and a draft of this chapter. I hoped that Dr. Cording could recall the details of the first flight covers that were sent 63 years earlier on the return survey flight of the Pan Am Clipper.

Then, I waited. As the days passed, I began to fear that Dr. Cording might be reluctant to answer my inquiry. Perhaps he didn't want to get involved with a stranger. Perhaps he was not feeling well. Perhaps he just couldn't remember what had happened so many years ago. As the days passed with no answer I became more and more concerned. Finally, in desperation I made another call to his former dental office in Michigan to see if Dr. Cording had received my materials and if he was going to contact me. Lena, was non-committal. "I forwarded the materials to him and if he wants to contact you, I am sure he will." I

*Cecil and Evelyn S. Cording – 1940s*

began to think that the mystery would not be solved - that I would come close, but fail. Then, after almost a two-week wait, I received the call! "Mr. Krupnick, this is Dr. Cording. I understand you have been looking for me." My fears were unnecessary. He was as anxious to tell me the rest of the story as I was to hear it from him.

So, now, after more than 60 years, I can share with you all the details of the newly discovered first survey flight covers from New Zealand to the United States.

As a young boy Robert Cording was always interested in aviation. In 1925, when he was only seven years old, he remembers hearing about the first attempt to fly from Australia to New Zealand that ended in tragedy with the plane never being found. Three years later he followed the progress of Kingsford-Smith in the Southern Cross, when it made the first successful flight from Australia to New Zealand.

When Robert's father, Cecil Cording, joined Cadbury Fry Hudson Ltd., the managing director, C.V. Smith, would stay with the family whenever he was visiting in the Auckland area. Mr. Smith was vitally interested in the development of airmail, because his mother lived in Scotland and it would shorten the time required to exchange letters with her. Smith was also a stamp collector, so he shared young Robert's interests in aviation and in first flight covers.

In 1937 Robert Cording recalls the tremendous excitement that he felt when word came that the first Pan Am Clipper would arrive by the end of March. He very much wanted to see the mighty airplane that he had read so much about and, if possible, to meet the crew. Perhaps he would even get a chance to have an envelope carried on the return flight and thereby add another first flight cover to his growing collection of flight covers.

Finally, on March 29, 1937 word came that the Clipper had departed Pago Pago, American Samoa, and that it would arrive in Auckland Harbor that afternoon. Robert Cording and his father Cecil were part of the huge crowd watching as the Clipper touched down.

Cecil Cording, as Auckland's representative for Cadbury Fry Hudson, Ltd. worked with Pan Am's agent, Harold Gatty, in regards to provisioning the Clipper for the return flight. Cording also knew Gatty through a shared interest in cricket, golf and the Masons. On the evening of the Clipper's arrival, Cording took the opportunity to ask Gatty if Captain Musick would mind carrying a first flight cover prepared by his son, Robert, back to the United States. When Gatty readily agreed, Cecil Cording also asked if he would carry a cover as a surprise gift for his boss, C.V. Smith. When Gatty agreed to this request as well, Cecil Cording gave Gatty the first flight covers that were prepared by himself and his son for delivery to Captain Musick for the return flight to the United States.

*Robert C. Cording and soon-to-be wife, Anne – May 1938*

In addressing the envelope for Mr. Smith, Cecil Cording put on the Auckland rather than the Dunedin address for Cadbury Fry, so that the flight cover, when mailed back from the United States, would come to him in Auckland, rather than go directly to Mr. Smith in Dunedin. At a later date, Cording planned to give the rare survey flight cover to his boss as a souvenir of the historic flight.

Traditionally, first flight covers are cancelled both in the city where the flight originates and in the city where the flight terminates to prove that the envelope flew on the first flight. Because Harold Gatty was a cover collector himself, he agreed to take the Cording and Smith covers to the main post office in Auckland on Queen Street, just three-blocks from the harbor. After Gatty had them properly cancelled with the Auckland postmark, Gatty gave them to Captain Musick for his signature and for the flight back to the United States.

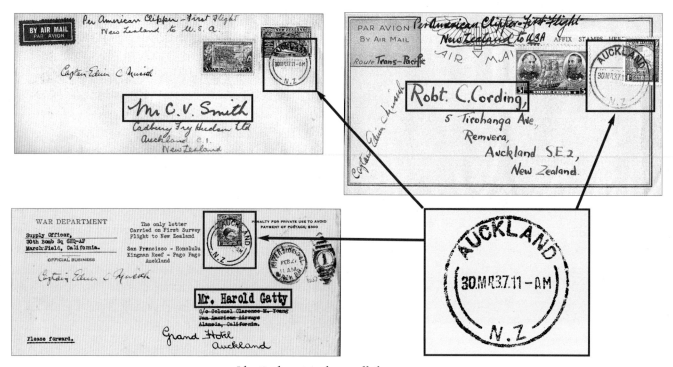

*Identical postmarks on all three covers*

If you examine the postmarks on these newly dicovered first flight covers addressed to Cording and Smith and if you compare the postmark on the single letter carried on the survey flight south to New Zealand that Captain Musick personally delivered to Harold Gatty, you will see that all three postmarks are identical – same post office (the main Auckland post office) – same time of the day – (11:00 a.m.) - same date – (March 30, 1937).

Therefore, when Harold Gatty took the Cording and Smith first flight covers to the Queen's Street post office to receive the Auckland postmark, he also had the same postmark applied to the single letter Captain Musick carried with him for Gatty on the flight south.

As in the past, unless authorized by the United States Post Office Department, Pan Am discouraged the carrying of souvenir mail on all survey flights. Mail had not been authorized by the United States Post Office on this flight. However, on this flight from New Zealand to the United States, the rules and regulations of the New Zealand postal authority were primary and the New Zealand government strictly prohibited any personal mail on this first survey flight to the United States.

However, both Harold Gatty and Edwin Musick knew that on the survey flights to Wake and Midway in 1935, Pan Am officials had conveniently looked the other way and allowed the crew to prepare a few souvenir covers for their friends and families for these pioneering flights. Gatty and Musick also thought that they were held in such high esteem by Pan Am that the company officials would not criticize them if they wanted to bend the rules and carry a few flight covers as souvenirs of this historic flight. Therefore, in spite of Pan Am's policy and in spite of the postal regulations of both New Zealand and the United States, Captain Musick told Harold Gatty that he would be happy to carry the flight covers back to San Francisco and, once properly cancelled, return them to Auckland for his son Robert Cording and his boss, C.V. Smith.

270

As promised, Captain Musick carried the first flight covers with him on the return flight of the Pan Am Clipper to Honolulu where he arrived on April 9, 1937. Several days later, on April 13, 1937, when Musick flew as a passenger from Honolulu to San Francisco, the first flight covers for Robert Cording and C.V. Smith were still safely tucked away in his flight bag. Captain Musick, however, never had them cancelled in San Francisco and he never mailed them back to the collectors in New Zealand as he promised. What could have prevented the highly reliable Captain Musick from keeping a promise that he had made to his good friend Gatty? What could have caused him to seriously disappoint Robert C. Cording, a young man who so loved aviation and wanted to add one more flight cover to his collection?

The answers to these troublesome questions are found in a handwritten note that was wrapped around the newly discovered survey flight covers for the first flight back to New Zealand that were given to me by Tim Young.

The note was written on a half sheet of Pan Am stationery by the father of Tim Young, the Pacific Division Manager, Colonel Clarence Young.

*Back of Colonel Young's handwritten note - "These are Valuable"*

*Front of Colonel Young's handwritten note*

> "*These covers were brought from Auckland to U.S. by Ed Musick on the initial <u>survey</u> flight from Australia (*) in 1937. They were to be mailed in U.S. thus authenticating the "first cover" character. However, they were intercepted in San Francisco and not deposited in the P.O. for cancellation stamp, and returned to addressees. Never-the-less they are the <u>first</u> covers to be flown to the U.S.*"
>
> Clarence M. Young.

*(*) Although Colonel Young mistakenly wrote "Australia", he clearly meant New Zealand.*

When Colonel Young wrote that "the covers were intercepted in San Francisco" he was undoubtedly talking about the action that he personally took when he learned that Captain Musick had violated both the regulations of the New Zealand postal authorities and the policies of Pan Am in carrying the souvenir mail on the survey flight from New Zealand to the United States. Young undoubtedly felt that if Musick's actions in carrying the flight covers were discovered, it would so anger the New Zealand authorities that the airmail contract with New Zealand could be placed in jeopardy.

Captain Musick was the chief pilot for Pan Am in the Pacific. He was world famous and he answered only to the head of the Pacific Division, Colonel Clarence M. Young. Therefore, no one other than Young had the opportunity and the authority to "intercept" the covers from Captain Musick.

On this flight Musick had been gone from home for over a month. Furthermore, the crew of the Clipper had experienced engine trouble, horrible weather and terribly dangerous landing areas on this survey flight. Musick had literally risked his life and the lives of the crew for the company and he was probably still exhausted from the grueling flight. He certainly would have been frustrated by Young's decision to take the first flight covers away from him that he had personally promised to have cancelled in the United States and returned to New Zealand.

Colonel Young, however, was strict on the enforcement of company rules. He was also known to have a quick temper. He probably told Musick that he had forbidden the Pan Am employees stationed on the North Wind at Kingman Reef from sending any souvenir covers or personal mail back to Honolulu with Musick on the return flight of the Clipper and he had to enforce the rules uniformly for all employees. Angry words were probably exchanged between the two strong willed men over this matter. However, as head of the Pacific Division, Young was very concerned about doing anything that might later be criticized by either the United States or the New Zealand postal authorities. It was clearly Young's responsibility to make certain that nothing happened that could possibly jeopardize the airmail contracts to carry mail to and from New Zealand. Therefore, Colonel Young felt duty bound to enforce the rules and confiscate or "intercept" the flight covers. Musick, as a loyal employee, was forced to reluctantly relinquish the first flight covers to Colonel Young. As Young explained in his handwritten note, the survey flight covers had been "intercepted in San Francisco" and they would not be sent back to the New Zealand collectors. Perhaps Colonel Young should have also destroyed the first flight covers that he had just taken away from Captain Musick. Instead, he bent the rules and added these rare and valuable covers to the collection of flight covers that he was saving for his own young son, Tim.

Even though the survey flight covers never received the San Francisco postmark that had been requested by Harold Gatty, Colonel Young correctly and accurately points out in his note found with the covers – "nevertheless, they are the first covers (from New Zealand) to be flown to the United States".

This flight, which should have been a triumph, must have been the low point in Captain Musick's long career with Pan Am. He was their first pilot and he had quickly established himself as a meticulous and exceptionally skilled aviator. Chosen as the chief pilot in the Pacific Division, he became a national hero. His modest, understated style made him a role model who led by example. On the survey flight to New Zealand, he had overcome danger and one frustration after another. The final indignation would have been the confiscation and "interception" by Colonel Young of the flight covers that Musick had promised to return to Robert Cording and his father.

Robert Cording told me that he had always wondered why Captain Musick had not returned to him the survey flight covers that he promised to carry back to the United States. Now, after 63 years, he finally understands what happened to prevent their return. Then Dr. Cording shared with me in a letter one of the most exciting and poignant moments that occurred in his young life. I'll let him explain in his own words:

# ROBERT C. CORDING. D.D.S.

February 21, 2000

Dear Mr. Krupnick:

It has been a pleasure to speak to you about the early flights of the Pan Am Clippers from the U.S.A. to New Zealand and their return and the philatelic covers that were carried.

I note that you have two covers, one addressed to Mr. C.V. Smith and one to me. I addressed my envelope and the one to Mr. C.V. Smith was addressed by my father. Mr. Smith was managing director of Cadbury, Fry, Hudson Ltd., a large chocolate candy and cookie company. My father was the Auckland district sales manager for the same company and Mr. Smith stayed at our home when he was in Auckland. My father knew that Mr. Smith collected stamps. On each of the envelopes my father added the notation "Per American Clipper First Flight – New Zealand to U.S.A.". The envelopes were handed by my father to Harold Gatty who said Captain Musick would carry them to the U.S.A. and mail them back to me in New Zealand.

At that time I was a university student and saw the Clipper land on Auckland harbor on the first flight in March of 1937. When the Clipper arrived back in Auckland the following December on its second flight to our country, I was working for the summer vacation at R. and E. Tingey, a paint and wallpaper chain founded by my grandfather and his twin brother. One morning I was called to the telephone with the comment "I think it is an American!" When I answered I heard, "This is Captain Ed Musick speaking. I wanted to contact you before we left again". After congratulating him on another great flight, I suggested he might like to visit my family for dinner and have a quiet evening away from all the turmoil. He replied, "I'd like to do that, but at this time I'm really busy making final arrangements for this return flight. We'll be back in about two weeks and I'd be pleased to accept your offer. I'd like you to come onboard the Clipper to see what it's like to work here!". That was an offer that was quite unexpected and I was thrilled to accept. The Samoan Clipper crashed on the next flight to New Zealand, so I never got to meet Captain Musick.

Later, I wondered why Captain Musick would seek out some one who had no previous contact with him. This question has remained unanswered for me for sixty-three years. Only after I read your article on the first survey flight to New Zealand, telling what had happened to the envelopes that had been given to him to carry on the return flight to the United States in April of 1937, did I realize that Captain Musick wanted to explain to me in person the situation about why the covers had not been returned as promised.

Thank you for your effort to contact me, and the privilege of reading your well researched book. And GOOD Luck with your new book.

*Robert C. Cording*

Robert C. Cording

After Captain Musick completed the first survey flight to New Zealand in April of 1937, he told Colonel Young that he was too exhausted to serve as captain on the initial flight to Hong Kong on April 21, 1937. Instead, he said, he was going to take a long vacation. Due to the weeks away from home and the grueling schedule, Musick also planned to discuss with his wife his future with the company. Perhaps it was time, after all, to consider the office job that he knew was available with Pan Am in Alameda. But, then again, perhaps after a good rest he would be refreshed and ready to renew the flights to New Zealand at the end of December of 1937.

*Pan Am's magazine for first flight to New Zealand*

Juan Trippe's plan of flying to New Zealand before suitable aircraft and bases were available was ill conceived and dangerous. It was pure folly on Pan Am's part to think that they could maintain regular air service through Kingman Reef using a boat as their station base. It was madness to consider the small Pago Pago Harbor, surrounded by high hills, as a suitable harbor for safe landings and take offs. But Trippe would not be deterred by these obvious obstacles. He wanted to extend Pan Am's sky routes to New Zealand before the British beat him there. He had his eyes on Australia as well.

Through the skill and good luck of the flight crew, the first flight was successfully completed on the route south through Kingman Reef and Pago Pago. With the oil leak, the bad weather, and the deadline imposed by the first flight to Hong Kong, Musick had taken risks to complete the survey flight that he would not otherwise have taken. The danger was constant, however, and fatigue was an ever present companion. Only one more successful flight would be completed over this torturous route. The third flight to New Zealand in January of 1938 would end in disaster, with the loss of the Samoan Clipper, with the loss of world famous Captain Musick and with the loss of his young and talented crew. The Pacific pioneers were about to pay a terrible price for Juan Trippe's impatience in establishing air service to New Zealand.

| Transfer Flight S-42B Honolulu to Manila | April 18 - 22, 1937 | S-42B Hong Kong Clipper | LaPorte / Nixon |
|---|---|---|---|

| Outbound Flight Schedule | | Inbound Flight Schedule | |
|---|---|---|---|
| Honolulu - Midway | April 18 | Manila - Guam | Dec. 9 |
| Midway - Wake | April 19-20* | Guam - Wake | Dec. 10 |
| Wake - Guam | April 21 | Wake - Midway | Dec. 11-10* |
| Guam - Manila | April 22 | Midway - Honolulu | Dec. 11 |

*Dateline - Gain day outbound - Lose day inbound

When the New Zealand survey flight was completed on March 9, 1937 the Sikorsky S-42B Pan American Clipper II NC 16734 remained in Honolulu for a complete overhaul overseen by Captain Musick and Phil Berst, Pacific section maintenance supervisor in Honolulu. Regular flights to New Zealand were not required under Pan Am's agreement with New Zealand until the end of the year.

Negotiations were, however, complete for Pan Am to fly regularly to Hong Kong starting April 21, 1937. Therefore, it was determined that the Pan Am Clipper II would be transferred to Manila to fly the Manila to Hong Kong shuttle flight. This would allow the passengers and mail to be transferred at Manila to the shuttle flight to Hong Kong, so that the outbound Clipper could immediately return to San Francisco. With the Hong Kong shuttle flights, Pan Am could maintain the regular schedule over the rest of the Pacific route.

*The former Pan Am American Clipper II - newly rechristened Hong Kong Clipper - April 1937 in Hong Kong*

Therefore, when maintenance on the Pan Am Clipper II was complete, Captain Musick formally turned the Clipper over to Captain A.E. LaPorte for the transfer flight to Manila.

---

**PAA** **PAN AMERICAN AIRWAYS COMPANY**

### MEMORANDUM

DATE __13 April 1937__

TO ___Mr Philip B. BERST___          FROM ___Division Engineer___

DEPT. ___Maintenance___          DEPT. ___Maintenance___

LOCATION ___Honolulu___          LOCATION ___Alameda.___

SUBJECT ___Travel orders for inspection of System bases and supervise initial work in conncetion with installation of base at Hong Kong.___

You are directed to proceed via the NC-34 from Honolulu to Manila on or about 14 April, 1937, and via such transportation as you may select from Manila to Hong Kong.

During the period covered by these orders you will make a general inspection of the Maintenance Departments of the System's bases at Midway, Wake, Guam, Manila, and Hong Kong. You will also supervise the initial work in connection with the installation of our base at Hong Kong.

Upon the completion of the above, you will return to your regular duties at Honolulu.

Please advise this office as to your prospective movements so that we may make requests on Reservations Control for your transportation.

Please submit your traveling expense account reports regularly and in accordance with current instructions.

John C. Leslie.

CC/ Airport Mgr. Honolulu.
    "    "    Manila.
    Chief Mech.  Manila.
    File.

---

Pacific maintenance supervisor, Phil Berst, was given orders to travel on the transfer flight to inspect the facilities at Midway, Wake, Guam and Manila on the westbound flight. His most important task, however, was to finalize the installation of Pan Am's new base at Hong Kong.

Pictured below is Phil Berst to the right of Colonel Bicknell, the station manager in Honolulu who previously held the same position at Wake. Berst was also supplied with business cards by Pan Am in both English and Chinese to assist him with his work while in Hong Kong.

On April 18, 1937 the Clipper, under the command of Captain LaPorte and First Officer Nixon, left Hawaii with Phil Berst and the rest of the crew to prepare for the shuttle flights from Manila to Hong Kong.

Captain Musick told his supervisors that the survey flight to New Zealand had been too grueling, and that he was far too exhausted to make the inaugural flight to Hong Kong as had been previously planned. Therefore, on the same day that the Pan Am Clipper II departed for its new assignment, April 18, 1937, he departed eastbound as one of the ten passengers on the Hawaii Clipper. This flight was under the command of Captain Leo Terletzky. By an ironic coincidence, within little more than a year both Captain Musick and Captain Terletzky would be killed in tragic accidents. Captain Musick perished in January of 1938 when the Sikorsky S-42B Hong Kong Clipper (renamed the Samoan Clipper) exploded while returning for an emergency landing at Pago Pago Harbor on the third flight to New Zealand. Captain Terletzky, in command of the Hawaii Clipper, disappeared under mysterious circumstances on the westbound flight from Guam on July 27, 1938.

*Honolulu station manager George Bicknell on left and Phil Berst*

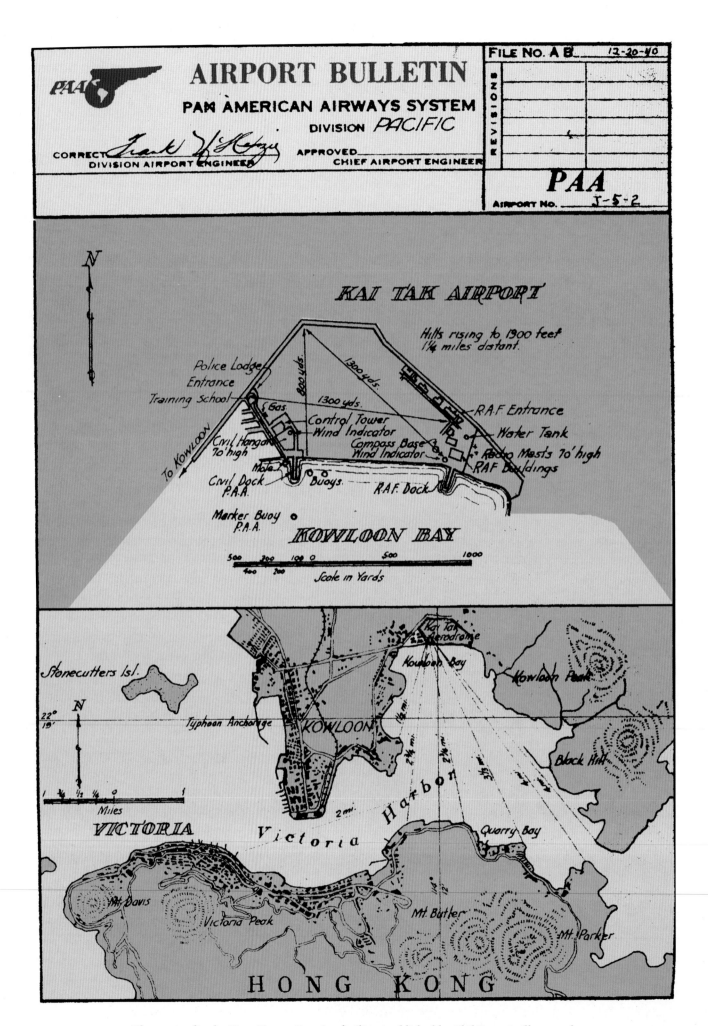

*The survey for the Hong Kong - Pan Am facility established by Phil Berst is illustrated*

*View across Kowloon Bay from Kai Tak Airport - 1945*

The Hong Kong Clipper remained based at Manila providing the shuttle service to Hong Kong until early December of 1937. Pan Am was still short of aircraft in the Pacific; therefore, in December of 1937, in order to fulfill Pan Am's promise of starting regularly scheduled air mail service to New Zealand by the end of 1937, the Hong Kong Clipper had to be transferred back from Hong Kong to Honolulu and it was renamed the Samoan Clipper.

A single flight cover is known to exist from the westbound portion of this transfer flight. Greg Schmidt shares his cover with us that was flown from Honolulu to Manila when the Hong Kong Clipper was flown to Manila in April of 1937. The back stamp confirms its arrival in Manila on April 21, 1937.

The year of 1937 was proving to be a successful year of continued expansion for Pan Am in the Pacific.

| Survey - Manila to Hong Kong | April 23 - 24, 1937 | S-42B Hong Kong Clipper | LaPorte/Briggs |
|---|---|---|---|

| Outbound Flight Schedule | | Inbound Flight Schedule | |
|---|---|---|---|
| Manila - Macao | April 23 | Hong Kong - Manila | April 24 |
| Macao - Hong Kong | April 23 | | |

After arriving in Manila, the Hong Kong Clipper made the first survey flight from Manila to Macao and back to Hong Kong where the crew spent the night. The refueling and maintenance facilities that were set up by Phil Berst were found to be adequate. Word was relayed to Alameda that all was finally in readiness for the inaugural airmail flight to Hong Kong.

*Hong Kong Clipper takes off from from Pan Am base at Kowloon Bay in Hong Kong*

No flown covers have been identified from this short survey flight. One unstamped envelope, with a corner logo of the China National Air Corporation (CNAC) that was controlled by Pan Am, was signed by the crew members when they were in Hong Kong. Because this cover does not contain any postmarks, we cannot tell if it was flown on this survey flight.

*In Hong Kong, the former Pan Am Clipper is formally re-christened as the Hong Kong Clipper - the American flag, the Hong Kong flag and the Chinese flag are proudly displayed on the Clipper's bow.*

*Flight brochure for Pan Am's CNAC Hong Kong connecting service*

廣 香 汕 廈 福 溫　　上 　　　　　　　廣 香 汕 廈 福 溫
州 港 頭 門 州 州　　海 　　　　　　　州 港 頭 門 州 州

二 啓 揭 鼓 德　龍 各　　　　四 　總 太 十 九 自 中 中
沙 德 陽 浪 士　華 處　　　　川 公 平 諸 龍 來 平 山
頭 飛 碼 嶼 古　　所 　地 　路 司 南 道 半 水 街 公
江 機 頭　　堆　電 飛 　事 　橋 　路 八 島 樓 一 園
面 場　 附 棧　話 機 　務 　北 　三 號 酒 內 二 中
　　　 近 　前　華 場 　所 　塊 　十 皇 店 太 三 山
　　　　　 江　界 地 　 　郵 　七 帝 三 原 號 橋
　　　　　 面　六 址 　 　政 　號 行 號 汽 福 堍
　　　　　　　 八 　 　 　局 　　 三 　車 達 花
　　　　　　　　二 　 　 　大 　　 樓 　公 汽 柳
　　　　　　　　二 　 　 　廈 　　　 　司 車 塘
　　　　　　　　二 　 　 　　 　　　 　 公 四
　　　　　　　　　 　 　 　售 　　　 　 司 一
　　　　　　　　　 　 　 　票 　　　 　 　號
　　　　　　　　　 　 　 　分

電 電 電 電 電 電　　　　電 電 電 電 電 電
話 話 話 話 話 話　　　　話 話 話 話 話 話

## HEAD OFFICE:

SHANGHAI  Post Office Building, corner of North  Phone  40040
          Szechuen and North Soochow Roads          40047-8-9
          No. 57 Nanking Rd, (Booking Office)  Phone  12955

## BRANCH OFFICES:

WENCHOW   41 Hwa Liu Tang, Near Chung       Phone  78
          Shan Park
FOOCHOW   Foochow Motor Sales Co.,     Phone 2890 & 2895
          123 Chung Ping Road
AMOY      Paramount Motors Co.,             Phone  989
          Amoy Waterwork Bldg
SWATOW    San Shing Co.,                    Phone  1352
          30 Chi Ping Road
HONGKONG  3 Peninsula Hotel Arcade, Kowloon Phone  50605
          King's Building, 8 Connaught Rd,  Phone  33131
CANTON    37 Tai Ping Road South            Phone  15004

## AERODROMES:--

SHANGHAI  Lunghwa              Chinese Phone  68222
WENCHOW   River side, in front of Txaco Installation
FOOCHOW   Ku Shan Point
AMOY      Near Yuan Tang Kon Kou
SWATOW    Chi Yang Mah Tao
HONGKONG  Kai Tak Airport
CANTON    River side, Erh Sha Tao

## AGENCIES IN FOREIGN COUNTRIES:

United States - American Express, Inc.
             - Pan American Airways Co,
             - Thos. Cook and Son, Ltd.
Europe       - Air France
             - American Express, Inc
             - Imperial Airways, Ltd
             - Thos. Cook and Son, Ltd

中 國 航 空 公 司
# China National Aviation Corp.

滬 粵 綫
## SHANGHAI-CANTON LINE

飛 航 時 刻 及 客 票 價 目 表
## Time Tables & Passenger Fare Rates

C. N. A. C. Air Routes.

電報掛號　中國
Cable Address  Chinese

二十六年五月五日起實行          Corrected to May 5, 1937

*Timetable for May 5, 1937 - Providing connecting service with Pan Am's Transpacific service to Hong Kong*

| 1st Scheduled Mail Flight to Hong Kong | April 21 - 27, 1937 | M-130 China Clipper (Alameda to Manila) | Cluthe/Cone |
| | April 28 - 29, 1937 | S-42B Hong Kong Clipper (Man- Macao ) (HK-Manila) | LaPorte/Briggs |
| | April 30 - May 3, 1937 | M-130 China Clipper (Manila - Honolulu) | Cluthe/Cone |
| | May 3 - 4, 1937 | M-130 China Clipper Honolulu-S.F | Lorber/Culbertson |

| Outbound Flight Schedule | | Inbound Flight Schedule | |
| --- | --- | --- | --- |
| San Francisco-Honolulu | April 21-22 | Hong Kong - Manila | April 29 |
| Honolulu - Midway | April 23 | Manila - Guam | April 30 |
| Midway - Wake | April 24-25* | Guam - Wake | May 1 |
| Wake - Guam | April 26 | Wake - Midway | May 2-1* |
| Guam - Manila | April 27 | Midway - Honolulu | May 2 |
| Manila - Macao | April 28 | Honolulu - San Francisco | May 3-4 |
| Macao - Hong Kong | April 28 | | |
| *Dateline - Gain day outbound - Lose day inbound | | | |

After long and complicated negotiations, permission was finally granted to complete the Manila to Hong Kong link in Transpacific travel, allowing for the connection to other airlines for flights to China, Singapore and onward to Europe.

The first flight to Hong Kong was scheduled to depart San Francisco on the afternoon of April 21, 1937, with the Martin M-130 China Clipper under the command of Captain Cluthe. By coincidence, at 10:00 a.m. on April 21 the Hawaii Clipper inbound from Honolulu completed Pan Am's 100th crossing of the Pacific Ocean. The inbound Hawaii Clipper is pictured at Alameda upon its arrival as it is about to be pulled out of the water. In 1937 one hundred Pacific crossings without an accident was a very significant accomplishment.

*Arrival of 100th crossing*

*Loading China Clipper for inaugural Hong Kong flight - Red stripes were added to wings of Clipper to commemorate Hong Kong service*

Pictured above is the China Clipper being loaded with air express parcels destined for Hong Kong. To the right of the floating walkway, **Movietone** photographers can be seen making movies of the event. Over 500 pounds of freight and 1100 pounds of mail were carried on the inaugural flight to Hong Kong.
At 3:30 p.m. the crew boarded the China Clipper for the Hong Kong inaugural flight. In the bottom picture Captain Cluthe, who took over as commander for the fatigued Captain Musick, can be seen at the top of the pier preceded by his crew on the lower walkway.

Captain Cluthe commanded the China Clipper to Manila, arriving April 27, 1937. In Manila the mail and cargo were off-loaded and put aboard the Hong Kong Clipper, which had just returned to Manila after successfully completing the survey flight to Hong Kong. Captain LaPorte, in the Sikorsky S-42, flew the Hong Kong Clipper on the last portion of the flight from Manila to Hong Kong.

*Banquet in Hong Kong in honor of Captain LaPorte and crew seated at right*

As was the custom, after the Hong Kong Clipper arrived in Hong Kong on April 28, 1937 the officials held a welcoming banquet in honor of the crew. Although Captain LaPorte and the other members of his crew had only flown the plane the short distance from Manila, they were the recipients of all the honors that were bestowed.

Captain LaPorte flew the Hong Kong Clipper back to Manila to the China Clipper waiting at Pan Am's Cavite base. Captain Cluthe then flew the China Clipper back to Honolulu, where Captain Lorber took over command and completed the final leg of the inaugural flight from Honolulu to San Francisco, arriving on May 4, 1937.

The post office in San Francisco advertised the new Hong Kong mail service in posters printed in both English and Chinese.

The cover craze was at its peak and literally hundreds of thousands of first flight covers were carried for collectors on this flight. Only a small sample of the special envelopes printed for this flight can be shown.

The most interesting cover in my collection for this flight was prepared for Rose VanDusen, the mother of Pan Am's public relations director. It is signed by each of the three captains who commanded a portion of the inaugural flight.

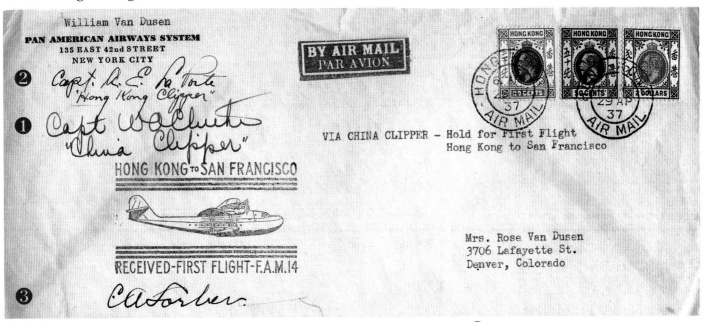

① *Captain Cluthe-San Francisco to Manila and Manila to Honolulu* ② *Captain LaPorte-Manila to Hong Kong-Macao and return to Manila* ③ *Captain Lorber-Honolulu to San Francisco*

Phil Berst, who had set up Pan Am's base in Hong Kong, sent a crew signed cover from Hong Kong to his young daughter Catherine back in Honolulu.

By completing the Manila to Hong Kong airmail route, Pan Am had filled the last remaining link for around the world airmail service. It was now possible, for the first time in history, to mail a letter from New York or Hong Kong and have it go completely around the world by scheduled airmail service. As part of Pan Am's promotion of the first flight to Hong Kong, Pan Am assisted collectors in creating these colorful souvenirs of around the world flight.

Pictured are three covers that were mailed around the world by collectors as part of the inauguration of airmail service to Hong Kong.

# FIRST TRANS-PACIFIC AIR MAIL TO CHINA
## NEWS-FEATURE BULLETIN

*(The Following News Matter Released for Wednesday, April 21 or thereafter)*

| No. 3-C | **Pan American Airways System, 135 East 42nd Street, New York City** | April 19, 1937 |
|---|---|---|

## First Air Mail Service to China Completes Last Link in 'Round-the-World Skyway

### FIRST CHINA AIR MAIL IS FIELD DAY FOR STAMP FANS

SAN FRANCISCO, Apr. 00 (Special)—The local postoffice is experiencing a "Christmas" mail rush. But with Santa Claus seven months ahead of time, and the famous China Clipper substituting for sleigh and reindee[r] ... tains of "first fligh[t] ... place of Yuletide ca[ndles]. A big crew of [han]dlers has been adde[d] ... ular postoffice depar[tment to] cope with the bigg[est] rush of mail this or[ any] office has had in yea[rs, and] of it all is the first a[ir mail] across the Pacific to [the] which is scheduled [to leave this] city next Wednesday.

Between them, [the national] and the local offices o[f the Ameri]can Airways have al[ready sold] nearly 100,000 specia[l stamps, with] prospects of twice th[at amount by] the time the Clippe[r gets under] way. The normal h[andling] has been doubled du[e to the fact] that a special Gover[nment rate] is being placed on a[ny] mail originating in [the United] States that is destin[ed for] Macao or Hong K[ong, ter]minals of the wor[ld-girdling] ocean airline that wi[ll link Amer]ica and Asia with a[ir serv]ice.

cially to mark this new service, have also stimulated the flood of first flight "covers." In denominations of 20 cents and 50 cents, the new Transpacific air mail stamps have been eagerly sought by col-

complete set, officials state, is made up of twenty-one separate covers and costs, in postage, $16.80. Experts estimate that the value of these covers, six months from now, will be "around $100"

[have] been able to secure a com- [for all first flight mail originating]

### First Air Mail Service Around the World Starts Today

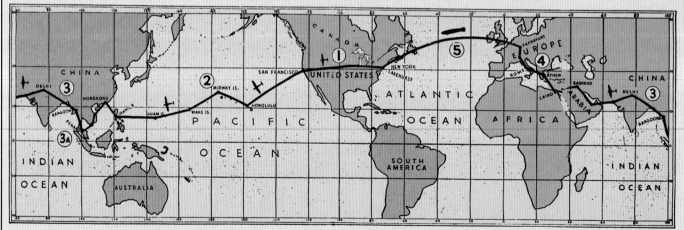

When the China Clipper Takes Off from San Francisco Today (Wednesday, April 21 for Hong Kong, China, the Last Link in a 24,000 Mile Airway Chain Extending Completely Around the Globe Will Be Completed. Here are the Steps That Will Now Take Air Mail and Passengers, On Regular Schedules, Around the World in Sixteen Days

1. New York to San Francisco, overnight, via United Air Lines. 2. San Francisco to Hong Kong, 5½ days, via Pan American Airways. 3. Hong Kong to Athens, 6 days, via Imperial Airways to Penang, Royal Dutch Airlines, Penang to Athens. Athens to Frankfort, ½ day, Alla Littoria, (Italian Airlines) and Deutsche Lufthansa. Frankfort to New York, 4 days, via Zeppelin Hindenburg.

*Shanghai, China - eastbound around the world*

*Around the world - west bound*

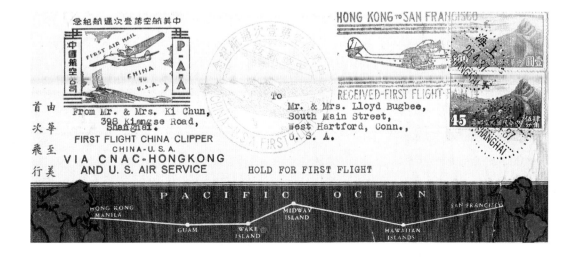

289

290

*Macao posting*

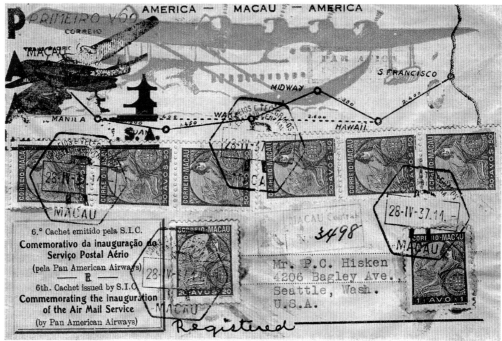

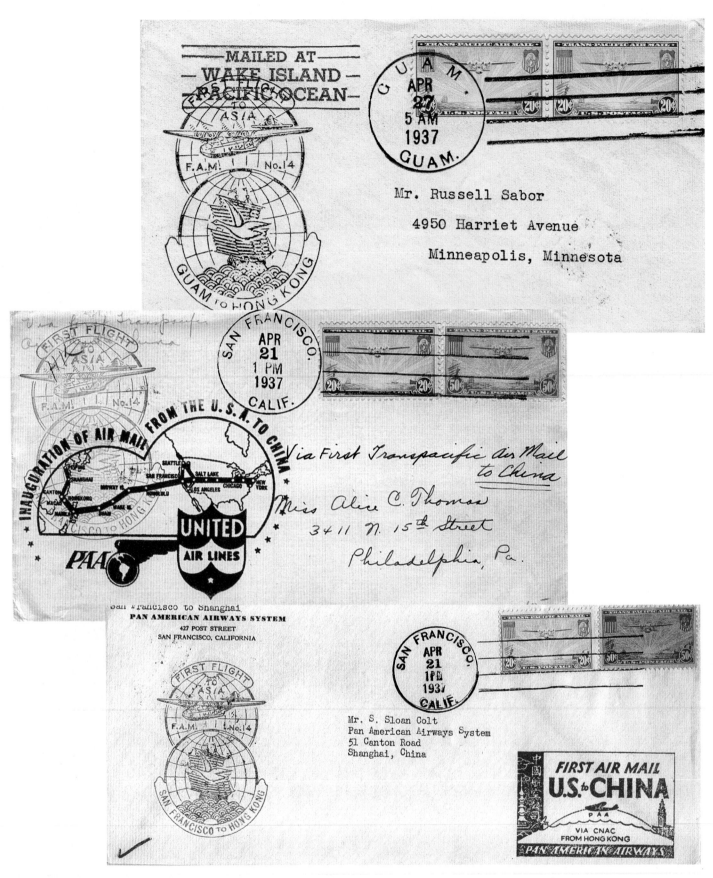

From Pan Am's first survey flight to Honolulu in April of 1935 to the opening of service to Hong Kong in April of l937, it had taken Pan Am one hundred Pacific crossings and two years to reach Juan Trippe's goal of regular service to China.

Pan Am had accomplished its goal without the loss of a single life or single aircraft. Now, Juan Trippe could rest and consolidate his empire. The Boeing 314s were due for delivery in little more than a year. Trippe envisioned regular flights to New Zealand and Australia in the near future. The future had never looked brighter for Pan Am than it did in April of l937. All of Juan Trippe's dreams for his airline were coming true.

| 1st Revenue Passenger Service to Hong Kong | April 29 - May 12, 1937 | M-130 Hawaii Clipper (to Manila) | Dahlstrom/Culbertson |
|---|---|---|---|
| | | S-42B Hong Kong Clipper | LaPorte/Nixon |

| Outbound Flight Schedule | | Inbound Flight Schedule | |
|---|---|---|---|
| San Francisco - Honolulu | April 29 - 30 | Hong Kong - Manila | May 7 |
| Honolulu - Midway | May 1 | Manila - Guam | May 8 |
| Midway - Wake | May 2 - 3* | Guam - Wake | May 9 |
| Wake - Guam | May 4 | Wake - Midway | May 10 - 9* |
| Guam - Manila | May 5 | Midway - Honolulu | May 10 |
| Manila - Hong Kong | May 6 | Honolulu - San Francisco | May 11 - 12 |
| *Dateline - Gain day outbound - Lose day inbound | | | |

Even before the China Clipper had returned to San Francisco from the first scheduled mail flight to Hong Kong, the Civil Aeronautics Authority had approved passenger service over the same route. Therefore, on April 29 the Hawaii Clipper left San Francisco outbound on the first scheduled passenger flight to Hong Kong. With this flight the last remaining gap in passenger air travel was closed and for the first time in history, passengers were able to fly around the world on regularly scheduled flights. The first two passengers to book around the world air travel were Frederick Emerson, a businessman from Auburn, New York, who claimed that he had conferences in 19 different countries and Ernest Haywood, an attorney from Raleigh, North Carolina. The picture of Ernest Haywood, taken in Bermuda in 1938, was sent to me by his grandson, who said in his letter that uncle Ernest was somewhat of a celebrity around Raleigh in the 1930s and 1940s and that:

*"He was a prominent attorney and inveterate traveler, who was also involved in a shoot-out on the steps of the county court house. The story goes that a brother of a young lady, whom Ernest had seen socially, wanted Ernest to set a wedding date. When Ernest refused, words were exchanged and guns were drawn. Uncle Ernest was found to have acted in self-defense and eventually exonerated."*

*Uncle Ernest in Bermuda waiting for clipper flight - 1938*

*First passenger to Hong Kong*

*Colonel Young and Captain Dahlstrom*

The two around the world travelers, however, were not the first to buy a passenger ticket to Hong Kong. That distinction went to Carlton E. Morris, the author of "One Man's Family". Pictured with Carlton Morris is Mr. V.A. Kropff, Pan Am's District Traffic Manager, for the Pacific Division, who sold him the first ticket to Hong Kong. Clara Adams, professional world traveler, missed out on this inaugural passenger flight.

Pictured just before takeoff from Pan Am's Alameda base is Colonel Clarence Young, Manager of Pan Am's Pacific Division and Captain R.A. Dahlstrom, Commander of the Hawaii Clipper. Captain Dahlstrom has just received a scroll of friendship from Young for delivery to the Governor of Hong Kong and Col. Young is also about to present him with two bronze plaques for delivery to Manila and Hong Kong commemorating the event. The entire proceedings were being broadcast live by radio to Hong Kong.

On the next page the Hawaii Clipper is pictured at the floating dock ready for its 3:00 p.m. departure. Pan Am added four broad bands of red color on the wings in honor of the Hong Kong flights, so by computer, we have added the color to our black and white photograph.

*Hawaii Clipper about to depart - Note the broad red stripes on the wings added by Pan Am to celebrate the opening of mail and passenger flights to the Orient*

The inauguration of Hong Kong passenger service fulfilled another of Juan Trippe's goals of around the world commercial air travel. Juan Trippe's series of successes in the Pacific remained unbroken.

| 1st Mail Flight from New Zealand (Mail on return only) | December 23, 1937 to January 3, 1938 January 5-6, 1938 | S-42B Samoan Clipper Honolulu-NZ-Honolulu M-130 Philippine Clipper (Honolulu - San Fran.) | Musick/Culbertson Cluthe |
|---|---|---|---|

| Outbound Flight Schedule | | Inbound Flight Schedule | |
|---|---|---|---|
| Honolulu - Kingman Reef | Dec. 23 | Auckland - Pago Pago | Jan. 2-1* |
| Kingman Reef - Pago Pago | Dec. 24 | Pago Pago - Kingman Reef | Jan. 2 |
| Pago Pago - Auckland | Dec. 25-26* | Kingman Reef - Honolulu | Jan. 3 |
| | | Honolulu - San Francisco | Jan. 5-6 |

*Dateline - Gain day outbound - Lose day inbound

Captain Musick was still on extended leave, but because he was Pan Am's most respected and skilled pilot, he was called back at the end of 1937 to start the difficult scheduled flights to New Zealand through Kingman Reef and Pago Pago, that, by agreement, had to be inaugurated by the end of the year if Pan Am was to keep its concession to fly mail to New Zealand.

*Samoan Clipper at mooring Pago Pago - December 24, 1937*

Pan Am also knew that Captain Burgess, of Imperial Airways Limited of Great Britain, was approaching New Zealand from the west on a survey flight with the flying boat Centaurus. Therefore, there was open competition between the two airlines to become the first to establish regular airmail service to New Zealand. Because of an equipment shortage, the Hong Kong Clipper that had been flying passengers and mail between Manila and Hong Kong had to be brought back to Honolulu for this December flight to New Zealand. It was rechristened the Samoan Clipper.

On December 23, 1937, the Samoan Clipper departed Honolulu for this, the second flight to New Zealand. Although no mail was authorized for the outbound flight south, regular mail would be carried inbound from New Zealand. The North Wind, which had been chartered to serve as the base at Kingman Reef, had been replaced by the four masted schooner Trade Wind, which had been purchased by Pan Am specifically to serve as the permanent Kingman Reef base on the regular New Zealand flights. Pictured is the Trade Wind at Kingman Reef welcoming the Samoan Clipper for its overnight stop on its second flight to New Zealand.

*Trade Wind at Kingman Reef*

*At mooring Pago Pago harbor- Pan Am Samoan Clipper*

*Pan Am's Samoan Clipper foreground-Imperial Airways Centaurus background-in Auckland Harbor December 26, 1937*

*Captain Musick and Captain Burgess are pictured shaking hands after the arrival of the Centaurus*

After stops at Kingman Reef and Pago Pago, the Clipper arrived in Auckland on December 26, 1937, a day ahead of Captain Burgess with the Imperial Airways flying boat, Centaurus. Once again the crowds at Auckland were tremendous. Two flying boats, one from the United States and one from Britain, were anchored in their harbor at the same time.

The meeting between Captain Burgess and Captain Musick was an emotional event for both of the famed flying boat captains.

*Captain Burgess on left and crew on Centaurus at Auckland - December 1937*

Captain Burgess completed six souvenir covers of his inaugural survey flight to New Zealand and one of the six known covers signed by his crew is illustrated.

*Only six covers flown*

*Reverse signed by crew of Centaurus*

*Engine maintenance in Auckland*

While in Auckland, regular maintenance was performed on the Clipper engines. Pictured is Pan Am's maintenance crew in Auckland servicing the outside port engine. On the next flight south one of these same engines developed an oil leak, which ultimately resulted in the loss of the Samoan Clipper.

*December 31, 1937 - Auckland, New Zealand*

This photograph of Captain Musick was taken in Auckland after the second flight. He did not like to be photographed out of uniform and he asked at the time that it not be published. It was one of the last photographs ever taken of him.

Because the United States Postal Service did not authorize the carrying of any mail to New Zealand, no souvenir flight covers from the southbound flight have surfaced over the years.

However, to complete its agreement with New Zealand, the Samoan Clipper carried a large volume of mostly souvenir mail northbound from New Zealand to Honolulu. In Honolulu the mail was off loaded from the Samoan Clipper, and placed on board the eastbound Philippine Clipper under the command of Captain Cluthe, for the remainder of the inaugural New Zealand mail flight from Honolulu to San Francisco.

A common cachet seen from this northbound flight is the small rectangular box - New Zealand to U.S.A. - which was applied to the mail by Pan Am as the standard souvenir flight cover. It is usually seen in red, but about 10% of the covers show a purple, rather than a red cachet. Over 35,000 letters were carried on the northbound flight with a total weight of 353 pounds.

Juan Trippe rarely signed flight covers. Because Captain Musick died a week after the completion of this flight, Juan Trippe undoubtedly signed this envelope after Musick's death. Therefore, it is surprising that he would agree to sign this cover – especially because it would be a constant reminder of the tragic price that was paid by Pan Am in trying to rush service to New Zealand over the dangerous route with aircraft unsuitable for the task.

*Red cachet*

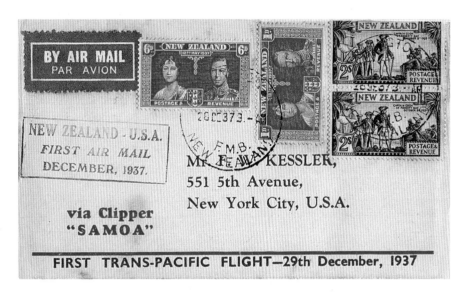

*Purple cachet*

*Cover signed by Juan Trippe*

301

In addition to the small rectangular cachet, Pan Am also prepared 200 to 300 sets of covers with a large black cachet for each of the three legs of the flight - New Zealand to American Samoa - New Zealand to Honolulu - New Zealand to the United States. All but one of the souvenir flight covers with the large black cachet are on large size Pan American Airways envelopes. The only exception I have seen is a souvenir cover on a New Zealand printed envelope that is illustrated below.

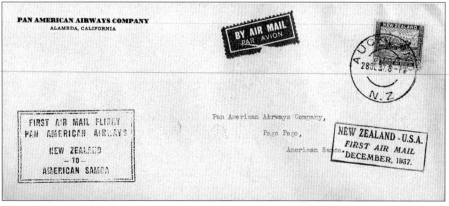

I have even found one cover that has both the common small red rectangular cachet and the far more scarce large black cachet.

*Both the common red cachet and rarer large black cachet*

As Pan Am's most senior pilot, and as the recognized dean of Transpacific flight, Captain Musick was expected to also make the third flight to New Zealand just four days after completing this flight. The first survey flight in March of 1937 had resulted in the loss of an engine on the San Francisco to Honolulu portion of the flight and the remainder of the first survey flight to New Zealand was made under terrible weather conditions. This second long flight to New Zealand kept Captain Musick away from home for the entire Christmas holiday and it was almost as difficult. The fact that he was expected to repeat the flight just four days later played heavily on his mind. Because of his fame and acknowledged skill, Pan Am had Captain Musick on a killing schedule. The long hours of flying and the months away from his wife and his home were beginning to take a toll.

Edwin C. Musick

This picture captures the fatigue that he felt as he completed the second round trip to New Zealand over the difficult route through Kingman Reef and Pago Pago. It is too bad at this time that he did not take the long vacation he promised his wife - it's too bad he didn't take the desk job that was available - it's tragic that he continued with one more flight of the Samoan Clipper to New Zealand.

## Flight Schedule

| Honolulu - Kingman Reef | January 9 |
| Kingman Reef - Pago Pago | January 10 |
| Pago Pago - Lost at Sea | January 11 |

---

### MAIL SCHEDULE

# Honolulu Star-Bulletin EXTRA

Evening Bulletin, Est. 1882, No. 19179
Hawaiian Star, Vol. XLV, No. 14140

16 PAGES—HONOLULU, TERRITORY OF HAWAII, U. S. A., WEDNESDAY, JANUARY 12, 1938—16 PAGES ★ PRICE FIVE CENTS

## 3 of Crew! Clipper That Crashed

CAPT. MUSICK     J. W. STICKROD    J. A. BROOKS

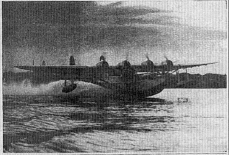

# CLIPPER BURNS, ALL CREW DEAD!

## Avocet, Searching Sea Near Tutuila, Recovering Parts

WASHINGTON, Jan. 12. (UP)--Pan American Airways announced today all members of the Samoan Clipper crew are dead.

WASHINGTON, Jan. 12. (AP)—Juan T. Trippe, president of Pan American Airways, said today it was "definitely established" that Capt. Edwin C. Musick and the other six crew members were killed in the wreck of the Samoan Clipper.

The craft was "destroyed by fire of unknown origin" near Pago Pago yesterday, Mr. Trippe said.

On the basis of radio reports from Samoa, Mr. Trippe said it was determined the seven were killed at approximately 8:30 a. m. Samoan time yesterday (9 a. m. Honolulu time.)

The Samoan Clipper was wrecked at sea yesterday morning with the loss of all aboard.

Pieces of wreckage, unmistakably identified were picked up early today by the USS Avocet about 11 miles northwest of the western point of Tutuila, American Samoa, and 12 1-2 miles from Pago Pago.

This information was received from the Avocet by radio at Pearl Harbor at 8:27 a. m. today from the governor of American Samoa

The message, addressed to the bureau of operations, navy department, Washington, with information for the commandant at Pearl Harbor, read:

"Avocet reports finding heavy oil slick at latitude 14-08-20, longitude 170-51 (approximately the location of Tutuila, near which the plane disappeared yesterday).

### Launch Recovers Parts

"Has motor launch recovering parts of wrecked plane. 'Identification satisfactory.'"

The message did not indicate whether the wreckage gave evidence that the plane had burned, as was thought possible.

Today's discovery solved the mystery of what became of the four-engined Sikorsky flying boat which Capt. Musick was taking from Honolulu to Auckland on the sec-

ond trip of the recently inaugurated New Zealand service.

At 7:50 a. m. Tuesday a radio message from the plane which had left Pago Pago for Auckland at 6:02 a. m., said it had developed oil trouble and was returning to the PAA base on Tutuila.

At 8:27 a second message said the clipper was but 3 minutes from Pago Pago and was dumping gasoline preparatory to landing.

Nothing was heard from the clipper afterwards.

### An Oil Slick Found

This morning an oil slick was found by the Avocet at about the spot where the last report was sent and at about the point where the dumping of fuel started.

It was also reported that natives had seen the clipper "flying in smoke" near the western point of Tutuila.

## Samoan Clipper Had Gallant Flight Record

A gallant flying record ended disastrously when the Samoan Clipper crashed into the South Pacific early Tuesday morning, only minutes removed from a haven of safety at Pago Pago.

The 19 ton, four engined flying boat won a lasting place in international aviation history when, in 1935, she pioneered the air path across the Pacific from California to the Orient. Appropriately, she found her way to New Zealand from Alameda via Honolulu.

### Lubricating Trouble
Lubricating trouble which is reported to have been responsible for the crash of the Samoan Clipper had been experienced before by the plane.

When the Sikorsky arrived at Pearl Harbor March 18 last year to prepare for her first test flight over the Antipodes route, she glided in with her No. 2 engine dead because of a leak in the oiling system.

At that time Capt. Musick is reported to have said:

"The engine trouble we had last night was not serious when we discovered it. It's always best to cut out the engine rather than risk serious developments. Our experience last night proves once more the value of multi-motored planes for transoceanic flying."

Her unparalleled exploit in spanning the earth's greatest ocean left her work and her triumphs still incomplete.

Pan American Airways selected the silver bullet seaplane to pioneer still another international air route, and in March, 1937, sent her skimming down the South Pacific

### End Heroic as Life
Her end, in a sense, was as heroic as her life, for she crashed on the route she had recently explored and which was still so new to air travel that passenger service had not yet been started.

She was claimed by waters which she had conquered thrice before—first, on her pioneer flight; and twice in recent weeks on voyages from Honolulu to New Zealand and return.

By tragic coincidence she carried with her into the sea her pilot, Capt. Edwin C. Musick, the self-effacing, sober faced veteran who had flown her on exploratory flights which marked the way for transpacific aviation of today and the future.

Service exclusively in the Orient for PAA followed her first exploratory flights. In that duty she carried the name of the Hongkong Clipper.

### Rechristened Here
Recently she flew back to Honolulu and was rechristened the Samoan Clipper.

She was the first transport airplane in the world to be designed specifically for transoceanic operation.

Within her hull and in wings and tail

**Turn to Page 4, Column 3**

## FEARS VOICED THAT CLIPPER FELL AFLAME

### Smoke Pall Reported Near Place Where Oil Was Found

PAGO PAGO, American Samoa, Jan. 12. (UP)—Fears were expressed today that the Pan American Airways Samoan Clipper, piloted by the veteran Capt. Edwin C. Musick and carrying a crew of six, may have caught fire after encountering motor trouble.

Finding of an oil slick on the ocean 12 miles from Tutuila followed a report that a smoke column was seen in the same vicinity

The plane, en route to New Zealand on the second successive flight she had caught fire while dumping gasoline for a landing with three motors.

### Dumping Gasoline

It was feared the plane might have caught fire while dumping gasoline for a landing with three motors.

Two ships and one airplane returned the search this morning for the flying boat.

The USS Avocet, an aircraft tender on temporary station in Pago Pago while the regular station ship Ontario is at Pearl Harbor, left this port last night for the search vicinity and a navy plane took off at 5:30 this morning.

The plane, piloted by Lt. T. B. Williamson, who is also commander of the Avocet, made a five hour search yesterday afternoon, returning at 6 p. m. and reporting no trace.

**Turn to Page 4, Column 2**

## Mrs. Musick Informed Of PAA Clipper's Loss

### Commander's Wife in Seclusion; Had Been Confident of Safety

SAN FRANCISCO, Jan. 12. (AP)—Mrs. Edwin C. Musick, wife of the commander of the Samoan Clipper, received news of the plane's loss in a secluded apartment today.

A short time before word of discovery of the Seline wreckage of Pago Pago was received she had expressed confidence that her husband was safe.

"Capt. Musick has been down before. I know that he is safe," she had asserted.

She recalled that her husband always remained calm under the most hazardous conditions.

Reporters recalled that on November, 1935, when he piloted the same clipper which later became the Samoan Clipper on the first survey flight across the Pacific to Honolulu, he was asked to send something colorful regarding the flight.

Musick answered the next with the following message:

"The sun set at 6:32 p. m. tonight."

Mrs. F. J. Meluan, wife of the navigator aboard the Samoan Clipper, was reported prostrated in Alameda.

## MUSICK RATED AMONG GREAT WORLD FLIERS

### No. 1 PAA Pilot Flew Pioneering Trips to Rio, Across Pacific

He carried with him in the crash of his Samoan Clipper a record of never before having had a serious accident befall any aircraft while he was piloting, and no injury ever occurring to one of his passengers.

When he was conducting acceptance tests of the Brazilian Clipper, first of the transoceanic type of aircraft developed for PAA, Capt. Musick piloted the four engine plane to 10 world records on a single test flight of 1,250 miles non-stop.

All world marks for speed and load for various distances up to 2,000 kilometers were broken.

Capt. Musick piloted the craft on its maiden flight to Rio de Janeiro and Buenos Aires and returned to the United States in five days.

Serious faced, square chinned, Capt. Musick then turned to his pioneering flights across the Pacific. In 1935 he piloted the Pan American Clipper on the first transpacific flight in history, and later blazed the trail on the Alameda-Hawaii-Auckland run on which he met disaster yesterday.

Capt. Musick's sober mien and slightly stooped figure were familiar.

**Turn to Page 2, Column 3**

### CLIPPER CREW COMPOSED OF ABLE GROUP

John W. Stickrod, 22, Flight Engineer, Had Been Engineer Here

John W. Stickrod, 22, flight engineer on the Samoan Clipper, was one of the youngest and ablest members of PAA's engineering staff.

He began his training for a flight engineer's position when he joined the clipper for the first survey flight to Auckland in March, 1937.

Prior to that time he had been the leading mechanic of the Pearl City PAA base staff.

At that time he had been devoted to piloting early type flying boats in the Florida area.

MEMPHIS, Tenn., Jan. 12. (AP)—Hamilton Sellers, a brother of Pilot C. G. Sellers, who was aboard the ill-fated Samoan Clipper, said today that Mr. Sellers was awarded the Distinguished Service Cross during the World war.

He won the award as the man of heroism displayed in bombing flights in France.

He was born in Memphis. At Sewanee university he became a football star.

After the World war he became a pilot for the Chinese National Aviation Co., he its Shanghai to Hankow run, and in 1936 served as personal pilot to Generalissimo Chiang Kai-shek.

### Native of Missouri

He was born in St. Louis, Mo., in 1894, became one of the "early birds" of American exhibition and commercial aviation and served through the war with American forces as civilian flying instructor training young American aviators for service overseas.

Before he joined Pan American Airways in 1927 he had already built up a record for piloting practically every known type of aircraft which had been developed in America.

Much of his time had been devoted to piloting early type flying boats in the Florida area.

Those years of experience supplied the foundation on which Capt. Musick steadily advanced to his eminence in world aviation.

Those years of experience gained at Wake, from which point he made several flights to Guam and Midway.

## Men Who Were Aboard Clipper On Last Flight

Crew members aboard the wrecked Samoan Clipper were: CAPT. EDWIN C. MUSICK, 44. His wife lives in San Francisco.

C. G. SELLERS, 44, first officer. Wife and child in Manila.

P. S. BRUNK, 33, junior flight officer.

F. J. McLEAN, navigator, 42. Has wife and two daughters.

J. W. STICKROD, engineer, 23, formerly of Honolulu.

J. W. BROOKS, assistant engineer, 38. Wife and child in Honolulu.

T. J. FINDLEY, operator, 37.

SAN FRANCISCO, Jan. 12. (AP)—The navy hydrographic department notified Pan American Airways today that a navy launch was recovering parts of the wreckage of the Samoan Clipper 12 miles west of Pago Pago.

There was no mention of survivors among the seven members of the crew on the clipper when it fell into the sea yesterday.

The unsigned message to the navy said "Identification (of the wreckage) satisfactory."

PAGO PAGO, American Samoa, Jan. 12. (UP)—The USS Avocet today located wreckage of a plane definitely identified as the Samoan about 14 miles northeast of Pago Pago.

# EXTRA!

## San Francisco Chronicle
### THE CITY'S ONLY HOME~OWNED NEWSPAPER

FOUNDED 1865 — VOL. CLI, NO. 182     CC     SAN FRANCISCO, THURSDAY, JANUARY 13, 1938     DAILY 5 CENTS, SUNDAY 10 CENTS.

COMPARATIVE TEMPERATURES

| | High Low | | High Low |
|---|---|---|---|
| San Francisco | 57  43 | Denver | 44  40 |
| San Jose | 64  34 | Salt Lake | 46  34 |
| Los Angeles | 76  53 | New York | 33  16 |
| Seattle | 48  42 | Chicago | 28  22 |
| Honolulu | 80  64 | New Orleans | 60  48 |

Chronicle Home Carrier Service

Weather
Fair,
Becoming
Cloudy
Complete Weather Report on Page 23

# CLIPPER EXPLODED IN AIR, CREW OF 7 DEAD

## Hoover Will Visit Belgium As Guest of Government

The Belgian Ambassador at Washington has transmitted from the Belgian government an invitation to former President Herbert Hoover to revisit the scene of his herculean labors during the World war, it was learned yesterday.

The former chief executive has accepted, and will sail from New York for Belgium February 8, it was announced at his home on the Stanford campus.

*(Continued on Page 12, Col. 8)*

### Chronicle Artist Magill's Conception of Tragedy

## Captain Musick Rated as One of World's Greatest Pilots

### By WILLIS O'BRIEN
Number One Pilot

That was the only title ever held or ever sought from Pan-American Airways by Captain Edwin C. Musick but it was title enough for any man. For it meant far more than being the chief pilot of a American commercial flying concern.

Captain Musick, who met his death in the South Pacific Tuesday morning, was officially recognized as

## Captain Musick Dies as Flaming Ship Falls in Sea

### Big Plane Destroyed by Blast While Dumping Gasoline, Charred Debris Hints

#### By HARRY VERNER

FIRE!
EXPLOSION!
DEATH!

Out of the tropical calm of the South Seas flashed those shocking answers yesterday to the fate of Captain Edwin C. Musick and six other members of the crew of Pan American Airways' Samoan Clipper.

Twenty-four hours of silence which followed the disappearance of the flying boat on the final leg of her second scheduled flight between Honolulu and New Zealand was broken by radio flashes from Pago Pago, American Samoa, carrying this frightful story.

The Clipper caught fire in midair while dumping gasoline in preparation for landing at her Pago Pago base.

She was then only six minutes away from the base, flying

*More Clipper News on Pages A, B, 4 and 5*

on three engines. The fourth had been cut out due to an oil line leak.

Apparently an explosion ripped the Clipper apart and she plummeted into the sea, killing everyone aboard.

**Fragments Found on Sea**

Charred fragments of the plane found floating on oil-smeared swells 14 miles northwest of Pago Pago marked the scene of the giant craft's death dive.

Remaining unanswered were two questions of prime importance.

Whether the bodies of Musick and the other six Clipper crew members had been recovered.

Whether the physical evidence at the scene yielded any information concerning the specific cause of the fire.

Navy and Pan American officials said there was no question that all seven aboard the plane lost their lives when it was destroyed—that death came instantaneously with the first realization of danger.

First report of the discovery of the Clipper's wreckage was received here shortly before noon yesterday from the aircraft tender Avocet, stationed at Samoa.

**Forced Back by Oil Leak**

The Avocet radioed to navy headquarters at Samoa that

*Continued on Page 12, Col. 2*

## Roster of Airmen Lost In Pacific Disaster

Here are thumb-nail sketches of the personnel of the lost Samoan Clipper

CAPTAIN EDWIN O. MUSICK, commander, born St. Louis, Mo., 1894; lived 1940 Washington street, San Francisco with wife; no children.

C. G. SELLERS, first officer, born September 5, 1893, at Dyersburg, Tenn.; wife and child in Manila.

PAUL S. BRUNK, junior flight officer, born November 13, 1907; ex-wife living in San Francisco; brother in Berkeley.

J. MacLean, navigator, born October 2, 1895, at Passaic, N. J.; lived 508 Lincoln avenue, Alameda.

J. W. STICKROD, first engi-

neering officer, born July 14, 1914, at Los Angeles; came from American Airlines, Fort Worth, Texas, in 1935; mother, Mrs. Lillian M. Stickrod, 15 North Beachwood drive, Los Angeles.

A. BROOKS, assistant engineering officer, born September 29, 1899, at Weiser, Minn.; wife and child in Honolulu.

T. J. FINDLEY, radio operator, 2172 Lincoln avenue, Alameda, born 1908, Mill Valley; joined Pan-American November 1936; detailed from company school to active service month ago.

The front pages of the *San Francisco Chronicle* and the *Honolulu Star-Bulletin* reflect the shock and sadness of the nation at the loss of Captain Musick and the crew of the Samoan Clipper. With a shortage of equipment and with personnel pushed to their physical limits, Pan Am was being stretched beyond its ability in its attempt to establish regular service to New Zealand.

The official report of the Bureau of Air Commerce filed June 6, 1938 made the following observations:

```
Captain Edwin C. Musick held a Federal transportation
pilot's license, class 3B land and sea. His last physical
examination was December 9, 1937 showing him to be in good
health. Captain Musick's record indicated that he had a
total of 13,200 hours of flying experience; 2,320 hours of
Transpacific operations. His total experience with the
Sikorsky S-42B in Transoceanic operations was 502 hours.

Departure from the dock at Pago Pago, American Samoa was
made at 5:32 a.m. local time on January 11, 1938. The
airplane actually rose from the water five minutes later.
The plane carried a total of 751 pounds of mail. It was
loaded to a gross weight of 41,936 pounds . . . radio
communications were of a routine nature until 6:37 a.m. Pago
Pago time (one hour after lift off), when the following
message was received: "We have oil leak in the right
outboard engine and are returning to Pago Pago." At 8:20
Pago Pago time: "The engine with the oil leak has been
stopped at 6:08 a.m. and some gasoline has subsequently been
dumped."

At 8:27 a.m.: "We are going to dump gas and we can't use
the radio during the dumping. Stand by."
. . .
The weight at take off was 2,000 pounds less than the
maximum. Over 7,000 pounds was represented by the 730
gallons of gasoline in the wing tanks. Fully loaded, it
would have been impossible to stop the aircraft quickly
enough upon landing to avoid going onto the reef, therefore
dumping the fuel was necessary before returning to Pago Pago
for the emergency landing.
. . .
After reviewing several alternatives for the accident, it is
the opinion of the investigating board that the probable
cause of the accident was an explosion associated with the
dumping of fuel. The precise cause of the ignition being
undeterminable.
```

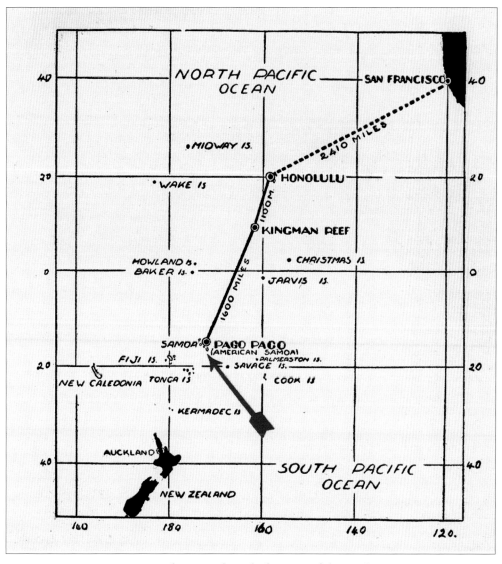

The maps show the location of the crash.

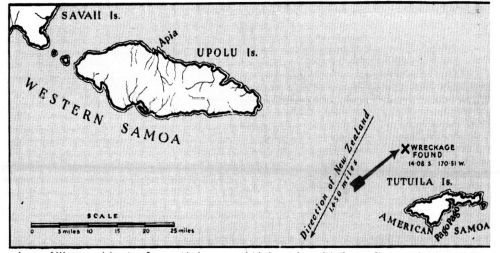

A map of Western and American Samoa, with the spot at which the wreckage of the Samoan Clipper was found marked with a cross.

## Plane Destroyed by Explosion Inside; Bits Picked up

PAGO PAGO, Jan. 13. (Ⓟ)—Examination of bits of wreckage clearly indicated today that an interior explosion sent the Samoan Clipper plunging into the ocean Tuesday with its crew of seven men.

The USS Avocet, which located the spot 12 miles west of Pago Pago where the clipper went down while attempting to return here with one motor stopped, reported the surface of the water was covered with hundreds of small fragments of the huge flying boat.

Natives who witnessed the last plunge of the clipper said it burned rapidly on the water, making a large volume of black smoke.

### No Hope of Recovery

The plane apparently sank in 6,000 feet of water in a section where there are many sharks, and officials held no hope for recovery of the bodies of Capt. Edwin C. Musick and other crew members or of parts of the clipper itself.

Fragments of the fuselage and of the coat of T. J. Findley, radio operator, showed evidence that holes had been blown through them by an explosion within the clipper. The coat was identified by a wing emblem.

The trousers of J. A. Brooks also were found and identified by a bent tie clasp in the pocket. All the fragments recovered were charred and burned and covered with aluminum powder. Many of them were small wood fragments from the inside of the plane.

Officials were forced to rely upon reports of natives in attempting to piece together the story of the wreck. Natives told of seeing heavy black smoke from the burning ship.

### By B. F. KNEUBUHL

PAGO PAGO, American Samoa, Jan. 13. (U.P)—Carrying bits of wreckage which indicated the Samoan Clipper was the victim of a terrific explosion, the USS Avocet returned to Pago Pago harbor last night.

I interviewed Chief Boatswain H. S. Bogan, who took the Avocet to the patch of wreckage 18 miles from Pago Pago while the vessel's commanding officer, Lt. T. B. Williamson, showed the way in the Avocet's seaplane.

Bogan said no bodies or signs of bodies were discovered in the large oil slick which marked the clipper's grave.

Surface of the sea was covered with small fragments from the interior of the plane, including bits of wood and paper.

The area was covered with aluminum powder, indicating drift bombs had blown apart in the crash.

Everything inspected was charred, indicating the plane was a mass of flame as it plunged into the sea at latitude 14 degrees 8 minutes south, longitude 170 degrees 51 minutes west.

No piece of wreckage recovered was large. Fragments varied from an inch or two square to six inches.

A section from the chart board, charts and a book of navigation tables were picked up.

The oil and debris probably were not floating over the exact spot where the plane went down, due to the drift and a light southwest wind.

307

*U.S.S. Avocet*

A seaplane tender, the U.S.S. Avocet, based in American Samoa, was dispatched immediately to the area where it was suspected that the Clipper had crashed. Pictured is the Avocet and the small seaplane carried aboard which participated in the search. The Avocet's launch picked up fragments of the Clipper that were found floating in an oil slick in the water. They filled several small bags with debris which is seen being offloaded at Pago Pago from the Avocet following their search.

*Seaplane and launch of Avocet during search*

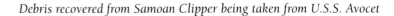

*Debris recovered from Samoan Clipper being taken from U.S.S. Avocet*

BULLETIN

1938.

WASHINGTON, JAN. 12 (UP).--JUAN T. TRIPPE, PRESIDENT OF

PAN-AMERICAN AIRWAYS, ANNOUNCED TODAY THAT HE WAS "DISTRESSED" TO

STATE THAT ON THE BASIS OF A RADIO MESSAGE RCEIVED FROM SAMOA "IT

HAS BEEN DEFINITELY ESTABLISHED THAT CAPT. EDWIN C. MUSICK AND SIX

OTHER MEMBERS OF HIS CREW MET DEATH TUESDAY MORNING AT APPROXIMATELY

8:30 O'CLOCK (SMOAN TIME) WHEN THE SAMOAN CLIPPER WAS DESTROYED

BY FIRE OF UNKNOWN ORIGIN."

JB341P

*Juan Trippe released a bulletin to the press*

# PAN AMERICAN AIRWAYS COMPANY

**PERSONAL**
for

1-13-1938
Copies of letter (handwritt
sent by Mr. John C. Leslie
to Mr. and Mrs. Stickrod (J.
at Los Angeles

COL. C. M. YOUNG
MR. C. T. RAMSEY
MR. P. MITCHELL
MR. ANDRE PRIESTER
MR. PHIL BERST

"My dear Mr. and Mrs. Stickrod -

There is nothing I can say which will repair
the loss we have all suffered in the death of your
son. I am sure you know that we who were associated with him in his work extend to you our
sincerest sympathy.

I think you will want to know how much of a
place he had made for himself during his relatively
short time with our Company. The position he held
was one of real importance, which is in itself
clear evidence of his proficiency. More than that,
he was notable always for irreproachable conduct
and enthusiastic loyalty to his organization.

Your loss, and ours, is a great one. I only
hope that we may all find comfort in the fact that
he died doing that which he most loved to do, and
in a project of manifest importance to our Nation.

Sincerely,

John C. Leslie.

San Francisco
January 14, 1938"

PAN AMERICAN AIRWAYS SYSTEM—GENERAL OFFICES—135 E. 42ND STREET, NEW YORK CITY

Particularly hard hit was the close knit Pan Am community at Honolulu. They intimately knew all of the crew members. John Stickrod, a young flight engineer from Honolulu, had made his first flight with Captain Musick in March of 1937 on the first survey flight to New Zealand. Because Stickrod was a mechanic, John C. Leslie, the chief engineer for the Pacific division, knew him best. Therefore he wrote a condolence letter to Stickrod's parents expressing the sympathy of the entire Pan Am staff in Honolulu on the loss of their young son.

*Pan American Airways*

Mrs. Alice Brooks:

We, the personnel of the Honolulu airport, extend to you our deepest sympathy for the loss of your husband and our friend "Jack", on the Samoan Clipper.

(January 11, 1938)

| | | |
|---|---|---|
| R. R. Banks | P. B. Berst | G. W. Bicknell |
| J. C. Bonamy | W. Breuer | G. B. Buhl |
| C. H. Carlyle | G. M. Conklin | A. J. Copeland |
| H. M. Danielson | L. E. Dickey | S. J. Feliz |
| H. O. Gentry | W. K. Harris | M. R. Hefty |
| W. W. Hobdy | M. C. Hons | J. A. Keanu |
| R. C. Lanik | D. E. Linebarger | H. M. Macomber |
| L. D. Paulson | H. K. Rothe | T. Sasaki |
| Y. Sato | E. V. Schoenberg | L. E. Shriver |
| S. K. Smith | H. J. Strickland | A. T. Taki |
| | G. W. Taylor | S. H. Warren |

Mr. J.A. Brooks was also a young flight mechanic from Honolulu aboard the Clipper. He was married with two young children. The Pan Am personnel in Honolulu sent a condolence card to his widow, Alice Brooks, expressing their sorrow at the loss of her husband, Jack.

*Jack Brooks with wife Alice and their children shortly before accident*

*Radio operator Findley on the left and Flight Engineer Stickrod were in the crew of last flight of the Samoan Clipper*

After the loss of the Samoan Clipper, the flags at Pan Am's office in New Zealand were flown at half mast.

The people of New Zealand and Samoa held a memorial service at sea at the site where the Clipper crashed.

*Pan Am's New Zealand office*

*A giant orchid wreath was prepared for the memorial service for the crew of the Samoan Clipper*

*Preparing to drop memorial wreath*

*On January 15, 1938 the M.V. Matua of the Union Steamship Company of New Zealand dropped the wreath at the crash site as part of a memorial service*

# UNION STEAM SHIP COMPANY OF NEW ZEALAND, LIMITED

M. V. "MATUA"

31st. January 1938

Dear Sir,

I am in receipt of your letter of 24th.inst. with regard to the service held aboard this vessel in memory of the crew of the "Samoan Clipper". The following is a copy of the entry in the ship's Log Book of the occasion: (15th.January 1938)

'3.52 pm.  Rang Stand By

3.56 pm.  Stop.

4.00 pm.  Smooth sea, mod.Nthly.Swell, Fine & Clear.

Memorial Service for crew of Pan-American flying boat "Samoan Clipper" held over spot where flying boat crashed and sank with all hands at 9am. 11th.Jan.1938

Lat.  14.08 S.
Long. 170.51 W.

4.12 pm.  Full Speed.'

Yours faithfully,

MASTER

*Letter from the Master of Matua confirming the memorial service for Samoan Clipper*

*Arrow - Nurse assisting Mrs. Musick*

In addition to the memorials that were held in New Zealand and at sea off Samoa in memory of Captain Musick and his crew, a memorial service attended by his wife and his fellow pilots was also held on January 24, 1938 in San Francisco in the rotunda at City Hall. Pictured immediately after the memorial service are Pan Am flight crew members outside City Hall. If you look closely you can see the cape of one of the two nurses and the doctor who assisted Mrs. Musick in coming down the steps following the emotional memorial for her husband and his fellow crew members.

WAIRARAPA DAILY NEWS.

# EXTRA

THURSDAY, JANUARY 13, 1938.

### SAMOAN CLIPPER LOST.

### WRECKAGE FOUND.

## NO NEWS OF CAPTAIN AND CREW.

United Press Association—By Electric
Telegraph—Copyright.
Extraordinary.
Received This Day, 8.40 a.m.
HONOLULU, This Day.

The Navy Department has received a report that s.s. Avocet has found wreckage and identified it as that of the Samoan Clipper.. There are no indications yet regarding the fate of the captain and crew.

### LATER.

### CREW ALL DEAD.

United Press Association—By Electric
Telegraph—Copyright.
Extraordinary.
Received This Day, 9.25 a.m.
WASHINGTON, Jan. 12.

The Pan-American Airways have announced that all the crew are dead.

As was the custom of the day, when news broke between editions of the newspaper, a printed handout would be prepared for posting in store windows. Illustrated above is the handbill from New Zealand following this tragedy.

# UNEXPLAINED EXPLOSION

## BLOWN TO FRAGMENTS

## WRECKAGE ON OCEAN

# NO TRACE OF ANY BODIES

Loss of the Samoan Clipper with her entire crew of seven was announced yesterday by Pan American Airways. The Clipper was making her first commercial flight from Pago Pago to Auckland on Wednesday, and is believed to have been blown to fragments by an explosion, the cause of which is not definitely known. Details of the dead are:—

**Captain Edwin C. Musick,** master of the Samoan Clipper, aged about 43 years, married, of San Francisco.

**Captain Cecil G. Sellers,** acting as first officer, married, with children, of Manila.

**Mr. P. S. Brunk,** second officer, of Honolulu.

**Mr. F. J. MacLean,** navigator, aged about 38 years, of Alameda.

**Mr. T. D. Findley,** radio operator, of Honolulu.

**Mr. J. W. Stickrod,** flight engineer, single, of Honolulu.

**Mr. J. A. Brooks,** flight mechanic, married, with two young sons, of Honolulu.

A Press Association cablegram from Pago Pago says:—

The U.S.S. Avocet has returned from her search for the Clipper, bringing bits of wreckage and burned clothing, the smallness of which is regarded as bearing out the belief that the Clipper was destroyed by a terrific explosion. No bodies were found, and it is believed they never will be found.

The chief boatswain, Mr. H. S. Bogan, said: "Bits of wood and paper covered the sea. Apparently they were fragments from the interior of the flying-boat, measuring from an inch or two square to six inches square. There were no large pieces. We found a pair of trousers containing a bent tie clasp, which it is believed belonged to the assistant engineering officer, Mr. J. A. Brooks. We also picked up a coat bearing the Pan American insignia, filled with holes, apparently due to the explosion, and a small section of the chart board, together with a book of navigation tables."

The **Auckland Herald** also reported the loss and carried this report on January 13, 1938.

315

*The crew stayed at the Sadie Thompson Inn, directly opposite Pan Am's pier and floating dock*

*Harbor Pago Pago, American Samoa January 1938*

Pictured is the dangerous harbor that required Captain Musick to discharge fuel before attempting the emergency landing. The approach to the harbor was in the direction marked by the arrow A over the 1,700 foot Mount Piva, also called the Rainmaker. The highest hill is the 2,150 Mount Matafao marked by the arrow C. The Clipper would be moored to a buoy and the crew taken off by ferry to the Pan Am dock marked by arrow B.

Dick Conley was the airport manager in American Samoa. Admiral Chamberlain, as his chief mechanic, was second in command. They took these remarkable photographs of the Samoan Clipper making its final approach to the beautiful but very restricted harbor at Pago Pago. The Clipper can be seen descending sharply after passing over Mount Piva as it approached the harbor.

The Samoan Clipper is just a few feet above the water, about to touch down safely for the last time.

After touching down at Pago Pago Harbor, the Clipper must quickly come to a stop. Otherwise, it would go up on the reef that protects the mouth of the harbor. The Samoan Clipper is seen taxiing slowly back to Pan Am's dock marked by the letter "B" in this photograph.

A member of the flight crew can be seen checking the aircraft after it is safely moored to the landing barge. Pan Am personnel, assisted by local Samoans, secured the craft.

*The Samoan Clipper is safely moored for the evening*

Admiral Chamberlain, the chief mechanic who took this picture, wrote in hand **Pago Pago, Jan 10, 1938.** **The last picture of the Samoan Clipper.** This photograph hung in Colonel Clarence Young's office at Alameda and later at Treasure Island, as a reminder of the sacrifice paid by Captain Musick and the crew of the Samoan Clipper in pioneering the air routes to New Zealand. It was a painful but respectful remembrance of their efforts. The picture was given to me by Colonel Young's son, Tim Young.

Although United States airmail had been authorized by the post office on this third flight to New Zealand, for some reason, at the last minute, Pan Am elected not to accept southbound mail. However, air express freight was carried. All mail, of course, was lost in the crash. But, some letters intended for the flight can be found. The cover illustrated arrived in Honolulu on January 3, 1938, in plenty of time to make the January 9 departure. However, once Pan Am decided not to accept southbound mail, a handwritten notation was placed on the envelope either by the post office or Pan Am and the mail was returned to the sender.

Collectors also sent mail to American Samoa by way of Apia, Western Samoa, to be placed on the southbound flight to New Zealand. It traveled by the vessel Pilot to Apia and then it was forwarded, again by ship, 50 miles to American Samoa to be placed on the Clipper for the American Samoa to New Zealand portion of the flight. When Pan Am refused to accept mail on this southbound flight, the envelopes were stamped at Pago Pago in purple with the words "service did not eventuate". What is surprising is that the mail was held in American Samoa from January 1938 until July 1940, almost two and a half years, before it was finally released by the post office for return to the sender. The reason for the long delay has never been explained, but it was undoubtedly due to the tragic loss of the Samoan Clipper and confusion as to what should be done with the mail.

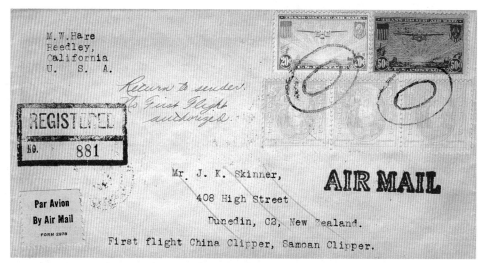

*Cover intended for flight*

*Mail refused by Pan Am at American Samoa*

*Posted January 10, 1938-Returned July 22, 1940*

Ed Musick's nephew, who lives in Connecticut, told me he had recently traveled to New Zealand and American Samoa to investigate the crash. While in American Samoa he met an elderly man, who as a young boy witnessed the explosion and participated in the failed rescue attempt. The old man's son is now the Minister of Samoan Affairs in American Samoa.

I used a cover from the December 1937 flight, typed in the explanation of what he had witnessed in 1938, and sent it to Sala Elisala to sign. His son assisted me in having his elderly father sign the envelope and then in signing the envelope himself as a witness.

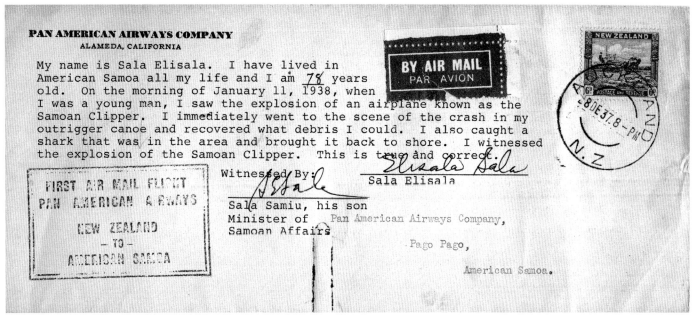

*Cover signed by witness to explosion of Samoan Clipper*

The shark that the young Samoan caught at the scene was the subject of the article in the New Zealand paper on January 16, 1938.

This cover signed by the surviving witness to the crash closes this tragic chapter in Pan Am's history when they tried to go too far, too fast, with too little equipment over too difficult a route to New Zealand. From the poorly conceived beginning, the frantic attempt to open service to New Zealand by December of 1937 was doomed.

After the crash, the Civil Aeronautics Authority closed the Pago Pago harbor to commercial flights. Pan Am withdrew from the South Pacific to await the delivery of the Boeing B-314s and the establishment of a new and far safer route by way of Canton Island and New Caledonia. The survey flights over the new route would not get under way until September of 1939 and because of a continuing shortage of clippers, regular airmail service to New Zealand would not be established until July of 1940.

## HUMAN REMAINS IN SHARK

### Found Near Where Samoan Clipper Crashed

(Received January 16, 6.30 p.m.)

Pango, Pango, January 15.

Human bones including a man's rib arm and thighbone and a man's shirt were taken from the stomach of a shark caught off the north shore of Tutulia Island, near where the Samoan Clipper met disaster.

The waters are infested with most ferocious, man-eating sharks.

*Article from **Auckland "Dominion"** January 16, 1938*

| Last Flight of Hawaii Clipper | July 23-29, 1938 | M-130 Hawaii Clipper | Terletzky/Walker |
|---|---|---|---|

### Flight Schedule

| | |
|---|---|
| San Francisco - Honolulu | July 23-24 |
| Honolulu - Midway | July 25 |
| Midway - Wake | July 26-27* |
| Wake - Guam | July 28 |
| Guam - Lost at Sea | July 29 |

*Dateline - Gain day outbound - Lose day inbound

# Honolulu Star-Bulletin EXTRA

MAIL SCHEDULE

Evening Bulletin, Est. 1882, No. 19179
Hawaiian Star, Vol. XLV, No. 14143

16 PAGES—HONOLULU, TERRITORY OF HAWAII, U. S. A., FRIDAY, JULY 29, 1938—16 PAGES

★ PRICE FIVE CENTS

# PLANES, SHIPS HUNT CLIPPER!

PACIFIC HOLDS FATE OF PAN AMERICAN PLANE

LAST MESSAGE FROM CLIPPER

**LAST HEARD FROM YESTERDAY** The giant transpacific Hawaii Clipper (above), with fifteen persons aboard, was reported missing early today on its 1,800-mile flight from Guam Island to Manila. The map shows the route of the plane and the point, 565 miles out of Manila, from which her last message was received late yesterday.—A. P.

# SUBMARINES JOIN SEARCH OVER PACIFIC

### Fear Felt for Safety of 15 Aboard Flying Boat, Missing Many Hours Between Guam Island and Manila

By Associated Press.

MANILA, Friday, July 29.—An intensive search by air, sea and underwater craft was ordered tonight for the Pan American Airways's giant Hawaii Clipper, which disappeared with fifteen men on a flight from Guam to Manila.

Within twelve hours after the last radio call was sent by the twenty-six-ton flying boat, the most intensive three-way search of the Pacific Ocean ever undertaken in the vicinity of the Philippines was ordered by Army and Navy commanders.

Seven planes, eight Navy ships, six submarines and an Army transport were thrown into the hunt for the $150,000 (Martin) flying boat, which literally vanished from the air midway on her 1,600-mile flight.

Admiral Harry E. Yarnell informed the Navy Department he had directed Rear Admiral George J. Myers at Manila to use all available ships in the search. Yarnell, commander of the Asiatic Fleet, is in China. Myers commands the 16th Naval District at Cavite, near Manila. The Navy has fourteen surface vessels and

(Continued on Page 2, Column 4.)

# MISSING ON CLIPPER IN PACIFIC

MAJ. HOWARD C. FRENCH

FIRST OFFICER M.A. WALKER

SECOND OFFICER G.M. DAVIS

THIRD OFFICER J.M. SAUCEDA

WAH SUN CHOY

DR. EARL B. McKINLEY

DR. FRED C. MEIER

STEWARD IVA PARKER

R. A. KENNEDY

an Am was still trying to recover from the loss of Captain Musick and the Samoan Clipper in January of 1938 when they were struck by another tragedy. On July 29, 1938, the Hawaii Clipper disappeared on a flight from Guam to Manila with six passengers and a crew of nine.

The *Guam Recorder* was a monthly magazine devoted to news of the island. In its issue for September of 1938 it gave a full report of the fateful flight of the Hawaii Clipper.

*September, 1938 -*

## The Guam Recorder
# Hawaii Clipper Search

The Hawaii Clipper, Captain Terletzky arrived Guam, 3:47 p.m. 28 July from Alameda carrying two bags of mail and one package air express and seven passengers. Francisco Limtiaco disembarked at Guam. The Hawaii Clipper left Guam at 6:00 a.m. July 29 on her regularly scheduled flight to Manila. Onboard were the following passengers and crew:

Choy Wah Sun, New York, (wealthy owner of the three Chinese restaurants)
Fred Meier, Washington, D.C. (Department of Agriculture)
Howard French, Portland, Oregon (Car dealer on vacation)
Edward Wyman, New York (formerly with Pan Am: export sales for Curtiss-Wright)
K.A. Kennedy, San Francisco, (Pan Am's Pacific Division Traffic Manager)
Earl McKinley, Washington D.C. (Department of Agriculture)

Captain Leo Terletzky
First Officer M. A. Walker
Engineer H. L. Cox
Second Officer G. M. Davis
Assistant Engineer B. Tatum
Third Officer J.M. Sauceda
Radio Officer W. McCarty
Fourth Officer J.W. Jewett
Steward I.H. Parker

At about 2:00 p.m. the last position was received by radio by the Guam station of Pan American Airways, after which communication ceased. It was believed at first that only the ship's radio equipment had gone out of commission. As a precaution, however, the Governor of Guam ordered the U.S.S. Penguin to stand by to search for the Clipper. At the time that radio contact was lost, the Hawaii Clipper was 565 miles from Manila and about 800 miles from Guam. The U.S.S. Meigs was the closest vessel to the Philippine Clipper's last reported position. They reached the last position about 10:00 p.m. on the evening of July 29. The search was fruitless until about 5:00 p.m. on July 30, when a large patch of oil about two ship lengths in diameter was found. A sample of the oil was obtained and one of the officers onboard the Meigs stated that the patch of oil in his opinion contained gasoline.

*U.S.S. Penguin*

*Captain Leo Terletzky*

*Eduardo Fernandez*

The last radio transmission with the Hawaii Clipper before its disappearance was made by Eduardo Fernandez of Manila. He was the radio operator stationed at Panay, the Pan Am radio facility in a village in the hills above Cavite, Pan Am's Philippine base.

# PAN AMERICAN AIR WAYS

Leo Terletzky          J. W. Jewett          William McCarty
M. A. Walker           H. L. Cox             Ivan H. Parker, Jr.
George M. Davis        Brooks T. Tatum       K. A. Kennedy
J. M. Sauceda

After days of intensive search we are regretfully forced to the assumption that the Hawaii Clipper, with all aboard, was lost at sea early in the afternoon of Thursday, July 28. The last report from the aircraft, received at 2:11 P. M. local time, gave her position as approximately 300 miles off the Philippine coast and 560 miles out of Manila. The aircraft was then proceeding on routine schedule, over the southern course used at this season, en route from Guam to Manila with six passengers, United States mails and air express.

Through the invaluable cooperation of the War and Navy departments, sixteen surface vessels and ten aircraft have made a systematic search covering an area of 160,000 square miles between the Clipper's last reported position and her scheduled destination, Manila.

Lacking recovery of any positive evidence it is impossible, at this time, to assign a cause for the Clipper's loss. Examination of all records indicates that nothing of an unusual character was apparent with regard either to the aircraft or to operating conditions, during the flight covered by the aircraft's reports. The radio log shows that the flight was being conducted in line with standard operating practice.

Captain Terletzky was one of Pan American's most distinguished flight commanders. He was one of the first to attain a Master's ranking in transoceanic air transport. Each of his flying officers was qualified by years of study and practice in the requirements of ocean transport operation.

An intensive investigation is being continued with the full cooperation of all interested government agencies.

*Pan Am newsletter - August 1938*

Soon after the loss, rumors arose that the Hawaii Clipper had been involved in a hijacking perpetrated by the Japanese. Passenger Choy Wah Sun, the businessman from New York, was carrying $3,000,000 in cash to give to the Chinese for their war efforts against the invading Japanese. It was speculated that the Japanese also wanted a Martin flying boat so that they could copy and manufacture it in preparation for their war efforts. The conspiracy theory involved two Japanese naval officers who allegedly snuck onto the Clipper at night while it was at Guam and hid in the luggage compartment that had direct access to the passenger compartment. During the hijacking attempt something went wrong and the plane was lost. A book published in 1980 entitled **"The China Clipper"** by Ronald W. Jackson sets out in detail this alleged hijacking. The hijacking theory was never substantiated by hard evidence, but it remains part of this sad chapter in Pan Am's history in the Pacific.

# Hope Fades As Clipper Hunt Goes On

## Sabotage Hinted By Aviation Expert

MANILA, P. I., Aug. 1.—(Monday)—(I.N.S.)—Although most of the searchers are convinced that the Hawaii Clipper with its fifteen occupants plunged to the bottom of the Pacific, ships and airplanes still zigzagged over the tropical seas today in the greatest ocean search in aviation history.

One aviation expert who asked that his name be kept secret, said:

"If the Hawaii Clipper blew up I am sure it was as a result of sabotage. Clipper flights are too carefully planned to permit accidents."

One ominous fact which some officials took to support the sabotage theory was the absolute radio silence—the lack of even a word shouted into the microphone after Captain Terletzky's last report of his position.

### PROBE PREPARATIONS

While the search went on, preparations for a rigorous investigation were being pushed. From Washington and from a Manila aviation expert came sinister hints the Clipper might have been deliberately sabotaged.

The sabotage theory hinged largely on reports that Choy Wah Sun, wealthy Chinese passenger aboard the Clipper, was carrying a large sum of money to the Chinese Nationalist government.

It recalled similar rumors of sabotage when the Samoa Clipper exploded in mid-Pacific last January.

Convinced that the film of oil and gasoline found on the ocean 525 miles south of here marks the grave of the huge Pan American flying boat, army and navy craft continued the hunt for possible wreckage which might provide a clue to the Clipper's fate.

### REMOTE CHANCE

And there was still a million-to-one chance that some or all of the fifteen men aboard might still be alive, clinging to floating debris — although ships and planes have already scanned and rescanned a vast area, under perfect weather and visibility conditions.

Navy destroyers and other craft were aiding the army transport Meigs in circling the area around the Clipper's last reported position, —the spot over the ocean from which Capt. Leo Terletzky dispatched his last routine report three days ago, before the Clipper's radio fell silent.

It was the transport Meigs which veered from its course and rushed to the spot as soon as word of the Clipper's distress was flashed over the air lanes, and it was the Meigs which discovered the ominous oil slick after a night and day of search.

*Honolulu Star-Bulletin - August 5, 1938*

*The Guam Recorder*

January 1938                                    10 Cents

It is very ironic that the cover of **The Guam Recorder** published just six months before the loss shows a Pan Am Clipper apparently heading into the sea. We know it was not intended as such, but it was an eerie predictor of what did happen to the Hawaii Clipper.

The year 1938 would be sadly remembered as the most tragic year in Pan Am's pioneering flights of the Pacific.

| First Flight to Treasure Island | January 24 - 31, 1939 | M-130 China Clipper | Nixon |
|---|---|---|---|

## Flight Schedule

| | |
|---|---|
| Hong Kong - Manila | January 24 |
| Manila - Guam | January 25 |
| Guam - Wake | January 27 |
| Wake - Midway | January 29-28* |
| Midway - Honolulu | January 29 |
| Honolulu - San Francisco | January 30-31 |

*Dateline - Gain day outbound - Lose day inbound

In January of 1939 Pan Am transferred their seaplane base from the old Navy station at Alameda across San Francisco Bay to Treasure Island. Treasure Island was a man-made island built in San Francisco Bay as the site of the 1939 Golden Gate International Exposition and as a future municipal airport for the San Francisco Bay area. The building project was undertaken by the U.S. Army Corps of Engineers at a cost of about $4,000,000, and it was funded by the Works Progress Administration, one of President Roosevelt's depression fighting programs. Pan Am would occupy a portion of Treasure Island as their seaplane base during and after the Exposition.

The 40 acre island was approximately a mile long and 2/3 of a mile wide. It was dredged up from the harbor floor to a height of about 13 feet above sea level. There was a main terminal and two hangars for maintenance and storage.

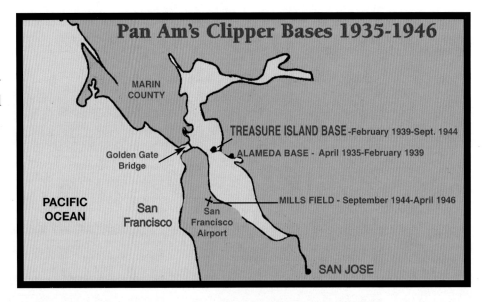

*Oakland Bay Bridge and Treasure Island in foreground and Golden Gate Bridge in background*

Treasure Island would remain Pan Am's home until September of 1944 when the Navy's need for the entire island forced Pan Am to move to Mills Field on San Francisco Bay, adjacent to the current San Francisco International Airport.

*Program for the Golden Gate Expo on Treasure Island-Pan Am's base January 1939*

*Left-*
*Postcard of Boeing Clipper high above new Treasure Island Base*
*Note - Clipper also at mooring*

*When the fair was over, Treasure Island was to become the city's airport*

The official brochure for the fair contained an artist's drawing of how Treasure Island was supposed to look after the fair closed.

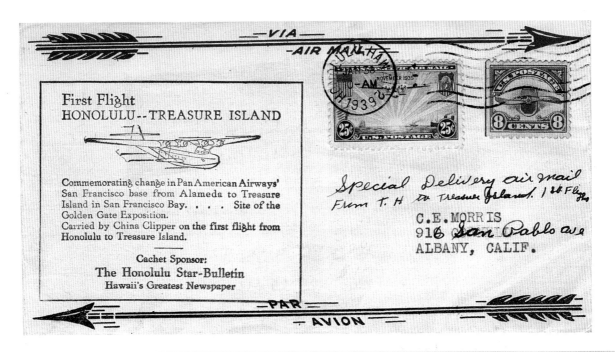

*Front*

*Reverse*

The China Clipper was inbound from Manila when Pan Am changed its facility to Treasure Island. The cover collectors were caught by surprise and the only souvenir covers that are seen are for the last inbound leg of the flight from Honolulu to San Francisco. The cachet prepared by the **Honolulu Star-Bulletin** is found in several colors. One of these covers shows Pan Am's received stamp with the word "Alameda" crossed off and the words "Treasure Island" handwritten below. This is the only evidence that it actually went to the new base.

| First Flight from Treasure Island | February 5 - 14, 1939 | M-130 China Clipper | Cluthe/Bierer |
|---|---|---|---|

### Flight Schedule

| | |
|---|---|
| San Francisco- Honolulu | February 5-6 |
| Honolulu - Midway | February 7 |
| Midway - Wake | February 8-9* |
| Wake - Guam | February 10 |
| Guam - Manila | February 13 |
| Manila - Macao | February 14 |
| Macao - Hong Kong | February 14 |

*Dateline - Gain day outbound

It was anticipated that the move from Alameda to Treasure Island would correspond with the delivery to Pan Am of the first of the Boeing B-314s. However, the first Boeing was not ready to make its maiden flight and the first flight from Treasure Island, under the command of Captain Cluthe, was in the Martin M-130 China Clipper.

Because cover collectors had anticipated the new aircraft would make the flight, a Boeing B-314 is depicted on the souvenir flight cover. Although the aircraft depicted is wrong, the wording on the cachet "China Clipper" is correct.

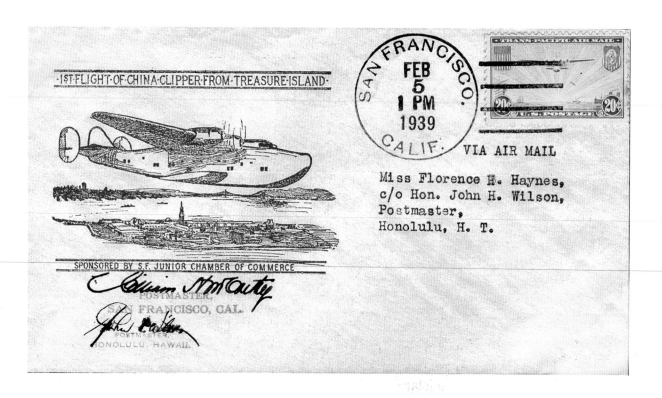

*Dedication flown cover from the new Treasure Island Base to Honolulu*

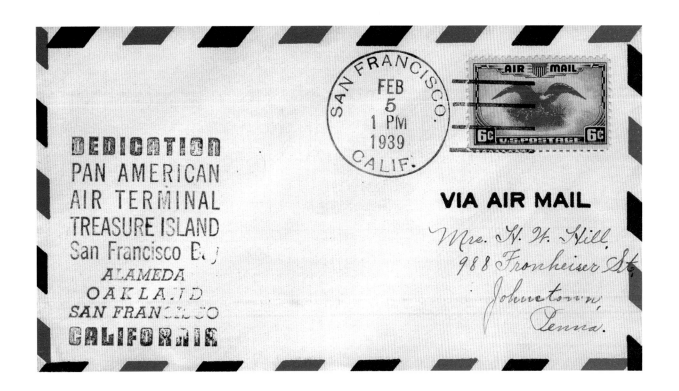

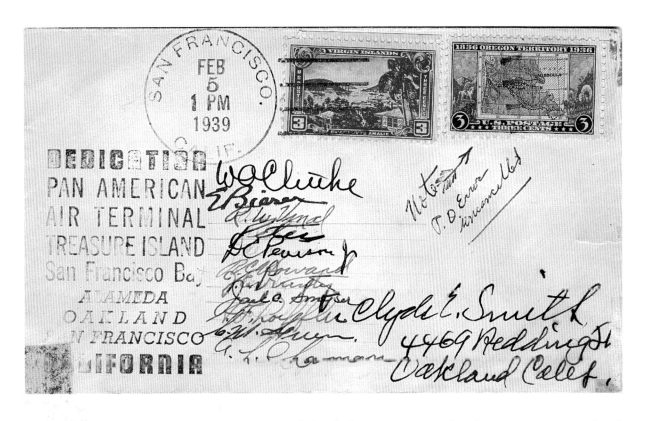

Captain Cluthe and his crew signed one of the dedication covers for the new Treasure Island base as a souvenir of the first flight departing from Pan Am's new base. The cover was not flown.

| First Flight California Clipper | Feb. 23 - March 14, 1939 | B-314 California Clipper | Cluthe/Bierer |
|---|---|---|---|

| Outbound Flight Schedule | | Inbound Flight Schedule | |
|---|---|---|---|
| San Francisco - Honolulu | February 23-24 | Hong Kong - Manila | March 4 |
| Honolulu - Midway | February 25 | Manila - Guam | March 7 |
| Midway - Wake | February 26-27* | Guam - Wake | March 8 |
| Wake - Guam | March 1 | Wake - Midway | March 12-11* |
| Guam - Manila | March 2 | Midway - Honolulu | March 12 |
| Manila - Macao | March 3 | Honolulu - San Francisco | March 13-14 |
| Macao - Hong Kong | March 3 | | |
| *Dateline - Gain day outbound - Lose day inbound | | | |

At last, by the end of January 1939, the long awaited first Boeing B-314 was ready for delivery to Pan Am. Before its christening, it was referred to as "Number 18". On January 27, 1939 it left Boeing's Seattle plant on Lake Washington for San Francisco. However, it made a planned stop at Astoria, Oregon, located on the Columbia River between Washington and Oregon, where Boeing formally made delivery to Pan Am on the Oregon side of the river in order to avoid the very high Washington state sales tax.

*NC18602 - Number 18 landing at Honolulu*

*First flight Boeing B-314 - California Clipper*

After formal delivery in Oregon, the Boeing Clipper continued its flight and on January 28, under the command of Captain Tilton, they arrived at San Francisco. Captain Tilton had become the senior pilot in the Pacific after the loss of Captain Musick. He was scheduled to be the commander of the first Transpacific flight of the Boeing Clipper, but he had an attack of appendicitis and had to turn the honor of making the inaugural flight over to Captain William A. Cluthe, the second ranking pilot for Pan Am in the Pacific.

After completing 16 trial runs, Boeing #18 was ready to make its inaugural flight. This first flight of what would later be christened the California Clipper was a celebration, not only for Pan Am, but also for Boeing. A crew of 12 under the command of Captain Cluthe and first officer Bierer departed San Francisco on February 23 along with 12 passengers representing Pan American Airways, the Boeing Company, Wright Aeronautical Company and the U.S. Government. Both Phil Berst and Almon Gray, whose families have shared with me their scrapbooks and flight covers were among the Pan Am employees who accompanied the crew on this epic flight.

The Boeing Clipper departed for Honolulu at 3:00 p.m. on February 23 and the cargo holds were well stocked with express packages and mail, much of it souvenir mail sent by collectors, who were also excited about the delivery of the super flying boat to Pan Am.

Note the wavy flag painted on the bow of the Boeing 314. This is the first time that the prominent wavy flag appeared on a Pan Am Clipper. Pan Am said it was for extra protection in foreign waters. This was obviously in response to the growing tensions that were building in the Pacific.

*Captain Cluthe has all the flower leis, but second officer Pearson is getting all the attention*

Upon arrival in Honolulu the crew received a traditional Hawaiian welcome. Captain Cluthe was smothered by a half dozen flower leis by the Hawaiian girl standing to his immediate right, but she appears to be far more interested in second officer Pearson standing on her right.

This large group photograph was taken shortly after arrival of the new Boeing in Honolulu. Standing left to right is: Al Loeffler, second engineer; Jim Prunty, first engineer; F.H. Stephen, Civil Aeronautics Authority; (C.A.A.) Lon Charman, second radio officer; B.E. Michael, third officer; L. R. Merrill, second steward; Harry La Porte, first steward; D.C. Pearson, second officer; Captain W.A. Cluthe; Jack Smyser, first radio officer; E. Bierer, first officer. Kneeling left to right is: Bill Miller, C.A.A.; Wellwood E. Beall,

*Father of the Boeing Clipper - Wellwood E. Beall*

Boeing Corporation (designer of the Boeing 314); F.J. Weigand, Curtiss-Wright Company; C.T. Ramsey, Pan Am; Andre A. Priester, chief engineer Pan Am; Joe Boudwin, C.A.A.; Herbert Ponceti, Boeing Company; John H. Caffery, Curtiss-Wright; G. Lossow, C.A.A.; Al Gray, assistant communications superintendent for Pan Am's Pacific Division. Absent from the photograph are crew members Sam Peters, navigator, Chick Weesner, third engineer and Phil Berst, Pacific maintenance superintendent who joined the flight in Honolulu.

Wellwood E. Beall, kneeling second from left, convinced Boeing to pursue the Pan Am bid. In fact, he convinced Pan Am to extend the period for bids for Boeing even though the deadline had passed. Because of his success on this project, he was later named chief engineer for Boeing.

After a night of festivities in Honolulu they departed the next morning on their westward journey.

# PAN AMERICAN AIRWAYS, INC.

GENERAL OFFICES   CHRYSLER BUILDING   NEW YORK CITY

*Assistant communications superintendent for the Pacific Division Almon Gray with his boss André A. Priester, chief engineer for Pan Am in Honolulu on first flight of Boeing Clipper*

Yours very truly,

PAN AMERICAN AIRWAYS, INC.

A. A. Priester,
Chief Engineer.

*The Boeing at Cavite, Philippines, on March 2, 1939*

On March 2 they arrived at Cavite, Pan Am's base near Manila. At Cavite a local photo studio took a picture of Boeing No. 18 being serviced and fueled in the harbor. The studio immediately processed the film and had the picture made into postcards to present to the officers and crew before their departure. Almon Gray had one of his souvenir postcards of the Boeing B-314 at Cavite stamped at Wake and Midway on the return flight to San Francisco.

*Postcard of Boeing at anchor at Cavite, Philippines*

It is not surprising that both Pan Am and Boeing wanted to prepare souvenir flight covers to commemorate the very successful inauguration of Boeing B-314's first flight in the Pacific. The colorful envelopes are not difficult for collectors to find. However, the souvenir envelope that Phil Berst prepared personally for his wife contained a short note and the envelope is signed by both the captain and first officer. This is the only cover I have seen with this style of cachet that is signed by any of the crew.

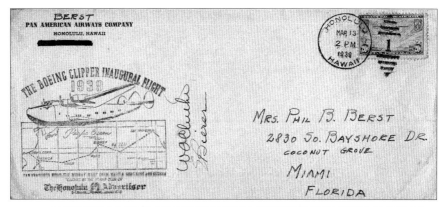

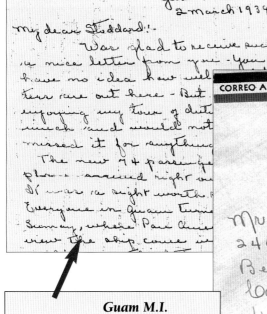

**Guam M.I.**
**8 March 1939**
**The new 74 passenger Boeing plane arrived right on schedule. It was a sight worth seeing - Everyone in Guam turned out to Sumay, where Pan Am is to view the ship come in. Am sending you this letter on their return trip to be stamped with the Guam seal and first flight of Boeing B-314.**

*Modified cachet used on this cover - with letter enclosed*

*Cachet created for National Airmail Week May 15 - 21, 1938*

*Left - portion of letter in first flight envelope*

To promote the use of airmail, President Roosevelt declared the week of May 15, 1938 as National Air Mail Week. To commemorate the occasion, the postmaster on Guam, James Underwood, designed a special cachet to be used on all airmail sent from Guam during National Air Mail Week. This cachet for National Air Mail Week was modified by Postmaster Underwood and used again to commemorate the first flight of the Boeing Clipper to Guam in March of 1939. This cachet, modified for the first flight of the Boeing Clipper, was used by the postmaster on mail flown from Guam on March 2 and March 8 of 1939.

Most of the souvenir mail sent from Manila for this first flight of the Boeing B-314 also contained a purple diamond shaped cachet that was designed and applied in Manila by the Philippine Department of Posts.

*Guam cachet applied by Pan Am base manager in Guam*

*Philippine Department of Posts cachet*

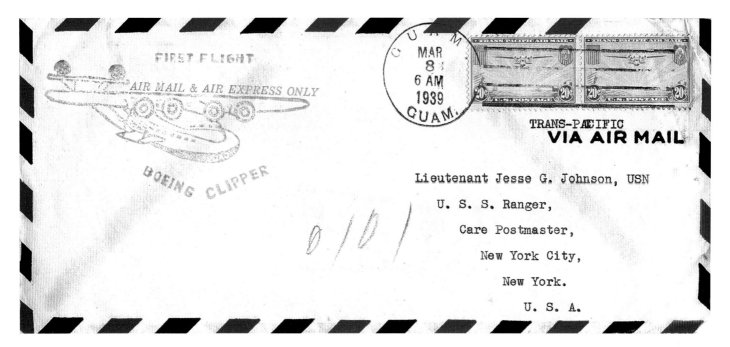

*Only 50 covers with this cachet from Guam were prepared*

The envelope posted on Guam, addressed to Lt. Jesse Johnson, illustrates the cachet that was prepared in Guam by a clerk working for the Navy. In a letter to Johnson contained inside the envelope he states that he applied this cachet of the Boeing Clipper to 50 letters that were mailed from Guam on the return flight of the Boeing Clipper. It is back stamped March 20, 1939, on the U.S.S. Ranger at Guantanamo Bay, Cuba where Lt. Johnson was undoubtedly based in early 1939. Lt. Johnson was such an avid collector and creator of first flight covers in the Pacific, that his absence from the Pacific may account for the fact that many of the first flights and historic flights after he left were not being commemorated with flight covers as they were when he was still stationed with the Navy in Honolulu.

*Cachet prepared by Boeing Corporation*

*Cachet prepared by **Honolulu Advertiser***

# CHRISTENING A CLIPPER
## 'Happy Landing to You!'

**MRS. SYDNEY WALTON**
"Happy landing," says Mrs. Sydney Walton (left) to Mrs. Clarence Young at Tuesday's christening of the Califor-

**MRS. CLARENCE YOUNG**
nia Clipper by Mrs. Wallace Alexander of Piedmont at the Treasure Island base of Pan-American Airways.

## WHEN CALIFORNIA CLIPPER WAS CHRISTENED

When Col. Clarence M. Young, manager of Pan American Airways' Pacific division, and Mrs. Young (left), looking on; Mrs. Wallace M. Alexander (center) christened the new 42-ton California Clipper at the Exposition yesterday. It was an orthodox "champagne ceremony." But at Honolulu, the rites were "dry" when the Honolulu Clipper was named. The captain and crew drank coconut milk in lieu of the bottle-smashing ceremony.
—Tribune photo.

# Clipper California Takes Wings

One of Pan American's big new flying boats yesterday officially became the California Clipper.

In colorful ceremonies conducted at the Pan American base on Treasure Island, Mrs. Wallace M. Alexander, wife of one of the directors of Pan American Airways, christened the 74-passenger ship, breaking a bottle of champagne across the blunt nose of the plane.

Flags fluttered briskly. The Exposition band played the "Star-Spangled Banner." And thousands stood on tiptoes as the name California was given wings.

Speakers during the half-hour ceremony, broadcast on a Nation wide radio hookup, included Leland Cutler, president of the Exposition Postmaster William H. McCarthy, Federal Exposition Commissioner George Creel, Mayor Rossi, Marshall Dill, president of the Chamber of Commerce, and Arthur J. Dolan Jr., president of the Junior Chamber of Commerce. Colonel Clarence M. Young, manager of the Pacific division of Pan American Airways, presided.

"As the clippers shuttle back and forth, week in and week out, they have brought the peoples of the West and the Orient closer, made for better relations and carried America's offers of trade and trade opportunities."

The youth of San Fancisco was represented by Dolan, who presented a bronze plaque to Colonel Young commemorating the first passenger flight of the California Clipper.

At conclusion of the ceremonies guests were permitted to inspect the new flying boat, whose sister ship, the Honolulu Clipper, will be christened today in Hawaii.

*Mrs. Wallace M. Alexander, center, christened the California Clipper - She is pictured with Mrs. Lois Moran Young and Colonel Clarence Young*

CALIFORNIA CLIPPER
CHRISTENING AT
TREASURE ISLAND, SAN FRANCISCO

*The California Clipper was christened two months after delivery*

SPONSORED BY S.F. JUNIOR CHAMBER OF COMMERCE

James Horgan
789 Morse St
San Francisco, Cal.

*Mrs. Wallace M.Alexander, wife of one of the Pan American's directors, christens "California Clipper" at the Treasure Island base with a bottle of California champagne*

## PROGRAM

CHRISTENING CEREMONIES
CALIFORNIA CLIPPER

Tuesday, April 25th, at 3 p. m. 1939
Treasure Island
San Francisco, Calif.

PAN AMERICAN AIRWAYS SYSTEM

The maiden flight of Boeing B-314 Number 18, was a complete success. It was a triumph for Pan Am, for Boeing and for everyone associated with the development of the revolutionary aircraft.

The Clipper was officially christened the California Clipper two months later after its flight on April 25, 1939.

With the arrival of the Boeing B-314 in the Pacific, the era of speed and luxury in air travel had arrived.

341

| First Flight of Honolulu Clipper | March 15 - April 5, 1939 | B-314 Honolulu Clipper | McGlohn |
|---|---|---|---|

| Outbound Flight Schedule | | Inbound Flight Schedule | |
|---|---|---|---|
| San Francisco - Honolulu | March 15-16 | Hong Kong - Manila | March. 28 |
| Honolulu - Midway | March 19 | Manila - Guam | April 1 |
| Midway - Wake | March 20-21* | Guam - Wake | April 2 |
| Wake - Guam | March 24 | Wake - Midway | April 3-2* |
| Guam - Manila | March 26 | Midway - Honolulu | April 3 |
| Manila - Macao | March 27 | Honolulu - San Francisco | April 4-5 |
| Macao- Hong Kong | March 27 | | |
| *Dateline - Gain day outbound - Lose day inbound | | | |

P an Am planned for the Atlantic Clipper in Baltimore, the California Clipper in San Francisco and the Honolulu Clipper in Hawaii to all be christened on the same day, Tuesday, April 25, 1939. Both the Atlantic Clipper and the California Clipper were christened as planned, but head winds delayed the Honolulu Clipper on its outbound flight from San Francisco and it arrived too late in the evening for the christening ceremonies.

*Christening Honolulu Clipper - April 26, 1939*

Therefore, to Pan Am's disappointment, the christening of the Honolulu Clipper had to be postponed until Wednesday, April 26, 1939 at Pan Am's Pearl City Base at Pearl Harbor. The ceremonies were carried out in the best Hawaiian tradition, with much coconut milk and many traditional Hawaiian costumes.

Surprisingly, no official or unofficial cachets were prepared as souvenirs commemorating the christening of the Honolulu Clipper.

*Helen Poindexter, daughter of Hawaii's governor assisted with christening*

*The crew receives flower leis*

| 1st Survey San Francisco to New Zealand | August 22 - Sept. 6, 1939 | B-314 California Clipper | Tilton/Cluthe Cluthe/Fleming** |
|---|---|---|---|

### Outbound Flight Schedule
| | |
|---|---|
| San Francisco - Honolulu | Aug. 22-23 |
| Honolulu - Canton Island | Aug. 24 |
| Canton Island - Noumea | Aug. 27-28* |
| Noumea - Auckland | Aug. 30 |

### Inbound Flight Schedule
| | |
|---|---|
| Auckland - Noumea | Sept. 2 |
| Noumea - Canton Island | Sept. 3-2* |
| Canton Island - Honolulu | Sept. 4 |
| Honolulu - San Francisco | Sept. 5-6** |

*Dateline - (Between Canton & Noumea) Gain day outbound - Lose day inbound
**Captain Cluthe/1st officer Fleming in command, Honolulu to San Francisco

After the loss of the Samoan Clipper the dangerous route through Kingman Reef and American Samoa was abandoned. Pan Am immediately began negotiating with the British for a suitable island with a lagoon between Honolulu and New Zealand to use for an overnight stopover for the Clippers. In May of 1938 Frank McKenzie, Pan Am's engineer in charge of building the bases on Wake and Midway in 1935, sailed aboard the U.S.S. Ontario to Canton Island and surveyed the lagoon as a possible seaplane base. Based upon his very favorable reports, Pan Am selected Canton Island as its mid-Pacific base.

*Aerial view Canton Island 1938*

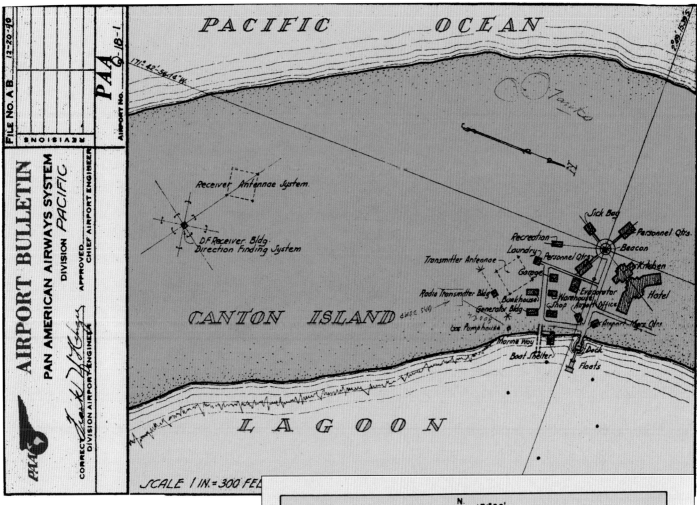

AIRPORT BULLETIN
PAN AMERICAN AIRWAYS SYSTEM
DIVISION PACIFIC

Map of Canton Island

With the worsening conditions in Europe, Great Britain needed the United States as an ally, so they quickly agreed to allow the United States to use uninhabited Canton Island jointly with them, as a Pacific flight stopover. France, for the same reason, similarly agreed to the use of the harbor at Noumea, in their colony of New Caledonia as a second stop. Karl Lueder, who had been the station manager at Midway during the building of the base in 1935, was sent to Canton Island in May of 1939 to again oversee the building of a seaplane base on a remote Pacific island.

The old Alaskan freighter, the North Haven, which had previously been chartered for the building of the Wake and Midway bases in 1935 and chartered again for the building of the hotels in 1936, was chartered a third time for the Canton Island construction project. The North Haven arrived at Canton Island on May 16, 1939 with the Pan Am staff and construction crew and with all the materials for building a base on this desert island.

When they arrived, they were greeted by Hawaiian high school boys who had been placed on the island by the United States Coast Guard and the Department of Interior to fly the flag and strengthen the U.S. claim to this uninhabited island. As before, when he had built bases at Wake and Midway, McKenzie first built a tent city on shore at Canton Island and the supplies were off loaded. The construction pace was frantic. By mid-August most of the work was completed.

*"Welcome to Blackville" - settlement of Hawaiian school boys - Three British colonists also had a settlement nearby*

*Construction begins
May 1939*

*Village takes shape
June 1939*

*June 1939*

*July 1939*

*Pier is ready
Canton Island - July 1939*

## PAN AMERICAN AIRWAYS' CANTON ISLAND BASE

As an intermediate stop for air mail, passenger and express service to New Zealand, Pan American Airways selected Canton Island in the Phoenix Group, an island held jointly by the United States and Great Britain. Canton was a barren coral atoll, with no human inhabitants and practically no vegetation, but it afforded a convenient location and a central lagoon furnishing an excellent harbor for the Clippers. To make an ocean air base, Pan American Airways established a community on the island—built quarters, installed a water supply system, electric power system, built a dock for disembarkation and a hotel for use of passengers in transit. Every item of materials and supplies had to go by ship from the United States, and the little village on Canton was constructed from the sand up. The illustration shows an early phase of construction.

*Card often found in envelope for first flight from Canton Island*

In late 1938, after Canton had been selected as the future mid-Pacific base, a survey crew returned to the island by boat to build a memorial lighthouse dedicated to Captain Musick and the crew of the Samoan Clipper who perished in the January l938 crash. The bronze plaque commemorating the crew had not yet been placed when these l938 photos were taken.

*Musick Lighthouse - 1938*

*Dedication of Musick Lighthouse - 1938*

In 1995, I sent a role of film to Canton Island and asked that the lighthouse be photographed. A passing yachtsman took pictures of the lighthouse and sent the film to me for developing. The lighthouse, in poor repair, is still standing. The bronze plaque, although slightly broken, still commemorates the tragic loss.

*Musick Lighthouse on Canton 1995*

*Bronze plaque at Musick Lighthouse dedicated to Samoan Clipper as it appears today*

DEDICATED BY THE UNITED STATES
DEPARTMENT OF THE INTERIOR
TO THE CREW OF
PAN AMERICAN AIRWAYS

"SAMOAN CLIPPER"

LOST AT SEA ON JANUARY 11, 1938
WHILE SURVEYING FIRST SOUTH
PACIFIC AERIAL TRADE ROUTE

CAPTAIN E. C. MUSICK
C. G. SELLERS                P. S. BRUNK, JR.
F. J. MacLEAN               S. W. STICKROD
J. A. BROOKS               T. J. FINDLEY

Just before boarding the California Clipper at Treasure Island to take-off for the survey flight to New Zealand, the crew posed for this photograph, in which there are, left to right in the front row: Division Chief Pilot J.H. Tilton, commanding the survey flight: Captain William A. Cluthe, First Officer: J.L. Fleming, Second Officer: V.A. Wright, Third Officer: B.E. Michael, Fourth Officer. Rear row, left to right: J.E. Prunty, First Engineering Officer: J.W. Zeigler, Asst. Engineering Officer: J.C. Smyser, Radio Officer: A.L. Charman, Second Radio Officer: T. Moffatt, Steward, and H.R. LaPorte, Flight Service Supervisor (in charge of stewards, serving as a steward for this flight).

The California Clipper, under the command of pilot John Tilton, departed Treasure Island on Tuesday, August 22, 1939. Ralph Young, the brother of Pacific division manager, Clarence Young, was on Canton Island as part of the crew building the new base. Young kept a log while on Canton Island from May of 1939 to February of 1940. Let's take a look at his log for the day when the Clipper arrived for the first time.

**Thursday, August 24:** The Clipper left Honolulu this morning at 4:20. The distance from here, 1,661 miles. By mid-afternoon all eyes were searching the northern horizon for the plane, which was first sighted at 4:35 p.m. She grew rapidly in size and soon was over the island. After several sweepings of the runway lengthwise and

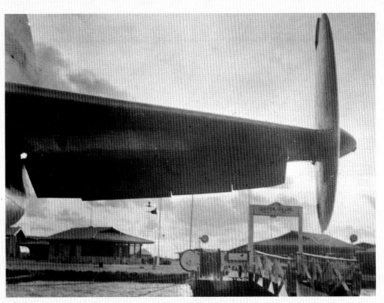

*Clipper at Canton - August 1939*

cross for surface survey, she took position and nosed eastward, into the wind, and entered the groove for a landing, either satisfied that all was well or that, regardless, there was no alternative. She troughed the cushioning lagoon water at 4:50 nestling safely. She had 20 aboard, including a crew of 11. Also mail and supplies. Captain Tilton reported an excellent trip. Time 12 hours 15 minutes - gas consumption -- gallon and a half per mile.

*Canton base - August 25, 1939*

**Saturday, August 26:** The plane didn't get away this morning owing to weather south in the line of travel and a faulty motor, either of which would have in itself been sufficient for postponement. Ball game in the p.m. between the flight crews and the Canton Flying Fish, won by the Flying Fish. To bed early as there is to be a 4 AM take off in the morning.

**Sunday, August 27:** The Clipper scheduled to take off at 5 AM this morning was delayed pending correction for an air condition, which corrected itself at sunrise. At 5:48 the plane lifted from the water after a run of approximately 3,650 feet. The preflight report from here to Treasure Island that the runway was clear and spacious enough to accommodate the plane has been proven justified. The Wright brothers really started something.

Noumea, New Caledonia, 1,700 miles southwest of Canton Island, was the Clipper's next stop on the flight to New Zealand. Thirteen hours after departing Canton and after crossing the dateline and picking up a day, the California Clipper arrived on August 28, 1939 at the new Pan Am base on an island in the harbor at Isle Nou, Noumea, New Caledonia.

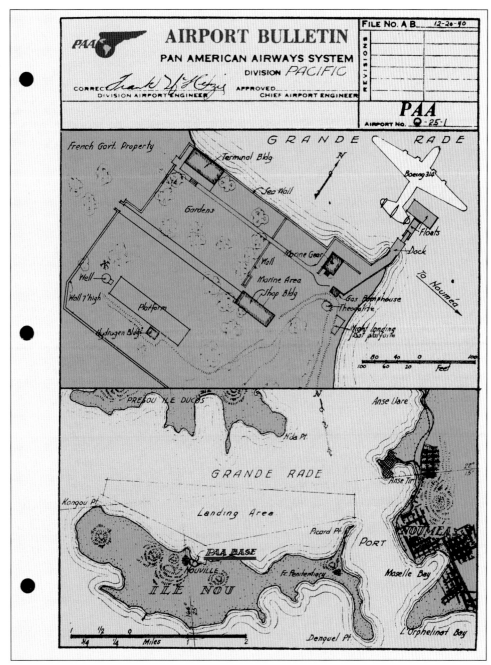

FILE No. A B \_\_\_\_ 12-20-40

AIRPORT BULLETIN
PAN AMERICAN AIRWAYS SYSTEM
DIVISION *PACIFIC*

REVISIONS

CORRECT *Frank H. Kitzi*
DIVISION AIRPORT ENGINEER

APPROVED \_\_\_\_
CHIEF AIRPORT ENGINEER

*PAA*
AIRPORT No. *Q-25-1*

French Govt. Property

GRANDE RADE

N

Boeing 314

Terminal Bldg

Sea Wall

Gardens

Floats

Dock

Marine Gear

To Noumea

Well

Mall

Marine Area

Wall 7' high

Shop Bldg

Gas Pumphouse

Theodolite

Platform

Night Landing Test Platform

Hydrogen Bldg

80 40 0 100
100 60 20 Feet

PRESQU'ILE DUCOS

N

Anse Uare

N'da Pt.

GRANDE RADE

Anse Tir

22° 15'

Kongou Pt.

Landing Area

NOUMEA

Picard Pt.

PAA BASE

PORT

NOUVILLE

ILE NOU

Fr. Penitentiary

Moselle Bay

Denquel Pt.

L'Orphelinat Bay

1 ½ 0
¾ ¼ Miles 1 2

*California Clipper at moorings Noumea, New Caledonia - September 1939*

353

*Looking west at mooring facilities New Caledonia - September 1939*

*View from airport manager's office looking east*

*Pan Am office at Noumea, New Caledonia before repair - May 1939*

*Pan Am offices after repair September 1939*

*Shop building*

In Noumea, Pan Am had converted a deserted prison on an island in the harbor into its new base.

*View of Noumea and Isle Nou - Cross indicates Pan Am base on Isle Nou. Arrow indicates landing area*

The photograph from the hill overlooking Noumea shows the location of the Pan Am base on Isle Nou, and the arrow indicates the landing path for the Clippers.

*General view Noumea and Island of Isle Nou, looking SW, showing shipping entrance to harbor*

After spending two days at a guesthouse in town, the passengers and crew flew on to a tremendous welcome in New Zealand. Just as Juan Trippe had used Macao to convince Hong Kong to open their harbor to Pan Am flights, he was counting on the flights to New Zealand to force Australia into permitting landing rights in Australia as well. He was pleased the New Zealanders gave the California Clipper such a warm welcome.

When Captain Musick flew to New Zealand on the first mail flight in December of 1937, he was met in Auckland Harbor by an Imperial Airways seaplane under the command of Captain J. W. Burgess. On this first flight of the Boeing B-314 to New Zealand, history repeated itself. Once

*Imperial Airways Aotearoa and California Clipper at Auckland - August 30, 1939*

again, Imperial Airways Captain J.W. Burgess made sure that a British Imperial Airways seaplane was in the harbor to greet Captain Tilton and the Pan Am crew upon their arrival in New Zealand in August of 1939.

Captain Burgess had arrived two days before the California Clipper on the flying boat Aotearoa on a survey flight from England by way of Sydney, Australia. It was more than a coincidence that every time Pan Am made a significant first flight to New Zealand, the British tried to be there to show that the competition was not over in the race to establish commercial flights to this part of the Pacific. Although Britain needed allies, their competitive spirit would not allow them to stand by idly without at least a challenge to the Americans' expansion of commercial routes into these British Commonwealth countries.

Due to the very short notice that preceded the California Clipper's flight to New Zealand, collectors were almost precluded from sending any souvenir mail on the southbound survey flight. Once again, postal contracts had not yet been signed and crew members were discouraged from carrying any souvenir mail with them on the survey flight.

*Captain J. Burgess (left) Commander of Aotearoa greets Captain J.H. Tilton, commander of the California Clipper - August 30, 1939 at Auckland*

*Cancel on arrival*

One letter has been found, however, that did make it from San Francisco to Honolulu as a souvenir envelope on the first leg of the survey flight to New Zealand and it is shown above.

*Rare covers from first flight to New Zealand over new route - 1939*

C.A. McDonald, owner of the Waikiki Drug Company, was a flight cover collector who was well known to the Pan Am flight crews. He was able to use his connections with the crew to get two souvenir envelopes carried aboard the southbound flight from Honolulu, addressed to Noumea, New Caledonia and two more envelopes addressed to New Zealand. These two rare southbound survey flight covers are illustrated.

When the California Clipper departed Auckland on September 2, 1939 on the return flight to Canton Island, Canton's station manager, Karl Lueder, was ready. As he had done on Midway Island for the first survey flight back in June of 1935 to Midway, he again hand carved out of a wooden block a cachet showing an outline of the island and the words "First Flight", for souvenir covers to commemorate the first northbound flight from Canton Island. Cachets were applied September 3 upon the Clipper's arrival at Canton Island, and the envelopes were carried back on the California Clipper and canceled September 5 upon their arrival in Honolulu.

*Gift for President Roosevelt from Pan Am*

Once again, President Roosevelt received a gift from Pan Am of a flight cover commemorating another important Pacific flight.

Also illustrated is a cover addressed to Frank Kenner, the commander of the Coast Guard Cutter Taney, that had brought Karl Lueder to Canton Island in May of 1939. Frank Kenner, as part of his Coast Guard duties, was in charge of taking water and supplies to the various Pacific islands where Hawaiian school boys had been placed to stake our government's claim to these remote and uninhabited islands that were now important to Pacific aviation. The plan to use the Coast Guard and the Hawaiian high school boys in this way is another example of the cooperation of the United States with Pan Am's expansion in the Pacific.

The Pan Am crew stayed at the St. Francis Hotel when they were in San Francisco and the cover illustrated was carried by the crew to John McDonald, the manager at the St. Francis. This envelope has the rarely seen purple cachet and was given to me as a gift by his son.

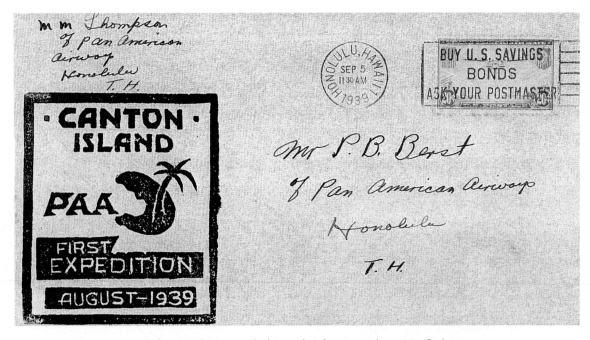

*Only cover known with this cachet for September 1939 flight*

The black cachet with the large palm tree commemorates the first expedition to Canton Island. It has only been seen on one souvenir cover from this August survey flight. Phil Berst, the Pacific division superintendent of maintenance was sent the cover by Mr. Thompson, who was Pan Am's chief mechanic on Canton. This cachet with the palm tree remained on Canton Island after this survey flight. It was used again on a very few covers in July of 1940 when the first regular scheduled mail took place. However, on all later occasions when it was used, it appears in red rather than black.

The new route through Canton Island and Noumea proved to be quite satisfactory. Not only were the Pacific stopovers safer, but the larger Boeing B-314 had a greater payload capacity and, therefore, was more suitable for making the flights than were the previous aircraft. However, with the opening of Atlantic service there were not enough Boeing B-314s to fly both the Atlantic and Pacific routes and the Atlantic service had the highest priority in 1939. Therefore, regularly scheduled flights to New Zealand would have to wait until July of 1940.

| 2nd Proving Flight San Francisco to New Zealand | November 19 - 30, 1939 | B-314 Honolulu Clipper | Cluthe/McGlohn |
|---|---|---|---|

| Outbound Flight Schedule | | Inbound Flight Schedule | |
|---|---|---|---|
| San Francisco. - Honolulu | Nov. 18-19 | Auckland - Noumea | Nov. 25 |
| Honolulu - Canton Island | Nov. 20 | Noumea - Canton Island | Nov. 27-26* |
| Canton Island - Noumea | Nov. 21-22* | Canton Island - Honolulu | Nov. 28 |
| Noumea - Auckland | Nov. 23 | Honolulu - San Francisco | Nov. 29-30 |

*Dateline - Gain day outbound - Lose day inbound

The second survey flight over the new route was flown by the Honolulu Clipper. It was called a "proving flight" by Pan Am and it was given little publicity by the company. Apparently no souvenir mail was carried. The flight went successfully but because of a continuing shortage of Boeing Clippers, scheduled service was not inaugurated to New Zealand until July of 1940.

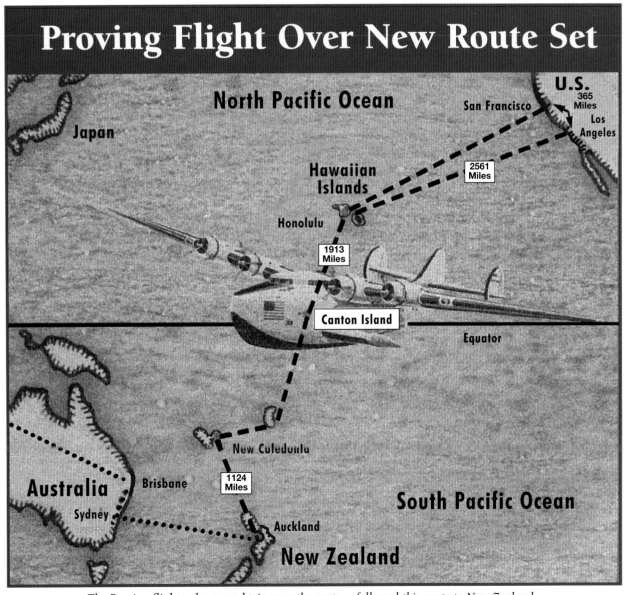

*The Proving flight - the second trip over the route - followed this route to New Zealand*

| 3rd Survey Flight Honolulu to Canton Island | February 16-17, 1940 | B-314 California Clipper | K. Beer |
|---|---|---|---|

| Outbound Flight Schedule | | Inbound Flight Schedule | |
|---|---|---|---|
| Honolulu - Canton Island | February 16 | Canton Island - Honolulu | February 17 |

Following the second survey flight over the new route to New Zealand in November of 1939, Pan Am anticipated starting the regular scheduled service before the end of the year. However, a shortage of aircraft and the Civil Aeronautics Administration's delay in granting final approval of the new route to New Zealand continued to plague the Pacific Division. Therefore, in spite of Pan Am's best intentions, scheduled mail service had to be indefinitely postponed.

Meanwhile, back on Canton Island, the workers who had arrived in May of 1939 to build the base were beginning to get restless to return home.

Ralph Young, the brother of Pacific Division Manager Clarence Young, had arrived at Canton onboard the North Haven on May 16, 1939. He expressed his growing

# Clipper Takes Off For Canton Island

On the first survey flight to Canton island in more than three months, the California Clipper took off at 5:55 this morning from Pearl Harbor in command of Capt. K. V. Beer. Purpose of the flight, which was ordered by the San Francisco office of Pan American Airways. is to familiarize the 11 crew members with Canton and to test the improved landing facilities at the island, Karl Leuder, PAA section superintendent, said.

The runways in the lagoon have been lengthened and new ones cleared since the Honolulu Clipper made the last flight to Canton in November. The California Clipper will remain at Canton until Friday morning, when it will take off for Pearl Harbor.

The plane will leave Sunday afternoon for San Francisco. Another purpose of the Canton flight is to provide a greater interval between clippers to the mainland. The China Clipper is to take off this afternoon for the coast.

No passengers are being carried to Canton. The California Clipper is taking two movie films and fresh food to Canton. The regular crew is aboard with the exception of a steward who was not needed because there are no passengers.
The same plane arrived at 4:30 Tuesday afternoon from the Orient.

*Newspaper article from the **Honolulu-Star Bulletin,** February 16, 1940*

frustration in the daily log he kept during the long months he had worked on Canton. By reading his detailed log, I discovered that a previously unreported third survey flight was made to Canton Island in early 1940. Furthermore, a reading of Ralph Young's log also reveals the reasons for this third and rather secretive final survey flight to Canton Island.

**January 29, 1940:** It is nine months ago that we left San Francisco. Less than half the expedition here now. I expected to be gone only about four months. I would like to get back before the tenth month is finished, but I have my misgivings. I hear nothing about a flight.

**February 1, 1940:** Glad January is out of the way. Hope to get back to the states late this month. Doubt it. Can't get any definite word as to just why planes aren't coming yet. Somehow feel they won't get underway in regular service before March, but hope I'm wrong. Life down here is getting a bit irksome and I want to get out. I have had enough of it.

**February 5, 1940:** Hurt my arm. It's so sore, it's difficult to bathe, shave or even write.

*Base at Canton was ready for Clipper Flights*

**February 6, 1940:** Radio to the island from Clarence M. Young. Said an investigating committee has recommended approval of this route to CAA It's the start anyway. So we may get a plane down here sometime late this month, but it could easily be much longer.

**February 10, 1940:** About 15 waiting to leave on the first plane down. I don't see how it can be done. My arm is still so sore, it's difficult to write.

**February 13, 1940:** The radio man said today the California Clipper, one of the two Boeings in the division (along with the Honolulu Clipper), was scheduled to leave Treasure Island tomorrow on a regular trip to China. Now the other is in China returning. Since only two Boeings can fly this line, this will mean a trip cannot be made down here before the first of March. I have my doubts that I'll get back to the states by April 1. My arm is still sore.

**February 17, 1940:** Left Canton on the Clipper, just before sunrise February 17. Arrived Honolulu shortly after sunset. X-rays in Honolulu showed a fracture in the wrist.

Based on his personal log, it appears that Ralph Young complained to his brother, Clarence Young in San Francisco, about his injured arm and his desire to leave the island and to get home. Clarence responded to his brother's requests by ordering the California Clipper, commanded by Kenneth V. Beer, to make a quick one day trip from Honolulu to Canton to bring his brother back for medical treatment. Because the injury was not life-threatening, Clarence Young could not justify the expense of the quick evacuation to company officials at Pan Am's home office. Therefore, the stated purpose of the trip was to "test the new longer runways at Canton Island," but the real reason for the trip was for Clarence Young to help his brother Ralph get back to Honolulu for medical treatment for his injured arm. Because of the personal nature of the trip, it is not surprising that this flight received no publicity from Pan Am. This was the final flight to Canton before regular airmail service was begun in July of 1940.

| 1st Mail Flight - New Zealand & 1st Flight American Clipper | July 12 - 24, 1940 | B-314 American Clipper | Tilton/Martin |
|---|---|---|---|

| Outbound Flight Schedule | | Inbound Flight Schedule | |
|---|---|---|---|
| San Francisco - Los Angeles | July 12 | Auckland - Noumea | July 20 |
| Los Angeles - Honolulu | July 12-13 | Noumea - Canton Island | July 21-20* |
| Honolulu - Canton Island | July 14 | Canton Island - Honolulu | July 22 |
| Canton Island - Noumea | July 15-16* | Honolulu - Los Angeles | July 23-24 |
| Noumea - Auckland | July 18 | Los Angeles - San Francisco | July 24 |

*Dateline - Gain day outbound - Lose day inbound

The first scheduled airmail flight to New Zealand was also the inaugural flight of the new Foreign Airmail Contract 19 (FAM 19) and the maiden flight of the newly christened American Clipper. The flight was scheduled for July 12, 1940. For the first time Pan Am planned to include a stop at Los Angeles, both outbound and inbound. Therefore, in order to increase publicity for the flight, they decided to christen the new Clipper at the Los Angeles seaplane base at San Pedro's Terminal Island. On Wednesday, July 5, 1940, Captain Tilton and first officer McGlohn and a crew of nine flew the American Clipper from San Francisco's Treasure Island to Los Angeles for the official christening. On July 6 the formal christening ceremonies were held at the landing barge just off Terminal Island. The newly painted large wavy American flag can clearly be seen on the bow. Mrs. Mark T. McKee, the wife of one of Pan Am's directors, did the honors.

*Christening at landing barge, July 6, 1940*

*Christening at landing barge, July 6, 1940*

*Mrs. McKee breaks the bottle of California champagne*

After the christening, the American Clipper was flown back to San Francisco for the scheduled July 12, 1940 departure and the crew met at Treasure Island to discuss the flight. Pictured seated left to right: radio officer, A.L. Chairman; Captain R.J. Nixon; Captain J.H. Tilton, chief pilot of the Pacific Division in command; first officer, F.C. Martin – standing left to right, steward, T. O'Leary; third radio operator, R.G. Dickson; second radio operator, J.A. Hrufky; first engineer, H.F. Loeffler, second engineer, G.B. Brimhall; second officer N.F. Searles and Steward C.C. Baleeby.

Juan Trippe is shown in San Francisco giving Captain John Tilton his official license under Foreign Airmail Contract 19 (FAM 19) to carry mail on this historic first flight.

*July 12, 1940*

After departing San Francisco, the Clipper headed south to Los Angeles, where additional mail was put on board. The American Clipper then immediately continued on to Honolulu, arriving the next morning.

In Honolulu the Pan Am flight crew and their guests received a traditional Hawaiian welcome. Although this was the first scheduled airmail flight and revenue passengers were not permitted, the American Clipper did carry 13 passengers in addition to the crew on the inaugural airmail flight.

Pictured above are 13 of the guests who were passengers on the first airmail flight. Leading the group was Colonel Clarence M. Young, director of Pan Am's Pacific division. He is in the center of the picture, to the right of the native Hawaiian, who has just welcomed him to the islands. On the left of the group is Harold Gatty and his wife. Mr. Gatty was the Pan Am representative in New Zealand, who worked for over five years to bring this flight about. After suffering through the loss of the Samoan Clipper in 1938, he was relieved and gratified to finally be making the trip to New Zealand on one of the new Boeing B-314s, the American Clipper. Also traveling as a passenger was W.T. Miller, one of the chief inspectors for the Civil Aeronautics Authority and General W.F. Frank of the Army Air Corps based at Hickam Field in Honolulu. He was flying as a military observer. After an enjoyable night's stay at the Royal Hawaiian Hotel, the group departed the next morning from Pan Am's Pearl City base on Clipper NC 18606 and headed for Canton Island.

This was the first group of passengers to visit this remote island where Pan Am had built a base in the summer of 1939. The little village was similar to the Pan Am bases at Wake and Midway. The hotel was almost identical to the hotels built on those islands. The hotel register for the first night shows Clarence Young as the first guest. The captain of the flight and the chief pilot in the Pacific, John Tilton, signed next. Other guests included W.F. Frank of the Army Air Corps and Mr. and Mrs. Harold Gatty.

Souvenir flight mail was most welcome and Pan Am prepared many different official cachets for each leg of the flight.

Pan Am bases at Wake and Midway did not have civilian post offices. But, Canton Island did have a civilian post office and Clarence Young made sure that his son, Tim, had the first letter ever cancelled by the Canton Island postmaster, H.K. Graves, who was also a Pan Am employee.

### HOTEL REGISTER

THIS HOTEL IS NOT RESPONSIBLE FOR LOSS OF MONEY, JEWELS OR OTHER VALUABLES UNLESS DEPOSITED IN THE SAFE PROVIDED FOR THAT PURPOSE IN THE OFFICE

JULY 14 1940

| NAME | ADDRESS | ROOM | TIME OF ARRIVAL | TIME OF DEPARTURE |
|------|---------|------|-----------------|-------------------|
| Clarence M. Young | San Francisco | 125 | 7-14 | 7-15 |
| John H. Tilton | " | 105 | 7-14 | 7-15 |
| W. T. Miller | Washington D.C. | 115 | 7-14 | 7-15 |
| R. J. Nixon | San Francisco | 105 | 7-14 | 7-15 |
| Maxwell | Los Angeles | 117 | 7-14 | 7-15 |
| F. H. Stephens | Los Angeles | 119 | 7-14 | 7-15 |
| W. Cornwell | N. & S. Pearl Harbor | 121 | 7-14 | 7-15 |
| Gen. W. F. Frank | Hickam Field, T.H. | 109 | 7-14 | 7-15 |
| Ramsey | Oakland, Cal | 123 SUITE "A" | 7-14 | 7-15 |
| | Treasure Island | 122-124 | 7-14 | 7-15 |
| George Gardner | Treasure Island | 101 | 7-14 | 7-15 |
| M. Angus | " | 101 SUITE "B" | 7-14 | 7-15 |
| Mr. & Mrs. H. Gatty | Auckland N.Z. | 109-111 | 7-14 | 7-15 |
| Fred Laidlaw | New York City | 103 | 7-14 | 7-15 |

*Canton Island hotel register for first flight*

UNITED STATES POST OFFICE
CANTON ISLAND, SOUTH PACIFIC
I hereby certify that this is the first envelope cancelled by this Post Office.
H.K. Graves
Acting Postmaster

CANTON ISLAND,
JUL 15 A.M. 1940
CANTON ISLAND.

VIA AIR MAIL

TIMOTHY M. YOUNG
1940 VALLEJO ST
SAN FRANCISCO
CALIFORNIA

*Cover prepared by Clarence Young for his son's collection of first flight covers*

An interesting cover was sent by passenger W.T. Miller, the C.A.A. inspector, to the director of the Division of Territories and Possessions with the Department of the Interior in Washington, D.C. The Department of the Interior was responsible for maintaining and supplying the Hawaiian school boys on the desert islands scattered over the Pacific that the United States was claiming as possible future air bases. This entire program involving school boys, the Navy and the Coast Guard, was another example of the excellent cooperation between Pan Am, the civilian government and the military that existed in the Pacific at this time.

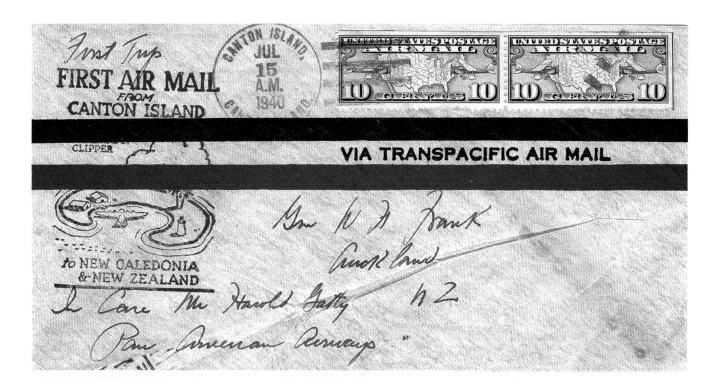

The Canton Island cover addressed to General W.F. Frank, care of Harold Gatty, was also posted on Canton Island on July 15. General Frank was also a non-revenue passenger observing the flight for the military. He addressed his souvenir cover to Harold Gatty, who was Pan Am's representative in New Zealand, and who was also flying with his wife on the first southbound flight with General Frank. Mrs. Gatty was probably the first woman ever to visit previously uninhabited Canton Island. The hotel register for July 14, 1940 documents her visit and the visit of the other passengers. A wide variety of official cachets were prepared by Pan Am for this flight.

Phil Berst also received a small souvenir cover from the manager of the base at New Caledonia, H.E. Jubinville.

Capt. J. Tilton

U.S. AIR MAIL
CANTON ISLAND

CANTON ISLAND,
JUL
A.M.
1940
CANTON ISLAND.

SAN FRANCISCO
HONOLULU
CANTON ISLAND
NOUMEA
AUCKLAND
F.A.M. 19
SOUTH PACIFIC SERVICE
FIRST FLIGHT

V

Mr. J. E. Lamiell,
2000 Yale Avenue, N. W.,
Canton, Ohio, U.S.A.

Canton Island to Noumea

ST AIR MAIL
FROM
NTON ISLAND

OPENED BY CENSOR
PASSED BY CENSOR

NEW CALEDONIA
NEW ZEALAND

CANTON ISLAND,
JUL
15
A.M.
1940
CANTON ISLAND.

UNITED STATES POSTAGE
AIR MAIL
10

VIA AIR MAIL

MR. ABRAHAM BOGIS,
522 PORTER ST.
PHILADELPHIA PA.
U.S.A.

EASTERN
Air Lines

NEW ZEALAND — U.S.A.
AIR MAIL SERVICE
VIA NEW CALEDONIA, CANTON IS.
AND HAWAII.

AUCKLAND C.1.
19 JUL 40 10 - AM
N.Z.

FOUR
4

UNITED STATES AIR MAIL

SAN FRANCISCO, CALIF.
JUL 12
11 - AM
1940

GOLDEN GATE
INTERNATIONAL
EXPOSITION
1940

UNITED STATES POSTAGE
50 CENTS 50

AIR MAIL
TOMORROW'S MAIL TODAY
EASTERN AIR LINES

GREETINGS VIA "HONOLULU CLIPPER"
FROM
THE GREAT SILVER FLEET
NEW ZEALAND

EASTERN Air Lines

FIRST FLIGHT F.A.M. 19
HONOLULU CANTON IS. NOUMEA AUCKLAND
SOUTH PACIFIC SERVICE
SAN FRANCISCO CALIFORNIA

MR. SAMUEL D. FUSON,
ARTHUR KUDNER INC.,
INTERNATIONAL BUILDING,
ROCKEFELLER CENTER, NEW YO
U.S.A.

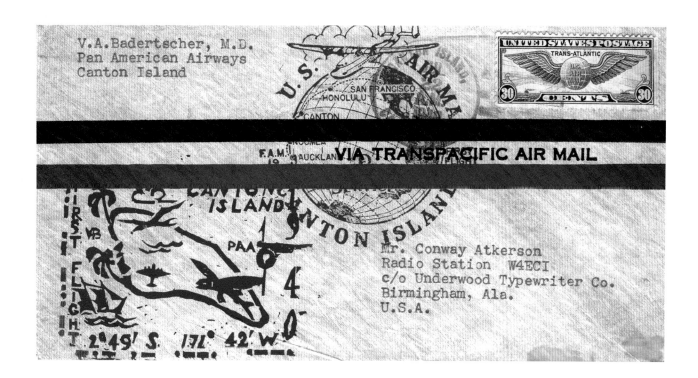

In addition to these official cachets, a medical doctor on Canton Island, Dr. V. Badertscher, designed and carved the cachet showing the Canton Island lagoon with the Clipper at anchor. In a letter contained in the envelope to his friend Conway Atkerson, he said: "The cachet stamp on the cover I designed and chiseled out of a block of wood".

The envelope from Dr. L.E. Shank to a nurse at San Diego County Hospital also has the wood block carved cachet done by Dr. Badertscher. Shortly after writing the letter, Dr. Shank left Canton Island for Wake to work for the civilian contractors building the Navy base on the island. When Wake fell to the Japanese, he was captured. Two years later he and 90 other prisoners were killed by the Japanese for supposedly sneaking military information to the American forces. There is a memorial on Wake Island to Dr. Shank and the other prisoners who were executed.

*Cachet from September 1939
survey flight - Canton to Honolulu*

*July 1940 first flight*

Also shown is the hand carved cachet that was previously seen on the one Canton Island survey flight cover from the September 1939 survey flight that was sent to Phil Berst. It is used again this time in red rather than black on this 1940 first flight cover.

It is interesting that the doctor who served a year later on Canton Island in July of 1941 also hand carved a cachet that was applied in July, 1941, onto the covers to celebrate the first anniversary of the July, 1940 first airmail flight to Canton Island.

After the first anniversary of Pan Am airmail flights to Canton Island had passed in July of 1941, the words "First Anniversary" were removed from the oval cachet and the cachet continued to be used on mail posted on Canton Island up until the war. It was applied in September of 1941 to this envelope from Dr. Franklin on Canton Island to a friend in California.

*Cancelled at both British and American post offices at Canton Island – December 11, 1941*

At the time that this cover was prepared and cancelled on Canton, all of the Pan Am personnel were about to be evacuated under wartime emergency conditions on the 130 foot tug "Mamo" bound for American Samoa. It was going to be a rough and dangerous trip with most of the Pan Am personnel being forced to travel in an open barge towed behind the tug. The men were only allowed to take with them the clothing that they wore and a small pillowcase filled with a few supplies for the trip. Why would anyone under these harsh and dangerous conditions prepare one last souvenir cover before fleeing for his life? It is hard to explain rationally. Once again this proves that cover collectors are indeed a strange breed.

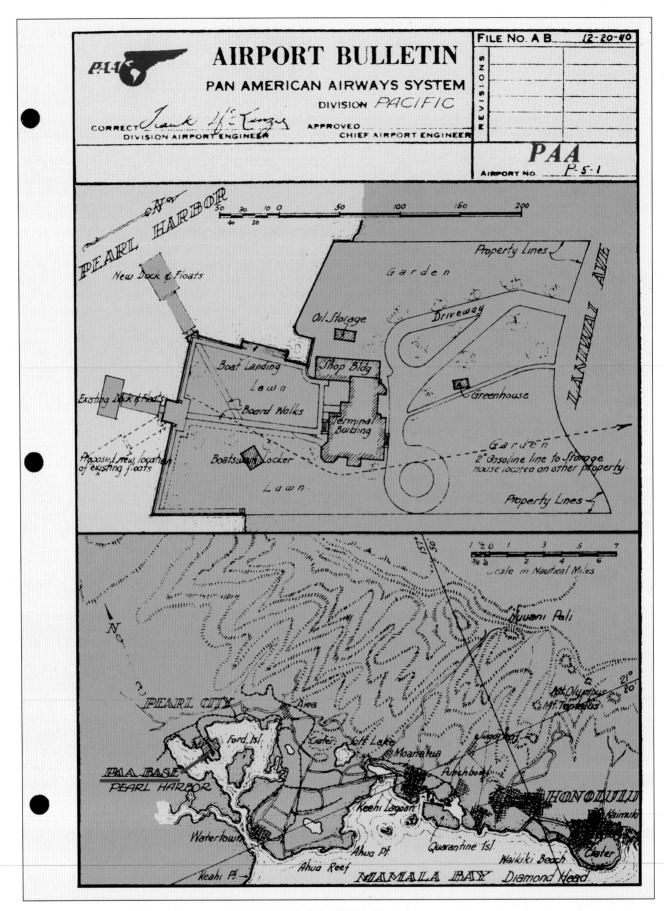

# AIRPORT BULLETIN

## PAN AMERICAN AIRWAYS SYSTEM

DIVISION *PACIFIC*

CORRECT _____ *Frank McKenzie*
DIVISION AIRPORT ENGINEER

APPROVED _____
CHIEF AIRPORT ENGINEER

*PAA*
AIRPORT NO. _____ P-5-1

*Pan Am's Pearl City base*

In preparation for this flight, Pan Am had improved the seaplane bases in Honolulu and New Zealand by adding large, floating docks. The new docks extended far into the harbor, so that the Clipper could be moored at the dock regardless of the condition of the water. Surveys of the bases at Honolulu and Auckland, New Zealand show the floating docks added specifically for the new Boeing B-314 aircraft.

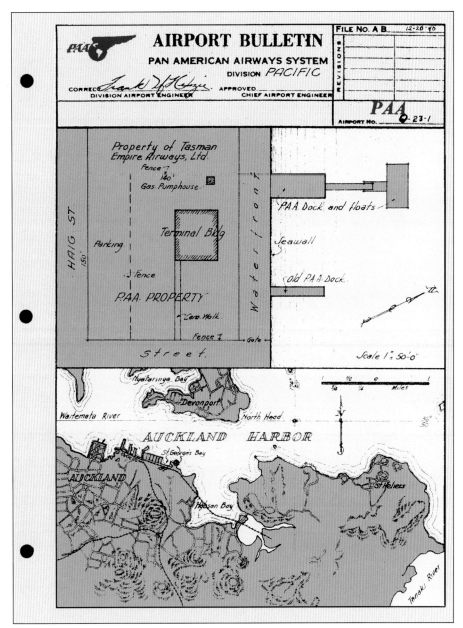

Pan Am's New Zealand base

*A Boeing clipper at new floating dock at Mechanics Bay, Auckland - July 18, 1940*

This rare color aerial photograph of Pan Am's New Zealand base was taken on July 18, 1940, after the arrival of the American Clipper on the first scheduled airmail flight to New Zealand. The Pan Am Clipper is berthed in the foreground at the floating dock at the Pan Am base on Mechanic's Bay, Auckland, New Zealand. The Tasman Airlines "Aotearoa" is tied up at the dock next to the American Clipper at the base of Tasman Empire Airways. Another Tasman aircraft, "Awarua", is at her mooring in the harbor.

Three years and three months after Pan Am's first survey flight to New Zealand, regular airmail service was successfully inaugurated. With the new Boeing 314 aircraft and with the new route through Canton Island, the difficulties faced by Captain Musick had been eliminated. Australia, however, would still not grant the landing rights Juan Trippe had hoped to achieve. Therefore, the New Zealand service never became profitable. But, once again, with the establishment of airmail service to New Zealand, Pan Am had achieved another long sought after goal.

| 1st Flight - Honolulu to Los Angeles | July 23-24, 1940 | B-314 - American Clipper | Tilton/ Martin |
|---|---|---|---|
| **Inbound Flight Schedule** **Honolulu - Los Angeles        July 23-24** | | | |

On the return flight of the first scheduled airmail flight to New Zealand, the American Clipper flew directly from Honolulu to Los Angeles. This was the first time that the Clipper had gone directly to Los Angeles from Honolulu and it was therefore the inauguration of direct service to the new Los Angeles seaplane base that was located at Terminal Island in San Pedro Harbor near Los Angeles.

*American Clipper's first flight from New Zealand to San Francisco landing at Los Angeles - July 24, 1940*

The American Clipper is shown landing on its first scheduled flight. Large crowds and welcoming bands were on shore to greet the inaugural flight from Honolulu.

*Pan Am office - 1940*
*Harbor side*

The Los
Angeles terminal
was a modest
building on the
harbor at San
Pedro. The
building is still
standing and it is
now used as an
office by the
California
Department of Fish
and Wildlife.

*Pan Am office - street side - 1940*

*Pan Am office in 1999 - now a state fish and wildlife office*

*Clipper approaching landing barge on first flight - July 24, 1940*

*The cover illustrated was flown to the new Los Angeles base and is signed by Capt. Tilton*

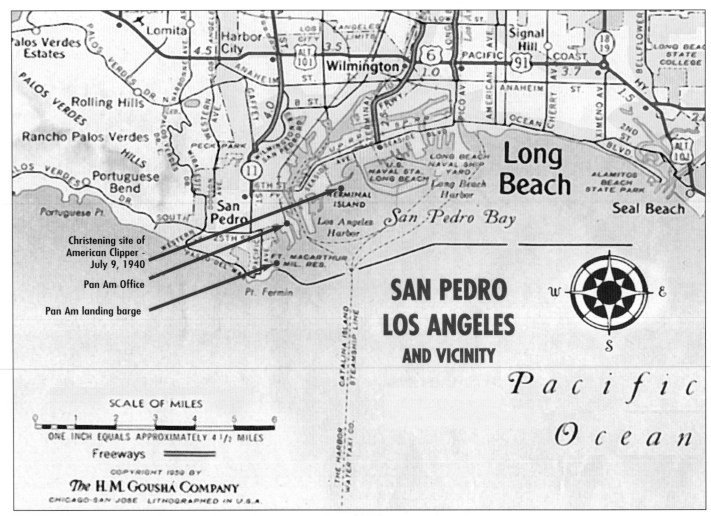

*Los Angeles landing barge*

*Map of Harbor*

| Preview Press Flight to New Zealand | August. 10 - 16, 1940 | B-314 California Clipper | Cluthe/Barrows |
|---|---|---|---|

| Outbound Flight Schedule | | Inbound Flight Schedule** | |
|---|---|---|---|
| San Francisco - Los Angeles | August 10 | Hong Kong - Manila | September 4 |
| Los Angeles - Honolulu | August 10-11 | Manila - Guam | September 6 |
| Honolulu - Canton Island | August 12 | Guam - Wake | September 7 |
| Canton Island - Noumea | August 14-15 | Wake - Midway | September 8-7 |
| Noumea - Auckland | August 16 | Midway - Honolulu | September 8 |
| | | Honolulu - San Francisco | September 9-10 |
| *Dateline - Gain day outbound - Lose day inbound | | **Inbound flight of China Clipper | |

Just as Pan Am had conducted a press flight shortly before the inauguration of the first revenue passenger flights across the north Pacific in October of 1936, a similar press flight was conducted a month before the first revenue passenger flight in the south Pacific to New Zealand.

The newspapermen departed on August 10, 1940 aboard the California Clipper under the command of Captain Cluthe from San Francisco by way of Los Angeles to Honolulu. In addition to the representatives of the American press, there were two newspapermen from Australia who were particularly important to Juan Trippe and Pan Am because Pan Am wanted the Australians to read all the details about the great success of the flight to their neighbor, New Zealand. Then, Trippe hoped, the business community in Australia would fear losing out on world trade and as a result grant Pan Am landing rights in Australia, which was, of course, Trippe's ultimate goal in inaugurating the South Pacific flights. Trippe used the same strategy successfully in playing Macao off of Hong Kong in 1937 to gain access to British Hong Kong when they initially denied him landing rights.

Everything went according to schedule on the press flight until they reached Canton Island. There the Clipper sustained some minor damage during the mooring operation and Captain Cluthe decided to remain a day longer at the remote coral atoll. This decision brought a cheer from the pressmen onboard for it gave them more time to rest from their hectic schedules and to go after some of the huge fish that they spotted in the lagoon.

tinued operations. AUG 14 1940

## CLIPPER AT CANTON, IS HELD FOR REPAIRS

### Minor Damage Gives the Party Time for Exploration

**By HAROLD CALLENDER**
Wireless to THE NEW YORK TIMES.

CANTON ISLAND, Aug. 13—As the Pan American Airways California Clipper, en route to New Zealand, drew from the pier for a take-off in the lagoon here as the sun peeped over the horizon at dawn today, it was discovered that during the mooring operation the launch's aerial had scraped the Clipper's left aileron.

Captain Cluthe decided to remain a day longer at this tiny coral atoll, occupied by the Pan American Airways station.

The decision brought a cheer from those on board, who had flown from New York to this island, 7,000 miles, in about forty-nine hours. The party was pleased, too, at the opportunity to go after some huge fish which were seen darting after their prey in the translucent water.

The ship carried twenty-four passengers and a crew of eleven.

Canton is a typical tropical island with a lagoon which Pan American developed as a base. The island's population of forty-two includes thirty-four of the line's staff.

On the flight from Honolulu the Clipper journeyed over scattered clouds and a calm sunlit sea at an altitude of 7,000 to 10,000 feet. Although near the equator, the temperature outside the plane at midday was 54 degrees Fahrenheit and the passengers, in tropical clothing, were chilly.

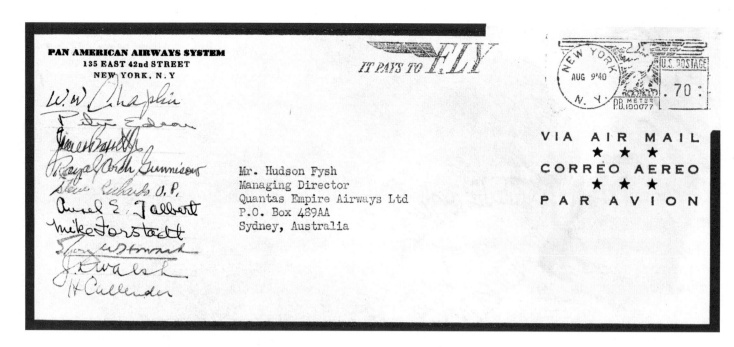

They arrived in Auckland, New Zealand on August 16 and after a short stopover they flew on to Australia on the Australian airline, Tasman Empire Airways. From Australia, they flew as guests of the Royal Dutch Airways to Java and Sumatra, where they were again guests of the government. They again flew by Royal Dutch Airways to Singapore and finally Hong Kong. The first group of seven reporters arrived in Hong Kong in time to catch the Clipper, under the command of Captain Chase, that departed Hong Kong on September 4, 1940. They reached San Francisco on September 10, 1940.

The only souvenir cover from this press flight that I have seen is on a metered mail envelope from New York that is from the collection of Greg Schmidt. It was carried to New Zealand on the press flight and it was autographed by the newsmen when they arrived in Australia.

When the newsmen flew on by other airlines from New Zealand to Hong Kong, Captain Cluthe and the crew returned immediately on the California Clipper to San Francisco. On the outbound press flight from San Francisco to New Zealand on the California Clipper, Theron Griffin was a member of the flight crew.

*Griffin's envelope mailed at Canton Island on return of California Clipper from press flight to New Zealand*

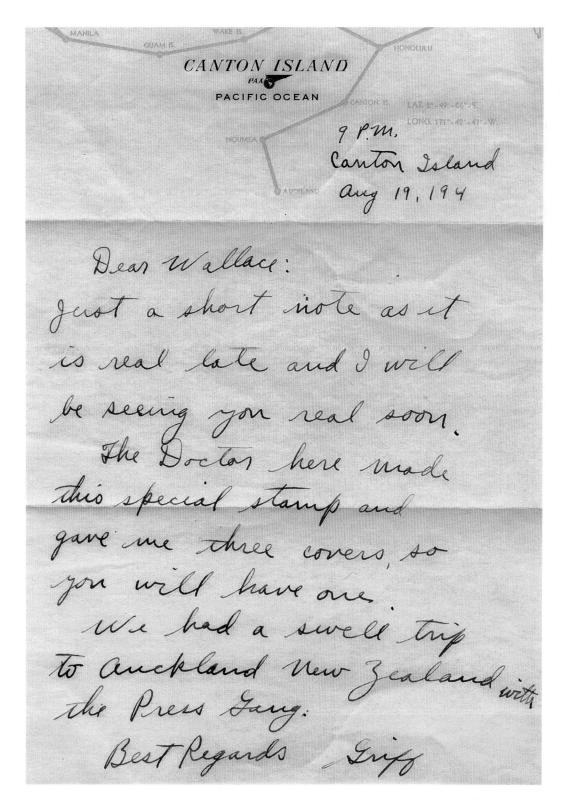

9 P.M.
Canton Island
Aug 19, 194

Dear Wallace:
Just a short note as it
is real late and I will
be seeing you real soon.
The Doctor here made
this special stamp and
gave me three covers, so
you will have one.
We had a swell trip
to Auckland New Zealand with
the Press Gang.
Best Regards   Griff

On the return flight of the California Clipper to San Francisco, crew member Griffin sent this letter and envelope from Canton Island to a friend in Oakland, California. He used one of the envelopes given to him by the doctor on Canton, with the hand carved cachet showing the island. He closed his letter with these words: "We had a swell trip to Auckland, New Zealand with the press gang". They probably were an entertaining group of travelers on this early flight to New Zealand before the inauguration of regular passenger service.

However, unlike Trippe's success in gaining landing rights in Hong Kong in response to the fear of the Hong Kong business community that they would lose world trade to Macao if Hong Kong was not opened to Pan Am, the officials in Australia were not so easily swayed. They remained firm that if Hawaii was not opened to commercial flights of the British and Australian airlines, Australia would remain closed to American interests, including Pan Am. Hawaii remained closed to all foreign commercial flights, so the stalemate remained and Pan Am was unable to fly to Australia.

| V.I.P. Flight to New Zealand | August 24 - September 7, 1940 | B-314 American Clipper | Nixon/Searles |
|---|---|---|---|

| Outbound Flight Schedule | | Inbound Flight Schedule | |
|---|---|---|---|
| Los Angeles - Honolulu | August 24-25 | Auckland - Noumea | September 2 |
| Honolulu - Canton Island | August 26 | Noumea - Canton Island | September 4-3* |
| Canton Island - Noumea | August 27-28* | Canton Island - Honolulu | September 5 |
| Noumea - Auckland | September 1 | Honolulu-San Francisco | September 7 |
| *Dateline - Gain day outbound - Lose day inbound | | | |

After the very successful press flight to New Zealand in August of 1940, which generated the desired news coverage in Australia and around the world, the VIP flight hosted by Pan Am's director, C.V. Whitney, departed San Francisco for Los Angeles and onward to Honolulu and New Zealand. Because this flight was hosted by one of the directors, rather than by charismatic Juan Trippe and his wife Betty, it did not generate the glamour and excitement that accompanied the VIP flight across the north Pacific in October of 1936.

The VIPs departed on August 24, 1940 aboard the American Clipper under the command of Captain R.J. Nixon. In Honolulu, they again stayed at the Royal Hawaiian Hotel, which was the customary overnight stop for Clipper passengers. On Canton Island they experienced a comfortable but spartan Pan Am hotel similar to the ones that had been built on both Wake and Midway for overnight Clipper passengers.

*Motor yacht Southern Seas - Floating hotel at Noumea, New Caledonia - August 1940*

When they arrived at Noumea, New Caledonia, they were in for a pleasant surprise. Because this remote and rarely visited French colony in the South Pacific did not have adequate facilities for overnight guests, Juan Trippe purchased a beautiful 200 foot yacht that had been owned by Cyrus Curtis, the publisher of the **Saturday Evening Post**, and had it converted into a luxurious floating hotel for the passengers and crew during their overnight stay at Noumea. Pan Am christened the yacht the Southern Seas. The VIP guests were the first Clipper passengers to stay in the refurbished staterooms on the yacht. The crew slept on the upper deck in small but pleasant rooms that had been added to the yacht during its conversion by Pan Am.

*Regular airmail carried on flight*

*Amon Carter souvenir cover –*
*Los Angeles to Canton Island*

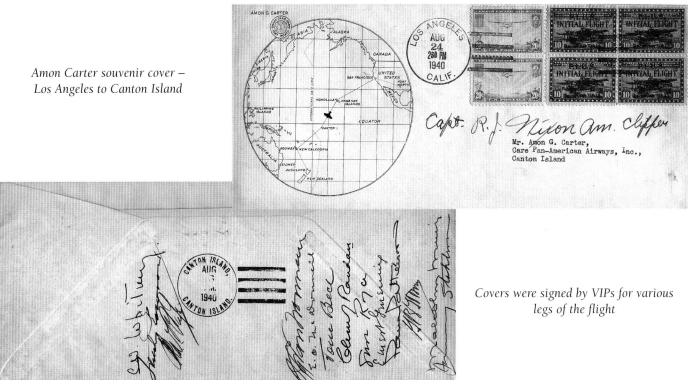

*Covers were signed by VIPs for various*
*legs of the flight*

Regular airmail was, of course, carried on this flight. Illustrated is an envelope that traveled in the mail compartment on the VIP flight.

The only souvenir mail that has been seen for this flight was prepared by Amon Carter, who had prepared all the flight covers for the VIP flight in October of 1936. He was not one of the guests on this VIP flight to New Zealand, so he asked Director C.V. Whitney to use the envelope he prepared, to have it signed by the flight captain, Nixon, and his VIP friends and then to send it back to him for his personal collection of flight covers. Pan Am Director Whitney was happy to accommodate his friend Amon Carter with the souvenir for his collection.

With the success of the press flight in August and the VIP flight in early September, all was in readiness for the first revenue passengers to New Zealand, who were about to depart San Francisco.

| 1st Revenue Passenger Flight to New Zealand | September 11 - 23, 1940 | B-314 American Clipper | Beer |
| --- | --- | --- | --- |

### Outbound Flight Schedule
| | |
| --- | --- |
| San Francisco - Los Angeles | Sept. 11 |
| Los Angeles - Honolulu | Sept. 11-12 |
| Honolulu - Canton Island | Sept. 13 |
| Canton Island - Noumea | Sept. 14-15* |
| Noumea - Auckland | Sept. 16 |

### Inbound Flight Schedule
| | |
| --- | --- |
| Auckland - Noumea | September 18 |
| Noumea - Canton Island | September 19-18* |
| Canton Island - Honolulu | September 20 |
| Honolulu - Los Angeles | September 22-23 |
| Los Angeles - San Francisco | September 23 |

*Dateline - Gain day outbound - Lose day inbound

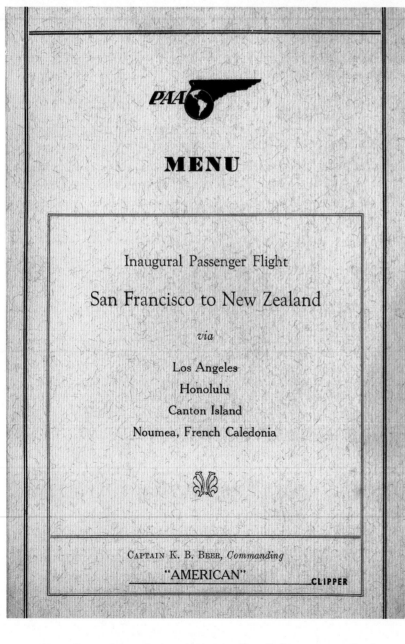

Menu for meal served to passengers on first flight to New Zealand

The long awaited first revenue passenger flight departed San Francisco on September 11, 1940 and after picking up additional passengers in Los Angeles, flew on the same day to Honolulu for the overnight stop before heading south by way of Canton Island and New Caledonia to New Zealand.

Clara Adams, the world traveler who had been among the first seven passengers on the first passenger flight across the North Pacific to Manila in October of 1936, was once again one of the first to book a ticket as a passenger on this inaugural flight to New Zealand.

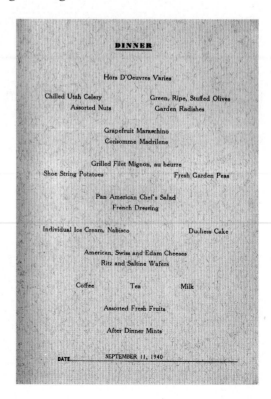

388

*Haere Mai
Ki Niu Tireni*

(which, in the Maori language means)

*welcome to
New Zealand!*

*1941 brochure for Pan Am
passenger service to New Zealand*

2. Deep Sea Fishing at Mayor Island, Tauranga, rivalling Russell's fishing attractions.

3. Unexcelled trout fishing at Rotorua Lake Taupo, Huka Falls, and district, October through April.

4. Winter sports at Tongariro National Park, staying at Chateau Tongariro on the slopes of Mount Ruapehu. June through September.

*A longer visit would enable you to see:*

1. Lake Waikaremoana, Napier, and District of Hawkes Bay, New Zealand's main wool-producing Province.

2. Taranaki and Mount Egmont, rich dairying district.

3. Wellington—Capital City and seat of Government.

*And in the South Island:*

1. The West Coast—via Scenic Lewis Pass or Otira Gorge, down to the Franz Joseph and Fox Glaciers, where a river of ice flows through sub-tropical forests.

2. Winter Sports at the Hermitage, Mt. Cook, New Zealand's highest peak.

3. Lake District of the South, in the midst of Southland's snow-capped mountains.

4. Milford Sound, in the heart of the Fiord District.

## Facts About New Zealand

Total population: 1,700,000.

Maori population: 90,000.

Area: Slightly larger than Great Britain, *i.e.*, 67,000,000 acres, 20,000,000 being under cultivation, with 60 farms more than 100 square miles in extent.

Total railway mileage: 3,319.

Mileage of main highways: 12,000.

220,000 Automobiles registered—equivalent to 1 to every 8 persons, a rate surpassed by the United States and Canada only.

One person in every 10 is a telephone subscriber, which ratio is exceeded only by the United States.

Wellington Radio (60 K.W.) is one of the most powerful stations in the Southern Hemisphere.

[ 14 ]

Printed by Whitcombe & Tombs Ltd

# Haere Mai-
# Welcome

389

*Covers signed by first New Zealand passenger Clara Adams*

Even the irrepressible Clara Adams must have been tiring of all the first flights because she did not produce anywhere near the variety of covers that she had created for the first passenger flight to Manila. The novelty of Transpacific flight had simply worn off and passengers and crew members were just not as interested in signing her souvenir mail as the first passengers had been in 1936 in the early days of Pacific travel. By now Transpacific flights were almost routine. She did, however, manage to create a few souvenir covers for her collection to commemorate the historic event.

Pictured above is the flight crew about to depart on the California Clipper for the first flight to Singapore. Leading up the gangplank from left to right: flight steward M.B. Chrisman, flight steward C.P. Relyea, fourth officer F. W. O'Hanlon, second engineering officer G.H. Schmidt, third officer J.W. Strickland, first radio officer Morton, second officer T.M. Wold, first engineering officer J.W. Zeigler, first officer R.C. Howard, and Captain J.W. Barrows.

Upon landing in Singapore, Captain Barrows told reporters: "We had a wonderful trip." The flight to Singapore took 6-1/2 days from San Francisco, rather than the five to six weeks it would have taken by steamer.

Speaking for the British community in Singapore, Air Marshal Sir Robert Brooke-Popham said to Captain Barrows upon his arrival:

*Captain J.W. Barrows*

"We have come to regard America and the Americans as our steadfast, warm-hearted friends in a season of trouble. Unless the world is utterly bad, its desire for the common decencies dead, its sympathy for those who wish to keep their integrity and independence and be at peace, smothered by fear or greed or sycophancy, Great Britain must have millions of friends. . . So, Captain Barrows, we greet you with a deep warmth of pleasure, hoping that you and all who steer these ships of the air over the estranging leagues of the sea have nothing but fair voyages and happy landings."

Because of the political turmoil in Singapore, it is not surprising that advance notice was not given to collectors for the Singapore first flights. As a result, most collectors did not have time to prepare souvenir envelopes.

Pan Am, however, anticipated the demand from first flight collectors and had a supply of large size envelopes cacheted and stamped along the first flight route. In a circular prepared by the company after the flight occurred, they offered collectors a complete set of eight Singapore first flight covers for $4.50.

## Pan American Airways Company
### (PHILATELIC SECTION)
### 135 East 42nd Street, New York, N. Y.

**ADDITIONAL FIRST FLIGHT COVER SERVICE • TRANSPACIFIC SERVICE**

**EXTENSION MANILA, PHILIPPINE ISLANDS TO SINGAPORE, STRAITS SETTLEMENTS**

On April 30, 1941 the Civil Aeronautics Board authorized Pan American Airways Company to extend the Transpacific Air Mail Service from Manila, Philippine Islands to Singapore, Straits Settlements. This service is to be operated on a fortnightly schedule from Manila to Singapore and return, in connection with the regular U. S. Transpacific Air Mail Service. *(See Postal Bulletin #18191 of May 6, 1941 for official announcement of this service).*

The inaugural flight on this new service was made from San Francisco, California on May 3, 1941 (covers cancelled by P.O. on May 2, 1941); from Honolulu, Hawaii on May 5, 1941; from Guam on May 9, 1941 and from Manila, P.I. on May 10, 1941 (covers cancelled by P.O. as of May 9, 1941), arriving at Singapore, S/S on May 10, 1941.

The return trip left Singapore, S/S on May 12, 1941 (covers cancelled as of May 10, 1941) and arrived in San Francisco, California on May 20, 1941.

Due to many reasons it was impossible for the Company to handle direct from Philatelists or Collectors their own individual first flight covers, as has been done on many previous first flights made by this Company. Under the circumstances the Company prepared and forwarded a sufficient number of first flight covers from each point on this route to meet the requirements of Philatelists and Collectors who might desire to obtain such first flight covers on this service.

All first flight covers forwarded are addressed to Pan American Airways, (address printed on cover) at point of destination. The covers are in large Pan American Airways air mail envelopes (9-1/2 x 4-1/8). No other covers or sizes were serviced by the Company on this flight.

These first flight covers have now been returned to the United States and are available to all who may be interested in obtaining same. Those available and cost of each cover are:

| | | | | | |
|---|---|---|---|---|---|
| San Francisco | to Singapore, S/S | $ .85 | Singapore, S/S to Manila | $ .30 |
| Honolulu | to Singapore, S/S | .65 | Singapore, S/S to Guam | .40 |
| Guam | to Singapore, S/S | .45 | Singapore, S/S to Honolulu | .65 |
| Manila | to Singapore, S/S | .35 | Singapore, S/S to San Francisco | .85 |

(Complete sets of these 8 covers are available at $4.50 per set)

These covers may be purchased from the Pan American Airways Company (Philatelic Sec[tion], [135] East 42nd Street, New York City, N. Y. All orders for these first flight covers must [be accom]panied by a money order or certified check made payable to Pan American Airways Company, [New York,] N. Y. in the exact amount required for the purchase of the covers desired.

In order to avoid any mistakes in the handling of these covers, a special order bla[nk is en]closed with this circular and it is requested that your order be made on these blanks. [The name] and address of the person to whom these covers are to be sent should be *printed* in the up[per right] hand space provided for this purpose.

United States postage is affixed to covers posted in San Francisco, Honolulu and Gu[am, Phil]ippine Commonwealth postage to those posted in Manila, and Straits Settlements postage [to those] posted in Singapore. All covers are backstamped by the Post Office at Point of destinati[on except] those from Singapore to Honolulu and San Francisco. The Singapore, Honolulu and San [Francisco] covers have been backstamped by a Company backstamp, indicating date of arrival there.

The Company has affixed a suitable cachet on each cover serviced on this flight. [The] Singapore covers bear the censorship stamp, indicating that these covers have been p[assed for] transmission by that Bureau.

**ORDER FOR FIRST FLIGHT COVERS**

| | First Name | Initial | Surname |
|---|---|---|---|
| Please Print Full Name & Address of Person to Whom covers are to be sent. | | | |
| | Address | | |
| | City | | State |

| Remarks | From | To | Quantity | Rate | Amount |
|---|---|---|---|---|---|
| | San Francisco | Singapore S/S | | .85 | |
| | Honolulu | " | | .65 | |
| | Guam | " | | .45 | |
| | Manila, P.I. | " | | .35 | |
| | Singapore S/S | Manila | | .30 | |
| | " | Guam | | .40 | |
| | " | Honolulu | | .65 | |
| | " | San Francisco | | .85 | |
| | | | | | |
| | Complete Set of Above Covers | | | 4.50 | |
| | | | | | |
| | Return Registration Fee (Optional) | | | .15 | |
| | TOTAL | | | xxx | |
| Amount Remitted | (P.O. Money Order (Ex. Money Order (Certified Check | | | | |
| | FOR P.A.A. USE ONLY Amt. Rec'd: Check ( ) M.O. ( ) $ | | | | |
| Received Verified and Check by: | | | | | |
| Covers Mailed | | | | | |

*Order form - Singapore first flight*

394

PAN AMERICAN AIRWAYS SYSTEM
GUAM, M. I.

GUAM
MAY
9
6 AM
1941
GUAM

UNITED STATES POSTAGE
TRANS-ATLANTIC
30 CENTS 30

**VIA AIR MAIL**

PAN AMERICAN AIRWAYS, INC.

SINGAPORE,

STRAITS SETTLEMENTS

PASSED FOR TRANSMISSION
93

FIRST FLIGHT COVER
GUAM - SINGAPORE

PAN AMERICAN AIRWAYS SYSTEM
SINGAPORE
STRAITS SETTLEMENTS

PASSED FOR TRANSMISSION
95

SINGAPORE
5 PM
10 MAY
1941

DON'T WORRY

ABOUT SHIPS

**VIA AIR MAIL**

PAN AMERICAN AIRWAYS, INC.

MANILA, P. I.

Singapore * Manila
FIRST FLIGHT AIR MAIL

FIRST FLIGHT COVER
SINGAPORE - MANILA

PAN AMERICAN AIRWAYS SYSTEM
SINGAPORE
STRAITS SETTLEMENTS

SINGAPORE
7 PM
10 MAY
1941

MALAYA  MALAYA  MALAYA

**VIA AIR MAIL**

PASSED FOR TRANSMISSION

PAN AMERICAN AIRWAYS, INC.

TREASURE ISLAND,

SAN FRANCISCO, CALIFORNIA

AIR MAIL
FIRST FLIGHT PAA

FIRST FLIGHT COVER
SINGAPORE - SAN FRANCISCO

Because they were sold in sets of eight covers by Pan Am, all of these large size Pan Am envelopes for the Singapore first flight that are shown on this on the previous two pages are quite common and reasonably priced.

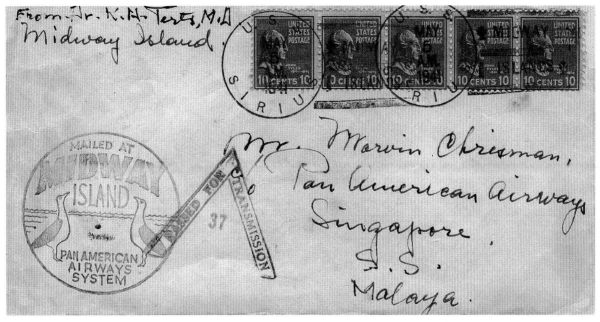

*Rare commercial cover flown from Midway to Singapore on first flight*

Any small size envelope, or any envelope from a different location such as Wake or Midway, or any covers signed by the pilot or the crew, are much more difficult to locate.

Many of the different cachets seen on small size envelopes were privately produced by a stamp and cover dealer from Manila, Walter Bruggmann. Being in Manila he learned on May 5 that the flight had departed San Francisco and he had several days to prepare his flight covers in time for the arrival of the California Clipper in Manila on May 9, 1941.

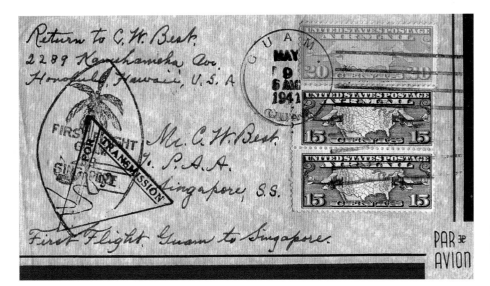

*Privately prepared Guam to Singapore cover*

*Midway to Singapore first flight cover*

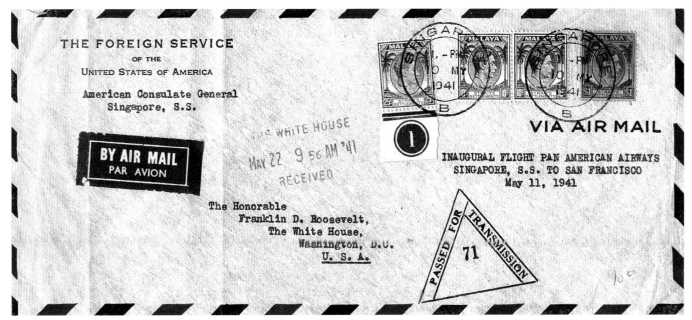

*President Roosevelt was an avid stamp collector and US diplomats delighted in sending him souvenir covers*

President Roosevelt was, of course, watching the political developments closely in this troubled part of the world. The War Department was also working with Pan Am to gather information on the conditions in the Pacific.

WAR DEPARTMENT
HEADQUARTERS OF THE ARMY AIR FORCES
WASHINGTON

RECEIVED
AUG 11 1941
DIVISION MANAGER'S OFFICE

OFFICE OF
THE CHIEF OF THE AIR STAFF

August 6, 1941.

Colonel Clarence Young,
Pan American Airways Company,
San Francisco, Calif.

Dear Clarence:

Acknowledging your letter of the 2nd I want to assure you of our appreciation of the information which you have given us. The critical situation requires that we have every bit of the latest information available on airdromes in the Pacific and we will appreciate any data which you may have on any bases of which you have information.

This place is a mad house but there is never a dull moment. Harold Lee George has just come up from Langley and is Chief of the War Plans Division of the Air Staff. At the present, we have only four officers in this Division but are trying to get it increased to a size that can take care of our problem.

As you are aware, it is undesirable that any emphasis be placed on the fact that we are endeavoring to get information as above noted.

Kindest personal regards.

Sincerely,

K. N. WALKER,
Lt. Col., A.C.,
War Plans Division.

In August of 1941, Clarence Young brought the War Department up to date on the Pacific bases served by Pan Am, which included the new Singapore base. Lt. Walker, of the War Plans Division, responded to the Pacific division manager's report and told him the importance of continuing to forward every bit of information being gather by Pan Am to the War Department during this critical period.

The close cooperation between the military and Pan Am, which started with the survey flights in 1935, continued in the troubled months before WW II.

In spite of the deteriorating conditions in the Pacific, Pan Am continued to expand its routes in the region.

| 1st Revenue Passenger Flight to Singapore & 1st Flight of Pacific Clipper | May 21 - June 4, 1941 | B-314A California Clipper (Pacific Clipper) | G.B. Blackmore |
|---|---|---|---|

| Outbound Flight Schedule | | Inbound Flight Schedule | |
|---|---|---|---|
| San Francisco - Honolulu | May 21-22 | Singapore - Manila | May 29 |
| Honolulu - Midway | May 23 | Manila - Guam | May 31 |
| Midway - Wake | May 24-25* | Guam - Wake | June 1 |
| Wake - Guam | May 26 | Wake - Midway | June 2-1* |
| Guam - Manila | May 27 | Midway - Honolulu | June 2 |
| Manila - Singapore | May 28 | Honolulu - San Francisco | June 3-4 |
| *Dateline - Gain day outbound - Lose day inbound | | | |

Captain Barrows did not experience any problems on the first mail flight to Singapore. Therefore, because of the flight's success, the Civil Aeronautics Administration immediately authorized passenger service for the next Singapore flight departing on May 21, 1941. The first passenger flight carried 15 passengers, five of whom were enroute to Singapore. The inaugural passenger flight to Singapore was also the first flight for the newly delivered Boeing B-314A – NC 18609.

It was at this point in time that the confusion over the names and aircraft numbers of the Pan Am Boeing Clippers flying in the Pacific first arose. This new Boeing Clipper, NC 18609, which ultimately became known as the Pacific Clipper, was first given the name "California Clipper" by Pan Am because the original California Clipper, NC 18602, was temporarily leaving Pacific service to be modified for Atlantic flights. Pan Am reported the naming of this new Clipper, NC 18609, in their *New Horizons* magazine for June 1941:

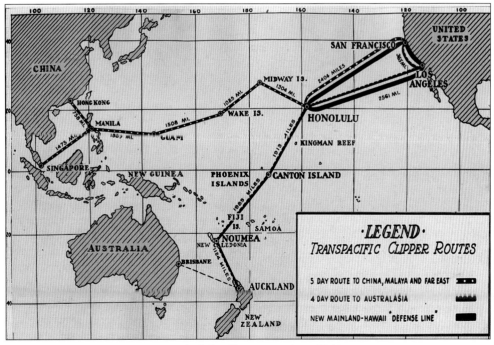

*Pan Am's Pacific routes - June 1941*

*The name of the airplane making the first passenger flight to Singapore was the California Clipper, a new airplane with an old name. The original California Clipper, NC 18602, on returning from the assignment of establishing airmail service to Singapore, went into the shop at Treasure Island to be made ready for transfer to the Atlantic operation. She gave up her name to the new NC 18609 that just arrived from the Boeing factory.*

*New Horizons - June 1941*

Within months, however, the old California Clipper returned from Atlantic service to once again fly the Pacific routes and the name California Clipper was restored to its rightful place on the old Boeing B-314, NC 18602. The newly delivered NC 18609 then received its new name, the Pacific Clipper. With the addition of passenger service to Singapore, Pan Am passenger service stretched 9,472 miles from San Francisco to Singapore.

| 1st Flight Anzac Clipper | July 15 - 29, 1941 | B-314A Anzac Clipper | Blackmore |
|---|---|---|---|

| Outbound Flight Schedule | | Inbound Flight Schedule | |
|---|---|---|---|
| San Francisco - Honolulu | July 15-16 | Singapore - Manila | July 23 |
| Honolulu  - Midway | July 17 | Manila  - Guam | July 25 |
| Midway - Wake | July 18-19* | Guam  - Wake | July 26 |
| Wake - Guam | July 20 | Wake - Midway | July 27-26* |
| Guam - Manila | July 21 | Midway  - Honolulu | July 27 |
| Manila -  Singapore | July 22 | Honolulu - San Francisco | July 28-29 |

*Dateline - Gain day outbound - Lose day inbound

The Anzac Clipper, B-314A, NC 18611, was the last of the five Boeing B-314s to enter regular Pacific service. It is pictured in this postcard at Clear Lake California, north of San Francisco in the wine country. Clear Lake was far enough inland that it escaped the coastal fog, which was quite common in northern California and the San Francisco Bay area. It was used by Pan Am as an alternative landing area when the Treasure Island base was fog bound.

No special cachets or envelopes were prepared for the first flight of the Anzac Clipper. Flight covers would have to be identified by postmarks.

Of the twelve Boeing B-314s ordered by Pan Am, five were placed in service in the Pacific, four were placed in service for the North Atlantic and Africa routes, and three were sold to the British to assist them in their war effort.

*Postcard of Anzac on Clear Lake, California*

| 1st Regular Shuttle Los Angeles - San Francisco - Honolulu | August 10 - 13, 1941 | B-314A Anzac Clipper | Tilton |
|---|---|---|---|
| **Outbound Flight Schedule** Los Angeles - San Francisco - Honolulu - August 10-11 | | **Inbound Flight Schedule** Honolulu - Los Angeles - San Francisco - August 12-13 | |

On August 10, 1941, Pan Am started regular shuttle service for passengers, mail and air freight between San Francisco, Los Angeles and Honolulu. Although the first Clipper flight to Los Angeles had occurred in July of 1940, regular scheduled service had not been established between the three cities. To serve the growing Honolulu market and to solve the bottleneck that existed between California and Hawaii, Pan Am shuttle service was scheduled with three flights every two weeks. With the new shuttle service there were three round trips weekly between California and Hawaii.

*Captain J.H. Tilton, Miss Doris Bowles and scroll - The scroll carried greetings to the mayor*

There was little fanfare when the shuttle service flights were inaugurated. However, when Captain Tilton landed in Honolulu at the end of the first shuttle flight, he did take part in an informal ceremony to mark the opening of the new service. He brought with him a scroll addressed to Honolulu Mayor Leslie Petrie from Los Angeles' Mayor Fletcher Bowron expressing the pride of Los Angeles in the new air link between "our two great cities". Captain Tilton is seen presenting the scroll in Honolulu to Pan Am's secretary Doris Bowles for delivery to Honolulu's mayor.

No special flight covers have been identified from this flight, but by watching postmarks on registered or special delivery letters, collectors should be able to identify mail that was carried on Pan Am's new service to Hawaii.

| 1st Flight Hong Kong Clipper II | Sept. 22 - 23, 1941 | S-42B Hong Kong Clipper II - Myrtle | Ralph/Strickland |
|---|---|---|---|

| Outbound Flight Schedule | | Inbound Flight Schedule | |
|---|---|---|---|
| Manila - Macao | Sept. 22 | Hong Kong - Manila | Sept. 23 |
| Macao - Hong Kong | Sept. 22 | | |

The original Hong Kong Clipper flew mail and passengers from Manila to Hong Kong from April of 1937 to December of 1937 when it was transferred back to Honolulu, renamed the Samoan Clipper, and put in service for the planned scheduled flights to New Zealand. The Clipper was lost in January of 1938 when it exploded while attempting to return to American Samoa for an emergency landing. Even with the delivery of the Boeing B-314s in 1939 and 1941, Pan Am was short of aircraft in the Pacific and they were therefore unable to reassign a Clipper to the shuttle flights between Manila and Hong Kong. Therefore, on any flights to Manila, the Clipper making the flight would have to go on to Hong Kong before returning to San Francisco.

With the extension of service to Singapore in May of 1941 the need for an additional aircraft on the shuttle service between Hong Kong and Manila became acute. Therefore, to meet the emergency, the Bermuda Clipper was transferred to Hong Kong to make the shuttle flights. The flight schedule called for two shuttle flights each week between Manila and Hong Kong.

The Bermuda Clipper, a Sikorsky S-42B was renamed the Hong Kong Clipper II and it acquired the affectionate name of "Myrtle". On September 22, 1941 the newly rechristened Hong Kong Clipper II made its first flight from Manila to Hong Kong, returning the next day. No special cachets were prepared for the flight, but mail carried on the flight could be identified by postmarks.

Its service in the Pacific would be brief. In less than three months the Japanese would attack Pearl Harbor and as an early casualty of the Pacific war, the Hong Kong Clipper II would be destroyed by enemy fire as it sat at its dock in Hong Kong.

*The Hong Kong Clipper II at Hong Kong*

| 1st Flight to Fiji | November 5 - 17, 1941 | B-314A Pacific Clipper | Tilton/Wilson |
| --- | --- | --- | --- |

| Outbound Flight Schedule | | Inbound Flight Schedule | |
| --- | --- | --- | --- |
| San Francisco - Los Angeles | Nov. 5 | Auckland - Noumea | Nov. 12 |
| Los Angeles - Honolulu | Nov. 5-6 | Noumea - Suva | Nov. 13 |
| Honolulu - Canton Island | Nov. 7 | Suva - Canton Island | Nov. 14-13* |
| Canton Island - Suva | Nov. 8-9* | Canton Island - Honolulu | Nov. 15 |
| Suva - Noumea | Nov. 10 | Honolulu - Los Angeles | Nov. 16-17 |
| Noumea - Auckland | Nov. 11 | Los Angeles - San Francisco | Nov. 17 |

*Dateline - Gain day outbound - Lose day Inbound

In November of 1941 Pan Am added Fiji as an overnight stop between Canton Island and Noumea, New Caledonia. Fiji was added primarily as an operating expediency to break up the long 2,000 mile flight from Canton Island to New Caledonia. The stopover provided Pan Am with an opportunity to refuel and, more importantly, because of the shorter distance that had to be traveled to the next layover, it also allowed them to greatly increase the payload on the flight from Honolulu to New Zealand. The company had determined that each pound of additional payload that could be carried by a Transpacific Clipper was worth approximately $95.00 per year in added revenue to Pan Am from passenger and freight service.

*The Clipper is shown resting in the harbor at Suva, Fiji on the first flight*

At the same time that Pan Am added Fiji as a refueling stop between Canton and Noumea, they surveyed and approved remote Palmyra Island as another fuel stop to break up the 1900 mile flight between Honolulu and Canton Island. Palmyra, an uninhabited, privately owned island 900 miles south of Honolulu, had many small islands scattered around its lagoon and it was a suitable fuel stop between

*Fiji*

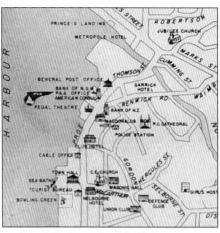

*Suva harbor*

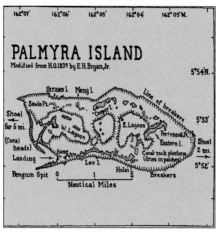

*Palmyra*

Honolulu and Canton that would also permit Pan Am to increase the payload to New Zealand. However, due to the outbreak of the war, Pan Am never utilized the option of refueling at Palmyra Island. Both Palmyra and Fiji were, however, shown as stopovers on the map of commercial air routes that Pan Am published in their annual report for 1943.

In late 1941, Pan Am also felt that Suva, Fiji definitely had potential for both passengers and freight, since it was not only the capital of Fiji, but also the headquarters of the British Empire for the islands of the western Pacific. Pan Am estimated that ten passengers a year would travel by Clipper from Auckland to Suva. The wartime activity in the Pacific, however, caused travel by Clipper to accelerate rapidly. On their second flight from Auckland, in late November of 1941, just before the outbreak of WW II, they carried 42 passengers to Fiji. In their news release they bragged that on this one flight Pan Am had exceeded their travel projections to Fiji for the next four years. Little did they know at that time that it would be their last flight to the Pacific before WW II shut down all operations west of Honolulu.

**From 1943,
PAN AM Annual Report
Route map for December 1941**

*Note that both Palmyra and Suva, Fiji are shown as stopovers to New Zealand*

As if Pan Am realized that this might be the last celebration for a long time, the airline gave the inaugural flight to Fiji the full first flight treatment. They prepared special cachets for each leg of the flight. Captain Tilton, assisted by first officer Wilson, headed up a crew of eleven. Almon Gray, whose family shared his scrapbooks and photos with me, was a crew member serving as a radio officer. Phil Berst, whose daughter Catherine also shared her father's scrapbooks and pictures with me, traveled along as the maintenance supervisor for the Pacific region to inspect the new base at Fiji.

*Flight crew to Fiji*

Pictured above at Treasure Island before departure is the entire crew. From left to right, steward R. Donharn, steward G.F. Burris, first radio officer P.T. Harper, third officer A.L. Terwilleger, second radio officer A.A. Gray, first engineer R.N. Goodson, Captain J.H. Tilton, fourth officer W.H. Grace, second officer J.A. Hrutky, second engineer J.B. Parish, and first officer J.A. Wilson.

The only flight cover I have seen signed by all the crew members is the one that Phil Berst, a passenger on the flight, had prepared and sent to his daughter, Catherine, as a souvenir of this last first flight before WW II. The cover is illustrated below.

*Gift for young Catherine Berst from her father*

Another unusual cover is the commercial letter mailed by Mrs. Ludden to her son at the Matson Navigation Corporation in Fiji. It made the first flight and was back stamped on arrival in Fiji on November 9, 1941. It is the only mail from the flight that I have seen that was not a souvenir of the first flight but a commercially used envelope with a letter enclosed.

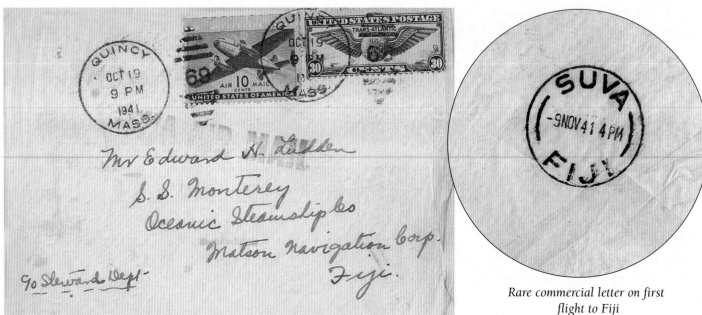

*Rare commercial letter on first flight to Fiji*

*Seldom seen envelopes printed by cachet manufacturer, L.W. Staehle of New York City.*

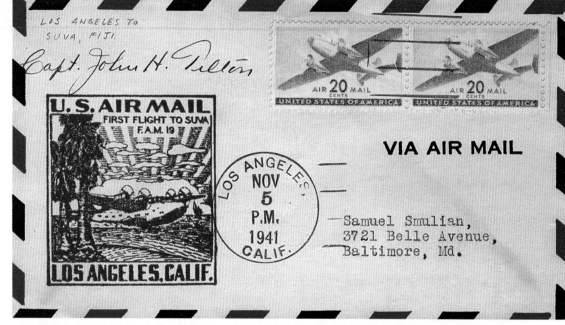

*Various cachets seen with Fiji first flights*

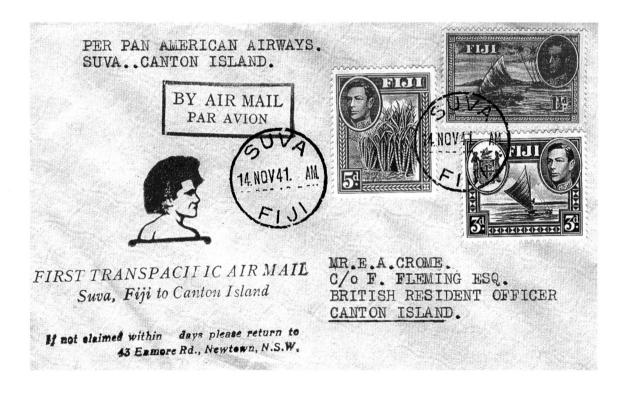

By mid-November of 1941, Pan Am's Pacific routes were operating smoothly. They finally had enough equipment to make the long flights to New Zealand and Singapore and the shuttle flights between Manila and Hong Kong. The great depression was nearly over. People were spending extra money for airmail, air express and even air travel. Although the business future was bright everyone knew the political climate was unstable. Pan Am did not realize, however, that they only had a few short weeks to operate in the Pacific before the outbreak of WWII.

# LAST PRE WAR FLIGHTS OF THE CLIPPERS

| Honolulu Clipper Last Prewar Flight | October 20 - 23, 1941 | B-314 Honolulu Clipper | Ford |
|---|---|---|---|
| **Outbound Flight Schedule** | | **Inbound Flight Schedule** | |
| Los Angeles - Honolulu    Oct. 20-21 | | Honolulu - San Francisco    Oct. 22-23 | |

The Boeing B-314 Honolulu Clipper, NC 18601, was flying the shuttle from Honolulu to the mainland just prior to the war and was in San Francisco undergoing regular maintenance from the end of October until after the attack on Pearl Harbor.

| California Clipper Last Prewar Flight | November 17 - 30, 1941 | B-314 California Clipper | Lodeesen |
|---|---|---|---|

| Outbound Flight Schedule | | Inbound Flight Schedule | |
|---|---|---|---|
| San Francisco - Los Angeles | Nov. 17 | Auckland - Noumea | Nov. 25 |
| Los Angeles  - Honolulu | Nov. 17-18 | Noumea  - Suva | Nov. 26 |
| Honolulu - Canton Island | Nov. 20 | Suva  - Canton Island | Nov. 27-26* |
| Canton Island - Suva | Nov. 21-22* | Canton Island  - Honolulu | Nov. 27 |
| Suva  - Noumea | Nov. 23 | Honolulu - Los Angeles | Nov. 29-30 |
| Noumea - Auckland | Nov. 24 | Los Angeles - San Francisco | Nov. 30 |
| *Dateline - Gain day outbound - Lose day inbound | | | |

On November 17, 1941 the California Clipper, NC 18602, departed San Francisco for Los Angeles and ultimately Honolulu to continue the bi-monthly service to New Zealand that had been established in July of 1940. The Clipper arrived in New Zealand on November 24 and the next day it left Auckland, New Zealand on the inbound flight, which included overnight stops at Noumea, Suva, Canton, Honolulu and finally San Francisco where it arrived November 30, 1941. It was then turned over to the maintenance crew for routine servicing which was still being performed at Treasure Island when the war broke out.

The illustrated registered cover was sent by the American Consulate in Sydney, Australia to the Secretary of State. The back stamp of November 28, 1941 in Honolulu proves that it was carried on the last inbound flight of the California Clipper from New Zealand before war was declared. On the back is a small message certifying that the envelope was part of Franklin D. Roosevelt's collection that was sold in 1946.

*Front*

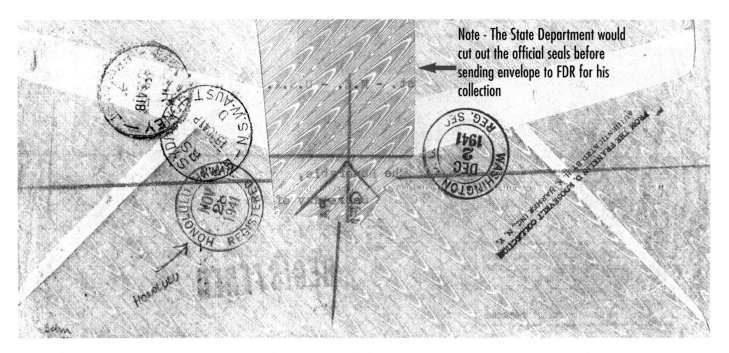

*Honolulu postmark November 28, 1941-This proves it was last flight before Dec 7, 1941- Cover is from President Roosevelt's collection*

The next illustrated cover was posted at Canton Island on November 25, 1941 in time for it to be placed on board the California Clipper on November 26, 1941 when the Clipper arrived at Canton on the last inbound flight before the war. The stamps showing the transport plane in flight had been introduced in the last half of 1941, and the twenty cent stamp was issued August 27, 1941. It is unusual to find a transport stamp used from remote Canton Island before the war to pay postage for the airmail letter.

| American Clipper Last Prewar Flight | December 2 - 5, 1941 | B-314 American Clipper | |
|---|---|---|---|
| **Outbound Flight Schedule** | | **Inbound Flight Schedule** | |
| **Los Angeles - Honolulu** | **December 2-3** | **Honolulu - San Francisco** | **Dec. 4-5** |

Shuttle service between San Francisco and Los Angeles and onward to Honolulu had been established in August of 1941. The Boeing B-314A American Clipper, NC 18606, was assigned to this shuttle service. At the time that war was declared the American Clipper was also at Treasure Island undergoing routine maintenance.

| Pacific Clipper Last Prewar Flight | December 1 - 8, 1941 to January 6,1942 | B-314A Pacific Clipper | Ford/Mack |
|---|---|---|---|

| Outbound Flight Schedule | | Inbound Flight Schedule | |
|---|---|---|---|
| San Francisco - Los Angeles | December 1 | Auckland – Noumea | December 15 |
| Los Angeles - Honolulu | December 2 - 3 | Noumea – Gladstone, Australia | December 16 |
| Honolulu - Canton Island | December 4 | Gladstone – Darwin, Australia | December 17 |
| Canton Island - Suva | December 5 - 6* | Darwin – Surabaya, Java | December 18 |
| Suva - Noumea | December 7 | Surabaya – Trincomalee, Ceylon | December 21 |
| Noumea - Auckland | December 8 | Trincomalee – Karachi, India | December 26 |
| | | Karachi – Bahrain, Saudi Arabia | December 28 |
| | | Bahrain – Khartoum, Sudan | December 29 |
| | | Khartoum – Leopoldville, Belgian Congo | January 1, 1942 |
| | | Leopoldville – Natal, Brazil | January 2, 1942 |
| | | Natal – Port of Spain, Trinidad | January 5, 1942 |
| *Dateline - Gain day outbound - Lose day inbound | | Port of Spain – LaGuardia, New York | January 5-6, 1942 |

The Pacific Clipper completed the first flight to Fiji with Captain Tilton in command on November 17, 1941. After routine servicing and a fresh crew under the command of Captain Ford and first officer Mack, the Pacific Clipper departed San Francisco on December 1, 1941 for Los Angeles, where they spent the night before flying on to Honolulu enroute to New Zealand. On December 5, after spending the evening at Canton Island, the crew flew on to the new stopover at Suva, Fiji before proceeding on to Noumea, New Caledonia. At Noumea they spent the night on the luxurious yacht, the Southern Seas, which continued to serve as a floating hotel for the passengers and crew. After an enjoyable evening aboard the yacht, they departed the next morning, December 8 – (December 7 in Honolulu) on the last leg of the flight to New Zealand. Just two hours out of Auckland, Captain Ford received the emergency message "Plan A" and he was told of the early morning attack on Pearl Harbor. He continued on to his destination under the cloud of war. Once in New Zealand, he awaited word from Pan Am's home office on what he should do. Finally, on December 14, 1941 Pan Am headquarters wired him that the only safe course for him to follow was to continue west across uncharted waters to New York.

An excellent book entitled **The Long Way Home** by Ed Dover has just been published. It recounts in detail Captain Ford's epic journey westward around the world. Even in this meticulously researched and nicely illustrated

*Captain Robert Ford*

book, Dover was unable to fully resolve the confusion over the correct aircraft number for the Pacific Clipper. Although he refers to the aircraft as NC 18602, the number generally assigned to the California Clipper, he readily acknowledges that there is a possibility that this number designation is incorrect. From my research, confirmed primarily by the June 1941 article in *New Horizons* that I discuss in Flight #32, I conclude that NC 18609, which was delivered to the Pacific in May of 1941, was temporarily given the

*The Pacific Clipper moored at New York's Marine Terminal - at the end of epic flight*

name of the California Clipper while the original California Clipper NC 18602 served temporarily in the Atlantic. Then, several months later when the California Clipper came back to the Pacific, it was given back its old name. The newly delivered Clipper, aircraft number NC 18609, became the Pacific Clipper. In spite of the confusion over the NC number of the aircraft, everyone does agree that the aircraft commanded by Captain Ford on his epic westward trip around the world was named the "Pacific Clipper" at the time of his remarkable flight. Let's not let this confusion over the correct aircraft number for the Pacific Clipper divert our attention from the exciting aviation adventure of Captain Ford's wartime escape from the expanding Pacific war.

Finally, after a nerve-wracking week waiting in Auckland for a flight plan from Pan Am, Captain Ford departed on the evening of December 15 for Noumea, New Caledonia to evacuate the Pan Am staff and to pick up two spare engines, one for delivery to the maintenance and repair facility that was being built in Karachi and the other as insurance for the Pacific Clipper on its long flight home. In Noumea, once loading was complete and all the Pan Am staff were safely aboard, they departed westward to Gladstone, Australia.

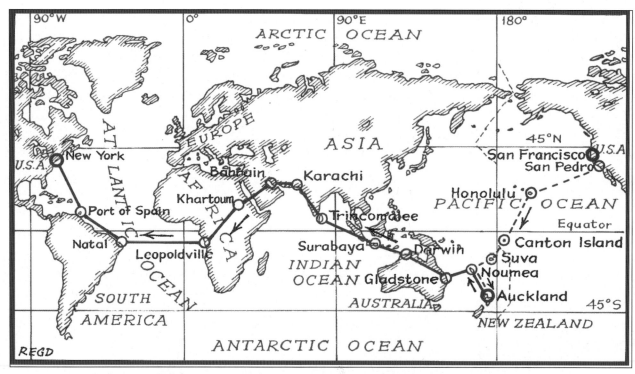

*Captain Ford's flight touched five continents (all except Europe and Antarctica) and crossed the equator four times*

The world map, used with permission from the book **The Long Way Home**, charts the Pacific Clipper's journey around the world. After departing Auckland, New Zealand, they flew to Noumea, Gladstone and Darwin in Australia; Surabaya, Java in the Dutch East Indies; Trincomalee, Ceylon; Karachi, India; Bahrain, Saudi Arabia; Khartoum, Sudan; Leopoldville, Belgian Congo; Natal, Brazil; Port Of Spain, Trinidad; and finally, at 5:54 a.m., on January 6, 1942, after an overnight flight from Port of Spain, Trinidad, Captain Ford radioed LaGuardia to tell them that he was a surprise visitor from the west requesting permission to land.

Because of the news blackout occasioned by the war, the traffic controllers at LaGuardia were taken totally by surprise. They had no record of overseas, inbound flights due at that time. The startled flight controller told Captain Ford that the seaplane channel was closed until daylight. Therefore, they would have to circle for about an hour before they could be cleared for landing. Finally, at daybreak, they brought the Pacific Clipper in and moored her to a docking buoy. They stepped out into a bitter New York winter day, but in spite of the cold, it was good to be home.

**The New York World Telegram** reported the Pacific Clipper's arrival as "the greatest achievement in the history of aviation since the Wright brothers flew at Kitty Hawk." **The New York Herald Tribune** wrote in their editorial, "The feat is one of which the pilot and crew and the Pan Am Airways may well be proud . . . but its significance will not be missed on either side of the Pacific."

Pictured is the crew on their arrival in New York, where the shock of Pearl Harbor was still very fresh in the minds of all of the people. Any triumph during

Roderick Norman
Brown-2nd officer

Verne C. Edwards
asst. flight steward

Oscar Hendrickson
2nd radio officer

James G. Henriksen
3rd officer

John Henry Mack
1st officer

John Bertrand Parish
2nd engineering officer

John D. Poindexter
1st radio officer

Homans K. Rothe
1st engineering officer

Barney Sawicki
flight steward

John Delmer Steers
4th officer

Captain Robert Ford - cover of New
Horizons magazine - January 1942

these early depressing days of the war was celebrated with great enthusiasm. Captain Ford and his crew became heroes.

Based on reports filed by Captain Ford, it has always been assumed that mail was not carried on the escape flight around the world on the Pacific Clipper. However, the airmail cover below, cancelled December 2, 1941 in Australia, and at 1:00 p.m. on January 6, 1942 at Shelby, Ohio, raises some very interesting questions.

This envelope would have been flown from Sydney, Australia to Auckland, New Zealand to meet the Pacific Clipper when it was scheduled to arrive in New Zealand from New Caledonia on December 8, 1941. If it had been carried on the Pacific Clipper on its around the world flight, it would have arrived in New York City at 6:00 a.m. on January 6, 1942, in time to be placed onboard the early morning mail flight to Cleveland, Ohio. Shelby, Ohio is a 90-minute drive from Cleveland. Therefore, based on its January 6, 1942 arrival in Ohio, it is possible that it was carried on the Pacific Clipper on its around the world flight. But, then again, perhaps it went by sea. The cover does raise some interesting and unanswered questions as to whether mail was carried by the Pacific Clipper on the flight to New York City. However, in the confusion of war, would the letter have reached Ohio by January 6, 1942 if it had traveled by sea? More research needs to be done on how long it would have taken by ship from Auckland to the United States.

*Was this cover carried by Pacific Clipper on its around the world flight?*

417

The secret report filed by Captain Ford, just two days after his return, concluded with these thoughts.

*"Throughout the trip the whole crew functioned very smoothly, every man doing his utmost at all times. There was no complaint from any crew member at any time during the trip. Around 50% of the credit for the successful completion of the trip should be accorded to the two engineers, Mr. Rothe and Mr. Parish. The other 50% should go to the navigating department headed by second officer, Mr. Brown, ably assisted on many occasions by Mr. James Henrikson, who was third officer during the trip. . . I felt at any time on the trip I could have turned over command to first officer John H. Mack with full confidence in the successful conclusion of the mission. Officer John Steers, CAA-trained pilot, showed that the civilian trained program is highly successful . . . There was nothing remarkable about the performance of the trip, to me. I could not help but notice how well received PAA was in every part of the world, and how everybody expected us to know exactly what we were doing and where we were going. They were amazed at the length of some of our flights, but did not seem to consider it unusual that we had thus far successfully negotiated all legs. The underlying credit for success of the whole operation should, of course, be given to the training that all hands have received in the organization of routine methods of handling practically every exigency that can arise in the course of long flights."*

*Robert Ford*

## PAN AMERICAN AIRWAYS SYSTEM

TRANSPACIFIC DIVISION, TREASURE ISLAND, SAN FRANCISCO, CALIFORNIA

February 3, 1942

Mr. H. Rothe
Pan American Airways, Inc.
Treasure Island
San Francisco
California

Dear Mr. Rothe:

Already I have expressed to you verbally my appreciation of your fine work on Trip 5073 to Auckland and thence via Africa to New York.

For the benefit of your personnel record I would like to address the following remarks to you:

I sincerely feel that I owe the Engineers on the round-the-world trip a great debt in gratitude for your remarkable demonstration of intelligence, industry, intimate knowledge of your job and devotion to duty over and above anything that could reasonably be expected.

Your ingenuity on several occasions saved the trip from failure if not disaster.

It is with great pleasure that I give you the highest recommendation possible.

Very truly yours,

R. Ford

RF:s

Marian Rothe, the widow of Homans (Swede) Rothe, flight engineer on this flight of the Pacific Clipper, shared with me her memories and her treasured mementoes of this flight. She was most proud of the personal letter of thanks her husband received from Captain Ford shortly after the flight.

*New Aviation Comics* for August of 1942 featured the story of Captain Ford's escape and the first commercial flight around the world. The first page of the comic traced his route and the last page recounted their landing at LaGuardia and the four world records set by their flight.

This was indeed a remarkable flight, made possible by the skill and training of a Pan Am crew, performing perfectly under wartime emergency conditions.

| Anzac Clipper Last Prewar Flight | December 6 - 8, 1941 | B-314A Anzac Clipper | Turner/Sommers |
|---|---|---|---|

| Outbound Flight Schedule | | Inbound Flight Schedule | |
|---|---|---|---|
| San Francisco - Hilo | December 6-7 | Hilo - San Francisco | December 7-8 |

Guy F. McCafferty was a young crew member on the last flight of the Anzac Clipper before WWII. In March of 1999, using his log book to refresh his memory, he wrote me a long letter detailing this flight. My account of the flight is based upon his remembrance.

On December 5, 1941, the Anzac Clipper Boeing B-314A departed San Francisco with a planned

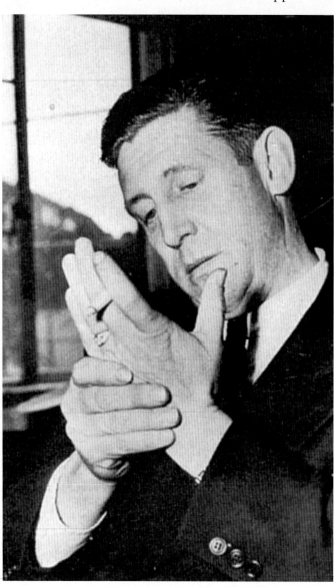

*Captain Lanier Turner - December 1941*

destination of Singapore. The flight was under the command of Lanier Turner and first officer Ed Sommers. McCafferty served as a relief pilot. There were 32 passengers plus mail and freight. The flight departed Treasure Island at 5:00 p.m. and an hour and 45 minutes into the flight the Clipper developed engine trouble, requiring an engine shut down and a return to the base. The flight was rescheduled for the same departure time the next day, December 6, 1941. The 5:00 p.m. departure was again delayed. According to one story, the delay was due to one of the passengers, who went to his daughter's dance recital and was held up in traffic. Therefore, the plane was held at Treasure Island for his arrival. Another report says that there was a minor maintenance problem on the Clipper took an hour to clear. Regardless of the reason, as a result of the delay, the Anzac Clipper departed an hour and a half behind schedule for Honolulu.

The Clipper was about an hour out of Honolulu on the morning of December 7, 1941, when Captain Turner received a coded message "Plan A" indicating that Pearl Harbor was under attack. The contingency war plans that had previously been worked out by Pan Am were immediately put into operation. The flight was diverted to an early morning river landing in Hilo on the island of Hawaii.

If the Anzac Clipper had not been delayed an hour and a half in its takeoff, it would have been landing at Pearl Harbor at the exact time of the Japanese attack. Therefore, the delay undoubtedly saved the passengers and crew from an uncertain fate and perhaps destruction.

In Hilo, Captain Turner was ordered by Pan Am to complete the required maintenance as quickly as possible, to offload the mail and to return immediately with any passengers who wanted to return to the security of San Francisco. Surprisingly, all the passengers voted to stay in Hawaii. Therefore, the Clipper without any passengers left the evening of December 7 and arrived at Treasure Island on December 8, 1941.

The mail that had been offloaded in Hilo was transferred to Honolulu where it was censored by the newly formed civilian censor board and if forward delivery was still possible under the wartime conditions, it was sent to its destination. If it could not be forwarded, it was returned to the sender.

The cover illustrated was mailed from Jersey City on December 3, 1941 and was aboard the Anzac Clipper as it approached Honolulu. It was among the items of mail that were offloaded at Hilo that were sent to Honolulu. Because this letter was intended to go westbound out of Honolulu, it had to be returned to the sender in New Jersey. Due to the confusion of handling mail during the early months of the war it took eight months to be returned.

With the outbreak of the war, all travel by Clipper was controlled by the military. Civilian mail, such as the illustrated envelope, had a low priority during these hectic and frightening days following the attack on Pearl Harbor.

| China Clipper Last Prewar Flight | November 19 - Dec. 6, 1941 | M-130 China Clipper | McGlohn |
|---|---|---|---|

| Outbound Flight Schedule | | Inbound Flight Schedule | |
|---|---|---|---|
| San Francisco - Honolulu | Nov. 19-20 | Singapore - Manila | November 30 |
| Honolulu - Midway | Nov. 24 | Manila - Guam | December 1 |
| Midway - Wake | Nov. 25-26* | Guam - Wake | December 2 |
| Wake - Guam | Nov. 27 | Wake - Midway | December 3-2* |
| Guam - Manila | Nov. 28 | Midway - Honolulu | December 4 |
| Manila - Singapore | Nov. 29 | Honolulu - San Francisco | December 5-6 |

*Dateline - Gain day outbound - Lose day inbound*

The last prewar flight of the China Clipper departed San Francisco for Singapore on November 19, 1941. The flight to Singapore was uneventful. On the inbound flight the China Clipper departed Singapore on November 30, 1941, and ultimately arrived at Wake the afternoon of December 2, 1941. After routine servicing and an overnight stay, the China Clipper left Wake for Midway on December 3, and after crossing the dateline and spending two nights at Midway, the Clipper arrived in Honolulu the afternoon of December 4, 1941.

The illustrated cover from Wake Island with the hard to read overlapping cancels appears worn and unattractive. Careful examination, however, reveals a fascinating story of the China Clipper's last flight before WW II.

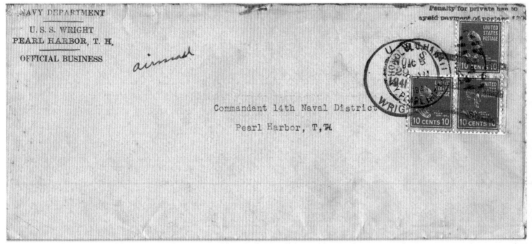

*Last mail off Wake Island- Last Prewar flight of China Clipper.*

In mid-November of 1941, the U.S.S. Wright, with Navy Lt. Winfield Cunningham onboard, received orders to proceed directly to Wake Island so that Lt. Cunningham could assume command of the Naval air station at Wake. The Wright arrived at Wake on the morning of November 28, 1941 and Lt. Cunningham departed the vessel, taking along his golf clubs for what he hoped would be a routine assignment.

The envelope illustrated was first cancelled onboard the Wright on the morning of November 29, 1941. Because the letter was addressed to the Navy Commandant in Honolulu, it was a high priority letter. Therefore, rather than carry it on the slow U.S.S. Wright to Honolulu it was held at Wake for the inbound China Clipper, which arrived on December 2, 1941. The envelope, cancelled on the U.S.S. Wright on November 29, 1941, was placed onboard the inbound China Clipper. On December 3, 1941 the Clipper departed Wake and, after crossing the dateline and an overnight stay on Midway, arrived at Honolulu on the afternoon of December 4, 1941, too late for the mail to be delivered to the post office. The next morning the envelope carried on the China Clipper, was cancelled at Pearl Harbor at 8:00 a.m., December 5, 1941. These double postmarks of November 29, 1941 onboard the Wright at Wake Island and at 8:00 a.m. on December 5, 1941 at Pearl Harbor provide absolute proof that this envelope traveled from Wake to Honolulu on the last prewar flight of the China Clipper.

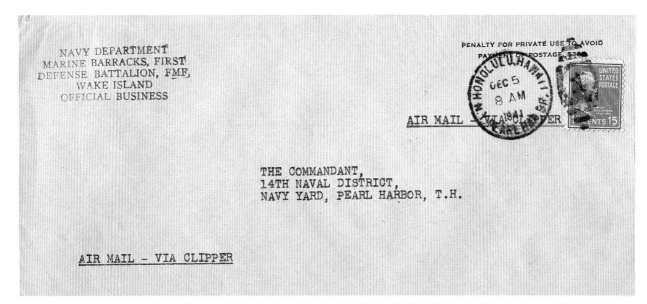

Illustrated is another cover from Wake that was also onboard the China Clipper on its last prewar flight. It was sent from the marine detachment at Wake that was under the command of Major Devereux. Because Wake did not have a post office, this Marine Corps envelope carried by the China Clipper was also postmarked at 8:00 a.m. on December 5, 1941 at Pearl Harbor.

After delivering Lt. Cunningham to the doomed island, the U.S.S. Wright departed Wake Island on November 30, 1941 and after a stop at Midway, it arrived at Pearl Harbor eleven days later, in the early morning of December 8, 1941, less than a day after the surprise Japanese attack.

Let us look at two unique pieces of mail from Wake Island that were not carried on the China Clipper on her last prewar flight, but were carried instead aboard the U.S.S. Wright from Wake to Honolulu.

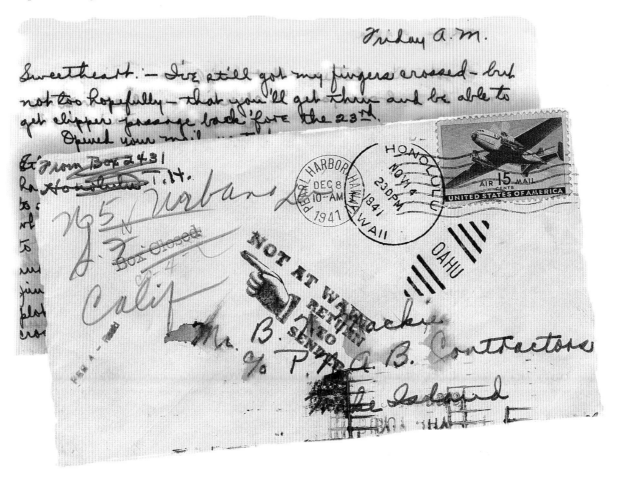

First, is the water stained envelope with a letter enclosed that tells a compelling tale of the last civilian construction worker to leave Wake Island before the Japanese attack. The envelope was mailed from Eleanor Mackie at Honolulu to her husband, B.W. Mackie, one of the 1200 men on Wake who were rushing to complete the naval base.

Based on the contents of her letter, B.W. Mackie had completed his work contract and was scheduled to leave Wake and return with his wife to California. If space was available, he had permission to fly from Wake to Honolulu on the inbound flight of the Philippine Clipper that was expected to arrive at Wake from Guam on November 23, 1941. However, with all the frantic prewar activity in the Pacific, Mackie and his wife were doubtful he could get a seat on the crowded Clipper. His wife, however, was anxious for his return when she wrote:

> **Friday A.M.**
> **(November 14, 1941)**
>
> ***Sweetheart,***
> ***I've still got my fingers crossed – but not too hopefully – that you'll get through and be able to get Clipper passage back 'fore the 23rd.***

On Friday afternoon, November 14, 1941 she mailed the letter, with the expectation that it would be placed on a Clipper in a day or so and carried to her husband on Wake by no later than November 22, 1941. The outbound China Clipper, however, did not arrive in Honolulu from San Francisco until November 20 and because of bad weather, it did not depart Honolulu for Midway until November 24, 1941. Therefore, Eleanor Mackie's letter to her husband that was carried by the China Clipper did not leave Hawaii until November 24, 1941 and did not arrive at Wake until November 26, 1941, twelve days after it had been mailed.

B.W. Mackie, however, had been very, very lucky! He had indeed gotten a seat on the inbound Philippine Clipper which arrived in Honolulu on Tuesday afternoon, November 25, 1941. A few days later the Mackies left Honolulu by boat for California, departing just days before the December 7 attack on Pearl Harbor.

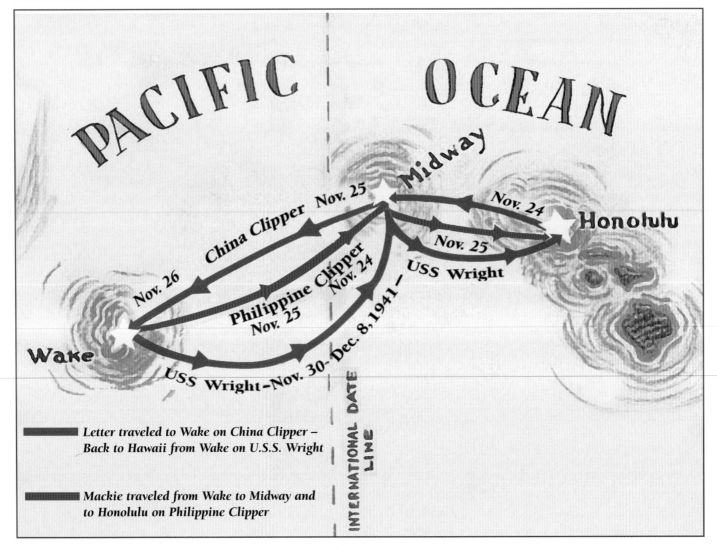

424

Meanwhile, the now unimportant letter from Eleanor Mackie to her husband had been delivered to Wake on November 26, 1941 by the outbound China Clipper. When the postal clerk on Wake checked to see if Mackie was still on the island he learned that he had departed Wake one day earlier on the Philippine Clipper for Honolulu. Therefore, the clerk applied the rubber stamp "Not at Wake Island". Before it was discovered on this envelope, this postal stamp "Not at Wake Island" had not been seen on any Wake Island mail.

Apparently postal regulations stated that Clipper mail that could not be delivered would be returned to the sender by sea, rather than by Clipper. **❶** Therefore, Eleanor Mackie's letter was <u>not</u> held for the next inbound Clipper flight, which would have been the return of the China Clipper to Wake on December 2. 1941. Instead, the envelope was sent back to Honolulu along with the other low priority non-airmail letters onboard the U.S.S. Wright, which departed Wake on November 30, 1941 for Midway and Honolulu.

The U.S.S. Wright, with the Mackie letter onboard, arrived in Honolulu on the early morning of December 8, 1941. The Mackie letter, along with other mail carried on the Wright from Wake, was cancelled at 10:00 a.m. December 8, 1941 at the Pearl Harbor branch of the Honolulu Post Office.

Days later, when the post office in Honolulu attempted to return the Mackie letter that had been sent back from Wake to Honolulu Post Office Box 2431 (Eleanor Mackie's box number in Honolulu), they discovered that the postal box had been closed several days earlier when the Mackies left Honolulu for California. **❷** Box Closed  So the Mackie letter was sent to the forwarding address they left with the post office when they closed their mailbox - 265 Urbano Street in San Francisco, California. The now well traveled Mackie letter left Honolulu by ship sometime after **❸** January 14, 1942. It was finally delivered to the Mackies in San Francisco on February 4, 1942. **❹** FEB 4 - Rec'd  In all the confusion the letter was never censored.

This rare letter carried on the last outbound pre-war flight of the China Clipper, is probably the only surviving piece of mail that arrived at Wake in late 1941. All the other mail sent to Wake during this period was destroyed when the Japanese landed in late December of 1941.

Another piece of mail carried with the Mackie letter on the U.S.S. Wright from Wake to Honolulu was a postcard that was also written on Friday, November 14, 1941, the same day as Eleanor Mackie's letter to her husband. When "Spike", a construction worker on Wake, mailed the postcard to his girlfriend, he did not want to spend 35¢ of his hard earned money to send it by Clipper to the States. Therefore, the card was carried on the U.S.S. Wright along with the other non-airmail letters. This postcard, which also arrived on the Wright in Honolulu on the morning of December 8, was also postmarked at 10:00 a.m. December 8, 1941 at Pearl Harbor. "Spike" was not as fortunate as Mackie and he, along with the other 1200 construction workers and the surviving marines and naval personnel, were taken prisoner when Wake fell to the Japanese.

In early December of 1941, the conditions in the Pacific had reached the boiling point. Everyone believed that war was inevitable. They only hoped that they had time to prepare. No one realized that the attack would come so soon or that the first strike would be so devastating. These last few pieces of mail that left Wake Island also show how unprepared they were for the surprise attack and how fate played a role on who escaped and who was trapped on remote Wake Island.

**GREETINGS
FROM
WAKE ISLAND
NORTH PACIFIC OCEAN**

*Left – Pearl Harbor postmark on Mackie letter – identical to the postmark on postcard from Spike.*

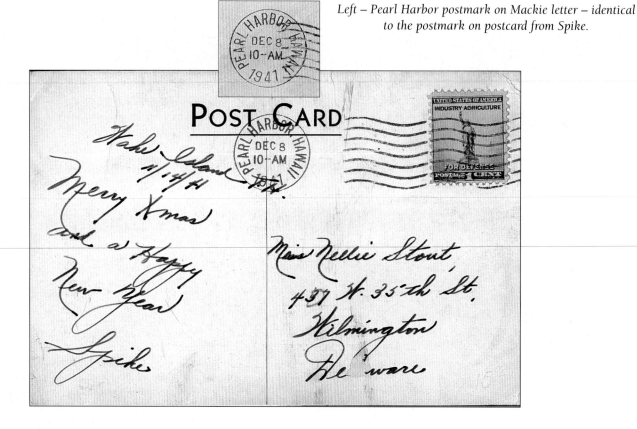

| Philippine Clipper Last Prewar Flight | Dec. 3 - 11, 1941 | M-130 Philippine Clipper | Hamilton/Moss |
|---|---|---|---|

| Outbound Flight Schedule | | Inbound Flight Schedule | |
|---|---|---|---|
| San Francisco - Honolulu | December 3 - 4 | | |
| Honolulu - Midway | December 5 | Wake to Midway | December 8 – 7* |
| Midway - Wake | December 6 – 7* | Midway to Honolulu | December 8 |
| Wake for Guam – Return to Wake | December 8 | Honolulu to San Francisco | December 10 – 11 |

*Dateline - Gain day outbound - Lose day inbound

Wake Island in early December of 1941 was a place of high activity and low preparedness. The 1200 civilian construction workers under the supervision of Dan Teeters were using their heavy equipment and manpower to build runways, shops, utilities and barracks, but no military defenses. They were, of course, unarmed. The 38 officers and 475 enlisted men stationed on Wake had only 12 recently arrived Grumman Wildcat fighters and a few three-inch and five inch artillery guns, machine guns, rifles and pistols. The marines had to build all military defenses with picks and shovels, aided by an occasional bulldozer borrowed from the civilian workers. They had no radar, no fueling facilities, no parking so as to disperse the aircraft and no bombproof bunkers. They even lacked an air raid siren to warn the island of approaching planes. Twenty percent of the troops were without firearms or field equipment. In the official report published by the Marine Corps after the war they stated:

> Wake in the autumn 1941 was literally an image of America: an island in the path of the inevitable war; an island vibrant with unceasing construction in an effort to recapture lost time; an island militarily naked.

Wake and the other Pacific bases got into this vulnerable position because Congress failed to act decisively on the recommendations of Rear Admiral A.J. Hepburn, who headed up the commission that reported to Congress in May of 1938 on defense base preparedness. The Hepburn report recommended $7,500,000 for the immediate construction of a naval air base at Wake and similar fortifications for Guam.

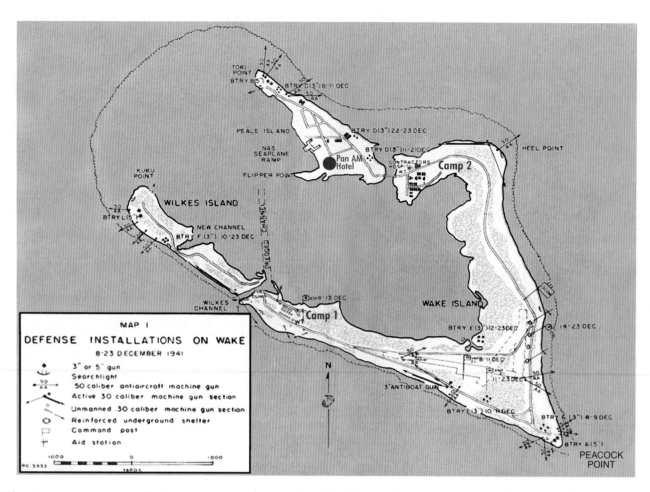

The Guam recommendations were never acted upon. The military strategists, however, felt that Wake should be fortified, even though they believed that it could not be long defended from an all out Japanese attack. If the Japanese were forced to mount a major air and sea attack against a well fortified Wake, they would be forced to expose a large portion of their fleet to an Allied counter attack in the open north Pacific. In short, in the event of war it was planned that a well equipped and defended Wake would be bait for a huge military trap. Therefore, in early 1941 the civilian contractors finally and belatedly began the work necessary to convert the remote island into a military fortress. As construction slowly advanced, troops were transferred to the island. On June 23, 1941, five officers and 173 marines of the 1st Defense Battalion, under the command of Major Louis Hohn, arrived.

On October 15, 1941 Major James P. S. Devereux became commander of the 1st Defense Battalion detachment when he relieved Major Hohn, who was transferred off the island. By virtue of his seniority, Devereux also became the temporary Wake Island commander. On November 2, 1941 an additional 200 marines and nine officers arrived. On November 19, 1941, 49 additional marines with the Marine Fighting Squadron 211 were transferred to Wake. All of the marines on Wake were based on the south side of the lagoon at Camp One.

On November 28, 1941 the U.S.S. Wright arrived and Lieutenant Winfield Scott Cunningham, came ashore to assume command of the naval air station at Wake Island. Although he only held the rank of lieutenant, as commander of the naval air station, he became the commander of all the forces on Wake Island. Also on board the Wright was navy Commander Campbell Keene with eight officers and 58 bluejackets for the new naval air station. They arrived without arms or field equipment. Naval Air Base Commander Cunningham and navy Commander Keene with his navy officers and men were located on the north side of the lagoon at Camp Two with the 1200 civilian construction workers. The physical distance by road between marine commander Devereux at Camp One and Wake Island's naval base. Commander Cunningham at Camp Two was approximately four miles. The emotional distance between the men, however, was even greater. Smoldering just below the surface was the unspoken belief that navy officer Cunningham lacked the combat training and toughness necessary for this assignment and when the invasion occurred, that he surrendered the island earlier than was necessary.

After the war, both Devereux and Cunningham wrote personal and emotional books defending their individual roles in the battle for Wake.

Cunningham's timing in arriving at Wake could not have been worse. Construction was far from complete, Wake had no airplanes, war was ten days away and Pearl Harbor had wired saying: "International situation indicates you should be on alert."

On December 4, 1941 twelve Grumman Wildcat fighters took off from the deck of the Enterprise and arrived at Wake to provide the island's sole air defense. They were under the command of Major Paul Putnam, who wrote in his December 3, 1941 letter to his commanding officer about his feelings as he was about to arrive at the unfortified and defenseless island with his twelve sleek new aircraft.

> "*The admiral . . . made it plain to me and to the whole ship that nothing should be overlooked or any trouble spared in order to insure that I will get ashore with twelve airplanes in as near perfect condition as possible. I immediately was given a full compliment of mechs and all hands aboard ship have continually vied with each other to see who could do the most for me. I feel a bit like the fatted calf, being groomed for whatever it is that happens to fatted calves. But it surely is nice while it lasts and the airplanes are pretty sleek and fat too.*"

*From Major Putnam's letter – December 3, 1941*

*Navy and Marine*
*Wake Island service pin-twice actual size*

*Commander Winfield S. Cunningham*
*U.S.N. Island commander of Wake*
*November 29 - December 23, 1941*

*Major James P. S. Devereux*
*commander the Marine defenders*
*of Wake*

*Major Paul A. Putnam*
*commander of Marine Fighting*
*Squadron 211*

But there was little that Commander Cunningham, Major Devereux and Major Putnam could do in the few days they had to prepare Wake for what was coming. In spite of the obvious emergency, the civilian contractors continued to work on projects for the naval air station, not the military defense installations. The twelve fighting aircraft were too few and the marine defense force too inadequate. The radar and other vital equipment was missing. All they could do was hope that any conflict was months away. They worked and they hoped.

In spite of the growing tensions, Pan Am continued to fly regular Transpacific flights through Wake. Other than to require the wives of the hotel and maintenance crews to remain in Honolulu, little changed for the Pan Am community. In early December of 1941 Pan Am personnel totalled 65. Twenty-seven men were from the states and the other 38 were Chamorros, natives of Guam, who worked at the hotel, the laundry and in other maintenance positions.

The Philippine Clipper (NC 14715) departed San Francisco on December 3, 1941 for its regular flight to Singapore. After overnight stops at Honolulu and Midway, it arrived with its four passengers at Wake on Sunday afternoon, December 7, 1941 (Saturday, December 6 in Honolulu).

Shortly after sunrise on Monday morning, December 8 (Sunday, December 7 in Honolulu) Pan Am's Captain Hamilton taxied the Philippine Clipper out onto the lagoon, took his take-off position and at 6:55 a.m. broke the surface of the water and soared west toward Guam. Just as the Clipper departed the Wake radio officer received a frantic, uncoded transmission that Pearl Harbor was under attack. While word of the attack was relayed to the Wake commanders, the Philippine Clipper was recalled about twenty minutes out of Wake. The Clipper circled and returned to the lagoon. Pan Am's Captain, J.H. Hamilton, arrived back to a scene of frantic activity. Four of the 12 Wildcat fighter aircraft had been sent out on patrol. Construction of protective berms that was necessary to permit the dispersal and camouflage of aircraft was scheduled to be completed later in the day. Therefore, to avoid possible damage from attempting to move the aircraft on rough ground, the squad commander made a decision that he would always regret – to leave the Wildcats in their regular, rather confined, unprotected parking area.

Meanwhile, Captain Hamilton received orders from Base Commander Cunningham to conduct a long-range southward search with fighter escorts later during the afternoon. He then met with Major Putnam to plan the afternoon scouting mission.

It was shortly before noon when a rain squall drifted across Peacock Point on the south side of Wake. The clouds hid the approach of 36 twin-tailed Japanese bombers of the 24th Air Flotilla, based at Roi, 720 miles to the south. Without radar and with the sound of the pounding surf drowning out the sound of the approaching aircraft and with the horizon covered by clouds, Wake Island had no warning of the approaching planes. The Japanese fighters flew in three 12-plane V formations and they dropped from the protective clouds at 11:58 a.m. Seconds later bombs and gunfire were striking Wake Island.

*Grumman F4F-3 fighter - of the type employed by VMF-211 to intercept daily Japanese raids on Wake as well as to bomb and strafe enemy naval vessels on December 11 and 12, 1941*

According to the official Marine Corps report:

> *"By 12:10 p.m. the enemy division had expended bombs and ammunition, turned away, rendezvous and commenced their climb back to cruising altitude. The pilots in every one of the planes were grinning widely. Everyone waggled his wings to signify 'BON ZAI'."*

The Japanese had escaped without the loss of a single aircraft. Admiral Inouye was proud of his 24th Air Flotilla for their devastating strike and their initial good fortune.

Of the eight Wildcats on the ground, seven were destroyed and one rendered inoperable. Of the four aircraft that were on patrol, three landed safely after the attack, but the fourth hit debris on the runway and was put out of commission. Worst of all, of the 55 Marine aviation personnel on the ground, 23 were killed and 11 were wounded, including two pilots killed and three injured. At one stroke, VMF-211 lost 75% of its aircraft and over 60% of its personnel.

*Eight Wildcats destroyed on initial attack - Japanese photo*

The Pan Am base also took a terrible pounding. Ten of the Chamorros from Guam were killed. The office was destroyed and the hotel was in flames. Shortly after the attack John B. Cooke, the manager of Pan Am's Wake base, wrote of his escape from Wake. Although his report reveals the prevailing racial prejudices of the time, it does capture the confusion and terror of the day:

# REPORT OF ATTACK ON WAKE

*After the bombing attack was over, I was bleeding some about the face and body, but a quick check assured me I had no injury of consequence.*

*I then left what was left of the building to see how others had fared, proceeding directly to the hotel about half a block distant. This framed building of 40 rooms and spacious lobby and dining room was badly battered and one wing was already ablaze. Several minutes search revealed no one there and in leaving I noted what appeared to be all of the white Pan Am personnel on the dock or approaching it and the Clipper's engines were being started.*

*At first it seemed to me to be a bit cowardly to think of leaving, but there would have been no purpose in remaining. Every Pan Am building had been hit and several were burning. Power was gone and radio was gone, all was gone. The station had been rendered useless.*

*Continued next page*

A check revealed 16 bullet holes in the Clipper, but miraculously, somehow, the gas tanks and engines were not damaged. To leave meant saving the airplane and ourselves so we left.

Thirty-five of us, plus fuel, made a terrific load for the Martin. The first try for take-off failed, as did the second. For a third, the safety factor was nil as already the engines had been full throttled longer than cylinders ordinarily stand. But Captain Hamilton promptly taxied back for another try. This time he kept full speed the entire length of the runway. When the point had been reached where it was either take off or crash, the plane lifted and retained sufficient altitude to cross the island. We then skimmed the water for several hours. Necessarily, and to better avoid detection. At nightfall we took a respectable altitude that remained well aloft until we neared Midway, which we reached at midnight.

Refueling was hurriedly accomplished at the established refueling barge anchored some distance out from shore. The Japs had attacked Midway from ships some distance out, and we could learn but little. One sizable building was in flames. In less than an hour, we were underway again. No trouble about take-off this time as

*Bullet riddled Philippine Clipper safely home -
December 11, 1941*

*Arrival of Captain Hamilton, officers John Hrutky and Ted Hrutky at Treasure Island on December 11, 1941. There were approximately 1750 men on Wake. Some 1200 were civilians and approximately 500 were connected with the construction of the naval air base.*

runway was unlimited. We reached Honolulu the next day at mid-afternoon. Patches of bombed and burned airplanes were observed as we neared our destination, and Pearl Harbor of course showed much evidence of the Jap's visit. Listing, smoldering vessels. We did not loiter as all were pretty much exhausted after 24 hours in the air, under strain and without sleep. Honolulu proper did not suffer except for a random bomb or two.

The Clipper took off for the mainland by next day. But due to the long trip, only the crew was aboard. The rest of us spent ten blacked out nights at the Moana Hotel before returning by ship to San Francisco.

When the Philippine Clipper, bound for Honolulu, lifted off Wake lagoon at 12:58 p.m., exactly one hour after the initial attack, the air patrol requested of Captain Hamilton, by Commander Cunningham, was forgotten. Also left behind at Wake were the 27 surviving Chamorros who worked for Pan Am on Wake. Two who tried to stow away were put off the aircraft. "It seemed", said Commander Cunningham, "an unfortunate time to draw the color line". A Pan Am mechanic, Waldo Raugust, was busy after the attack helping to get the wounded Chammorros to the hospital at Camp 2 and he didn't get word about the flight. Neither did Mr. H.P. Hoevenor, an employee with the Bureau of Budget. He too somehow missed seeing the departure notice. Both men became prisoners when Wake surrendered 16 days later. This caused Colonel Devereux to comment, "It struck me as a rather drastic lesson in the wisdom of punctuality".

*Insignia for Wake Island*

The fighting men and the civilian workers on Wake knew that their only hope for survival lay in a relief force being sent out with fresh troops and replacement aircraft. What they didn't know was that the chaos and devastation caused by the Pearl Harbor attack had made a large rescue force an impossibility. Hawaii was worried about its own safety and survival. No one knew where the aircraft carriers for the attacking planes at Pearl Harbor were located and whether they or a Japanese landing force was going to follow up the initial Pearl Harbor air attack.

Finally, on December 15, 1941, a token contingent of relief vessels departed Honolulu for Wake. The carrier Saratoga, three cruisers, nine destroyers and a squadron of planes and about 200 marines, were assigned to the mission. Due to the slow oiler that accompanied the vessels, the convoy could only make 12 knots. At this slow pace they could not expect to reach Wake until December 24, 1941.

On December 20, 1941, a single navy PBY patrol bomber, the first outside physical contact with Wake since the attack, dropped out of the clouds and onto the Wake lagoon, bringing the tentative plans for Wake's relief and reinforcement. Major Walter Baylor, who had arrived with Commander Cunningham on the Wright on November 28, 1941, also had orders to be transferred to Midway on the PBY's return flight from Wake. There was also space on board the aircraft for both the Pan Am passenger, H.P. Hoevenor, and Pan Am employee, Waldo Raugust, the two men who had missed the Philippine Clipper's departure 12 days earlier. However, parachutes and "Mae West" life preservers required by navy regulations could not be found. So they missed the flight of the PBY and their last chance to escape. Before leaving Wake, Major Baylor visited the hospital and took a personal message from each of the wounded men that he promised to telegraph to their families when he reached Honolulu. He also gathered the official reports from Commander Cunningham, Major Devereux, Major Putnam and Lt. Commander Greey, who was the navy officer in charge of the civilian construction projects.

*Major Baylor at work*

7 JAP WARSHIPS
I CRUISER
4 DESTROYERS
I SUBMARINE
I GUNBOAT
9 JAP PLANES

*Cartoon: "Semper Fidelis" by Jerry Doyle*

But time was running out on the island. The final two aircraft, that had been kept flying by cannibalizing salvage from wrecked aircraft, took off for the last time on December 22. One crashed on landing, the other was lost in battle. That was the end of the air battle for Wake; VMF-211 ceased to exist and Major Putnam and his remaining men reported to the infantry and awaited the invasion from the Japanese force that now surrounded the island in warships.

The relief force was still two days away and worse, Admiral Kimmel, who had approved and planned the Wake rescue operation, had been relieved of duty and Admiral Chester A. Nimitz was the new commander of the crippled Pacific Fleet. Nimitz was still in Washington and would not arrive in Honolulu until Christmas Day. Neither the navy nor the country could afford another naval disaster. The Saratoga was too valuable to lose. For these reasons, the relief force was called back to Honolulu. The Japanese landing force attacked Wake at 10:00 p.m. December 22, 1941.

By 2:30 a.m. on December 23 the Japanese landing barges hit the beach. By 3:00 a.m. Japanese forces had landed at several points on the island. With daylight, the defenders of Wake counted 16 Japanese vessels completely ringing the atoll. They cruised just out of range of the few guns that remained operational. At 7:00 a.m. the Japanese launched an air strike. The anti-aircraft battery at Peacock Point opened fire on the planes as a final gesture from the only remaining intact anti-aircraft battery on the island.

Shortly after 7:00 a.m. Major Devereux reported to Commander Cunningham that the situation was critical. It was agreed that there was nothing that could be done and that it was senseless to keep spending lives when there would be nothing gained in return. Furthermore, to continue fighting would also risk the lives of the civilian construction workers. Word was passed to the few remaining positions held by the Americans that they should surrender. By 8:00 a.m. on December 23, 1941 it was over.

It was a defeat, but to many it was a victory, because in the early dark days of the war it showed Americans the will of their fighting men. "Remember Wake Island" became a slogan that rallied the troops and the country throughout the war. Later there were questions and controversies over who was in command, whether it was Devereux or Cunningham. There was controversy over whether or not the relief force should have been called back without even attempting a rescue. There was, however, never any question that a small, poorly equipped force with basically three patched up aircraft held off far superior Japanese forces for 16 days and that the Japanese were forced to pay a heavy price, including seven war ships, one cruiser, four destroyers, one submarine, one gunboat and nine planes, not to mention hundreds of casualties to defeat the out gunned and out manned Americans.

THE WHITE HOUSE
WASHINGTON

Citation by

THE PRESIDENT OF THE UNITED STATES

"The courageous conduct of the officers and men who defended Wake Island against an overwhelming superiority of enemy air, sea, and land attacks from December 8 to 22, 1941, has been noted with admiration by their fellow countrymen and the civilized world, and will not be forgotten so long as gallantry and heroism are respected and honored. They are commended for their devotion to duty and splendid conduct at their battle stations under most adverse conditions. With limited defensive means against attacks in great force, they manned their shore installations and flew their aircraft so well that five enemy warships were either sunk or severely damaged, many hostile planes shot down, and an unknown number of land troops destroyed."

*Franklin D. Roosevelt*

Wake prisoners on board Nitta Maru. Naval Air Base Commander Cunningham (seated in uniform at right) finds smiles of group inexplicable. He guesses that the photographer suddenly asked for a smile and each individual responded instinctively. Wake civilian boss Dan Teeters on Commander Cunningham's right.
(From Japanese propaganda magazine Freedom)

Waldo Raugust, the mechanic who did not make the flight, remained in Japanese prison camps for the remainder of the war. When the 12 Pan Am employees who were captured in December of 1941 at Guam and Wake were released, their stories were featured in the Pan Am monthly newsletter. Waldo Raugust signed his picture from the newspaper article that is in my collection.

On the morning of the attack on Pearl Harbor, when the Philippine Clipper returned to the Wake lagoon to pick up the Pan Am employees, in order to lighten the load for the Clipper, all of the air express packages and all of the mail was left on the dock. Some reports say it was burned, but that has never been substantiated. Most likely the now unimportant mail was still on Wake when the Japanese captured the island 16 days later. In any event, none of the mail carried on the Philippine Clipper on this flight was ever recovered.

Other than the clothing worn by those being evacuated, the only item brought from Wake by the Pan Am staff was the U.S. flag that was flying at Pan Am's office. The rescued flag was presented by the Pan Am crew to Pan Am's public relations director, William VanDusen. He left the Wake flag to his wife, who gave it to aviation historian Don Thomas. I obtained the flag from Don Thomas when I obtained his extensive collection of Pan Am memorabilia in 1995.

## GUAM-WAKE INTERNEES SAFE; AWAITING TRANSPORTATION HOME

Twelve fellow PAA employees captured in December, 1941, on Guam and Wake are reported safe and good health. Eleven of them—Richard Arvidson, George Blackett, Max Brodofsky, George M. Conklin, Charles F. Gregg, Alfred Hammelef, Fred Oppenborn, Everett Penning, James Thomas, Robert Vaughan, and Grant Wells, were in Yokohama a week ago on September 9, awaiting transportation home, according to Ken Frazer, fellow internee who was captured along with Panam men at Guam. (Mr. Frazer was with a construction company building air bases there in December, 1941.)

W. RAUGUST    C. GREGG    G. CONKLIN    G. WELLS

*U.S. flag and Pan Am flag flying over Pan Am's Wake Island office*
*December 1941*

*Pan Am's Wake Island flag brought back aboard the Philippine Clipper*
*December 8, 1941*

Once Wake Island came under attack, no personal mail left the island. Wives and sweethearts, however, desperately tried to write their loved ones who were trapped on the doomed island. In December of 1941 the sweetheart of Ensign Belmont M. Williams on Wake wrote him a letter. She obviously had been following the developing story of the attack. She, along with the rest of America, hoped that a rescue force was on the way to save her boyfriend and the garrison. She, of course, had no way of knowing if personal mail was being flown by the Navy to the besieged island. Hopefully she wrote to her loved one and even after the passage of almost 60 years, the letter is so loving and intimate that it would be inappropriate to include all the romantic passages. Its very intimacy reminds us once again of the lives that were at risk, the lives that were disrupted and the lives that were lost, not only in this battle, but throughout the war. It truly was a time when people gave everything for the love and protection of their country. In her letter she writes:

"Thursday, 8:30 p.m., December 18, 1941

Hello sweetheart:

Today is our day. Happy anniversary my darling. You have made these two years the happiest ones in my life. It has been wonderful being your sweetheart and sharing my love with you. . . Although you have only been gone four months, it seems like an eternity and I will never be truly happy until we are together again.

My last letter from you was postmarked in Pearl Harbor on December 5. The last day you wrote was December 3. I received it on December 8. Darling, so many things have happened since that time. What a comfort it would be to know that you are safe. A letter or a telegram right now would be the nicest xmas present I could receive. I pray for you every night and in between times too and everyone else is saying a prayer for you, my dearest one. I know that God is watching over you and will keep you safe for me. I have spent most of my time since a week ago Sunday sitting by the radio listening for news. . .

We have just started our lives together and we have so much happiness in store for us in the future and so many plans to complete . . . Before I go to sleep, I will ask God to take care of you and keep you safe. I hope, dear, that I may receive a letter soon.

With all my love,

Helen"

By the time the letter was returned from Honolulu, with the cold, uncaring words,

she knew that Wake had surrendered to the Japanese on December 23, 1941. The best she could hope for was that her loved one was a prisoner of war and not one of the early casualties of war. Ensign Williams did survive the attack on Wake and as 1941 ended, he was a prisoner of war bound for Japan.

The envelope with the cold message "missing in action" tells a story that we should not forget. As author Tom Brokaw says in his recent book, **The Greatest Generation,** we should all remember and take strength from the sacrifices that were made by our parents and grandparents during the war. They really were the greatest generation of our lifetime.

After the surrender of Wake on December 23, 1941, the American flag did not fly over the island again until September 7, 1945. Colonel Walter L.

*Raising Japanese flag –*
*December 23, 1941*

Baylor, who was the last American to leave Wake when he departed on December 21, 1941 on a flying boat to Midway, was given the honor of being the first American to step back ashore at the end of the war on September 7, 1945. Pictured is the Japanese contingent surrendering to the U.S. Marines on September 7, 1945, while the colors are once again proudly raised over Wake.

*U.S. colors being hoisted over Wake once again by Marines as Japanese*
*officers salute - September 7, 1945*

After the Philippine Clipper's dramatic escape from Wake, while it was being repaired at Treasure Island, a portion of the aircraft struck by Japanese gunfire was removed and mounted on a plaque and presented to Colonel Young, Pan Am's Pacific manager. Recently his son, Tim Young, shared with me his father's treasured memento that was proudly kept in his father's office throughout his long and distinguished career with Pan Am.

It is remarkable that the Philippine Clipper was hit 16 times by Japanese gunfire and was still able to make it safely back across the Pacific. This last prewar flight of the Philippine Clipper is a poignant reminder of the risks faced by the Pacific pioneers, first in establishing the routes across the Pacific, and then in surviving the attack upon the far flung Pan Am base. The escape of the Philippine Clipper from Wake was a little bit of good news for a country struggling with the many early defeats of the war.

*Bullet riddled portion of the Philippine Clipper*

Fragment of
bullet-scarred
interior wainscoting
from the hull of the

**PHILIPPINE
CLIPPER**

shelled by Japanese at
Wake Island,
December 7, 1941

| Hong Kong Clipper II Last Prewar Flight | December 6, 1941 | S-42B Hong Kong Clipper II | Ralph/Strickland |
|---|---|---|---|

The Hong Kong Clipper II, formerly the Bermuda Clipper, started flying the Manila-Macao-Hong Kong-Manila shuttle flights September 22, 1941. Affectionately nicknamed "Myrtle" by the crew, the plane completed her last eastbound flight on November 30, 1941 from Hong Kong to Manila, connecting with the China Clipper inbound from Singapore to San Francisco on the China Clipper's last flight before World War II.

On December 6, 1941 the Hong Kong Clipper II completed her last flight from Macao to Hong Kong.

*The Hong Kong Clipper II at Hong Kong*

On December 8, 1941 (December 7 Honolulu time) the crew was preparing to depart Hong Kong harbor for Manila to meet the Philippine Clipper due in Manila on December 10 from San Francisco. Captain Fred S. Ralph and his six man crew planned an early morning takeoff from Hong Kong's Kai Tak Airport when they heard that Japan had declared war on Great Britain. Captain Ralph directed his men to remove their belongings from the Clipper and as they started to do so, Japanese fighter planes appeared over the hills surrounding the harbor. The crew raced for cover. Captain Ralph leaped from the dock into three feet of water to seek the protection of a large concrete post.

*Captain Ralph safely back in New York*

Captain Ralph and the crew were evacuated from Hong Kong at night by the China National Airways Corporation. Flying over war torn China, they eventually reached Calcutta by way of Chungking, China. In Calcutta, the Pan Am Clipper, Capetown, that had just inaugurated service to Capetown, South Africa, picked up Captain Ralph and his crew and flew them back to New York. The remarkable escape had taken over a month and there was no loss of life.

Pictured is a scale model of Pan Am's Hong Kong office under enemy attack. The picture is a still shot from a movie prepared by Pan Am during the war.

The Hong Kong Clipper II was sunk at the dock in Hong Kong. She had only been in service seven weeks in the Pacific.

Mail that was intended to depart on the Hong Kong Clipper on December 8, 1941 was confiscated by the Japanese and was not released until September of 1945 after the war's end.

The Hong Kong Clipper II was the only clipper destroyed by enemy gunfire during the war years.

*Above - Scale model used in movie*

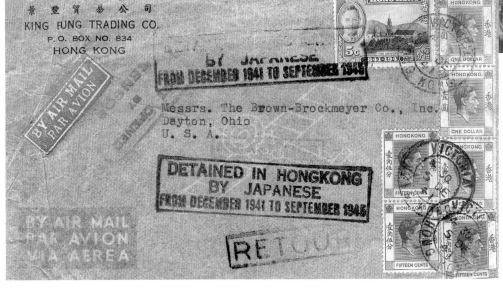

*Left - Mail held in Hong Kong for duration of war*

| NATS Pacific Survey | Mid - August (south) September. 2 -18, 1942 | PBM-3R Martin Mariner | Tilton/Chase |
| --- | --- | --- | --- |

| Outbound Flight Schedule (South) | | Inbound Flight Schedule (North) | |
| --- | --- | --- | --- |
| Honolulu - Palmyra | | Brisbane - New Zealand | September 2 |
| Palmyra - Canton | | New Zealand - Tonga | September 7 |
| Canton - Fiji | | Tonga - American Samoa | September 8 |
| Fiji - Noumea | | American Samoa - Penrhyn | September 10 |
| Noumea - Brisbane, Australia | | Penrhyn - Palmyra | September 12 |
| | | Palmyra - Honolulu | September 14 |
| | | Honolulu - Oakland | September 15-16 |
| | | Oakland - Honolulu | September 18-19 |

At the outbreak of WW II the Navy moved quickly to establish war time transportation routes across the Pacific. In June of 1942 a Naval Air Transport Service (NATS) contract was entered into between Pan Am and the Navy whereby Pan Am would use their own crews to fly the Navy planes for essential military travel. By September of 1942 Pan Am and the Navy were ready to establish a regular South Pacific service from Australia to the United States using bases at various islands along the way.

*Flight information booklet for NATS flights*

*NATS badge worn by Pan Am personnel*

*Official NATS logo*

*Martin Mariner used on Pacific survey flight*

The aircraft selected for South Pacific transport was the new seaplane built by the Glenn Martin Company of Baltimore, Maryland, the PBM-3R Martin Mariner.

This gull winged, twin engine craft carried a crew of nine and 14 to 20 passengers. It weighed 40,000 pounds and could carry a payload of 15-20,000 pounds. The first purpose of the survey flight was to see if the new craft designed for short flights was capable of carrying mail and personnel over the long distances required. The second purpose was to evaluate the suitability of the landing areas on the islands.

Captain John Tilton, Pan Am's chief pilot in the Pacific, was in charge of the Pan Am flight crew of officers Turner, Chase and Fleming. William Mullahey, who was blowing up coral heads at Wake in 1935 was now Pan Am's Operations Chief in the Pacific and he was in charge of the Pan Am engineers and mechanics travelling with the survey crews. The Army and Navy also had personnel aboard.

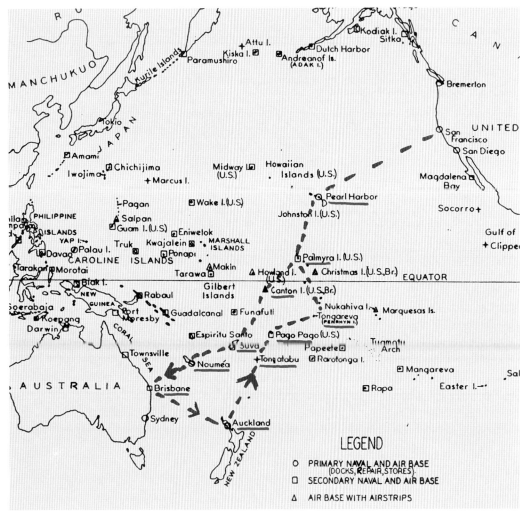

*Route of Pan Am's Naval Air Transport Service (NATS) Survey flight September 1942*

*Martin Mariner at dock in Noumea*

On the south bound trip no flight covers were prepared. Harold Gatty, however, was stationed in Brisbane, Australia, headquarters for the Allied High Command and General McArthur. Gatty was an avid cover collector. He didn't want to miss a chance to add to his Pan Am first flight collection. Therefore, when the Mariner arrived in Brisbane on the survey flight of the Pacific Islands, he imposed on Bill Mullahey to carry flight covers back on the North bound survey flight to be posted from the various islands. Gatty agreed to divide the covers with well known Australian flight cover collector Ernie Crome.

*In addition to the two engine Martin Mariner transport, Pan Am crews also flew the four engine Coronado transport - Pictured is the Coronado at Brisbane, Australia - headquarters of Allied Command in the Pacific*

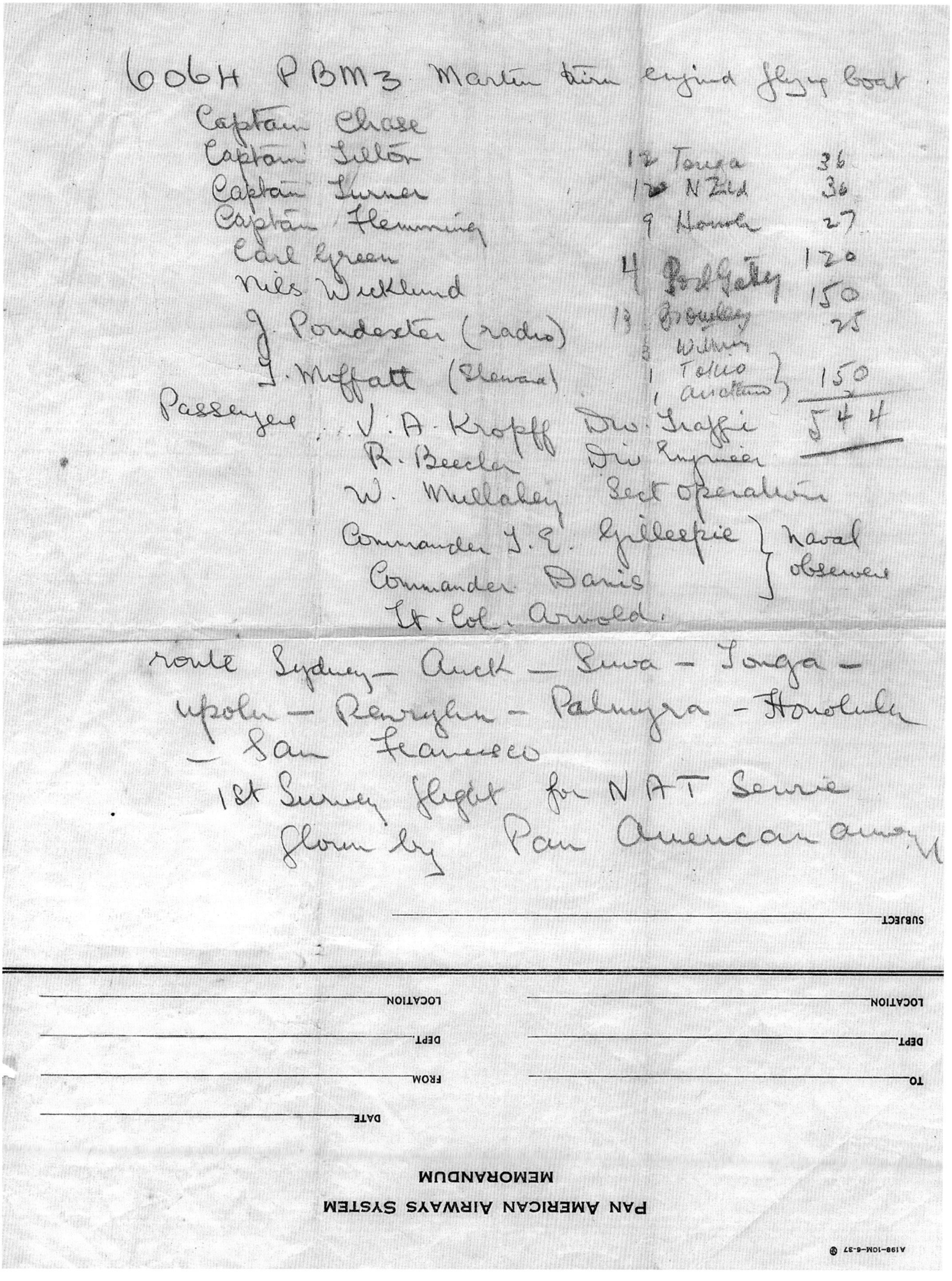

606H PBM3 Martin twin engine flying boat

Captain Chase
Captain Sillor
Captain Turner
Captain Flemming
Carl Green
Nils Wicklund
J. Poindexter (radio)
J. Moffatt (Steward)

Passengers   J. A. Kropff   Div. Traffic
             R. Beecler     Div. Engineer
             W. Mullahey    Sect Operation
             Commander J. E. Gillespie } Naval
             Commander Davis           } observers
             Lt. Col. Arnold

12 Tonga        36
12 N Zld        36
9 Honol         27
4 Port Getty   120
13 Broughley   150
  Wilkin        25
  Toko    }
  (Auckland)   150
Div. Traffic   544

route Sydney - Auck - Suva - Tonga -
Upolu - Penrhyn - Palmyra - Honolulu
- San Francisco
1st Survey flight for NAT Service
flown by Pan American airways

Harold Gatty's handwritten note on Pan Am stationery giving William Mullahey his instructions on how to post the covers was found in one of the envelopes. It appears that twelve sets of covers were prepared - six sets for Crome and six for Gatty.

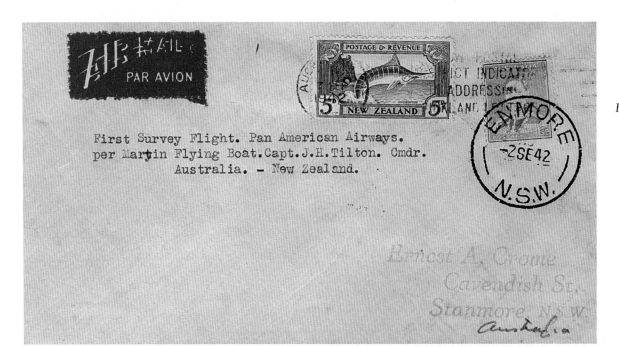

First Survey Flight. Pan American Airways.
per Martin Flying Boat. Capt. J. H. Tilton. Cmdr.
Australia. - New Zealand.

*Flown Australia to
New Zealand*

First Survey Flight.
Pan American Airways.
per Martin Flying Boat.
Capt. J. H. Tilton. Cmdr.
Australia... Tonga.

*Flown Australia,
New Zealand, Tonga*

PASSED

W.W./2.

Ernest A. Crome
Cavendish St.
Stanmore, N.S.W.
Australia

*Flown Australia,
New Zealand,
Penrhyn,
Cook Island*

U.S CENSORSHIP
EXAMINED
By 2771

*Flown Australia to Oakland then back to William Mullahey Pan Am's operation manager at Pearl City, Hawaii*

**Allied Ferry Command Survey Flight**

Sidney - Suva -
Tonga - Upola -
Pemrhyn
Palmyra
Hawaii
Oakland

*Card found in one of the flight envelopes*

**First Survey Flight for N.A.T. Service**
**flown by Pan American Surveys**
**September 2, 1942**
**by Martin Flying Boat 6064 - PBM 3.**

Captains:  Tilton, Chase, Turner and Flemming.
Observers: Commanders Gillespie and Davies for U.S. Navy
Lt. Col. Arnold for U.S. Army.

Route:  Sidney - Auckland - Suva - Tonga - Upola -
Penryhn - Palmyra, Honolulu and Oakland, California.

Eighteen (18) letters were carried from Sidney to points
underscored.

Phil Chase, one of the four Pan Am pilots on the South Pacific Survey flight, was attached to the NATS Pacific squadron VR-2 based in Alameda California. His naval address was NATS Pacific-202 FPO San Francisco, California.

Putting the stamps on the envelope upside down meant that the sender loved the person receiving the letter.

*Letter from Pan Am pilot attached to VR-2 of NATS*

*Cartoon from NATS information booklet*

Was the survey flown by a Pan Am crew for NATS in a Martin Mariner really a Pan Am flight or a Navy Flight? I'll let you decide, but for Pan Am cover collectors and historians it is an interesting and little known chapter in Pan Am's remarkable history of Pacific flights.

| 2nd Flight Around the World | January 14 to February 23,1943 | B-314A Capetown Clipper** B-314A Anzac Clipper*** | Masland/Auten**** Vaughn/Atterbury***** |
|---|---|---|---|
| New York – Miami – Port-of-Spain, Trinidad | | | January 14, 1943 |
| Port-of-Spain – Natal, Brazil | | | January 15, 1943 |
| Natal – Fish Lake, Liberia | | | January 17, 1943 |
| Fish Lake – Lagos, Nigeria | | | January 18, 1943 |
| Lagos – Khartoum, Sudan | | | January 20, 1943 |
| Khartoum – Bahrain, Persian Gulf | | | January 26, 1943 |
| Bahrain – Trincomalee, Ceylon | | | February 10, 1943 |
| Trincomalee – Exmouth Gulf, Australia | | | February 14, 1943 |
| Exmouth Gulf – Perth, Australia | | | February 15, 1943 |
| Perth – Brisbane, Australia | | | February 16, 1943 |
| Brisbane – Noumea, New Caledonia | | | February 18, 1943 |
| Noumea – Suva, Fiji  * | | | February 19 –18, 1943* |
| Suva – Canton Island | | | February 19, 1943 |
| Canton – Honolulu | | | February 20, 1943 |
| Honolulu – San Francisco | | | February 21 – 22, 1943 |
| San Francisco – New York City | | | February 23, 1943 |

 

| | |
|---|---|
| * | Dateline – loss of one day inbound |
| ** | Capetown Clipper flew New York – Ceylon and return |
| *** | Anzac Clipper flew around the world |
| **** | Masland / Auten commanded Capetown Clipper – New York to Bahrain and Anzac Clipper – Bahrain to New York around world |
| ***** | Vaughn/Atterbury commanded Anzac Clipper – New York to Bahrain Capetown Clipper – Bahrain to Ceylon and back to New York |

At the outbreak of the war, December 7, 1941, there were only fourteen aircraft in the world capable of flying the oceans with a useful payload. All of them were Pan Am Clippers. The military decided to leave the two Martin M-130s in the Pacific to be flown by the Navy on the Honolulu to San Francisco shuttle flights. Of the remaining twelve Boeing B-314s, three had already been sold to the British. The remaining nine Boeings were allocated: four to the Army for strategic transport and special missions; and five were assigned to the Navy for passenger and cargo flights in both the North Atlantic and the Pacific regions. The planes assigned to the Navy were flown by the Naval Air Transport Service (NATS) and, in most cases, the crews were experienced Pan Am crews who had flown the Clippers for Pan Am before the outbreak of the war. The Boeings assigned to the Army, however, were flown by both Army personnel and civilians on special assignment to the Army for specific flights.

*Boeing in war paint - taking off*

449

Each Army Air Transport special flight was referred to as a "Special Mission" and assigned an SM number. For example, Special Missions 70 and 71, in January and February of 1943 flown by the Army Air Transport in a Boeing Clipper, were Presidential flights to and from the Casablanca Conference in Morocco. This was the first flight by a President of the United States while in office. Even though it was flown under wartime conditions, it was completed without incident.

Special Mission 72 (SM-72) was one of the most remarkable flights of the wartime period, yet it received virtually no publicity. It was the second flight around the world by any commercial airplane. The first flight around the world by a commercial aircraft was Captain Ford's escape flight from Australia to New York at the outbreak of the war.

Special Mission 72 was anything but routine. It started with a call from Colonel Milton Arnold at the Pentagon to Pan Am's New York base on January 7, 1943, requesting a Pan Am pilot to come to the Pentagon to discuss a very difficult and very secretive mission. Pan Am Captain William Masland was next

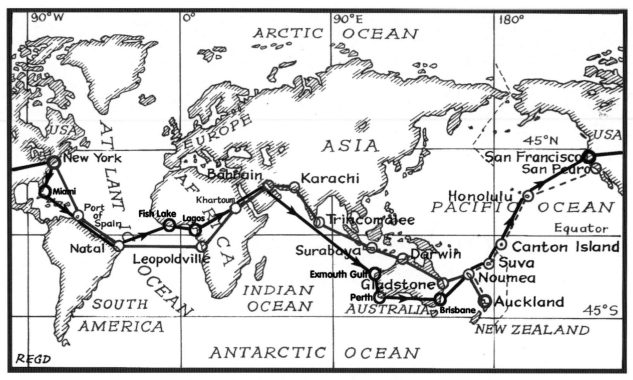

*Map showing the 1st and 2nd around the world clipper flights*
*Captain Ford's flight shown in red* ▬▬ *and Captain Masland's flight shown in green* ▬▬

up on the assignment board so he was assigned to SM-72. He traveled by train from New York to meet Colonel Arnold at the Pentagon in Washington to discuss the mission. He was told that SM-72 would involve carrying 1,000 pounds of "cargo" from the Royal Air Force seaplane base in Ceylon, non-stop to Australia, a distance greater than New York to Lisbon. The proposed non-stop flight would push the Boeing B-314 to its limit. Captain Masland was only told that the cargo weight would be allocated to three men and that the cabin configuration would have three seats and one bunk. When Masland asked how he could allocate one bunk among three men on the 20-hour flight, he was told he would have no difficulty in making that determination. The exact purpose of the trip was not revealed.

This flight was so important to the Army that two Clippers would be assigned to fly to Ceylon, with the backup Clipper returning from Ceylon the way it had come. The other Clipper, under the command of Captain Masland would continue the journey to Australia and continue east, stopping at the prewar Pan Am island bases of Noumea, Fiji, Canton, and Honolulu. From Honolulu, the Clipper would fly to San Francisco and back to New York City.

Although Captain Ford's flight with the Boeing B-314 Pacific Clipper in December of 1941 had been called an "around the world flight", in reality, because it started in California and returned only to New York, it did not complete the trip, around the world by flying from New York to California. Therefore, this

*Captain William Masland*

flight, if it were completed, would be the first around the world trip by any commercial aircraft.

Although Captain Masland was still a civilian, he was told that he would be flying on SM-72 in the uniform of the Army Air Transport Command and that Pan Am would not receive any credit for the flight. After receiving his orders, Masland immediately returned to Pan Am's North Beach base outside of New York and studied the few available charts for the epic flight.

The only aircraft available for the scheduled departure was the Capetown Clipper, which had a well-deserved reputation as a "clunker". It was a low performance plane that had difficulty maintaining altitude at optimum cruising speed. It was questionable if it could successfully complete the long non-stop flight from Ceylon to Australia.

The much more reliable Anzac Clipper would not be back in New York for servicing in time for the January 14, 1943 departure date. Therefore, it was decided that as soon as the Anzac Clipper came in and could be serviced, it would follow the Capetown Clipper out to Bahrain and, if it caught up in time, the crews would exchange aircraft and the Anzac Clipper would be flown by Captain Masland from Bahrain to Ceylon and from Ceylon to Australia, on the most difficult portions of the planned flight. Captain Masland was still not told who his passengers would be, but he was told he had to be in Bahrain no later than January 26, 1943.

As scheduled, on January 14, 1943, the Capetown Clipper, under the command of Captain Masland and First Officer Auten, departed New York for Miami to pick up spare parts before proceeding to Port-of-Spain, Trinidad. After an overnight stop, the Clipper flew on to Natal, Brazil; followed by stops at Fish Lake, Liberia; Lagos, Nigeria; Khartoum, Sudan; and Bahrain, on the Persian Gulf, where the Cape Town Clipper arrived as scheduled on January 26, 1943. Its performance was not acceptable to Masland – it was still a clunker.

The backup Anzac Clipper, under the command of Captain Chili Vaughn and First Officer Atterbury departed three days after the Capetown. They caught up with the Capetown Clipper in Bahrain on January 27, 1943.

With the two Pan Am crews at Bahrain, they were told that they would not depart until the Casablanca Conference in Morocco was concluded. It was at this point that they first heard rumors that their 1,000 pounds of cargo would be President Roosevelt, Prime Minister Churchill and perhaps even Joseph Stalin. If things went according to plan, the Anzac Clipper would carry the world leaders to Brisbane, Australia to meet with China's Generalismo Chiang Kai-Shek and General Douglas McArthur, the Allied Supreme Commander in the Pacific. On their forced long layover at Bahrain, Captain Masland took the opportunity to check the performance of the Anzac Clipper, and, as expected, found that it was far superior to the Capetown clunker. He moved his crew to the Anzac Clipper in preparation for the remainder of the trip around the world.

During the two week stay at Bahrain, Masland found out, to his great disappointment, that Roosevelt would not be returning from the Casablanca Conference by way of Australia. A security leak made the flight too dangerous, as enemy fighters would be looking for the Clipper. Instead, Franklin Roosevelt flew the Dixie Clipper back to New York. Roosevelt acknowledged the cancelled plans to fly to Australia on the Boeing in his "fireside chat" upon his return, when he said he was sorry he was "unable to meet with the troops in the Pacific after the conference". In spite of the change of passengers, SM-72 went on as planned with a far less famous "cargo" – three Army generals. On February 10, 1943, the Anzac Clipper, now under the command of Captain Masland and the Capetown Clipper, under the command of Vaughn, finally left Bahrain for Trincomalee, Ceylon, where they faced another six day delay.

From Ceylon, Captain Vaughn and First Officer Atterbury returned to New York the way they had come with the Capetown Clipper. Captain Masland in the Anzac Clipper, continued east with his three passengers, successfully completed the long flight from Ceylon to Exmouth Gulf, Australia before continuing south to Perth, Australia.

In Perth, Captain Masland, who was a civilian, got into a heated argument with Colonel Milton Arnold, who had flown on military aircraft from Washington, D.C. by way of Honolulu to meet Masland's flight that was planned to have been carrying the President. Arnold wanted Masland to return to Ceylon and fly back to New York the way he had come. Masland wanted to carry a heavier payload than was possible if he turned back. He definitely wanted to complete the eastward flight around the world.

In Captain Masland's book, **Through the Back Doors of the World in a Ship that had Wings,** he recounted his dispute with the Colonel and their disagreement about the route to be followed on the return flight:

> *The argument turned warm. I was puzzled. There seemed no reason to the colonel's insistence on the repetition of the dangerous flight in order to take the longer way home, carrying light cabin loads and exceeding the time limitation on ship and engines. Whatever his reasons, the colonel had it in for Pan Am, and intended to take it out on me, now that the crossing had been accomplished.*
>
> *I stood my ground and the Colonel finally acceded, but someone saw to it that no public disclosure of this flight was ever made. Even after the war was over and Pan Am's Public Relations Department, looking about for something to say, found that the three Pan Am divisions agreed that this was their most outstanding flight during the war, and nothing at all came of the public relation's efforts to make grist for their publicity mill out of this first commercial circumnavigation. Their project was quashed somewhere in the mists that surrounds the Pentagon.*

As a result of the argument and Masland's stubborn insistence, he was given permission to continue east around the world, but his flight was never publicized by the military or Pan Am.

After an overnight stay at Perth, Captain Masland and the Anzac Clipper departed with 26 U.S. Naval officers who were happy to have the luxurious flight home by way of the South Pacific.

After an overnight stay at Brisbane, the Anzac Clipper flew on to Noumea, New Caledonia; Fiji and Canton Island. They were now crossing old Pan Am territory that had not seen a Clipper since the outbreak of the war. They arrived back in New York on February 27, 1943, only 16 hours after Vaughn and the Capetown Clipper returned to New York from the east.

*Anzac Clipper landing at Perth*

I recently found an 80 page mimeographed report prepared by Pan Am in 1944 entitled ***"The Contribution to the United States War Effort Made by Government-owned Boeing Clippers Operated by Pan American Airways"***. A Pan Am map of the world identified the routes followed by Boeing Clippers during the war. In the report, the Special Missions flown by the Army are covered in detail. The Special Missions 70 and 71 to take President Roosevelt to the Casablanca Conference may have been the most important Special Mission to the war effort, but SM-72 which flew around the world was the most technically difficult. However, even in this detailed Pan Am publication Captain Masland is never mentioned by name and, considering the importance of his accomplishments, the oversight appears to have been intentional.

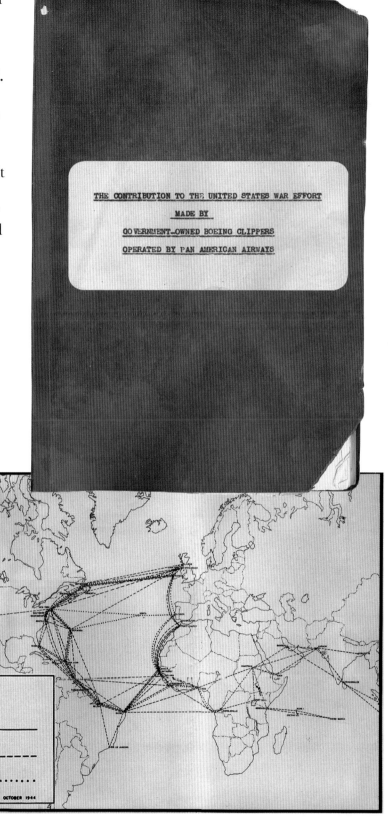

*14x28 inch fold-out chart in Pan Am 80 page wartime report*

For the rest of his life Captain William Masland remained bitter about the lack of publicity for his epic flight. The around the world flight commanded by Captain Masland on the Capetown Clipper and the Anzac Clipper was a remarkable aviation feat under the best of conditions. Because it was successfully completed under dangerous wartime conditions, it deserved much more recognition than it did receive. It was actually the first flight around the world by commercial aircraft and it was essentially ignored by the military and by his employer, Pan Am. By including it in the 50 historic and memorable flights pioneered by Pan Am in the Pacific, I have tried, in a small measure, to give his remarkable record setting accomplishment the recognition that it deserves.

| Last Flight Philippine Clipper | January 20 - 21, 1943 | M-130 Philippine Clipper | Elzey/Judd |
| --- | --- | --- | --- |

**Inbound Flight Schedule**

Honolulu - Not Completed        January 20-21

The Philippine Clipper had been turned over to the Navy at the outbreak of WWII and it was making regular shuttle flights between Honolulu and the mainland under a Navy Air Transport contract, using crews provided by Pan Am. An admiral based in Honolulu had to be in San Francisco for a top secret meeting to discuss troop landing areas for a planned invasion of various Japanese controlled Pacific islands. He was carrying confidential photographs and reports that were essential to the Pacific campaign.

Captain Robert M. Elzey told the admiral that the weather reports for San Francisco were so bad that it was unlikely that a landing could be attempted at Treasure Island in the bay. However, in response to the admiral's insistence, he agreed to fly over the area and make an attempt to land before heading south to fog-free San Diego. Due to the bad weather, dense fog and navigational errors, the Philippine Clipper crashed into the side of a mountain near Ukiah, California, north of San Francisco, killing the nine crewmen and the ten Navy passengers.

Pictured is the heat exchange unit from the Philippine Clipper that was recovered from the crash site. It was given to me by one of the people involved in the salvage and recovery of the Clipper's remains.

After 14,628 hours and 16 bullet holes from a strafing at Wake Island, the Philippine Clipper was gone. This left only the China Clipper from the original three Martin M-130s delivered to Pan Am in 1935 and 1936. The China Clipper continued to provide shuttle service between Honolulu and San Francisco until June of 1943, when it was transferred to Miami to fly the route to Leopoldville, Belgian Congo. On January 8, 1945 the China Clipper also had a tragic end when it hit a submerged object while attempting a landing at Port of Spain, Trinidad, with the loss of nine of the twelve crewmen and 14 of the 18 passengers. With the loss of the China Clipper in 1945, the Martin M-130s that had truly pioneered Pacific flight were gone less than ten years after their first historic flights across the Pacific.

*Recovered from the Philippine Clipper*

| Transfer from Treasure Island to Mills Field | Sept. 15, 1944 (approximate) |
|---|---|

Treasure Island had been Pan Am's San Francisco base from January 1939, when it was proudly opened as part of the Golden Gate Exposition, until September of 1944 when the Navy expanded its wartime operations at Treasure Island, forcing Pan Am to relocate its seaplane base to the bay adjacent to Mills Field, which is now San Francisco International Airport. The actual transfer took place gradually over approximately a two week period in mid-September of 1944. Due to wartime considerations, flight information is difficult to obtain.

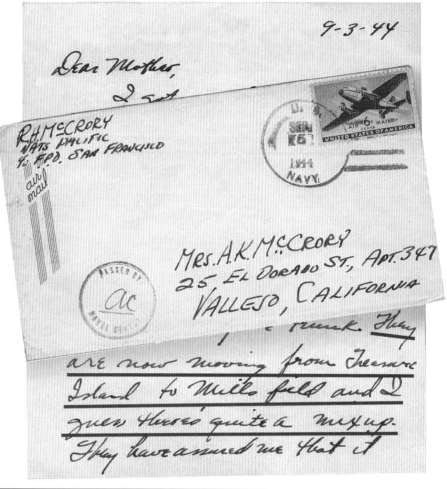

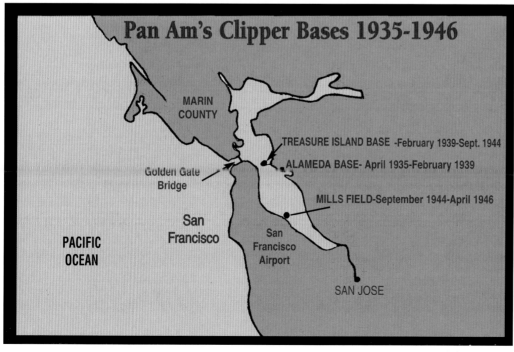

The illustrated envelope from Pan Am mechanic, R.H. McCrory, who was serving as a mechanic based in Honolulu for the Naval Air Transport Service (NATS), contained a letter to his mother postmarked September 6, 1944 where he tells her:
*"They are now moving from Treasure Island to Mills Field and I guess there's quite a mix up."*

*Harbor at Mills Field - 1944*

Pictured above is one of the Boeing B-314s anchored in the harbor at Mills Field with the Pan Am service buildings visible in the background. An aerial photo of the same building is also shown. Due to wartime secrecy there were no commemorative or special flight envelopes to mark the transfer.

*Mills Field - October 1944*

| Last Flight Honolulu Clipper | November 3 - 4, 1945 | B-314 - Honolulu Clipper | Robbins/Reid |
|---|---|---|---|

**Inbound Flight Schedule**
**Honolulu - Not Completed          November 3-4**

When the Philippine Clipper was lost in the tragic accident of January 21, 1943 and the China Clipper was transferred to Miami in June of 1943, the Boeing B-314 Honolulu Clipper was transferred to the San Francisco to Honolulu shuttle service. On November 3, 1945 the Honolulu Clipper departed Honolulu for California with 13 naval personnel and a naval crew of ten. The Clipper was under the command of Captain Sannis E. (Robby) Robbins and first officer Wallace W. Reid. Departing 90 minutes behind the Honolulu Clipper was Captain Fred Richards in the Dixie Clipper. About 650 miles east of Honolulu, the Honolulu Clipper began to experience a serious loss of power. The cargo and 500 pounds of mail were heaved out of the plane to lighten the load. When the Clipper failed to gain altitude, at 11:00 p.m., Captain Robbins brought the plane in for an emergency mid-ocean landing. Captain Richards, in the trailing Dixie Clipper, circled over the Honolulu Clipper that was now wallowing in 8 to 10 foot seas and he made sure by radio contact that all vessels in the area were aware of the emergency so they could come to the aid of the downed Clipper.

A Navy transport, the U.S.S. John Henry Payne, was 35 miles away and the U.S.S. Manila Bay was 60 miles away and they altered their courses to assist in the rescue. At 5:30 a.m. the Payne came into sight of the Honolulu Clipper. By 8:00 a.m. the Manila Bay had also arrived and all passengers were evacuated to the Payne. For the next three hours mechanics from the Manila Bay tried to fix the engines. When that failed, it was decided that the Manila Bay would attempt to tow the Clipper back to Honolulu. For the first few hours, the towing operation went slowly, but successfully. Then the tow lines broke and the Clipper was adrift. For the next two days the Manila Bay followed the Clipper that was drifting slowly westward.

The San Pablo, a seaplane tender, was in the area and it too was called in to attempt the recovery. Lines were secured and they attempted to lift the Clipper onto the San Pablo, but the Clipper was just too heavy to lift and she crashed into the fantail of the San Pablo, destroying the Clipper's wing and one of its engines. The crippled Boeing was again adrift, 500 miles from Honolulu. The captain of the San Pablo reluctantly received permission to sink the aircraft with gunfire. From about a mile away the guns of the San Pablo blasted the Clipper for over 30 minutes. With smoke and fire coming from the battered hull, she finally slipped below the waves.

*Downed by engine failure a still sturdy Honolulu Clipper is pictured wallowing in wind-tossed Pacific*

*The Honolulu Clipper adrift with U.S.S. San Pablo standing by*

Six and a half years earlier the Honolulu Clipper had been christened with coconut milk at Pearl Harbor. She had flown over 18,000 hours and 11,000 of those hours were conducted by Pan Am crews under the military contracts with NATS. The final tribute to her strength and endurance was the fact that no one was injured or lost during the night time ditching at sea and that she withstood three days of pounding in the open sea before having to be put under by gunfire. The Clippers' days for flying the Pacific with Pan Am were numbered. Military operations were being phased out, the old Pan Am Clippers were wearing out and land planes that were faster and more reliable were poised to take over transoceanic flight from the aging seaplanes.

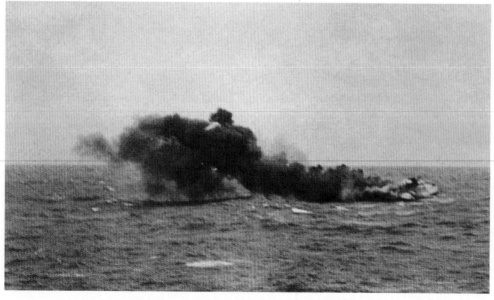

*Honolulu Clipper being shelled prior to sinking*

| Last Clipper Flight | April 8 - 9, 1946 | B-314 - American Clipper | Terrell |
|---|---|---|---|

**Inbound Flight Schedule**
**Honolulu - San Francisco        April 8-9**

Unfasten your seat belt – stretch your legs!  Pan Am's last Clipper flight in the Pacific has just touched down at Mills Field on San Francisco Bay.  This exciting and romantic chapter in aviation history ended quietly.  On the morning of April 9, 1946 Captain Dent Terrell with a crew of 9 landed the American Clipper at Pan Am's Mills Field seaplane base, near the site of the current San Francisco International Airport.

*Pictured above is the crew of the last Clipper flight with Captain Terrell on the far left*

*Shorty Greenough - the chief mechanic who had served throughout the Pacific since the first Clipper flights in 1935 - takes off his hat in respect for the final Clipper flight*

The "End of the Line Achievement Award" was also presented by Pan Am to Captain Terrell. Land based aircraft had proven to be superior to the Clippers and airports had been built as part of the war effort to accommodate the large land based planes.

Pan Am's public relations director, William VanDusen, sent a souvenir envelope and letter that had been carried from Honolulu aboard the American Clipper on this last flight to the newspaper reporters around the country to salute this historic end of Pan Am's flying boat service. Let's read for one last time his final and fitting tribute to the end of the era of Pan Am's Pacific Clippers:

*Captain Terrell shows Shorty Greenough the "End of the Line Achievement Award" presented to Captain Terrell at the end of the flight*

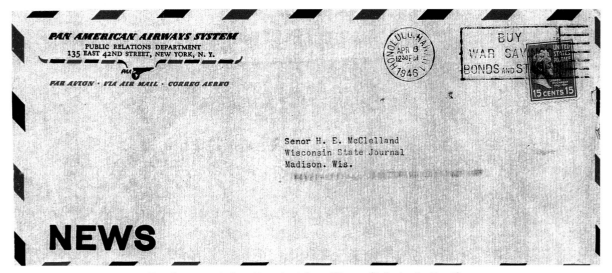

*Envelope carried on Pan Am's last Clipper flight in the Pacific*

*. . . We couldn't let those grand old ladies pass out of the picture without a little visit. We're going to miss them! Why, they had more sex and glamour in five minutes than we can build into a land plane in five years!*

*They contributed a chapter in the annals of flying that will still be thrilling reading for generations to come. They bred a new breed of airmen - - who talked and thought and worked in the lingo of the air-sea. They left an indelible mark. And they'll take with them some of that glory, some of that sense of accomplishment, some of that excitement of the "first", some of the thrill of the "man against the sea", some of that bold adventure of the explorer and the pioneer. Yes, some of the faith and the hope and the courage of all those who fly . . .So Hail, old timers, Hail and farewell . . ."*

*William VanDusen – April 1946*

After its last flight, the American Clipper joined two other Clippers in the backwaters of San Francisco Bay awaiting their final fate.

In August of 1946 the War Asset Administration sold all seven of the surviving Pan Am Clippers, including all the spare parts and engines, to Universal Airlines for $325,000. By 1951 these remaining relics would be gone as well to scrap heaps or watery graves.

Almost eleven years earlier, in April of 1935, Pan Am's Transpacific flights began with excitement and anticipation. The public's interest increased with each new success as Pan Am extended its air routes from Manila to Hong Kong to New Zealand and finally to Singapore and Fiji. But, with the end of the war, and with advances in land based aircraft, the era passed with little or no press coverage. The romantic Clipper era that revolutionized air travel had ended. The Pacific pioneers had done their job well. The future belonged to land based planes and the new pilots who would fly them. I hope you have enjoyed our flight back in history as much as I have enjoyed sharing it with you.

*Harbor at Mills Field - once proud clippers await sale as war surplus*

# CHAPTER FOUR
# PAN AM AT WAR

When Pearl Harbor was attacked on December 7, 1941, all of Pan Am's operations in the Pacific were terminated and all of Pan Am's aircraft were placed under the direction of the military and transferred to either the Army Air Transport Command or the newly formed Naval Air Transport Service (NATS). All Pan Am aircraft in the Pacific were operated by NATS. Whenever possible Pan Am personnel were kept together by NATS in order to provide the most experienced air and ground crews possible for the aircraft.

*Captain C. H. Schildhauer*

TEN THOUSAND TIMES

How 17 years' experience
made possible the story of
THE CLIPPERS AT WAR

AROUND THE WORLD

*Pan Am booklet - 1943*

Navy Captain C. H. "Dutch" Schildhauer was credited with creating the concept for NATS. In June of 1934, Dutch Schildhauer, a former Navy pilot and flying boat devotee, became Juan Trippe's agent to accumulate the knowledge needed to begin the Pacific operations. He was instrumental in getting the Navy to take control of Midway and Wake so that leases could be given to Pan Am so they could build the bases necessary to cross the Pacific. Therefore, he was quite close to Pan Am and he had great respect for the organization. On December 12, 1941, just five days after the bombing of Pearl Harbor, Dutch Schildhauer's plan for a naval air transport program was given in detail to the Secretary of the Navy, Colonel Frank Knox. NATS was immediately given the mission of utilizing the existing military and Pan Am aircraft into a scheduled transport operation capable of supporting the military and naval operations with the speedy movement of essential personnel and material.

In creating its military airline, the Navy sought the aid of those most experienced in aviation, Pan Am and the other commercial airlines in the United States. Using the experience of Pan Am in the Pacific, the Navy developed NATS along the lines of a commercial airline modified to the demands of a wartime military operation.

Initially NATS had three squadrons, VR-1 in Norfolk, Virginia for the East Coast - VR-2 in Alameda, California for the West Coast and the Pacific region - VR-3 in Olathe, Kansas for the continental United States. A branch of VR-2, the Pacific squadron, was maintained in Honolulu. The two surviving Martin M-130s that were in the Pacific at the outbreak of the war, the Philippine Clipper, and the China Clipper, were turned over to NATS and flown by experienced Pan Am crews between Honolulu and California. The five Boeing B-314s that were in the Pacific were likewise turned over to NATS and were also operated by Pan Am crews. The Boeings were freely shifted between the Atlantic and Pacific as changing needs dictated.

Both the Martin M-130s and the five Boeing B-314s lost their shiny silver color and took on the camouflage colors of dull gray for wartime service.

*Martin M-130 in war time gray*

463

*Boeing B-314 in camouflage*

*Consolidated PB2Y-3R Coronado at Pearl City Base, Honolulu – Pan Am base escaped damage from the Pearl Harbor attack*

# CHART OF NATS FLYING BOATS IN THE PACIFIC

## Martin PBM-3R MARINER

The Glenn L. Martin Company of Baltimore, Maryland began the design of the gull winged, twin engine Mariner in 1937 and a prototype flew in February of 1939. The Navy contracts placed in late 1940 called for 379 PBM-3s. Fifty of these Mariners were converted to transports by the Glenn Martin Company with the designation PBM-3R (R for Transport). The Mariner had a wing span of 118 feet - length of 80 feet - maximum speed of over 200 m.p.h. - cruising speed of 127 m.p.h. - - range of 2,240 miles - weight of 33,000 pounds empty and 52,000 pounds loaded. It could carry 20 passengers in addition to the crew of eight or nine, giving it a payload of between 4,000 and 5,000 pounds.

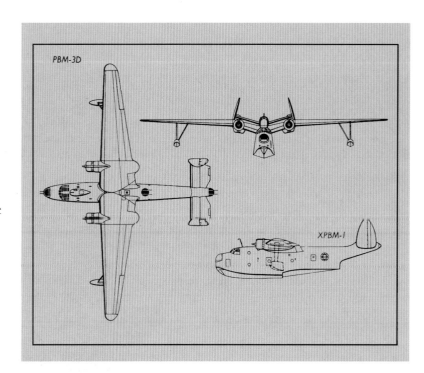

## Consolidated PB2Y-3R CORONADO

In July of 1936 the Consolidated Aircraft Corporation was awarded a contract for the design and construction of a large four-engine maritime reconnaissance bomber flying boat. The prototype flew in December of 1937. The first Coronado was delivered to the Navy in December of 1940. A total of 210 PB2Y-3 Coronados were eventually built. Thirty-one of these were converted to PB2Y-3R, or PB2Y-5R transports by the Rohr Aircraft Corporation with the first transports delivered to the Pacific in late 1943. The Coronado had a wingspan of 115 feet - length of 79 feet - maximum speed of 200 m.p.h. - cruising speed of 141 m.p.h. - range of well over 3,000 miles. It was powered by four 1200 horsepower Pratt & Whitney Twin Wasp engines and it could carry a payload in excess of 10,000 pounds, more than twice that of the Mariner.

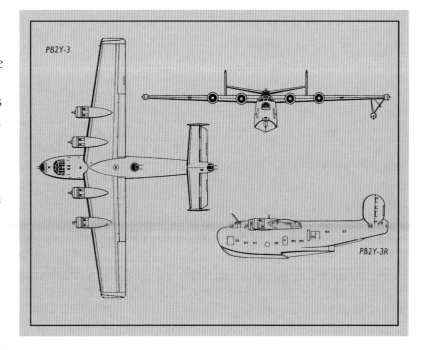

Because they were too valuable to the war effort after December 7, 1941, the Clippers never flew west of Honolulu. At the outbreak of the war, the only aircraft readily available for the transport of mail, material and men west of Hawaii were the gull winged, short range, twin engine Martin Mariners. The engines of these aircraft made a distinctive grinding sound which announced their arrival long before they came into sight. The Martin Mariner transports were designated as PBM-3R: PB standing for patrol bomber; M for Martin, 3 for the third modification of the design, and R for Transport. The Mariners were converted to transports by the plane's manufacturer, the Glenn Martin Aircraft Corporation of Baltimore, Maryland. The Mariner PBM-3R truly pioneered the wartime routes throughout the South Pacific. The Mariners filled the gap until the larger four engine planes, the Coronados, with longer flight ranges and greater payloads, could be built and made operational. The Martin Mariners also established the air links between Honolulu and Brisbane, Australia, site of the headquarters for the Allied Pacific Command where General McArthur was based after the fall of the Philippines.

The Mariner's survey flight of September 1942, flown with Pan Am crews, took the aircraft to the most remote areas of the Pacific where they landed in isolated, uncharted harbors and where the flight crews did their own loading and unloading.

*Martin PBM Mariner*

*Conversion of Martin Mariner to a transport at Glenn Martin Company plant near Baltimore - Note the removal of the gunner's bay*

*Combat version of Martin Mariner*

The most dramatic air/sea rescue in the Pacific involved a Martin Mariner with Pan Am Captain W.W. Moss in command. Captain Moss had been the first officer on the last flight of the Philippine Clipper before World War II when the Clipper returned to Wake to successfully evacuate Pan Am personnel as the island was under heavy air attack from Japanese fighters. When Pan Am Captain Moss, flying the twin engine Martin Mariner for NATS, arrived at a remote Pacific island, word came that a nearby troop transport, the Cape San Juan, had been torpedoed and was sinking. After unloading the Mariner, Captain Moss asked for volunteers to return with him to the site of the sinking in an attempt to save the drowning Navy seamen. The seas were running 10 to 15 feet when he spotted survivors clinging to pieces of wreckage. By judging the angles of the waves, he managed to bring the Mariner in for a rough, open water landing. Rafts were tossed overboard that were tied to the plane and they taxied slowly as survivors desperately swam to the trailing life rafts. Forty-eight exhausted, oil smeared men climbed onboard the plane from the rafts. Unfortunately, many doomed sailors had to be left in the water so that the heavily overloaded seaplane could even attempt a take off. Captain Moss maneuvered the plane into position and when a wave lifted it, he managed to bounce off the first swell to a height of 30 feet. After five or six bounces the Mariner was finally airborne. For this successful rescue Captain Moss received a commendation by the Navy for praise worthy judgment, courage and airmanship. The experience of this Pan Am captain had saved the lives of 48 seamen under the most difficult rescue circumstances imaginable. After 24 months of hard service, the Martin Mariners were retired.

*Illustration from advertising for Glenn Martin Company depicted rescue accomplished by Captain Moss*

*Captain W.W. Moss
Pan American pilot flying for the Naval Air Transport Service, whose skill in a stormy sea effected the rescue of 48 survivors of a troop ship sinking*

In late 1943, the Consolidated-Vultee PB2Y-3R (or 5R), the famed Coronados were finally delivered to the Pacific to fill the Mariners' role of carrying the vital men and material to the Pacific outposts. The conversion of the Coronados from bombers to transports was done by the Rohr Aircraft Corporation of California and they were so proud of their work for the Navy that they ran advertisements featuring the modified Coronados with the Pan Am logo proudly displayed on the nose. To convert to a transport, the engines had to be removed. Then all the control cables had to be rerouted to the cabin ceiling to provide more interior cargo space. Strengthened wood and aluminum flooring was substituted for the standard corrugated aluminum decking. A much wider cargo door was added to the left side of the aircraft. The entire modification package resulted in an 8,000 pound weight loss for the plane, due mainly to the removal of armor, gun turrets and bomber-related equipment. These changes, along with changes in the engines, increased the range from 2,400 miles to over 3,000 miles, so that the Coronados could easily fly from Honolulu to the mainland.

The regular flights of the long range Coronado from Honolulu to Brisbane, Australia became known as the "Brisbane Bullet". The six stops required by the Martin Mariners were replaced by only two or three stops for the Coronados.

However, by the end of 1944 even the Coronados were being phased out of Pacific service by the arrival of the colossal Martin Mars flying boat. Pan Am crews never flew the Mars because the Navy's contracts with Pan Am were being phased out and the Pan Am aircraft and crews were being returned to civilian control.

*Advertisement for Rohr Corporation, featuring their conversions of Coronados - Note logo on airplane*

*Now detached from NATS with a well earned "Well done," the Consolidated Vultee "Coronado," and the Martin "Mariner" distinguished themselves early in the war when the going was roughest and toughest*

*Coronado transport taking off*

Coronado being loaded by Pan Am crew at Treasure Island base
– Oakland Bay Bridge in the background

Coronado being loaded by Pan Am crew

*The Coronado with Pan Am logo*

*Pan Am's busy Treasure Island base – 1943*

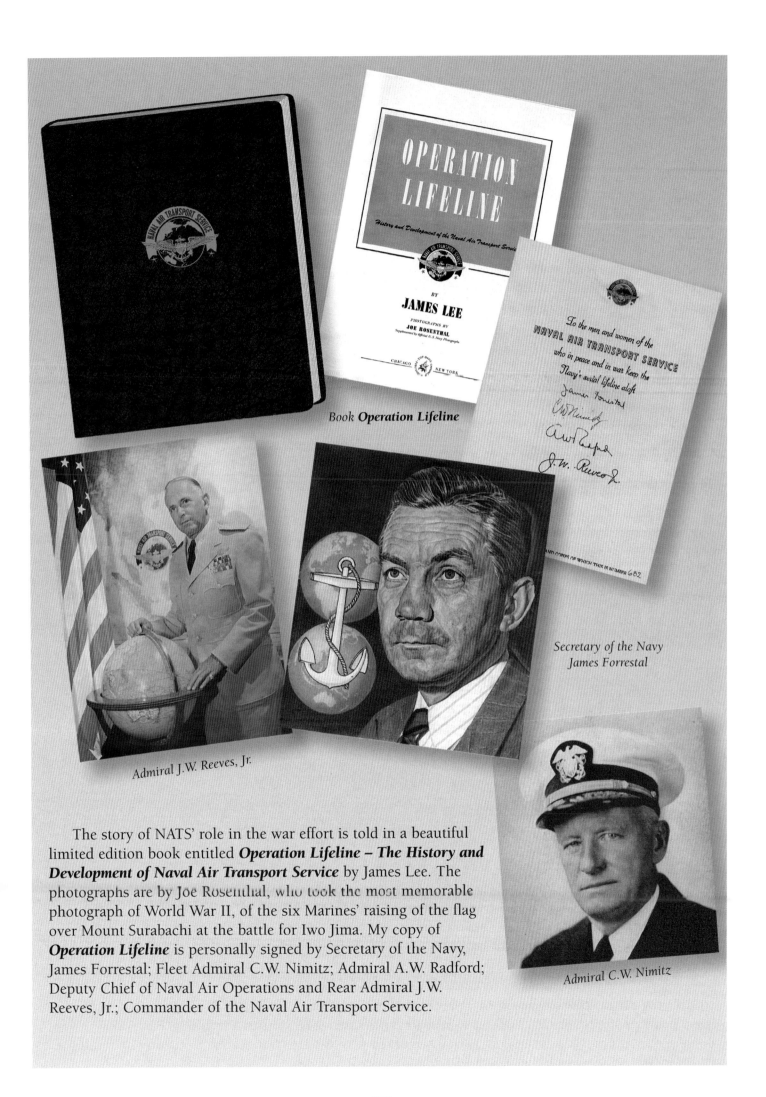

Book **Operation Lifeline**

To the men and women of the
NAVAL AIR TRANSPORT SERVICE
who in peace and in war keep the
Navy's aerial lifeline aloft

*James Forrestal*
*C.W. Nimitz*
*A.W. Radford*
*J.W. Reeves Jr.*

AND CORPS OF WHICH THIS IS NUMBER 682

Admiral J.W. Reeves, Jr.

Secretary of the Navy
James Forrestal

Admiral C.W. Nimitz

The story of NATS' role in the war effort is told in a beautiful limited edition book entitled **Operation Lifeline – The History and Development of Naval Air Transport Service** by James Lee. The photographs are by Joe Rosenthal, who took the most memorable photograph of World War II, of the six Marines' raising of the flag over Mount Surabachi at the battle for Iwo Jima. My copy of **Operation Lifeline** is personally signed by Secretary of the Navy, James Forrestal; Fleet Admiral C.W. Nimitz; Admiral A.W. Radford; Deputy Chief of Naval Air Operations and Rear Admiral J.W. Reeves, Jr.; Commander of the Naval Air Transport Service.

*Red Cross assists Pan Am in loading medical supplies for transoceanic flight*

*112,000 letters destined for U.S. troops overseas being readied for loading aboard a B-314 Clipper - weighed nearly 3,000 pounds*

Carrying the mail was always a vital part of Pan Am's wartime activity. It was determined that 80,000 letters made up approximately one ton of airmail. Therefore, as far back as the 1930s, Pan Am in cooperation with the British Imperial Airways, worked with the Eastman Kodak Company to develop a system to drastically shrink the weight and volume of military mail.

Under the system they developed military mail would be sent to a central processing laboratory.  Five thousand  letters would be copied onto a single roll of 16-millimeter film.  This accomplished, the letters would be destroyed, the roll of 16 millimeter film would be sent across the ocean to another processing center closer to the final destination, where the letters would be reproduced on special paper and put into special envelopes with windows so that the letter address itself became the outside address. Mail from military personnel based in the Pacific would be sent to Honolulu and copied onto film. The film would then be sent to San Francisco where it would be printed and placed in envelopes for the final destination. The system was originally called  "Airgraph", but when it was adopted by the military postal system it was called "Victory Mail", abbreviated "V...  MAIL" (three dots and a dash are Morse code for the letter V). The Eastman Kodak Company was so proud of its partnership with Pan Am they featured the V Mail process in its war time magazine advertising.

Pictured are two letters.  One originated on Midway Island, the other at Pago Pago, American Samoa They were copied on film in Honolulu and the film was sent to the mainland to be converted back into mail for the folks at home.

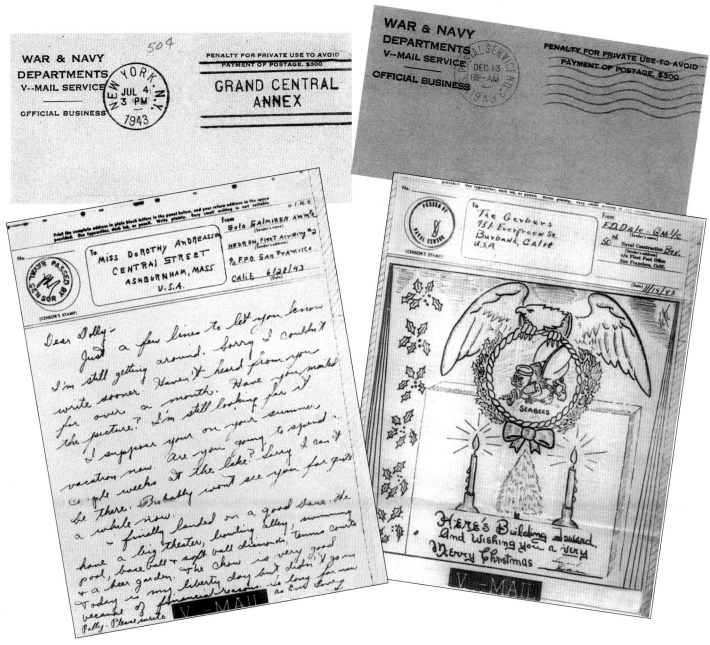

*Soldier's letter sent from Midway to home by V-mail*

*Letter sent from American Samoa by V-mail*

A—You read a letter in your boy's own writing, like that above (actual size).
B—The three small boxes in the photograph contain over 5000 of these letters—in the form of photographic film. C—On this one roll of 16-mm. film—shown in slightly reduced size—1700 letters have been photographed.

# Kodak created, U.S. Government adopts "V····-MAIL"... for communication with our men on distant fronts

YOUR BOY writes you a letter on a sheet of paper — regular letter size. This is photographed on Kodak microfilm — is reduced in size to about a quarter of a square inch ... Now it has only 1/100 of the weight of normal mail.

With thousands of other letters — 85,000 letters weighing 2000 pounds weigh only 20 when reduced to microfilm — it is swiftly flown from his distant outpost to America.

Here, again through photography, the letter addressed to you is "blown up" to readable size — folded, sealed in an envelope, and forwarded to you. It is as clear as the original writing. It really *is* the writing of your boy because it's a photographic print.

And your letters to him, which you write on special forms, go by the same space-saving, time-saving V···· — Mail.

Kodak developed and perfected the process ... Pan American Airways and British Overseas Airways, the two great pioneers in transoceanic air transport, blazed the air trails ... and the three companies, as Airgraphs, Ltd., offered the service to the American and British governments.

IN APRIL, 1941, under the trademark "Airgraph," England first employed the system to solve the problem of getting mail to and from the forces in the Near East. The Airgraph System was gradually expanded until it knits the British Empire together with about a million letters a week — personal and official.

And now the men serving overseas in the American armed forces also have the benefits of this form of speedy correspondence.

Airgraph, or V···· — Mail as it is called here, is an adaptation of Kodak's *Recordak System* which has revolutionized the record-keeping methods of thousands of banks and business houses. Many records of the U.S. Census, Social Security, and Army Selective Service are on microfilm — error-proof, tamper-proof, lasting photographic copies of the original bulky records ... Eastman Kodak Company, Rochester, N. Y.

**SERVING HUMAN PROGRESS THROUGH PHOTOGRAPHY**

*Kodak magazine advertisemnt showing the V-mail process and Kodak's partnership with Pan Am - Each small roll of 16mm film held 5,000 letters*

In addition to carrying the V-mail to the troops, Pan Am personnel attached to NATS used mailing addresses assigned by the Navy for their personal mail. Phil Chase was one of Pan Am's pilots who, along with the chief Pan Am pilot, John Tilton, made the survey flight in the Martin Mariner in September of 1942. In Chase's January 5, 1943 letter to his girlfriend, he explains to her that although he is part of the NATS squadron VR-2 based in Honolulu, his mail must still be addressed to VR-2 headquarters in Alameda - - NATS Pacific, Navy 202 FPO, San Francisco, California.

*Letter from Phil Chase - one of the pilots on the survey flight*

Robert H. McCrory joined Pan Am in 1943 in San Francisco as a young mechanic and almost immediately joined NATS. After several months he was transferred to Honolulu to service the Boeing B-314s. While still at Treasure Island he was given a round stainless steel badge, which gave him access to the tool locker for servicing the Boeing Clippers. He gave me this Pan Am service badge as well as his NATS service pin.

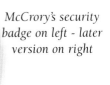

*McCrory's security badge on left - later version on right*

*McCrory's NATS pin - 1943*                1942                1944

He also made sure that the Clippers flown for the Navy contained a new Pan Am in-flight safety pamphlet. This four page pamphlet illustrated the escape doors from the Clipper and had instructions for inflating and using the emergency life rafts. In an almost humorous vein, the pamphlet stated: Hints to life raft skippers – ***"No Pan Am passenger has ever had a chance to occupy, let alone command, one of our life rafts and we hope that you never will. And yet it is just good sense that you should know the facts of life rafts"***. This may be the earliest inflight safety card carried by a Pan Am Clipper in the Pacific.

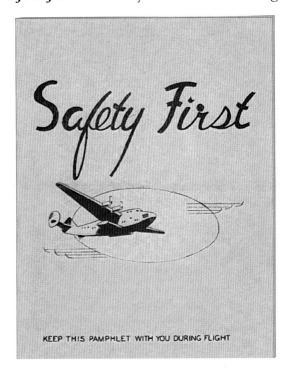

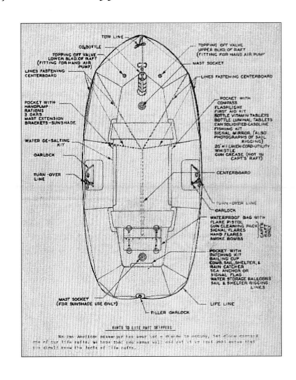

*Safety brochure for Boeing 314*

He also provided to traveling servicemen the cartoon booklet *"Flying the Pacific Made Easy"*.

# CHIC SALES DEPARTMENT

NATS planes are equipped with heads, but you should take advantage of ground facilities wherever possible. The Orderly will direct you to the head and weeping post and instruct on its proper use. The head should never be used while the plane is not in flight or during landing or takeoff.

# WHEN DO WE EAT?

NATS' military mission is so urgent that little space is available on NATS planes for the bulky and heavy cooking equipment which is necessary for preparing the sort of meals NATS would like to serve. The Orderly will serve you with food during regular meal hours. There is a charge of 50¢ per meal.

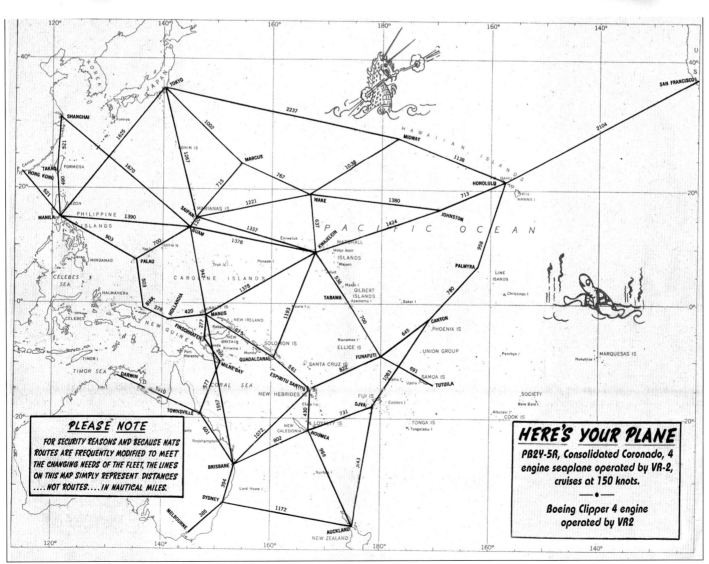

**PLEASE NOTE**

FOR SECURITY REASONS AND BECAUSE NATS ROUTES ARE FREQUENTLY MODIFIED TO MEET THE CHANGING NEEDS OF THE FLEET, THE LINES ON THIS MAP SIMPLY REPRESENT DISTANCES ....NOT ROUTES....IN NAUTICAL MILES.

**HERE'S YOUR PLANE**

PB2Y-5R, Consolidated Coronado, 4 engine seaplane operated by VR-2, cruises at 150 knots.

—•—

Boeing Clipper 4 engine operated by VR2

*Lois Moran Young, the wife of Pacific Division manager Clarence Young, supported the war effort by promoting the purchase of war bonds*

# WINGS OF DEMOCRACY

THE EYES of the world are focused on the sky today. Supremacy there is the key to victory it has been proven, and it is there that America and her allied and friendly nations possess overwhelming advantages.

Those advantages are not limited to existing and potential military air might. Peerless commercial airlines, turned to the task at hand, play a heartening role. In the last war, the nerve centers and outposts of the Allies were linked merely by slow and often uncertain surface transport.

Not so today. Across the international skyways, on 90,000 miles of aerial lifelines, the Flying Clippers shuttle with frequency and dependability. Military, industrial and diplomatic couriers are sped on vital missions. A steady stream of mail, materials and merchandise is kept flowing. Those lines have not and will not be cut.

Pan American Airways blazed its trails as an instrument of friendly international travel, trade and communication. Today it has undertaken additional and more important assignments pursuant to the successful prosecution of the war. The clock around it is meeting emergencies with skill and resourcefulness giving ever more and better service in the interests of all that democracy stands for.

**PAA PAN AMERICAN AIRWAYS SYSTEM**

All of Pan Am's advertising during the war years had a decidedly patriotic theme and many of the brochures dealt with the problems of secrecy and travel priorities for passengers and war materials.

# WINGS OF VICTORY AND PEACE

BLAZED by the Flying Clipper Ships in 15 years of pioneering international air transport, some 100,000 miles of established world skyway routes are today serving as aerial life lines of the United Nations. Tomorrow their ever-broadening wings will, in peace-time's commerce, span those global routes with a frequency and capacity such as to fundamentally affect all foreign trade. The boldest practical visions ever conceived by men with wings will, to the beat of Pan American propellers, be translated into a saga of fact.

PAA PAN AMERICAN AIRWAYS SYSTEM

Since December 7...

Pan American Clippers, huge as they are, can carry only so much weight. In this emergency, with normal transportation facilities curtailed, the value of every pound of every patriotic American we are equipping keeping with the desire so that they may best serve the needs of everyone. By eliminating some of the former luxury features of our service, we are effecting a weight saving sufficient to accommodate several additional passengers or shipments of cargo which could not otherwise be transported * This means you are asked to sacrifice berth facilities, a portion of your former baggage allowance and certain other comforts. We feel sure you will be willing to make this important contribution to the maximum use of war time ocean air transportation.

**PAN AMERICAN AIRWAYS SYSTEM**
TRANSPACIFIC DIVISION

*Notice to Priority Passengers*

Your attention is directed to the priority coupon attached to your ticket. On the flight(s) on which you are about to embark, as covered by your ticket, the normal gross weight of the aircraft, including its passengers and cargo, will be exceeded in aid of the war effort, as authorized by regulations of the Civil Aeronautics Board.

**PAN AMERICAN AIRWAYS**
*System*

*Brochures dealing with secrecy and priorities of passengers and war materials*

**WINGS OF DEMOCRACY**

*Summary of*
**WARTIME INTERNATIONAL TRAVEL REQUIREMENTS**

*For departure from*
NEW YORK • MIAMI
NEW ORLEANS • BROWNSVILLE
LAREDO • LOS ANGELES
SAN FRANCISCO • SEATTLE

**PAA**

*Via*
**PAN AMERICAN WORLD AIRWAYS**

THIS INFORMATION IS EXCLUSIVELY FOR PAN AMERICAN PASSENGERS
Issued April 25, 1945

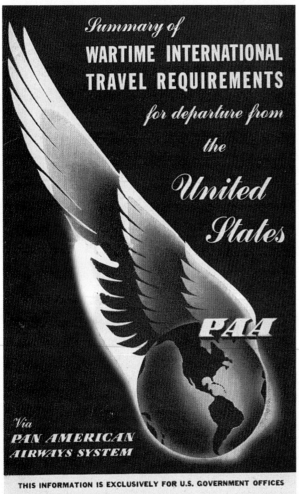

*Summary of*
**WARTIME INTERNATIONAL TRAVEL REQUIREMENTS**
*for departure from*
*the*
*United States*

**PAA**

*Via*
**PAN AMERICAN AIRWAYS SYSTEM**

THIS INFORMATION IS EXCLUSIVELY FOR U.S. GOVERNMENT OFFICES
Issued March 15, 1944

UN **PROBLEMA** DE **GUERRA**

A **WAR PROBLEM**

**PAN AMERICAN** PAA **AIRWAYS SYSTEM**

Because of the increasing complexity of wartime currency regulations, Pan Am in 1944 introduced Pan Am flying money in $50 booklets of ten $1 certificates and eight $5 certificates. The money was underwritten by American Express, so even though Pan Am is gone, the unused Pan Am money is still good. The picture shows Pan Am's vice president and general traffic manager, V.E. Chenea at the White House presenting Pan Am's first flying money booklet to Eleanor Roosevelt in March of 1944.

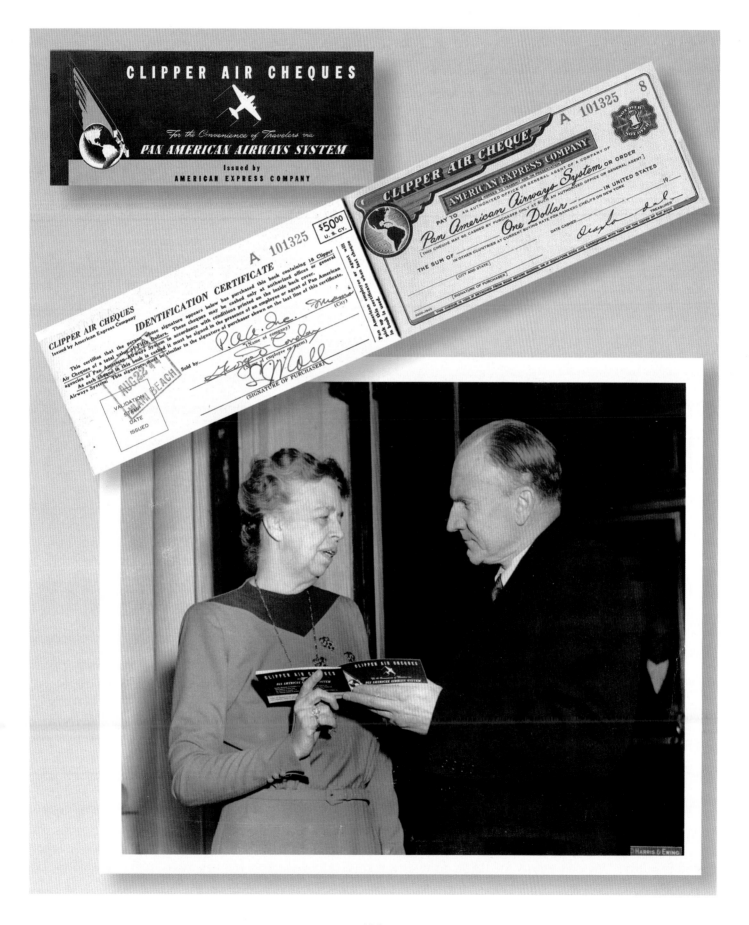

485

NEWS LETTER FOR THE TRANSPACIFIC DIVISION FAMILY, PAN AMERICAN WORLD AIRWAYS

VOL. II No. 3      TREASURE ISLAND      DECEMBER 1, 1943

# NO CASUALTIES FROM NIP BOMBINGS AT PAN AMERICAN BASE

HNL...Nov.30. SOPAC dispatches bring news of two November bombings of a certain island base of Pan American operations. Twice during the month, Pan American personnel had to dash for the slit trenches while the Nip bombers roared overhead.

The list of our men at this "front

## 5,000 OCEAN CROSSINGS BY PAN AMERICAN FLIGHT CREWS SINCE PEARL HARBOR

TSL...Nov. 18. While di⸻⸻⸻d of bombs dropping at o⸻⸻⸻es, Pan American ⸻⸻⸻rly yesterda⸻⸻⸻⸻an cre⸻⸻⸻w

**ATTENTION: PAA JUNIORS**

That good looking pin on the Pic Page is waiting for you. If your Dad is in PAA and you want to let your friends know he's fighting for Victory by keeping 'em flying, just fill out this coupon and have Dad turn it in to his Shop Foreman, Max Friedman in Smoking Room or at the Information Booth in the Ad Bldg. (This means "daughters" too.)

My name is _____
My Dad works in _____ Dept.
of PAA at _____

Oak⸻
of ⸻
IN ⸻
Of sp⸻
vision⸻
Pacifi⸻ ⸻⸻⸻ ⸻or PAA
crews h⸻⸻⸻d 1221 cros-
sings o⸻ ⸻ North Pacific between the Hawaiian Islands and
the Mainland, including both
Clipper schedules and crossings
made with the Naval Air Transport aircraft, operated for
(continued on Page 5)

THIS ISSUE
Presents

Hawaii Calls
Our Own Cross-
word Puz:
Letters to
Editor
Sports News
TRANSPAC P:

John Boyle, S⸻
and viewed a t⸻
tainment by the ⸻
band and vocal tal⸻

**"MY DAD WORKS FOR P.A.A. IN VITAL WAR SERVICE"**
*This was the theme of a pin that Pan Am dads were able to give to their kids during the war years. Pictured above is Raymond Shields, fire chief at Treasure Island pinning his son Raymond Shields Jr.*

## TOTALLY AT WAR UNTIL VICTORY

In mid-1942 the Pan Am Pacific Division started a newsletter dedicated to the war effort. The issue for December, 1943 had an article on an air attack at one of the Pacific bases staffed by Pan Am employees. An article on the picture page showed a new pin issued by Pan Am for the children of Pan Am employees that stated proudly: "My dad works for P.A.A. in vital war service". A coupon was enclosed in the newsletter so that children could write in for one of the pins.

Juan Trippe's annual report always started and concluded with a patriotic message and his particular concern for the Pan Am employees who had died in the line of duty and those that were still in Japanese prison camps.

1941 Annual Report

## The Wings of Democracy

On behalf of the war effort, Pan American has been privilaged to undertake assignments which the President of the United States has characterized as of an importance which "cannot" be over estimated."

That Pan Am today is able to serve the United Nations throughout the world, is due in large measure to the fourteen years of pioneering and scientific progress which has gone into the development of it's facilities and the training of it's personnel.

On all fronts, the test of war emergency has been met with courage and resourcefulness. Management, technical staffs, flight crews and ground forces are cooperating in making this organization an effective instrument in the war effort.

May 2, 1942

*Juan Trippe*

President

---

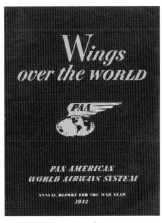

1942 Annual Report

When the Japanese attacked Pearl Harbor on December 7, 1941, the United States had at it's command in Pan American Airways the only air transport system world-wide in scope. Your system was providing commercial air transportation to all continents, serving 62 countries and colonies. In addition, Pan American had just organized a modern air route across Africa under arrangements with the War Department and the British Government.

Enemy occupation of Wake, Guam and the Philippines cut the trans-Pacific line to the Orient. But the alternate military air route to China via the South Atlantic was available, serving Africa, the Middle East, Russia and India as well. Bombers and military supplies were enroute to our allies. Critical materials from the Orient, the Middle East, Africa and South America necessary for our munitions plants at home were soon on their way. Worl-wide communications for vital mails and important passengers were maintained.

Personally and on behalf of our directors, I wish in this fifteenth annual report, to record appreciation for the loyalty, teamwork and patriotism of the entire organization.

June 16, 1943

*Juan Trippe*

President

---

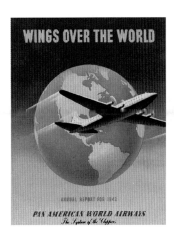

1943 Annual Report

## The Wings of Democracy

The record of Pan American Airway Systems during 1943 is again one of devotion to the war effort.

The legislative and executive departments of our Government have the final responsibilty for this decision. Your company has placed it's knowledge and experiece at their disposal.

In the meantime, the men and women of Pan American Airways are concentrating on the job of speeding victory by mainaining the system's wartime transport services abroad and by operating military cargo services for both the Air Transport Command and the Naval Air Transport Service.

Ninety of the system's personnel have given their lives in performance during the war period. Forty five are still interned in Japanese prison camps.

The system's war contribution has been made possible only by the gallantry, loyalty and teamwork of Pan American emplyees throughout the world.

June 1, 1944

*Juan Trippe*

President

# The Wings of Democracy

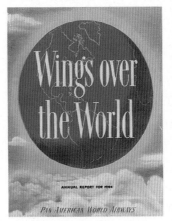

**1944 Annual Report**

Again in 1944, the record of Pan American Airways is one of devotion to the war effort. The system's war contribution has been made possible only by the patriotism, loyalty and teamwork of Pan American employees throughout the world.

*Juan Trippe*

June 1, 1945                                    President

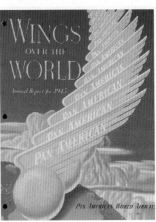

**1945 Annual Report**

The year 1945 witnessed the resumption of commercial service over most of the system's routes which had been transferred to military control during the war. Limited commercial service to Europe was re-established in November upon termination of military operations under the Navy contract. Sevices to Australasia and the Orient have necessarily been deferred pending delivery of additional flight equipment in 1946.

At the time of Pearl Harbor, Pan American was the world's largest international air transport system, serving 62 countries and colonies on 5 continents. As contrasted with domestic carriers in the United States, who were able to continue commercial service because their routes did not extend to war areas, over half of Pan American's system was converted to military service. Pan American's net earnings during the war years, therefore, ran contrary to the domestic industry's consistantly upward trend.

*Pan American flying boat "Clippers"- once the latest word in transocean flying equipment - have now been retired after valiant war service - Here one of the newer, faster, more economical DC- 4 transports is taking off as the crew of the flying boat waves a "Bon Voyage"*

*Boeing B-314 – moored in harbor at recently captured Saipan - March 1945*

*At Saipan - March 1945*

As the tide of battle turned and allied victories in the Pacific began to mount, Pan Am Clippers were once again allowed to carry key military personnel and equipment west of Hawaii. These rare pictures of the California Clipper were taken in Saipan shortly after the defeat of the Japanese in March of 1945.

By the end of 1945, all of Pan Am's contracts with the Navy had been terminated and all of the Pan Am aircraft that survived were returned to civilian service. The widow of Swede Rothe, the flight engineer on the epic around the world escape flight of the Pacific Clipper, shared with me the certificate given to her husband by Pan Am in recognition of his service with NATS. The war experience of her husband Homans Kinsman Rothe is typical of the military service by the flight crews and ground personnel who served Pan Am in the Pacific. He enlisted as a flight engineer in San Francisco in September of 1942. He held various assignments, including shop superintendent, in both San Francisco and Honolulu. On November 15, 1945 his contract was terminated and he returned as a flight engineer to Pan Am.

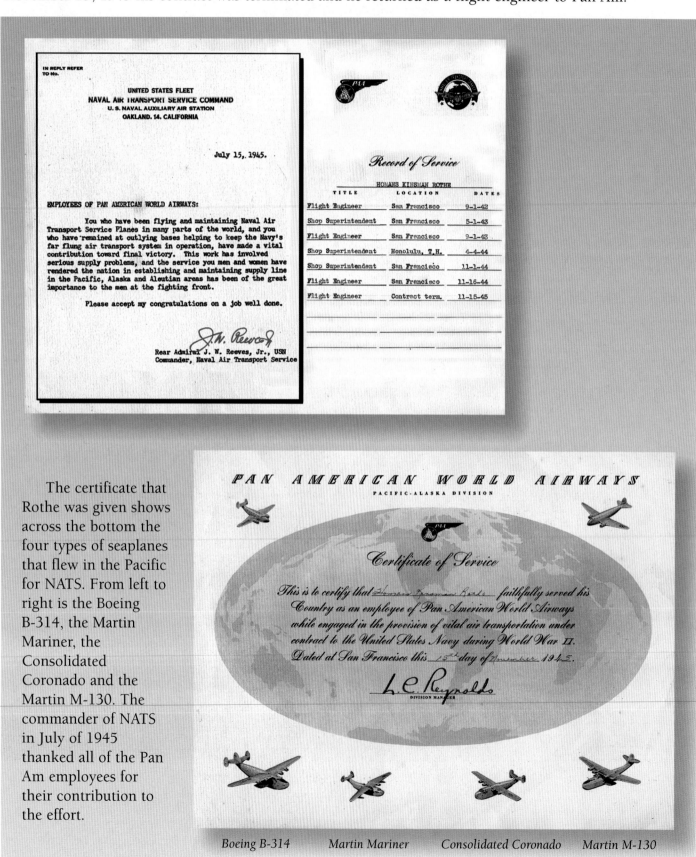

The certificate that Rothe was given shows across the bottom the four types of seaplanes that flew in the Pacific for NATS. From left to right is the Boeing B-314, the Martin Mariner, the Consolidated Coronado and the Martin M-130. The commander of NATS in July of 1945 thanked all of the Pan Am employees for their contribution to the effort.

Boeing B-314          Martin Mariner          Consolidated Coronado          Martin M-130

In 1945, Pan Am's documentary film entitled, "Clippers at War", stated:

*Every Clipper route was now a war route. Pan Am's worldwide system of 239 radio stations from New York to Singapore relayed the orders of the Army and the Navy. There were many war heroes in the Pan American family. Two hundred gave their lives in performance of war duty. The Japs interred forty-five more in prison camps. There were hundreds of heroic acts. Over 80,000 Pan Am men and women served in the war effort. To all parts of the globe, over the victory routes they pioneered, they flew to the fronts where our boys gave their lives so that democracy could live. Now that victory has been won, the wartime trails which Pan Am blazed to the world's most distant lands have become America's great peacetime highways.*

*Secretary of War, Robert Patterson, on behalf of President Truman, presents the Medal of Merit, the highest civilian award, to Juan T. Trippe, 1946*

Without question, Pan American aircraft and personnel made significant contributions to the successful war effort in the Pacific. In 1946, Juan Trippe, both individually and on behalf of all the Pan Am employees, received the well deserved Medal of Merit, the highest award given for civilian service.

# CHAPTER FIVE
# SUPPLY SHIPS OF PAN AMERICAN

Pan Am Clipper ships never could have flown the Pacific without the assistance and support of vessels, that were either owned or chartered by Pan Am or provided by the military for Pan Am's benefit. Never before has the full story of these ships been told.

# S.S. NORTH HAVEN

The best known supply ship used by Pan Am in the Pacific was the S.S. North Haven. The 300 foot, 5,000 ton Alaskan freighter from the home port of Seattle was chartered three times by the Pan American Aviation Supply Corporation, a corporation set up by Pan Am specifically to provide services for the Pacific islands.

*The North Haven, Pier 22, San Francisco - March 1935*

The first charter from March 27, 1935 to August 1, 1935 was to build bases on Midway, Wake, and Guam. This charter of the North Haven attracted national and even worldwide attention because the men and material it carried would make possible the first commercial flights in history across the Pacific to the Philippines.

The second charter of the North Haven from January 14, 1936 until May 17, 1936 was to build the prefabricated hotels on Wake and Midway in preparation for the first passenger flights that were scheduled for later in 1936.

The third and final charter of the North Haven, from April 29, 1939 to July 1, 1939, was to build the Pan Am base at uninhabited Canton Island in the South Pacific for the flights to New Zealand that started in July of 1940.

*Loading a tractor for Wake*

*A launch for Midway being loaded - March 1935*

*A launch for Midway*

*A gasoline tank for Guam*

*Officers on first cruise, 1935 - Captain A.J. Borklund in the center standing; first officer Pederson to his left*

On the first two charters of the North Haven, Captain Borklund was in command and Oscar Pederson was the first officer. On the North Haven's third charter from April through June of 1939, Oscar Pederson was the captain.

William S. Grooch was Pan Am's executive officer of the first two cruises of the North Haven. He was a naval flyer during the first world war and he joined Pan Am in 1928 and resigned in 1937. He was also the author of three books about this exciting period in Pan Am's history and the first book, **Skyway to Asia** recounts in detail the first cruise of the North Haven in 1935 when the bases were built on Wake and Midway.

The first charter of the North Haven left pier 22 in San Francisco on March 27, 1935 and arrived in Honolulu on April 4, 1935. In Honolulu, after a few additional workmen were hired, the ship proceeded on to Midway, Wake, Guam and on June 16, 1935 finally arrived in Manila, its final destination.

*Captain Borklund, Bill Grooch, executive director of the cruise, being congratulated at the end of the cruise by Colonel Young, director of the Pacific division. - August 1935*

*Pan Am construction workers on the deck of the North Haven*
*March 26, 1935 - about to depart on cruise*

Danilo "Dan" Vucetich served in the capacity of supercargo on all three of the North Haven's cruises. As supercargo, he was in charge of all matters dealing with obtaining supplies and loading and off loading of freight. According to Will Trout, a worker on the expedition that built the hotels on Wake and Midway, Dan Vucetich was a good man to work for - always happy and out going.

*Dan Vucetich,*
*supercargo on cruise*

*North Haven laying off Wake Island - June 1935*

*North Haven laying off Wake Island - June 1935*

The barge loaded with supplies from the North Haven, is seen heading towards the landing at Wake. Supplies would then be taken off the barge and taken by the short railroad to the lagoon and barged again across the water to Pan Am's base on Peale Island.

*Off loading aviation fuel on Wake Island*

In Manila, ten souvenir covers intended for collectors were delivered to the captain of the North Haven with the request that, after leaving Manila, the letters be posted at sea and placed into the regular mail when the North Haven arrived at Guam on its return voyage to San Francisco.

Any letter posted at sea is referred to as "paquebot" mail. Under international postal regulations, regardless of what country's stamps are affixed to ship mail, the postmaster is required to accept the mail for posting. When the North Haven arrived at Guam, these ten envelopes with Philippine stamps were taken to Guam's postmaster, J.H. Underwood, to receive the official paquebot markings before they were cancelled with the Guam postmark and placed into the regular U.S. mail at Guam for delivery to the United States. Postmaster Underwood, however, was not prepared to handle ship mail and he did not have the required rubber stamp with the word "PAQUEBOT", indicating that the mail had been posted at sea. Therefore, he did the best he could to accommodate the mail from the North Haven by using loose individual letters to make up the word "PAQUEBOT". His limited supply of alphabet letters did not include the letter "U", so he had to crudely fashion one by using an "I" and a "J" to form a letter "U" in PAQUEBOT. These ten paquebot covers from the North Haven are the only postal history items associated with the North Haven on its first charter. The illustrated cover with Philippine stamps was postmarked in Guam and forwarded to Chicago. The letter inside the cover explained postmaster Underwood's problems with trying to make a paquebot mark on Guam in order to properly cancel the envelope.

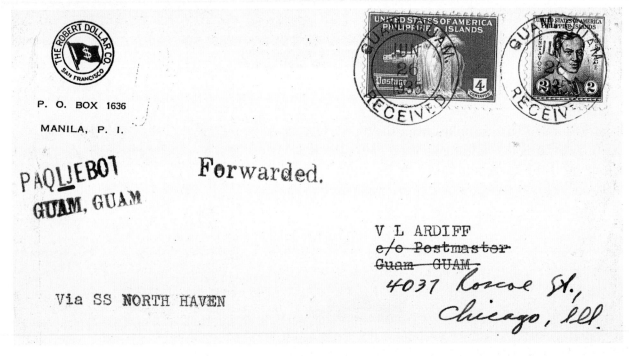

*One of the Paquebot covers posted on North Haven while at Guam June 26,1935 - Note letter U in Paquebot*

*Midway Island as seen from the deck of the North Haven - July 1935*

By the time the North Haven reached Honolulu on August, 9, 1935, on its return trip at the end of the first charter, the men of the construction crew had been away from civilization and their families for almost four months. In Honolulu, the return of the North Haven made headline news. From the picture in the newspaper, it is nice to see that some things, like a warm welcome home from a wife or sweetheart, has not been improved upon over the years.

# NORTH HAVEN RETURNS; AIR BASES LAID DOWN

## HERE'S HOW THEY WELCOME PAA MEN

Typical of the welcome given to other lucky members of the party, Tex Underwood, a Honolulu boy with the Pan American construction expedition which returned to Honolulu on the North Haven today as greeted by his wife exactly as shown here. And wouldn't you do the same thing if you hadn't seen your wife for 14 weeks? Tex was a plumber who helped install equipment at Midway and Wake islands

## 45 REMAIN AT TINY ISLES TO AWAIT PLANES

### Pan American Ship In Brief Call On Way To the West Coast With Big Job Done

### Stations Ready For Use By Passenger Clippers, Is Announcement Here

BALTIMORE, July 18. (AP) — Lifting a load, including her own weight, of 51,300 pounds to an altitude of 18,200 feet, the flying Clipper No. 7, which will carry the first passengers across the Pacific ocean for Pan American Airways, established an unofficial world record today. The Clipper carried a pay load of 24,000 pounds with 10 persons aboard.

With signal achievement to its credit, the Pan American pioneering construction party, which has established airports at Midway, Wake and Guam islands for use in the transpacific airline from California to China, via Hawaii, returned to Honolulu today in its chartered freighter North Haven.

The expedition, after battling nature's obstacles of sea and land, is only seven days behind a tentative work schedule drafted months ago before the North Haven left the Pacific coast.

"Radio direction, transmitting and receiving equipment, workshops and living quarters for the permanent employes have been completely installed at the islands and are ready for immediate use," said Cmdr. William S. Grooch, the company's senior representative with the party.

"Thus are added 3,630 more fully equipped miles to Pan American's transpacific route — Hawaii to Midway, 1,130 miles, Midway to Wake, 1,200 and Wake to Guam, 1,300.

"This has been accomplished with only one death that of William F. Young, of pneumonia at Guam, without any accident, except for minor cuts, and without any sickness beyond inevitable boils among men unaccustomed to working in the tropics. We are behind a very tentative schedule only because we encountered difficulties which could not be foreseen in making exploratory plans in a mainland office.

### Wake Job Tough One

"Our most serious setback was on the Wake island group, which consists of three islands — Wilkie, Peale and Wake. To establish our base on Peale we had to make a hazardous landing with all the heavy equipment on Wilke and then ferry it across a lagoon to Peale. This unexpected series of transhipment put us back seven days.

While the bases were being established, the North Haven continued to Manila to leave equipment and three men to work in the establishment of the base there when permission is given by the Philippine government.

### 45 Left Behind

A total of 45 men have been left at the various islands, permanent crews who will be replaced probably once a year or once every two years, according to how they individually stand up to the life of exile.

Thirteen men, who joined the North Haven on its way westward in Honolulu, disembarked today and the remainder of the party, 58 men, will continue to the mainland when the North Haven sails at 2 o'clock today from Pier 26.

The men on arrival were suntanned and as "fit as fiddles," eager to be ashore after their absence of three and a half months. Honolulu was left on April 7.

### Correspondent Here

Prominent among them was Junius P. Wood, veteran newspaper correspondent who accompanied the expedition, appeared nonchalant, smoking an old corn cob pipe, wear-

(Continued on Page 9. Col. 1)

On the second charter of the North Haven to build the hotels at Wake and Midway, which lasted from January 14, 1936 to May 17, 1936, Dan Vucetich mailed the nicely illustrated envelope from Midway Island to his young son, Sandy back home in San Francisco.

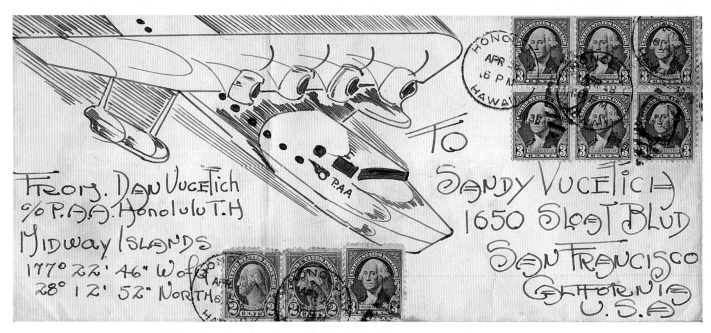

*Dan Vucetich drew the Sikorsky S-42 on this cover for his son - mailed from Midway - April 28, 1936*

My friend, Wil Trout, who is now in his 80's and living in Oregon, sent me this picture taken in front of the Wake Hotel during construction in early 1936. Left to right are Wilber Trout, Walter Klinger, Don Meyers, unknown and Dan Vhyormeyer.

*Midway Hotel under construction*

*End of the second cruise of the North Haven - May 1936. Captain Borklund, Frank McKenzie, chief airport engineer and Colonel Young, director of the Pacific division meet with newspaper reporter on the right*

*Left:*
*Colonel Young in the center meets with Captain Pederson and Frank McKenzie before Pederson and McKenzie depart on the third cruise of the North Haven to build the base on Canton Island in the spring of 1939*

The third and final charter of the North Haven left San Francisco for Honolulu on April 29, 1939 loaded with supplies for Canton Island. In Honolulu additional supplies were loaded before departing for Canton Island. While enroute to Canton, the North Haven crossed the equator for the first time while on a Pan Am charter. Therefore, the captain and crew prepared an elaborate initiation ceremony, presided over by His Nautical Majesty, Rex Neptune, played by Frank McKenzie, Pan Am's chief airport engineer. Dan Vucetich had his picture taken as he was being dumped into the salt water pool, while receiving a swat with the paddle on his backside. The picture was mailed to him from Canton Island by the airport manager, R.W. Fraser.

*Left: Men awaiting initiation*

Canton Island.

Oct. 10th-39

Hell-o Dan:

Enclosing a shot of you being thrown into the water as we crossed the Equator, now you know who hit you on the 'ars' with the paddle. Have some good shots of the initiation so when I return to the mainland will be glad to show them to you.

My best to Freddie, hope this finds you in good health and spirits. We all missed you on the last unloading.

Your friend,

R W Fraser.

Dan saved both the certificate issued to him after the initiation and the official proclamation of the **Ancient Order of the Deep**. The same type of Jupiter Rex certificate was given by Pan Am to passengers in the Caribbean when they crossed the equator. Up until this point in time, however, the certificate had not been used in the Pacific because passenger flights in the Pacific had not yet crossed the equator.

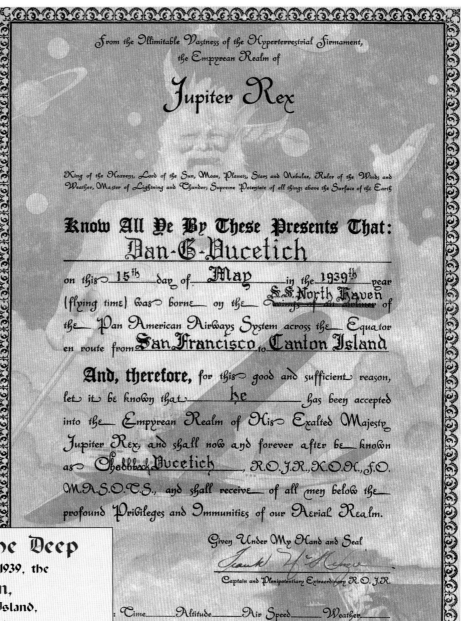

*Above. Jupiter Rex certificate*

## Ancient Order of the Deep

In the forenoon of May 15, 1939, the

### S.S. North Haven,

On her journey to Canton Island,
cross the equatorial line.
Ye age old tradition of the sea was religiously observed
By the members of the Pan American Airways expedition
aboard in commemoration of this event.
On this day all candidates were initiated into the realm of the

## Ancient Order of the Deep

During the ceremony, his

## Nautical Majesty, Rex Neptune,

presided with his consort and scribe by his side. Among
other punishments inflicted to the culprits by his majesty's
order, the severe paddling of their seats was one of the
outstanding spectacles.
All bewhiskered gazebos were committed to
the royal tonsorial parlor for a clean shave
and to have their faces lathered with a cup of
grease and thick machine oil.
Tossed into the huge salt water tank, the dunking completed
the ritual, admitting the candidates thereby into the
membership of the

## Ancient Order of the Deep

The S.S. North Haven served Pan Am well during her three charters. Without the Pacific bases and without the hotels built as a result of her cruises, flights across the Pacific would not have been possible.

# S.S. NORTH WIND

The second vessel placed under charter by Pan Am, The S.S. North Wind, was the sister ship to the North Haven and also part of the fleet of the Northland Transportation Company of Seattle, Washington.

## Aviation Supply Vessel

**UNIQUE JOB** — *The Seattle steamship North Wind, which is used to freight supplies to the various "stepping stones"* || *on the trans-Pacific route of the Pan American Airways. She will return here in June to enter into the Alaskan trade.*
—(Photo by Fisher's Studio.)

*North Wind departing Seattle for San Francisco to start charter - October 1936*

The North Wind's first Pan Am charter started in October of 1936, when it was dispatched to the bases at Wake and Midway to resupply them with aviation fuel, food, and supplies. Once that was completed, the North Wind picked up the station manager at Wake Island, Mr. Stewart A. Saunders, and sailed to Kingman Reef where they arrived on December 28, 1936. The crew spent several days surveying the lagoon to determine if it could be used as the first overnight stop for the Clippers on the planned route to New Zealand. The North Wind completed its survey on January 2, 1937 and left Kingman Reef for American Samoa, where they surveyed Pago Pago harbor as a possible landing site for the second stop for the Clipper. On January 26, 1937 the North Wind arrived back in Honolulu.

In his detailed report to Pan Am's operations manager, Mr. Saunders noted that Kingman Reef had previously been visited in 1935 by Harold Gatty, Pan Am's representative to New Zealand. Mr. Saunders concluded his somewhat pessimistic survey report by saying that, if Kingman Reef was to be used, the only satisfactory arrangement for a base would be the anchoring of a station ship in the lagoon for the convenience of passengers and crew and for the housing of maintenance, communications and personnel necessary to support the Clipper on its overnight stop.

In spite of the obstacles noted by Saunders in his report, Pan Am decided to forge ahead with the survey flight to New Zealand, using both Kingman Reef and American Samoa as overnight layovers. Therefore, the North Wind was outfitted in Honolulu to serve as Pan Am's Clipper base at Kingman Reef and the ship left Honolulu on March 11, 1937 to take up its position in the middle of Kingman Reef, to await the arrival of the Clipper. Buoys were placed in the lagoon to mark the start and stop points for the Clipper on its landing and take off.

*Dan Vucetich on the left, with airport engineer Frank McKenzie in front of Wake Hotel on the first cruise of the North Wind – December 1936*

Stewart Saunders filed this report from Kingman Reef:

"The day before the Clipper was supposed to arrive, the lagoon was as calm as a mill pond. However, on the next day visibility was near zero with heavy rain, overcast and choppy waters. Weather reports to the Clipper were disheartening as well. But Captain Edwin C. Musick and his crew came steadily onward. Suddenly through the rain we heard the roar of the motors. The Clipper passed overhead at about 200 feet. Captain Musick couldn't see us but the goniometer told him where he was. Visibility was about 500 feet and it was still raining when the Clipper landed in the lagoon and taxied alongside".

The North Wind remained at Kingman Reef until the Clipper and Captain Musick returned from New Zealand in early April. After the Clipper departed for Honolulu on April 9, 1937, the North Wind pulled anchor and returned to Honolulu, arriving on April 14, 1937. Days later, the North Wind departed for San Francisco to end Pan Am's first charter of the North Wind.

Let's examine three of the envelopes that Dan Vucetich mailed home from the first charter of the North Wind that lasted seven long months, from October of 1936 to May of 1937. Remember, Dan Vucetich had been in charge of the cargo for Pan Am on the **FIRST** expedition of the North Haven to build the bases in 1935. He served again as supercargo on the **SECOND** expedition of the North Haven to build the hotels on Wake and Midway in 1936. Therefore, the first charter of the North Wind, when he served again as supercargo, was the **THIRD** Pan Am expedition for both Pan Am and Dan Vucetich in the north Pacific. Therefore, for this charter of the North Wind, he made up rubber stamp to use on his personal mail for this **THIRD** expedition-"S.S. North Wind" S. S. North Wind 3rd Expedition. He also made up four other rubber stamps to use on his envelopes that read DAN VUCETICH, WAKE, MIDWAY and SAN FRANCISCO.

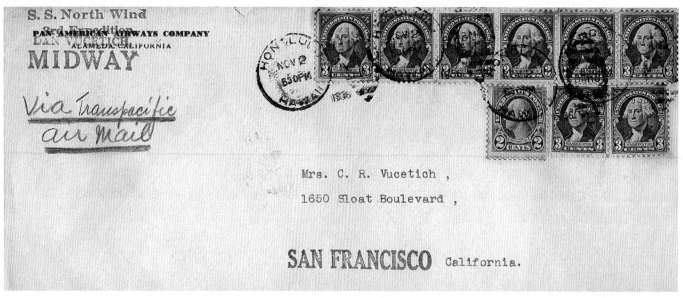

*Mailed from the North Wind while at Midway to Dan Vucetich's wife*

The first envelope was addressed to his wife and it was mailed from Midway in late October of 1936 and postmarked at Honolulu on November 2, 1936.

The second envelope from the North Wind was mailed in December of 1936 when the ship visited Wake to pick up the station manager, Stewart Saunders, to take him to the lagoon at Kingman Reef to determine if it was suitable as an overnight stop for the Clipper ship's survey flight to New Zealand that Pan Am planned for early 1937. The envelope contained a hand drawn Christmas greeting from Dan Vucetich to his boss, Colonel Clarence Young, who was the manager of the Pacific division for Pan Am.

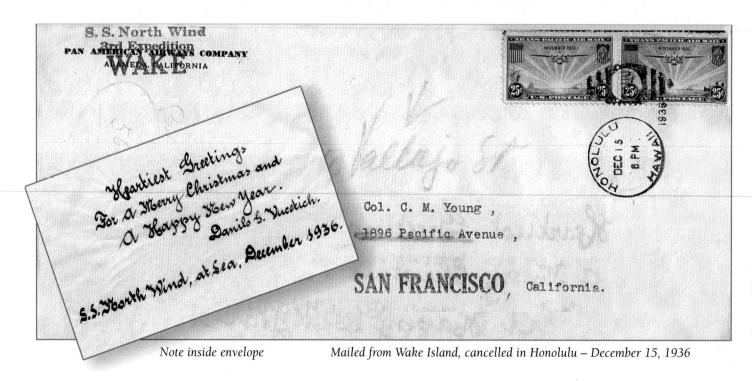

*Note inside envelope*          *Mailed from Wake Island, cancelled in Honolulu – December 15, 1936*

The third and last envelope from this first charter of the North Wind is the souvenir letter Dan Vucetich sent to his son. This envelope was supposed to be flown on the Pan Am's Clipper's return flight from Kingman Reef to Honolulu. Company regulations however, prohibited it being flown back to Honolulu by Captain Musick. Therefore, the envelope was carried onboard the North Wind to Honolulu where it was mailed and flown by Clipper back to San Francisco. The first charter of the North Wind, which started in October of 1936, ended in May of 1937.

*Was supposed to be the souvenir flight cover - air mail was prohibited*

*Gooney bird at Midway*

*Rare Pacific seal pup on Midway beach*

The second and last charter of the North Wind for Pan Am started October 15, 1937 and ended in late December of 1937. On October 21, 1937, at the beginning of the second charter period for the North Wind, Clarence M. Young wrote a letter to Dan Vucetich setting out his duties as supercargo. With his letter Young also enclosed the charter agreement which is shown on the next page.

PAA **PAN AMERICAN AIRWAYS COMPANY**

PACIFIC DIVISION

P.O. BOX 445 · ALAMEDA · CALIFORNIA

October 21, 1937

To: Master S.S. "NORTH WIND"
Mr. Dan Vucetich
Fred Olsen Line Agency, Ltd.
All Pan American Airways Company Personnel aboard "NORTH WIND"

Subject: Instructions concerning current charter trip of the
S.S. "NORTH WIND"

    The purpose of the current charter trip of the S.S. "NORTH WIND" is the distribution of cargo, fuel, provisions, etcetera, to the various Pacific bases of Pan American Airways Company, including all duties and functions in connection therewith.

    Mr. Dan Vucetich is hereby designated the Senior Representative of Pan American Airways Company aboard ship, and his authority will be respected accordingly in all matters, other than those pertaining to the actual operation and navigation of the vessel itself.

    The transfer of cargo from ship to shore at the various bases, and the functions aboard ship and at the bases will be handled in the manner and by the personnel designated in the attached copy of a memorandum from the Assistant Airport Maintenance Engineer to the Division Engineer, dated October 20, 1937.

    Fred Olsen Line Agency, Ltd. will attend to all matters pertaining to entry and clearance of the vessel, including refueling, etcetera.

    The present schedule of the vessel is to proceed from San Francisco to Honolulu, thence Midway, Wake and Guam, returning from Guam to the mainland via Wake, Midway and Honolulu, discharging and/or loading cargo at each point in accordance with instructions now in possession of Mr. Vucetich. The schedule is subject to change in accordance with instructions which may be issued by the undersigned through Mr. Vucetich.

    For the information and guidance of Mr. Vucetich a photostatic copy of the Charter Party is attached to his copy of this memorandum.

Yours very truly,

Clarence M. Young
Clarence M. Young
Manager, Pacific Division

CMY/eb

PAN AMERICAN AIRWAYS SYSTEM—GENERAL OFFICES—135 E. 42ND STREET, NEW YORK CITY

FRED OLSEN LINE

GENERAL AGENTS
PACIFIC COAST
FRED. OLSEN LINE AGENCY, LTD.
FINANCIAL CENTER BUILDING
CABLE ADDRESS
OLSENLINE

REGULAR FREIGHT AND
REFRIGERATOR SERVICE
NORTH PACIFIC TO U. K. & NORWAY
NORWAY/ANTWERP TO NORTH PACIFIC
PASSENGER ACCOMMODATIONS

NORTH PACIFIC SERVICE

SAN FRANCISCO

Oct. 21, 1937.

Mr. Dan Vucetich,
Supercargo, S/S "NORTH WIND"

Dear Mr. Vucetich:

We enclose herewith for your files, a photostatic copy of the Charter Party of the present voyage of the S/S "NORTH WIND."

Very truly yours,

FRED. OLSEN LINE AGENCY, LTD.

By [signature]

HM/EC

**ISBRANDTSEN-MOLLER COMPANY, Inc.**

CABLE ADDRESS:
"ISMOLCO"
CODES:
WATKINS, SCOTTS 10TH
A. B. C. 5TH, BOE CODE

26 BROADWAY — NEW YORK, N. Y.

TIME CHARTER
PRODUCE GOVERNMENT FORM
APPROVED BY THE
NEW YORK PRODUCE EXCHANGE
NOVEMBER 6TH, 1913
AMENDED OCTOBER 20TH, 1921

**This Charter Party** made and concluded upon in the City of New York, the fifteenth day of October 1937
Between NORTHLAND TRANSPORTATION COMPANY
Owners of the good American Screw Steamship "NORTH WIND" of
of 2448 tons gross register, and 1465 tons net register, having engines of nominal horse power
and with hull, machinery and equipment in a thoroughly efficient state, and classed First Class
at Amer. Bureau of Shipping of about cubic feet grain capacity, and 4000 tons
dead weight capacity (cargo and bunkers, including stores not exceeding fifty tons) on Lloyd's Summer freeboard, inclusive of permanent bunkers, which are of the capacity of about 5000 bbls. fuel oil ~~tons of coal~~ now trading

and PAN AMERICAN AVIATION SUPPLY CORPORATION, Charterers of the City of New York

**Witnesseth,** That the said Owners agree to let, and the said Charterers agree to hire the said Steamship from the time of delivery, for about 45 days to about 4 months

Charterers to have liberty to sublet the Steamer for all or any part of the time covered by this Charter, but Charterers remaining responsible for the fulfillment of this Charter Party.

Steamer to be placed at the disposal of the Charterers, at Seattle, Washington, any time between October 16th and October 18th, 1937
in such dock or at such wharf or place (where she may always safely lie afloat, at all times of tide), as the Charterers may direct, and being on her delivery ready to receive cargo with clean-swept holds and tight, staunch, strong and in every way fitted for the service, having water ballast, steam winches and donkey boiler with capacity to run all the steam winches at one and the same time (and with full complement of officers, seamen, engineers and firemen for a vessel of her tonnage), to be employed, in carrying lawful merchandise, including petroleum or its products, and passengers so far as accommodations will allow (but any expense necessary to fit the steamer to comply with United States Passenger Inspection laws to be borne by ~~Charterers~~ Owners) in such lawful trades, ~~between safe port and/or ports in British North America, and/or United States of America, and/or West Indies, and/or Central America, and/or Caribbean Sea, and/or Gulf of Mexico, and/or Mexico, and/or South America~~
As per attached clause ~~and/or Europe, and/or Africa, and/or Asia, and/or Australia~~, excluding ~~River St. Lawrence from October 1st to May 1st, White Sea, Black Sea and the Baltic out of season, Magdalena River, and~~ all unsafe ports:

It is further understood and agreed that the charter hire of Three Hundred Fifty Dollars ($350.00) per day is based on the present seamen's wage scale and should the seamen's wage scale be increased during the term of the charter, hire will be increased proportionately. Or the increased wages over present wage scale to be paid for by the charterers on presentation of payrolls covering additional wages.

Understood twelve (12) persons

Fueloil

vessel is described as capable of steaming ten (10)/ten onehalf (10½) knots speed per hour in service fully loaded on a consumption of about one hundred and five (105) barrels fuel oil per day of 24 hours in calm weather and smooth sea.
Understood vessel has heavy lift capacity boom of twenty (20) tons but gear and expense for rigging to be for charterers account.
Wherever the word "coal" appears in this charter the word "fueloil" to apply.

WITNESS:

PAN AMERICAN AVIATION SUPPLY CORPORATION

M. S. Peters — [signature]
V. Pres

NORTHLAND TRANSPORTATION COMPANY

[signature] — [signature]
Sec.

*Portion of charter agreement*

In Dan Vucetich's letters to his wife and family, sent during this long cruise, you can almost feel his fatigue and frustration at being away from his family for the better part of another year. By reading his letters home, you can better understand the hardships and loneliness he faced.

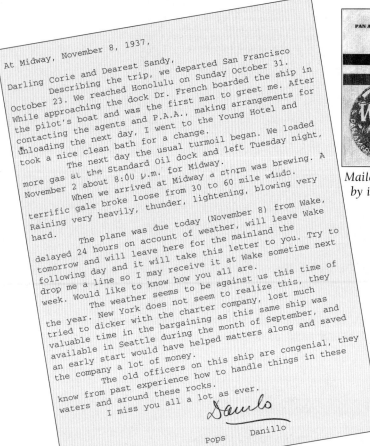

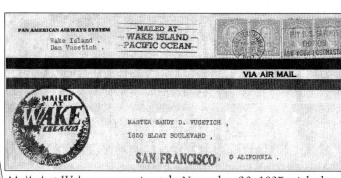

*Mailed at Wake -- approximately November 20, 1937, picked up by inbound Clipper -- approximately November 23, 1937, and postmarked at Honolulu – November 25, 1937.*

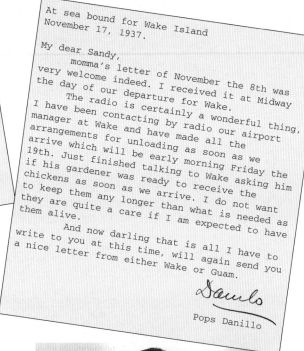

Midway November 27, 1937

Darling Corie, Dearest Sandy:

It was certainly nice to receive your letter of November 16th. The mail was delayed on account of weather. It was a long time between planes for the past two weeks.

Will certainly place 40 cents from now on on my letters, I realize that the envelope was marked Midway. Our trip at Midway was tough, that is the work with the unloading, equipment shot to pieces, a lot of incompetency as well (keep that to yourself of course). At Wake I found the equipment in very good shape but a storm played havoc with it two days after we got here. Barges were busted, landing docks smashed up, the launch which does the towing lost its propeller because it had hit the rocks, a lot of worry and grief, could not do anything else but stand by, so we lost three days standing by and repairing the damage, this afternoon we got started again and hope to finish today towards the evening and shove off for Guam. Our worries will be over for awhile until we return to both Wake and Midway, weather is the principal thing for both places.

Thanksgiving came and is gone. No one thought of it. We had turkey aboard, such as it was. I have been feeling fine. The leg is in fine shape. No more swelling.

It is very hard to foretell when this tub will be back, maybe around the end of the year, we will celebrate New Year's Eve together, I'm certainly rushing things, the men are loyal and certainly work hard, the airport managers are doing their very best to cooperate with me, I have their fullest support and respect, their cooperation is needed to speed up the work. My next mail will be from Guam. This letter will be picked up here by one of the planes returning from Manila just about the time we get to Guam.

Sandy darling, be sure to do your homework, study is very important, I know you will. He wants his boy to making the grades all the time.
Love and kisses to all. Pops misses you all indeed.

Pops   Danillo

*Vucetich with souvenirs of voyage*

After the second charter of the North Wind was completed in December of 1937, the ship was not chartered again by Pan Am. Dan Vucetich was assigned to other duties with the company that did not keep him at sea and away from his home for months at a time.

# SCHOONER TRADE WIND

The short term charter of the large freighters North Haven and North Wind by Pan Am proved to be costly. Therefore, when station manager Stu Saunders determined that a permanent supply ship would have to be anchored at Kingman Reef to serve as a base for the Clipper on the flights to New Zealand, the Pacific division manager, Clarence Young, obtained a smaller less expensive vessel on a long term charter basis, to use as the Kingman Reef base ship.

THE FOUR-MASTED SCHOONER "TRADE WIND," COMMISSIONED IN SEPTEMBER, AS THE SUPPLY SHIP FOR THE SYSTEM'S MID-PACIFIC AIR BASES

*Photo from Pan Am annual report for 1937*

Therefore, in October of 1937, Pan Am chartered a four-masted schooner, formerly known as the Margaret F. Sterling, and had it modified to fit their needs. Staterooms were added for the Samoan Clipper's crew and sophisticated navigational equipment was installed to assist the Clipper in locating the vessel at tiny Kingman Reef. When the outfitting was completed, the schooner was re-christened by Pan Am with a more appropriate name, the Schooner Trade Wind.

*Trade Wind at sunset at Kingman Reef - December 1937*

The vessel had been launched in Vancouver in 1919. Her four wooden masts were constructed of Douglas fir – 37 inches in diameter and 106 feet tall. Pan Am installed auxiliary power so the vessel could get in and out of Kingman Reef without difficulty. A crew of twelve, under the command of Captain Halvor Mikkelsen, of the United States Naval Reserve, was assigned to the Trade Wind. Captain Mikkelsen, a native of Denmark who lived in New York, was considered a master seaman. He also held the record time of fourteen days for sailing from Honolulu to Seattle. Donovan Mackay, from Denver, Colorado, served as the radio officer on the Trade Wind to direct the Clipper to the mid-Pacific base.

Because the planned flights to New Zealand were to start by the end of 1937, the Trade Wind was rushed into service. It sailed immediately to Kingman Reef and took up a position in the lagoon in time to meet the newly re-christened Samoan Clipper, under the command of Captain Musick, on the Clipper's second flight to New Zealand in December, 1937.

*Trade Wind at Wake*

512

*Left:*
*Trade Wind at Guam*
*1938*

*Right:*
*Captain Mikkelsen on*
*left with guest -*
*Note - Pan Am logo*
*on stack*

*Left:*
*Wheel of Trade Wind*

  The Samoan Clipper's third trip south to New Zealand by way of Kingman Reef in early January of 1938, ended in disaster. On this tragic third flight, Captain Musick and the crew spent a restless evening onboard the Trade Wind at Kingman Reef before departing for Pago Pago, American Samoa on January 10, 1938. The next morning, January 11, 1938, after they took off from American Samoa for New Zealand, engine trouble required the Clipper to turn back. In attempting to jettison fuel, the Samoan Clipper exploded.

After the accident, the route through Kingman Reef and American Samoa was abandoned. Even though it was no longer needed as a base ship at Kingman Reef, the Trade Wind was still under a long term charter to Pan Am, so to utilize the vessel for the rest of the charter period, it was used as a supply ship for the mid-Pacific bases, sailing between Honolulu, Wake, Midway and Guam.

In September of 1939 the **Guam Recorder** reported a visit by the Trade Wind to Guam:

> *Our island was visited this month by the schooner Trade Wind, commanded by Captain Halvor Mikkelsen. This vessel is one of the few commercial sailing craft left in the world sailing the high seas. Captain Mikkelsen is generally accompanied by his charming wife, herself a veteran of 68,000 miles under sail. "I have been in the best hotels in Florida, New York, Seattle and Honolulu, but none have rooms that are better, nor nearly so comfortable, as those aboard the Trade Wind", says Mrs. Mikkelsen.*
>
> *They were at Kingman Reef and saw Captain Musick with his brave companions fly away into the blue, never to return. "Always before, when the pilots and crews had flown in and out of the bases where we were stationed, I had said, "we'll be seeing you soon", Mrs. Mikkelsen reflected, but that day, after the Clipper had become a speck that vanished in the steaming dawn, I remembered that I had shaken hands and said "good-bye".*
>
> *It's puzzled me all day. Why had I said simply "good-bye"? The next day, when the radio cracked with the sad news of their disappearance, I remembered my farewell. I am puzzled still.*
>
> *A few years more and the sailing ships will be gone. Undoubtedly freight ships will finish the pioneer work of the Trade Wind that started three years ago.*

Mail has been found that traveled both to and from the Trade Wind while it was on one of its supply missions for the Pacific bases. The wife of Donovan Mackay, the radio operator on the Trade Wind, addressed a July 11, 1938 letter to her husband with instructions that the letter be held at Guam for the Trade Wind's arrival.

*Mail sent to Trade Wind - 1938*

Donovan Mackay also sent a letter from the Trade Wind to his wife from Midway Island on March 24, 1938 and from Wake on July 8, 1938, as the Trade Wind made its slow passage toward Guam.

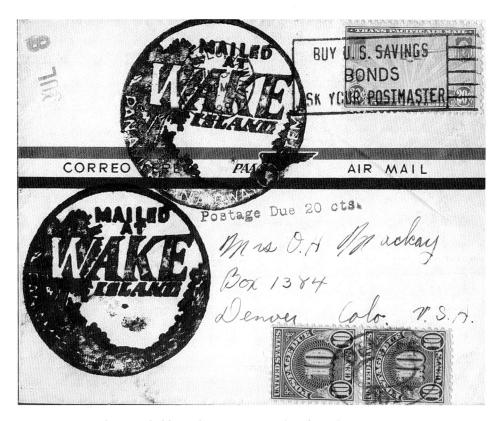

*Envelope mailed by radio operator Mackay from the Trade Wind*

The Trade Wind was one of the last commercial sailing vessels in the Pacific. With a good wind it could make 12 knots – considerably faster than the Alaskan freighters, North Haven and North Wind. It is fitting that a four-masted schooner, very similar to the famous China Clippers of the late 1800s, served as a supply vessel for the "China Clippers" of the air. However, within a few years, all of the great Pacific sailing vessels were gone and the romantic era of four-masted sailing ships came to an end. In seven more short years, by 1946, the era of Pan Am's great flying Clippers would also pass into history.

# M.Y. SOUTHERN SEAS

The last months of 1939 were heady days for Pan Am. They had welcomed the Boeing B-314s in March of 1939, the survey flights to Europe were completed and regular mail and passenger flights were crisscrossing the Atlantic. Pan Am was beginning to make real money and Juan Trippe's tendency to spend lavishly when times were good was quite evident.

By September of 1939 Pan Am was once again surveying flights to New Zealand. The dangerous route through Kingman Reef and American Samoa had, of course, been abandoned with the loss of the Samoan Clipper. The new route took the Boeing B-314 from Honolulu south 1900 miles to remote Canton island. A little village had been built by Pan Am at Canton and there were facilities for the crew and the passengers.

The next stop on the new route was New Caledonia, a French possession lying only 900 miles east of Brisbane, Australia. This sleepy French colony did not have adequate facilities for either a Pan Am flight crew or wealthy and influential passengers. Therefore, Juan Trippe came up with a plan to cater to the fancy tastes of his well-heeled passengers, and at the same time provide accommodations for the crew. He purchased the steam yacht Lyndonia that was owned by Cyrus H. K. Curtis, the owner and publisher of **The Saturday Evening Post.** After extensive renovation by Pan Am, the yacht was rechristened the Southern Seas and sailed to the Pan Am base at New Caledonia where it became a luxurious floating hotel for the overnight stay of the clipper passengers and crew.

Trippe also planned to have the Southern Seas make a fast trip from New Caledonia to Brisbane for passengers who wanted to go to Australia rather than to fly on by Clipper to New Zealand and then have to fly over to Australia on a different airline.

*A 24 page pamphlet describing the Yacht Lyndonia was given to every passenger boarding the vessel*

516

*Dining Room looking forward*
←

*Study*
→

*Owner's Room looking forward*
←

*Photographs from brochure for Lyndonia*

The Lyndonia was a spectacular vessel. Its overall length was 230 feet with a 200-foot waterline. The beam was 30 feet with a draft of 12 feet 8 inches. Cruising range was over 6,000 miles. The hull was entirely of steel with decks, bulwark, rails and exterior work all in teak. There were three decks. The boat deck, the main deck and the lower deck. The owner, Cyrus Curtis, had a beautiful brochure prepared to present to his guests, and it showed the true grandeur of the vessel.

*M/V Southern Seas-in the yards of the Consolidated Shipbuilding Corp.*
*June 1940*

For Pan Am's purposes, however, they wanted to convert it from steam to diesel; they wanted to reduce the size of the spacious state rooms so there would be enough separate rooms for the crew and passengers of the Clippers stopping at New Caledonia. Therefore, the Lyndonia was taken to the Consolidated Ship Building Corporation Yards at Morris Heights, New York for complete renovation. Dan Vucetich, who served as Pan Am's supercargo in charge of all provisioning on the North Haven and North Wind, was given the job of overseeing the conversion of the Lyndonia to a floating hotel for the Pan Am. Work was scheduled to be completed in time for the vessel to serve as the hotel for the first planned flight over the new route scheduled for mid-1940. Progress was slower than was anticipated and by July 14, 1940, when the California Clipper made the first flight to New Zealand, the yacht had not yet arrived in the Pacific. So on July 16, 1940 when the crew and guests arrived at New Caledonia they had to be put up at a boarding house in town.

Finally by early July 1940, the conversion work was completed and she sailed down the East River to New York Harbor where she was re-christened the Motor Yacht Southern Seas. Under the command of J. L. O'Connell, the Southern Seas left New York for the South Pacific by way of the Panama Canal.

The refurbished yacht was even more luxurious than it had been under the ownership of Cyrus Curtis. The dining salon was supplied with the finest Irish linen and crystal goblets, the lounge and the bar were paneled in mahogany and equipped with a record player and short-wave radio and provided with hardwood dance floors which rolled up when not in use. To insure that the finest food would be served, Pan Am hired a cook and pastry chef from one of New York's finest restaurants. Juan Trippe certainly knew how to spend money and how to pamper his wealthy guests and passengers.

*Yacht Lyndonia in drydock -*
*February 28, 1940*

The Southern Seas made the voyage from New York to New Caledonia by way of the Panama Canal and Tahiti encountering a typhoon in route. There was no serious damage but it lost a great deal of paint from the bow. When it finally arrived off New Caledonia, the Captain was surprised that there was not a pilot ship or a welcoming craft to lead it into the harbor. The terrified French in New Caledonia thought it was one of the dreaded German Raiders that was playing havoc with shipping in the South Pacific during l940. When they finally satisfied themselves that it was a friendly vessel there to serve the Pan Am passengers and not to endanger their shipping, they led her to the Pan Am flying boat base at Isle Nou in Noumea Harbor.

Captain O'Connell gave these signed photographs of himself and the Southern Seas to Sandy Vucetich, the young son of Dan Vucetich who was in charge of the yacht's renovation.

Captain J.L.
O'Connell

*Motor Yacht the Southern Seas*

SOUTHERN SEAS - AUGUST 1940

Pan Am's floating hotel proudly displayed the Pan Am flag and the Pan Am logo painted prominently on its smokestack. The Southern Seas arrived in New Caledonia in time to serve as an elegant hotel for the VIPs including C. B. Whitney, one of Pan Am's Directors, who acted as host for the group when they stayed overnight on August 29, 1940 before flying on to New Zealand. As the first passengers to stay on the Southern Seas, the VIPs sent a souvenir cover to their friend, Amon Carter, the owner of the **Fort Worth Star-Telegram,** who was also a good friend of Juan Trippe.

Later, the yacht sailed to Sydney to be repaired and reconditioned. While there the activities of the German submarines and surface raiders in the waters between Australia and New Caledonia forced the company to abandon the planned shuttle service between Noumea and Sydney.

*Left - Recently discovered rare cover from Captain J.L. O'Connell "ON BOARD M.V. SOUTHERN SEAS" at New Caledonia to Pan Am's Treasure Island headquarters - March 14, 1941*

Once the Southern Seas had safely sailed back to Noumea, she stayed permanently in the harbor as a floating hotel for passengers and flight crews. The passengers stayed in the regular and refurbished staterooms and the crew was satisfied with the small rooms built on the top deck.

*Southern Seas in wartime - 1943*

With the outbreak of the war the Southern Seas was first taken over by the Army, and then by the Navy. It served as a troop transport and as a rest and recreation vessel for the battle-weary soldiers and sailors in that area of the Pacific. At war's end while she was at Okinawa tied up to some other vessels, a cyclone came through and the regal vessel was crushed and sank at the dock.

The Southern Seas is a fitting memorial to the glory days of Pan Am in the Pacific when the luxury in air travel reached its highest level. For a short time, she played a little known and romantic part in Pan Am's pioneering flights to New Zealand.

# SCHOONER KINKAJOU

One of the five vessels chartered by Pan Am in the Pacific was the schooner Kinkajou. Built in 1924 by the J.F. James Boatyard in Essex, Massachusetts, the 90 foot, two-masted fishing schooner was designed by the famous naval architect, John G. Alden. Her high freeboard made her suitable for offshore heavy weather sailing.

In 1935 Pan Am wanted to explore the islands between Hawaii and Australia as potential seaplane bases. But they wanted to conceal their intentions from the press, potentially competing airlines, and the British, who also claimed the uninhabited Pacific islands. Therefore, to cover its involvement, Pan Am formed the Oceanic Nitrate Company and incorporated it for the stated purpose of looking for deposits of guano on these remote islands. In the early 1900s, guano (bird droppings) was commonly used as fertilizer.

*Two masted schooner Kinkajou - 1935*

In order to give the expedition some credence as a scientific trip, Dr. Dana Coman, a psychiatrist on the staff of Johns-Hopkins Medical School and a veteran of an Antarctic expedition, was put in charge of the Pan Am expedition. Captain Constantine Flink, who held a master seaman's license from Russia, Norway and the United States, was in command of the vessel. A mate, three sailors and a cook completed the small ship's crew.

The United States government not only assisted Pan Am in this effort, but they hid the true purpose of the expedition and went along with the guise that it was a scientific mission.

The Kinkajou's first cruise departed Honolulu on July 24, 1935 for the mid-Pacific. Six Hawaiians were onboard who had agreed to serve as colonists on Howland, Baker and Jarvis Islands. These same islands were also being colonized by Hawaiians with the support of the Coast Guard, in cooperation with the Navy and the Department of the Interior. Although Dr. Coman weakly disclaimed that his trip on the Kinkajou was sponsored by Pan Am, he did admit that "information collected would be made available to commercial air companies if they wanted".

After delivering two colonists each to Howland, Baker and Jarvis Islands, the Kinkajou sailed on to Christmas Island to also explore it as a possible air base. Although Christmas Island had a lagoon suitable for seaplanes, they learned, to their disappointment, that the British ran a successful coconut plantation on the island for the production of copra. Therefore, British sovereignty would prevent using Christmas Island as an air base.

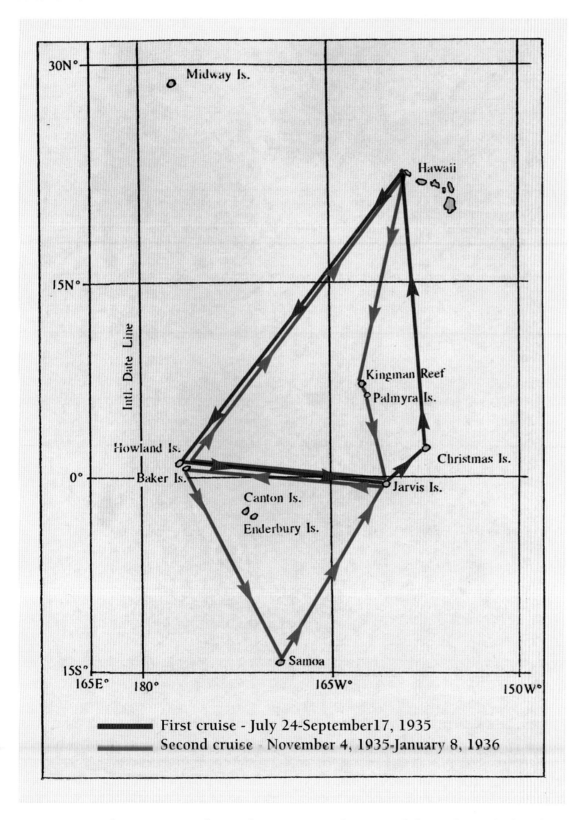

### Voyages of Schooner Kinkajou for Pan Am

▬▬▬▬▬▬

First Cruise
July 24 – September 17, 1935
Honolulu, Howland, Baker, Jarvis, Christmas Island, Honolulu

▬▬▬▬▬▬

Second Cruise with Harold Gatty to American Samoa November 4, 1935-January 8, 1936.
Outbound:
Kingman Reef – Palmyra – Jarvis Howland, Baker – American Samoa.
Inbound:
Jarvis, Howland, Baker, Honolulu

On September 17, 1935, the Kinkajou returned to Honolulu at the end of its first cruise on behalf of Pan Am. By October the crew was rested and ready to depart on their second voyage. However, they had to wait for one more member to arrive. Harold Gatty, the representative of Pan Am, was still in New Zealand, where he was negotiating with the government for terminal and landing rights in Auckland for the Pan Am Airways planned flights to New Zealand.

On November 4, 1935, with Harold Gatty onboard, the Kinkajou departed Honolulu on the second and final portion of the Pan Am sponsored expedition. After examining Palmyra Island and Kingman Reef to determine their suitability as seaplane bases, Gatty went on to Baker Island. At Baker, Captain Flink and Gatty attempted to land in a lifeboat through the heavy surf and a wave caught the boat about 200 yards offshore and turned it over. The colonists on the island were able to save them and no one was seriously injured.

From his inspection, Gatty confirmed that Howland, Baker and Jarvis did not have lagoons and therefore, could not be used for seaplanes. Furthermore, Palmyra needed too much work to be quickly readied as a seaplane base. However, if a base ship were anchored in the lagoon,

U.S. DEPARTMENT OF COMMERCE
BUREAU OF AIR COMMERCE

Honolulu, T.H.
July 22, 1935

From:    W.T. Miller.
To:      Henry Ahia,
         In Charge at Jarvis Island
Via:     Doctor Francis Dana Coman, in Yacht KINKAJOU

Subject:    Jarvis Island.

1.    Be advised that Doctor Coman has been granted permission to land two American citizens on Jarvis Island, for the purpose of remaining and living thereon for a short period of time, to make a scientific study of the island and to investigate the guano conditions.

2.    The following personnel will continue to remain under your supervision:

        Daniel Toomey,
        Geo. West,
        Frank Cockett.

3.    You are requested to extend Doctor Coman your co-operation, assisting him in landing and extend such courtesies as he may request.

4.    The Coman expedition will supply and provide their own equipment, provisions, supplies and water, and it will not be necessary to utilize Government assistance. The present food, water and medical supplies under your control are not to be dispensed with, unless in case of emergencies. The establishing of the Coman camp in close proximity to the present camp will be satisfactory.

5.    It is expected that the present personnel of Jarvis Island will cooperate, coordinate and make a special effort to maintain a high standard of morale with the newcomers.

W. T. MILLER,
Supt. of Airways.

Kingman Reef might serve as the first overnight stop on the flights to New Zealand.

After Gatty had examined Howland and Baker, the Kinkajou sailed south to examine the harbor at Pago Pago, American Samoa.

It was a rough trip and by the time the vessel arrived at American Samoa, Gatty had seen enough. He left the Kinkajou and returned to California by commercial liner. Based upon his personal inspections, Gatty determined that the harbor at Kingman Reef was the only possible overnight stop for the first night's flight from Honolulu. The harbor at Pago Pago, American Samoa, although surrounded by high hills, could serve as the second stop for the Clipper, before the final portion of the flight to Auckland. By using these two mid-South Pacific bases, Pan Am could reach Auckland, New Zealand in three days from Honolulu.

After Gatty left, the the vessel at American Samoa, the Kinkajou sailed back to Jarvis, Howland and Baker Islands to pick up the six colonists. On January 8, 1936 it returned to Honolulu ending the second and final voyage of the Kinkajou for Pan Am.

# J. H. U. Psychiatrist To Lead Expedition To South Sea Isles

## Dr. Francis D. Coman Says Experts Will Study Natural Life On Three Equatorial Land Dots On Air Route To Antipodes

[By the Associated Press]

Honolulu, July 20—America's colonization of three Pacific islands in key positions on any air line which may be started to the antipodes will be increased soon by members of a scientific expedition sailing from here Tuesday.

The party, headed by Dr. Francis D. Coman, psychiatrist of Johns Hopkins University, was to land two men each on Howland, Baker and Jarvis Islands. The United States Department of Commerce already has four Hawaiians on each of these islands studying aeronautical data.

"Our work will be to consolidate America's possession and occupation of the islands," Dr. Coman said.

### To Study Natural Life

The 40-year-old psychiatrist said a study would be made of natural life, guano deposits and soil on the three islands.

Dr. Coman disclaimed any connection with Pan-American Airlines, which is preparing to start a trans-pacific air service in the near future, and with other air lines, but said information collected by his expedition would be made available to commer-

Dr. Coman at wheel of Kinkajou

cial air companies if they want it. The Pan-American Line assisted Dr. Coman in preparing the yacht Kinkajou for the expedition.

Complete camping equipment will be carried, and it was arranged to land a portable radio set and a radio operator on each island.

### Will Return In September

The Kinkajou will return to Honolulu in September and leave two weeks later to pick up the men previously left on the islands.

Harold Gatty, around-the-world flyer now in Australia, will accompany the party on the second trip.

Capt. Constantine Flink, who served with the Beebe expedition, will be master of the Kinkajou, a two-masted schooner equipped with an auxiliary motor. Dr. Coman was medical director of Rear-Admiral Richard E. Byrd's first Antarctic expedition.

Howland and Baker islands are tiny dots of land just north of the Phœnix Island group and almost on the equator. Jarvis Island lies south of the Fanning islands and also close to the equator. All three are almost directly south of the Hawaiian group.

*New York Times -- January 8, 1936*

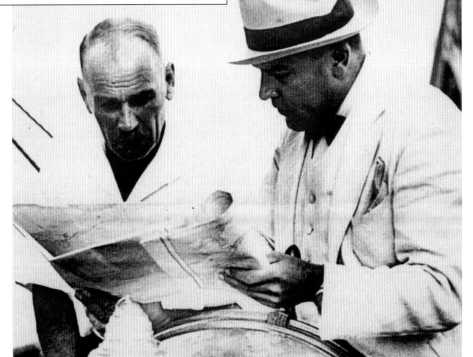

*Captain Constantine Flink on left confers with Dr. Coman on route to be followed*

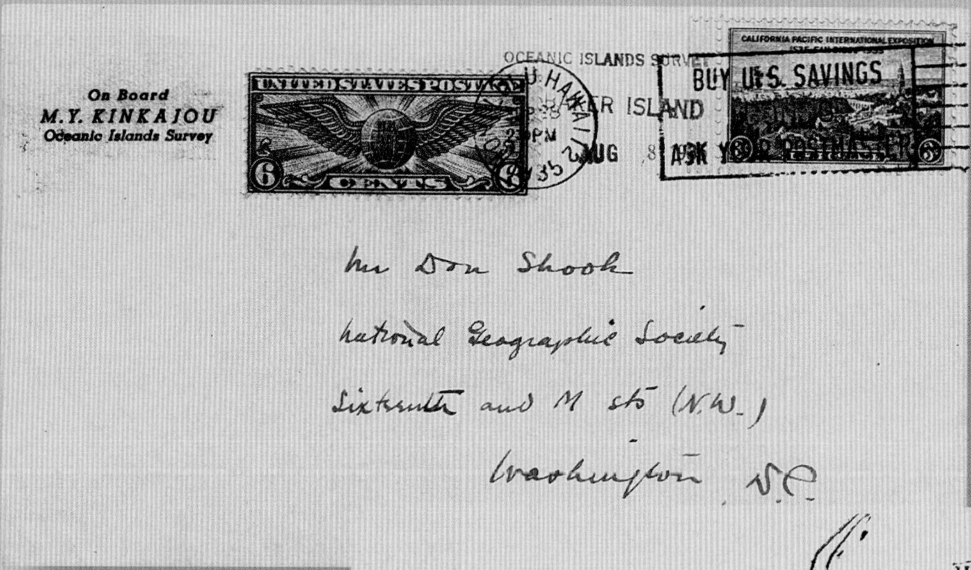

On Board
**M.Y. KINKAJOU**
*Oceanic Islands Survey*

UNITED STATES POSTAGE
6 CENTS

OCEANIC ISLANDS SURVEY
U. HAWAII
BAKER ISLAND
AUG 8 1935

BUY U.S. SAVINGS
ASK YOUR POSTMASTER

CALIFORNIA PACIFIC INTERNATIONAL EXPOSITION

Mr Don Shook

National Geographic Society

Sixteenth and M sts (N.W.)

Washington, D.C.

*Posted from Baker Island
August 8, 1935 received in
Washington D.C. on
October 7, 1935*

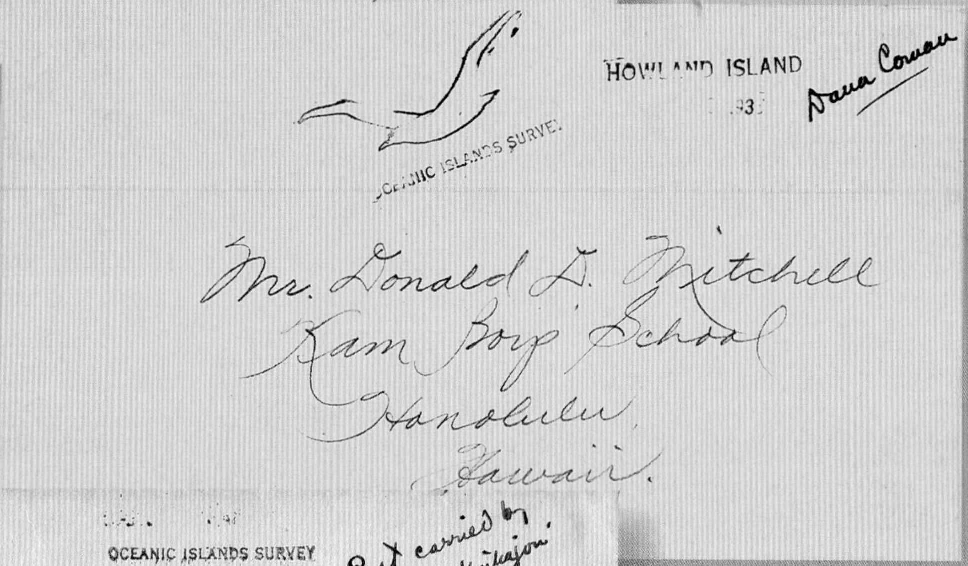

HOWLAND ISLAND
193
Dana Coman

OCEANIC ISLANDS SURVEY

*Posted Howland Island
November 30, 1935 signed
by Dr. Coman*

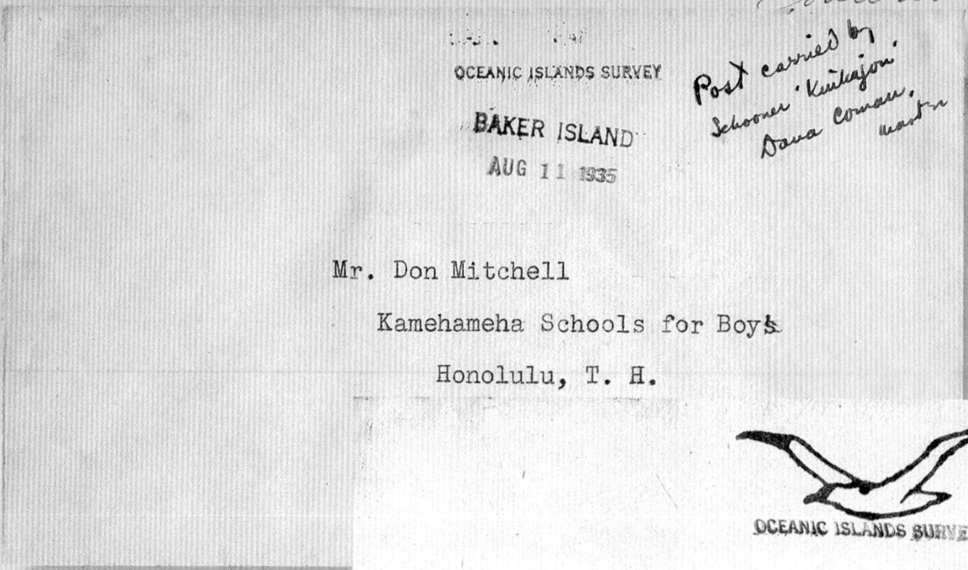

Mr. Donald D. Mitchell
Kam Boys School
Honolulu,
Hawaii.

OCEANIC ISLANDS SURVEY

BAKER ISLAND

AUG 11 1935

Post carried by
Schooner 'Kinkajou'
Dana Coman. master

Mr. Don Mitchell

Kamehameha Schools for Boys

Honolulu, T. H.

*From Baker Island*

OCEANIC ISLANDS SURVEY

JARVIS ISLAND
Coman
DEC 1935

Don Mitchell
Kam Boys School

*Right:
From Jarvis Island*

Crew

## COMAN COMPLETES CRUISE.

### Returns to Honolulu After Survey of Pacific Islands.

**Wireless to THE NEW YORK TIMES.**

HONOLULU, Jan. 8.—Completing his second survey cruise to Baker, Howland and Jarvis Islands aboard the schooner yacht Kinkajou, Dr. Dana Coman has returned to Honolulu, bringing with him six boys from Kamchameha schools who had been stationed on the three islands just below the Equator since last July as meteorological observers.

When the party sailed from Honolulu on Nov. 4 Harold Gatty, as representative of Pan American Airways was aboard, but he left the Kinkajou at Pago Pago, Samoa, and returned to California by commercial liner.

The party experienced heavy weather in the vicinity of Baker Island and was forced to lie off the island six days. The surf capsized a small boat party going ashore, but no one was injured.

Dr. Coman expects to spend a month in Honolulu winding up the affairs of the expedition before sailing for the United States.

*New York Times -- July 20, 1935*

Captain Flink at end of cruise

Crew and colonists at end of cruise

In December of 1935, the Kinkajou was sold for $8,000 to Donald W. Douglas of Douglas Aircraft Corporation, who was also a director with Pan Am. After several more changes of ownership, the Kinkajou was turned over to the Coast Guard in 1942 for wartime duty. At war's end she was in poor condition and she ended her days as a shark fishing boat off the coast of Costa Rica.

Although Pan Am did its best to conceal its charter of the Kinkajou and to deny that its cruises in 1935 were for the benefit of Pan Am, nonetheless the secretive Kinkajou was one of the five vessels chartered by Pan Am that helped make possible the later flights of the Pacific pioneers.

# U.S.S. NITRO

The first government vessel to assist Pan Am in the Pacific was the 480 foot ammunition carrier, the U.S.S. Nitro. When Pan Am decided to fly the Pacific, virtually nothing was known about Wake Island, the uninhabited island between Midway and Guam, which the Clippers needed for an overnight base.

*U.S.S. Nitro - note platform over bow*

*Loening seaplane*

Therefore, to accommodate Pan Am, the Navy agreed to survey Wake and report back to Pan Am as to whether or not there was a lagoon that could be used by the Clippers. A young naval aviator, Lt. Jesse G. Johnson, flew the plane for the photographer taking the survey photographs. A platform was built over the bow of the Nitro to accommodate the Loening amphibian OL-9 airplane.

In February of 1935, the Nitro sailed from Pearl Harbor to obtain the information needed by Pan Am to plan the first Pacific flights. Lt. Johnson reported that it was a very enjoyable cruise. At Guam, Johnson and the photographer flew around the island surveying prospective bases for Pan Am. From Guam the Nitro sailed to Manila where they spent two weeks flying around the island taking aerial photographs. After leaving Manila, they stopped again for a short time at Guam before proceeding on to Wake. They arrived at Wake early on the morning of March 8, 1935. Lt. Johnson wrote:

> "There was no place to anchor; the survey party went ashore in small boats at daylight and after the sun was up for about two hours, I was hoisted over the side in the Loening amphibian airplane OL-9 #9210. Accompanying me was Mr. Carroll, a Navy photographer, who did an excellent job in working his camera while I was flying back and forth across the island to make the pictures.
>
> You can imagine my surprise at the appearance of this island coral reef. It was only four and a half miles long and one and a half miles wide. . . I would call it the pearl of the Pacific. The coral heads in the lagoon made it look like a dotted gem of variegated marine colors inside its land rim, which certainly would not allow an airplane to land. However, during the course of the morning flight, the camera got out of order and Mr. Carroll asked me to land in order to repair it, which I did and found that the coral heads were deeper than I had expected and that there was ample room for a seaplane to land inside the reef, in wonderfully calm and protected waters".

By making the flight, Lt. Johnson had become the first person to ever fly over Wake or to land in its lagoon. Lt. Johnson was also an avid collector of flight covers and this interest continued throughout his life. Johnson reported:

> *"On both days I carried with me 500 large sized envelopes, which I know now, according to the best cover collecting procedure, was the wrong thing to do (too many covers for them to become valuable). However, they were carried, which is the important thing! I do not regret that there were so many of them, because they have given me an opportunity to make many friends, and it certainly has helped to show us the importance of this island. . . The cachet was from a wood cut by Mr. Archie Erickson, who is the manual training instructor at the McKinley High School in Honolulu. In preparing his souvenir covers we ran out of stamps and 432 covers are all that were prepared for the Wake Island flight."*

At the end of the survey flight the small two-seater amphibian landed in the ocean near the Nitro, a boom was lowered and the plane was lifted back to its storage area on the bow of the ship. The Nitro, carrying the seaplane, returned to Pearl Harbor on March 18, 1935 after surveying Wake for Pan Am.

The first cover illustrated is signed by the pilot, Jesse Johnson, and is typical of the Wake Island survey covers. The postmarks trace the route traveled by the Nitro from Manila back to Guam, before stopping at Wake on March 8, 1935.

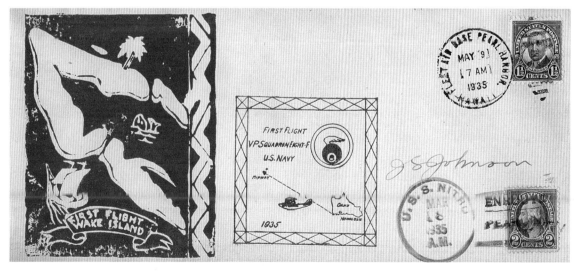

The next cover with the red cachet is far more rare. Lt. Johnson also used the cover again for the Navy survey flights to Midway that took place in May of 1935.

The Nitro's survey of potential seaplane bases at Wake and Guam is typical of the close cooperation that existed between the Navy and Pan Am throughout Pan Am's pioneer flights of the Pacific. Without this cooperation, Pan Am's Pacific flights could never have taken place.

# U.S.S RAMAPO

Another supply vessel that deserves mention is the 480 foot U.S.S. Ramapo. Even though it was a U.S. Navy oiler it was used by Pan Am to supply aviation fuel to Wake and Midway during this period.

U.S.S. Ramapo

In January of 1936 one of the officers on the Ramapo was permitted by Colonel George Bicknell, station manager at Wake, to use the hand made cachet that had been carved for the Wake Island survey flights in August of 1935.

*Lt. Cooper of the U.S.S. Ramapo used the hand carved cachet from August 1935 Wake survey flight on his letter*

Although Colonel Bicknell, had reported that this cachet was destroyed immediately after the survey flights, it apparently was still on hand six months later when Lt. Cooper on board the Ramapo used it to mail a souvenir cover to himself and to several others. The cover is also unusual because the mailing took place in January of 1936 as a so called Clipper flight. This was during the period when flights were suspended while the engines were being reworked. Therefore the cover either sat at Wake for a month and a half before the next Clipper flight or it was placed on a vessel and carried back to Honolulu for posting.

# U.S.S. AVOCET

It all started innocently enough in the spring of 1937 when the U.S.S. Avocet, a seaplane tender, departed Honolulu on May 16, 1937 with a group of scientists for Canton Island to view the total eclipse of the sun. The "innocent" scientific expedition quickly escalated into what became known as the "Canton Island Affair", which eventually involved the United States in a serious political dispute with Great Britain, New Zealand and Australia.

Canton Island was the only land mass that was in a position to view the June 8, 1937 total eclipse of the sun, which would last on Canton for three minutes, 33 seconds. A total eclipse of similarly long duration would not occur for another 18 years.

No sooner had the Avocet departed Honolulu on this "purely scientific mission", when the State Department received an irate cable from the British counsel in Australia complaining about the actions of the Americans. He pointed out that the British vessel, the H.M.S. Leith, had visited the Phoenix group in 1937 to formally claim the remote islands, including Canton, as part of the British colony of the Gilbert and Ellis Islands. Therefore, the Australians and the British forcefully informed the Americans that prior notification and permission was necessary before the U.S. vessel could land the scientists at this British colony. Clearly, the British argued, the mission was not "purely scientific" and they claimed that it had, as one of its primary objectives, the surveying of Canton Island as a potential base for both seaplanes and land based aircraft. The State Department was in an embarrassing

The U.S.S. Avocet, a 180 foot minesweeper, seaplane tender, was built in 1917

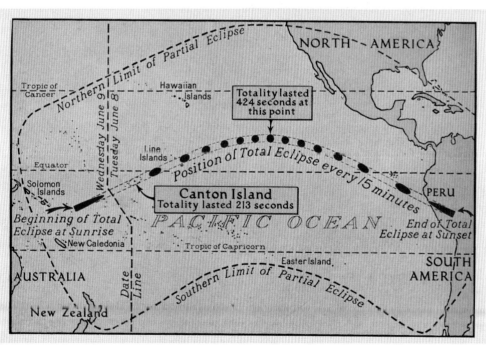

Path of eclipse

position. If they asked the British for permission to land, they would be conceding sovereignty to the British. If they didn't ask for permission, a serious international incident could result. After some quick legal research by the State Department, it was determined that the United States had a very weak, but none-the-less plausible claim to Canton Island. Therefore, the United States elected to do nothing. They would not ask for permission, and they would hope for the best.

On May 26, 1937, the Avocet arrived at Canton and moored just outside the pass to the lagoon. On May 26, 1937 the H.M.S. Wellington also arrived at Canton with the New Zealand scientists to view the eclipse. The New Zealand newspapers angrily reported that the Avocet had moored at the only available anchorage and had refused to move when the New Zealand vessel arrived. The article correctly pointed out that Canton's primary importance was not as an eclipse observing point, but as a vital link in Transpacific air service.

Although Pan Am had used Kingman Reef and Pago Pago Harbor as mid-ocean layovers on the survey flight to New Zealand, the airline was aware that these bases were difficult at best and impossible and dangerous at worst. Therefore, the Navy knew that the Canton Island lagoon was desperately needed by Pan Am as a mid-Pacific seaplane base. The British, backed up by New Zealand and Australia, did not want Canton Island used by Pan Am, unless reciprocal landing rights were granted to the British in Honolulu, which our government would not consider. The British were particularly upset that the scientific expedition was used as a cover to press the Americans' questionable claim to ownership of Canton. When the crew of the Avocet also erected on Canton Island a monument with a large stainless

*Navy Captain J.F. Hellweg, in charge of the expedition - Dr. S.A. Mitchell, the scientific leader of the expedition - radio announcer George Hicks*

steel American flag, the British were furious. The British notice of ownership, put up in January of 1937 by the crew of the Leith, was still intact on the island. The Americans' monument was an insult and, in the view of the British, a clear violation of international law.

The navy observers traveling with the scientists to view the eclipse had determined, however, that Canton Island was perfect for both land and seaplanes. Therefore, to strengthen our government's claim, the Navy was willing to create an international incident by immediately stationing young Hawaiian colonists on the island similar to those colonists already occupying Baker, Jarvis and Howland Islands.

President Roosevelt, however, did not favor such a direct confrontation with the British, so he vetoed the plan to immediately colonize Canton Island. The President wanted to try negotiation before confrontation. The British, however, refused to discuss the issue of an American seaplane base on Canton, so Roosevelt's strategy of negotiation without occupation ultimately failed.

*Monument 1995*

*Camp of 13 scientists and 13 navy assistants*

*Live radio broadcast of eclipse - The Avocet can be seen in the distance - The weather was perfect*

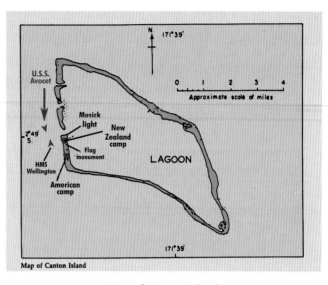

Map of Canton Island

*Map of Canton Island*

After completing the eclipse expedition in June of 1937, the Avocet was transferred to American Samoa where she served as the station ship. When the Samoan Clipper was lost on January 11, 1938 on the third flight to New Zealand, the crew of the Avocet recovered the charred remains of the Clipper and returned the debris to Pago Pago. The Avocet was caught at Pearl Harbor on December 7, 1941 and she received a battle star for her participation in the defense of the fleet. She served out the war in the North Pacific.

*Spectacular eclipse photo taken during the three minutes and thirty-three seconds of totality. Canton Island - June 8, 1937 at 8:03 a.m.*

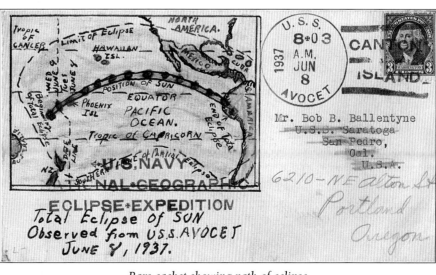

*Rare cachet showing path of eclipse*

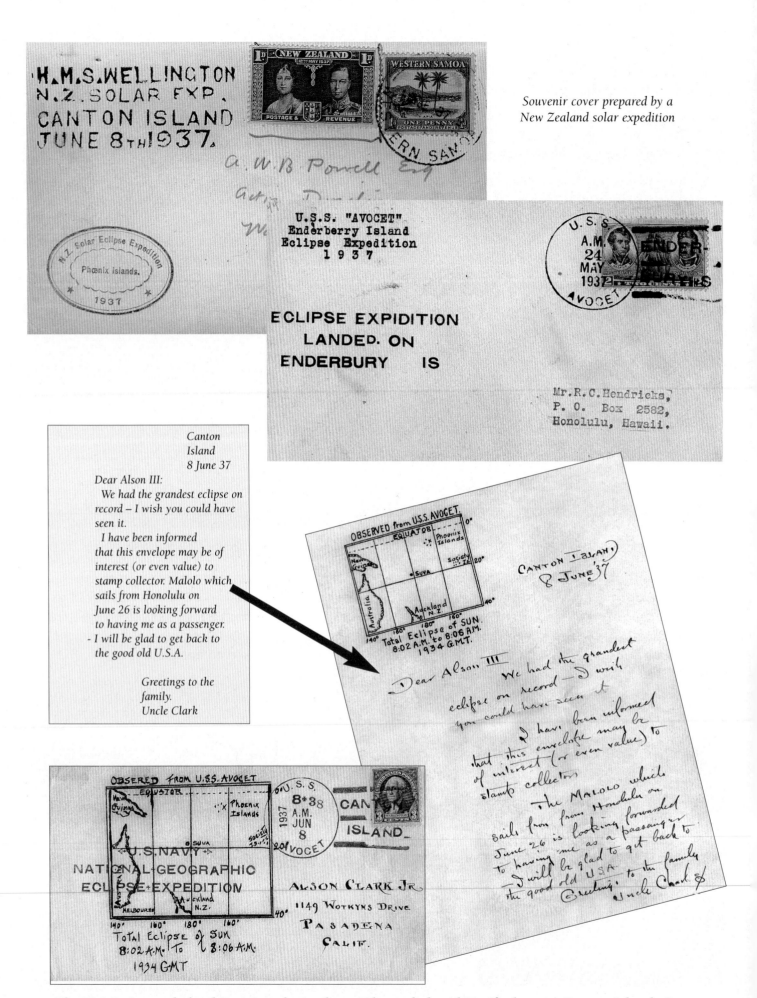

*Souvenir cover prepared by a New Zealand solar expedition*

Canton
Island
8 June 37

Dear Alson III:
   We had the grandest eclipse on record – I wish you could have seen it.
   I have been informed that this envelope may be of interest (or even value) to stamp collector. Malolo which sails from Honolulu on June 26 is looking forward to having me as a passenger. - I will be glad to get back to the good old U.S.A.

   Greetings to the family.
   Uncle Clark

   The U.S.S. Avocet helped Pan Am obtain the much needed mid-Pacific base at Canton Island. Once again, the close relationship between Pan Am and the Navy in the Pacific helped Pan Am in pioneering the Pacific flights.

# U.S.S. ONTARIO

The U.S.S. Ontario also played a role in Pan Am's development of Pacific air routes. After the loss of the Samoan Clipper in January of 1938, the harbor at Pago Pago was closed to Clipper flights. Pan Am began an active search for an island with a lagoon, suitable for the Clippers.

*U.S.S. Ontario at Pago Pago*

The Avocet had taken a party of scientists and naval observers to Canton Island to view the eclipse and make a preliminary survey for Pan Am as to whether or not the lagoon could be used as a seaplane base. Pan Am, however, had not had their own engineers examine the island. Therefore, Frank McKenzie, who was Pan Am's engineer who had been in charge of building the bases at Wake and Midway in 1935, was given the task of surveying Canton Island for Pan Am. In May of 1938, he took a steamer to Pago Pago, American Samoa. On May 22, 1938 he departed Pago Pago harbor aboard the U.S.S. Ontario, a 185 foot coal burning tug, which served as the station ship at the American possession in the South Pacific.

On May 28, 1938, McKenzie and two fellow Pan Am employees, accompanied by Captain W.S. Howard, commander of the Ontario, went ashore at Canton for the official inspection of the island.

They were met by Mr. H.T. Towill of the U.S. Department of the Interior, Mr. Landsdale, the British custodian and administrator, and Mr. Manning, the British wireless operator. Towill was preparing the island for the arrival of the Hawaiian colonists who were going to remain permanently on the island to strengthen the American's claim to the disputed territory.

As a peace offering to the British representative Mr. Landsdale and his Fijian helper, McKenzie delivered potatoes, lard, bread, coffee, and cigarettes – all compliments of Pan Am. The crotchety and rather formal British administrator was not overjoyed at the prospect of the planned American occupation.

*British representative Landsdale on Canton Island with Fijian helper*

Based upon the survey already completed by Towill, McKenzie confirmed that, with a little blasting of coral heads, the lagoon at Canton would be ideal for a mid-Pacific base. The Pan Am employees left the next day and returned to Pago Pago aboard the Ontario. On their return on June 2, 1938, Captain Howard posted a souvenir envelope to commemorate the trip.

*Posted day after Ontario returned from survey cruise to Canton Island*

Meanwhile, Frank McKenzie returned by steamer from American Samoa to Honolulu and arranged for the expedition of the North Haven to return to Canton in the spring of 1939, with supplies to build the Pan Am base.

The voyage of the Ontario provides another interesting footnote to the history of Pan Am's Pacific flights.

# COAST GUARD CUTTERS ITASCA AND TANEY

In early 1935 the Department of Air Commerce was faced with a special problem. With Pan Am's stated intention to fly the Pacific, there was suddenly great interest in the future development of air routes to China and Australia. Stopovers at Midway, Wake and Guam were adequate for the planned flights to Manila and Hong Kong. However, little was known about the islands that lay between Honolulu and Australia. Were any of them suitable for land planes or seaplanes and, more importantly, what country owned these various remote and mostly uninhabited islands?

These mid-Pacific islands are quite arid and over the years bird droppings, called guano, had accumulated, sometimes to a great depth. Up until the mid-1930s guano was virtually the only fertilizer available to farmers and it was a valuable commodity on the world market. To assist American fertilizer companies and farmers to obtain guano, the United States passed the Guano Act of 1856, which allowed our country to claim as U.S. territory any uninhabited island that contained guano deposits.

Under the Guano Act of 1856, U.S. citizens could claim any uninhabited island for guano mining and many of these mid-Pacific islands had at one time or another been claimed by Americans for mining. However, once the best quality and most accessible guano had been dug and shipped away, the Americans left and the islands were once again uninhabited. Over the years British interests had also mined guano on the same islands. Therefore, both the Americans and the British asserted ownership claims to these inhospitable specks of land in the mid-Pacific. Therefore, the immediate colonization of the disputed islands by Americans would strengthen our country's claim to these potential air bases that were now important to both the United States military and to Pan Am.

William T. Miller from the Bureau of Air Commerce was in charge of the colonization project. He attacked his new assignment with great enthusiasm. Secretly he quickly coordinated the efforts of several government departments. The United States Coast Guard, a part of the Treasury Department, made Coast Guard Cutters based in Honolulu available to transport the colonists to the islands and to keep them supplied with food and water. The Navy furnished a broad range of supplies, including fuel for the ships and thousands of gallons of water in 50-gallon drums. The United States Army Air Corps helped establish the island camps by providing both equipment and personnel.

*Coast Guard Cutter Itasca*

So as not to alarm the Japanese, Harold A. Meyer, the army's coordinator on the project, felt it was important that the mission appear to be a civilian undertaking. Therefore, rather than soldiers, young native Hawaiian men, who were either students or graduates of the Kamehameha School for Boys in Honolulu, were enlisted to serve as members of the colonization parties.

The Coast Guard initially assigned the Cutter Itasca to serve as the supply vessel for the expedition. The Itasca was a 250-foot Lake class cutter built in 1929 in Oakland, California at a cost of $900,000. She had a maximum speed of 17 knots and carried 12 officers and 85 men. Supply trips to the islands were made every three months and the Itasca served as the supply vessel on eight of the first ten expeditions.

The first cruise to colonize the islands was aboard the Itasca under the command of Commander W.N. Derby in March of 1935. Also on board was the expedition leader, William T. Miller from the Bureau of Air Commerce and Harold A. Meyer of the Army Air Corps, who served as his assistant. Five colonists were settled on Jarvis Island, six colonists on Howland Island and five colonists on Baker Island. These three islands chosen for the initial colonization, Jarvis, Howland and Baker, were adequate for air strips for land based aircraft, but they lacked lagoons for seaplanes. The immediate future of aviation in the Pacific was clearly Pan Am type seaplanes. Canton Island, with its large lagoon was the preferred island, but the British refused to permit its use so colonists were not sent to Canton during the first three years of the project.

*Cutter Itasca*

*Richard B. Black, expedition leader with U.S. Army assistance*

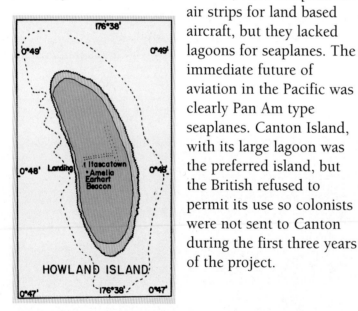

*Howland Island*

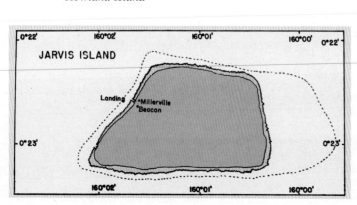

*Jarvis Island*

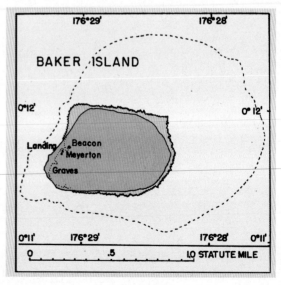

*Baker Island*

538

William T. Miller on deck of Itasca

Colonists on Jarvis as Itasca departs island - 1936

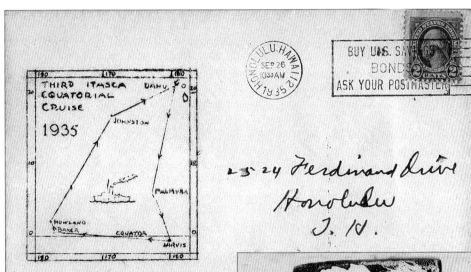

Souvenir cover from the third
cruise to resupply
the colonists

Souvenir cover from the fourth
cruise of the Itasca signed by
William Miller

*Cutter Taney*

By the end of 1937, the Taney had replaced the Itasca as the primary Coast Guard supply vessel for the colonists. Built in 1936 in Philadelphia at a cost of $2,500,000, the 327-foot cutter of the Secretary class had a top speed of 19 knots and a cruising speed of 13 knots. She normally carried 16 officers and 107 men.

In January of 1938, the Samoan Clipper was lost on its third flight to New Zealand and the Civil Aeronautics Administration closed the Pago Pago harbor as a landing area for commercial aircraft. Because of this closing, the need to secure Canton Island as a seaplane base became critical. Regardless of the British position, quick, aggressive action had to be taken to strengthen the American's claim. Therefore, on February 28, 1938 the Taney took colonists for the first time to both Canton Island and nearby Enderbury Island.

From the time colonists were landed on Canton Island in March of 1938, until the British finally agreed to the use of Canton as a seaplane base in late 1939, the entire focus of the government supported colonist expedition was to serve the interests of Pan Am. During this period the Taney, in effect, became a support and supply vessel for Pan Am. For example, on the sixteenth cruise, which departed from Honolulu on May 20, 1939, Pan Am Station Manager Karl Lueder and five other Pan Am employees were transported directly to Canton Island. After reaching Canton, the Taney, at Pan Am's request, went to American Samoa to pick up radio equipment that was no longer needed in Samoa and delivered it directly back to Canton for the Pan Am base.

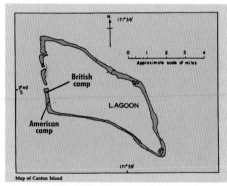

*Canton Island*

On the next cruise in October of 1939 the Taney carried nine Pan Am employees and a large shipment of dynamite to Canton and returned 11 workers to Hawaii.

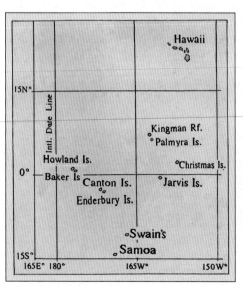

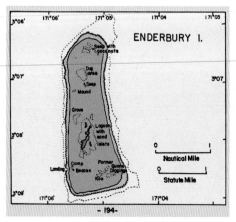

*Enderbury Island*

Traveling aboard the Taney was not hardship duty. In the interesting book, **Panala'au Memoirs**, by E.H. Bryan, Jr. is a full account of the colonization expeditions. In the book, conditions aboard the Taney were documented by one of the government observers:

> *"First, a word about our vessel, the U.S. Coast Guard cutter Taney. No private yacht could have been more comfortable. In fact, one might say that we traveled on a $2,500,000 private yacht, manned by 108 courteous and efficient officers and men. Passengers at the maximum numbered 34, bringing the population of our floating hotel up to 142. Excellent food, movies every evening, careful consideration given to our slightest wish, no cruise could have been more delightful. Our host, Commander E.A. Coffin, did everything within his power to facilitate our making the most of the trip, landing us here, rowing us there, routing and timing the course of the vessel so that we were at the right spot at just the right time".*

All of this pressure brought by the United States Government by placing colonists on Canton Island, finally paid off. In August of 1939, just days before Pan Am's first survey flight to Canton and New Zealand, Great Britain formally recognized Pan Am's right to operate a seaplane base on Canton Island. The agreement called for joint U.S. and British control of the island, open to the air interests of either country. This was accomplished without the United States giving the British reciprocal landing rights in Honolulu. Once again, the close working relationship between Pan Am and the Navy in the Pacific paid big dividends for the airline.

*Settlement at Canton Island - U.S. flag on the left - British flag on the right - March 1938*

*Settlement of colonists at Baker Island*

Regular mail flights were established through Canton Island in July of 1940 and the next cruise of the Taney in October of 1940 removed the colonists from Canton. At the outbreak of the war, Howland, Baker, Enderbury and Jarvis Islands were still being colonized. Unfortunately, the war would not bypass these remote and defenseless islands. On January 18, 1942 the Japanese attacked Howland Island, killing two of the Hawaiian colonists and destroying the lighthouse built for Amelia Earhart's failed trip around the world. The Taney had the sad task of removing the last of the colonists in February of 1942.

*Landing at Jarvis Island – Cutter Taney anchored offshore*

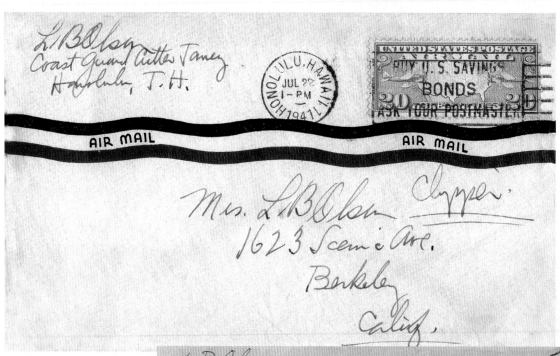

*Letter from Commander of the Taney postmarked July 22, 1941 in Honolulu written while on the twenty-second supply expedition*

*Letter from the Commander of the Taney written on the last cruise to pick up the colonists who survived the Japanese attack and return them to Honolulu*

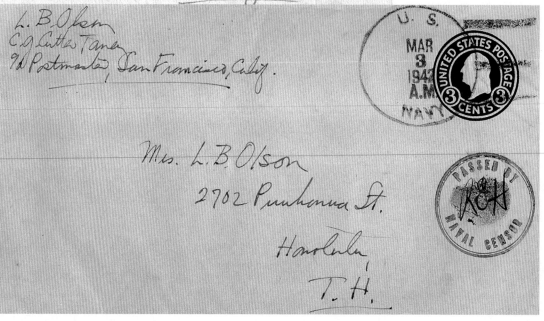

Not only did the Coast Guard assist Pan Am during this period, they also supported Amelia Earhart's unsuccessful attempt to become the first woman to fly around the world. In preparation for Earhart's flight, a tractor was landed on Howland Island and two crude runways were scraped on the rough coral rock. For her comfort, colonists even built an outdoor shower. Amelia had purchased a $75,000 twin engine Lockheed Electra 10E for the flight. To help finance the trip, Earhart, in cooperation with the stamp department at Gimbels Department Store in New York, sold flight covers for $2.50 unsigned and $5.00 signed. Of the 10,000 covers available for purchase, 6,000 were sold. The advertisement for the covers stated that a special cachet would be applied at "Howland Island cachet – the first one in its history".

With the 6,000 flight covers stowed aboard the Electra, Amelia Earhart and her navigator, Fred Noonan, and additional crew members Paul Mantz and and Harry Manning, departed the Oakland Airport at 4:30 p.m. on March 17, 1937. Captain Edwin Musick had departed an hour earlier in the Sikorsky S-42 Pan American Clipper on the first leg of the survey flight to New Zealand and the Martin M-130 Philippine Clipper had also departed at the same time on a regular flight to Honolulu. For three aircraft to be flying to Honolulu a few minutes apart was an historic event.

*Amelia Earhart at 25 in 1923*

*Brochure for Amelia Earhart souvenir covers - note that a special cachet would be applied at Howland Island*

*Very rare cover signed by Amelia Earhart that was left out of the group of covers that she carried*

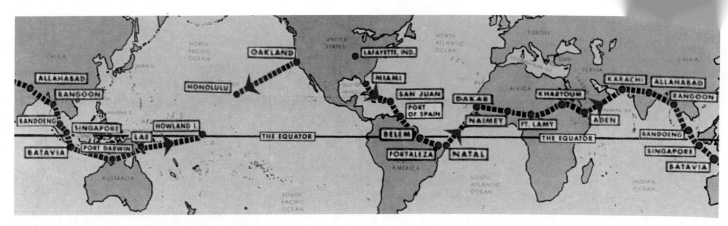

*Earhart first departed March 17, 1937 westbound from Oakland, California - After her aircraft was repaired, she departed the second time June 1, 1937 eastbound from Miami*

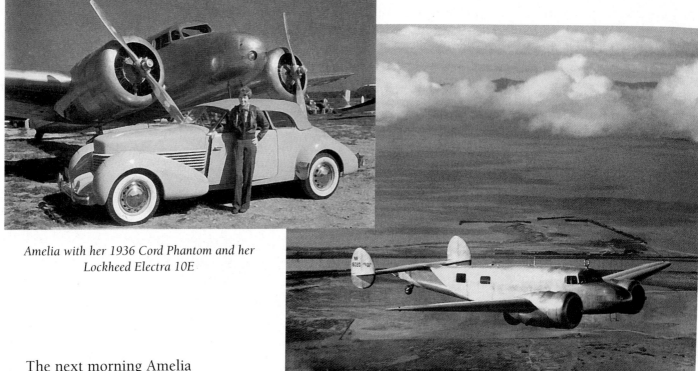

*Amelia with her 1936 Cord Phantom and her Lockheed Electra 10E*

*Earhart's Lockheed Electra*

The next morning Amelia successfully landed in Honolulu, setting a record time for the Pacific crossing. Two days later, while attempting a take off for Howland Island, Earhart crashed. Although she was unhurt, the damaged aircraft had to be shipped back to California for repairs. The 6,000 flight covers on board were initially held by the Honolulu Post Office and later returned to Oakland for repacking for the eastbound flight on the repaired Electra.

On June 1, 1937 Amelia Earhart and Fred Noonan departed the Miami Municipal Airport eastward for Brazil before flying the Atlantic to West Africa. From there the route around the world basically followed the equator.

*Amelia Earhart confers with her navigator, Fred Noonan, before departure*

On June 29, 1937, after a 7 hour 43 minute flight from Port Darwin, Australia, Earhart and navigator Noonan landed the Lockheed Electra at Lae, New Guinea. They spent the next two days packing the plane and discarding everything that was not absolutely necessary for the long flight. Unfortunately, Earhart had elected not to install a trailing antenna that would have assisted her in communicating with Howland Island, on the next and most difficult leg of her flight. Finally, on July 2, 1937 at 10:00 a.m. Noonan and Earhart departed for Howland Island. The flight was scheduled to take 18 hours. Because she was traveling with the sun and across the date line, she was scheduled to arrive at Howland shortly after daybreak on July 2, 1937.

At 2:45 a.m. the Itasca heard the first transmission from Earhart. An hour later, at 3:45 a.m. her voice was heard again. At 5:00 a.m. a garbled message was heard. At 6:14 a.m., her transmission was received: **"Want bearing on 3105 kilocycles on hour. Will whistle into microphone"**. An hour later, at 6:45 a.m. Earhart said, **"please take bearing on us and report in a half hour. I will make noise in microphone about 100 miles out"**. Though her voice was clear, the message was not long enough for the Itasca to take a bearing. Desperately the Itasca radioed back, **"Cannot take bearing on 3105 very good. Please send on 500 or do you wish to take bearing on us?"** There was no answer. At 7:42 she radioed, **"we must be on you but cannot see you, but gas is running low. Been unable to reach you by radio. We are flying at altitude 1,000 feet"**.

The Itasca began transmitting and she responded immediately, **"Earhart calling Itasca. We are circling but cannot hear you. Go ahead on 7500 either now or on the scheduled time of half hour"**. At 8:00 a.m. Earhart acknowledged the Itasca for the first time, **"KHAQQ calling Itasca. We received your signals, but unable to get a minimum. Please take bearing on us and answer on 3105 with voice"**. The Itasca answered that they couldn't take a bearing on that frequency because the direction finder worked only up to 500 kilocycles. At 8:44 a.m. the Itasca received its last desperate message, **"We are running north and south"**. The Itasca responded immediately by listening to every frequency she might use, but there was no answer. Not once in her messages had she given the Itasca her position, her course, her speed or her estimated time of arrival.

Amelia Earhart and Fred Noonan were the object of the greatest rescue search ever made for a single lost plane. Four thousand men in ten ships and 65 airplanes searched an area the size of Texas for 16 days. The battleship Colorado and the aircraft carrier Lexington joined the Itasca. No trace of the Electra was ever found. On July 16, 1937, naval authorities ended the search for Amelia Earhart.

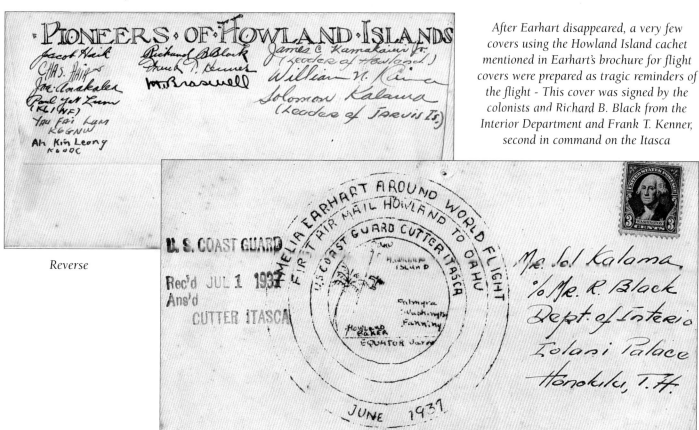

*After Earhart disappeared, a very few covers using the Howland Island cachet mentioned in Earhart's brochure for flight covers were prepared as tragic reminders of the flight - This cover was signed by the colonists and Richard B. Black from the Interior Department and Frank T. Kenner, second in command on the Itasca*

*Reverse*

# Miss Earhart, Her Plane And Navigator Noonan

MAIL SCHEDULE
BOAT MAIL
From Coast—Coolidge, Tues., a. m.
From Coast—Lurline, Sat. 11 a. m.
From Orient—Hoover, July 9
From Orient—Chichibu, July 6
From Australia—Monterey, July 7
For Australia—Maneer, July 14
AIR MAIL
For Coast—Phil. Clip., July 8
For Coast—China Clip., July 5
From Orient—China Clip., July 4
For Orient—Phil. Clip., July 8

# Honolulu Star-Bulletin

**LAST EDITION**

Evening Bulletin, Est. 1882, No. 15014
Hawaiian Star, Vol. XLV, No. 14155

20 PAGES—HONOLULU, TERRITORY OF HAWAII, U. S. A., FRIDAY, JULY 2, 1937—20 PAGES ★ ★ ★ PRICE FIVE CENTS

# AMELIA LOST! HUNT ON

## Cutter Prepares For Search; Flier's Fuel Supply Is Exhausted

### Chance For Safe Landing At Sea Is Described As 'Desperate' By Fliers

### Say Buoyancy of Plane Depends On Whether It Is Damaged Alighting

LOS ANGELES, July 2. (U.P.)—If Amelia Earhart exhausted the fuel supply of her plane and the sea was calm when she presumably was forced down en route to Howland island, the craft is capable of floating indefinitely, builders of the plane said.

A low winged monoplane, the ship was designed with particular view to such an emergency, according to executives of the Lockheed Aircraft Co.

How long Amelia Earhart and Fred Noonan can survive if forced down at sea is a question so surrounded by "ifs" that its answer is inevitably conjecture.

But fliers who know her type of plane and the hazards of a sea landing frankly shook their heads when asked that question today. The chance of survival, they said, was almost non existent.

They pointed out these facts:

The Earhart plane is heavy and fast. It lands at 65 to 70 miles an hour. By stalling it just above the waves and "dropping it in," Miss Earhart could hit the water at about 50 miles an hour.

The open sea is a desperate place to put down any plane, especially a
(Continued on Page 4, Col. 4)

### Amelia's Route On Attempted World Flight

Itinerary of Amelia Earhart's world flight:

June 1—Left Miami, Fla., and landed in San Juan, Puerto Rico, the same day.

June 2—Landed at Caripito, Venezuela.

June 3—Landed at Paramaribo, Dutch Guiana.

June 4—Landed in Fortaleza, Brazil.

June 7—Landed at St. Louis, Senegal, Africa, from Natal, Brazil.

June 10—Reached Gao, French Senegal, from Dakar, Africa.

June 11—Landed at Ft. Lamy, Chad Territory, from Gao.

June 12—Landed at El Fasher, Anglo-Egyptian Sudan.

June 14—Flew to Massawa, Eritrea, and Assab, Eritrea.

June 15—Reached Karachi, India, from Assab.

June 17—Arrived in Calcutta.

June 18—Took off for Bangkok but was forced to turn back, landing in Akyab, India.

June 19—Reached Rangoon, Burma.

June 20—Continued to Bangkok, and Singapore.

June 21—Reached Bandoeng, Dutch East Indies.

June 24—Proceeded to Batavia and Sourabaya, Java.

June 25—Returned to Batavia for repairs to her plane.

June 28—Landed in Port Darwin, Australia, after touching at Koepang, Timor.

June 29—Landed in Lae, New Guinea.

July 1—Left Lae for Howland island.

### Last Word From Plane Indicates Gas Nearly Gone, No Land In Sight

### Was Due At Howland Island At Noon On 2,550 Mile Hop From New Guinea

**By The Associated Press**

Amelia Earhart, America's foremost woman flier and her navigator, Fred J. Noonan, were lost at sea today in the desolate wastes of the central Pacific after apparently overshooting tiny Howland island at the end of a 2,550 mile flight from New Guinea and running out of gasoline.

A brief message from the coast guard cutter Itasca at Howland, coming after five and a half hours of radio silence, brought the news

SAN FRANCISCO, July 2. (P)—Amelia Earhart carried a rubber lifeboat and life belts for herself and Navigator Fred Noonan. The gasoline tanks are so equipped as to float the plane when empty.

that Miss Earhart, at 9:15 Honolulu time this morning, reported she had only 30 minutes' fuel supply left and was flying out of sight of land.

This message was followed by another period of radio silence which lasted until past 2 this afternoon as the Itasca cut off communicaitons with the Honolulu coast guard headquarters, apparently keeping its radio clear on the possibility of picking up further word from the flier.

**May Have Passed Isle**

In its first message the Itasca advised coast guard headquarters that it was leaving at 1:30 Howland time to search "northwest of the island," indicating that Miss Earhart and Noonan had flown past it in the early morning hours.

The Itasca reported that one hour before her last message Miss Earhart said she was 100 miles from Howland but had been unable to sight the mile long strip of land or the Itasca.

The only other land in the vicinity is Baker island, 30 miles south of Howland and almost on the equator. A group of Hawaiian colonists living on Baker have equipment for radio transmission and if Miss Earhart had landed there it was believed the information would have been relayed to the Itasca.

Coast guard officials here hurriedly consulted with army and navy officers regarding plans for sending additional vessels to aid the Itasca in the search. The cutter Taney, which is equipped with an airplane, is in drydock here for repairs which are not scheduled to be completed for a month.

**Has Safety Devices**

Anticipating the possibility of a
(Continued on Page 4, Col. 5)

Frank Kenner, the second in command on the Itasca, heard Earhart's last transmissions. His widow shared with me the mementos he had saved from his cruises that colonized the Pacific islands from 1935 to 1942. Included was an interesting letter that he wrote to his sister shortly after Amelia disappeared.

Although Kenner's letter basically supports the overwhelming evidence that Earhart merely lost her way, ran out of gas and crashed into the Pacific, those who want to believe that she somehow survived and fell into enemy hands, found his letter intriguing. When Kenner wrote, "she asked us to do the impossible, knowing ahead of time that we could not furnish her with the services that she wanted" those who think she survived the flight argue that the "services" she wanted was to be rescued from the Japanese. Books have been written in support of the theory that she did survive, but hard evidence proves otherwise. She simply got lost and ran out of fuel.

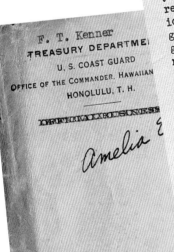

**TREASURY DEPARTMENT**

UNITED STATES COAST GUARD

HONOLULU, HAWAII

10 August.

OFFICE OF COMMANDER
HAWAIIAN SECTION
SAN FRANCISCO DIVISION

Dear EVE-

While some free time is available, will drop you a line, and thank you for your letter. I guess Betty's letters informed you that I had once again returned to Honolulu. It was some cruise to say the least. In spite of the tragic events that took place it was filled with interesting moments. I did enjoy getting back in the South Pacific, with old ITASCA crowd. Doebler and Nelson wre gone but the others were still on her. Our cruise lasted 36 days cruised nearly nine thousand miles.

As to Amelia losing herself, she had only herself to blame. We all admired her nerve and pluck to attempt such a flight, but we can not admire her good sense and judgement in her conduct of it. She was too sure of herself, and too casual. She devoted no effort to the details at all. When it was too late and she was going down she hollered for our aid but that was too late. We did all we could. She never gave us any of her positions as we repeatedly requested of her to do, she never answered or acknowledged any of our messages. She gave us no information as to her plans, what plans she had for communications she changed in the middle of the flight. All in all it was a mess. I heard her last broadcasts myself. She realized too late that fact, by the desperate note in her transmissions. Her voice plainly indicated that she was in trouble, then she went to pieces. She asked us to do the impossible, knowing ahead of time that we could not furnish her with the services that she wanted. She clearly indicated throughout the flight that she was not familiar with her radio equipment. If she had only answered our messages earlier in the flight we might have had some idea where to look for her, and might have been able to save her. It would take hours to write the whole story, some day will tell it all to you, for it is interesting. There is so much that we had to assume, that we really can not find all the answers. Do No more news so will close for this time. Give my best to all. Do write again soon. Take care of yourself, don't work too hard. Life is too short to rush things. ( the tropics have me). If you need or want anything, just holler.

With much love Frank

*Frank Kenner's letter to his sister - 1937*

At the time of her death, Amelia Earhart was one of the most famous women in the world. She helped make the public aware of aviation, while also promoting international peace and the ideals of equality for women. She died at the height of her fame.

The plan to place colonists on the uninhabited islands in the mid Pacific clearly promoted Pan Am's interests in the Pacific. The securing of Canton Island was crucial for the further expansion of Pan Am. The Itasca and the Taney as well as the other Coast Guard cutters that helped supply the colonists on those islands were important to Pan Am's success in establishing regular service to New Zealand. Because they played such an important role, they deserve to be included along with the other vessels that helped Pan Am pioneer the air routes across the Pacific.

# U.S.S. BUSHNELL

The U.S.S. Bushnell was launched in 1915 and for the next 22 years the 350-foot vessel served as a submarine support ship and survey ship in both the Atlantic and the Pacific.

In December of 1937 the Bushnell was transferred to duty performing hydrographic surveys in the Pacific. It was during this period that she assisted Pan Am by conducting a survey of Canton Island and other nearby islands to determine their suitability as seaplane bases. The cruise to survey the central Pacific islands departed San Diego, California on April 1, 1939 and arrived off Canton on April 23, 1939.

*Canton Island – April 1939*

At Canton, the Bushnell's photographer photographed the small homes and offices of the British and American representatives living on the island in 1939. The same buildings were sketched approximately a year earlier on this rare cover that was mailed from Canton in June of 1938. This cover was signed by all of the people then living on Canton Island.

*Hand drawn on Canton Island - July 1938*

*Sketch of Canton Island settlement July 1938*

The Bushnell completed its preliminary surveying work and departed Canton Island in April of 1939 to survey the other nearby islands. She returned to Honolulu on July 27, 1939, completing the first half of the voyage.

After a week in port for fresh supplies, the Bushnell returned to the South Pacific to survey other potential seaplane bases. In August of 1939 she was stationed at Canton Island when the new Boeing B-314, the California Clipper, landed in the Canton lagoon on its outbound survey flight from Honolulu to New Zealand.

U.S.S. Bushnell at Hull Island, South Pacific
17 August '39

My Dear Marjorie,
    This is the note I promised mailed at Canton Island. We arrive there tomorrow morning. We recently received word from there that the clipper plane will be down about 24 August so that this note may arrive in Santa Monica before you do.
    With all best wishes for your happiness, I am sincerely,
    David Hubbard

Mailed at Canton Island

The doctor on board the Bushnell mailed this envelope and letter from Canton to a friend and, although it violated the regulations of both Pan Am and the post office to carry mail on the survey flights, it was carried by the Boeing Clipper on its return flight from Canton to Honolulu and onward by Clipper to the United States.

In August of 1941 the name of the Bushnell was changed to the U.S.S. Summer. After the war she surveyed the Bikini Atoll prior to the atomic tests. She was decommissioned in September of 1946.

# CHAPTER SIX
# A TRIP ON THE PHILIPPINE CLIPPER

W hen Transpacific passenger service was inaugurated in October of 1936, the first passengers were wealthy adventurers, seeking the publicity of being among the first to travel by air on the Pacific route. A one way ticket to Manila cost about $800. In the middle of the depression it was thought that only movie stars and the heads of large corporations could afford the price of a ticket.

As time passed however, the advantages of air travel became so obvious that ordinary business people began to fly on Pan Am's Transpacific flights.

Professor Fritiof N. Fryxell was typical of the Transpacific passenger of the late 1930s. Let's examine his trip and try to recapture the excitement experienced by one of the early passengers across the Pacific.

Professor Fryxell was born in Moline, Illinois in 1900. He graduated from Augustana College in Rock Island, Illinois in 1922 and after getting his Ph.D. he returned to Augustana to teach geology.

*Professor Fryxell - 1939*

In May of 1939 he was asked by the Commonwealth of the Philippines to spend a year surveying the Philippines to determine the oil possibilities of the area. They wanted him to start work in the Philippines immediately after he finished his school year in May. However, he wrote back to them saying that he had commitments through the summer to the National Park Service, where he worked as a geologist, and that the earliest he could leave was on August 25th on the steam ship President Coolidge, getting him to the Philippines 24 days later, on September 17th. This was later than the Government of the Philippines wanted him to report, so they offered him a very interesting proposal.

CLASS OF SERVICE

This is a full-rate Telegram or Cablegram unless its deferred character is indicated by a suitable symbol above or preceding the address.

# WESTERN UNION

1220

:(31)

R. B. WHITE
PRESIDENT

NEWCOMB CARLTON
CHAIRMAN OF THE BOARD

J. C. WILLEVER
FIRST VICE-PRESIDENT

SYMBOLS

DL = Day Letter

NL = Night Letter

LC = Deferred Cable

NLT = Cable Night Letter

Ship Radiogram

The filing time shown in the date line on telegrams and day letters is STANDARD TIME at point of origin. Time of receipt is STANDARD TIME at point of destination

Received at

1939 APR 26 PM 4 33

C162 165/167 DLC=RF LOSANGELES CALIF 26 108P

FRITIOF M FRYXELL, DEPT OF GEOLOGY=
AUGUSTANA COLLEGE

PHILIPPINE WORK ONE YEAR SALARY 500 DOLLARS PER MONTH WORK
TO BE RECONNAISSANCE TO DETERMINE OIL POSSIBILITIES OF THE
ISLANDS FOR THE GOVERNMENT STOP WORK TO BE UNDER MY
SUPERVISION BUT EACH FIELD GEOLOGIST WILL BE ASSIGNED
AND BE RESPONSIBLE FOR HIS OWN AREA STOP WORKING CONDITIONS
MILD AVERAGE TEMPERATURE 82 DEGREES BUT RAIN EVERY DAY
STOP COMPLETE CAMP AND COOK AND HELPERS PROVIDED WITH
EACH PARTY AND ALL TRANSPORTATION AND EXPENSES STOP YOU
WILL FIND WORK VERY INTERESTING AS COUNTRY ENTIRELY NEW
STOP YOUR TRANSPORTATION TO BE PAID FROM YOUR LOCATION
TO PHILIPPINES WITH FULL SALARY FROM DATE OF DEPARTURE
PROVIDED YOU  FLY CLIPPER ACROSS PACIFIC OTHERWISE ONE
HALF SALARY FOR BOAT TRAVEL STOP THIS IS NOT DIRECT
OFFER AS HAVE A NUMBER OF INQUIRIES OUT AND WILL ACCEPT
FIRST OFFER AS AM LEAVING FOR PHILIPPINES MAY ONE AND
AM DESIROUS OF COMPLETING PARTIES BEFORE LEAVING STOP
WOULD LIKE TO HAVE YOUR DEPARTURE FROM STATES AS CLOSE
TO JULY ONE OR EARLIER IF POSSIBLE WIRE YOUR REPLY
WESTERNUNION=
        GRANT W CORBY
        500 82.

THE COMPANY WILL APPRECIATE SUGGESTIONS FROM ITS PATRONS CONCERNING ITS SERVICE

*Telegram asking Dr. Fryxell to fly the Clipper to Manila*

They told him that if he would agree to fly on the Philippine Clipper departing on August 23, 1939 getting him to Manila on August 30, 1939 rather than go by the slow steamship President Coolidge, they would start paying him his salary on August 23. However, if he insisted on travelling by steamer, they would only pay one-half of his salary during the period of his transit. This meant about a $300 difference to him based on the $500 per month salary he was to earn for working in the Philippines for a year. With the pay incentive, Professor Fryxell agreed to fly on the Philippine Clipper getting him to the Philippines approximately three weeks earlier than if he took the steamer.

Let's join Professor Fryxell as he makes his plans to fly the Philippine Clipper from San Francisco to Manila. Let's try to recreate the trip visually with items from his scrapbook of his trip and other brochures and time tables of the period from my collection.

*Small Pocket Sea / Air Brochures*

Travel brochures in 1939 published by Pan Am heavily advertise the combined sea/air travel to Manila and Hong Kong. Such trips were popular because they kept the overall travel expenses to a somewhat more reasonable level. One way passage on the steamer was approximately $250 compared to the $800 one-way fare for the Clipper. Professor Fryxell undoubtedly saw similar brochures to the ones illustrated on sea/air travel and they would have helped him to plan his trip.

*Map inside Sea/Air brochure*

At this time in the late 1930s Pan Am was also publishing a series of small pocket brochures that provided additional information on sea/air travel. These pocket travel brochures would have been available from Pan Am's Chicago ticket office.

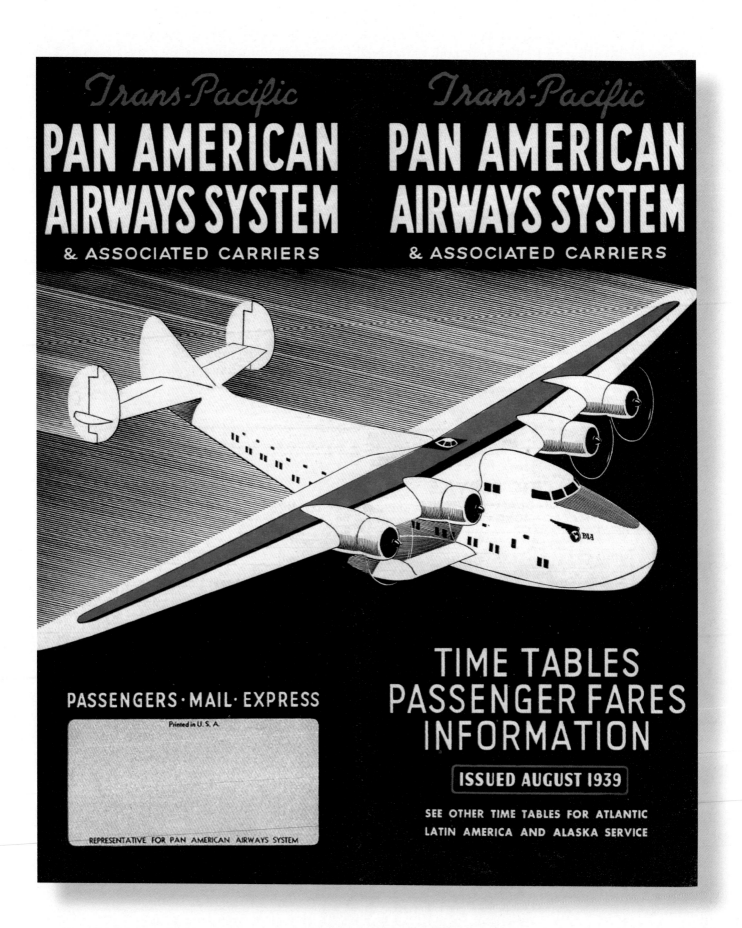

Pan Am also issued timetables for the Pacific routes several times a year. The timetable for August 1939 would have given Professor Fryxell the actual flight schedule for his August 23, 1939 departure.

A small fold out brochure entitled "Shortcuts to Sunshine" explained to him the stops along the way in Honolulu and Guam. The brochure even touted Midway and Wake Island as having "all the comforts of home, including crystal clear water and great fishing. "

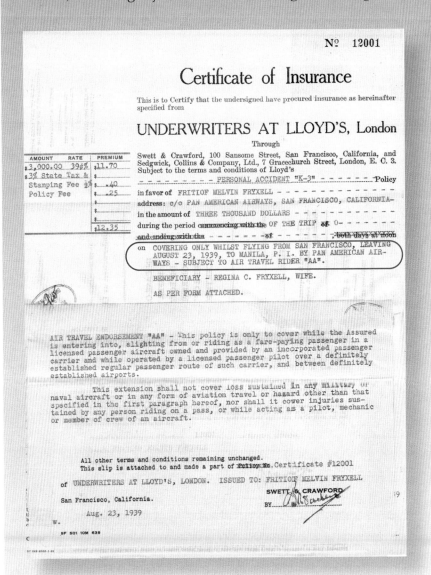

As the time for his departure grew closer, he realized that his life insurance policy contained an exclusion for air travel because such travel was considered too risky to be insured under a normal life policy. Therefore, for $12.35 he bought a Lloyds of London policy with his wife as the beneficiary in the amount of $3,000 specifically covering himself for the August 23, 1939 departure on the Philippine Clipper to Manila. He felt that the policy was good protection for his wife and two children who remained behind in Rock Island during the year he was to be in the Philippines.

The AIR TRAVELER
*Across the Pacific*

SAN FRANCISCO · HONOLULU · MIDWAY · WAKE · GUAM · MANILA · HO
*Your Official Guide Book - - Keep It With You*

*Via* PAN AMERICAN

**HOW TO MAKE RESERVATIONS**
for a
**CLIPPER CRUISE**

For your convenience, Pan American Airways System has made special arrangements with the Travel Agent whose name appears below, to provide full information about these or other Clipper Cruises. He can relieve you of further details and start you off with arrangements prepared in advance for complete enjoyment of your trip. Write, phone or call on your agent personally, and you will be taken care of by one who is an expert in Travel and ready to assist you.

*Routes of the Flying Clipper Ships*

Booklet 1-B. 11-36                    Printed in U.S.A.

WORLD'S STANDARD FOR AIR TRANSPORTATION

Once he purchased his ticket, Pan Am gave him a small handbook entitled ***"The Air Traveler Across the Pacific"*** which gave him additional information on each of his stops along the way. It also contained advertising of the businesses and services available in Honolulu and in Manila. This pamphlet also gave him glowing reports of the vacation virtues of the Midway and Wake Island stop overs. In fact, as to Wake, it made specific mention of the beautiful beaches and the alleged treasure of $1,000,000 in gold that was on the vessel Libelle which broke up on the reef at Wake Island and the brochure held out possibilities that a lucky traveler might find gold on Wake's beaches.

The most visually beautiful brochure provided by Pan Am was entilled **"Transpacific"**. It had a colorful map of his entire route and it showed a color cutaway view of the Martin M-130.

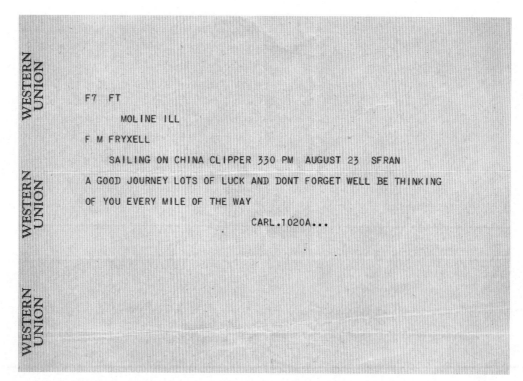

```
F7  FT
       MOLINE ILL
F M FRYXELL
       SAILING ON CHINA CLIPPER 330 PM  AUGUST 23  SFRAN
A GOOD JOURNEY LOTS OF LUCK AND DONT FORGET WELL BE THINKING
OF YOU EVERY MILE OF THE WAY
                              CARL.1020A...
```

His friends back home in Moline, Illinois sent him a telegram in San Francisco, wishing him a safe trip

Ministers living near San Francisco came to Pan Am's new Treasure Island base on August 23, 1939 to wish him well and to see him off.

## PAA

### BERMUDA • WEST INDIES • MEXICO
### CENTRAL & SOUTH AMERICA
### ALASKA • HAWAII • PHILIPPINES • CHINA

*1939 Ticket envelope*

**PAA PAN AMERICAN AIRWAYS**
TRANSPACIFIC SERVICE

NAME Mr. FRYXELL

DESTINATION

## IDENTIFICATION TAG
### SEE OTHER SIDE

*He checked his four bags and the baggage tag indicated he was just under the 50 pound limit*

## BAGGAGE CHECK
### PAN AMERICAN AIRWAYS SYSTEM
& Associated Carriers

TO **MANILA**

| No. Pcs. | Total Weight |
|---|---|
| 4 | 4 9 |

Delivery of Baggage will be made to the bearer of the corresponding Baggage Claim Check.

| Passenger Ticket No. | Seat or Comp. No. |
|---|---|
| | |

Form B. No. **11-32-83**

*Stationery with S-42 design on cover*

THE LARGEST
AIR MAIL SYSTEM
IN THE WORLD

With the same speed and dependability which accompanies you whenever you travel over the 40,000 mile routes of the Pan American Airways System, your air mail and the air mail of all nations of the world is daily sped to its destination.

Directly serving more than 170 cities in 44 countries and colonies of the West Indies, Mexico, Central and South America, Alaska, Hawaii, the Philippines, and the Orient, and with connections to all the continents of the world, your correspondence may be carried with all the advantages of rapid, reliable service which you

*Flying Clipper Ships*

CORREO AEREO   PAA

CORREO AEREO   PAA

KEEP IN TOUCH WITH
HOME AND OFFICE
BY AIR MAIL
**Fast-Economical-Convenient**

Pan American Airways is proud of its record for mastery of detail of which the provision of this special AIR MAIL STATIONERY is but one example. For your convenience it has been prepared to afford a maximum of "writing space", with a minimum of weight and postage. For instance:

Two sheets and an envelope
weigh under 5 grams
Six sheets and an envelope
weigh under ½ ounce
Thus, at very little additional cost it is now possible to deliver your letters at a time-saving often as great as twenty days.

Aboard the Flying Clipper Ships, Pursers will gladly provide complete and detailed information regarding rates, schedules and the best connections so that your letters may reach their destination promptly. He will also furnish or obtain stamps at prevailing charges and mail your letters at the earliest possible moment.

PAA

MAIL BY AIR EVERYWHERE
EL CORREO AEREO LLEGA PRIMERO

*Contained via airmail stickers*

PAN AMERICAN
AIRWAYS SYSTEM

When he got on board, airmail stationery was provided to him. Pan Am was using two different designs of stationery packets at the time, one of them showed the S-42 Sikorsky flying over the Pacific route and the other pictured the Martin M-130.

The photograph displays the map from the brochure entitled **"Transpacific"** along with other items that were available to Professor Fryxell as mementoes of his flight.

After flying over 20 hours from San Francisco he arrived in Honolulu and was put up overnight at the Royal Hawaiian Hotel. His bags were checked with the hotel overnight yellow tag.

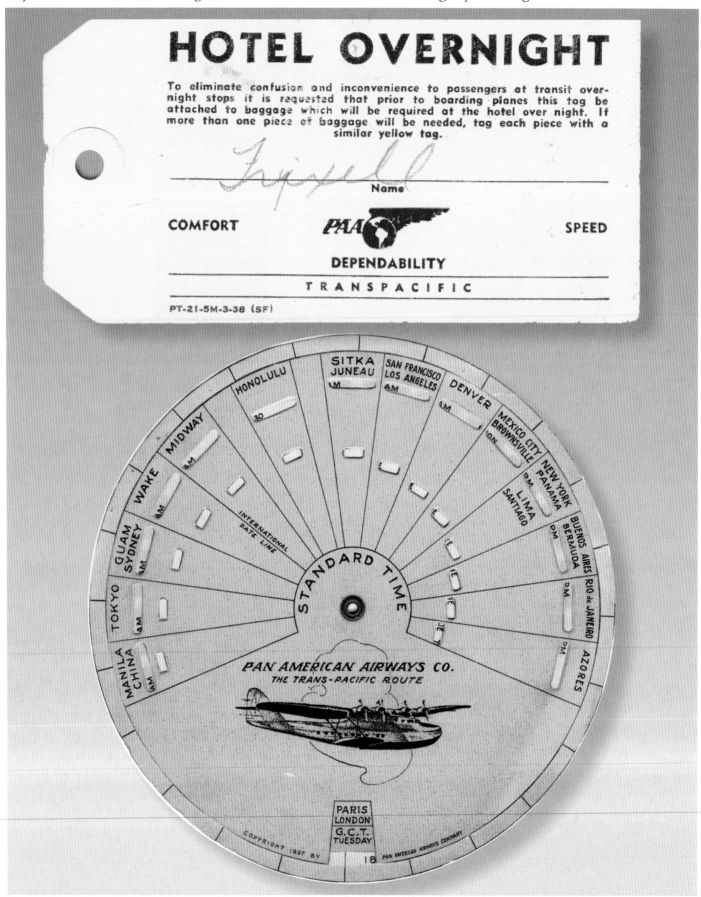

Pan Am also provided him with a large wheel that allowed him to keep track of the date and time back home as he crossed various time zones and ultimately the International date line. The Martin M-130 Clipper is illustrated on the wheel. The wheel had been designed by Almon Gray, the radio operator on Wake in 1935.

When he arrived at Honolulu, he was given a brochure for the city by Pan Am's general agent, the Inter-Island Steam Navigation Company. However, he was scheduled to leave early the following morning and unless there was a sudden change in the weather he would not have a chance to explore the sights in Honolulu.

The weather remained good, so before dawn he was taken back to Pan Am's Pearl City base where the Philippine Clipper was waiting for an early morning departure.

Pictured is the Philippine Clipper approaching the landing barge at Midway after an easy nine hour flight from Honolulu.

*Philippine Clipper approaching barge at Midway*

Once at the landing barge, the passengers were put aboard a launch, the Panair V-P, for the short trip to the dock. This launch, manufactured by the Wheeler Boat Company of Brooklyn, New York, was similar to the launches used at all of Pan Am's Pacific bases. Juan Trippe liked to do business with local merchants, which was one of the reasons he selected the Brooklyn boat builder to build the Pan Am launches. In the late 1930's Wheeler boats were well know because Ernest Hemingway in 1934 had selected a 38-foot Wheeler "Playmate model" cruiser, which he named the "Pilar", as his fishing boat for Key West.

*Midway passengers and supplies are taken from the landing barge to the dock*

*Arriving passenger at Midway leaving boat for station wagon ride to hotel*

*Clean modern houses made Midway a small city - 1939*

*Main street Midway - 1939*

*Photographing and filming the natives on Midway*

*Concrete plaque at Goofy Gooney Club*

On Midway, the island staff invited Dr. Fryxell to the Goofy Gooney Club for a cold beer.  He was told to follow the signs to Gooneyville in order to visit the club. He declined the invitation and settled for an iced tea in the hotel dining room instead.

*At Midway, even golf was available at low tide for the adventuresome traveler.*

*Midway Hotel - on postcard available for passengers - front of card*

At Lat. 28°13′ N. Long. 177°22′ W. (F...
Ocean), on Midway Island, Pan Americar...
ways has built this spacious airway inn, cc...
to discriminating travelers. It represents *he*...
ernization which has come to this mid-P...
coral isle in the development of Pan Am...
Airways transpacific airline.

*Back of card*

*On road from Midway dock to Hotel - Note Pan Am license plate*

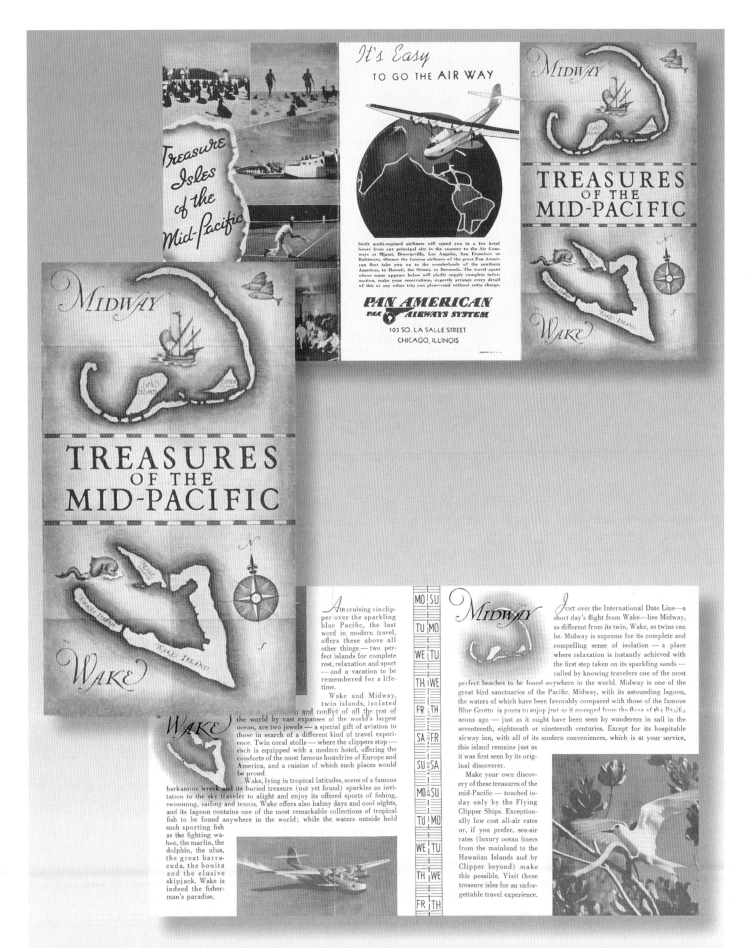

At Midway a small pocket brochure entitled "Treasures of the Mid Pacific" again highlighted Midway and Wake as travel destinations. At Midway he was able to see if the desert island lived up to its billing as a resort. Although Pan Am promoted Wake and Midway as vacation stopovers, virtually all of the passengers continued on with their flight without spending extra time at either island.

*Postcard - Midway Hotel dining room*

*Postcard - Midway beach*

*Gooney birds were everywhere on Midway*

In addition to the brochures, Pan Am had available at Midway four company issued postcards - one each of the gooney bird - the hotel - the hotel dining room - the gooney birds on the beach. The next morning Dr. Fryxell flew to Wake across the international date line.

*Wake had a large hydroponic garden to provide fresh vegetables for hotel guests*

*Postcard showing Pacific Tern at Wake*

*Postcard showing Wake Pier with Martin M-130 in lagoon*

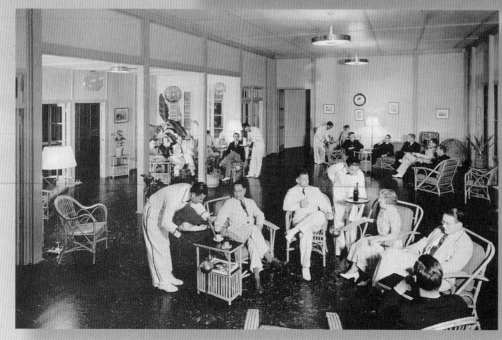

*Postcard of lobby at Wake Hotel*

Fritiof Fryxell:                                          #6

The "Philippine Clipper" will depart at 7:00 A.M.
tomorrow from the float.  You will be called at
5:45 A.M., and your breakfast will be ready
immediately upon your appearance in the lobby.
Will you kindly have your baggage ready to
dispatch to plane at 6:15 A.M.

We desire to make your short stay at Wake a
comfortable and enjoyable one.

                    WAKE ISLAND
                   PACIFIC OCEAN
                 August 27, 1939

*Typical room at
Wake Hotel
Professor Fryxell
was in room #6*

When he retired to his room on Wake a small typewritten card was awaiting him advising him of the 7:00 a.m. departure of the Philippine Clipper for Guam.

As scheduled he arrived in Manila on August 29, 1939. He had not only earned an extra $300 in salary by flying the Clipper, but also saved 18 days of boring sea travel. He also had a memorable journey that he would never forget.

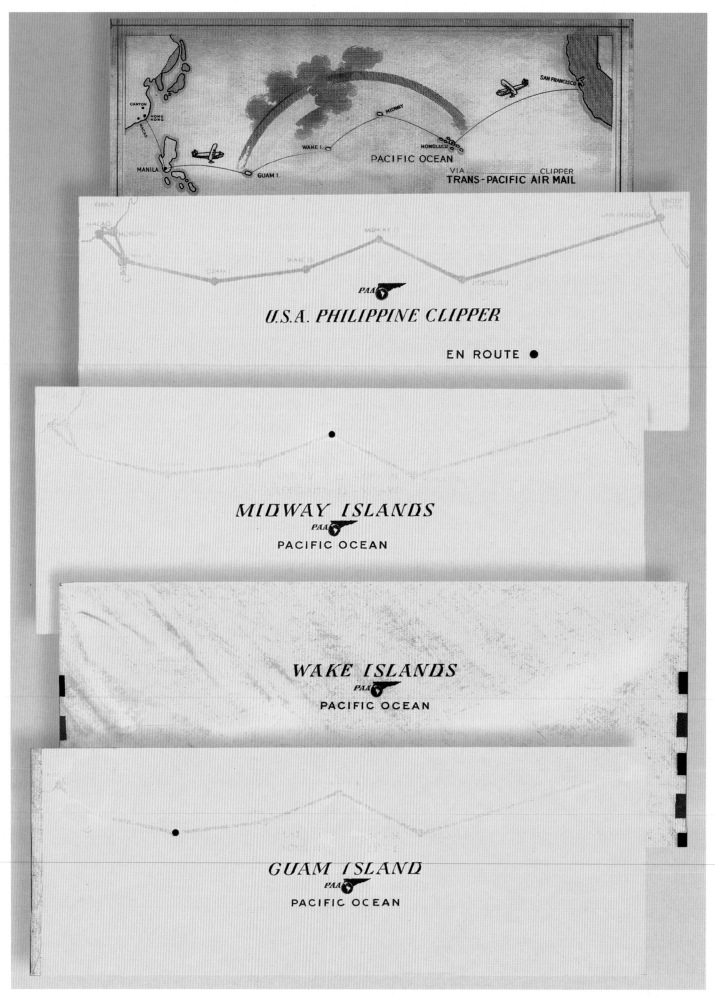

*Stationery provided to Professor Fryxell*

V. E. Chenea
General Traffic Manager
Pan American Airways System
Chrysler Building
New York, N. Y.

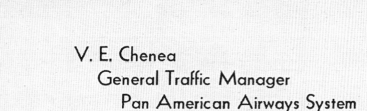

## "IF I WERE *Manager, I'd____!*"

How often one hears that phrase followed by cryptic exclamations referring to the service given by large organizations . . . Here is an opportunity to place yourself in the position of "Manager" for the moment and tell us what you would do to make your trip more enjoyable.

Too frequently transportation lines see things only from their point of view, but you as one of our valued guests can help to broaden our perspective. Perhaps you have some ideas you would like to jot down on the other side.

**We invite your suggestions.**

He never used the comment card that was provided to him and we can only assume that he was pleased with his flight

575

# PAN AMERICAN AIRWAYS COMPANY

GENERAL OFFICE—TREASURE ISLAND—SAN FRANCISCO, CALIFORNIA

DIVISION TRAFFIC OFFICE
427 POST STREET
SAN FRANCISCO, CALIFORNIA

"IT PAYS TO FLY"

October 2, 1939

Mr. Fritiof Fryxell,
1331 42nd Avenue,
Rock Island, Illinois

Dear Mr. Fryxell:

You will recall that when you crossed
the International Date Line on your recent flight in the
PHILIPPINE CLIPPER, Father Time played another of his in-
genious pranks on you. In order that you may have an
accredited document which may sometime be invaluable in
accounting for this confusing discrepancy in your span of
time, we are mailing you under separate cover your Certificate of Phoebus Apollo. It is now in the mail, and should
reach you shortly.

We sincerely hope that you enjoyed your
flight with us, and we trust that we may have the pleasure of serving you again on your next trip across the
Pacific.

Sincerely yours,

V. A. Kropff,
Division Traffic Manager

VAK/mlc

125 E. 42ND STREET, NEW YORK CITY

*Type of certificate
sent by Pan Am
11"x14"*

In October of 1939, when Pan Am wrote to Dr. Fryxell in Rock Island, he was still in Manila so his wife received the certificate that was presented to him to commemorate his crossing of the international date line on his Clipper flight. Unfortunately his certificate has been lost, but it was similar to the one given Dan Vucetich in 1938.

At the end of his year in Manila he returned home on the slow S.S. President Cleveland. He was again greeted by telegrams and postcards from his friends back in Rock Island, welcoming him back.

*Dr. Fryxell on slow trip back to California*

CA196 8=MOLINE ILL 25 410P            1940 AUG 25 PM 2 44

F M FRYXELL, CARE S S PRESIDENT CLEVELAND=

=AMERICAN PRESIDENT LINE ARRIVING TONIGHT OR TOMORROW

MORNING SFRAN=

WELCOME HOME AND BEST WISHES FROM US ALL=

=CARL.

FRYXELL.

Welcome home,
Esther
Philip
Hildegarde
Lawrence
Margaret

Professor Fryxell continued to teach at Augustana College until 1973, when after completing 50 years of teaching, he retired. He passed away in Rock Island at age 86 in 1986.

There is no question that his trip across the Pacific by Philippine Clipper was one of the most memorable experiences of his life.

I am also sure that Pan Am hoped that their brochures, postcards, timetables and stationery made his trip more enjoyable and memorable.

# CHAPTER SEVEN
# CHINA CLIPPER - THE MOVIE

As a result of the tremendous favorable publicity Pan Am obtained with the China Clipper's first flight to Manila, Warner Brothers rushed into production a very forgettable movie entitled *"China Clipper"*. Although Pan Am stated that the movie was not intended as the representation of the company, the plot is almost identical to Pan Am's corporate history up until the mid l930s.

In the movie a successful businessman, who is frustrated with slow steamship travel, quits his job and establishes the "Trans-Ocean Airways". He bids successfully for the international airmail route between Key West and Havana. After conquering the Caribbean with the Sikorsky S-42, the company turns its attention to the Pacific. In these sequences the Martin M-l30 China Clipper was used for background shots.

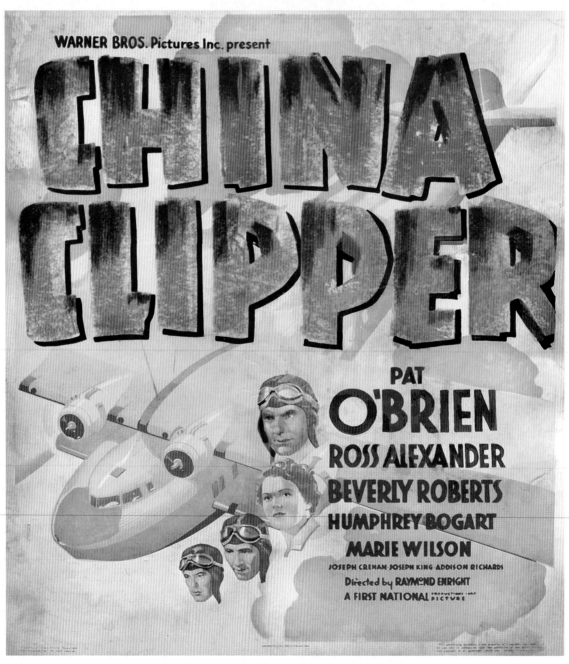

*Graphics from store window card for China Clipper movie*

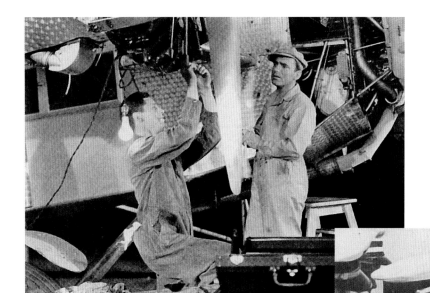

The 1936 motion picture **"China Clipper"** starred Pat O'Brien, Humphrey Bogart, Ross Alexander and Beverly Roberts. Produced by First National Productions Corporation, this was the first aviation feature to be made without a flight-related loss of life being part of the story line. Pan Am's China Clipper appeared in several of the film's sequences.

*Right – Bogart on left talking to crew*

*The China Clipper in the movies, a Warner Brothers location crew at Alameda, California, pictured as they photograph scenes of the giant Clipper ship for sequences in the air-thriller "China Clipper." The four engines on the huge airship were turning as the picture was made preparatory for a short flight across San Francisco Bay. Members of the cast of the picture who went to Alameda to appear in atmospheric scenes bringing in the airplane include Pat O'Brien, Beverly Roberts, Ross Alexander, Humphrey Bogart, Marie Wilson and H.B. Walthall.*

*News release on back of photo*

Actor Pat O'Brien received top billing along with Ross Alexander. The leading ladies were Beverly Roberts and Marie Wilson. A new actor in Hollywood, Humphrey Bogart, was also mentioned as a supporting actor.

The movie was hailed as a breakthrough, setting a new high standard for motion picture photoplays based upon modern commercial aviation. Both Warner Brothers and Pan Am were proud of the fact that it was the first aviation picture without a "crash". Pan Am's public relations director, William Van Dusen served as technical advisor to Warner Brothers, and flight officers Lodeesen and Lewis from the Pacific Division served as advisors for the scenes where the Clipper was depicted in flight.

*Left to right - Pat O'Brien, Humphrey Bogart, Joseph Crehan and Ross Alexander with Sikorsky S-42 in background*

*Cast and film crew with Martin M-130 China Clipper in background*

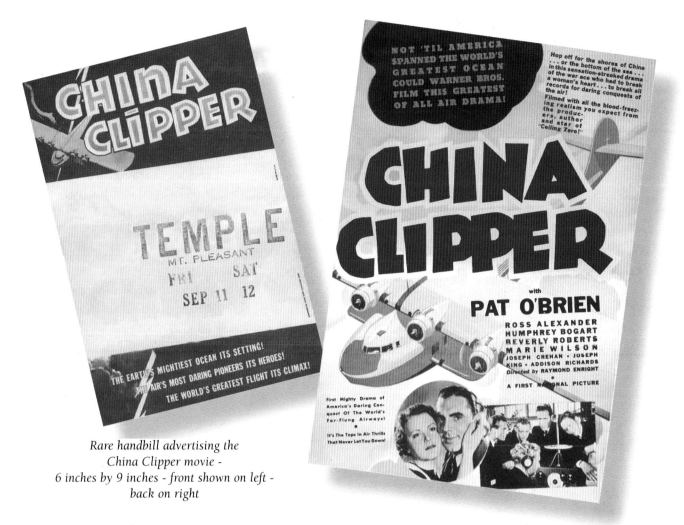

*Rare handbill advertising the*
*China Clipper movie -*
*6 inches by 9 inches - front shown on left -*
*back on right*

*On the set the Sikorsky S-42 in background*

*Left to right: Pat O'Brien, Beverly Roberts, Humphrey Bogart, Marie*
*Wilson and Ross Alexander*

The photographs shot on location at Pan Am's Alameda base are from the Pan Am newsletter. Both the Sikorsky S-42 (with round windows) and the Martin M-130 China Clipper were used in the movie. Humphrey Bogart, of course, went on to become the leading actor of his day and he was recently named as the male actor of the 20th Century. His work as a supporting actor in China Clipper did not earn him any special recognition.

In the late 1930s the success of Pan Am in crossing both the Pacific and the Atlantic is comparable to our Nation's success in the space program in the late 1960s and early 1970s. The interest in Pan Am and their flying accomplishments was at its peak.

# CHAPTER EIGHT
# FRANKLIN DELANO ROOSEVELT

B ecause so many of my favorite flight covers are from the personal collection of Franklin D. Roosevelt, it seems fitting to pay tribute to President Roosevelt and his remarkable career and to also examine his lifelong hobby of stamp collecting.

His interest in the hobby began as a young boy, many years before he was stricken with polio. After his illness and after he completed his treatment, he was wheelchair bound and stamp collecting was one of the few hobbies that he could still actively pursue. He once said *"I owe my life to my hobbies, especially stamp collecting"*. His interest was never passive or casual. He believed thoroughly in the hobby and because of his enthusiasm and example, stamp collecting became a national obsession in the 1930s and early 1940s. In April of 1945, on the eve of victory in the war, he passed away.

*May 5, 1936 – An early color photograph of the president working with his stamp collection in the White House study*

Rather than donate his collection to a museum, the family decided that it was more fitting to sell it at auction so that other collectors could enjoy the pleasure of owning a piece of the President's collection.

His wife Eleanor Roosevelt wrote in 1946 at the time his collection was sold, *"Anything my husband did, everywhere he went, and every position he held served the purpose of increasing his collection, since he never forgot this hobby of his which filled a great many leisure hours"*.

Roosevelt referred to stamp collecting as *"the science of human relationships"*. His collection filled over 150 volumes.

The sale of his collection was conducted by H.R. Harmer, Inc. in New York City in two sessions, the first on Monday, February 4-5, 1946 and the second on April 1–2, 1946.

*President at his Hyde Park home library*

*Catalog from Roosevelt sale*

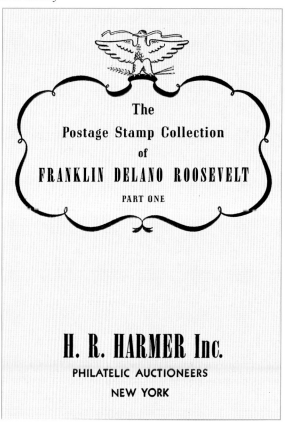

*Catalog for sale - 1946*

Many of the unique flight covers that appear in this book from the President's collection were contained in lot 425, which the catalog described as follows: "Lot 425 – 1934 to 1942 – Collection of 151 various first flight covers for special events, all with cachets printed or hand stamped, all addressed to the president, in a large ring binder with card pages". His entire collection of flight covers in lot 425 sold for $400.

THE WHITE HOUSE
WASHINGTON

Our late President was this country's number one stamp collector. It is difficult to estimate what part his hobby of stamp collecting from boyhood played in the shaping of his international views but we do know that as a stamp collector he constantly dealt with and considered the peoples of the entire world. The Franklin D. Roosevelt Stamp Collection is tangible evidence of the international consciousness of a great leader.

*Harry Truman*

*Letter from President Truman contained in catalog*

In 1946 the auction catalog for President Roosevelt's collection proudly stated, *"Philately reigns supreme among all hobbies. It has aptly been termed the king of hobbies and it has likewise been the hobby of kings and presidents."* This was undoubtedly true in 1946. Although the hobby will never again attract the following of the general public as it did in the 1930s and 1940s, it still remains an enjoyable way to gain knowledge of our world.

The Roosevelt collection had an appraised value of $80,000 and Harmer's was quite proud that the sale realized $210,855.00.

**MRS. F. D. ROOSEVELT**
**342 MADISON AVENUE**
**NEW YORK 17, NEW YORK**

I am very glad to write a short foreword to go with this booklet on my husband's stamp collection. He derived so much pleasure and relaxation from working with his stamps, I feel rather sad that he never had time to develop in any of his children or grandchildren the same interest and love for stamp collecting that he had himself.

This collection is largely valuable because my husband started it as a very small boy, and then acquired a collection which belonged to his mother, much of which was given her by her uncle who had travelled widely in the days when few people travelled. After that start, everything my husband did, everywhere he went and every position he held, served the purpose of increasing his collection since he never forgot this hobby of his which filled a great many leisure hours.

It had its serious purpose, however, in that through it he learned the most extraordinary amount of geography and history and never forgot any item that he learned. He knew where all of the small islands were that our men had to occupy in the Pacific, and I doubt that most of us in this country ever heard of the great majority of them. He knew the history of far flung places and somehow through his long association with stamps, he had absorbed a world picture which included a knowledge of birds and beasts and agriculture and weather such as few of us have.

All of this was grist to his mill when it came to understanding what was happening to our servicemen all over the world.

Whether this collection is sold intact or broken up, I hope that whoever acquires the stamps, will acquire with them some of my husband's interest and power to lose himself in the occupation of the moment, which is the secret of complete relaxation. These stamps gave my husband great pleasure and I hope they will continue to bring pleasure and good luck to those who may handle them in the days to come.

*Eleanor Roosevelt*

THE WHITE HOUSE

WASHINGTON

November 28, 1941

Dear Mr. Trippe:

The President has asked me to
thank you ever so much for that extremely
interesting cover of the first Pacific
Air Mail. He is delighted to have it for
his collection and sends you his very best
wishes and grateful thanks.

Very sincerely yours,

Grace G. Tull

Mr. Juan Trippe,
Chrysler Building,
135 East 42nd Street,
New York, N.Y

*The world changed between
November 28, 1941 and December 8, 1941-
first flight covers became unimportant*

THE WHITE HOUSE

WASHINGTON

December 8,
1941
CONFIDENTIAL MEMORANDUM FOR THE PRESIDENT:
COPIES TO:   GENERAL WATSON
             CAPTAIN BEARDALL

The postmaster General reports
receipt of the following from Pan American
Airways:

One of the clipper ships, S-42, has
been lost through bombing at Hong Kong.

Base at Guam lost.

Gasoline at Guam and Wake Island
destroyed.

Clipper now probably on its way from
Wake Island coming East toward San
Francisco according to radio from Captain
of clipper two miles out to Wake Island.

One clipper plane at last report was
proceeding on way from Suva, Fiji Islands
to Auckland, New Zealand.

Plane for South Africa which departed
from Florida December sixth is proceeding
on journey.

(Steve Early)
S.T.E.

*President Roosevelt returning from the Casablanca conference - Admiral Leahy to the president's right, Harry Hopkins, his aide, across from the president, Pan Am Captain Howard Cone, commander of the Boeing Clipper*

*Aboard the Dixie Clipper celebrating president's birthday - January 1943*

It is also interesting that President Roosevelt was the first American president to fly while he was in office and his history making flight was on board a Pan Am Clipper. In late January of 1943 the Dixie Clipper, under the command of Pan Am Captain Howard M. Cone, flew Roosevelt to the Casablanca conference held in Morocco. Winston Churchill, Joseph Stalin and Charles DeGaulle also attended. On the return flight of January 30, 1943 a very tired looking Roosevelt celebrated his 61st birthday. He passed away two years later in the spring of 1945 when victory in the war was close at hand. Unfortunately he did not live to celebrate the hard won triumph.

*Twenty-two men who served their Commander-in-Chief - The two eleven-man crews of the Atlantic Clipper and the Dixie Clipper which carried President Roosevelt and his party on the ocean part of his Casablanca trip - The two men seated in the center, front, are (left) Captain R. Vinal of the Atlantic Clipper, and next to him, right, Captain H.M. Cone of the Dixie Clipper*

All of the Roosevelt pictures were generously provided by the Franklin D. Roosevelt Library at Hyde Park, New York.

*Exhausted President Roosevelt returning from Casablanca January 30, 1943*

Stamp collecting has given me a lifetime of pleasure and along the way it has also helped me to acquire a good working knowledge of geography, history and politics. I have particularly enjoyed collecting the entire envelopes, rather than just the stamps, because the envelopes and the letters that they sometimes hold can tell some wonderful stories. Collectors call these envelopes "covers". For the past 25 years I have concentrated on collecting airmail covers flown across the Pacific by the Pan Am Clippers from 1935 to 1946.

*First flight to Hong Kong – April 1937*   *Survey flight to Honolulu – April 1935*

Some of these flight covers were prepared solely for collectors as souvenirs to commemorate a particular flight or a particular historic event. These souvenir covers usually had a cachet applied to the left side of the envelope which related to the event being celebrated. A typical example of a souvenir first flight cover is the flight cover Pan Am prepared for the survey flight to Hawaii in April of 1935. For some of the flights, like the first flight to Manila in November of 1935 and the first flight to Hong Kong in April of 1937, literally hundreds of thousands of covers were sent by collectors as souvenir first flight mail. Most of this first flight mail is purely philatelic, meaning it was created solely for its souvenir value for collectors.

*Front of commercial airmail cover*

Some collectors of flight covers ignore these philatelic covers and concentrate solely on commercial, or non-philatelic mail. These collectors are primarily interested in the various routes that mail had to travel in reaching its final destination and in the postal rates charged for the letter. Many times, due to political unrest or a change in airline schedules, the mail could not travel by the most direct route. By examining the postmarks and by knowing the aviation history, knowledgeable collectors can determine the route that was traveled by airmail letters posted more than sixty years ago.

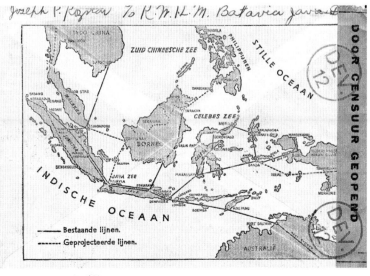

*Back of cover*

In these days of e-mail and faxes, it is hard to imagine how revolutionary airmail was in the 1920s and 1930s in speeding up communication around the world. In 1929 it could take three to four months to send a letter to the Orient and to get a reply. It could easily take six weeks or more to exchange a letter between New York and Europe. Pan Am's pioneering flights to Manila in 1935 and to Hong Kong in 1937 shortened the time for delivery and greatly increased the speed of communication in the world.

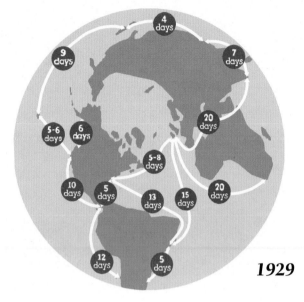

**1929**

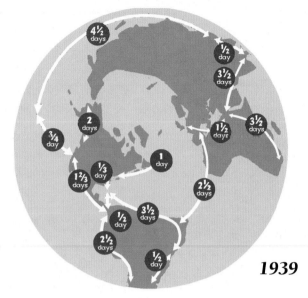

**1939**

*In 1929:* The pace of world's trade routes, geared to the speed of the ocean steamer, was slow indeed. Mail took two weeks, six weeks, eight weeks to bring an answer to a query. A business trip to another continent consumed a month, perhaps a season.

*In 1939:* The world of trade, now scaled to the swift flight of the transport plane, has shrunk to a sixth of it's former size. By the year's end the American business man will be able to reach any city in Europe, Latin America or Alaska within the time he could cross the United States by train. Asia is now less than a week away: New Zealand and Australia soon will be no more distant.

With the inauguration of airmail service to Manila in 1935, Pan Am prepared a booklet highlighting airmail service in the world. By studying the booklet you can determine the frequency of airmail flights and the rates charged for airmail to various countries.

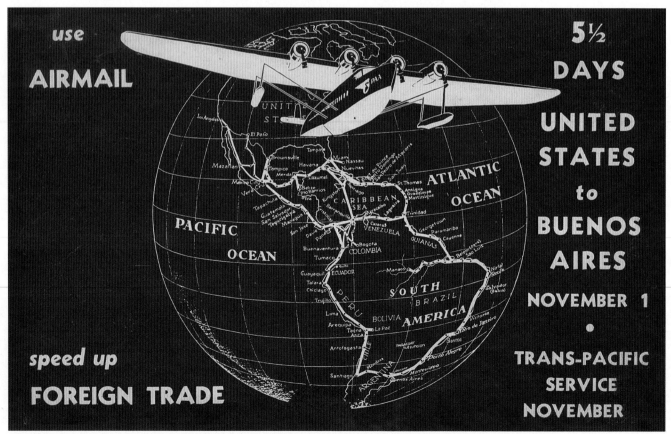

*Cover of November 1, 1935 Pan Am airmail brochure*

# USE AIR MAIL TO SPEED TRADE

## UNITED STATES — ARGENTINA — NOW ONLY 5½ DAYS
## FASTER SERVICE TO ALL POINTS SOUTH
## HAWAII — GUAM — PHILIPPINES — CHINA

REDUCING communications time to a fraction of that heretofore required, United States foreign air mail places at the command of American business the fastest international transport service in the world.

In this continued period of adjustment, the air mail service provides a rapid means of maintaining contacts in quickly changing markets, the instrument by which turn-of-the-market opportunities can be made into sales.

### Transit Time to Rio Cut by 2 Days—Replies Can Now Be Received in 12 Days

Firms maintaining contacts with Brazil will be glad to learn that this tremendous increase in speed of service will cut down the time it takes to receive a reply by 4 days. Likewise there is time between arrivals and departures to enable answers to be drafted without rush.

### Faster Schedules To and From Central and South America via Brownsville

Particular attention is directed to faster service through Central America which reduces transit time between Brownsville, Texas and the Canal Zone by an entire day. Two-day service between these points twice weekly now becomes effective which will greatly increase the value of foreign air mail for those many individuals and business concerns who are relying more than ever on this fast and dependable means of communication.

Direct connections at Cristobal for South American cities also provides a speedier service for those located in the middle and far western sections of the United States who value the closer contact with their South American markets which this improved service provides.

Connections with other air mail carriers at Brownsville is also greatly improved so that service via either Brownsville or Miami is now equally fast from all cities in the United States served by air mail routes.

### Use Envelope Routing Stickers To Speed Air Mail

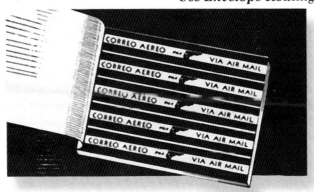

At the request of a great number of business firms we have prepared a series of envelope stickers. The routing stamp, in red, white and blue, is in the form of a strip, weighs less than the former routing stamps and carries instructions in both Spanish and English.

These stickers are in booklets of 50 strips each. They are gummed, and bound between wax-paper sheets to prevent adhesion. We are prepared to supply reasonable quantities of these booklets upon request.

*Inside cover of 1935 Pan Am airmail brochure*

# SOUTH AND WEST BOUND FOREIGN AIR MAIL CLOSINGS AND RATES

## EFFECTIVE OCTOBER 31 AND NOVEMBER 1, 1935
### To Hawaii, Guam, Philippines, China, beginning in November
## To all Latin American Countries and the Far East directly connected by United States Domestic Air Mail Lines

### GENERAL INFORMATION

Rates shown are all-inclusive and cover air transportation from any U. S. Post Office to any point in Latin America, Hawaii, Guam and Philippines. Cities not on air mail routes will be served by the fastest existing means to and from the airline.

Your letters may be deposited in any mail receptacle, but must be in time to be included in the dispatch of air mail for Latin America or the Far East. Your Postmaster will be glad to furnish you with the latest closing time at your nearest mail box.

Air mail stamps are recommended, but any postage stamps may be used if the total amount of postage is correct. Use the International Blue Label "Par Avion" (by air mail), procurable free from your post office. Ask for Form No. 2978.

*Schedule below refers to principal Latin American and Trans-Pacific ports only. Consult your Postmaster for more detailed information on Foreign Air Mail Service. Subject to change without notice.*

| Country—City | Rate per ½ oz. or Fraction | FINAL Closing Days (See "Important" Notice at Bottom) | Due Destination (Delivery same day or next morning) | Days in Transit | Days Saved |
|---|---|---|---|---|---|
| Antigua, St. Johns | 20 Cents | Wed-Thurs | Fri-Mon | 2, 4 | 4 |
| Argentina, Buenos Aires | 55 " | Mon-Wed-Thurs | Sun-Tues Wed | 5½ | 13 |
| Bahamas, Nassau | 10 " | Sun-Thurs (1) | Mon-Fri (A.M.) | overnight | 2 |
| Bolivia, La Paz | 40 " | Mon-Thurs | Air to Arequipa, Peru | 6 | 10 |
| Brazil, Belem (Para) | 50 " | Wednesday | Saturday | 3 | 12 |
| Brazil, Rio de Janeiro | 50 " | Wednesday | Monday | 5 | 9 |
| Brazil, Santos (Sao Paulo) | 50 " | Wednesday | Tuesday | 5¼ | 10 |
| British Guiana, Georgetown | 30 " | Wednesday | Saturday | 2¼ | 12 |
| British Honduras, Belize | 15 " | Thursday | Saturday | 1½ | 4 |
| Canal Zone, Cristobal | 20 " | Mon-Thurs | Wed-Sat | 2 | 5 |
| Chile, Arica, Antofagasta | 50 " | Mon-Thurs | Sat-Tues | 5 | 11 |
| Chile, Santiago | 50 " | Mon-Thurs | Sat-Tues | 5 | 11 |
| Colombia, Barranquilla | 35 " | Mon-Thurs | Wed-Sat | 2 | 6 |
| Colombia, Buenaventura | 35 " | Mon-Thurs | Thurs-Sun | 2½ | 6 |
| Colombia, Bogota, Medellin | 35 " | Mon-Thurs | Wed-Sat | 2 | 7 |
| Costa Rica, San Jose | 20 " | Mon-Thurs | Wed-Sat | 1½ | 7 |
| Cuba, Havana (2) | 10 " | Daily | Next Morning | overnight | 2 |
| Cuba, Santiago and Interior | 10 " | Daily | Next Afternoon | 1 | 3 |
| Dom. Rep., San Pedro (Sto. Do.) | 10 " | Mon-Wed-Fri | Tues-Thurs-Sat | 1 | 5 |
| Dutch Guiana, Paramaribo | 30 " | Wednesday | Saturday | 2½ | 13 |
| Dutch West Indies, Curacao | 30 " | Mon-Thurs | Air to Maracaibo | 3 | 5 |
| Ecuador, Guayaquil | 30 " | Mon-Thurs | Thurs-Sun | 3 | 7 |
| French Guiana, Cayenne | 30 " | Wednesday | Saturday | 2½ | 14 |
| Guam | 50 " | (5) | (5) | 7 | 21 |
| Guatemala, Guatemala City | 15 " | Mon-Thurs | Tues-Fri | 1 | 6 |
| Haiti, Port au Prince | 10 " | Mon-Wed-Fri | Tues-Thurs-Sat | 1 | 4 |
| Hawaii, Honolulu | 25 " | (5) | (5) | 1 | 6 |
| Honduras, Tegucigalpa | 15 " | Mon-Thurs | Wed-Sat | 1½ | 6 |
| Jamaica, Kingston | 10 " | Mon-Thurs | Tues-Fri | 1 | 4 |
| Mexico, D. F., Tampico | 10 " | Daily | Next Morning | overnight | 5 |
| Mexico, Merida | 10 " | Thurs (3) | Friday | 1 | 4 |
| Nicaragua, Managua | 15 " | Mon-Thurs | Wed-Sat | 1½ | 9 |
| Panama, Rep. of | 20 " | Mon-Thurs | Wed-Sat | 2 | 5 |
| Paraguay, Asuncion | 55 " | Mon-Wed-Thurs | Air to Buenos Aires | 7 | 13 |
| Peru, Lima | 40 " | Mon-Thurs | Fri-Mon | 3½ | 8 |
| Philippine Islands, Manila | 75 " | (5) | (5) | 8 | 25 |
| Puerto Rico, San Juan | 10 " | Mon-Wed-Fri | Tues-Thurs-Sat | 1 | 3 |
| Salvador, San Salvador | 15 " | Mon-Thurs | Wed-Sat | 1¼ | 6 |
| Trinidad, Port of Spain | 20 " | Mon-Wed-Thurs | Thurs-Fri-Sun | 2, 3 | 10 |
| Uruguay, Montevideo | 55 " | Wed-Thurs | Tues-Wed | 5½ | 13 |
| Venezuela, Caracas, La Guaira | 30 (4) " | Mon-Wed-Thurs | Thurs-Sat-Sun | 2½ | 5 |
| Venezuela, Cumarebo, Caripito | 30 (4) " | Mon-Wed-Thurs | Thurs-Sat-Sun | 2½ | 8 |
| Venezuela, Maracaibo | 30 (4) " | Mon-Wed-Thurs | Wed-Sat | 2 | 8 |
| Virgin Islands, St. Thomas | 10 " | Wednesday | Friday | 1¼ | 4 |

## IMPORTANT
Mail early, insure connections at Miami or Brownsville. Absolute final closing days shown above apply to cities enjoying fastest service to these points. Consult your Postmaster for final closing days and hours which in your City may be 1 to 2 days before those shown, depending upon whether the city where your mail is posted is served directly by an air mail line.

1 Daily except Saturday, January 1st to April 30th, inclusive. Thursdays only after April 30th, 1936.

2 Connecting Air Service to All Principal Cities via Cuban Domestic Air Lines.

3 Closing day via Brownsville is same. Arrival in Merida is on 2nd day.

4 The rate for dispatch of air mail by the U. S. foreign air mail routes to Venezuela and by the Venezuelan domestic air mail routes is 45¢ per half ounce or fraction. The Venezuelan cities so served are Coro, Chichiriviche (optional stop), Maracay, San Fernando, Ciudad Bolivar, Guasipati, Tumeremo. Your Postmaster will furnish information about time of delivery at destination.

5 Call the Post Office or any Pan American Office. Departures from San Francisco effective early November and once every two weeks until January, 1936. Weekly thereafter.

### PLEASE DESTROY PREVIOUS ISSUES
*Receipt of this issue assures you of subsequent issues when mailed*

*5. Call the Post Office or any Pan American Office. Departures from San Francisco effective early November and once every two weeks until January, 1936. Weekly thereafter.*

The week of May 15 through May 21, 1938 was declared National Airmail Week in the United States. The date marked the twentieth anniversary of the inauguration of airmail service in our country. Pan Am participated in Airmail Week by applying a special cachet to their airmail letters sent from Honolulu.

Before the commencement of airmail service in November of 1935, Guam was so isolated from the United States that a letter could literally take months to reach the island. In honor of National Airmail Week, Guam's postmaster, James H. Underwood, had one of the native men carve a special cachet from a linoleum block to apply to airmail sent from the island during National Airmail Week.

OFFICE NO. X3000                                    THIRD CLASS

**United States Post Office**

GUAM, GUAM

JAMES H. UNDERWOOD, POSTMASTER
ANTONIA I. MARTINEZ, ASSISTANT                May 15, 1938.

Honorable John E. Lamiell,
Director International Postal Service,
Post Office Department,
Washington, D.C.

Dear Mr. Lamiell:

I am sure that you will be interested in learning what Guam has done to commemorate the Twentieth Anniversary of the inauguration of the air mail service which has finally been extended to our formerly isolated Island.

The enclosed copies of notices published in "THE GUAM EAGLE", with some added foot notes, will serve as a brief statement of the efforts we have made to fittingly observe the anniversay of a service which means so much to Guam.

This souvenir letter will also serve as a very belated acknowledgement of your kind Christmas greetings for which I am exceedingly grateful.

Sincerely yours,

James H. Underwood
Postmaster.

*Cachet prepared by Guam postmaster for National Airmail Week – May 1938*

From:
James H. Underwood,
Postmaster, Guam, Guam.

VIA AIR MAIL

Honorable John E. Lamiell,
Director,
International Postal Service,
Post Office Department,
Washington, D. C.

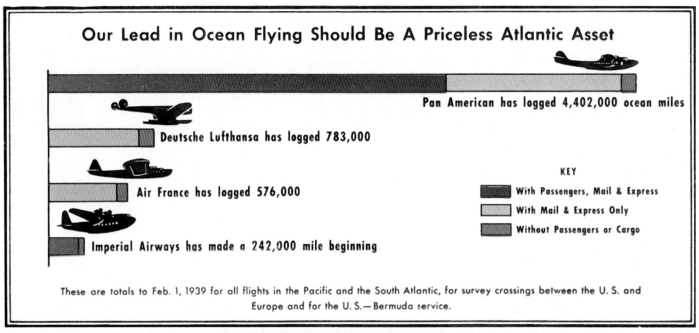

## Our Lead in Ocean Flying Should Be A Priceless Atlantic Asset

Pan American has logged 4,402,000 ocean miles

Deutsche Lufthansa has logged 783,000

Air France has logged 576,000

Imperial Airways has made a 242,000 mile beginning

**KEY**
- With Passengers, Mail & Express
- With Mail & Express Only
- Without Passengers or Cargo

These are totals to Feb. 1, 1939 for all flights in the Pacific and the South Atlantic, for survey crossings between the U. S. and Europe and for the U. S. — Bermuda service.

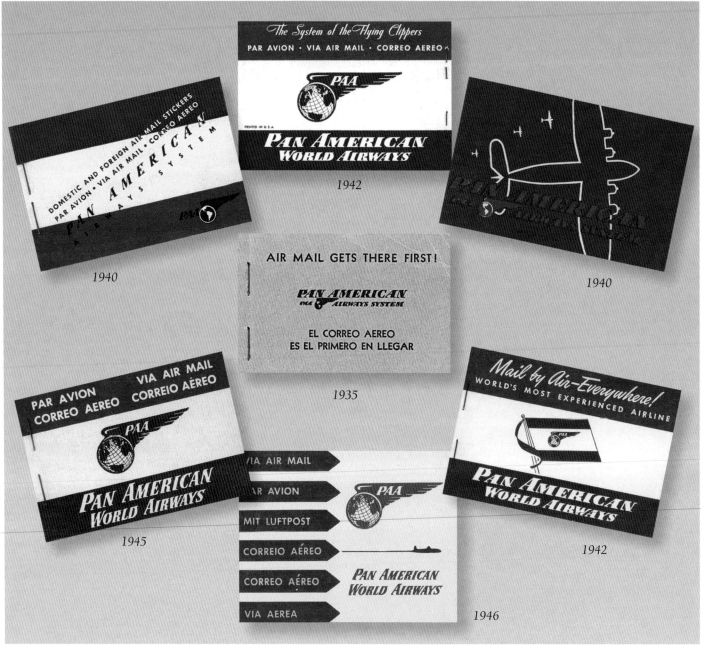

*1942*

*1940*

*1940*

*1935*

*1945*

*1942*

*1946*

Although the cover and stickers designs changed through the years, Pan Am, in order to encourage airmail, continued to provide the airmail stickers booklets free to the public.

*January 1938 airmail brochure*

In January of 1938, after service had been extended to Hong Kong, Pan Am, published another airmail brochure showing the updated postal rates and departure times for various flights.

# LATIN AMERICAN AIR MAIL

| OUTGOING FROM U.S.A. | | | | | JANUARY, 1938 | INCOMING TO U.S.A. | | | |
|---|---|---|---|---|---|---|---|---|---|
| Closing Days Principal U.S. Cities (See "Closing" Information) | Due at Country of Destination | Minimum Days in Transit | Days Saved | Total Postage per ½ Oz. | Countries | Departure from Country of Origin | Arrival Principal U.S. Cities | Local Rate (All Inclusive for Weight Shown) | Weight (For Rate Shown) |
| Tu-We | Th-Sa | 1½ | 4 | 15 Cents | Antigua—St. Johns | Sa-Th | Mo-Sa | 1/3 | ½ oz. |
| Mo-Fr-Sa | Sa-We-Fr | 4½ | 12 | 40 " | Argentina—Buenos Aires | We-Fr-Sa | Mo-We-Th | 1.10 | 5 gr. |
| Su-Th¹ | Next Day¹ | ¾ | 2 | 10 " | Bahamas—Nassau | Mo-Fr¹ | Next Day¹ | 0/8 | ½ oz. |
| Mo-Fr | Fr-Tu | 3 | 11 | 35 " | Bolivia—La Paz | Th-Fr | Mo-Th | 1.75 | 5 gr. |
| Tu-Sa | Sa-We | 3½ | 11 | 40 " | Brazil—Northern | Mo-Th | We-Sa | 5$000 | 5 gr. |
| Tu-Sa | Su-Th | 4¾ | 9 | 40 " | Brazil—Rio de Janeiro | Tu-Sa | Sa-We | 5$000 | 5 gr. |
| Tuesday | Friday | 2½ | 11 | 30 " | British Guiana—Georgetown | Thursday | Saturday | 0.38 | ½ oz. |
| Wednesday | Friday | 1½ | 4 | 12 " | British Honduras—Belize | Friday | Sunday | 0.20 | ½ oz. |
| Su-Mo-Tu-Th-Fr | Tu-We-Th-Sa-Sa | 1 | 5 | 15 " | Canal Zone—Cristobal | Su-Su-We-We-Fr | Mo-Tu-Th-Fr-Su | 0.15 | ½ oz. |
| Mo-Fr | Fr-Tu | 3 | 11 | 40 " | Chile—Santiago | Su-Th | Th-Mo | 7.80 | 5 gr. |
| Mo-We-Fr | Tu-Th-Su | 1 | 7 | 35 " | Colombia—North | We-Fr-Su | Th-Sa-Mo | 0.35 | 10 gr. |
| Mo-We-Fr | We-Fr-Su | 1½ | 8 | 35 " | Colombia—Interior Cities | Tu-Th-Sa | Th-Sa-Mo | 0.35 | 10 gr. |
| Su-Mo-Tu-Th-Fr | Tu-We-Th-Sa-Su | 1½ | 7 | 15 " | Costa Rica—San Jose | Su-Tu-We-Fr-Sa | Tu-Th-Fr-Su-Mo | 0.60 | 5 gr. |
| Daily | Next Day | ¾ | 2 | 10 " | Cuba—Havana and Interior | Daily | Next Day | 0.10 | ½ oz. |
| Tu-Th-Sa | Next Day | ¾ | 4 | 10 " | Dominican Republic—San Pedro | Su-Tu-Fr | Next Day | 0.13 | 15 gr. |
| Mo-Fr | We-Su | 1¾ | 8 | 30 " | Ecuador—Guayaquil | Tu-Sa | Th-Mo | 1.55 | 5 gr. |
| Tuesday | Friday | 2¾ | 11 | 30 " | French Guiana—Cayenne | Thursday | Saturday | 5.00 | 5 gr. |
| Tu-We | Th-Sa | 1¾ | 4 | 15 " | Guadeloupe—Pt. a Pitre | Sa-Th | Mo-Sa | .... | ..... |
| Su-Mo-Tu-Th-Fr | Mo-We-We-Fr-Su | 1 | 6 | 12 " | Guatemala—Guatemala City | Mo-Tu-Th-Sa-Sa | Tu-Th-Fr-Su-Mo | 0.18 | 10 gr. |
| Tu-Th-Sa | Next Day | ¾ | 4 | 10 " | Haiti—Port au Prince | Su-Tu-Fr | Next Day | 0.12 | 10 gr. |
| Su-Mo-Tu-Th-Fr | Tu-We-Th-Sa-Su | 1½ | 6 | 12 " | Honduras—Tegucigalpa | Su-Tu-We-Sa-Fr | Tu-Th-Fr-Su-Mo | 0.46 | 15 gr. |
| Mo-We-Fr | Next Day | ¾ | 4 | 10 " | Jamaica—Kingston | Su-We-Fr | Next Day | 0/9 | ½ oz. |
| Tu-We | Th-Sa | 1¾ | 4 | 15 " | Martinique—Ft. de France | Sa-Th | Mo-Sa | .... | ..... |
| Daily | Next Day | ¾ | 4 | 10 " | Mexico, D. F. and Interior | Daily | Next Day | 0.20 | 5 gr. |
| Tu-Sa | Fr-Tu | 2½ | 11 | 30 " | Neth. Guiana—Paramaribo | Mo-Th | We-Sa | 0.55 | 5 gr. |
| Mo-We-Sa | We-Fr-Tu | 1½ | 5 | 25 " | Netherlands, W. I.—Curacao | Mo-We | Th-Sa | 0.40 | 5 gr. |
| Su-Mo-Tu-Th-Fr | Tu-We-Th-Sa-Su | 1½ | 7 | 12 " | Nicaragua—Managua | Su-Tu-We-Fr-Sa | Tu-Th-Fr-Su-Mo | 0.15 | 5 gr. |
| Su-Mo-Tu-Th-Fr | Tu-We-Th-Sa-Sa | 1 | 6 | 15 " | Panama—Republic of | Su-Su-We-We-Fr | Mo-Tu-Th-Fr-Su | 0.08 | 5 gr. |
| Mo-Tu-Sa | Mo-Mo-Mo | 4½ | 12 | 40 " | Paraguay—Asuncion | From B.A. | Mo-We-Th | 87.00 | 5 gr. |
| Mo-Fr | Th-Mo | 2½ | 10 | 30 " | Peru—Major Cities | Mo-Fr | Th-Mo | 1.45 | 5 gr. |
| Tu-Th-Sa | Next Day | | 3 | 10 " | Puerto Rico—San Juan | Su-Tu-Fr | Next Day | 0.10 | ½ oz. |
| Su-Mo-Tu-Th-Fr | Tu-We-Th-Sa-Su | 1½ | 6 | 12 " | Salvador—San Salvador | Su-Tu-We-Sa-Fr | Tu-Th-Fr-Su-Mo | 0.38 | 10 gr. |
| Mo-Tu-We-Sa | We-Th-Fr-Mo | 1½ | 7 | 15 " | Trinidad—Port of Spain | Tu-Th-Fr-Sa | We-Sa-Sa-Mo | 0.27 | ½ oz. |
| Mo-Fr-Sa | Su-We-Fr | 4¾ | 12 | 40 " | Uruguay—Montevideo | We-Fr-Sa | Mo-We-Th | 0.42 | 5 gr. |
| Mo-We-Sa | We-Fr-Tu | 1½ | 6 | 25² " | Venezuela—Major Cities | Mo-Tu-Th-Fr | We-Th-Sa-Mo | 1.30 | 10 gr. |
| Tu-We | Th-Sa | 1½ | 4 | 10 " | Virgin Islands—St. Thomas | Sa-Th | Mo-Sa | 0.10 | ½ oz. |

# TRANS-PACIFIC AIR MAIL

| | | | | | | | | | |
|---|---|---|---|---|---|---|---|---|---|
| Tuesday A.M. | Weekly | 20 | 4 | 70 Cents | Australia | Weekly | Thursday | .... | ..... |
| Tuesday A.M. | Weekly | 8 | 12 | 70 " | China | Weekly | Thursday | .... | ..... |
| Tuesday A.M. | Monday | 5 | 20 | 40 " | Guam | Weekly | Thursday | 0.40 | ½ oz. |
| Tuesday A.M. | Thursday | 1½ | 6 | 20 " | Hawaii | Weekly | Thursday | 0.20 | ½ oz. |
| Tuesday A.M. | Weekly | 7 | 15 | 70 " | Hongkong | Weekly | Thursday | $2.80 | ½ oz. |
| Tuesday A.M. | Weekly | 13 | 13 | 70 " | India | Weekly | Thursday | .... | ..... |
| Tuesday A.M. | Weekly | 11 | 16 | 70 " | Indo-China | Weekly | Thursday | .... | ..... |
| Tuesday A.M. | Air to H'Kong | 13 | 4 | 70 " | Japan | Weekly | Thursday | .... | ..... |
| Tuesday A.M. | Weekly | 7 | 17 | 70 " | Macao | Weekly | Thursday | $3.05 | ½ oz. |
| Tuesday A.M. | Weekly | 17 | 16 | 70 " | Netherlands East Indies | Weekly | Thursday | .... | ..... |
| Tuesday A.M. | Via Australia | 25 | | 70 " | New Zealand | Weekly | Thursday | .... | ..... |
| Tuesday A.M. | Tuesday | 6 | 16 | 50 " | Philippines | Weekly | Thursday | $1.00 | ½ oz. |
| Tuesday A.M. | Weekly | 12 | 19 | 70 " | Siam | Weekly | Thursday | .... | ..... |
| Tuesday A.M. | Weekly | 16 | 16 | 70 " | Straits Settlements | Weekly | Thursday | | |

NOTES:

¹Daily January through April.

²Add 15 cents per ½ oz. for service via Venezuelan domestic air mail lines to Chichiriviche, Calabozo, San Fernando, Bolivar, Guasipati, Tumeremo.

*In 1938 Pan Am was not flying to Australia or New Zealand, so the mail would be carried to Hong Kong and transferred to other airlines to reach Australia - Inside cover 1938 airmail brochure*

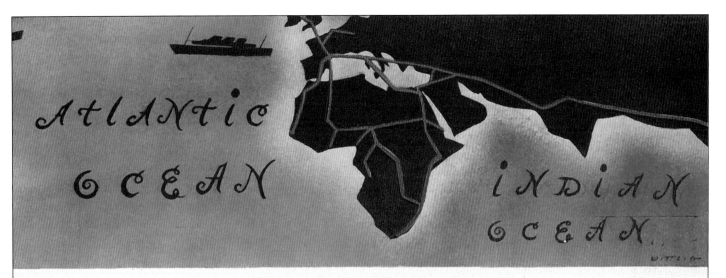

# AIR MAIL SERVICE IN EUROPE

Daily air mail service is available throughout all countries of Europe at the following U.S. postage rates, which are all-inclusive for the service indicated.

| Class of Service Desired | Necessary Endorsement on Envelope | ½ oz. | 1 oz. | 1½ oz. | 2 oz. | 2½ oz. | 3 oz. |
|---|---|---|---|---|---|---|---|
| By ordinary means in U. S. A. and by air in Europe. | "Air in Europe"..................... | 8c | 11c | 17c | 20c | 26c | 29c |
| By air mail in U. S. A. and by air in Europe..... | "Par Avion" Labels and add "Air in Europe"......................... | 11c | 14c | 25c | 28c | 39c | 42c |

★    ★    ★

# AIR MAIL SERVICE IN ASIA AND AFRICA

Frequent air mail service to important commercial centers in Asia and Africa is also available at the following U.S. postage rates from the United States, which are all-inclusive for the service indicated.

| Destination | Necessary Endorsement on Envelope — To "Par Avion" Labels Add | By Ordinary Means in U. S. A. and by Air from Europe to Destination | | | | | | By Air Mail in U. S. A. and by Air from Europe to Destination | | | | | |
|---|---|---|---|---|---|---|---|---|---|---|---|---|---|
| | | ½ oz. | 1 oz. | 1½ oz. | 2 oz. | 2½ oz. | 3 oz. | ½ oz. | 1 oz. | 1½ oz. | 2 oz. | 2½ oz. | 3 oz. |
| Belgian Congo......... | "From Paris"......... | 25c | 45c | 68c | 88c | $1.11 | $1.31 | 28c | 48c | 76c | 96c | $1.24 | $1.44 |
| Ceylon.............. | "From London"....... | 27c | 49c | 74c | 96c | $1.21 | $1.43 | 30c | 52c | 82c | $1.04 | $1.34 | $1.56 |
| Egypt............... | "From London"....... | 11c | 17c | 26c | 32c | 41c | 47c | 14c | 20c | 34c | 40c | 54c | 60c |
| Northern Rhodesia..... | "From London"....... | 27c | 49c | 74c | 96c | $1.21 | $1.43 | 30c | 52c | 82c | $1.04 | $1.34 | $1.56 |
| Portuguese East Africa.. | "From London"....... | 27c | 49c | 74c | 96c | $1.21 | $1.43 | 30c | 52c | 82c | $1.04 | $1.34 | $1.56 |
| Southern Rhodesia..... | "From London"....... | 27c | 49c | 74c | 96c | $1.21 | $1.43 | 30c | 52c | 82c | $1.04 | $1.34 | $1.56 |
| Southwest Africa....... | "From London"....... | 32c | 59c | 89c | $1.16 | $1.46 | $1.73 | 35c | 62c | 97c | $1.24 | $1.59 | $1.86 |
| Syria............... | "From London"....... | 11c | 17c | 26c | 32c | 41c | 47c | 14c | 20c | 34c | 40c | 54c | 60c |
| U. S. S. R. (in Asia).... | "From Europe"........ | 32c | 59c | 89c | $1.16 | $1.46 | $1.73 | 35c | 62c | 97c | $1.24 | $1.59 | $1.86 |
| Union of South Africa... | "From London" | 32c | 59c | 89c | $1.16 | $1.46 | $1.73 | 35c | 62c | 97c | $1.24 | $1.59 | $1.86 |

★    ★    ★

# AIR MAIL TIPS

CLOSING hours in your locality should be obtained from your Postmaster and applied to the days appearing in the column entitled "Closing Days."

LABELS or stickers should be affixed front and back of each air mail envelope. Use the "Par Avion." Form 2978 obtainable free from your local Post Office. Or obtain handy booklet of "Air Mail Stickers" from any Pan American Airways office.

POST your air mail letters in any United States mail box.

RATES are all inclusive for each ½ ounce or fraction and provide transportation to any destination in countries served from anywhere in the United States.

REGISTRATION of air mail is available to all foreign countries.

STAMPS especially designed for air mail are recommended but ordinary stamps are acceptable.

STATIONERY for air mail should be distinctive to assure preferred attention.

★    ★    ★

**Receipt by mail of this schedule assures you of future issues.**

Subject to change without notice.                                            Printed in U. S. A.

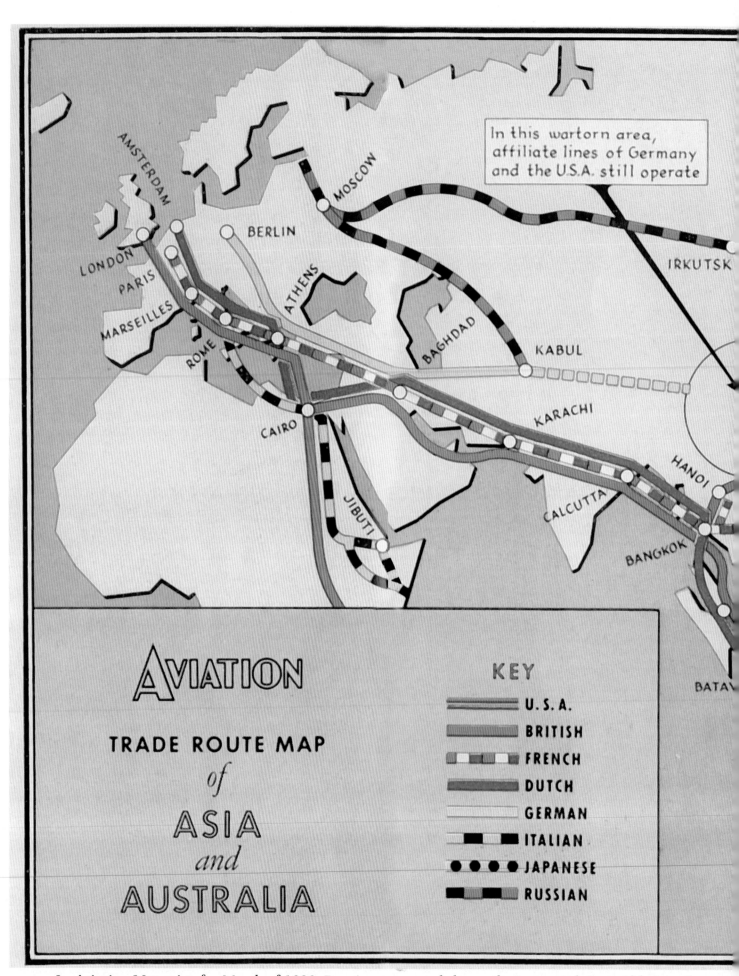

In this wartorn area, affiliate lines of Germany and the U.S.A. still operate

**AVIATION**

**TRADE ROUTE MAP**

*of*

**ASIA**

*and*

**AUSTRALIA**

**KEY**

| | |
|---|---|
| ═══════ | U.S.A. |
| ═══════ | BRITISH |
| ═══════ | FRENCH |
| ═══════ | DUTCH |
| ─────── | GERMAN |
| ███████ | ITALIAN |
| ●●●●●● | JAPANESE |
| ███████ | RUSSIAN |

In *Aviation Magazine* for March of 1939, Pan Am recounted the explosive growth in world airmail during the previous ten years. The charts and graphs in the article depicted the airmail routes as they existed in mid-1939, when Pan Am started Transatlantic airmail service.

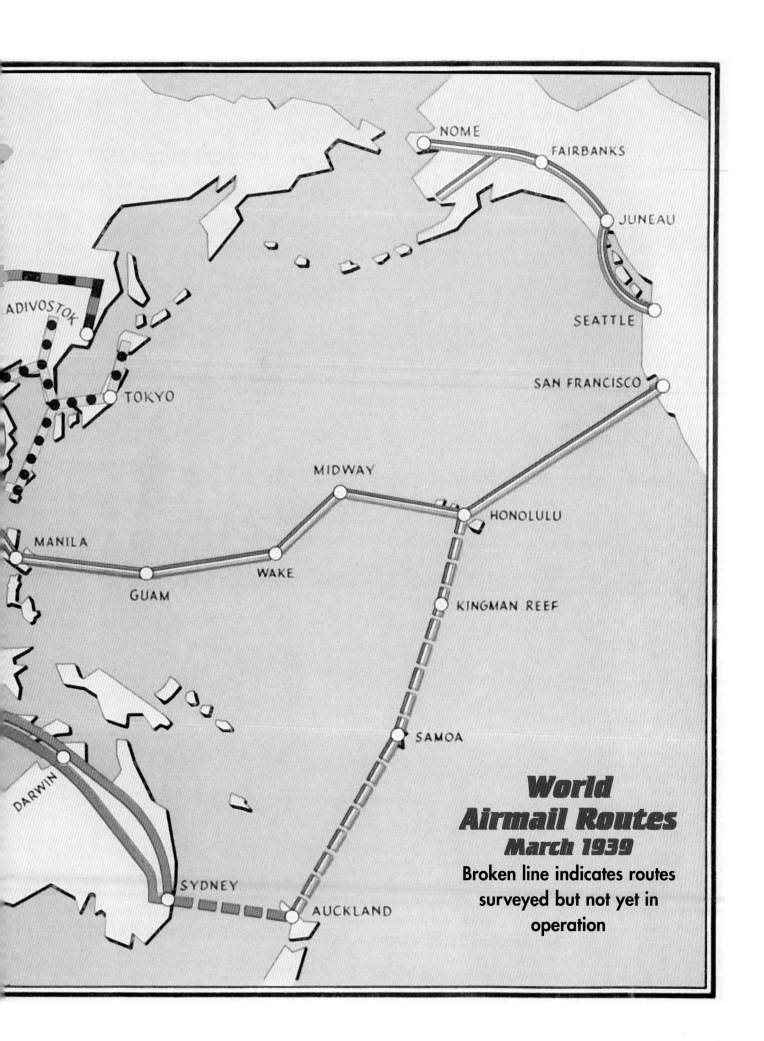

NOME
FAIRBANKS
JUNEAU
SEATTLE
SAN FRANCISCO
VLADIVOSTOK
TOKYO
MIDWAY
HONOLULU
MANILA
WAKE
GUAM
KINGMAN REEF
SAMOA
DARWIN
SYDNEY
AUCKLAND

**World Airmail Routes**
**March 1939**
Broken line indicates routes surveyed but not yet in operation

599

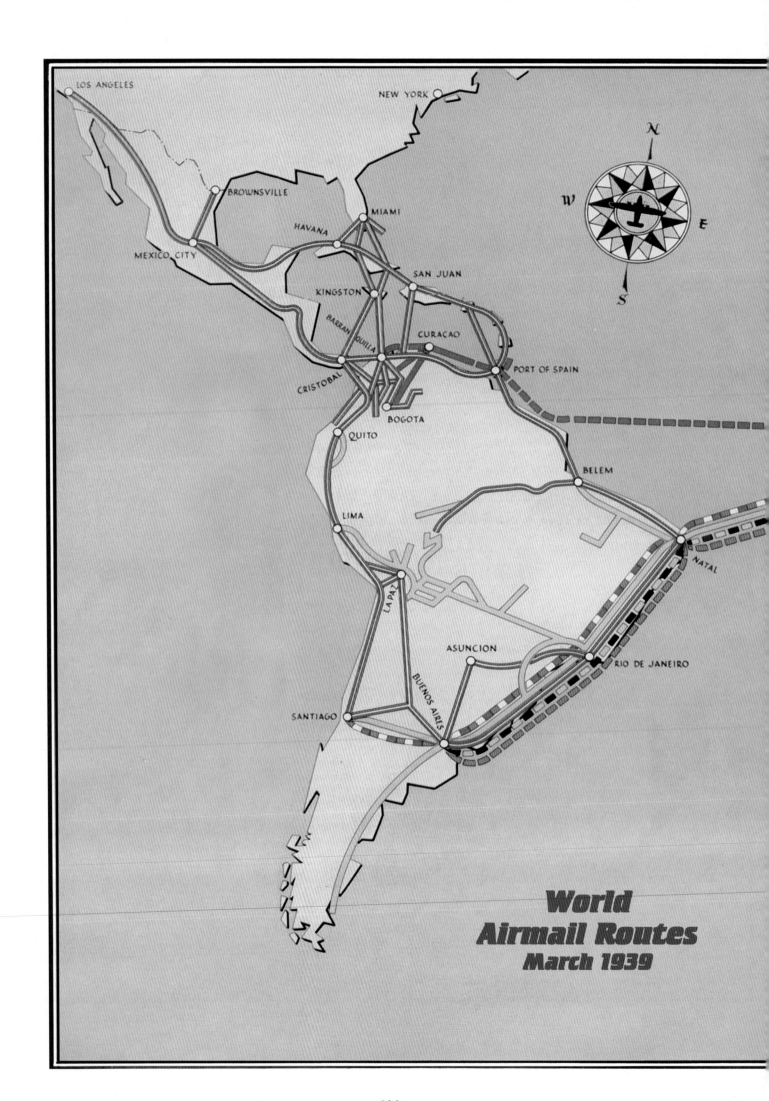

LOS ANGELES

NEW YORK

BROWNSVILLE

MIAMI

HAVANA

SAN JUAN

MEXICO CITY

KINGSTON

BARRANQUILLA

CURACAO

CRISTOBAL

PORT OF SPAIN

BOGOTA

QUITO

BELEM

LIMA

NATAL

LA PAZ

ASUNCION

RIO DE JANEIRO

SANTIAGO

BUENOS AIRES

N

W E

S

**World
Airmail Routes**
March 1939

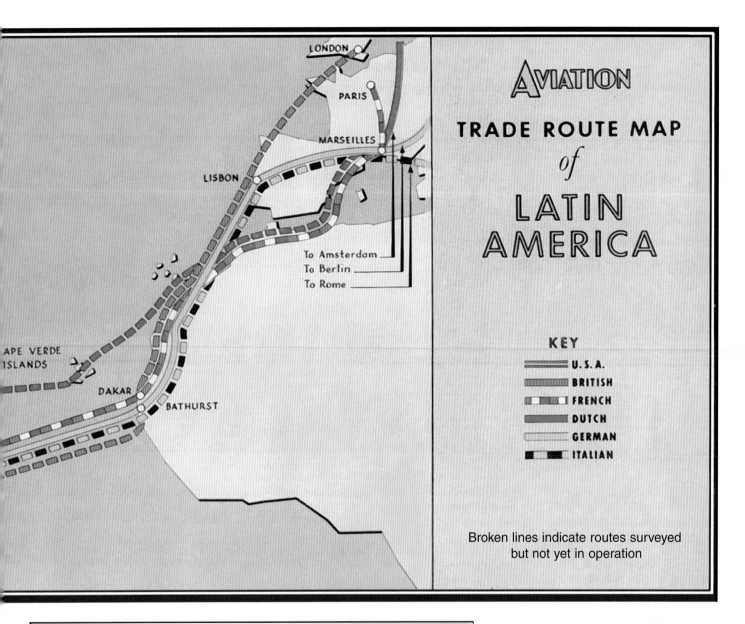

# AVIATION

## TRADE ROUTE MAP
## *of*
## LATIN AMERICA

LONDON

PARIS

MARSEILLES

LISBON

To Amsterdam
To Berlin
To Rome

CAPE VERDE
ISLANDS

DAKAR

BATHURST

### KEY

U.S.A.
BRITISH
FRENCH
DUTCH
GERMAN
ITALIAN

Broken lines indicate routes surveyed
but not yet in operation

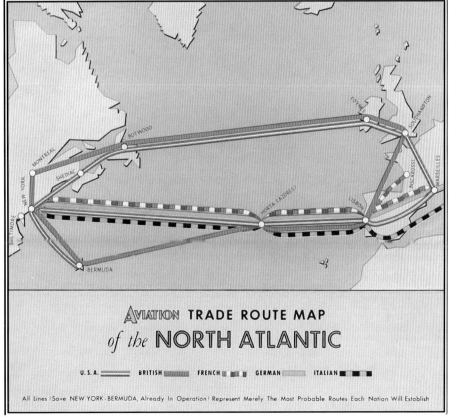

FOYNES

SOUTHAMPTON

BISCAROSSE

MARSEILLES

BOTWOOD

MONTREAL

SHEDIAC

NEW YORK

BALTIMORE

HORTA (AZORES)

LISBON

BERMUDA

### AVIATION TRADE ROUTE MAP
### *of the* NORTH ATLANTIC

U.S.A.    BRITISH    FRENCH    GERMAN    ITALIAN

All Lines (Save NEW YORK - BERMUDA, Already In Operation) Represent Merely The Most Probable Routes Each Nation Will Establish

In early 1939 the airline map illustrated shows U.S. routes reaching every important Latin American city. Germany, through aggressive development of affiliated companies, approached complete coverage. In 1939 Germany added a passenger service to its trans-Atlantic mail run and France did likewise. That same year Italy and Great Britain opened brand new air routes to North America.

# Airmail Rates from the Continental United States by Pan Am Clipper Service
## November 1935 to February 1945

| Continental U.S.A. to Destination | November 22 1935 to Manila FAM 14 | April 21 1937 to Hong Kong FAM 14 | July 12 1940 to New Zealand FAM 19 | May 3 1941 to Singapore FAM 19 | November 5 1941 to Fiji FAM 19 | January 15 1945 Rate reduction |
|---|---|---|---|---|---|---|
| Hawaii | 25¢ | 20¢ | → | | | 15¢ |
| Midway | 50¢ | 40¢ | 30¢ (#2) | → | | |
| Wake | 50¢ | 40¢ | 35¢ (#2) | → | | |
| Guam | 50¢ | 40¢ | 40¢ | → | | |
| Philippines | 75¢ | 50¢ | 50¢ | → | | |
| Hong Kong | | 70¢ | 70¢ | → | | |
| Canton Island | | | 30¢ | → | | |
| New Caledonia | | | 40¢ | → | | |
| New Zealand | | | 50¢ | → | | |
| Singapore | | | | 70¢ | → | |
| Fiji | | | | | 40¢ → | |

## Notes - Regarding Airmail Rates

1. Rates shown above are for 1/2 ounce letters.

2. From November 1935 until June 1939 mail to or from Wake and Midway required the same postage as mail to or from Guam. In approximately June of 1939 the rate was lowered to Wake and Midway. The new rate required only 10¢ additional postage between Midway and Honolulu and 15¢ additional postage between Wake and Honolulu. The earliest dates found with the lower postage rates are June 14, 1939 for Midway and August 21, 1939 for Wake.

3. During 1939 much of the mail to and from Midway and Wake was overfranked (carried more postage than was required). This occurred because of the confusion over the new lower rates and the unavailability of stamps in the correct denomination at these remote islands.

4. On December 7, 1941 all civilian airmail west of Honolulu ceased.

5. From 1935 until December 7, 1941, when airmail service was not available beyond the termination point of the Pan Am airmail route -- other airlines, when available, would carry the mail to its final destination without an additional airmail postage charge.

6. Mail going to the Continental United States from west of Honolulu by Pan Am Clipper that did not carry the full airmail postage to the west coast was off loaded at Honolulu and sent onward by sea at no additional postage charge.

7. With the opening of Pan American Clipper airmail service to Hong Kong on April 21, 1937, it was possible, for the first time to send an airmail letter to Hong Kong and onward by airmail on other carriers to the other major countries of the world. From the Continental United States to Hong Kong, the postage rate of 70¢ - per 1/2 ounce paid the airmail rate to Hong Kong and on to the final destination by connecting airmail service. Therefore, mail to the following destinations through Hong Kong from the U.S. was 70¢ - per 1/2 ounce: Australia, Burma, China, Malaysia, India, Indochina, Japan, East Indies, New Zealand, and Thailand.

8. By 1940 the war in Europe had disrupted airmail routes across the Mediterranean. Therefore, mail that had formerly gone to the United States across the Atlantic by way of Lisbon was, in some cases, routed on the long eastern route through Hong Kong and Singapore to connect with the Pan Am Clipper to cross the Pacific to the United States. The postage rate for mail sent on this long route to the United States was the same as the rate for the far shorter route crossing the Atlantic, which was 70¢ - per 1/2 ounce. This rate for mail from Europe over the Pacific route began on August 6, 1940.

9. On December 7, 1941, all Clipper service west of Honolulu ceased until the end of the war in the Pacific. Throughout the war, any service man's non-airmail letter could be sent home at no charge. However, airmail letters were charged at 6¢ - per 1/2 ounce. Thus, in the Pacific, if a service man wanted airmail service from Hawaii to the Continental United States, it could be sent by Pan Am Clippers for 6¢ - per 1/2 ounce.

10. After December 7, 1941 it appears that non-military airmail was sometimes carried along with military airmail beyond Honolulu by NATS to and from American Samoa. A letter has been seen dated August 1942 to American Samoa with 30¢ postage. Non-military airmail from American Samoa during this period usually carried 40¢ postage. Details of the service and the rates charged have not been determined.

11. On January 15, 1945 the airmail rate was reduced to 15¢ per 1/2 ounce on airmail to and from Hawaii.

*August 1942 - 30¢ rate to Samoa*

*April 1944 - 40¢ rate from Samoa*

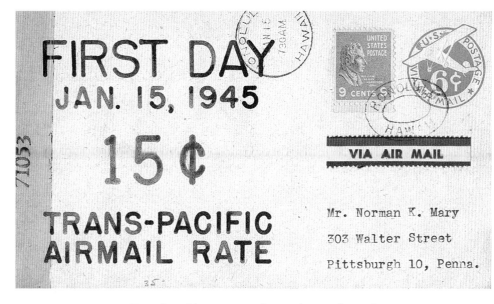

*First day of lower airmail rates for Pacific mail*

# Pan Am Flight Numbers for Collectors

| Flight | Name | Date | Crampon # | TO # | FAM # |
|---|---|---|---|---|---|
| 1. | Survey 1-Honolulu | April 16-23, 1935 | 29 - 30 | 1230 | |
| 2. | Survey 2-Midway | June 12-22, 1935 | 32 | 1236 | |
| 3. | Survey 3-Wake | August 19-28, 1935 | 33 | 1240 | |
| 4. | Survey 4-Guam | October 5-24, 1935 | 34 | 1243 | |
| 5. | 1st Flight to Manila | Nov. 22-Dec.6, 1935 | 37 - 38 | | 14 (1 - 6) |
| 12. | 1st Survey Flight to New Zealand | March 17-April 9, 1937 | 51 | | |
| 15. | 1st Flight to Hong Kong | April 21-May 4, 1937 | 58 | | 14 (10 - 16) |
| 17. | 1st Mail Flight to New Zealand | Dec. 23,1937-Jan. 4, 1938 | 61 | 1292 | |
| 24. | 1st Survey - New Zealand New Route | August 22-Sept. 6, 1939 | 75 | 1329 | |
| 26. | First Mail Flight New Zealand | July 12-24, 1940 | 78 - 79 | | 19 (1 - 9) |
| 31. | First Flight to Singapore | May 3-20, 1941 | 81 | | 14 (20 - 27) |
| 36. | First Flight to Fiji | November 5-17, 1941 | 91 | | 19 (15 - 23) |
| 50. | Last Clipper Flight | April 8-9. 1946 | 103 | | |

## References:

**CRAMPON #: -** *Aerophilatelic Flights Hawaii & Central Pacific, 1913 – 1946*, by L.J. Crampon, lists, in chronological order, most of the significant military and civilian flights of the Pacific from 1913 to1946.

**TO # : -** The Trans-Oceanic (TO) records flights listed in chronological order in the *American Air Mail Catalog*, Volume I, 1966. This is the official catalog of the American Air Mail Society.

**FAM #: -** Foreign Airmail Contracts (FAM) of the United States Post Office. FAM 14 was the first Pacific route inaugurated in November of 1935 to Manila. FAM 19, was inaugurated in July of 1940 to New Zealand. Information on foreign air mail contracts is included in Volume III of the *American Air Mail Catalog*, published in 1970.

### If you are interested in collecting flight covers, contact:

| | | |
|---|---|---|
| American Philatelic Society<br>Post Office Box 8000<br>State College, PA 16803 | American Airmail Society<br>Post Office Box 110<br>Mineola, NY 11501 | Metro Air Post Society<br>25 Brington Road<br>Brookline, MA 02445 |

### If you are interested in Pan Am history or collectibles, contact:

| | |
|---|---|
| Pan Am Historical Foundation<br>52 Vanderbilt Ave., New York, New York 10017<br>Email: foundation@panam.org | World Airline Historical Society<br>13739 Picarsa Drive<br>Jacksonville, Florida 32225 |

So, my message is simple. If you have enjoyed the flight covers that are shown throughout this book and if you have enjoyed learning more about the geography, history and politics behind those covers, I encourage you to find an area of special interest and to start a small collection of airmail covers. You will quickly meet other people who share your interest and you will soon have something to share with your children or grandchildren that isn't tied to the television or to a computer.

Stamp and cover collecting is a link with a simpler time, when the radio, the newspaper and the Saturday newsreel provided our news and entertainment. Hopefully the stories in this book have sparked an interest in collecting and if you follow it, the hobby can give you enjoyment all of your life. "Via Air Mail" can lead you to anywhere you want to travel.

# CHAPTER TEN

## PAN AM'S MEMORABILIA - 1935 - 1946

Throughout this book are illustrated items of Pan Am history that are not only visually pleasing, but also provide much historical information. With very few exceptions, the items illustrated are from my collection and they relate directly to Pan Am's Pacific operations during the 1935 - 1946 era of the Clipper ships. I hope these relics and treasures from the past help you recapture the spirit and excitement of the early Pacific pioneer flights. Enjoy!

# PAN AMERICAN'S ANNUAL REPORTS

## 1935 To 1946

Pan Am's annual reports during the era of the Pacific Clippers between 1935 and 1946 provide significant information on the development, growth and profitability of the Pacific operation.

From 1929 through 1942 the initials "P.A.A." had appeared to the left of the winged globe. In 1942 the annual report shows the corporate logo for the first time with the initials P.A.A. in the wing, rather than to the left of the winged globe. The name Pan Am World Airways also appeared for the first time in 1942.

From 1929 through 1939 the design, size and format of the annual reports remained unchanged.

# PAN AM STOCK CERTIFICATES

On June 2, 1927, Juan Trippe convinced twelve of his wealthy friends to invest a total of $300,000 in the future of commercial aviation. As a result, the Aviation Corporation of the Americas was created with Trippe becoming the Managing Director.

His new Board of Directors authorized him to bid on any airmail contracts that became available. The newly formed Pan American Airways Corporation had the inside track for the Key West to Havana airmail contract and it was awarded to Pan Am on September 8, 1927. By early October of 1927 Trippe had maneuvered the Aviation Corporation of the Americas into full control of Pan American Airlines Corporation and on October 18, 1927 the Aviation Corporation of the Americas' new subsidiary, Pan Am, was flying the mail daily to Key West.

The Aviation Corporation of the Americas remained the parent corporation owning all of Pan American's stock until 1931 when Pan American Airways became the primary company. Therefore, stock issued by the Aviation Corporation of the Americas from 1928 through early 1931 included Pan American Airways as a wholly owned operating subsidiary. Starting in 1931 shares in the Aviation Corporation of the Americas were converted to stock in Pan American Airways, Inc. and Pan American Airways remained as the sole surviving stock issuing corporation.

*Stock certificate #12 issued July 12, 1928 to Cornelius Whitney -*
*Whitney was a director of Aviation Corporation of the Americas*

*Juan Trippe was issued 100 shares of Aviation Corporation of the Americas stock on June 10, 1930*

*In June of 1934 Trippe was issued 100 shares of the new Pan American Airways stock - He sold it just two months later - During the early days of the company, Juan Trippe needed cash more than he needed stock*

This stock certificate issued to Cleo L. Musick, the widow of the famous Pan Am pilot Ed Musick, tells a sad story. Edwin Musick was one of the most popular and best known aviators in the country. He died tragically on January 11, 1938 in the crash of the Samoan Clipper on his third flight to New Zealand.

*Edwin and Cleo Musick - 1937*

*Former crew members Harry Canaday and W.T. Jarboe with
Mrs. Musick - 1958*

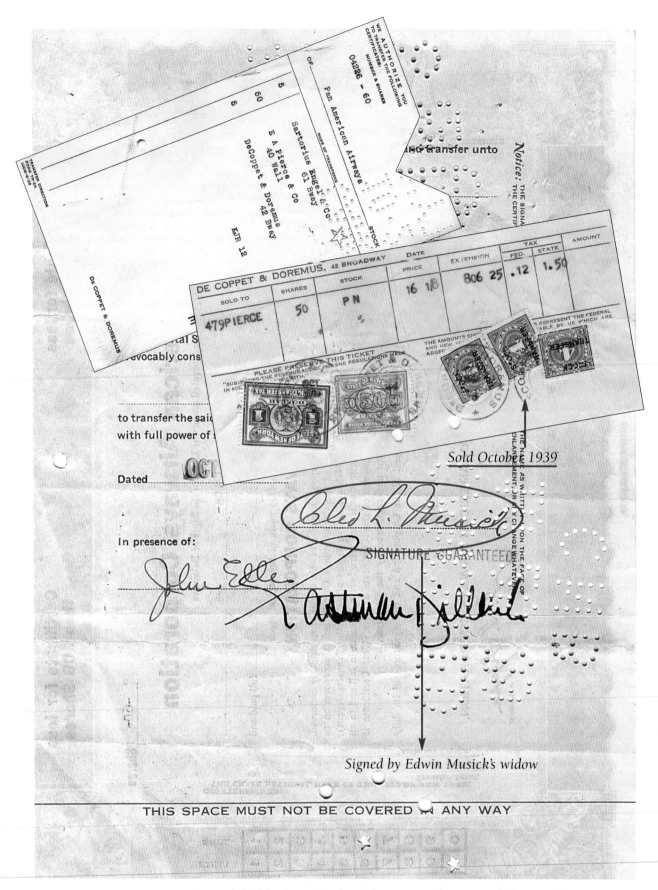

*Sold October 1939*

*Signed by Edwin Musick's widow*

THIS SPACE MUST NOT BE COVERED IN ANY WAY

*Cleo Musick sold 50 shares of the stock in October of 1939 for $16 per share, netting her $806*

Company benefits in the 1930s were either exceedingly small or non-existent. Therefore, in recognition of her husband's great service to the airline, Pan Am in March of 1938 gave Mrs. Musick 60 shares of Pan Am stock.

Pan Am stock certificates give an interesting view of the operations of the corporation and they also contain some hard to find signatures of not only the corporate officers, but also the pilots and other people who were involved with Pan Am during its formative years.

# PAN AM POSTER ART OF THE PACIFIC
## 1935 - 1946

Color photography was not highly developed or widely employed in advertising until approximately 1940. Therefore, color paintings or illustrations were often used by Pan Am to promote their early Pacific flights.

In 1939 Pan Am commissioned Gordon Grant to do a painting of the new Boeing B-314 Clipper flying over the sailing Clippers of old. At the time Grant was one of America's most popular artists. The painting, entitled "The Yankee Clippers Sail Again" is probably the most famous painting commissioned by Pan Am during this period.

The poster of the painting was printed on high-grade paper. On the original posters the Pan Am Clipper was embossed into the print by a steel plate, slightly raising the Clipper's outline from the rest of the poster.

# FLY TO SOUTH SEA ISLES

# Via PAN AMERICAN

Artist P.G. Lawler also created a wonderful series of art deco posters depicting various travel destinations of Pan Am around the world. One of Lawler's most popular and visually pleasing posters depicts the Boeing B-314 approaching a lagoon for a landing. In the background there is a mountain reminiscent of French Polynesia. Pan Am, however, did not fly to Tahiti and therefore it might be a stylized rendering of Diamond Head in Honolulu.

# ACROSS *the* PACIFIC

## IN FIVE DAYS
## *Via* PAN AMERICAN

*Another of Lawler's illustrations captures the Boeing B-314 over Hong Kong Harbor*

The next poster illustrated *(following page)* from this series by Lawler is from my collection. It depicts the Boeing B-314 arriving at Pan Am's Pearl City base in Honolulu. It truly captures the romance and excitement of Transpacific travel. In my first book I attributed this unsigned poster to artist, Frank McIntosh, who did a lot of work for the Matson Steamship Line. However, additional research has determined that this poster was also done by Lawler. The great visual impact captured by Lawler has made this beautiful poster a true art deco classic.

The 1944 Pan Am calendar contained six large poster-quality pictures of Pan Am destinations around the world painted by illustrator Steven Dohavon. The painting entitled "Wings Over the Pacific" for July of 1944 shows the Hong Kong Harbor with the Boeing B-314 at its mooring. This was the only illustration in the calendar series showing the Clipper in the Pacific region.

616

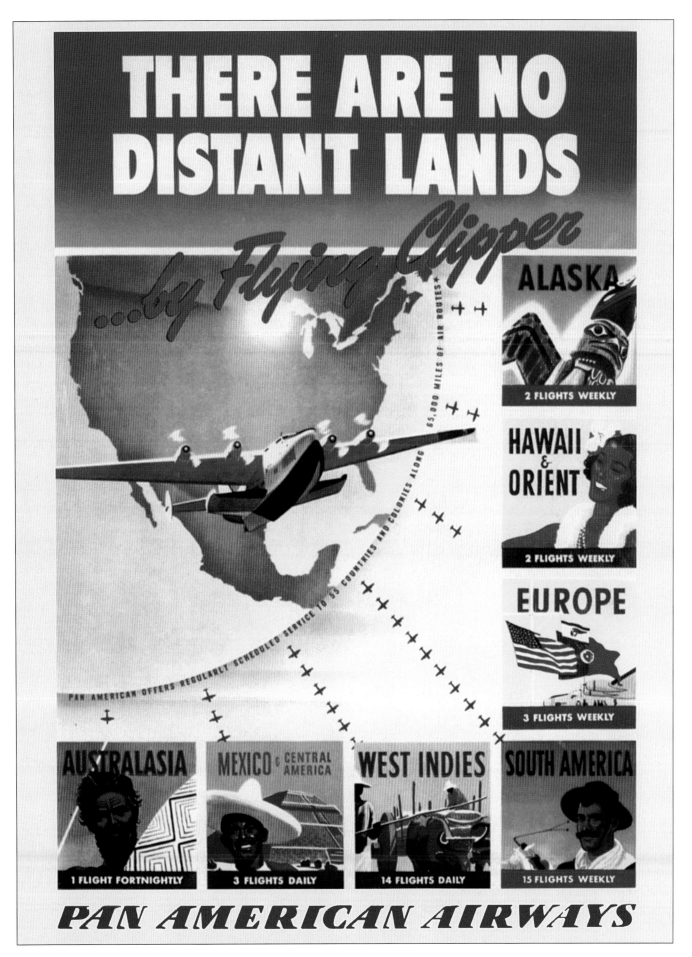

By the time New Zealand was added as a travel destination by Pan Am in September of 1940, the company's poster art had started to move away from the romantic art deco style of the 1930s to a slicker and more modern, commercial look. This 1940 poster advertising the South Pacific as a new travel destination is a good example of the new style. This poster format was also used by Pan Am in magazine advertising.

The most recent poster addition to my collection is the beautiful, large painting of Pan Am's routes, done by master illustrator, Leon Helguera. Helguera was a member of the prestigious Society of Illustrators in New York. Pan Am commissioned this poster in 1942 and the poster states that it shows the air routes: "As of December 7, 1941 - subsequent wartime changes censored".

Because these beautiful posters were intended for travel agents' offices, most of them were destroyed or discarded. Therefore, original posters from this prewar period are among the rarest and most valuable of Pan Am collectibles. Pan Am's poster art of the 1930s and early 1940s effectively captured the romance and excitement of Transpacific flight.

A recently discovered poster promoting international air express is actually a 21 inch by 14 inch cardboard counter sign with a fold out base. The illustration was designed in 1938 by artist Wittlig and it depicts the Boeing B-314 with a single vertical tail fin. This was the original design of the Boeing B-314. The final design for the Boeing had three tail fins. Air Express started in the Pacific in early 1936. This poster was undoubtedly prepared in anticipation of the Atlantic flights, which became a reality in mid-1939.

# PAN AMERICAN TIMETABLES FOR THE
# PACIFIC ROUTES - 1935 To 1946

September 1935

May 1936

July 1937

January 1939

April 1939

August 1939

September–November 1940

The timetables for the Pacific routes were updated and reprinted four times per year. In addition to providing information on the arrival and departure times for the early Pacific flights, the timetables also contain ticket prices and route maps that reflect changes in the Pacific operation.

Reverse of July 1937 timetable

Reverse of January 1938 timetable

June - August 1941

September 1945

Ironically the Martin M-130 China Clipper, Pan American's most famous Clipper in the Pacific, never appeared on a Pacific timetable

# PAN AM TICKETS AND TICKET ENVELOPES

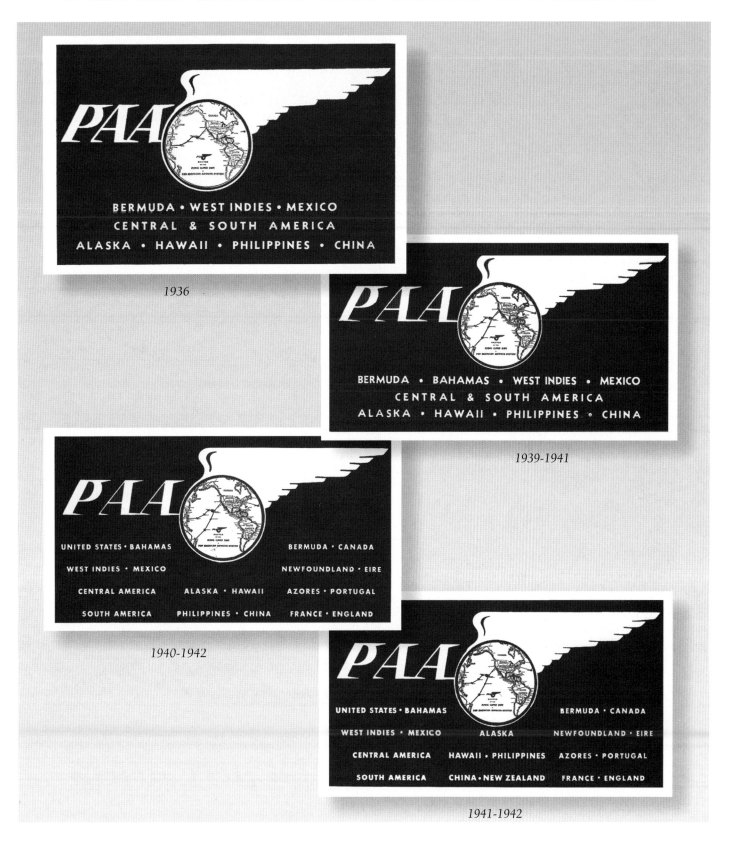

1936

1939-1941

1940-1942

1941-1942

During the 1930s, as Pan Am extended air service from one country to the next, ticket envelopes and route maps shown on the ticket envelopes were changed and the new destinations were added to those listed on the envelope.

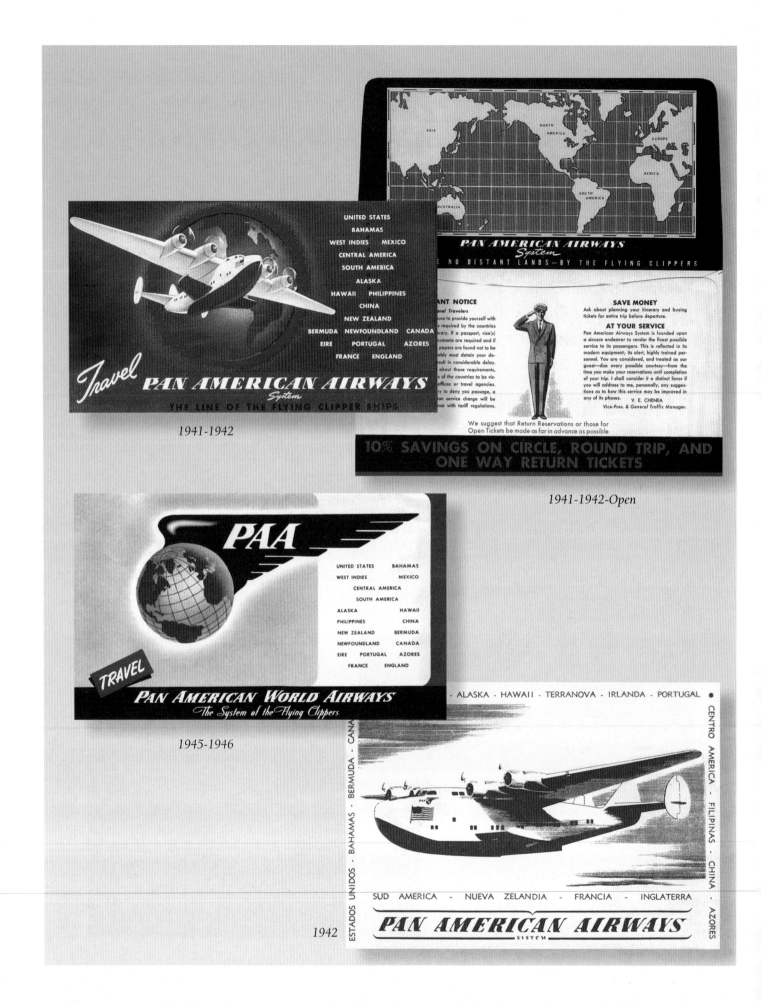

1941-1942

1941-1942-Open

1945-1946

1942

Illustrated are all of Pan Am's various styles of envelopes available during the period of the Pacific Clippers from 1935 to 1946.

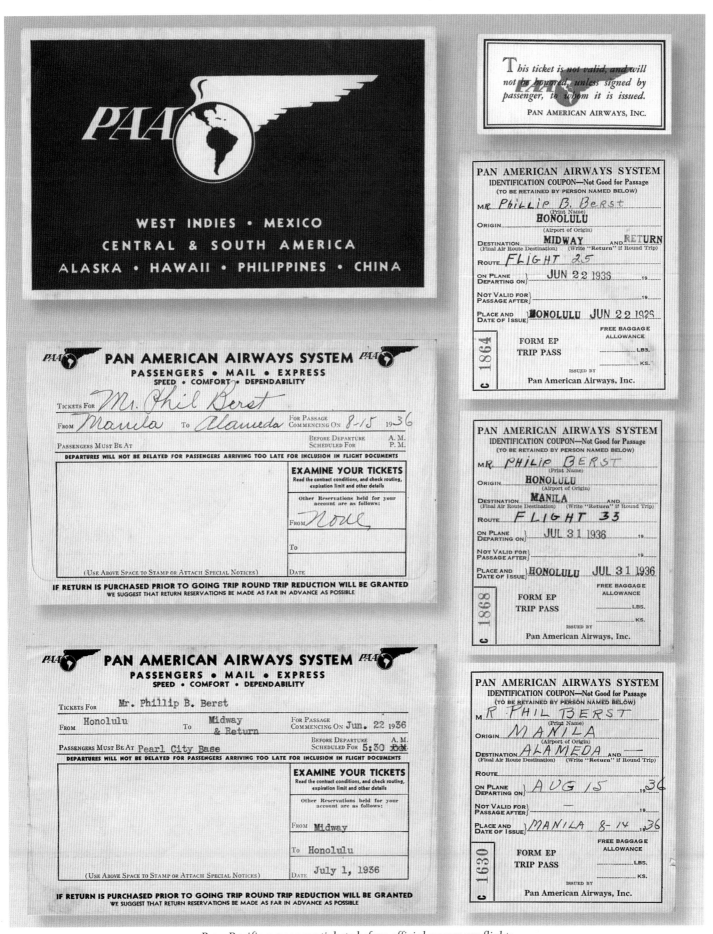

*Rare Pacific passenger tickets before official passenger flights*

Phil Berst, maintenance supervisor for Pan Am in the Pacific, flew frequently on the Clipper before regular passenger flights were inaugurated in October of 1936. In June of 1936 he flew on flight #25 from Honolulu to Midway. Later the same year, on flight #33, he flew from Honolulu to Manila and on August 15, 1936 he returned from Manila to Alameda.

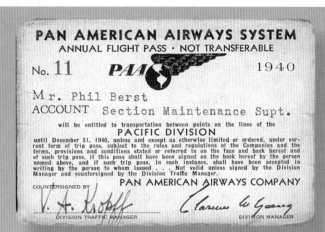

*The ultimate ticket - a pass issued to Pacific maintenance supervisor Phil Berst*

Illustrated below is the ticket (trip pass) issued to employee Max Brodofsky from San Francisco to Midway in November of 1940. Later the same year, Brodofsky was transferred to Guam, where he was captured at the outbreak of WW II. He remained a prisoner throughout the war.

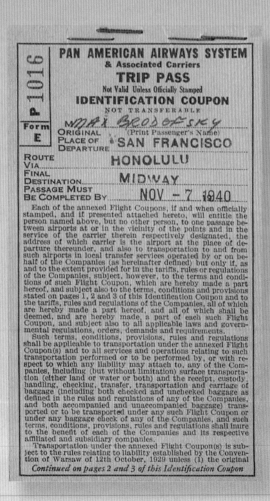

*Max Brodofsky's ticket*

*Pan Am commercial transportation certificate issued to O. Pruessman of General Electric Co.*

Contractors doing business with Pan Am were issued a "Letter of Identification" so they could travel free while working on Pan Am's contract.

# PAN AM BAGGAGE LABELS

1940 - 1941

Front

Reverse

1936- 1940

1940 - 1946

1936 - 1940

1942 - 1946

PAN AMERICAN WORLD AIRWAYS
PAA
The System of the Flying Clippers

*1942 - 1952*

CLIPPER EXPRESS
C.O.D.
PAN AMERICAN WORLD AIRWAYS
The System of the Flying Clippers
PAA
Form 33-26A

*1945 - 1955*

SHIPPED VIA
PAA
CLIPPER EXPRESS
PAN AMERICAN WORLD AIRWAYS

*1945 - 1955*

The System of the Flying Clippers
PAA
PAN AMERICAN WORLD AIRWAYS

*1942 - 1946*

*Additional baggage stickers used from 1942 to 1955*

1938 - 1941

1943

1945

# EMPLOYEE UNIFORMS AND PATCHES

Uniform patches were worn on Pan Am uniforms since the 1930s. At first the initials "PAA" were embossed into the fabric of the work clothes, such as mechanic's overalls that Joe Copeland wore while working on Kingman Reef in March of 1937. Later a patch with the "PAA" logo was given to the workmen to sew onto their work overalls. Pan Am told the mechanics to wear the white overalls whenever they were doing anything that could be seen by passengers or sightseers who visited at the bases and to wear the khaki overalls when they were out of public sight.

*Joe Copeland working at Kingman Reef - 1937*
*Note the PAA logo on the uniform that was embroidered onto the garment at that time.*

Robert H. McCrory, who now lives in Oklahoma, worked for Pan Am as a ground mechanic in Honolulu and San Francisco in the early 1940s. He provided me with both his brown and white Pan Am overalls, which he wore while working at Pan Am's Treasure Island base.

*The PAA logo sewn on workers uniforms*

*White uniform with PAA patch employees wore in public*

*1944 - 1960*

*1944 - 1960*

*1940 - 1945*

In approximately 1940, Pan Am shoulder patches appeared, such as the one being worn by the men loading cargo for one of the Clipper flights during the war.

*Pan Am souvenir patch - 1940's*

*1940 - 1945*

*1945 - 1960*

Cloth patches supplemented, but never took the place of the more traditional pins worn with pride by Pan Am employees.

# PAN AM SOUVENIRS AND MEMENTOES

In addition to the official company pins issued by Pan Am during this period, a wide variety of items were produced for Pan Am, using the Pan Am logo of the time. Money clips, belt buckles, earrings and cuff links are just a few of the items that can be found. Because they are so closely associated with the company, they are highly collectible and welcome additions to any collection.

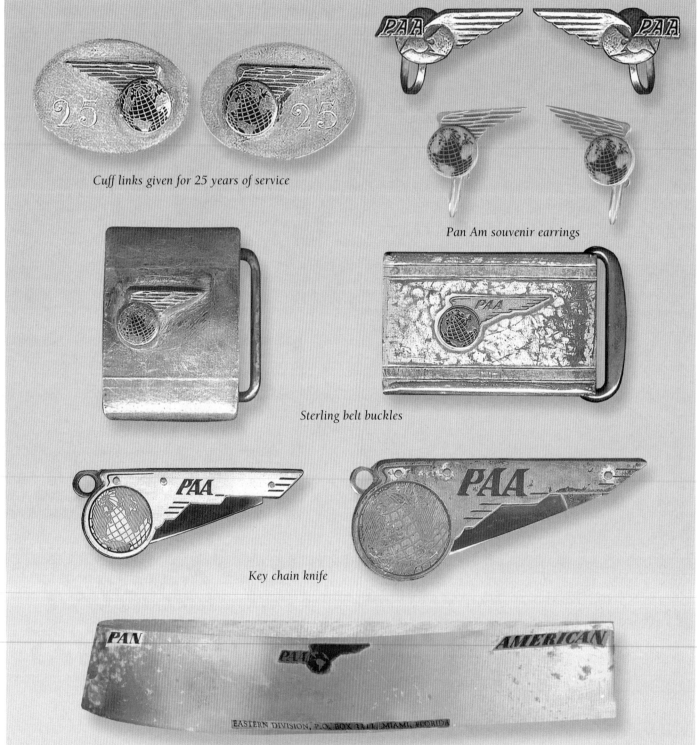

*Cuff links given for 25 years of service*

*Pan Am souvenir earrings*

*Sterling belt buckles*

*Key chain knife*

*In the 1940s, the last of the Sikorsky S-42s were being scrapped in Miami – station manager, Overton Snyder, had one of the wing support struts cut into one inch wide pieces, the Pan Am logo applied, and he gave the pieces of the S-42 away as souvenir paper weights to friends and business associates - paper weight is seven inches in length*

Money clip
1946 - 1960

*Souvenir medal commemorating the loss of Captain Edwin Musick on January 11, 1938 - a large bronze copy of this medal was presented by Mrs. Musick to New Zealand in 1954*

1946 - 1960

*Souvenir cigarette lighter*

*Pan Am porter's pin 1940 - 1955*

*Longines wrist watch presented to Phil Berst in April 1943 by "Transpacific gang" when he was transferred to the Alaskan Division*

*Cereal premiums - 1936-1941*

*1943*

# PAN AMERICAN EMPLOYEE PINS

Juan Trippe believed that Pan American should be run much like a military organization. Therefore, service pins and insignias were always quite important to the company. Pan Am's first flight pins appeared shortly after the company was founded in 1927.

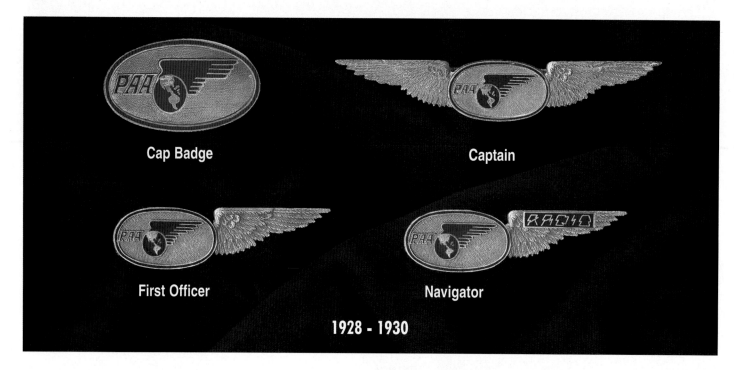

Cap Badge

Captain

First Officer

Navigator

1928 - 1930

Pictured in full size are the four varieties of flight pins worn from 1927 through 1929. The oval pin was worn as the cap badge and the other badges were worn as breast pocket insignias.

Pictured is Ed Musick in 1929 wearing the oval cap badge and double winged breast pocket captain's badge of the earliest Pan Am design.

The origin of the employee's service pin is also an interesting story. In the early days of Pan Am, the traffic department used to give passengers either a small double winged pin with a shield in the center, or a round blue pin, so as to identify the person as a Pan Am traveler.

Employees at Pan Am started to wear these passenger pins. So, Juan Trippe designed a new pin

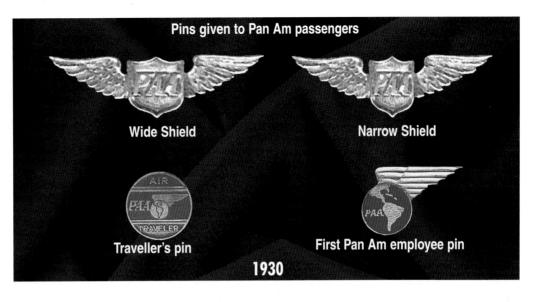

Pins given to Pan Am passengers

**Wide Shield**

**Narrow Shield**

**Traveller's pin**

**First Pan Am employee pin**

**1930**

specifically for the employees to wear, showing the round map of North and South America with the single wing extending to the right.

In September of 1935, Pan Am started the practice of adding stars to this employee service pin: a silver pin signifying up to three years of service; a gold pin for three to five years of service; a gold pin with a star signifying five years of service; two gold stars for ten years; three stars for fifteen years; and four stars for twenty years of service.

Phil Berst was one of the first employees to receive the gold five-year service pin with the single star. In most instances, both the manager of the division where the employee served and Pan Am's President, Juan Trippe would send a congratulatory letter along with the new pin.

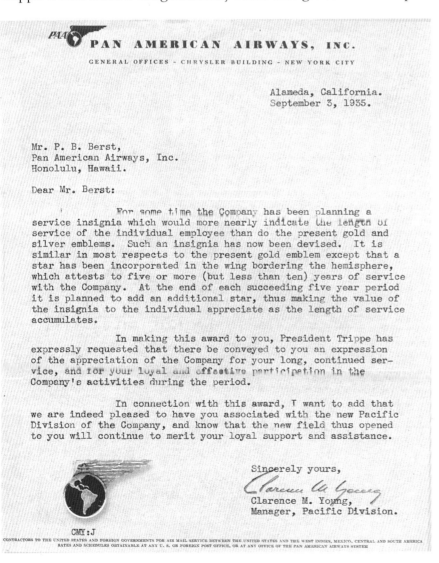

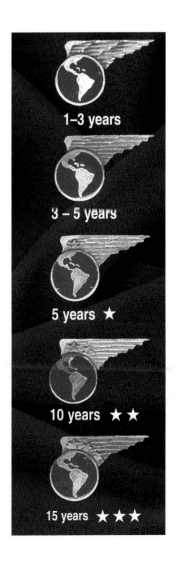

1–3 years

3 – 5 years

5 years ★

10 years ★ ★

15 years ★ ★ ★

In 1930, when employee service pins were instituted, pin designs were also approved for the various departments of the airline. The original globe showing only the western hemisphere remained part of Pan Am's logo until October of 1944 when the globe was modified to show the world from Europe to Asia. All of the pins are shown slightly larger than their actual size.

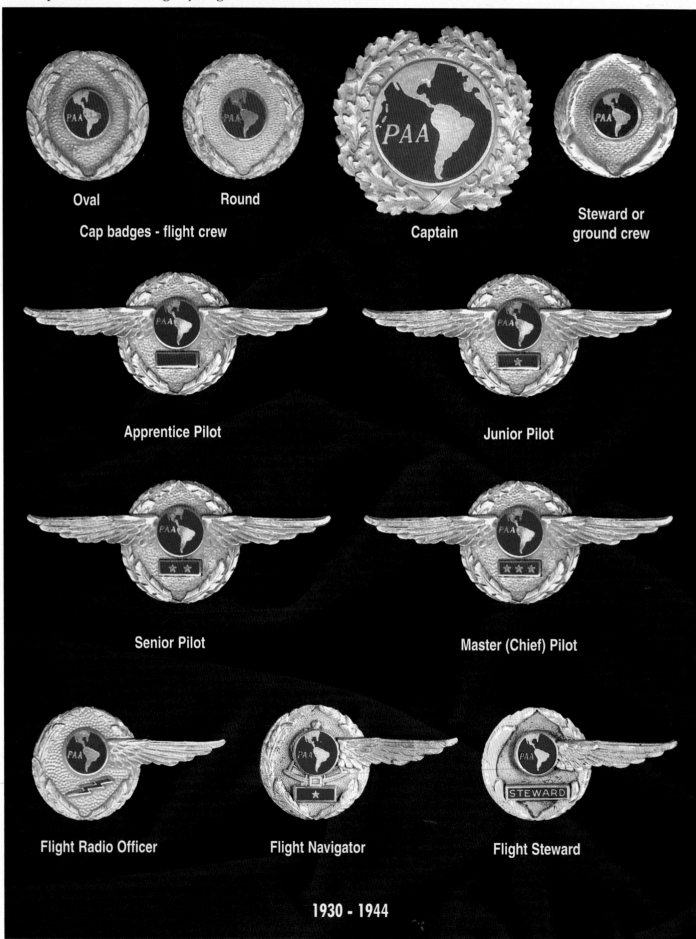

Oval      Round

Cap badges - flight crew

Captain

Steward or
ground crew

Apprentice Pilot

Junior Pilot

Senior Pilot

Master (Chief) Pilot

Flight Radio Officer

Flight Navigator

Flight Steward

**1930 - 1944**

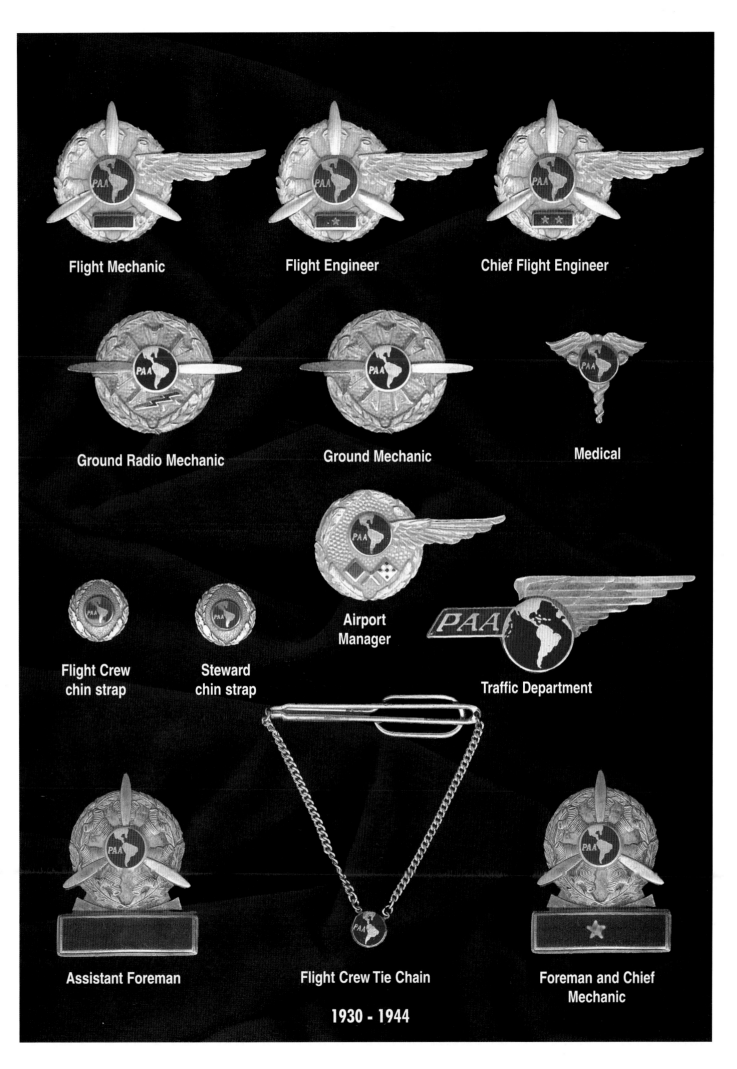

Flight Mechanic

Flight Engineer

Chief Flight Engineer

Ground Radio Mechanic

Ground Mechanic

Medical

Flight Crew
chin strap

Steward
chin strap

Airport
Manager

Traffic Department

Assistant Foreman

Flight Crew Tie Chain

Foreman and Chief
Mechanic

**1930 - 1944**

The original wing globed design of 1930, with the globe showing only North and South America, remained until 1944. In October of 1944, in recognition of the Pacific and European flights, the map on the globe was changed to include the world map from Europe on the east to the Orient on the west. During this period the company's name was also changed from Pan American Airways to Pan American World Airways. This new logo remained until January of 1958 when it was replaced by the light blue more modern round globe that existed for the rest of Pan Am's history

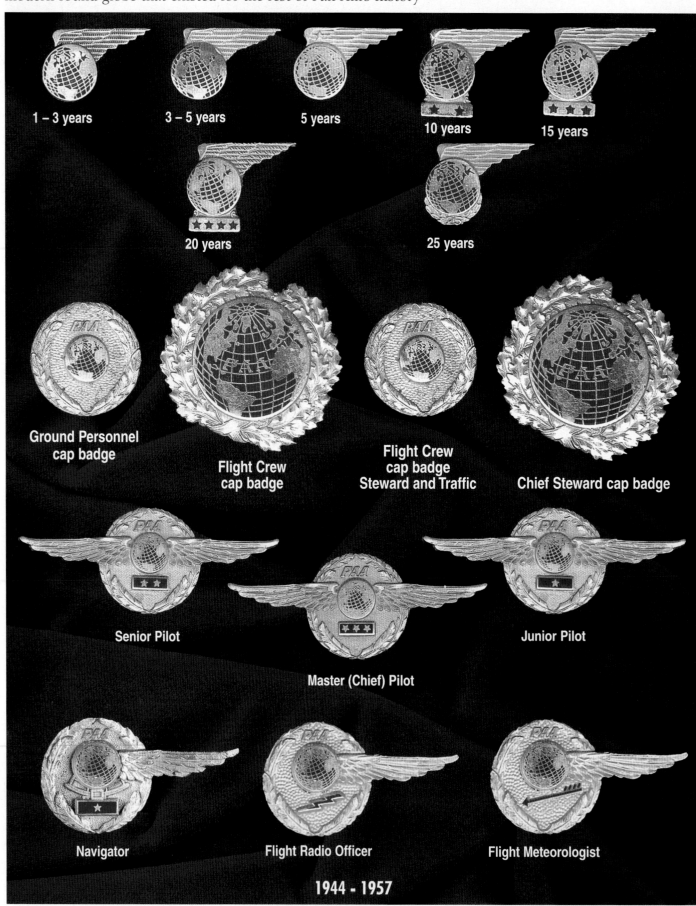

1 – 3 years

3 – 5 years

5 years

10 years

15 years

20 years

25 years

Ground Personnel
cap badge

Flight Crew
cap badge

Flight Crew
cap badge
Steward and Traffic

Chief Steward cap badge

Senior Pilot

Master (Chief) Pilot

Junior Pilot

Navigator

Flight Radio Officer

Flight Meteorologist

1944 - 1957

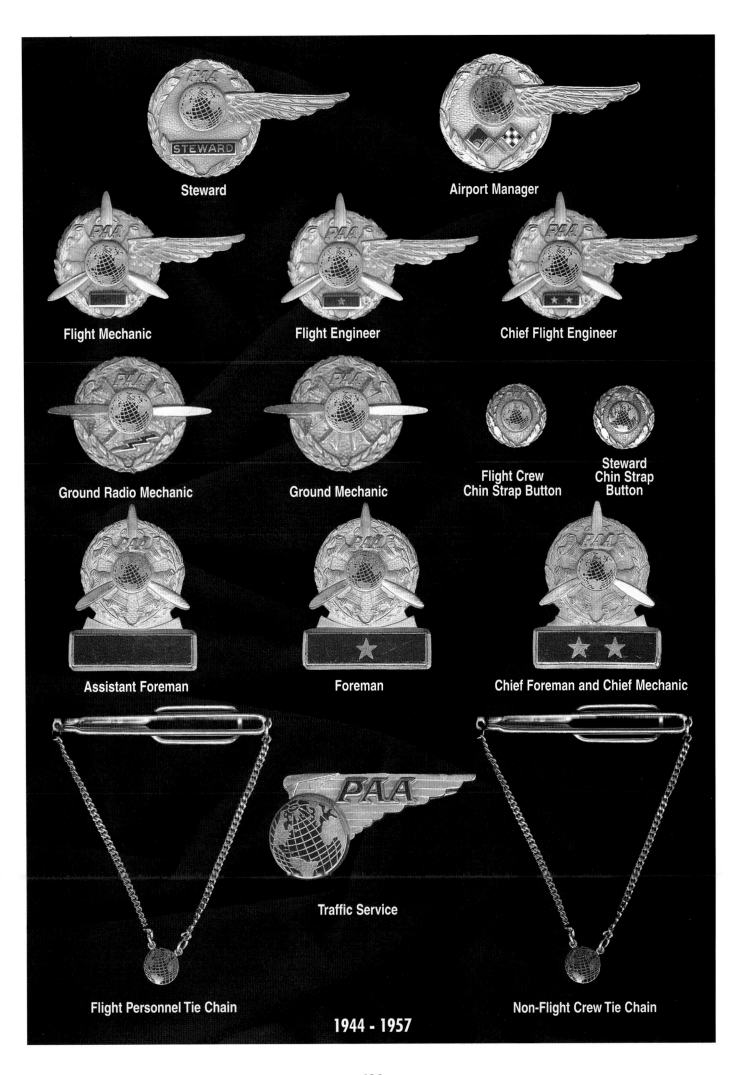

Steward

Airport Manager

Flight Mechanic

Flight Engineer

Chief Flight Engineer

Ground Radio Mechanic

Ground Mechanic

Flight Crew
Chin Strap Button

Steward
Chin Strap
Button

Assistant Foreman

Foreman

Chief Foreman and Chief Mechanic

Flight Personnel Tie Chain

Traffic Service

Non-Flight Crew Tie Chain

**1944 - 1957**

**Stores Group Head**

**Stores Assistant**

**Stores Clerk**

| Master Pilot | Senior Pilot | Junior Pilot or Navigator | Chief Flight Engineer | Flight Engineer | Flight Mechanic |
|---|---|---|---|---|---|

| Chief Flight Radio Officer | Flight Radio Officer | Asst. Flight Radio Officer | Ground Radio Operator | Flight Meteorologist |
|---|---|---|---|---|

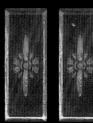   

| Chief Mechanic | Airport Manager | Traffic Personnel | Ground and Flight Steward |
|---|---|---|---|

## Collar Bars

**1944 - 1957**

Whenever an employee celebrated a five year anniversary with the company, both the division manager and Pan Am's president, Juan Trippe, would send letters of congratulations. Shown below are a series of letters received by Marvel Brown during her first twenty years with Pan Am.

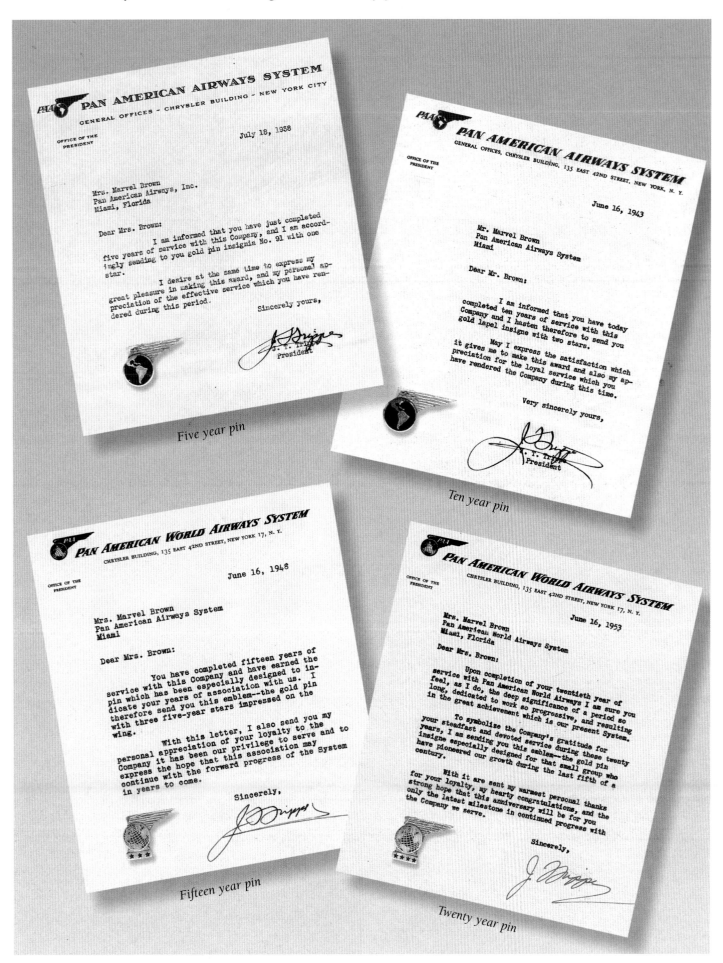

Five year pin

Ten year pin

Fifteen year pin

Twenty year pin

In April of 1944 Pan Am's first group of stewardesses graduated and the company prepared a new pin to identify the new Pan Am stewardesses. Although some of them served on the Clippers in the Caribbean, stewardesses did not serve on Transpacific Clipper flights. Below, one of the early stewardesses, Marvel Brown, is shown getting her flight wings from the manager of the Eastern Division, Overton Snyder.

*Seven (count 'em) pretty air stewardesses - first to fly the Caribbean Clippers - line up for review. Left to right they are: Dorothy Larsen, Atlanta; Elsbeth Exhart, Omaha; Louise Taylor, Lancaster, Pa.; Lois Smith, Peoria, Ill.; Dorothy Mills, Staatsburg, N.Y.; Gloria Smith, Detroit; and Doris Stimson, Chicago.*

# Girls Join the Crew Of Miami Clippers

First of their sex to "win their wings" and become members of Pan American's highly-trained flying crews, seven stewardesses are now serving aboard the big Clippers operating out of Miami.

Introduction of the girls to flying jobs marks another "first" for PAA; previously unwritten but long-standing tradition had resulted in all-male crews. Since the girls will supplement the present staff of male stewards they will in effect "relieve men for war duty elsewhere." They fly to Nassau, to Havana, and to Merida, Mexico.

The "ideal" PAA stewardess (on the basis of average characteristics of the seven girls) is:

Blue-eyed with brown hair, poised, self-pssessed, slender, 5'3", weighs 115, is 23, active in sports, a high-school graduate with business training, and — pretty.

Each girl is a graduate of the same general "background" course in Traffic as are the stewards (who, incidentally, continue to serve on the longer flights) and must know the intricacies of passports, manifests, clearance papers, immigration laws, etc.

Stewardesses are required to meet the same high physical standards as do stewards, then must prove their efficiency in swimming, life saving, and first aid. Ability to meet and serve the traveling public is a "must."

Finally, after this fundamental grounding, come flight tests under expert Flight Service Manager Arthur Nugent, Raymond Suarez, his chief assistant, and Chief Steward Alfred Scarafone.

Each stewardess wears a trim, powder-blue collarless tailored coat, a matching skirt, wide soft-collared shirtwaist, brown shoes, a powder-blue Robinhood-type cap, and stewardess insignia pin on the jacket coat.

A high school education and a background of business training are prerequisites for job applicants.

When Pan Am flights were extended in April of 1937 to Hong Kong, it allowed Pan Am to connect with their only airline affiliate in the Pacific, the China National Air Corporation (CNAC). Pictured below are the very rare fabric pins worn by the captain and the first officer.

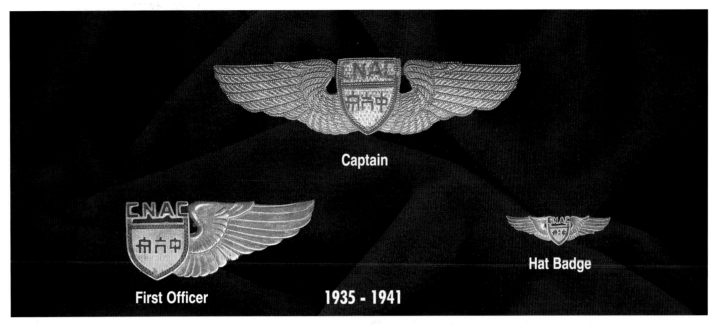

Captain

First Officer     1935 - 1941     Hat Badge

In the late 1930s, young children began to fly Clippers with some frequency and souvenir pins called "kiddie wings" were introduced. A small pin depicting the Martin M-130 in flight looks like it is an early kiddie pin, but it is believed to have been a sales premium for Kellogg cereal. The earliest documented kiddie pins were in 1940 for the Boeing B-314s and these pins are exceedingly rare. Starting in 1946, kiddie wings became standard gifts for children flying with Pan Am and they are relatively easy to find for both junior pilots and junior stewardesses.

The two small kiddie wings at the bottom were made of plastic, all the other kiddie wings were made of tin.

Cereal Premium 1935 - 1940     B-314 Kiddie Wing 1939 - 1941

Kiddie Wings 1945 - 1955

Kiddie Wings
1950 - 1957

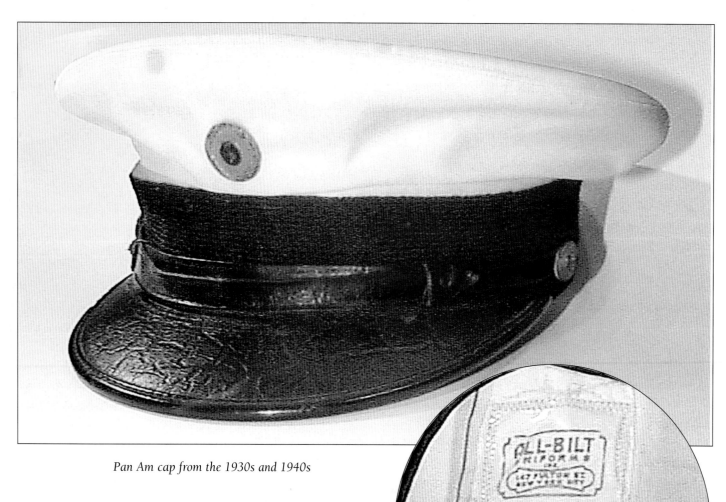

*Pan Am cap from the 1930s and 1940s*

The ground crews and stewards would wear a black leather strap above the brim. The flight captain, first officer and navigator would have double gold braid above the brim.

*Label showing New York manufacturer of Pan Am cap*

All of Pan Am's pins were manufactured by the L.G. Balfour Company of Attleboro, Massachusetts. Your high school or college ring was probably also manufactured by this well-known company.

Pan Am's employees wore their pins with pride. They were badges of honor within the company. Because they are so closely associated with the early pioneer flights, and, because they were never issued in large numbers, the pins and badges are among the most collectible mementoes of Pan Am's early history. Each pin or badge gives silent testimony to an employee who dedicated his or her life to the great airline.

# PAN AM CHINA

Glassware and china are among the most sought after mementoes of the flying boat era. Because china and glassware are fragile and because the conditions on the flying boats were harsh, very few pieces have survived. They are, however, reminders of an elegant and more leisurely time when aircraft meals were served in a separate dining room on white linen.

Pan Am's best known china was manufactured from approximately 1935-1942 by the Homer-Laughlin China Company of Newell, West Virginia.

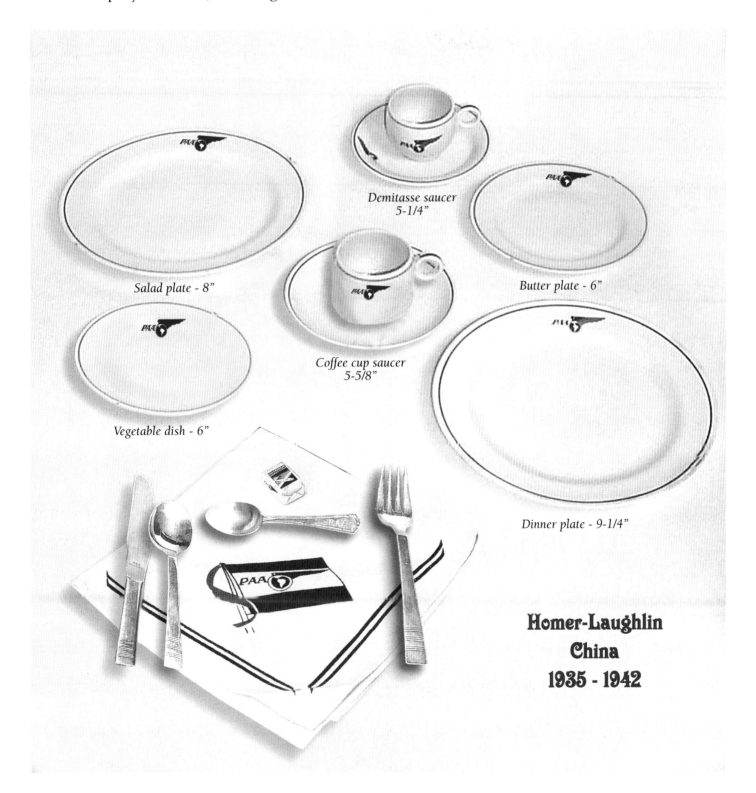

Salad plate - 8"

Demitasse saucer 5-1/4"

Butter plate - 6"

Vegetable dish - 6"

Coffee cup saucer 5-5/8"

Dinner plate - 9-1/4"

**Homer-Laughlin China 1935 - 1942**

*Menu from Martin M-130 - 1938*

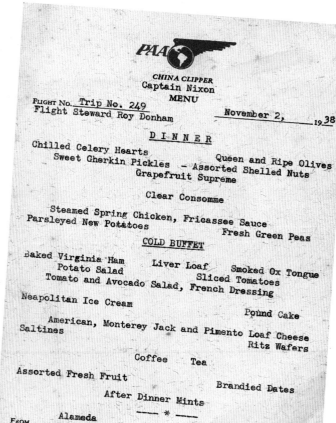

PAA

CHINA CLIPPER
Captain Nixon
MENU

FLIGHT No. Trip No. 249
Flight Steward Roy Donham                November 2,    1938

D I N N E R

Chilled Celery Hearts              Queen and Ripe Olives
    Sweet Gherkin Pickles  – Assorted Shelled Nuts
              Grapefruit Supreme

              Clear Consomme

    Steamed Spring Chicken, Fricassee Sauce
Parsleyed New Potatoes              Fresh Green Peas

              COLD BUFFET

Baked Virginia Ham        Liver Loaf      Smoked Ox Tongue
    Potato Salad                    Sliced Tomatoes
    Tomato and Avocado Salad, French Dressing

Neapolitan Ice Cream
                                  Pound Cake
    American, Monterey Jack and Pimento Loaf Cheese
Saltines
                                  Ritz Wafers

              Coffee      Tea
Assorted Fresh Fruit
                        Brandied Dates
          After Dinner Mints
                ——— * ———
FROM      Alameda
                        To      Honolulu

*Menu China Clipper - 1938*

*Galley on Boeing B-314*
*1940*

*Dining on Boeing B-314*
*1940*

*Dining on Martin M-130*
*1938*

Homer-Laughlin started making pottery in the late 1800s. For many years their plant was in East Liverpool, Ohio. In 1905 they expanded their operations and moved the company to Newell, West Virginia. Today, Homer-Laughlin China produces the largest volume of commercial china in the United States.

Pictured are examples of Homer-Laughlin china made for Pan Am. Three different versions of the company's hallmark, complete with date coding, appear on the back of different pieces of Pan Am china.

Although all of the china is extremely rare, undamaged examples of the demitasse cup and saucer are more frequently found. Cynics would say that the demitasse cup and saucer survived because they fit most easily into the pocket of the traveler as they departed the aircraft. Alex Vucetich, the son of Danilo Vucetich, however, has another explanation. He recalls going to Treasure Island during the Golden Gate Exhibition of 1939 and seeing the demitasse cup and saucer being sold by Pan Am as souvenirs to the fair goers.

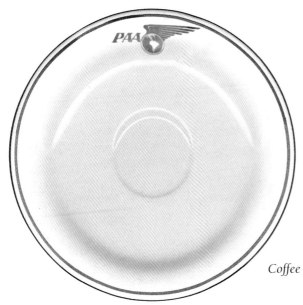

Recently, while liquidating an estate of a former Pan Am pilot, an antique dealer from Baltimore located 60 pieces of Pan Am china. Although much of the china was badly cracked and chipped, the collection did contain a never before seen variety of Pan Am china with a yellow-gold logo, rather than a traditional blue Pan Am logo. It appears that the gold color rubbed off rather easily and for that reason it was probably discontinued shortly after it was introduced.

*Coffee cup saucer with gold logo*

*Hallmark - November (K) 1937*　　　*Hallmark - February (B) 1938*　　　*Hallmark - June (F) 1939*

*Homer-Laughlin hallmarks with date of manufacture*

Another recently discovered piece of Pan Am china is the plate with four sections showing the China Clipper in flight. The plate was manufactured by the Bailey-Walker China Company in 1935 or 1936 for use on the new Martin M-130 aircraft. Harry Bailey and Albert Walker formed the china company in 1923 and they made china under the Bailey-Walker trademark from 1923 until 1942. During this period the company was located in Jersey City, New Jersey. Juan Trippe frequently chose suppliers for Pan Am who were close to the New York headquarters of the company and that might account for the choice of Bailey-Walker China Company of nearby New Jersey to make the china for the Martin M-130 Clippers.

In 1942 Walker bought out Bailey and the name was changed to the Walker China Company and Walker moved the company to Bedford, Ohio. In the mid 1940s the Walker China Company again made china for Pan Am with the new logo of Pan Am that had the initials PAA on the wing of the globe. This heavy china was used by Pan Am up until the Pan Am corporate logo changed to the round globe in 1959. Walker China ceased to exist in 1981.

*Bailey-Walker plate 1935 - 1936*

*Bailey-Walker hallmark - 1935*

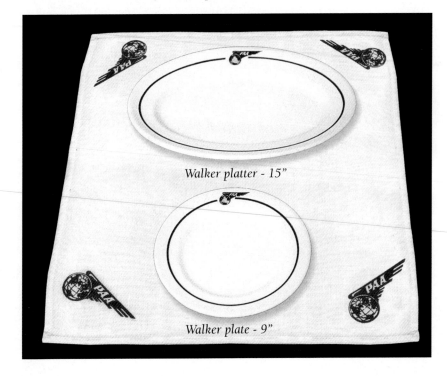

*Walker platter - 15"*

*Walker plate - 9"*

*Walker hallmark 1945 - 1960*

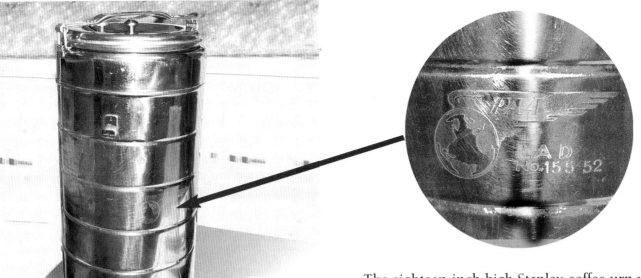

The eighteen-inch high Stanley coffee urn was used in the 1940s and 1950s. The logo on the urn with the initials PAA in the wing is similar to the logo on the china made by the Walker China Company during the same period.

*Hallmark on demitasse spoon*

*Hallmarks and Pan Am logos on stainless silverware*

The plain looking stainless knife, fork and spoon was used on the Clippers from the 1930s to the 1940s. It was manufactured by the International Silver Company and there is a small PAA on the back of each of the three pieces. The demitasse spoon with the PAA on the front of the handle is from a different unidentified manufacturer.

The manufacturers of the glassware from the 1930s have also not been identified.

*Served on Clippers 1936 - 1941*

# PAN AM MODEL AIRPLANES - 1935-1946

Unlike toy airplanes that were designed to be played with by young children, model airplanes were for display and several varieties of model airplanes have found their way into my collection of Pan Am Clippers.

By far the best known model airplane is the solid wood model of the Martin M-130 produced by the Strombecker Company of Moline, Illinois. Quite naturally they called their model the China Clipper. It was their first airplane kit and it received the designated number A-51. It was produced from late 1936 until 1956. Instead of the balsa wood usually used in model airplane kits, the model was made of pre-carved parts of white pine. It had a wingspan of 12-1/8 inches. Because it was easy to assemble and visually pleasing, the Strombecker model was an immediate success. Therefore, the company also produced a Boeing B-314, model kit number C-6 and a Sikorsky S-43 number C-3. I have not yet been able to locate examples of either of these models for my collection.

Strombecker discontinued the production of wooden kits in 1956 in favor of the more popular snap together plastic kits. In the 1980s Strombecker plastic kits with improved decals were reissued by Glenco.

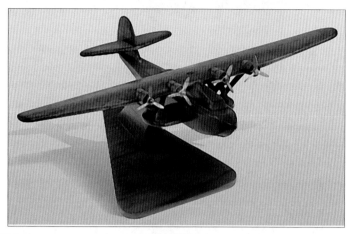

*Strombecker model signed by crew - March 1937*

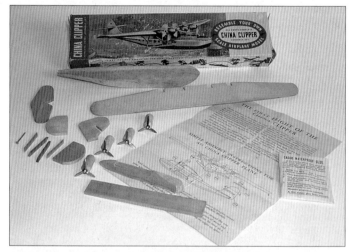

*Strombecker kit - 1936 - 1940*

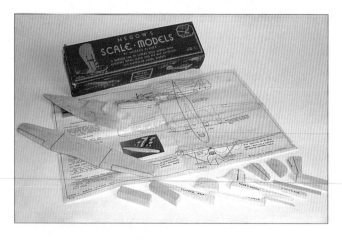

*1935 Megow kit - Glenn Martin Clipper*

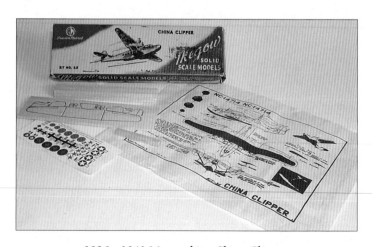

*1936 - 1941 Megow kit - China Clipper*

In early 1935 Frank W. Megow of Philadelphia, Pennsylvania, produced a balsa wood model kit that he called the Glenn L. Martin Clipper Ship. Later when Pan Am christened the new aircraft the China Clipper, he, of course, changed the name of his model to the "China Clipper". Both models had a 12 inch wingspan.

The most recent addition to my collection is the model manufactured by the Comet Model Airplane Company of Chicago in 1936, with the designation of kit number A-169. The model also had a wingspan of 12 inches and it was sold as a premium by Quaker Oats for a cereal box top and ten cents.

Also illustrated again is a die cast model of the Sikorsky S-42 with a 24 inch wingspan. The model was electrified so a soft glow would come out of the windows of the aircraft as it sat on the counters of travel agents. The bronze base had a map of North and South America. Similar travel agent models were made for the Martin M-130s and the Boeing B-314s. All travel agent models manufactured for Pan Am are extremely valuable and difficult to find.

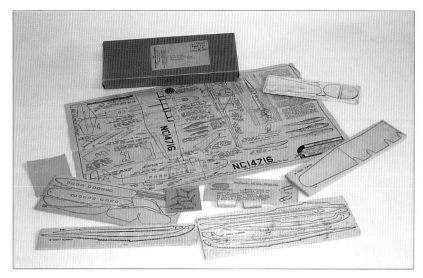

*Quaker Oats premium*

*Travel agent model*

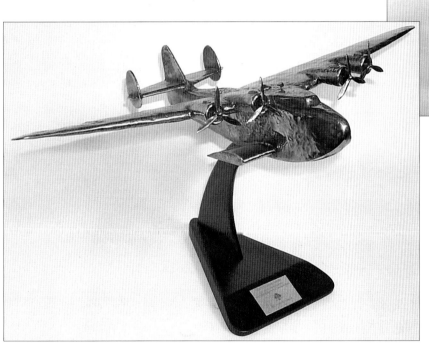

*This large copper model of the Boeing B-314 has a wingspan of 26" by Roy Butler*

*Boeing B 314 model by Dick Sobczak*

The large Boeing B-314 with the 26-inch wingspan was sculpted by the nationally known metal sculptor Roy Butler at his studio in Fort Lauderdale. Roy and I have been good friends for more than 20 years. My partners commissioned Roy to do the model as a surprise gift for me on the 25th anniversary of the founding of my law firm.

Another model in my collection is the Boeing B-314 with the 14-1/2 inch wingspan. It was carved for me by my good friend, Dick Sobczak.

All of the model aircraft of the Clippers helped to bring to life this romantic period in aviation history.

# PAN AM PUBLICATIONS 1930-1946

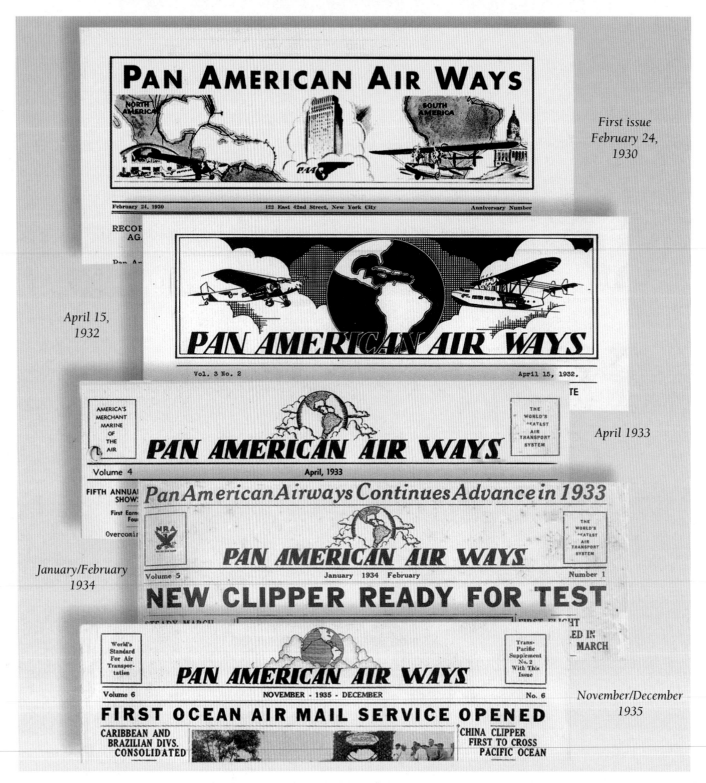

*First issue February 24, 1930*

*April 15, 1932*

*April 1933*

*January/February 1934*

*November/December 1935*

In doing research for this book, whenever possible I have used primary sources of information. These have included interviews with employees and the children of employees, personal logs of former employees, and company newsletters and magazines.

One of the most helpful sources of information has been the Pan Am company newsletter first published in 1928. Pictured at the top is the masthead from the first issue, which commemorated the first year anniversary of the company's founding. The masthead changed over the years as the company expanded its routes to Central and South America, to the Pacific in 1935 and finally to Europe in 1939.

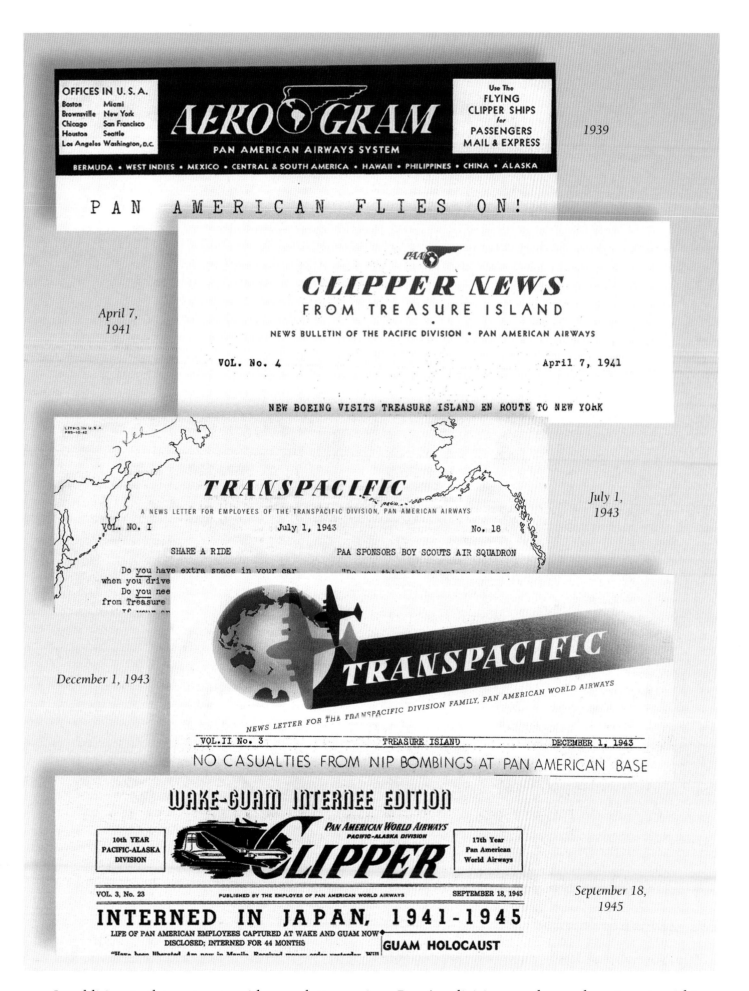

**OFFICES IN U.S.A.**
Boston   Miami
Brownsville   New York
Chicago   San Francisco
Houston   Seattle
Los Angeles   Washington, D.C.

# AERO GRAM
### PAN AMERICAN AIRWAYS SYSTEM

Use The
**FLYING
CLIPPER SHIPS**
*for*
**PASSENGERS
MAIL & EXPRESS**

*1939*

BERMUDA • WEST INDIES • MEXICO • CENTRAL & SOUTH AMERICA • HAWAII • PHILIPPINES • CHINA • ALASKA

## PAN AMERICAN FLIES ON!

*April 7, 1941*

# CLIPPER NEWS
### FROM TREASURE ISLAND
NEWS BULLETIN OF THE PACIFIC DIVISION • PAN AMERICAN AIRWAYS

VOL. No. 4        April 7, 1941

NEW BOEING VISITS TREASURE ISLAND EN ROUTE TO NEW YORK

LITHO IN U.S.A.
PRS-10-42

# TRANSPACIFIC
A NEWS LETTER FOR EMPLOYEES OF THE TRANSPACIFIC DIVISION, PAN AMERICAN AIRWAYS

VOL. NO. I     July 1, 1943     No. 18

*July 1, 1943*

SHARE A RIDE        PAA SPONSORS BOY SCOUTS AIR SQUADRON

Do you have extra space in your car
when you drive
Do you nee
from Treasure

*December 1, 1943*

# TRANSPACIFIC
NEWS LETTER FOR THE TRANSPACIFIC DIVISION FAMILY, PAN AMERICAN WORLD AIRWAYS

VOL.II No. 3     TREASURE ISLAND     DECEMBER 1, 1943

## NO CASUALTIES FROM NIP BOMBINGS AT PAN AMERICAN BASE

# WAKE-GUAM INTERNEE EDITION

PAN AMERICAN WORLD AIRWAYS
PACIFIC-ALASKA DIVISION

10th YEAR
PACIFIC-ALASKA
DIVISION

# CLIPPER

17th Year
Pan American
World Airways

VOL. 3, No. 23    PUBLISHED BY THE EMPLOYES OF PAN AMERICAN WORLD AIRWAYS    SEPTEMBER 18, 1945

*September 18, 1945*

## INTERNED IN JAPAN, 1941-1945
LIFE OF PAN AMERICAN EMPLOYEES CAPTURED AT WAKE AND GUAM NOW
DISCLOSED; INTERNED FOR 44 MONTHS
"Have been liberated. Am now in Manila. Received money order yesterday. Will

**GUAM HOLOCAUST**

In addition to the company-wide newsletter, various Pan Am divisions, and even departments within divisions had their own publications. Because this book concentrates on the Pacific division, I have only included publications that covered the Pacific area during the period of the flying boats.

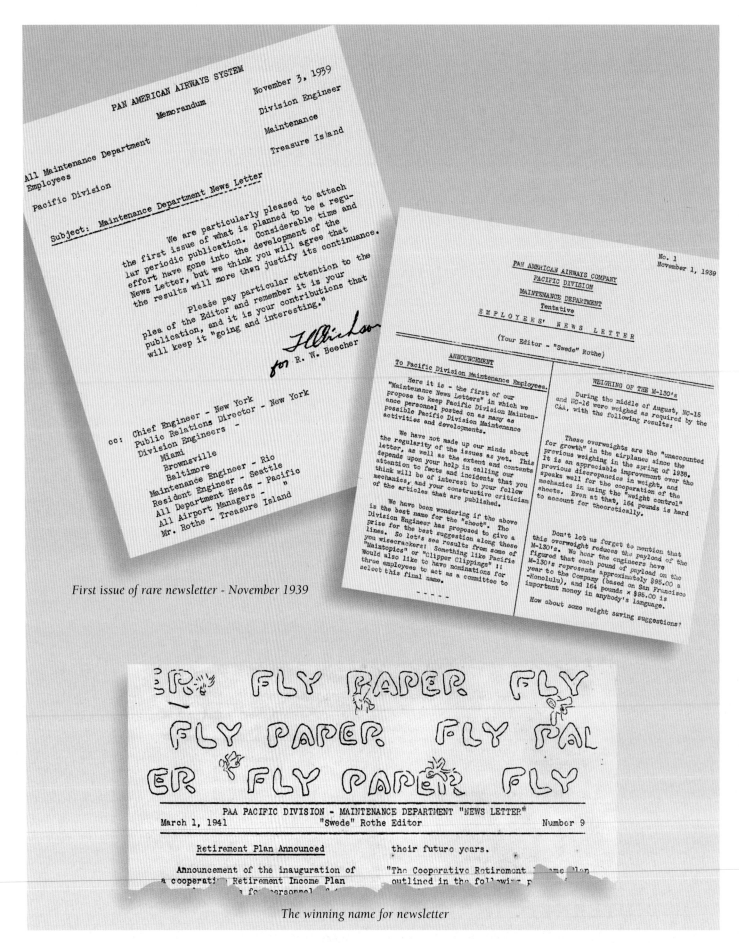

*First issue of rare newsletter - November 1939*

*The winning name for newsletter*

In November of 1939, "Swede" Rothe, the flight engineer on the Pacific Clipper's escape flight around the world in December of 1941, started a newsletter for the maintenance department of the Pacific Division. A contest was held to name the new publication and in early 1940 it was christened the ***"Fly Paper"***. "Swede's" widow, Marian Rothe, gave me a complete set of these rare Pan Am maintenance department newsletters.

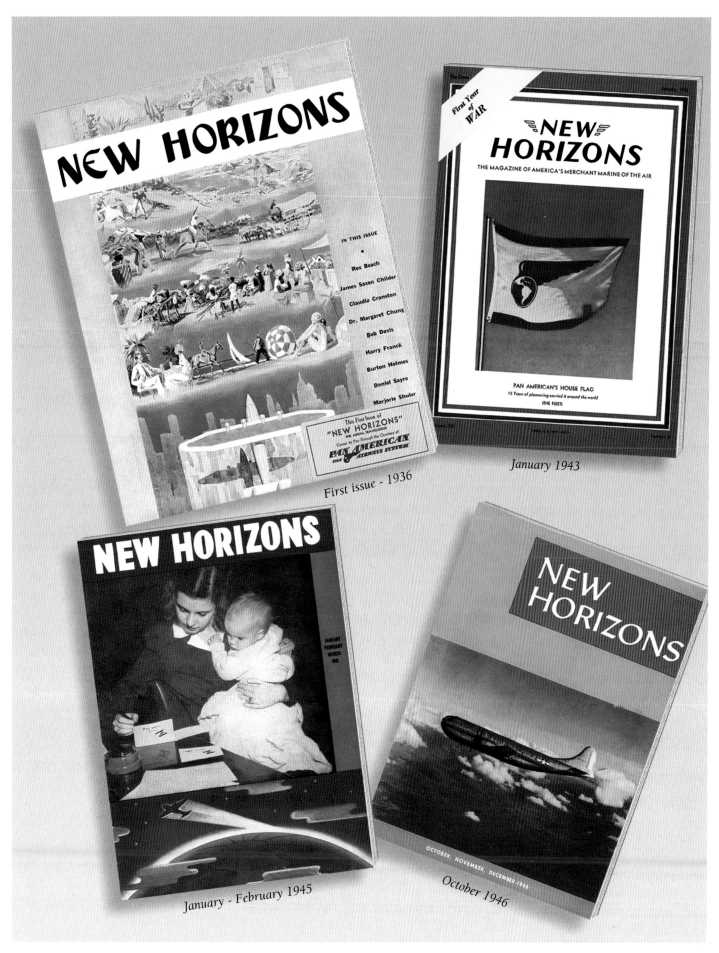

First issue - 1936

January 1943

January - February 1945

October 1946

In addition to newsletters, a monthly magazine was published by Pan Am, entitled **New Horizons**. The inaugural issue in 1936 was basically a Pan Am published travel magazine. However, by the late 1930s, the magazine had evolved into an aviation news magazine that concentrated on Pan Am activities, but also included articles on aviation news in general.

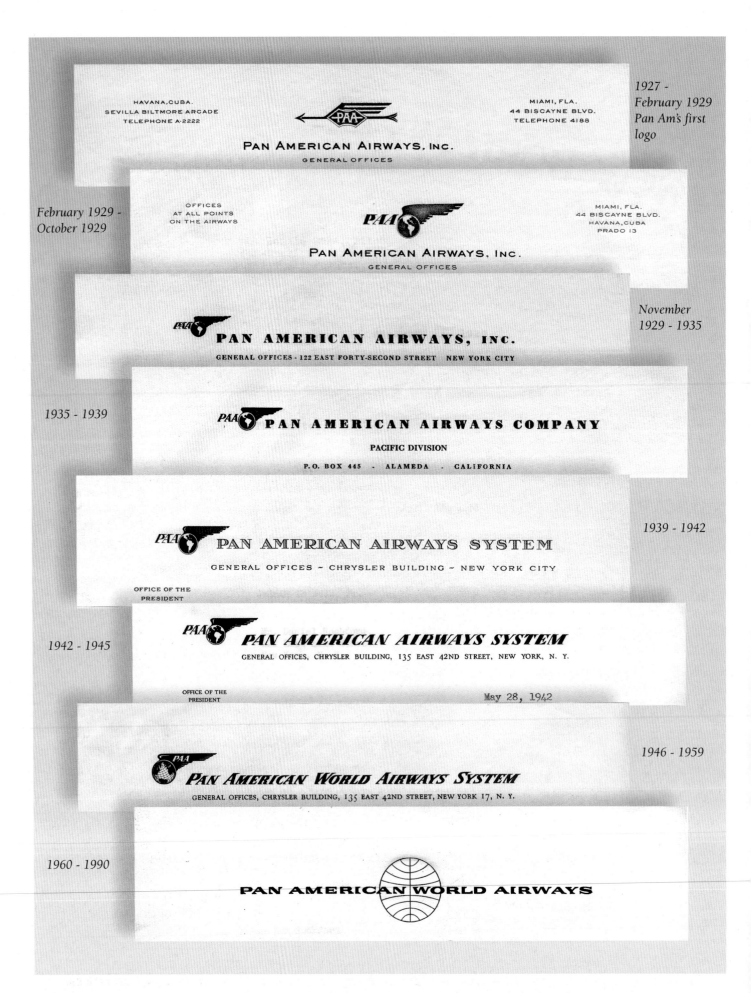

*1927 - February 1929 Pan Am's first logo*

HAVANA, CUBA.
SEVILLA BILTMORE ARCADE
TELEPHONE A-2222

MIAMI, FLA.
44 BISCAYNE BLVD.
TELEPHONE 4188

PAN AMERICAN AIRWAYS, INC.
GENERAL OFFICES

*February 1929 - October 1929*

OFFICES
AT ALL POINTS
ON THE AIRWAYS

MIAMI, FLA.
44 BISCAYNE BLVD.
HAVANA, CUBA
PRADO 13

PAN AMERICAN AIRWAYS, INC.
GENERAL OFFICES

*November 1929 - 1935*

PAN AMERICAN AIRWAYS, INC.
GENERAL OFFICES - 122 EAST FORTY-SECOND STREET   NEW YORK CITY

*1935 - 1939*

PAN AMERICAN AIRWAYS COMPANY

PACIFIC DIVISION

P.O. BOX 445  -  ALAMEDA  .  CALIFORNIA

*1939 - 1942*

PAN AMERICAN AIRWAYS SYSTEM
GENERAL OFFICES ~ CHRYSLER BUILDING ~ NEW YORK CITY

OFFICE OF THE
PRESIDENT

*1942 - 1945*

PAN AMERICAN AIRWAYS SYSTEM
GENERAL OFFICES, CHRYSLER BUILDING, 135 EAST 42ND STREET, NEW YORK, N. Y.

OFFICE OF THE
PRESIDENT                                        May 28, 1942

*1946 - 1959*

PAN AMERICAN WORLD AIRWAYS SYSTEM
GENERAL OFFICES, CHRYSLER BUILDING, 135 EAST 42ND STREET, NEW YORK 17, N. Y.

*1960 - 1990*

PAN AMERICAN WORLD AIRWAYS

Much of my research was done from the original company correspondence and it was interesting to see how the design of the logo changed through the years. Also note that Pan Am's name changed from letterhead to letterhead.

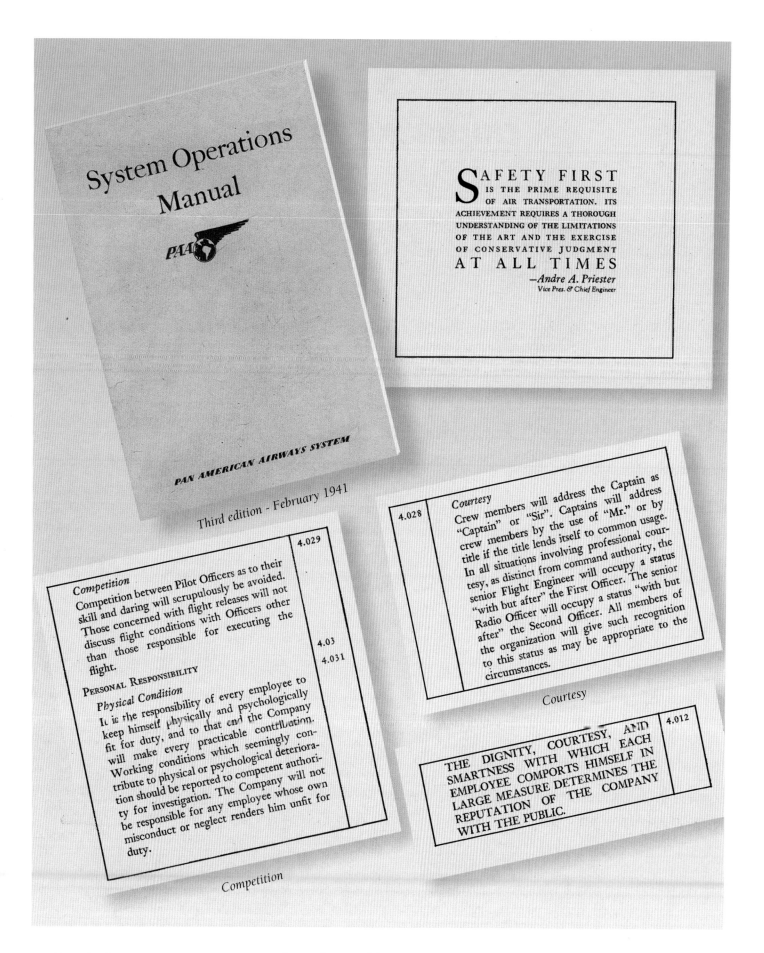

System Operations Manual

PAA

PAN AMERICAN AIRWAYS SYSTEM

*Third edition - February 1941*

**S**AFETY FIRST IS THE PRIME REQUISITE OF AIR TRANSPORTATION. ITS ACHIEVEMENT REQUIRES A THOROUGH UNDERSTANDING OF THE LIMITATIONS OF THE ART AND THE EXERCISE OF CONSERVATIVE JUDGMENT AT ALL TIMES

—*Andre A. Priester*
*Vice Pres. & Chief Engineer*

**Competition**

4.029

Competition between Pilot Officers as to their skill and daring will scrupulously be avoided. Those concerned with flight releases will not discuss flight conditions with Officers other than those responsible for executing the flight.

4.03

PERSONAL RESPONSIBILITY

4.031

*Physical Condition*

It is the responsibility of every employee to keep himself physically and psychologically fit for duty, and to that end the Company will make every practicable contribution. Working conditions which seemingly contribute to physical or psychological deterioration should be reported to competent authority for investigation. The Company will not be responsible for any employee whose own misconduct or neglect renders him unfit for duty.

Competition

4.028

*Courtesy*

Crew members will address the Captain as "Captain" or "Sir". Captains will address crew members by the use of "Mr." or by title if the title lends itself to common usage. In all situations involving professional courtesy, as distinct from command authority, the senior Flight Engineer will occupy a status "with but after" the First Officer. The senior Radio Officer will occupy a status "with but after" the Second Officer. All members of the organization will give such recognition to this status as may be appropriate to the circumstances.

Courtesy

4.012

THE DIGNITY, COURTESY, AND SMARTNESS WITH WHICH EACH EMPLOYEE COMPORTS HIMSELF IN LARGE MEASURE DETERMINES THE REPUTATION OF THE COMPANY WITH THE PUBLIC.

Pan Am's system operations manual was first published in November of 1929. The second edition was March 1931 and the third edition illustrated above is from February 1941. A few interesting sections are shown from the 48-page booklet.

All of these original source materials have allowed me to tell **"The Rest of the Story"** of Pan Am's Pacific Pioneers.

# CHILDRENS' BOOKS

1939

1939

Children's books featured stories about the Clipper ships during the late 1930's and early 1940's. The stories appealed equally to young girls and boys.

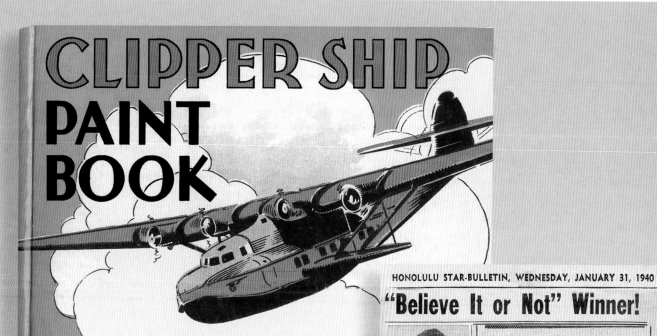

1937

Catherine Berst was given the coloring book when she flew on the China Clipper in 1938. She made the *Honolulu Star-Bulletin's* "Believe it or Not" section as a result of her air travel.

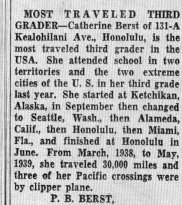

HONOLULU STAR-BULLETIN, WEDNESDAY, JANUARY 31, 1940

## "Believe It or Not" Winner!

### THIRD PRIZE WINNER

MOST TRAVELED THIRD GRADER—Catherine Berst of 131-A Kealohilani Ave., Honolulu, is the most traveled third grader in the USA. She attended school in two territories and the two extreme cities of the U. S. in her third grade last year. She started at Ketchikan, Alaska, in September then changed to Seattle, Wash., then Alameda, Calif., then Honolulu, then Miami, Fla., and finished at Honolulu in June. From March, 1938, to May, 1939, she traveled 30,000 miles and three of her Pacific crossings were by clipper plane.

P. B. BERST,
C/o Pan-American Airways.

Front - 1940

Back

feet, and accommodations are provided for thirty-two passengers and a crew of five. The four motors are Wright Cyclones of 1,120 horsepower each. They give the ship a speed of nearly 250 m.p.h. when fully loaded.

Another extra-size design by this same manufacturer is the Boeing 314 or *Yankee Clipper*. This ship is by far the largest flying boat yet constructed in this country. It has an enormous single wing of 152-foot span. The weight fully loaded is forty two tons! Four motors give 6,000 horsepower. All-metal construction is used throughout.

Luxurious cabins, on two deck levels, accommodate seventy-two passengers and a crew of eight. Cargo space in the wing carries 5,000 pounds of mail and express. The living quarters for the crew are also located in the spacious wing interior. The speed is stated to be 200 m.p.h.

This leviathan is now in the transatlantic service of Pan-American Airways, plying between the United States and Europe. Thus, constant progress has provided the American air transport operators with the world's finest aircraft and equipment. It has given our country the leadership in commercial aviation, and has won for our air lines the title of "the world's finest."

The development in American military aircraft has been equally impressive. Here again the influence of the record breaker is reflected in the details of design which contribute to efficiency and performance—elements all-important to the fighting craft of our air services. So swift is the pace of progress that the ships we now regard as the "last word" may be obsolete a few months hence.

The North American O-47 is an all-metal, mid-wing monoplane with retractable landing gear.

BOEING CLIPPER

1939

---

## PAN AMERICAN CLIPPER INAUGURATES AMERICA'S FIRST TRANSATLANTIC AIR TRANSPORT SERVICE

With the sweep of its wings the first *China Clipper* ripped out weeks of slow surface travel to the rich markets of the Far East. By 1936 a trip from this country to China was measured by a matter of sixty or seventy flight hours instead of by weeks.

It was not the big clipper planes alone that built the far-flung Pan American Airways. Juan Trippe visualized his world airways system and then picked the finest experts in every field to carry out his plans. Former diplomats covered the proposed routes long before the Clippers flew them. There was, of course, no freedom of the air. No plane could fly over a foreign country without permission. Trippe's emissaries had to get franchises. Germany, France, Britain, and Holland were after franchises in South America too. There, as in the Far East, they got the rights to fly, not by government pressure, but by selling aviation as a valuable business asset to any nation.

Once Trippe had his franchises, he sent experts to explore and lay out routes. They carved airports out of jungles and Arctic wastes, and in places where no white man ever had penetrated. The supply problems overcome and the engineering marvels performed by Trippe's advance men would furnish plots for a dozen movie thrillers. In laying out the bases at Wake and Guam on the Pacific route, more than one million separate items were bought, shipped, and installed before the first *China Clipper* took off from San Francisco.

Pan American's map added another blue line after the Pacific route was under way. This time it was to Alaska, and another distant travel time could be reckoned in flight hours rather than ocean days.

Then came the Atlantic and the giant Boeing 314 Pan American *Clippers*.

1939 - 1945

WINGSPAN 152 FEET
LENGTH 106 FEET

THE HUGE LONG-RANGE BOEING *CLIPPER* WEIGHED 41-TONS.

POWER

FOUR 14-CYLINDER 1,500-HP RADIAL ENGINES

FOUR 3-BLADED PROPELLERS WITH A DIAMETER OF 14 FEET FURNISHED THE *THRUST* FOR THE PLANE.

SPEED ONE HOUR
175 MILES

THE BOEING *CLIPPER* HAD A TOP SPEED OF 190 MILES PER HOUR AND COULD FLY NON-STOP FOR 3,100 MILES WITH 40 PASSENGERS. IT WAS OF ALL-METAL CONSTRUCTION AND DIVIDED INTO ELEVEN SECTIONS BY BULK-HEADS. IT HAD AN UPPER DECK FOR THE FLIGHT CREW AND STORAGE SPACE. THE MAIN DECK WAS DIVIDED INTO TEN COMPARTMENTS FOR PASSENGERS. BELOW THIS DECK WERE A SERIES OF WATERTIGHT COMPARTMENTS. A PASSAGE THROUGH THE WINGS PERMITTED THE SERVICING OF THE ENGINES DURING FLIGHT.

RANGE 3,100 MILES

CEILING 15,000+ FEET

PAYLOAD
74 DAY PASSENGERS. OR 40 SLEEPER PASSENGERS.
A CREW OF 8 TO 15 PLUS 2 TONS OF MAIL

THE FIRST BOEING *CLIPPER* TO SPAN THE ATLANTIC WAS THE LARGEST COMMERCIAL AIRPLANE IN THE WORLD. THE *CLIPPER* WAS EQUIPPED WITH EVERY AVAILABLE SAFETY DEVICE AND LUXURIOUSLY FITTED FOR THE DAY AND NIGHT COMFORT OF THE PASSENGERS. THE STURDY, SAFE *CLIPPERS* OPENED A NEW ERA OF AIR TRAVEL.

Boeing achieved such excellent results with its two-engined planes that its engineers went on to plan four-engined super-planes. When Juan Trippe wanted a plane for his Atlantic service, Boeing was ready with the 41-ton Boeing 314. The 314 *Atlantic Clippers* carried 74 passengers and boasted of compartments that could be converted into berths, dressing rooms, a dining salon, and a real kitchen for serving hot meals aloft. On May 20, 1939, just twenty years after the first transatlantic flight of the Navy NC's, the *Atlantic Clipper* took off on the trip that inaugurated Pan American Airways service to Europe. Juan Trippe's dream was reaching around the world.

*The Story of American Aviation - 1946*

TRAVEL BY AIR

1099

TRAVEL BY AIR

By

Dorothy Judd Sickels

WHITMAN PUBLISHING COMPANY
Copyright 1940 by
RACINE, WISCONSIN
Printed in the United States of America

*1940*

FAMOUS PLANES
*and*
FAMOUS FLIGHTS

IRVIN L HOLCOMBE

PR. MCMXL THE PLATT & MUNK CO., INC.          MADE IN U.S.

FAMOUS PLANES
*and*
FAMOUS FLIGHTS

*By*
JOHN WINSLOW

*Illustrations by*
IRVIN L. HOLCOMBE

·NEW·YORK·
·THE·PLATT·&·MUNK·CO·INC·
·PUBLISHERS·

SIKORSKY S-42 BERMUDA CLIPPER

*1940*

661

STORIES ABOUT YOUNG AMERICANS

# ATLANTIC CLIPPER

ELLEN K. DONOHUE, B.S.

Director of Speech Education and Remedial Reading
Midtown Branch, Ethical Culture School, New York

OXFORD UNIVERSITY PRESS · NEW YORK

THIS IS A STORY ABOUT BILL. BILL
LIVES IN A BEAUTIFUL APARTMENT AT THE TOP
OF AN APARTMENT HOUSE. BILL'S FATHER HAS BIG
... THE SEA SHORE. BUT
... THESE THINGS. WE
... ON IN THE AIR—ON A
... CAN TAKE A TRIP IN
... EXCITED ABOUT IT.

... DONOHUE, 1940

STORIES ABOUT YOUNG AMERICANS

# ATLANTIC CLIPPER

By ELLEN K. DONOHUE

ILLUSTRATED BY JOHN USHLER

OXFORD UNIVERSITY PRESS · NEW YORK

*Given by Pan Am on Atlantic flights - 1940-1941*

# Allan and Brenda on a Clipper

By Joyce Newbill Martin

Illustrated by Hal Forrest

*1942*

"Oh boy!" shouted Allan, "we're going to fly!"

# Allan and Brenda on a Clipper

By Joyce Newbill M...
Illustrated by Hal Fo...

Santa Barbara
Wallace Hebberd, Publisher
1942

1936

1938

### Flyer Killed

WILLIAM S. GROOCH.

* * *

## GROOCHES DIE IN MEXICO PLANE CRASH

### Pan American Trail-blazer Down in Snow

Word was received here today of the deaths in tn airplane accident in Mexico of William S. Grooch, former Pan-American Airways engineer and writer, and his wife and a Mexican pilot.

They were killed Monday night 70 miles east of Mazatlan when their plane crashed during a snowstorm on the Sierra Madre range. Mr. Grooch was surveying a route for Lineas Aereas Mineras, a Mexican airways system.

A naval flyer during the World War, he joined Pan-American Airways in 1928 and worked for it until 1937. He was executive officer of the crew which built the base on Wake Island. He wrote "From Crate to Clipper," a biography of Captain Edwin Musick, Pan-America pilot lost near Pago Pago last year.

Surprisingly few contemporary books were written about Pan Am during the 1935 - 1946 period. By far the best known are the three books written by William S. Grooch, who was in charge of the expedition that built the bases on Wake and Midway. In his foreword to **Skyway to Asia**, he explains that it is the story of his personal experiences, not an official company record of the expedition.

---

*"This book will come as a great surprise to my associates who were not consulted in its preparation. The last thing they and the Company would expect from me would be a book! This book salutes them all in my name".*

**William Steven Grooch**

---

1939

1941

His second book, **Winged Highway** tells of the part he played in the development of Pan Am in South America and China. It was described as lively reading and well illustrated.

His last book **From Crate to Clipper, with Captain Musick, Pioneer Pilot,** recounts the life of the famed pilot, Edwin Musick. The book was written in 1939, just the year after Musick died on the third flight to New Zealand.

**Over and Above our Pacific**, by Charles Paar, tells the story of a New York businessman who flew on the Clipper to Hong Kong in September of 1940. The book was published in 1941 before Pearl Harbor. The book was described as giving an exciting and comprehensive picture of the Pacific area on the eve of war.

1947

1943

Front

1937

Back

**Wings Over Wake** by Dorothy Kaucher recounts her flight in August of 1937 when she flew on the Hawaii Clipper with Captain Edwin Musick to Hong Kong. She apparently had a crush on Edwin Musick.

**Empire of the Air – Juan Trippe and the Struggle for World Airways** was written by Matthew Josephson in 1943. The publisher claims that: "In the spirit of candor, Mr. Josephson has taken up the many controversial issues raised by Juan Trippe's career". The book is interesting because it is the first book that deals with Trippe's rise to power in the field of commercial aviation.

Also included is the booklet, **My Ride on the China Clipper's Trans-Pacific Flight** published by Luther Y.P. Chang. It recounts his trip across the Pacific on the China Clipper in February of 1937.

# MAGAZINES FEATURING PAN AM

August 23, 1937

October 20, 1941

July 31, 1933

December 2, 1935

August 1939

April 1937

December 1936

Pan Am Pacific flights were the talk of the nation in the late 1930s. Therefore it is not surprising that the popular magazines of the day featured the airline's most recent accomplishments. Illustrated is a small selection of the contemporary magazines featuring Pan Am.

*December 1936*

CAN THEY BOMB US? By FLETCHER PRATT

*December 2, 1939*

*April 27, 1935*

*October 1938*

*December 1938*

**New York Times Magazine**

*April 27, 1935*

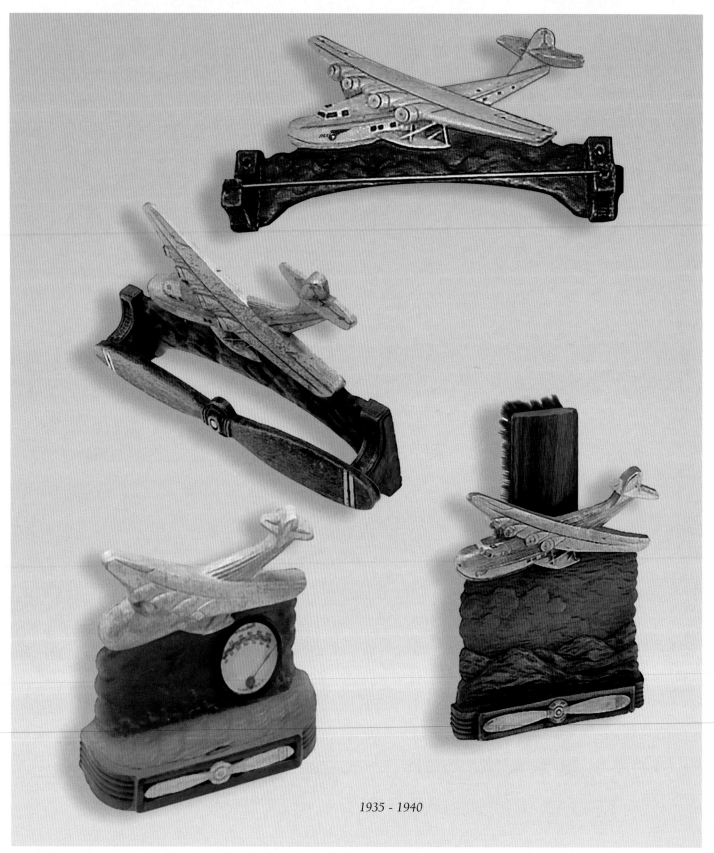

*1935 - 1940*

To capitalize on the popularity of Clipper Ships, tie racks, hair brushes and thermometers all carried the likeness of the Martin M-130. The table clock has the Pan Am logo.

Notebook - 1940

Coaster - wood burn design 1936

Ashtray - 1944-1950

1935 - 1940

1940

An album of International Air Liners distributed by
John Player & Sons -
Illustrated is the front cover of the album and page 17
showing Pan Am's Glenn Martin Flying-boat "China Clipper"

1940s

1940

1940

1936

In 1935 the Heinz Company of Pittsburgh produced as a sales promotion a series of 25 cards featuring various aircraft of the period - The Sikorsky S-42 was featured on the cover and on card number 3

Card number 3

Rare 1932 playing card

1950 - 1960

1943 - 1955

1945 - 1960

Aircraft Beverage of Stratford Conn.
used the Sikorsky S-42 for its logo -
The beverage company was located
close to the Sikorsky aircraft factory
in Bridgeport Conn. - 1935

Martin M-130 - 1936 - the end of the stereoview era

Because of the popularity of the Pan Am clipper ships at that time, many
manufacturers of different products would lift Pan Am's graphics for their
packaging as the illustrated example below shows

1935

# PAN AM ADVERTISING

Before 1940 Pan Am's magazine advertising was exclusively in black and white. In this section I have only included color advertising done by the company that related, at least in part, to the Pacific Clipper flights. I would welcome seeing examples of other color advertising done by Pan Am that I have failed to include.

# AMERICA'S PIONEERING GOE

IF some composer could capture the march of America in one
great symphony, this is what you would hear:

The war-whoop of Indians, the creaking of covered wagons,
the ring of the woodsman's axe, the clank of the surveyor's
chain. You'd hear the wind whistling through the rigging
of Clipper Ships, the deep-throated snort of the iron horse, the
staccato roar of the first automobile and airplane engines.

Blending with those sounds and rising above them all would
be a *new* note—the whir of Pan American propellers. Today
those propellers speed America's flag of aerial commerce—passen-

gers, express and mail—to 55 countries and colonies over
miles of air routes. *But only twelve years ago—*

A group of young Americans set out—some by foot,
muleback. They carved air bases from jungles; colonized
islands; built radio stations and developed navigationa
Designers created new-type planes, the multi-motored
Clippers. Pilots were trained in ocean flying. There we
liant achievements in engineering, meteorology, mainte

With a precision that thrilled the world, those trail-b
Pan American Clippers took whole continents and oce

674

# ON . . . . BY FLYING CLIPPERS

# It is a small world... by Pan A

LOOK carefully at the map above. Notice the short air route joining the United States and Cuba. Twelve years ago that route—90 miles—was the entire Pan American Airways System. Compare that distance on the map with the total network regularly flown by Pan American Clippers *today* ... 65,000 miles of skyways joining fifty-five countries and colonies!

Think what this change signifies. It means a world shrunk to one-sixth its former size by the magic of air transportation. It means that those great silver shuttles, the Flying Clipper Ships, are weaving a new fabric of friendly relations with once-distant peoples who are now our neighbors.

It means a new American leadership in this changing world! Those Flying Clipper Ships are America's Merchant Marine of the Air. They are recapturing,

on international trade routes, a prestige that has been lost to this cou since the days of sail.

Yankee enterprise has had to struggle against big odds. In the fac keen foreign-flag competition there were complex franchises to be ne ated, routes to be blazed, new-type planes to be developed. There were to be trained, radio and weather stations to be established, desert island be colonized for air bases. Mile by mile the routes of the Clippers advanced through the Latin Americas ... then across the Pacific, ove Atlantic, up to Alaska, down to Australasia. The story isn't ended. Yet tod

Pan American speeds passengers, merchandise and mail between n 250 points, makes connections with other transportation lines to hund

## ...rican

## ...NT MARINE OF THE AIR

Pan American planes have flown 1,400,000 persons 525,000,000 miles. ...than 2,300,000 tons of express cargo and mails have been carried! A ...f 130 Clippers maintains schedules at better than 98% regularity. ...herever you live in America, a Pan American terminal city is quickly ...ible. You can get passenger details at any travel bureau or transportation ...ffice; express information at any Railway Express office; air mail data ...post office... and all three at any Pan American office. ...hether you want to see fascinating lands, reach new markets with sales... ...nd merchandise, or give wings to your letters, the Flying Clippers are ... They have shortened travel weeks to days, and days to ... Truly, it is a small world today... by Pan American. *IT PAYS TO FLY*

The Pan American Airways System
### ROUTES OF THE
### FLYING CLIPPER SHIPS

===== SERVICE ACTIVELY OPERATED
===== SERVICE PLANNED AND PENDING
===== SERVICE TEMPORARILY SUSPENDED
----- PRINCIPAL U.S. CONNECTING AIRLINES

America's Merchant Marine of the Air
serving 55 countries, colonies and islands
along 65,000 miles of airplanes

## PAA

# PAN AMERICAN
### AIRWAYS SYSTEM

677

# ~~saved~~ *aaved a century*

## ...when Pan American Clippers brought China modern air-transport services ten years ago

~~s~~ IT USED TO BE in the United States before ~~~~ 1830, China's main arteries of travel, up ~~l~~ 1933, were her rivers. The *Yangtze Kiang* ~~~~ her Mississippi and the *Grand Canal* her ~~~~ Canal.

~~B~~ut China skipped the railway age which ~~~~had in North America. When Pan Ameri-World Airways, in 1933 joined the Chinese ~~~~vernment in ownership and operation of ~~~~ then 4-year old China National Aviation ~~~~poration, that country had only 6,000 ~~~~s of railway routes.

Very shortly after that, starting with 3,000 ~~~~s of air routes, the total of China's *air ~~te mileage* came to surpass the total of ~~~~na's *railroad mileage*. Days of slow, up-~~~~am river travel were cut to *hours*. Moun-~~~~ barriers vanished. A 14-day journey by ~~~~n chair from Chungking to Chengtu was ~~~~ed into an easy, 2-hour flight.

*China had saved a century!*

* * *

~~~~Since then, with the Burma road closed by Japanese, planes flown by American and ~~P~~an American-trained Chinese pilots of the ~~~~na National Aviation Corporation* have been ~~~~na's only link between Chungking and the ~~~~side world.

Modern air transport may yet turn out to

have saved China something more precious than a century . . . It may turn out, with the help of more fighting planes, that air transport will have been a great factor in saving Chinese civilization itself.

* * *

*For the record:* Pan American inaugurated its trans-Pacific Clipper service to the Philippines in 1935—but two years after effecting its association with China National Aviation Corporation.

This historic victory over the vast spaces of the world's largest ocean *preceded* by four years Pan American's conquest of the Atlantic. Scheduled flight over the route from San Francisco, to Midway, to Wake, to Guam, to Manila represents the establishment of the first over-ocean air transport service in the world's history.

In 1937, as illustrated to the left, this service was extended to Hong Kong, China. A new chapter in U. S.-China trade and cultural relations had begun!

Interrupted by the outrage of Pearl Harbor, this service forecast a brilliant post-war future for air travel between the two great republics. Victory for the United Nations means that this forecast will become reality, with Chungking only 20 hours by air from the U.S. West Coast.

### *8,616 People* safe out of Burma by air

Together with the U.S. Army Air Forces and the R.A.F., *China National Aviation Corporation* evacuated 8,616 soldiers, civilians, women and children out of Burma by air in 1942.

Much of the flying (to avoid Jap Zeros) had to be done at night. Overloaded planes had to climb above the 8,000-foot mountains which lie between Burma and India. Ice formation on aircraft was a regular occurrence . . . But C.N.A.C. pilots, trained by Pan American, got their unarmed planes through!

•

Of C.N.A.C. an American major said at that time (quoted from an AP dispatch), "*This is the best damned airline in the world. They fly only at night and in stinko weather.*"

*Daily and Sundays*, over a choice of routes, Pan American Clippers have long ~~~~n "rolling down to Rio"... *Tomorrow's* Clippers, far larger, faster and finer, will bring ~~~~ lovely Brazilian capital within 10½ hours of the United States for business or pleasure.

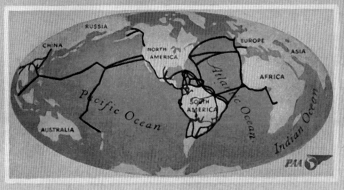

*The Routes of the Flying Clipper Ships*

THE PAN AMERICAN SYSTEM AS OF DEC. 7TH, 1941

# PAN AMERICAN WORLD AIRWAYS
## *Wings of Democracy*

# TOY CLIPPERS 1935 - 1946

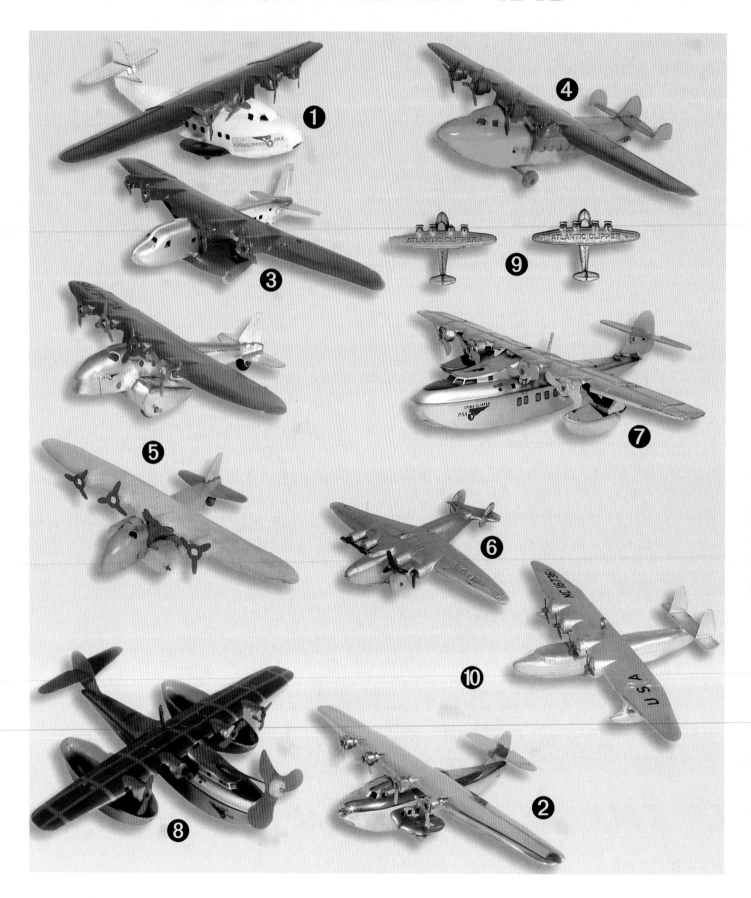

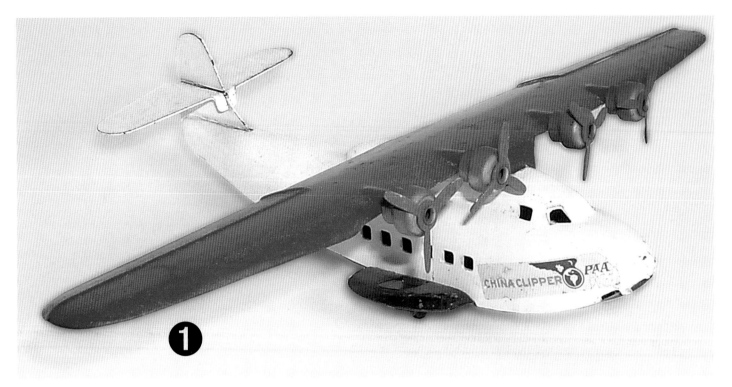

Childrens' toys have always reflected the adult world. Therefore, it is not surprising that in the late 1930s toy manufacturers began to produce toy Pan Am Clipper ships.

❶The most popular toy Clipper ships were manufactured by the Wyandotte Toy Company of Wyandotte, Michigan. The company was founded in the mid-1920s and went out of business in 1956. They were best known for their pressed steel, simply built, streamlined, art deco cars, trucks and airplanes. By far the most commonly seen toy airplane at toy shows and on eBay auctions is the China Clipper with a 13-inch wing span. It is usually seen with red wings and a white body, although the same airplane with blue wings is not uncommon. ❷By far the rarest version of this aircraft is the chrome-plated model, which is much more sturdily built than the simple pressed steel models. Almost 70 years after it was manufactured, it still looks as fresh as the day it was purchased for some excited young child.

❸The Martin M-130 toy airplane with the silver body and the 14-1/2 inch red wings appears to have been manufactured by the Wyandotte Company. It has not, however, been seen in toy catalogs, so it was possibly manufactured by a different company.

❹When the Boeing B-314 was introduced in 1939, the Wyandotte Company merely added two small vertical fins to the tail of the China Clipper and turned the China Clipper into a toy Boeing B-314.

**❺**The Marks Toy Company was founded in 1921 by Louis Marks who was formerly the managing director of the Ferdinand Strauss Toy Company. Marks specialized in low priced, quality toys. In April of 1972 he sold his company to the Quaker Oats Company, who in turn sold it to the European manufacturer, Dunbee-Combex-Marks. The company went bankrupt in 1980. Louis Marks died in 1982 at age 85.

The Martin Clipper with the 9-inch wingspan, manufactured by Marks, is seen in both the multicolored yellow, blue and pink variety and in the much more realistic silver with orange wings variety. The decals on the silver-bodied airplane are so small that they are barely readable, but with a magnifying glass the words "China Clipper 14716" can be read.

**❻**The Auburn Rubber Company was founded in 1913 in Auburn, Indiana as the Double Fabric Tire Corporation, making tires for model-Ts. It manufactured its first toys in 1935. The toy business went so well that approximately half of the company's 400 employees were devoted to toy making during the late 1930s. Although they are best known for their soldiers, they produced a Boeing B-314 NC 18601 in 1939. Probably for ease of construction they selected the twin tail fin version of the Boeing, rather than the triple fin tail, which was the final version manufactured by the Boeing Company. Unfortunately, rubber deteriorates over the years and the toy plane is always found with drooping wings and tail.

In 1960 the toy portion of the Auburn Rubber Company was purchased by the town of Deming, New Mexico. The company remained in New Mexico until it went out of business in 1969.

**❼**Probably the rarest toy airplane in my collection is the tin China Clipper with the eleven inch wingspan manufactured by J. Chein & Company in the late 1930s. Julius Chein was a one armed immigrant who founded his toy company in 1903 and who went on to become a leader in the toy making industry in America. In the 1930s the toy plant had 250 employees and was located in Harrison, New Jersey. In 1950 they moved the operation to Burlington, New Jersey. By the late 1970s, the business had gone into decline and it was sold to the Atlantic Products Company in 1987. They filed for bankruptcy in 1992.

**❽**In a beautifully produced book, *J. Chein & Company – A Collector's Guide*, a slightly different version of the China Clipper is pictured. The wind-up toy was capable of skimming across the water while being played with by a child. Although the China Clippers were beautifully made, the light tin construction and the wind-up mechanisms made them quite fragile. Today a Chein version of the China Clipper is difficult to locate in any condition.

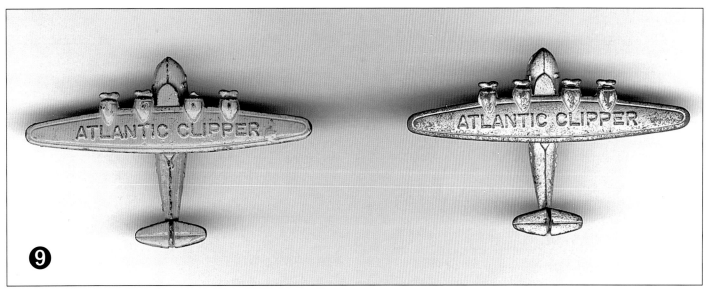

**❾** ❾The Tootsietoy Company was founded in 1893 by Samuel Daust and in 1911 he produced his first toy limousine. In 1922 a line of doll furniture was developed with the trade name Tootsietoy named after the daughter of the president, Tootsie Daust. Many of the oldest Tootsietoy vehicles were made in such large numbers and for so long a period of time that they are not hard to find today. The company has become the Strombecker Corporation, and it continues to make toys such as the metal marker pieces used in Monopoly games.

Although the company made a large variety of toy airplanes, the only Pan Am Clipper by Tootsietoy is the small diecast model with a 2-1/4 inch wingspan marked the Atlantic Clipper.

❿Dinky Toys were first made in England in 1932 under the name Modeled Miniatures. Production stopped during the war years and after several changes of ownership the company went out of business in 1988. The company's specialty was cars and airplanes. In the late 1930s they made the Pan Am Clipper, the Sikorsky S-42.

Illustrated is a well-detailed diecast model with a 6-1/2 inch wingspan. It carries a manufacturer's designation of 60W. In the pre-war version, the words "Pan American Clipper III Flying Boat" appear underneath the wing. An eyelet extends above the craft so that children could string the plane on a wire secured off the ground and push the plane along the wire so that it could "fly". Versions of this toy made after the war do not have the eyelet for flying the model. The Dinky toy was manufactured to a 1/212 scale, close to the common airliner scale of 1/200 that is popular today.

# CHRISTMAS CARDS

Pan Am personnel produced some colorful and unique Christmas cards during the short era of the flying boats in the Pacific. On the right is the earliest Christmas greeting in my collection. The Pan Am radiogram was sent by Captain Sullivan to the Pacific Division Manager Clarence Young in December of 1936.

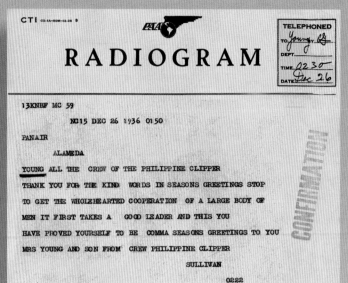

*December 1936*

In 1938 Theron E. Griffin, a flight engineer, produced by far the most interesting Pan Am Christmas card. While traveling as a crewmember on the China Clipper in December of 1938, he had the station manager at each stop apply a distinctive cachet to the card as the Clipper crossed the Pacific.

*December 1938*

Heartiest
Christmas and New Year
Greetings

*Juan Trippe sent out this greeting in 1936*

In December of 1939 Pan Am sent a calendar for 1940 showing the China Clipper heading for the new Treasure Island base.

Merry Christmas

Greetings on'wing from Hawaii!
Soaring to you thru' the night
Into the dawn--from over the sea
Acclaiming this epochal flight.

Distance afar now diminished
From the Isles of Paradise
Will hasten messages cherished
By man's triumph of the skies.

R.P.S.

Care with Envelope.    Dad

*Card from Honolulu - 1936*

SEASONS GREETINGS

January - 1940

Sun - Mon - Tue - Wed - Thu - Fri - Sat

|  |  | 1 | 2 | 3 | 4 | 5 | 6 |
| 7 | 8 | 9 | 10 | 11 | 12 | 13 |
| 14 | 15 | 16 | 17 | 18 | 19 | 20 |
| 21 | 22 | 23 | 24 | 25 | 26 | 27 |
| 28 | 29 | 30 | 31 |  |  |  |

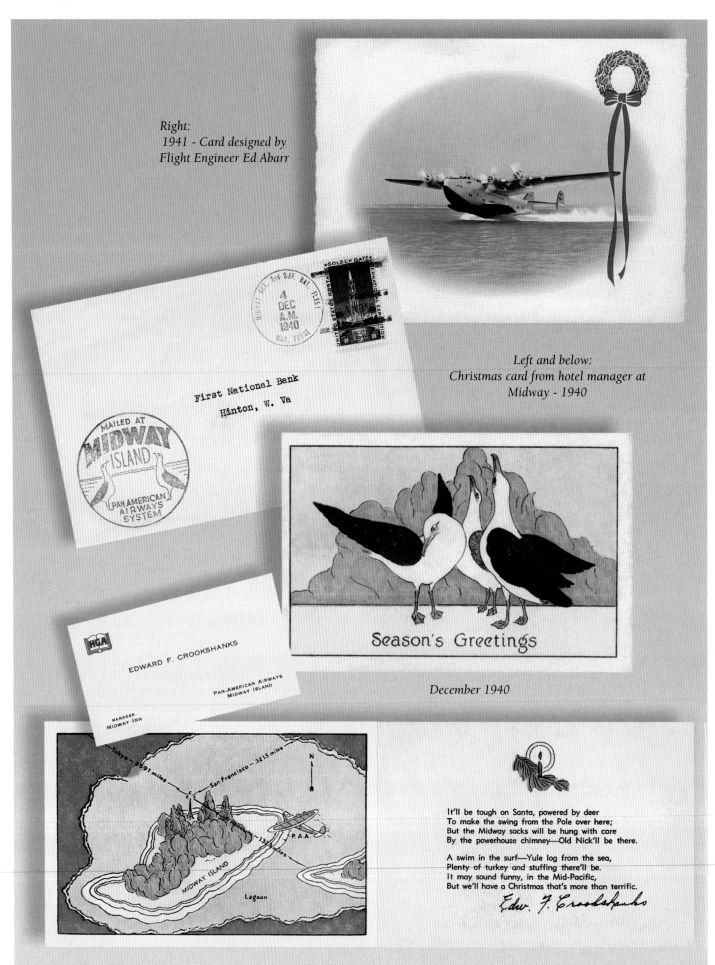

*Right:*
*1941 - Card designed by*
*Flight Engineer Ed Abarr*

First National Bank
Hinton, W. Va

MAILED AT
MIDWAY
ISLAND
PAN AMERICAN
AIRWAYS
SYSTEM

*Left and below:*
*Christmas card from hotel manager at*
*Midway - 1940*

Season's Greetings

HGA

EDWARD F. CROOKSHANKS

PAN-AMERICAN AIRWAYS
MIDWAY ISLAND

MANAGER
MIDWAY INN

*December 1940*

It'll be tough on Santa, powered by deer
To make the swing from the Pole over here;
But the Midway socks will be hung with care
By the powerhouse chimney—Old Nick'll be there.

A swim in the surf—Yule log from the sea,
Plenty of turkey and stuffing there'll be.
It may sound funny, in the Mid-Pacific,
But we'll have a Christmas that's more than terrific.

Edw. F. Crookshanks

In December of 1940 the manager of Pan Am's hotel on Midway Island sent a Christmas greeting to his friends. It is interesting that he mailed his card using slow sea mail, rather than the more expensive but much faster Clipper mail

*Front of card - 1943*

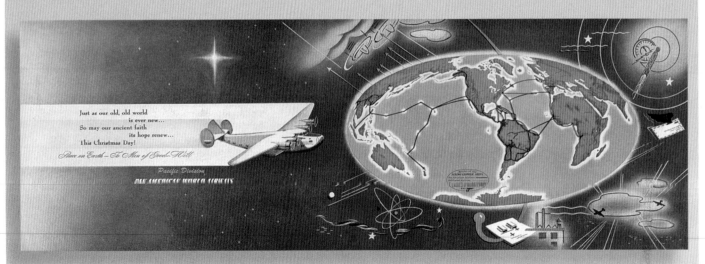

*Inside of card - 1943*

The last Christmas card in my collection was sent by the Pacific Division in December of 1943. It is surprising that they would send such an elaborate card during the austere war years.

# ARTIST

*Bob Jenny with President Bush - 1990*

The renowned aviation artist, Bob Jenny, produced the paintings used for both the cover of this book and the cover of the first book published by Jon Krupnick. Bob's remarkable career spans over forty years. He enjoys a national reputation as a muralist and aviation artist. His works have been hung in both Camp David and the White House. He is pictured presenting a painting to then - President George Bush of the TBF torpedo plane Bush flew in WW II.

Prints of Bob Jenny's paintings of the Pan Am Clipper ships are on permanent exhibit at the San Francisco Airport Museum, the University of Miami Richter Library and, before its demise, the corporate offices of Pan Am in Miami. Bob's work captures the romance and excitement of Pan Am's Clipper ships. The beautiful 40 inch by 60 inch original oil painting on canvas used for the cover of this book is available. For details, contact the author.

# POSTERS

Four beautiful posters featured in **Pacific Pioneers - The Rest of the Story** are available from **Aviationposters.com.** Two of the posters were produced from Bob Jenny's original paintings. They are available both in regular and in a limited edition of 1500 artist signed and numbered prints. The other two prints were provided from original posters in the author's collection. **Aviationposters.com** also offers many of the Clyde Sunderland photographs produced from the original negatives. Visit **Aviationposters.com** web site at **www.aviationposters.com.** There is a $15.00 shipping and handling charge on all poster orders.

| Clippers Unite the Pacific | The Last Clipper | Hawaii Overnight | Yankee Clippers |
|---|---|---|---|
|  |  |  |  |
| Image - 16" x 24"<br>Paper - 20" x 26"<br>•<br>PAA 3 - $65.00<br>(Artist signed 1500 limited)<br>•<br>PAA 4 - $40.00 | Image - 16" x 24"<br>Paper - 20" x 26"<br>•<br>PAA 5 - $65.00<br>(Artist signed 1500 limited)<br>•<br>PAA 6 - $40.00 | Image - 19" x 34"<br>Paper - 25" x 39"<br>•<br>PAA 7 - $50.00 | Image - 20" x 16"<br>Paper - 26" x 20"<br>•<br>PAA 8 - $40.00 |

**Aviationposters.com**
P.O. Box 30567, Santa Barbara, California 93130-0567
Phone: (800) 962-3373 • Fax: (805) 884-0409
E-mail: sales@aviationposters.com
Web page: www.aviationposters.com

*SHIPPING U.S.A. $15.00*
*PER ORDER*
OUTSIDE U.S.A. charged at cost
Sales tax where applicable

# SPECIAL LIMITED EDITION

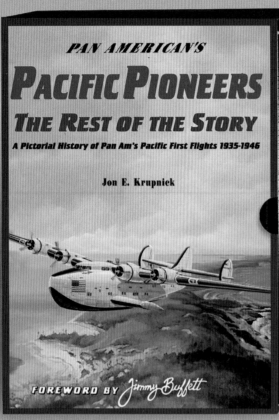
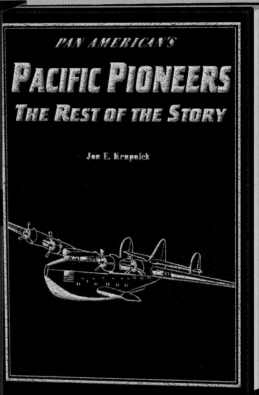

- Limited to 250 author signed and numbered books
- Leather-bound - Silver embossed cover
- Cloth cover slipcase
- Purchase price includes certificate for selection of one FREE poster from the posters illustrated on page 690

(Add $15.00 shipping charge for free poster)

## TO ORDER

| | |
|---|---|
| **Leather-bound Limited Edition..............$250.00**<br>Shipping and handling-add...............$6.00 | **Regular Hard Cover Book with Dust Jacket...$59.95**<br>Shipping and handling-add.....................$6.00 |

Please add sales tax where applicable - Shipping outside U.S. charged at cost

## Pictorial Histories Publishing Company Inc.

713 South Third Street West, Missoula, Montana 59801

Telephone: 888-763-8350 • FAX: 406-728-9280 • e-mail: phpc@montana.com

Web site: http://www.montana.com/phpc/stancvr.htm

# ACKNOWLEDGEMENTS

So many people have helped me with the research and production of this book, that I must, by necessity, keep my acknowledgements very short, or else this section would take several pages as well.

Fred Wolfe, who did the computer graphics on my first book, worked tirelessly to produce this new book. Without his goodwill the project could never have been completed.

To the extent humanly possible, I wanted to eliminate both typographical and factual errors. To this end Dr. Sally Moreman, a Ph.D. in English, provided much appreciated guidance and support. She also wrote the text for the flyleaf of the dust jacket.

As we neared completion James A. Tierney, an aerospace sales engineer, aviation historian and proof reader extraordinaire, went over the final drafts and caught and corrected literally hundreds of items. He gave me great confidence and I am extremely appreciative for his outstanding help.

Collector John Johnson has an unsurpassed knowledge of Pan Am history, particularly in the Pacific, and he shared this knowledge with me unselfishly. Tremendous help was also received from all of the following people and organizations and I thank them all for their assistance. They are acknowledged in no particular order and to each of them I extend my sincere thank you: Alan Klein (flight covers); Captain Al Raithel (naval research); Julius Grigore (aviation historian); Bryan A. Jones (postal historian – Fiji); Robert Caldwell (photographs); Leon Callaway (Los Angeles photographs); Miriam Rothe (widow of flight mechanic "Swede" Rothe); DeSoto Brown (Bishop Museum, Honolulu); Ted Drum (cigarette book); Fred Chan (playing cards); Keith Giles (researcher – Auckland City Library); Alistair Carlisle (Auckland War Memorial Museum); Museum of Transport, Technology and Social History – Auckland; Richard R. Wallin (Pan Am china); Richard W. Luckin (Pan Am china); George K. Sioras (Pan Am historian); R. Teichman (Franklin D. Roosevelt Library); E. Burke Haywood (passenger flight to Hong Kong); George Constantini (V-mail); Dr. Roger Schnell (postal rates and flight schedules); Diane Billingsley (Almon Gray's scrapbooks); Alex Vucetich (Danilo Vucetich's scrapbooks); Catherine Berst Lytton (Phil Berst's scrapbooks); David M. Abarr (David Abarr's scrapbooks); Tim Young (Clarence Young's scrapbooks); Wayne E. Moyer (model airplanes); Ted Bahry (Wake Island); Dan McGlaun (eclipse photo at Canton Island); Geoffrey Brewster (Philippines); Heinz Gappe (outstanding cover dealer – located FDR cover on back of dust jacket); Ken Snyder (Emil Buehler Naval Aviation Library); David H. Grover (Schooner Kinkajou); Robert Browning (U.S. Coast Guard historian); William E. Brown, Jr. (head of archives and special collections, including the Pan Am archives – Otto Richter Library of the University of Miami); Stan Baumwald (flight pins and badges); Greg Schmitt (flight covers); Art Pesin (fellow collector); Emillie G. Johnston (Guam Recorder); Robert Wilcsek (flight covers); Allen Crockwell (memorabilia); Roselyn Kenler (Dr. Ken Kenler's scrapbook); Judy Belan (Augustana College – Dr. Fryxell's papers); R.H. McCrory (mechanic on the Clippers in the early 1940s); Wil Trout (construction worker on North Haven); Capt. Guy McCaffrey (Pan Am Clipper pilot); Taitano Research Library, Micronesia Research Center – Guam; Judy Mazurek and Debbie Marema (two of my secretaries who provided valuable assistance).

A special thanks to Barbara and Bob Eggleson, my sister and brother-in-law, for their encouragement and help. Barbara, a postcard dealer in Port St. Lucie, Florida (561-466-7305) not only found postcards for my collection, but also found several Pan Am people who have shared their fathers' mementoes and whose stories I have now told in this new book.

Once again, a very, very special thanks to Cheryl Bauer, who typed and retyped this text. She is a true professional with a wonderful, helping attitude. I never could have completed the project without her help.

# BIBLIOGRAPHY

## BOOKS
Baylor, Lt. Col. Walter L.J., **The Last Man Off Wake Island:** The Bobbs-Merrill Co., New York, 1943
Bender, Marylin and Altschul, Selig, **The Chosen Instrument:** Juan Trippe, Pan Am: Simon & Schuster, New York, 1982
Brock, Horace, **Flying the Oceans: A Pilot's Story of Pan Am, 1935-55:** Stinehour Press, Lunenburg, Vermont, 1980
Bryan, E. H., Jr., **Panala'au Memoirs:** Bishop Museum, Honolulu, Hawaii, 1974
Cleveland, Reginald, **Air Transport at War:** M. Harper & Brothers Publishing, New York, 1946
Cohen, Stan, **Wings to the Orient: Pan American Clipper Planes, 1935-45:** Pictorial Histories Publishing Co., Missoula, Montana, 1985
Cunningham, W. Scott, **Wake Island Command:** Little Brown & Co., Boston, 1961
Daley, Robert, **An American Saga:** Juan Trippe and his Pan Am Empire: Random House, New York, 1980
Davies, R.E.G., **Pan Am - An Airlines and Its Aircraft:** Orion Books, New York, 1987
Dover, Ed, **The Long Way Home:** Ed Dover & Paladwr Press, McLean, Virginia, 1999
Driscoll, Ian H., **Flight Paths of South Pacific:** Whitcombe & Tombs, Ltd., Christchurch, N.Z., 1972
Gandt, Robert L., **China Clipper – The Age of the Great Flying Boats:** Naval Institute Press, Annapolis, Maryland, 1991
Grooch, Stephen, **From Crate to Clipper - with Captain Musick, Pioneer Pilot:** Longmans, Green & Co., New York, 1939
Grooch, Stephen, **Skyway to Asia:** Longmans, Green & Co., New York, 1936
Gwynn-Jones, Terry, **Wings Across the Pacific:** Orion Books, New York, 1991
Heinl, Lt. Col. R.D., **The Defense of Wake:** Division of Information, U.S. Marine Corps., Washington D.C., 1947
Holbrook, Francis X., **United States National Defense and Transpacific Commercial Aviation Routes,1933-41;**
    Fordham University, Doctorate Dissertation, 1969
Jackson, Ronald W., **China Clipper:** Everest House, New York, 1979
Kauffman, Sanford, **Pan American Pioneer:** Texas Tech Press, Lubbock, Texas, 1995
Klaás, M.D., **Last of the Flying Clippers:** Schiffer Publishing, Atglen, Pennsylvania, 1997
Krupnick, Jon E., **Pan Am's Pacific Pioneers:** Pictorial Histories Publishing Co., Missoula, Montana, 1997
Levering, Robert, **The Clipper Heritage:** Inter-Collegiate Press, New York, 1984
Masland, William M., **Through the Back Doors of the World in a Ship that had Wings:** Vintage Press, New York, 1984
Rich, Doris L., **Amelia Earhart:** Smithsonian Institution, Washington D.C.,1989
Sikorsky, Igor, **The Story of the Winged-S:** Dodd Mead & Co., New York, 1938
Trippe, Betty Stettinius, **Pan Am's First Lady - The Diary of Betty Stettinius Trippe:** Paladwr Press, McLean, Va, 1996

## MAGAZINES
**Guam Recorder:** (Monthly news magazine from Guam published by the Navy), 1935-1941

## PAN AM PUBLICATIONS
**Clipper News from Treasure Island** - 1941
**Flypaper** – periodic newsletter, maintenance department – November 1939 – December 1941
**New Horizons** – 1936-46
**Pan American Newsletter** – 1934 - 1939
**Transpacific Newsletter for the Transpacific Division** – 1941-44

## UNPUBLISHED LOGS & DIARIES
Berst, Phillip: Maintenance Superintendent – Pacific Division - Scrapbook and Logs - 1935-1943
Boyle, John: Manager at Wake Island - 1941
French, Dr. William O.: Doctor at Kingman Reef - Log at Kingman Reef - 1937
Gray, Almon: Radio operator at Wake Island – Radio flight officer – 1935-40
Kenler, Dr. Myron: Doctor at Wake Island - Scrapbook and Logs - 1935
Vucetich, Danilo: Supercargo – North Haven – North Wind - 1935-1941
Young, Clarence M.: – Manager of Pacific Division 1935 – 1953 - unpublished recollections - 1966
Young, Ralph: Log at Canton Island – April 1939 to February 1940

## INTERVIEWS
Canaday, Harry: Crew member on first survey flight and many historic flights thereafter - 1935-1937
Johnson, Admiral Jesse: Naval aviator in Pacific - 1934-1939
Kenler, Dr. Myron: Physician at Wake Island – 1935
Lytton, Catherine Berst: Daughter of Phil Berst, maintenance supervisor in Pacific – 1935-43
McCafferty, Guy: Crew member Anzac Clipper – last prewar flight - 1941
McCrory, Robert: Pan Am ground mechanic – 1943-46
Rothe, Marion: Widow of "Swede" Rothe, flight engineer on Pacific Clipper's flight around the world - 1940-1946
Trout, Wilbert: Construction crew at Wake – 1936
Vucetich, Alex: Son of Danilo Vucetich "Supercargo" – North Haven and North Wind – 1935-41
Young, Timothy: Son of Pacific Division manager Clarence Young – 1935-53

**Maps in Blue**

**Maps in Blue**